Ex Africa semper aliquid novi.
Out of Africa there is always something new

– Pliny the Elder
AD 23-79

You cannot hope to bribe or twist
Thank God, a British journalist;
But seeing what the man will do
Unbribed, there's no occasion to.

– Humbert Wolfe

Avoid clichés like the plague

Notice in newsroom of the
Daily Express, London

Christopher Munnion was the African correspondent for *The Daily Telegraph* of London for more than 20 years, covering most of the wars, revolutions, coups and upheavals on the continent during that period. Born in Essex, England, he became a foreign correspondent by following what he calls the 'traditional route' to Fleet Street, working for weekly and daily provincial newspapers before joining the *Telegraph* at the age of 21. He worked on foreign assignments in America and the Middle East before being posted to Africa in 1967. He is now a freelancer, writing for British and American publications and specialising in wildlife, conservation and environmental affairs. He is also co-author, with Randall Jay Moore, of another book, *Back to Africa*.

BANANA SUNDAY

Datelines • From • Africa

CHRIS MUNNION

WILLIAM WATERMAN PUBLICATIONS

To those colleagues worldwide who did not make it back.

Published in 1993 by William Waterman Publications
A division of William Waterman Publications (Pty) Ltd
PO Box 5091, Rivonia 2128

First edition, first impression 1993

ISBN 0 9583751 7 8

© Christopher Munnion, 1993

Book Design: Photo-Prints, Cape Town
Typesetting and Reproduction: Photo-Prints, Cape Town
Printed and bound by: Creda Press, Cape Town

CONTENTS

INTRODUCTION VII

GLOSSARY X

Chapter One
APOCRYPHA NOW! 1

Chapter Two
SONS OF SCOOP 25

Chapter Three
WHOSE UHURU? 51

Chapter Four
WINDS OF FLATULENCE 77

Chapter Five
HEART OF DARKNESS 99

Chapter Six
WHY YOU UNSHOT? 123

Chapter Seven
THE BROODING COLOSSUS 153

Chapter Eight
THE SCOURGE OF THE FLY WHISK 172

CHAPTER NINE
ARMAGEDDON IN THE ARMPIT 202

CHAPTER TEN
REBELLION AND REDOUBT 232

CHAPTER ELEVEN
'TELL THE QUEEN I LOVE HER' 256

CHAPTER TWELVE
CALIBAN'S CONTINENT 285

CHAPTER THIRTEEN
SOLDIERS OF MISFORTUNE 316

CHAPTER FOURTEEN
A LUTA CONTINUA 348

CHAPTER FIFTEEN
SUNSET IN THE SERGEANTS' MESS 376

CHAPTER SIXTEEN
FINAL EDITION 411

ACKNOWLEDGEMENTS 429
BIBLIOGRAPHY 431
INDEX 433

INTRODUCTION

When Al J Venter, publisher and adventurer, called from the Middle East I was not surprised. He is an inveterate, compulsive traveller, particularly to regions of human folly and conflict. As usual, it was more of a cursory command than a conversation. 'Drop everything! Put it all on one side...I've got a great idea that will take you all over Africa, probably all around the world. Right up your street.' The idea was the genesis of this book: the story of foreign correspondents in post-colonial Africa.

Having devoted the greater portion of my working life to reporting on Africa, the commission was inviting. My initial reluctance to undertake it was rooted in the firm knowledge that the seminal work on the foreign journalist unleashed on the Dark Continent, *Scoop*, had been written by Evelyn Waugh in 1936. All subsequent attempts at what the trade calls a 'matcher' failed or faltered.

Waugh's classic was written as a novel but that fooled no one, least of all his contemporary colleagues with whom he covered the Italian invasion of Abyssinia in 1935. It was a brilliant, biting satire of both Fleet Street and of Africa. To the foreign hack, however, *Scoop* had an almost eerie prescience; the chaos and confusion of the setting, the eccentricities, blunders and buffoonery of the central characters and even the *modus operandi* (and *vivendi*) were to prove an accurate reflection of the journalist at work in any given African situation in the ensuing 50 years.

This account does not presume to update *Scoop*. Indeed, I have drawn heavily on Waugh's novel, and on the memories of the men on whom he based his characters, as a starting point for this yarn. In my research, I developed a strong feeling that many of my own colleagues had modelled themselves on Waugh's supposedly fictional heroes to formulate their own approach to the job and professional techniques.

Another inhibition in accepting the assignment was an acute awareness that I was a belated and relatively minor player in the drama of Africa's transition from colonial rule to 'freedom' and 'independence'. There were others far better qualified than I to record the hack's Africa of that period. I contacted several of them. They were unanimous: 'If you really feel brave enough to write up those silly stories about your friends and colleagues in those crazy days, then go ahead.'

This account is no attempt at any form of history of the three decades of decolonisation in Africa. Nor does it pretend in any way to be a serious analysis of the way in which foreign correspondents covered that era. It is merely a nostalgic frolic, related by anecdote, reminiscence and observation, of only a small part of a story that was often hilarious, sometimes sad, occasionally tragic, but always absorbing.

The choice of Zimbabwe's independence in 1980 as a conclusion to this narrative is not entirely arbitrary. That event coincided, roughly speaking, with the coming-of-age of the microchip media revolution which has transformed the ethos and traditions of journalism (and, incidentally, caused the death of Fleet Street itself as London's newspaper village). From the first report from a remote frontier to the final printing and distribution of the newspaper, the computer rules. In the ever more pervasive world of television reportage, electronic news gathering technology and satellites ensure that the world and his wife are eyewitnesses to instant, unfolding history.

The quantity and, in most cases, the quality of the news product has increased immeasurably but I, for one, do not envy the young journalist whose nostrils will never be assailed by the mucky magic of printer's ink, whose feet will never vibrate as the rotary presses start to thunder out the first edition in the basement and whose fingers will dance over a lunchtime laptop PC instead of grasping a rusty tinful of banana gin in a Rwandan shebeen.

Gone for good are the days of the foreign correspondent hero, braving a night ride through hostile Zulu territory to get out his despatch by fast packet steamer or swimming a crocodile-infested river to reach the rebel camp by daybreak. Nowadays, the TV cameraman will zoom in on the advancing tanks as the beleaguered dictator is interviewed by satellite hook-up from New York in a live transmission watched by millions sitting on suburban sofas.

Lest I might appear to be suggesting there is a lesser element of danger in today's journalism let me add, hastily, with humility and sadness, that life has never been more dangerous for the reporters, photographers and TV crews than it is in the 1990s. According to the International Federation of Journalists in Brussels and Reporters

Sans Frontières in Paris, at least 61 journalists were killed in 1992 for coming too close to the truth. Some 130 were languishing in prisons from China to Chile. South Africa's painful and protracted transition to democracy is being accompanied by an ugly increase in threats and assaults – and worse – against journalists doing their job. As I write this – it is International Press Freedom Day – I hear that a TV reporter, Calvin Thusago, has just been stabbed to death and his colleague, Dudley Saunders, critically injured, by a mob in Sharpeville.

In the 30-year period covered by this account, a dozen colleagues died in the course of reporting Africa at its most turbulent. Three times as many colleagues have been killed in two years of reporting in Europe – specifically in covering the conflict ravaging the former Yugoslavia. No false bravado or spurious heroics here.

Africa's sanguine saga begins to appear positively benign by comparison. To be sure, the continent will, at any given time, suggest to the observer that it is wracked perennially by war, famine, fear, folly, disease, corruption and self-destruction. Throughout this book I quote the old Africa hand's cynical imprecation, when the going gets rough, 'AWA' – Africa Wins Again. To misquote Pliny the Elder, there is always news out of Africa, most of it bad. And yet I share a faith with many who love the continent that Africa and its people, having always demonstrated an amazing capacity for survival against enormous odds, will eventually win. Again.

Christopher Munnion, Johannesburg, June 1993.

GLOSSARY

Black – Originally a carbon copy of your dispatch kept for your own reference, or passed on to tardy colleagues for theirs. Still used to describe any duplication of your story.

Byline – Your name published above your story; after the expense account, the reporter's most prized possession.

Cablese – Now dated journalistic code by which the cost per word cables or telegrams to the office was reduced by running words together; e.g. 'Onwarding Chadwise Procover Prezpresser' would tell the editor that you intended to proceed to Chad to cover an impending presidential press conference.

Copy – Any written material intended to be set for publication.

Copytakers – Men and women employed at head office to take dictated copy on the telephone from the reporter on the spot. A special breed who, in the middle of recording your graphic eye-witness account of the coup, might yawn loudly and ask 'Much more of this, old boy?' Fortunately still extant and invaluable despite computerised communications.

Copytaster – Senior sub-editor (qv) who 'samples' all copy as it arrives to determine its relative value against the rest of the day's news.

Dateline – The practice of adding the name of the place from which you are sending the dispatch to your byline. A dateline also used to give the day on which a dispatch is sent, as opposed to received, at head office; eg. 'From Peter Peel, Banana, Sunday.'

Deadline – The time by which copy must be received by head office to be processed for publication.

Dispatch – The copy as sent to the office and used in the newspaper. These days more commonly described by hacks as the 'file' or the 'piece'.

File – As a verb, to send your dispatch by whatever means to the office. As a noun, the copy you have sent.

Hack – Once derogatory term now in common use self-mockingly by journalists to describe themselves and their colleagues. If you can 'hack it' you can manage to get in and out of any difficult situation and deal with it competently.

Health warning – An indication to the office that your copy is being censored or influenced in some way by extraneous circumstances. Also used by the foreign desk to convey to the reader that a dispatch has been subjected to censorship.

Herogram – Message of congratulation from head office on your file. Conversely a 'blast', a 'rocket' or just 'flack' from the desk means you are out of favour with the editor.

Intro – The first and most important paragraph of a news story which should arrestingly give the gist as well as the what, when, where, how and why of any event.

Lead – The main front-page story in the newspaper. As a verb, 'They led with my piece today' indicates to envious colleagues that your story is the most prominent in the newspaper.

Linage – System of payment by the word, line or length to part-time correspondents and freelancers.

Moonlighting – Contributing cladestinely to a newspaper or publication other than your own.

Mugshot – Passport-style photograph, carried at all times in quantity by the foreign correspondent to obtain press accreditation, passes and permits, genuine or spurious.

Newsprint – The low-grade paper on which newspapers are printed.

Pigeon – An obliging third party, usually found in airport departure halls, who agrees to ferry copy or film to your office.

Scoop – Used more outside journalism than within to describe a major story obtained by a reporter exclusively for his newspaper.

Shorts – Brief, hopefully pithy, items occasionally demanded by the desk to fill pages on 'slow days' when there appears to be a scarcity of other news.

Smalls – Journalists' term for the classified advertisements.

Splash – The lead (qv), or main story, on the front page.

Stringer – Foreign correspondent who may work for several publications on a payment-by-results basis.

Sub-editor – Not, as many seem to believe, the assistant or deputy editor but the head office desk men who check incoming copy, adjust it to fit a given space and write the headline.

Takes – Short sections of copy, probably of only two or three paragraphs, sent separately but in sequence to facilitate speedy handling at the other end.

CHAPTER ONE

APOCRYPHA NOW!

*T*he rifle pointed shakily at my head was less worrying than the eyes of the man holding it. The dilated pupils were fearful and encased in bloodshot whites. We were that close. Even in those naive days, I knew it was an automatic rifle capable of shredding me and, probably, the dusty, stunted trees behind me. I knew, also, that the Nigerian soldier whose uneasy acquaintance I was then making would have already switched his rifle to 'automatic' thereby rendering his nervous tremor immaterial to his aim should he pull the trigger. The one thought flashing through my mind was the same as that which many of my foreign correspondent colleagues had reflected on in dozens of such situations in different parts of the world. That thought, simply put, was 'What the fuck am I doing here?'

Behind the sights was a very young member of Nigeria's hastily assembled Third Marine Federal Commando Division, a unit bolstered with many thousands of teenaged recruits to counter the Biafran secession in the east. He seemed more frightened than I hope I appeared, but that mattered little as he had the gun, and I had not.

The situation resolved itself before we had a chance to exchange pleasantries. A beefy Nigerian sergeant who had accompanied Angus McDermid of the BBC and myself to the Biafran 'front' emerged from the bushes and spat an order at my would-be adversary. The young man's eyes widened still further with horror. He dropped the rifle to his feet and clasped his hands in front of him in a very unmilitary gesture. The sergeant picked up a hefty dead branch lying nearby and immediately set about the young soldier, beating him viciously about the head, neck and shoulders and cursing him all the while in Yoruba. He then turned to us, still heaving with his exertions, and said in impeccable English: 'We have had to train them so quickly…they have no discipline!'

I felt somewhat guilty, having caused the incident by wandering away from the press party to investigate what looked like an

appetising orange tree in a war zone. 'I'm sorry,' I said to the
sergeant and to the prone, bloody and blubbering figure at his feet.
'It was my fault,' I added, trying to express, ineffectually, my guilt. I
pointed to the orange tree. We had not had a drink for five hours.

'You want oranges?' asked the sergeant rhetorically. 'Stand
back!' He then ordered his men, including my friend who had scram-
bled to his feet, to fire on the tree. They did so for an ear-splitting
two minutes. From close range. On full automatic. As we quenched
our thirst on fresh, bullet-shredded oranges Angus gave me a friendly nudge. 'Welcome to war in Africa,' he muttered.

Thus, in that steamy West African summer of 1969 when the
civil war in Nigeria was building to its bloody climax, was I blooded
as an 'Africa hand', the supposed apogee of a career as a foreign correspondent. As an earlier, more distinguished colleague, Winston
Churchill, might have said 'Some apogee! Some career!'

To generations of journalistic hopefuls, the title 'foreign correspondent' was the most desired, the most glamorous and the most
difficult to attain. The accolade was more sought after than that of
Editor. That species, in those days, was more often than not drawn
from the ranks of the sub-editors, the grey production men who put
the newspapers together at arc-lit desks and in inky printing rooms.
They were figures of derision and scorn, we thought, to the swash-
buckling heroes of frontline journalism, the men who braved shot,
shell and danger in exotic places with unlikely names, scribbling a
dramatic despatch whilst sipping a martini, boarding airliners with
a blonde and disembarking with a redhead and occasionally dropping in on Fleet Street to recount, off-handedly to awed home-based
colleagues, tales of derring-do.

Surely the foreign correspondent was a breed apart? Glorious
independence, a confidence and courage that was taken for granted,
an ability to think, act and make decisions within the unforgiving
minute and to draft, in deathless prose, a vivid report of world shattering events which would be swiftly transmitted to head office by
the most ingenious methods under impossible circumstances?

Surely here was a man who remembered instinctively to fill the
bath before the siege started and the water supply was cut off, a
man who would be able to identify the pregnant anopheles mosquito
as the malaria-carrier, a man with the local knowledge and contacts
to acquire a bottle of Scotch in a drought, a working telex in a
typhoon or a racing camel in the desert?

Passports and constantly updated international health certifi-
cates were borne religiously to the office every day by the ambitious
young reporter, always hoping that his previous day's piece on the

Hounslow stabbing would have caught the eye of the Foreign Editor, that the command would come down to drop the London Bridge tide table and hot-foot it to the Levant.

Romance apart, there was always the whispered word of untold riches to be had on the foreign beat. The then meagre salary cheque could be banked offshore while Our Man in Manila lived on unquestioned, unlimited expenses. The tab for a suite at the nearest five-star hotel and the best restaurants in town would be sent directly to head office. And what about the chaps who had made enough on the thriving black money market in the Congo to pay off the mortgages and buy second homes in Wales?

The dream was only slightly dimmed when visiting foreign correspondents were buttonholed in the pub on brief returns to base. Of course, old boy, any posting away from this dump is a good posting. Naturally, old boy, there is no shortage of female company, even in the hairiest of spots. In fact, the more dangerous the situation the more readily the girls crave male company. Sure thing, old boy, you can make a bit on expenses and on the black exchange market as well, if you're lucky. But? Ah well, old boy, just had to come back to sort out the latest divorce. She ran off with my bloody lawyer, would you believe, so she's got the house, the car, the furniture, the bloody lot!

Eavesdropping on a group of foreign men reminiscing at the bar could also sound a cautionary note. There would be the exchange of enthralling, hilarious anecdotes and wonderful gossip about colleagues, tight as newts in the tightest of spots. Then, as the yarns dried up, a sipping of silent toasts before the sullen exchange of notes on alimony and maintenance and the names of good divorce lawyers. This was the bitter-sweet brotherhood of the men Fleet Street came to call the 'professional strangers'. There was a standing joke in journalism. The automatic response of someone learning what you did for a living was 'Oh, you must meet such interesting people!' We did, but most of them were our colleagues.

Take, for instance, Angus McDermid one of the most respected foreign correspondents of the day. Mention anywhere in Africa and he had been there and back numerous times, east, west, north and south.

He knew the terrain, the personalities, the politics and, above all, the labyrinthine modus operandi by which correspondents had to obtain their information and, more importantly, to file it – to get it back to the office.

Better still he was a Genuine Old Africa Hand – a GOAH, if you like. A rotund, carroty Welshman, McDermid was ready at all times to assist younger, less experienced hands. He was also possessed of that greatest of assets for a foreign correspondent, particularly those assigned to emergent Africa: a great sense of humour. His ability to find amusement in the many, frequently dangerous situations in which we found ourselves, at the huge dilemmas of finding the story and the even greater ones of getting it out, was always a source of great comfort. Above all, he had long since learned to laugh at himself.

Angus had been in Biafra when he secured, exclusively, the news that an important general had been assassinated. Censorship, including the monitoring of all telephone calls, was being strictly enforced by the authorities. McDermid booked what seemed like a routine call to his wife, Myfanwy, who knew and understood the exigencies of his job. After a few brief pleasantries, Angus switched to his fluent Welsh and began to dictate the story to his wife. A suspicious censor interrupted the call. He was breaking the rules by not communicating in his native tongue. 'My dear chap,' retorted Angus. 'This is my native tongue.' He completed his story without further interruptions. Myfanwy, dutiful as ever, relayed the translation to the BBC on the turn.

In the time we worked together in Nigeria, Angus convinced me that Africa could not only be fascinating to cover but fun as well...'If you can work a story on this continent, then you can hack it anywhere in the world,' Angus once said, referring to the logistical difficulties of operating amid the turmoil, tumult and confusion prevailing then (and now!) throughout most of the continent. I did not volunteer but the thought translated itself to S R 'Pop' Pawley, then Managing Editor of *The Daily Telegraph*, and to E H 'Ricky' Marsh, the Foreign Editor. I was posted to Africa for a two-year stint that turned into a 25-year assignment for that newspaper and a permanent one for me.

To my colleagues, the story of how I came to be despatched to the Dark Continent became a small part of Fleet Street apocrypha. It is worth recording perhaps if only to demonstrate the wonderful – and sorely missed – eccentricity of life on *The Daily Telegraph* under the Berry dynasty.

As a keen 21-year-old working for the *Yorkshire Post* I had heard on the grapevine that the *Telegraph's* Manchester office was recruiting a few reporters. I applied and duly travelled to Manchester for an interview with the late Tom Cooper, the Assistant Editor. Tall, silvery-haired and distinguished-looking, Tom was one of that city's more endearing characters. He had never been further west than Liverpool but had written a series of moderately successful novels about the Wild West under the name of Hart Cooper. The interview was conducted in The Swan With Two Necks, a newspaper watering hole beneath the old Withy Grove publishing house.

The only credential Tom appeared to seek from me was an ability to sink and hold pints of mild-and-bitter ale.

My taproom training in Yorkshire stood me in good stead. Tom appeared suitably impressed. There had been many applications, of course, but mine would be considered. If I had not received a letter by the end of the month 'keep in touch and better luck next time.' At my Bradford flat I fielded the post eagerly day after day. There was nothing. On the last day of the month I caught the mail as it dropped through the door. Nothing! The doorbell rang. It was the postman. 'Threepence to pay on this one,' he said. 'No stamp.' It was a letter offering me a staff job on *The Daily Telegraph*. That I had been obliged to pay the postage seemed to set the pattern for the whole of my career with that newspaper.

Only a few months later I was sent to London for a stint of holiday relief in the newsroom. Modest accommodation was booked for me and I was informed I would be on the 6 p.m. to 1 a.m. reporting shift. I duly reported, bright-eyed and bushy-tailed, to 135 Fleet Street, with its imposing, preserved facade and its lavatorial interior. The newsroom was a formidable sight. Everyone appeared to be very old, very brusque and all were donning coats and hats to go home or to the pub.

There were distinguished-looking men like Sir Henry Bate, Air-Commodore Teddy Donaldson, the air correspondent, John Prince, the health correspondent, Norman Riley and Jim Dawson, the education correspondent. In those days, the specialists cultivated the demeanour of top members of the professions they reported on: Prince looked like a Harley Street surgeon and Dawson had the manner and voice of a headmaster at a very strict public school. It was very intimidating but soon they were gone. Nobody could tell me to whom I should report or even where I should sit. I found a vacant desk and tried to look keen by scanning the newspapers and journals lying around.

It was about 8 p.m. before the door linking the newsroom to the sub-editor's room swung open and in walked Harry Winslade holding a slip of paper. Harry, ex-RN with the bearing of one used to a warship bridge and with a ward-room complexion, approached me quizzically.

'Are you with us, old boy?' he drawled, implying that if I wasn't I would be against him and THEM, the night top-brass that, I was vaguely aware, were running the show from the inner precinct. I leapt to my feet and introduced myself.

'Munnion...Manchester office...on relief duty.' I nearly added 'Sir!' in the military manner that the *Telegraph* seemed to foster.

'Good! good!' said Harry, dropping the piece of paper he was holding from shoulder height so that it fluttered onto the desk. It was another Telegraph mannerism, I was soon to learn. I read the note. It was a news tip, telephoned in from a hopeful in Potters Bar who would get a fiver if the story held up. It said, briefly, that the tipster understood the Aga Khan had lost millions of pounds in the collapse of some Middle Eastern oil venture. It named the company but that was all. Harry beamed.

'Get hold of the Aga Khan and see if there's anything in that, old boy,' he said, turning and disappearing through the door. Get hold of the Aga Khan! Late on a Sunday evening! In panic I looked around for a friendly face. There were none.

On a central desk I finally found well-thumbed copies of Kelly's, Debrett's Peerage and other guides to aristocracy. There were no references to the Aga Khan but there was listed a Princess Joan Aly Khan, a sister. Better still, there was a home telephone number in Belgravia. I dialled with some trepidation. After some while, an imperious but not unfriendly female voice answered.

'Is that the Princess Aly Khan?'

'Speaking...who is this?' I launched into an apologetic introduction.

'This is *The Daily Telegraph*...so sorry to bother you at this time but...'

She cut me short. 'Who?' she demanded, sharply.

'*The Daily Telegraph* newspaper...sorry to...' She cut me short again. 'I know it's a newspaper. Who are you?' I stuttered out my name and lowly rank. (I would have added a serial number had they given me one.) Her tone was more relaxed as she asked why I was calling. I gave her the gist of the message. 'Good heavens!' she exclaimed. 'That's very interesting. Of course you must get hold of my brother...you have his numbers, of course?' Well, no...that was why I was calling.

Exasperated voice: 'Do you have a pencil, Mr...Munnion?' I did. 'Well...what time is it?...good heavens...you'll be lucky to catch him at the Sardinia villa. He's due to leave in his own aircraft for his home in Paris. Try Sardinia first. He may have been delayed. You know what the weather's like down there at this time of year. If not try his home in Paris in two hours or so.' She rattled off the numbers and wished me luck.

I immediately asked the switchboard to book a call to Sardinia, failing which there would be a couple to Paris. I sat back, thinking 'Fleet Street? A doddle...get hold of the Aga Khan, indeed...just ring the Princess, get his whereabouts and numbers and here we go! What on earth is the weather like in Sardinia at this time of year?'

My smugness was short-lived. No more than five minutes elapsed before the door burst open to admit a troupe of even more formidable looking gentlemen, all seemingly with angry, raised eyebrows and all calling out different versions of my name. I was ushered to a desk where, I was told, Lord Camrose's secretary wanted to speak to me on one line and Lord Camrose's personal assistant was asking for me on the other. Now, Lord Camrose was a totally remote figure in my mind. I was vaguely aware that he was the older brother of The Proprietor (always referred to in upper-case) Michael Berry. Michael ran the newspaper from the lofty, barely accessible heights of the Fifth Floor (also always referred to in upper-case). Lord Camrose rarely, if ever, involved himself in the day-to-day running of *The Daily Telegraph*, hence the amazement when he had contacted the night editor to ask after a totally unknown young reporter.

The Back Bench phalanx gathered at the desk as I was finally put through to His Lordship. 'Minnion, is it?' he asked, pleasantly enough. I didn't correct his pronunciation. The way I was feeling, he had it absolutely right. 'Understand you've been trying to get hold of the Aga Khan...what's it all about?' I gave him chapter and verse of the events of the evening and read him the full text of the tipster's message.

I saw Harry Winslade, standing amid the glowering heavies, wince as I told His Lordship that 'a gentleman purporting to be the night news editor' had instructed me to get hold of the Aga to check the story right away. 'Good heavens,' exclaimed His Lordship. 'Know the family fairly well, you know, Minnion, but hadn't heard about this...tell you what, tell your chap...Green is it? [Maurice Green was then Editor of *The Daily Telegraph*, to me an equally remote figure]...tell him that I'll look into this and if there's anything in it I'll let him know.' I was now in a daze.

'Yes, of course, sir...thank you very much, sir...I'll let Green...er...Mr Green know right away.' Lord Camrose was now chummy. 'Thank you...er ...Minnion...G'night.'

I bade him a reciprocal 'G'night, sir,' and put down the telephone respectfully. The Back Bench descended upon me like a pack of wolves. Who the hell was I? Why on earth was The Owner calling me of all people? Who had I contacted and why? When I finally managed to splutter out an explanation, heads were clasped in hands and there was, among these angry men, much wailing and gnashing of teeth.

I was bemused, bewildered and a little concerned until one kind soul took me aside to explain that Princess Aly Khan had been living with Lord Camrose for some time, that it was supposed to be one of London's best-kept social secrets and that, in any event, His Lordship was under no circumstances to be disturbed after 7 p.m. in the evening.

It was an inauspicious start to my career. As the *Telegraph*'s teeming apocrypha has it, to this day, that very first assignment led to the command from on high, i.e. the Fifth Floor, 'I think we must send Minnion to Africa'. Typical *Telegraph* policy: send one of our smaller reporters to one of the larger continents, preferably a troublesome one.

I repeat 'apocryphal', only because there was a five-year gap between my dubious rapport with Lord Camrose and my first African assignment. Betwixt and between I was despatched to many parts of Britain and then to what we used to call, affectionately, the globe. There were memorable, long stints in America and the Middle East where, in Aden in particular, I learned the hard way just how painful was Britain's rapid retreat from imperial status.

When the call came from the Foreign Desk to pack my bags for a long-term assignment based in Africa it was accompanied by the offhand instruction to, inter alia, 'cover the end of this Rhodesian story, old boy'. The Rhodesian story, of course, was the Unilateral Declaration of Independence made less than a couple of years earlier by Ian Douglas Smith and his Rhodesian Front party. That story was to run for another 14 years before I was able to cover its end. But that was the *Telegraph* style. Correspondents were expected to get to any given trouble spot first and to remain long, long after the last opposition colleague had pulled out. It was a policy that paid off frequently.

Far from being regarded as a punishment posting, an African assignment was regarded with envy by colleagues. The *Telegraph*, after all, had long associations with Africa. With the *New York Herald,* it had co-sponsored Henry Morton Stanley's great east-to-west expedition across Africa from 1874 to 1877. The *Telegraph*'s then News Editor, John le Sage, had travelled to Marseilles to sign him up after his legendary expedition to locate Livingstone at Ujiji in what is now Tanzania. His immortal (apocryphal?): 'Dr Livingstone, I presume?' remains a masterpiece of understatement.

Moreover, Stanley (born John Rowlands, illegitimate son of a Welsh parlourmaid) embodied all the attributes any foreign correspondent required, then and now. He was, in the words of one biographer, 'a flamboyant rogue, braggart, bully and cheat, ruthless and unscrupulous in pursuit of his own interests and a prodigious liar.' He obtained his first scoop by bribing a telegraph operator to transmit his dispatches before those of his rivals, a practice employed by many of his foreign correspondent successors, including current, very distinguished members of *The Daily Telegraph* staff. He was also a man of immense courage, resourcefulness and foresight and thoroughly deserved the Gold Medal the Royal Geographical Society finally and reluctantly bestowed upon him. He was, without doubt, the first Genuine Old Africa Hand.

More deserving, perhaps, of the title 'First GOAH' was the amazing Archibald Forbes, a Scot who drifted into journalism when ill-health obliged him to leave the army. He covered the Franco-Prussian war for the *Morning Advertiser* and, with characteristic opportunism, was one of two reporters on the spot when Napoleon signed the formal French surrender.

For the *Daily News,* he covered the Zulu War in 1879 with his friend and mentor, William Howard Russell, covering for the *Telegraph.* It was the first African war to be covered by Fleet Street and, when Lord Chelmsford's forces finally routed the Zulu impis at Ulundi, Forbes made journalistic history with a remarkable feat of courage and ingenuity. Learning that Chelmsford did not intend to send his official despatch of the victory until the following day, Forbes saddled up and rode for 25 hours through hostile, still-smouldering Zululand to break the good news to an anxious empire. His despatch on the Battle of Ulundi was read in both the House of Commons and the House of Lords.

By absorbing the *Morning Post* in 1937, the *Telegraph* strengthened its historical links with Africa. The *Post* had employed Rudyard Kipling, the imperial muse, a winner of the Nobel Prize for Literature and a balladeer of the Boer War who had witnessed and experienced the continent at its worst but conveyed in his verse, indelibly, his love of the land and its people.

The *Post* had also been cajoled by a 25-year-old upstart named Winston Spencer Churchill into sending him as a correspondent to South Africa to cover the Boer War. He had used similar bludgeoning tactics two years earlier in the Sudan, where Kitchener was subduing bloodily the Mahdi's Dervishes. Churchill had persuaded the War Office to attach him to Kitchener's forces as a lieutenant – on condition that he paid for himself. Churchill knew he could get by with contributions to the *Morning Post.* He did so, but incurred the wrath of Kitchener who showed his disdain for this string-pulling, arrogant young man by making him suffer the same deprivations as his troops and limiting his telegraphic facilities to 200 words a day. Churchill was later able to reciprocate, but with affectionate hindsight, much later, wrote of Kitchener's gory march on Khartoum, that the general was 'consumed with matters of greater concern'.

In South Africa, young Winston was at it again. He was bullying, pushing and using every family connection to get a post as war correspondent for the confrontation with the Boers. He wanted action that he could observe, possibly participate in but certainly write about. His problem in his legendary assignment in South Africa during the Boer War seemed to be his great difficulty in deciding whether he should be correspondent or combatant.

There was to be a tragic, similar sequel some 70 years later when Lord Richard Cecil, second son of the Marquis of Salisbury, was killed while working as a journalist – but participating as an ex-British SAS officer – in action with the Rhodesian African Rifles against ZANLA guerrillas during the Rhodesian bush war. Richard, a good friend and colleague, had written for *The Daily Telegraph* some of the precious few frontline accounts of that nasty little war.

Edgar Wallace, covering the Boer War for the *London Daily Mail,* established another journalistic legend, securing a world scoop on the signing of the peace treaty at Vereeniging with a flair and ingenuity that has still to be matched. Lord Kitchener had gone to great lengths to keep secret the peace deliberations, barring correspondents from the camp and placing armed guards and barbed wire around the compound.

Wallace befriended one of the guards who happened to be in earshot of the proceedings. No doubt deploying an early variety of cheque-book journalism, he persuaded the man to carry three handkerchiefs – red (signifying nothing happening), blue (making progress) and white (treaty about to be signed). To the bemusement of his colleagues, Wallace took to making frequent train trips to and from Pretoria, a line which conveniently passed close to the wire of the peace encampment.

One crisp May evening in 1902, as the up train passed the camp, the guard emerged to blow his nose vigorously with a white handkerchief. Wallace had his exclusive and, true to form, a pre-arranged, encoded method of transmitting the news to London. He merely sent one line 'Have bought you 1 000 Rand Collieries 40s 6d' which indicated to the excited editors of the *Daily Mail* that peace was 'absolutely assured'.

So there were some distinguished, formidable footprints to be trod in my African posting. My base was to be Salisbury, the capital of the rebellious Rhodesia, as it was considered to be the centre of the main African story of the day, i.e. that with the most British interest.

Just how British the place was I could see from the airliner window as we prepared to land. I was reminded immediately of a caustic description of the Rhodesian capital by the BBC's James Mossman: 'The most ghastly place on earth...miles and miles of bloody suburbia.' The laconic Larry Fellowes of the *New York Times,* asked how he had enjoyed his first visit to Salisbury, drawled 'It's okay – but too far from town.'

The points made by both men were valid in a way, though I quickly found the place to be most congenial. The sub-tropical climate was tempered by the crispness of an altitude of several thousand feet. Despite the rebellion, the people, black and white, were relaxed, open and friendly. Better still, the *Telegraph* was renting for their correspondent a sunny bungalow in four acres of grounds with a swimming pool and tennis court. Suburban it may have been, but Carshalton was never like this, I thought as I settled down poolside to 'read in' to the story.

There was, of course, a lot of sympathy for Good Ol' Smithy upstairs at 135 Fleet Street. The Proprietor and the leader writers knew a lot more about Africa's disastrous post-independence record than I did at that stage. My first suggestion to the office was an in-depth look at the myriad liberation movements operating in a dozen African states and, of course, several European capitals.

My idea was received enthusiastically and immediately projected into a large three-part serial for the new *Sunday Telegraph*. The research took me from the Cape to Cairo, a journey which led to an unmemorable series of articles but personal experiences which gave me valuable exposure to the double standards applied to Africa that were practised and preached not so much by Fleet Street and the rest of the world's press, but by the retreating colonial governments in London, Paris and Lisbon.

It was soon apparent that, with very few exceptions, independent African states had managed merely to substitute colonial authority for a much more oppressive and fearsome rule by corrupt elites, more often than not created by tribal nepotism. The ordinary people, the 'masses', the *povo* or the *wananchi,* were manifestly faring worse as the leadership, invariably espousing spurious versions of Marxism, indulged in unbridled self-aggrandizement with 'aid money' poured in by guilty Western nations. 'Independence' for most Africans meant compulsory attendance at interminable rallies, usually in the new 'independence' stadia which would be reached by passing beneath some grotesque but expensive 'independence' arch.

There would be long-winded exhortations by visiting fellow-despots from neighbouring states who would expect rent-a-masses to cheer and ululate as they arrived at the new international airport to be whisked to the new multi-storey 'independence hotel' in the presidential fleet of expensive Mercedes-Benzes. I had to agree with Jomo Kenyatta who once wrote 'The African is conditioned...to a freedom of which Europe has little conception.'

News-gathering for the visiting correspondent started with a basic routine: a formal call on the Information Ministry for accreditation followed by the diplomatic rounds, dropping in on every foreign embassy and mission to exchange gossip and views with diplomats in the hope of getting a lead on a good story. I quickly established that I could leave the British diplomats until last. They were the least helpful and sometimes downright obstructive. Visiting journalists were, they made it clear, an embarrassment to Her Majesty's excellent relations with President Tillfinger's government.

I shall never forget the purple indignation of a young Foreign Office prig in Dar es Salaam when I called to ask what the British High Commission in Tanzania thought of the activities in that once romantic capital of such organisations as Rhodesia's ZAPU and ZANU, South Africa's ANC and PAC, Mozambique's Frelimo and Angola's FNLA, Unita and MPLA.

'You can't go around asking questions like that!' he expostulated. 'Don't you realise these people are very sensitive? Do you realise we have a very important contract to supply British bicycles to this country and people like you could jeopardise that?' It was the first I had heard of the bicycle contract but I pointed out that our readers might be interested in the activities of organisations that could affect British policy towards Africa. 'That's their business,' he snapped. 'We are trying to do business with these people. That is much more important to Britain.'

It was an attitude I was to find time and time again at British embassies and high commissions throughout Africa. Prying journalists were 'trouble-makers' to be discouraged at every turn from making inquiries and encouraged at every stage to catch the next aircraft out. On the three occasions I found myself incarcerated in gaol in Africa – in the course of journalistic duty – I was lucky enough to have American correspondents as cell-mates. The State Department raised Cain and invariably got us out intact. The FO, conscious no doubt of its bicycle contracts, wrung its hands and did precious little. Foreign correspondents were an embarrassment. There were a few notable exceptions in the British embassies and high commissions. Most of them were former Commonwealth Office types who had had long experience on the ground in far-flung corners of the empire.

By contrast, officials at other diplomatic missions were invariably welcoming, helpful and hospitable. The Americans were open and honest, even if they got it horribly wrong at most junctures. The French were as shrewd and manipulative as their foreign policy. The West Germans were loud, outspoken and very knowledgeable. The Russians laughed at themselves and their system. The Israelis, while they were still *persona grata* in African capitals, had incredible sources of good information. So had the Chinese, both offshore and mainland, if you could get to them. The Japanese, who always had much bigger bicycle – and many other contracts – were reserved but hospitable. All foreign diplomats, with the exception of the FO and the East Germans, had a nudge and a wink about the absurdity of any given situation.

I have a vivid memory of accompanying Steve Harper, then of the *Daily Express,* to waylay the Indian High Commissioner to Kampala when Idi Amin uttered his first threats against Uganda's Asian community. Steve, a tall man who believed in displaying a certain Victorian arrogance when in Third World situations, was irritated when we were kept waiting for more than an hour. I crouched beside him in the waiting room, grunting automatic agreement with his tirades. I was suffering from a hangover and grateful for the respite. The Indian diplomat arrived, a large gentleman exuding bonhomie and apologies for his tardiness.

'Don't tell me, gentlemen!' he exclaimed. 'I can tell you both have Fleet Street written all over you.' Steve was deflated. I was flattered. The Indian High Commissioner was extremely helpful on facts, background and outlook. Down the road, however, officials of the British High Commission were wringing their hands over the prospect of thousands of 'Asians' flooding the country. We tried to explain to the great British public, as gently as we could, that an influx of East African people of Asian descent could be a welcome development. They were a cultured, civilised body of people whose entrepreneurial spirit has long since proved itself in Britain, where many of them landed penniless and humiliated.

The reaction in Britain at the time reflected the xenophobia based on the unrestricted influx of fairly wild hill-dwellers from Kashmir. Having worked in places like Bradford where they were lured by their fellow-countrymen to work the still dark, satanic mills, I understood the adverse reaction in Britain to a new influx of 'Asians'. But on the ground, in Uganda, we could sense that a holocaust was on the way.

That first swing through Africa was educational. I had been brought up in a journalistic school that demanded that 'both sides' of any given story had to be presented fully and fairly with equal strength. It is a principle in which I still believe, although the idea of the 'journalism of commitment' took over soon after. This propounded that the best newspaper writing came from those who really felt and identified with causes, who became involved in some way.

To my great dismay, James Cameron, writing then for the *London Evening Standard,* justified this personalised standpoint after an enterprising visit to Hanoi to report on the Vietcong view of the Vietnam war. Like most things that Cameron wrote, they were 'great pieces' – the highest accolade you can get from fellow journalists. They read well, but they were far from 'balanced'. Cameron, perhaps the one journalist universally admired by his colleagues, went one further and wrote a memorable piece for *Punch* in defence of the 'journalism of commitment'.

It was, he argued, the only way to report events faithfully. I think he meant that subjectivity was the easiest way of reporting events that were intrinsically complex. Take a side, write well and it flows easily. The problem is that there are no 'both sides' to report – but many sides. Newspapers did not – do not – have the time or the patience to record the complexities of any given situation and thus tend to give prominence – and totally spurious awards – to those whose graphic accounts purport to give the accurate version of any event.

I was to learn this basic lesson much later in my career. The old *Telegraph* did not expect from me any 'commitment' and they did not get it. I arrived in Africa imbued with the concept of getting 'both sides' of the story. I had to learn the hard way that objectivity is difficult, if not unattainable, especially in an African situation.

Africa is a continent which leaves little room for indifference. It is a place of extremes filled with ironies and sharp contrasts. There are great spaces washed with myriad shades of yellows and greens. There is dust and damp, stink and fragrance. There are people, of all hues, who can switch from extremes of inhumanity and unbridled brutality to warm compassion and natural politeness with the speed of a cheetah after its prey.

I was swiftly drawn to the place, warts and all. So much so that I found myself missing it when I was elsewhere. I suppose it's the same kind of love-hate relationship that forms the basis of a passionate affair.

One of the most endearing aspects was the great camaraderie among the resident foreign press corps. Perhaps because of the difficulties of operating as a journalist, or possibly because of the frequently bizarre situations in which hacks would find themselves, the Africa hands tended to be great characters. The personalities could not have been more disparate, but all seemed to share a Boy's Own Paper sense of adventure and a Goon Show sense of fun. The rivalry was keen, sometimes hilariously so, yet there was much affection and many enduring friendships. There is nothing more cheering than arriving in a tense, rather dicey, post-coup African state and finding the familiar, friendly faces of colleagues with whom one has shared past dangers and will no doubt share future ones. There is no more powerful bond than that between people who have together undergone shot and shell, peril and threat.

As with any other peer group, one had to earn one's spurs. With the Africa corps, you knew you had arrived and been accepted once you had been accorded a sobriquet. Your nickname would be, invariably, unflattering. It would illustrate vividly some point of your character and demeanour that you were anxious to hide. Your Africa corps colleagues would pick up the weakness on the turn. Once they knew your nickname and used it regularly, in a way that indicated they did not recall your real name, you knew you had 'arrived' for all your faults.

The chief nicknamer was an Australian, Michael Keats, who was to become a senior executive of United Press International – UPI – but in those days headed the UPI bureau in Johannesburg. I have searched in vain for an antonym to 'lantern-jawed' to describe Mike's huge, jutting jowl. He was a role model for the cartoon character, Barry Mackenzie, the Private Eye parody of the 1960s Aussie in London's Earls Court, perpetually and unsuccessfully in quest of a Pommie Sheila to lay. Keats tried to lay only the ghost of Barry Mackenzie, never wearing a hat of any sort, certainly not one with dangling corks to dissuade the pervasive flies of his native island. His jaw was topped by a pair of sparkling eyes and a burly, rolling gait that suggested aggression but, to his friends, was always a welcome sight to colleagues in trouble spots. A studiously cultivated cynicism masked a warm and generous soul who would move mountains to help colleagues. His defence mechanism for this weakness was to create apt – and rather cruel – nicknames for his colleagues.

Thus Ken Whiting, the tall, languid and laconic head of the Associated Press bureau who had lost a couple of fingers in a childhood accident, was known as 'Fingers'. John Bulloch, a highly-competitive Welshman, was 'Sheepy'. John Monks, a portly, fair-skinned Australian, was 'Piggy' and Angus McDermid was 'Anxious'. A distinguished British correspondent with an effeminate demeanour and a sexual preference for young boys and young Zambian army officers was 'The African Queen'. Among our American colleagues were 'Colonel' Lee Griggs and 'Uncle' Jack Foisey. A later generation included John 'Shithead' Edlin, Holger 'Captain Wilderness' Jensen and Paul 'Paranoid' Ellman. Ellman was so proud of his sobriquet that he proudly wore a tee-shirt designed by his colleagues which bore the inscription 'Paranoid? Who Me?' You were not supposed to enjoy your monicker but once you had one you knew you were part of the regular corps.

I had been responsible for my own nickname in a chance remark to Keats shortly after I arrived. From that moment I was indelibly 'The Novice', or with the inevitable antipodean abbreviation 'Novvo'. At one stage I became the 'Australian jockey', having been twice mysteriously mistaken for one, once by a lady in a Mauritian hotel and again, a few weeks later, at a cocktail party in Cape Town. Years later, the Rhodesian press corps renamed me 'Sneaky Balls' because, I was assured, of my highly unorthodox manner of playing tennis. The nicknames were, by and large, used affectionately and tended to reinforce the camaraderie.

The journalistic practice of 'running with the pack', i.e. of operating with a group of colleagues from rival newspapers and swapping or sharing information, has its detractors. Certainly, some of the finest copy to emerge from Africa came from correspondents who preferred to work alone but, to my certain knowledge, there were graphic, award-winning dispatches from the occasional 'loners' which were totally fictitious. That's not to say that 'pack journalism' ensured accuracy. But the difficulties of getting anywhere near the truth in so many African situations were such that information shared, swapped and double-checked often helped to give readers a much fairer picture of whatever was going on.

There were other advantages. Correspondents often found themselves in dangerous situations where they would be threatened with arrest, violence or death. The greater the number of hacks, the less the risk (or so it was hoped). There were other circumstances in which concerted action by the pack would get everyone's stories out where individual efforts failed.

There was an unwritten understanding in the African press corps. If a colleague used his, or her, initiative and contacts to get an exclusive story, well and good. It so happened that most colleagues would pass on the information to other members of the pack after his first edition had appeared. This would ease the pain of the inevitable call-backs from rival offices. But if two or more correspondents obtained a story and kept it from the others it was regarded as 'a carve-up' which would create very bad blood. We had several examples of scoops that backfired: the story could not be substantiated or was disproved by the course of events. This would lead to that most dreaded of cables from the office asking 'WHY YOUR EXCLUSIVE STILL EXCLUSIVE?'

Good contacts could sometimes prove an embarrassment. Over lunch in Salisbury one day, the deputy head of Ian Smith's Central Intelligence Organisation told me of a diplomatic mission to neighbouring Mozambique. He immediately added the dispiriting words

'But that's strictly off the record of course', meaning that I could not write a word about it. Unbeknown to me, James MacManus of *The Guardian* had been told the same thing by another member of the CIO who had imposed no such restriction. He filed his story while I was hamstrung by the rule of confidence.

There were correspondents who preferred to work entirely on their own, using their own contacts and disdaining any form of pack journalism. On the whole, they tended to be early members of the 'journalism of commitment' school. Their modus operandi was to attach themselves to one or other of Africa's charming but fraudulent 'statesmen', like Julius Nyerere of Tanzania or Kenneth Kaunda of Zambia, and obsequiously reflect their views, spurious ideologies and prejudices in their dispatches.

They were often received as personal guests in state houses in Lusaka and Dar es Salaam. They would fly in presidential aircraft to the innumerable conferences, 'summits' and other junkets so beloved of the continent's strongmen. Their copy would be invariably a thinly veiled rationale for the rhetoric of their hosts. Occasionally, of course, they would be fed genuine stories of moment – when it suited the proclivities or prejudices of their hosts. They were, fortunately, few in number and were known, with some justification, to the cynics of the Africa corps as 'The Apologists'.

More robust members of the corps, usually under a drink or two, would refer to one or other of the female members of this group as 'the world's greatest horizontal reporter'. An element of chauvinistic jealousy was doubtless the cause of such remarks, yet there is much evidence to suggest that some of the more winsome of our female colleagues were not beyond bestowing favours in influential African bedrooms to get to the nub of the story, so to speak.

The unequal advantages of our women colleagues was brought home to me in the port of Beira in pre-independence Mozambique. With several colleagues I had been trying for a week to secure an interview with an extremely wealthy Portuguese businessman whom we knew to have great influence on the political future of the country. He had flatly refused to see us or even answer our calls. He did not like the press, a haughty aide informed us, and had nothing to say to any *journalista*. One evening we were joined for supper by a lady colleague from an eminently respectable journal.

She was hardly prim but her reputation as a formidable competitor with a wide range of contacts throughout Africa seemed to preclude anything other than professional intercourse. And yet I noticed a twinkle in her eye as we got around to complaining about the inaccessible man. She emerged at the hotel a day later to inform us, quite casually, that her exclusive interview with Mr Big of Beira had appeared in her newspaper that morning. 'You just haven't got the right approach,' she told us, smilingly. Later she had the grace to admit that the subject had insisted on being 'interviewed' by her at 2 a.m. in his private villa.

At the other extreme, there were the few correspondents who fed shamelessly off the goodwill of the pack without ever stirring to contribute in any way. In the words of balladeer Tom Lehrer, they let no one's work 'evade their eyes...they plagiarise, plagiarise, plagiarise...'

This mercifully small contingent included a British correspondent who, for some reason, had affected a public school drawl and demeanour despite his very humble origins and his lowly status on the scurrilous tabloid for which he worked. I shall call him 'Jimson'. His day would start with a leisurely bath and late breakfast in the best hotel in town, followed by a couple of stiff aperitifs as soon as the bar opened. There he would waylay colleagues with an ingratiating smile and the casual question, 'Anything going on, old boy?' If this ploy failed to produce a line for his evening despatch, he would put in an appearance, after an afternoon nap and high tea, at whatever communications centre the pack was using at the time, shiftily moving from desk to desk to scan surreptitiously his colleague's copy emerging from the typewriter or telex machine. 'What's the word, old man?'

When the legendary Donald Wise of the *Daily Mirror* heard that 'Jimson' had arrived in a particularly troubled capital, he exploded: 'Jimson? Jimson?...the only bomb that will get Jimson will have to negotiate the swing doors of the nearest five-star hotel, catch the lift to the penthouse floor and explode under his bed at 11 a.m!' Keats immediately dubbed Jimson 'The Lavatory Rat'. As always the name caught on.

Keats was 'talking live' to a colleague on the telex machine to advise him on a good, upcoming story when his friend jokingly came back on the machine to say, 'Be careful...the lavatory rat is behind you'. Instinctively Keats looked around. Sure enough, there behind him and peering over his shoulder, was Jimson. 'Anything going on, old boy?'

The 'Jimsons' were harmless enough. A much more dangerous 'visiting fireman' was the correspondent who would drop in for a few days, talk to a few people and then leave for a neighbouring capital, or London, or New York, to file a 'definitive' piece on the situation in which confidences would be cheerfully broken, embargoes ignored, key figures misquoted and the sinister security police chief heavily libelled. Our butterfly colleague would, no doubt, be back at El Vino in Fleet Street boasting about his experiences in Amnezia while, back at the revolution, we would be hanging by our thumbs or toe-nails.

Some of the firemen – as the transient hacks sent out from home base were called – felt compelled to compete with the resident correspondents with vivid displays of imagination. One of these highly observant souls managed to spot the fact that an Angolan Mig which buzzed the airliner in which he was travelling was Cuban. When challenged by those who know that jet fighters buzzing an airliner are, at best, a streak of greased lightning, rarely even visible to the ordinary passenger, he explained that he had seen the pilot 'wearing a Castro hat and puffing a large cigar'.

Another fireman decided to treat his readers to a graphic description of a Congolese soldier, guarding the room in which he was being held briefly, 'masturbating violently while grinning at me lasciviously'. His colleagues, then and now, had never viewed him as being that exciting. Yet another who found his way through some 'dense African jungle' had been assisted by 'the gleam of tigers' eyes in the darkness'. Zoologists, after years of searching for an African tiger, finally deduced that our man had been on a different continent.

A couple of others were in constant receipt of 'top-secret documents' which had been made available to them by 'top-level sources' within minutes of their arrival in Xenophobia, or wherever. All this was a massive joke to their colleagues back in Africa but, amazingly, the copy of these make-it-up artists was frequently used by their newspapers, deadpan and unquestioned.

In general, though, African hands were a merry, sociable and adventurous bunch who tried to combine the job with enjoying themselves in the most unlikely locations once the story had been obtained and filed. There was rivalry, of course, particularly at the time when the then great Fleet Street newspapers like the *Daily Mail* and the *Daily Express* were in earnest and deadly competition to get their Man On The Spot first and his highly personalised file, preferably emphasising the great danger undergone to get there, on the front page, as fast as possible.

In that era, the first-person intro. – such as 'Last night I swam the crocodile-infested waters of the Blue Nile to reach the blood-stained rebel headquarters of the cannibal Baluba tribesmen...' became a stock-in-trade and a source of much African journalistic legend. As shall be seen, there were correspondents who did swim waters that were infested by crocodiles and, sometimes, sharks.

When they did so, it was more likely to be in the course of winning a post-prandial wager than in making the front page. There were few who braved tiger-infested jungles, possibly because true jungle, or rain forest, is found only in pockets of West Africa. If tackled about such travesties, our heroes would wink and say, 'Never let the facts get in the way of a good story, old man.'

Peter 'Bigfoot' Younghusband, a massive South African who worked for many years as the *Daily Mail*'s correspondent in Africa, would roar with laughter at his colleague's discomfort and rancour. Big Pete had been the subject of a parody in the *New York Times*, written by Anthony Lewis, who had 'exposed' the foreign correspondent in Africa and his misdemeanours and misrepresentations with a personal attack on a character he called, with American subtlety, 'Peter Oldwife'. I was lunching with Peter Webb, the erudite and distinguished *Newsweek* correspondent in Nairobi when Bigfoot joined us, fresh from a Sudanese expedition, to be shown Lewis's critique. Another roar of giant laughter from the big man.

He produced a photograph of himself flanked by enormous, spear-wielding warriors of the Dinka tribe, the ferocious Southern Sudanese people then, as now, in rebellion against a Muslim central regime in one of the ghastly post-colonial ethnic quilts stitched together by the British. The Dinkas made Peter, some 6' 7" tall with the build of a Springbok lock, look like an Australian jockey. 'I'll send Lewis this to show him just how intrepid the Oldwife tribe can be', Peter promised. And he did, but with no response from the distinguished American commentator who, as far as we knew, had never even stood on the banks of a crocodile-infested river, let alone plunged into one.

Younghusband could be a ruthless opponent in quest of a story. The stories of his exploits – and exploitation – are legion. He could also be the kindest, most courageous and most compassionate of friends and colleagues if he suspected that you were under threat or in trouble. I had met him a few years earlier in Aden where, on the first of many similar occasions to follow, we had crouched together in shelter from incoming machine-gun fire to question each other's motives for choosing such a career and to exchange, in the blackness and fear, our hopes and dreams of some idyllic rural retreat.

Later, in the relative safety of a bar or a hotel terrace, we would join other colleagues in outdoing each other with tales of our cowardice under fire. They were conversations that turned invariably to melancholy exchanges about the toll that a foreign hack's existence took on marriage and family life. I was learning the hard way, as

many colleagues had before and since, that being a foreign correspondent could have tragic side-effects, emotional and other.

Bigfoot Younghusband had given me an early lesson of just what
friendship can mean on a foreign assignment. In Aden, during the
humiliating and costly British retreat, my daily beat for *The Daily
Telegraph* had been disrupted by an urgent request from the *Sunday
Telegraph* for a feature on the South Arabian Army. It meant a full
day's trip in a four-wheel drive vehicle into the middle of the desert
and a long and dangerous haul back to Aden at night. I reached the
oasis of the Crescent Hotel's bar for a restorative tincture.

Younghusband and Steve Harper of the *Express* questioned me
suspiciously. Where had I been and why? I poured out the sorry tale
of my day's exploits, accompanied by the usual expletives about trying to satisfy two foreign desks at the same time. Satisfied that I
had not been trying to pull my own exclusive, Bigfoot reached into
his pocket and tossed to me a copy of a story he had filed to the *Mail*
earlier. By good old foot-in-the-door enterprise, he and Harper had
talked their way into a hospital to interview a young British soldier
who had been the sole survivor of a grisly massacre in the Crater
district a few days earlier. The hospital had been declared strictly
out of bounds by the British military authorities but these two old
hands had blustered their way in and had emerged with graphic
descriptions of what had happened.

'You'd better file it quickly,' said Younghusband. Brimming with
panic and gratitude I drove to the cable office and, loosely rewriting
his copy, made the first edition. My story earned me far greater
prominence in the *Telegraph* than Peter's original did in the *Mail*. I
received an undeserved 'herogram' – or message of congratulation
on my file. Back in Africa, I like to think I was able, on occasion, to
repay his generosity.

It was that kind of spirit that made the Africa corps of the time
the most congenial company in which to work. The faces were friendly, the combined experience educational and the cynical companionship great fun. The bonds were strengthened by the difficulties we
had in those days of getting in and out of different African countries,
of talking, cajoling or bribing our way through border posts and road
blocks, of improvising when there were no facilities, food or sometimes (God forbid!) booze. And, as always most important, no way of
communicating our copy, commentary and trenchant analyses to the
great outside world as personified by deskbound wallahs in London,
Paris, New York and Washington who, we always thought, would be
munching a sandwich in a cosy office muttering to the night editor:
'I've put a dozen calls in to him...he's probably on the piss again.'

Some desk-men have had foreign experience which is supposed to make them more sympathetic to your given plight. Some have not. It was just my luck to get, more often than not, the latter when the going got rough.

An Ethiopian airliner had just taken off from Addis Ababa's international airport en route to London when the gentlemen of the Eritrean Liberation Front whipped out their pistols and hand-grenades and attempted to hijack the plane. The passengers were outnumbered by Ethiopian security men who immediately drew their weapons to retaliate – at 18 000 feet. As the battle raged, the pilot managed brilliantly to bring the aircraft back to Addis airport for a safe landing, despite a couple of grenade holes in the fuselage, a few bodies in the gangway and a lot of disconcerted passengers, many of whom were British bird-watchers fresh from an exotic expedition. A great story. The trouble was that I was in Nairobi nursing a freshly expired Ethiopian visa.

'How quickly can you get back to Addis to interview these Brit bird-watchers, old boy?' Well, if I managed to get to my much-bribed friend at the Ethiopian embassy in Kenya on the morrow I might be able to get another visa by the end of the day which would mean I could catch the following day's flight to Addis. A long pause.

'We think you should pop up there by car, old boy. It's a good story.' I pointed out, as gently as I could, that to drive from Nairobi to Addis was to negotiate 700 miles of rough bush, desert and mountains and therefore might take a few days.

'Are you sure about that, old boy?' asked the deskman suspiciously. 'It doesn't look that far.'

He, of course, was looking at *The Daily Telegraph* Wall Map Of Africa which showed the distance to be no more than a couple of inches.

Following Page Clockwise: ⮕

The Novice explores Africa – The author (right) travels up the Blue Nile in 1969 with (left) Alan Gordon, then racing editor of the Daily Mirror *who happened to be the only man available when trouble erupted in the southern Sudan.*

Peter 'Bigfoot' Younghusband of the Daily Mail.

Michael Keats of UPI – the chief nicknamer of the Africa press corps.

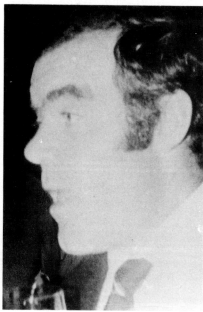

'This must be the wind of change' from left Peter Younghusband,
Daily Mail, John Monks, Daily Express, and Donald Wise, Daily
Mirror.

Angus McDermid
of the BBC, doyen
of the Genuine
Old Africa Hands.
He dictated his
stories in Welsh to
confound the
Nigerian
censors.

CHAPTER TWO

SONS OF SCOOP

Many Hollywood producers and not a few novelists have essayed caricatures of the 'typical' reporter, mostly without success. You could have scoured Fleet Street in vain for a shabby raincoat and battered trilby and the haunts of foreign correspondents would be unlikely to yield any James Bond-like figure. The fact is that there is no archetype for the breed. Journalism by its essence is a refuge of individuals. All human nature and form is to be found there.

Take, for instance, any given group of GOAHs assembled in the bar of Nairobi's Norfolk Hotel. There would be the long, the short and the tall. The burly chap with the broken nose and pug face is from *The Times* of London. His companion, the tall, elegantly dressed man with a military bearing and a fresh carnation in his buttonhole is from the tabloid *Daily Mirror*. The slightly built, bespectacled youngster, looking for all the world as if he has just started shaving, is full of shrapnel from five years of frontline coverage in Vietnam and Cambodia for *Time* magazine. He is sharing a joke with an elderly, ruddy-faced, bull-necked Canadian in a safari-suit – a veteran correspondent for *The Melbourne Age*. They are joined by a tall blonde, alluringly clad in tight denims and see-through blouse. She is with the *Christian Science Monitor*.

All would accord a warm and effusive greeting to the sprightly octogenarian who bounces into the bar with the confidence and gentlemanly demeanour of a born aristocrat. A chorus of 'What'll it be, Bill?' might give some indication that this could be Lord Deedes of Aldington, PC, MC, former Cabinet Minister, former Editor of *The Daily Telegraph* and, in his third career, a widely travelled and read columnist for that newspaper. Egregious he may appear, with pink socks peeping from half-mast trousers, but this is one of the longest surviving GOAHs.

Only if you tuned in to the conversations would you guess at their trade. (Unless, of course, they were joined by photographers whose need to carry dozens of items of equipment and rolls of film obliges them, almost to a man, to wear multi-pocketed fishing or combat jackets as a kind of uniform.) If you hoped to hear an exchange of erudition on the given political situation you would be disappointed. The talks would consist mainly of banter, bitching about the editors back on the desk and, as always, gossip.

The one word you would be unlikely to hear would be 'scoop', even if someone had beaten the rest of the pack with one. Very seldom do professional journalists use the word among themselves. When they do, it is usually emphasised with self-mockery. Outsiders who ask a reporter if he is looking for a scoop are regarded as patronising and pompous. Within the craft, 'exclusive' is acceptable but more often than not, a hack will boast of a story to his desk or colleagues: 'We've got it to ourselves.' I'm not sure why there should be such inhibition towards it. Perhaps it is because of its origins in dated American slang.

Where you will hear the word used by journalists – particularly foreign correspondents – with some respect it will be in reference to the title of the novel *Scoop* written by Evelyn Waugh in 1938. If Bill Deedes is in the group it is bound to crop up. As a young reporter for the *Morning Post* he was sent to cover the Italian invasion of Abyssinia in 1935 on which Waugh based his classic satire of Fleet Street. *Scoop*, Bill would agree, should be compulsory reading for any journalist thinking of volunteering for an African posting, or one in any other Third World region.

Waugh, a Roman Catholic convert, had been hired by the *Daily Mail* in 1935 to cover the invasion of Abyssinia, now Ethiopia. Son of a publisher and literary critic and author of several works of black comedy, Waugh had travelled extensively in Europe, the Middle East, Central America and Africa.

Scoop is a biting send-up of the foreign correspondent at work in Africa based on his own experiences in that still strange land as one of 'the pack'. He certainly had the measure of his colleagues, of Fleet Street and its proprietors, Ethiopia and its Emperor and Africa and its inhabitants. All this is evident in the novel, which was written only as fiction, thinly disguised fiction at that, to protect the author from the then – as now – fashionable libel actions against writers and journalists. His fictional country was 'Ishmaelia', quite clearly the then Empire of Abyssinia. His Fleet Street newspaper proprietor was 'Lord Copper', manifestly a parody of the late Lord Beaverbrook, the intrusive and abrasive Canadian owner of the *Daily Express,* a newspaper which is the closest we come to Waugh's *Daily Beast* in *Scoop*. Waugh's hero, or anti-hero as the

genre was later to become known, was William Boot, the rather
dotty offspring of an eccentric landed English family somewhere in
the shires. William eked out his generous living allowance by writing the weekly nature notes for the *Daily Beast:* 'Feather-footed
through the plashy fens passes the questing vole...' he was writing
when the summons came from Fleet Street to meet Lord Copper
himself. On the train to the metropolis he loathed, he worked out an
elaborate defence of a controversial note he had written about the
great crested grebe. Lord Copper was painted as an impetuous
tyrant. The nearest his staff would dare come to challenging him
was to mutter 'Up to a point, Lord Copper'. It was to remain a
phrase used frequently by hacks in and of conversations with their
ennobled proprietors. I used it on occasion in conversations with my
proprietor, Lord Hartwell, during periodic visits to London. It was
not that he was a tyrant. I simply could not understand his questions posed through an embarrassing, nervous stammer.

Back to Waugh's fiction. Lord Copper of the *Beast* had been
advised by a lady socialite of what she considered a great writing talent, one John Courteney Boot, an ambitious young man of letters. In
discussing with his foreign editor who the *Beast* was going to send to
the imminent crisis in Ishmaelia, Lord Copper remembered only the
surname 'Boot'. With classic Fleet Street bungling, it was William
Boot, he of the feather-footed vole inclination, who was sent to the
Ishmaelian front instead of James Courteney Boot, the 'writer' whose
character and background as described by Waugh resembles, as so
much else in the book, his own experiences. It was a brilliant, if not
original, literary device. The innocent, inexperienced and totally
unwilling nature correspondent suddenly finds himself competing
against the world's most famous – and notorious – war correspondents in a totally alien environment in what is clearly, though
unstated, Africa. He bumbles ingenuously through intrigues, political
machinations, corruption, squalor, lies, cheating, ignorance and
hilarious peer-group rivalry to find himself, inadvertently, with the
only real scoop of the war. He returns to London to a hero's welcome
but spurns Fleet Street fame for the plashy fens in the shires.

I first read *Scoop* as a schoolboy and found it very funny. I read
it for the second time in Addis Ababa while covering the 'creeping
coup' which led to the final – and very bloody – demise of Emperor
Haile Selassie of Ethiopia, Lion of Judah and King of Kings, and his
ramshackle empire in 1973.

Waugh's wonderful story had been based on his experiences as a
correspondent for the *London Daily Mail* in Addis Ababa in 1935. It
was still an amusing book, but tempered now by the realisation that

little had changed in those 38 years, either in the country or the conduct of the foreign correspondents and their editors.Waugh was
picked by the *Daily Mail* because he was one of the few writers
around who knew where Abyssinia was. He had been there before,
to cover the coronation of Haile Selassie for *The Times*. It was a ploy
hatched between himself and his publisher to persuade a Fleet
Street newspaper or two to sponsor his travelling and expenses to a
given spot where he would spend less time covering news and more
researching and preparing a couple of books – a novel and usually a
travelogue.

It had worked well in 1930. 'I had no fixed home and no possessions which would not conveniently go on a porter's barrow...now,
while I had the strength, I would go to the wild lands where man
had deserted his post and the jungle was creeping back to its old
strongholds. We turned our backs on civilization,' he was to write 15
years later. 'Had we known that all that seeming-solid, patiently
built, gorgeously ornamented structure of Western life was to melt
overnight like an ice-castle, leaving only a puddle of mud...we might
have lingered.' Since then, he wrote 'most of us had marched and
made camp, gone hungry and thirsty, lived where pistols are flourished and fired...at that time it seemed an ordeal, an initiation to
manhood'. Trenchant and prophetic words. They sum up, in a few
sentences, the motivation of many of the foreign correspondents who
were to follow Waugh to Africa and the abject misery, the 'puddle of
mud', to which most of that continent would be reduced in a short 50
years.

Abyssinians, particularly those who regarded themselves possessed of noble blood (long since spilled over the streets of Addis
Ababa), were loathe to regard themselves as Africans or even to
regard themselves as part of that dark and menacing continent.

The Empire of Ethiopia was remote, mystical and for the large
part pretty inaccessible to 19th-century travellers. Its ruling
Amharic people believed their ancestry was rooted in the Bible.
Indeed its Emperors, according to its early constitutions, were
descended directly from the union of Solomon and Sheba. One of the
titles assumed by Haile Selassie, who first ascended to power in
1916 as regent was 'Elect of God'.

It was an ancient Christian empire, originally based on the now
ruined city of Axum and, to European eyes, a romantic, isolated 'civilization' which, in the Middle Ages, had given rise to such legends
as those which had the legendary kingdom of Prester John located
in the misty highlands on the tableland of the Abyssinian plateau.
The power and wealth of the ruling Amharas resided in the influ-

ence of Coptic Christianity and its elaborate network of monasteries and shrines and the total awe with which its emperors were endowed through a system of patriarchal dispensation and aristocratic patronage. Little wonder that writers like Waugh were attracted to the place. Its bizarre rituals, its perpetuation of slavery while insisting on the maintenance of its ancient Christian traditions, its very remoteness must have been irresistible to young English writers of cynical bent. Waugh accepted both his publisher's suggestion and the ready cash put up by *The Times* and another Fleet Street newspaper to sponsor his visit to Addis Ababa in 1930 to cover the coronation of Haile Selassie as Emperor of Ethiopia. In his 'Remote People' Waugh recalls a weekend in a manor in Ireland. 'One of the party was on leave from Cairo; he knew something of the coming coronation. Further information was contributed from less reliable sources; that the Abyssinian church had canonised Pontius Pilate, and consecrated their bishops by spitting on their heads; that the real heir to the throne was hidden in the mountains, fettered with chains of solid gold; that the people lived on raw meat and mead; we looked up the royal family in the Almanach de Gotha and traced their descent from Solomon and the Queen of Sheba; we found a history which began: "The first certain knowledge which we have of Ethiopian history is when Cush ascended to the throne immediately after the Deluge." Another reference informed the company that "though nominally Christian, the Abyssinians are deplorably lax in their morals, polygamy and drunkenness being common even among the highest classes in the monasteries."'

Within weeks, Waugh had arranged his sponsorship and was making his way to Abyssinia by the then only viable route: he caught a boat train to Marseilles and boarded a small but jolly steamer which navigated the Mediterranean to Port Said, the Suez Canal and thence to Aden and Djibouti in French Somaliland. A rather erratic three-day railway journey followed from Djibouti to Addis Ababa, winding from the steaming coastal lowlands to the heights of the Ethiopian plateau and, eventually to the capital. It was a trip he was to make, with dozens of other foreign correspondents, five years later for the Italian invasion of Haile Selassie's empire.

That railway journey, amusing if the passenger was possessed of a sense of humour, was a slow but romantic and rather glamorous introduction to the Abyssinia of the 1930s. It remained so for many years.

Robin Stafford of the *Daily Express*, inspired by Waugh's early descriptions but frustrated by the railway authorities' inability to grasp the urgency of his mission, hired the entire engine and rolling stock to get him to Addis Ababa to cover one of the many attempted coups d'état against Haile Selassie in 1960. John Osman, the bouncing, perennial Boy Scout roving reporter for the BBC and his intrepid wife, Virginia, a first-class journalist in her own right, felt they had to 'take the Djibouti train' to Addis 15 years later, even though an airliner would have got them there far more quickly. Stafford and the Osmans have admitted that their decision to travel the rail route was inspired by the nostalgic desire to follow the traditional journalistic route of Evelyn Waugh and his colleagues.

Waugh attended the colourful but comic coronation of Haile Selassie in 1930 to record his observations not only in *Remote People* but, more memorably in *Black Mischief,* one of his first satirical novels of some mythical African empire. It was not that mythical. It was based clearly on his first experiences in Abyssinia. He deployed the licence that many of his colleagues to follow him, in Ethiopia as well as the rest of Africa, were to imitate in various ways. Waugh's descriptions of his African experiences, factual and fictional, were to reflect and echo, uncannily, my own and those of many of my colleagues in the demented decades that were to follow.

Take his description of Addis Ababa in 1930. 'Addis Ababa is a new town; so new, indeed, that not a single piece of it appears to be really finished...at every corner were half-finished buildings; some had already been abandoned; on others gangs of ragged Guraghi were at work.' It was the same in 1970 and again in 1980 and, no doubt, in 1990. The city is scattered over hills and ridges with groves of eucalyptus trees, the exotic Australian blue gums, breaking up the bleak skylines. The old imperial palaces and the latter-day additions like the ghastly Addis Hilton Hotel stand in what seems to be deliberate contrast to the sprawling mountainside shacks and huts in which the vast majority of the population live – and attempt to scratch a living. A great source of income for these miserable families was child prostitution. Addis, at one fairly recent time, could boast more child prostitutes than any other capital on earth. Suffering and poverty were as endemic to Abyssinia then as they are to 'modern' Ethiopia today. Waugh did not record any prostitutes in 1930 but lepers, eunuchs and slaves were in abundance.

It was his experience at the Emperor's coronation – rather than his journalistic flair – which persuaded the *Daily Mail* to hire him to cover the impending war with Italy in 1935. Literature, not journalism, was to be the beneficiary of his presence.

Italy had been Europe's loser in the carve-up of Africa which followed the First World War. There was rumoured to be a secret treaty promising Rome economic and other control of Abyssinia, and Mussolini had furtively furthered his ambitions in Africa by signing a treaty of friendship with Haile Selassie in 1928. It was his design to use some spurious breach of this treaty as a pretext to go to war.

In Addis Ababa, where great pride resided in the fact that it was one of the few African countries that had never been subjected to European colonisation, the treaty was regarded with disdain, something more to do with European politics than with African realities. In any case, Abyssinia was a member of the League of Nations which had guaranteed its territorial integrity and lulled its government into a false sense of security. When Mussolini announced his intention of 'reasserting his rights' in Abyssinia, the Emperor cheerfully and half-heartedly prepared for a war he thought the League of Nations would prevent.

In the United States, most of Europe and Britain in particular, the sympathy lay with the Emperor and his mystic but primitive 'civilisation'. Mussolini had already established himself as a bully and a braggart and his swaggering designs on this remote corner of Africa made him few friends. Italy shipped in helmeted troops, guns and armour to the African coast while Haile Selassie's men were pictured preparing themselves in the hills, barefooted with daggers and spears and building lion-pits to trap the unsuspecting invaders. This romantic vision of the impending war was quickly picked up in Fleet Street and other newspaper centres. Editors vied with each other to pick the right correspondent for the job.

There was an appalling lack of information about Abyssinia, its history, demography and climate in newspaper offices. Evelyn Waugh wrote that few editors could find the country on the map or had the faintest idea of its character. George Deakin, the admirably honest Foreign Editor of *The Times*, wrote to his correspondent, George Steer, 'There is little known about this dispute and even we must admit to our deficiency in this area.' At least one Fleet Street editor thought the inhabitants spoke classical Greek. Others, depending on what few travel books on the area were extant, thought that there were ancient palaces built on glaciers or in caves or on trackless, waterless plains below sea level. Correspondents were duly kitted out.

George Steer of *The Times* and O'Dowd Gallagher of the *Daily Express* were chosen as putative war correspondents for Abyssinia because they were South Africans and were thus deemed to have 'some knowledge of the terrain'. (Addis Ababa is closer to London than to Cape Town.) Stuart Emeny of the *News Chronicle,* whose zeal and industry as a reporter Waugh found a 'standing reproach',

wore silk pyjamas under his clothes, his editor having advised him
that such a precaution would prevent typhus. Emeny, according to
Waugh, also carried with him an iodine pencil with which he painted flea bites and scratches 'so that he soon presented a somewhat
macabre piebald spectacle.'

Waugh himself, despite his brief experience of Abyssinia,
indulged himself in London's tropical outfitters at the expense of the
Daily Mail. 'I trod miasmic pavements between cartographers and
consulates. In the hall of my club, a growing pile of packing cases,
marked for Djibouti, began to constitute a serious inconvenience to
the other members. There are few other pleasures more complete, or
to me more rare, than that of shopping extravagantly at someone
else's expense. I thought I had treated myself with reasonable generosity until I saw the luggage of my professional competitors –
their rifles and telescopes and ant-proof trunks, medicine chests,
gas-masks, pack saddles and vast wardrobes of costume suitable for
every conceivable social or climatic emergency.' All this, Waugh
later admits with admirable if cynical honesty, gave him an inkling
'of what later became abundantly clear to all, that I did not know
the first thing about being a war correspondent.' The weekly steamers out of Marseilles to Djibouti via Port Said in the summer of 1935
were ferrying a motley crew of correspondents in response to
rumour of war in Africa – Waugh, Emeny and a correspondent for
'the most important newspaper in Spain' who boasted of his
revolver, snake-proof boots and his lengthy dispatches composed
from his own translation of a history of Africa in German. Also on
board was a British businessman, Bill Rickett, also bound for Addis
Ababa. Rickett was to provide a couple of correspondents with the
only real scoop of the Abyssinian misadventure – one which was
missed by both Waugh and Emeny.

Ahead of them, already in Addis, were O'Dowd Gallagher for
the *Daily Express* and Noel Monks, an adventurous young Australian freelance journalist who took his chances on this promising
war story with only ten pounds in his pocket. George Steer, the
other South African, was the only other correspondent who had
reached Addis first. To Monks and Gallagher's amazement, the only
conveniently central hotel, The Imperial, was fully booked. Rooms
were reserved for such experienced old hands as Hearst newspaper's
famous H R 'Red' Knickerbocker and Sir Percival Phillips of *The
Daily Telegraph* due on the next fast packet out of Marseilles.

Monks recalled: 'We, of course, hadn't booked; hadn't even
thought about it and right there I learnt lesson number one on the
logistics side of being a foreign correspondent.' The Greek proprietor

of The Imperial put up the two disgruntled colonials in a 'converted' stable. 'It couldn't have been long converted, for donkeys and cows kept homing there every night,' wrote Monks. Apart from their unwelcome companions, Monks and Gallagher were to be disturbed by nocturnal drumbeats and the roaring of the Emperor's caged lions 'twenty of them, in rows of ten, in the palace driveway'.

Back in London, another young Englishman was preparing for his first assignment as a war correspondent in Ethiopia. W F 'Bill' Deedes, a 22-year-old reporter for the *Morning Post* and scion of an old and very distinguished landowning family in Kent, had been selected by his editor, H A Gwynne, as their man for Abyssinia.

'I didn't volunteer. I suppose as I was young and unmarried my insurance policy would have been lower than others. The *Post* had made it clear that it was the kind of war you might get into without being able to get out of.' Gwynne had been a war correspondent himself – with Winston Churchill in South Africa – and had three pieces of advice for Deedes: to remember he represented the *Morning Post* and therefore to kit himself well out at the best outfitters before leaving, to remember that 'a dead correspondent is of no value at all' and therefore to take no unnecessary risks and to ensure 'a finger of whisky at the bottom of a water bottle to destroy the microbes'.

His proprietor, Edward Russell, wished him Godspeed in a note and added, 'If the Emperor tells you – as he told me years ago – that the London policemen are marvellous you needn't bother to cable it.' Deedes took the first piece of advice very seriously and went on a five-day shopping spree. A leading London outfitter supplied a zinc-lined cedar trunk with his name engraved on the lid. It had compartments for uniforms. This was then crammed with about half-a-ton of clothing and kit to cater for what the shop assistants thought might be any Abyssinian contingency. There were three pairs of riding breeches (thick, heavy duty), three pairs of riding breeches (thin, tropical), a solar topee, a dozen bush shirts, cleft sticks, a double-brimmed terai (described on the label as a hat for white gentlemen travelling in the subtropics) and a medicine chest supplied by what Bill Deedes describes as 'the medicine man at the Army and Navy stores'.

This gentleman, unlike many Fleet Street editors at the time, knew that the train journey from Djibouti to Addis involved an overnight stop at a place called Awash which was in the middle of a malarial swamp. 'He assured me that all the mosquitoes in East Africa held a permanent convention there. I was therefore equipped with enormous quantities of quinine tablets. I remember that I swallowed enough of these things to turn me almost deaf. My hearing has been affected to this day,' Deedes recalled some 55 years later. Unlike other correspondents, however, the young Deedes did not catch malaria or any other of the unpleasant afflictions that hit some of his colleagues. Wilfred Barber, of the *Chicago Tribune,* was the only press casualty of the Abyssinian campaign. He died of kidney failure brought on by successive bouts of malaria, blackwater fever and pneumonia. Several others succumbed to severe disease and illness, much of which derived from malaria.

The young Deedes, heavily laden but shrewd enough to have acquired that most important piece of equipment – the only extant, modern map of Abyssinia – sailed on the SS *General Metzinger* from Marseilles in August 1935. His excitement, enjoyment and the inevitable frustrations of this, his first foreign assignment, are clearly reflected in the regular letters he wrote to his mother and to his foreign editor. Showing those admirable qualities of enterprise and use of contacts (his family had provided him with an introduction to the Chief of Police in Port Said where the ship docked), Deedes filed a story about Italian war materiel being shipped to East Africa.

The Suez Canal was 'interesting but infernally hot...camels and mirages and things all over the place'. But fellow journalists from six nations had boarded at Port Said, including 'the American writer Knickerbocker', and 'life is much brighter with Fleet Street chaps on board'. Like Evelyn Waugh on an earlier ship, Deedes found his foreign colleagues on their way to Addis most amusing. His German friend collapsed with sea-sickness. His Spanish colleague had to travel third-class 'where the heat is positively unspeakable' and the Japanese war correspondent 'skips hither and thither with little dictionaries translating all our conversations mentally into native tongue'. The Japanese correspondent plied steadily away at a diet of grapes and iced water but eventually passed out on deck from heat exhaustion. Bill helped to revive him but could only agree with his groggy assertion that it was 'Verra, verra hort'.

The largely young press corps on board the *General Metzinger* was also entertained by a Mr Glass of Cable and Wireless, an old imperial hand who regaled the journalists with horror stories of travel in the tropics. 'He makes us drink lemon juice until sundown when he insists on one large whisky and soda and one before going to bed. I shan't easily forget his face when one slightly ignorant and thirsty journalist ordered a whisky at tea-time. 'Drinkin' before sundown? Dammit, sir. Silly thing to do.'

Glass went on to recall 'a feller Aden way' who drank whisky at breakfast, a good rugby player though who nonetheless had died an early death. Despite the heat, the young Deedes developed what was to become a long life's devotion to golf.

'Our main occupation when it's not too hot is deck golf. None of the French or other foreign species play any game at all so we have the sports deck all to ourselves.'

Deedes, plus zinc-lined trunk, landed at Djibouti, 'a frightful spot', in 110 degrees in the shade. He was luckier with the famous train as Red Knickerbocker and his colleague, Carl von Weigan, of Hearst Newspapers, bought up a wagon-lit. 'We had the only private compartment on the train and brought with us two dozen bottles of iced Vichy in huge thermos flasks. So while the others got reduced to a pretty bad state elsewhere we were pretty comfortable.' At the stop at Awash, he didn't even see a mosquito, let alone be troubled by one. As the train wound its way up the escarpment towards Addis the scenery was 'not so different from Switzerland, only on a bigger scale and bits of it really queer.'

Deedes was met at Addis Ababa's railway station by Emeny, Waugh and Patrick Balfour, the *Evening Standard* correspondent, who whisked him to the Deutsches Haus, a pension alongside the overbooked Hotel Imperial. The Deutsches Haus, despite its name, was run by another 'grasping Greek'. It was to be their home for the next few, rather bizarre, months.

Devotees of *Scoop* will recognise Waugh's description of this establishment as the 'Pension Dressler' as they will acknowledge Waugh's reception of Deedes when he unpacked his zinc-lined cedar trunk. Probably the idea of the hapless William Boot of the *Daily Beast* in *Scoop* was formed in Waugh's mind with the arrival of the young Deedes. He joined Waugh and Emeny in their hilarity as he unpacked his half-ton of provisions and equipment for 'tropical emergencies' and spread them over the floor of his room at the Deutches Haus.

'Addis Ababa is at some 10 000 feet above sea level and that September it was singularly chilly,' recalled Deedes. 'Happily, I had started my journey in a thick suit for which I was very grateful. I wore it for most of the time in Addis.'

Even more elaborate were the supplies imported by the Fox-Movietone film crew (satirised in the novel as the 'Excelsior Move-Sound Expeditionary Unit To The Ishmaelite Ideological Front'). This team had brought an inexhaustible supply of cleft sticks and a folding canoe. Fox-Movietone's correspondent, Laurence Stalling, imported a large Red Indian motorcycle with a sidecar. He hoped this would get him to 'the front' but he succeeded only in terrorising the denizens of the capital. Ernest Hemingway had been responsible

in part for the overadequate supplies of the American correspondents. He had warned them before they left that Abyssinian vultures would 'peck out your eyes before devouring your livers'.

As it was, the only hazards encountered by the correspondents
in those early days in Abyssinia were those on the streets of Addis.
Legations and ministries were scattered over the range of hills on
which the city is built. To get around, Deedes hired an enormous
Chrysler saloon with a Sikh driver.

'A drive through Addis is just a nightmare,' he wrote to his family. 'They don't much mind killing natives here with motor cars and as
for dogs and cattle, it's not a good day unless you hit one.'

One wet day, Deedes' driver 'knocked an Ethiop for several
sixes'. A policeman arrived at the scene and apologised to the *Morning Post* correspondent 'for all the trouble caused to white man'.
Deedes wrote: 'It will, I fancy, be much safer when war starts and
we leave Addis.'

For most of the correspondents, there was to be no war coverage
– and not much travel beyond the capital. The Abyssinian authorities, politely but firmly, made it clear early on that they were quite
happy to have the correspondents spending large sums of money in
Addis Ababa but were not going to allow them anywhere near the
'front' wherever and whenever there was going to be one.

The hacks convinced themselves that Mussolini would launch
his offensive with a bomb and gas attack on Addis itself. Some of the
more nervous bribed themselves access to bomb shelters in the outskirts of town or slept with gas masks beside their beds. The wily
'Ethiops' had realised that this motley, wildly eccentric bunch of
Europeans had seemingly unlimited funds which they would lavish
on anyone who might help them with the two things they most needed – information and a means of getting it out.

Many African capitals were due to experience similar influxes
during the next fifty years. Many dubious pockets were to be lined
in remote corners – and, of course, detailed on equally dubious
expense sheets which were to infuriate foreign editors and bemuse
accountants for generations to come. In Abyssinia, as anywhere else,
the foreign correspondent is only as good as his communications. It
is axiomatic that the most sensational story in the world is useless
unless the correspondent can get it to his newspaper (or these days
his studio or satellite feed). Thus the more experienced correspondents arriving in Addis Ababa in 1935 lost little time in finding the
cable office and making themselves known to the staff. The wireless
station in Addis was, like most other official buildings in the capital,
a ramshackle affair which worked intermittently and whimsically.

It was, however, the only link between Addis and the outside world and the hacks were stuck with it.

The first shock they got was the charge per word: half-a-crown for the 'express rate' by which they all had to file. When Noel Monks came to send a dispatch to his native Melbourne, the charge was five shillings and sixpence a word. 'Haile Selassie was also emperor of the radio station,' Monks recalled bitterly. 'He owned it. From our dispatches to the world's newspapers totalling millions of words, the little dignified emperor collected a tidy fortune with which to while away his exile in Britain.'

In an attempt to cut costs, the correspondents abbreviated and codified their messages into a language known as 'cablese'. 'As long as', for instance, became 'Slongs' – meaning one paid 2s 6d for the one word instead of 7s 6d for the three. Forms of cablese had been in use since the late 19th century but the Addis press corps in 1935 refined it to a fine art.

The bemused Abyssinian operators, already trying to tap out thousands of words in a dozen foreign tongues, found the cablese of the English-speaking correspondents even more confusing. As a result, many dispatches arriving in London and New York were unintelligible.

Ralph Deakin, the foreign editor of *The Times*, wrongly blamed the influence of the American foreign correspondents for the strange new language. Cablese, however, was to remain a standard part of the foreign correspondents' repertoire for several decades. It remained in use, as a tradition, in messages between offices and correspondents in the field until the 1980s. It also provided journalism with some of its funniest and most legendary exchanges. My favourite (not to Abyssinia, although it might just as well have been) was the message from an impatient editor demanding 'WHEN WAR OUTBREAK LIKELY?' which elicited from a tired and emotional correspondent the reply 'MY BALLS UNMADE CRYSTAL!'

In Addis Ababa, the system of distributing incoming messages was even more haphazard. The wireless office would accumulate enough incoming messages to justify sending a messenger to the Hotel Imperial where they would be solemnly handed over to the first European he met for distribution. Inevitably this method led to the contents of any given message becoming known to all other newspapermen – and to many others, including the authorities. Inevitably, too, it led to numerous practical jokes among the assembled hackery. One, played by O'Dowd Gallagher on his fellow South African, George Steer, backfired. Gallagher slipped a fake message into the bundle purporting to be signed by Lord Astor, then proprietor of *The Times*.

'NATION PROUD OF YOUR WORK STOP CARRY ON IN NAME OF KING AND COUNTRY', it read. The message was also intercepted by palace staff who were so impressed that the Emperor invited Steer for a private audience, an exclusive interview and gave him a free run of all his ministries.

Each train that chugged up from the coast brought a new batch of correspondents, as well as the assortment of adventurers, mercenaries, confidence tricksters and spies that ritually attend any rumour of war. Waugh recorded a Sudanese travelling on a Brazilian passport and supposedly working for a Brazilian newspaper, a monocled Latvian colonel who had been a circus ring-master and a German who travelled under the name of 'Haroun al Raschid'. His head was completely hairless; his wife shaved it for him, emphasising 'the frequent slips of her razor with tufts of cotton wool'.

A rag-bag of would-be 'spies', interpreters, informants and rumour-mongers gathered at Addis station to waylay the incoming pressmen and tout their services. Some of these 'Armenian spies and others of like kidney', as Bill Deedes described them, occasionally provided reliable information. Most did not. All charged handsomely for their 'services'. Unbeknown to his closest colleagues, Waugh hired his own 'spy', a seemingly well-informed Abyssinian named Wazir Ali Bey. He paid him handsomely – until he discovered that Ali Bey was also 'secretly' in the pay of most other correspondents in town.

By the end of September, there were about 100 correspondents in Addis Ababa, crammed into every available hotel room and clamouring at government offices for 'news'. Each had to go through an absurd ritual of 'accreditation' at a little tin shack at the end of the main street which was proclaimed the 'Press Bureau'. 'Here morning and afternoon for the first six weeks, until everyone, even its organisers, despaired of it ever performing any helpful function, might be found a dozen or so exasperated journalists of both sexes and almost all nationalities,' Waugh wrote. The nominal head – never seen in the Press Bureau – was the 'suave, beady-eyed Dr Lorenzo Taesas' who was also head of the secret police, a judge of the special court and a personal adviser to the Emperor. Dr Lorenzo became in *Scoop* the scheming 'Dr Benito'.

Noel Monks was luckier. He and O D Gallagher were actually sought out at the Imperial by an English-educated Abyssinian foreign office official. When he learned that Monks had no strings, he handed over a sheaf of cables from newspapers around the world asking for assistance in finding a correspondent. Soon Monks had seven busy and lucrative strings.

As the weeks dragged on with no outbreak of hostilities, newspapers became increasingly shrill in their demands for local colour, background – anything in fact to justify the cost of having Our Man in Abyssinia. The *Daily Mail* finally aroused Evelyn Waugh from his sick-bed (he was suffering from mild dysentery) with a series of cables on the lines of 'REQUIRE COMPREHENSIVE CABLE GOOD COLOURFUL STUFF' and 'PLEASE INDICATE WHEN CAN EXPECT COMPREHENSIVE CABLE'. Fitter correspondents like Bill Deedes amused themselves by riding the surrounding hills on horses rented (for half the sum of one cabled word to London) by the day, seeking out the remaining caviare and pâté de foie gras in Italian shops and acquiring pet monkeys.

Deedes, in fact, was determined to enjoy himself to the full. When an invitation arrived to attend a banquet at the palace, Bill retrieved from the bottom of his half-ton trunk black tie and tails. He was the only correspondent properly dressed for the occasion 'although I failed to cut the dash I had hoped as the lights kept going out during the meal'. The Hotel Imperial press corps over-indulged on the Emperor's tej – a foul but potent Abyssinian concoction – and later found themselves locked into their rooms. The hypochondriacal Stuart Emeny of the *News Chronicle* 'forgot himself so far as to throw a rock through the Imperial window'.

Deedes persuaded Waugh from his bed to join him for some wine in a night club. They were approached by a lady called Esmé Barton, daughter of the head of the British Legation in Addis, Sir Sidney Barton. Without saying a word, she picked up a glass of wine and dashed the contents in Waugh's face. According to Deedes 'Esmé evidently thought that Waugh had used her as the character of Prudence in *Black Mischief* and resented being portrayed as a tart'. Esmé's resentment did not extend to other pressmen. She later married George Steer, *The Times* correspondent.

On his own admission, Waugh regarded the business of news-gathering with absolute disdain and the antics of his colleagues as wonderful grist for the novelist's mill. There was so much material, as evidenced by *Scoop*.

His character Sir Jocelyn Hitchcock, who, in the novel, invents a massacre in a remote city in Ishmaelia, is a precise portrait of the distinguished Sir Percival Phillips, the *Telegraph*'s man in Addis in 1935. Sir Percival had been knighted for his services as a war correspondent in World War I. In Addis Ababa, he had pre-booked at the Hotel Imperial the best room from which he rarely emerged. He worked in tandem with one of the most formidable agency reporters of the time, Jim Mills of Associated Press, known to his colleagues as the 'silver fox' because of his silver hair and professional cunning. Between them they hired a team of six of the most reliable 'spies' who reported to them regularly.

This joint operation produced a steady flow of colourful and informative copy which had the rest of the correspondents running around in desperation. O D Gallagher received a daily stream of 'call-backs' from the *Daily Express*: 'PHILLIPS IN *TELEGRAPH* SAYS ABYSSINIAN SPEARSMEN MASSING ON TIGRE FRONT STOP WHAT FOLLOW UP EXYOU' and 'PHILLIPS DESCRIBES HAILE SELASSIE SQUARE AS PICCADILLY CIRCUS OF ADDIS STOP THIS GREAT STUFF STOP LETS HAVE YOUR COMPAR-ISONS HAILE SELASSIES CAPITAL WITH LONDON' and finally, in desperation, from his foreign editor: 'BEG YOU EMULATE PHILLIPS STOP YOUR LACK CABLES MOST DISCONCERTING STOP NOT ONLY YOUR JOB BUT MINE AT STAKE SAYS CHRISTIANSEN [Arthur Christiansen, the editor] BECAUSE EYE SENT YOU ABYSSINIA.'

Gallagher knew full well that *The Daily Telegraph* man was exercising his fertile imagination from the fastness of his hotel suite. He and Monks, using a little colonial cunning of their own, established that much of Phillips' colour was being filched from an early travel book called *In the Country of the Blue Nile* by Colonel C F Rey.

They borrowed the book and, using the good Colonel's descrip-tions of the interior, sent some imaginative dispatches of their own. Gallagher finally received the accolade he had waited for: 'PHILLIPS BRILLIANT IN *TELEGRAPH* BUT YOU EXCEL HIM STOP KEEP IT UP'. Despite this jolly rivalry, there was little acri-mony among the correspondents. Sir Percival remained the respect-ed and beloved doyen of the press corps, so much so that when he got the only genuine scoop of the Abyssinian war his young col-leagues threw a lavish dinner party for him.

The fun and games came to an abrupt halt when, on October 2nd, the Italian forces under General Emilio de Bono, launched their offensive from Italian Somaliland. Webb Miller of United Press, one of two correspondents who had made the unfashionable choice of covering the war from the Italian side, broke the news to the world in a six-word cable. Soon Asmara was besieged with as motley and diverse a crew of international reporters as Addis had been some six weeks earlier.

Initially, they fared little better than their colleagues on the other side. The Italians imposed strict military censorship. General de Bono told correspondents: 'I don't like newspapermen or the

press but I suppose we will have to get along with each other.'
Matthews recalled that 'the stupid censorship, bad living conditions,
the altitude, the crazy climate, the strain on the heart, lungs and
nerves, all combined to create a colony of half-mad correspondents
rushing frantically about in a state of chronic hysteria.' Despite the
restrictions imposed by the Italians it was obvious to Webb and
other correspondents in Asmara that Mussolini's drilled and mechanised forces would quickly overwhelm the Emperor's eager but ill-
trained tribal forces. What price antiquated firearms, spears,
shields and lion-pits against tanks and bombers? But this was an
unpopular view in New York and London. Newspapers loved the
romantic notion of a beleaguered feudal Emperor repelling from his
mystical mountain kingdom the brutal might of an unpopular European fascist. Besides, the glamourised, not to say fictional, accounts
emanating from Sir Percy Phillips' bedroom at the Hotel Imperial
were a much better read than the stunted, censored reports coming
from Asmara.

In Addis Ababa, most correspondents, despite the frustrations,
had become emotionally involved with the Emperor and his cause.
Bill Deedes, in a letter to his family three weeks after the Italian
offensive, wrote: 'Sooner or later Mussolini is going to take a frightful crack from these people, and that perhaps will put him more in
the mood for negotiating. I will lay five pounds to a thaler (the
Abyssinian currency) that he mucks himself up completely and
takes a crashing hiding from the Ethiops on one front or another.
They have it waiting for him.' So committed had the Addis press
corps become to the Emperor's cause that they took the extraordinary and unprecedented step of suggesting to the authorities that
some form of military censorship be imposed on their dispatches.

Noel Monks attempted to explain the move: 'The very hopeless-
ness of Abyssinia's plight won one's natural sympathy so that one
would have to be very hard-baked indeed not to have any private
feelings about it...naturally we were assessing in our dispatches the
chances of Abyssinia should it come to a shooting war...all Italian
intelligence officers had to do was to read their newspapers.' The
correspondents got their censor – but he could read only French. 'In
a body we went to the Emperor, feeling so cross that we snarled
back at the lions as we passed between the cages...we obtained an
English-speaking censor, too, though we had to educate him on just
what was security.'

The one correspondent in Addis who not only saw the futility of
the Abyssinian cause but had undisguised sympathy for Mussolini
and his designs was, of course, Evelyn Waugh. (In 1935 the odium

attached to such sympathy was not as great as it was to become within a few years, so much so that many of Waugh's pro-Mussolini sentiments were excised from his travelogue *Waugh in Abyssinia.*)

The *Daily Mail* man found the demands of Fleet Street 'more and more fantastically inappropriate to the situation'. Waugh's spy-cum-interpreter, Wazir Ali Bey, fed daily reports to his clients of the heavy casualties being suffered by the Italians. 'Wazir Ali Bey's news service formed an ever-increasing part of the morning reading of French, English and American newspaper publics.' At this point, Waugh and most other correspondents were smarting from having missed the one major scoop of the Abyssinian campaign. It had been staring him in the face since he boarded the steamer at Marseilles. One of his fellow passengers, also on his way to Addis Ababa, was an English businessman named F W 'Bill' Rickett. Waugh mentally dismissed him as an arms dealer but found him a congenial travelling companion with whom to while away many convivial hours. No such illusions about Rickett were harboured by Sir Percival Phillips and the wily Jim Mills. They watched Rickett like a hawk, checking his background and his credentials and pumping him at every opportunity.

They were soon rewarded. Rickett was representing major American oil interests and was negotiating directly with the Emperor for an exclusive contract to prospect over vast tracts of Abyssinia, including land which the Italians would have to traverse in the course of their invasion. The international implications of such a deal were staggering. It would have put America in direct conflict with Italy and put a totally different complexion on the Emperor's chances of survival. When Sir Percy's story appeared in the *Telegraph,* swiftly followed by Mills's AP dispatch, the wires hummed between Washington, London and Paris. The deal was swiftly killed after urgent consultations between the three governments at the highest level.

If the diplomatic wires hummed, the press wires sang out loud. Every other newspaper and wire service in the world wanted to know why their man had not got the story and demanded immediate follow-ups. But they had been beaten fairly and squarely and they knew it, none more so than Waugh. He had been upcountry in Harar when the story broke, only to receive a cable from the *Mail* demanding 'BADLY LEFT OIL CONCESSION STOP SUGGEST YOUR RETURN ADDIS IMMEDIATELY'.

Waugh was already in bad odour with the *Mail* who were making arrangements to replace him. He was typically unconcerned, with good reason. The Rickett concession – the sensational story that should have been his from the start – was to form the basis for the plot of *Scoop*, a novel that has been reprinted more than 30 times since it was first published in 1938. The first Abyssinian communiqué of the war asserted that the first Italian bomb had destroyed 'the hospital at Adowa' killing many women and children. It was assiduously filed by most of the correspondents and given due prominence as an Italian atrocity by their newspapers. From the start Waugh, who knew the country better than most of his colleagues, was sceptical. He soon established that there wasn't, and never had been, a hospital at Adowa. When the *Daily Mail* demanded of him 'REQUIRE EARLIEST NAME LIFE STORY PHOTOGRAPH AMERICAN NURSE UPBLOWN ADOWA' he took great delight in cabling back 'NURSE UNUPBLOWN'.

The correspondents, who had been effectively confined to Addis since they arrived two months earlier, now began to agitate furiously to get to the fighting. There were two fronts – to the north and south – but the problem for the hacks was not which one to choose but to persuade the Abyssinians to allow them to leave town. The Emperor, or rather Dr Lorenzo, had calculated, probably correctly, that there were numerous spies among the foreign press. Apart from which some correspondents might just be able to establish that the communiqués put out by the Press Bureau bore absolutely no relation to the truth. The correspondents were only partially assuaged by promises that the Emperor would shortly be heading towards the northern front to bolster the morale of his warriors at Dessye. The foreign press would, of course, be invited to accompany him.

Haile Selassie's visit was repeatedly postponed, causing intense frustration among the correspondents. Waugh, sublimely indifferent to attempts by the *Mail* to recall him, decided with Deedes and Emeny to 'proceed frontwards' on their own. They acquired a truck, a driver, some retainers, a tent and provisions and sneaked out of the capital at 4 a.m. on the road to Dessye.

Aware that the authorities would alert officials to be on the lookout for unauthorised Europeans on the road, our three distinguished correspondents hid under a tarpaulin in the back of the truck. 'We hadn't realised that the tarmac road ended only four miles out of town and we were suddenly on a rough track,' Deedes recalled. 'It was extremely hot and uncomfortable.' At one point they emerged to cut the telephone line to prevent Addis alerting anyone ahead. 'A bit mischievous,' Deedes admitted. 'I don't know why one does these things in the heat of the moment.'

They got through the first checkpoint by bribing the official in charge with a tumbler full of whisky. That night, in an uncomfortable camp, Waugh insisted on three-handed bridge. 'I did not play the game and Waugh became extremely irritated,' Deedes recalled. The following day the vehicle came to a halt in a village and the three correspondents, huddled under their sheet in the back, were advised by their driver to get out 'as there are some people here who wish to shoot us'. The village headman clearly had his instructions from Addis. He proved impervious to the whisky trick and hemmed the three in with armed men. They finally returned to Addis in disgrace. Sir Sydney Barton received them 'more in sorrow than anger' and told them they had reduced the reputation of Britain. Sir Sydney, an amiable if sorely-tried diplomat, had been inundated with telegrams asking after 'three correspondents missing in the north'. The Abyssinians had fielded an angry protest from the French newsmen to the effect that preferential treatment was being afforded the British correspondents. An American had filed a graphic story which had the three being led away in chains by the Italians. Waugh found it all very amusing.

'On the whole it had been an enjoyable excursion,' he wrote, again making a mental note to include the incident in *Scoop*.

H R 'Red' Knickerbocker, the famed Hearst correspondent, had also been stung by Sir Percy's coup, although he had been the first to congratulate him. Knickerbocker was working feverishly to regain some lost ground. At dinner one evening he talked glibly about getting to the war and happily accepted large bets from Waugh and Deedes that he would not get within fifteen miles of the shooting.

They did not know that Knickerbocker had arranged for an aircraft to pick him up. He flew to the northern front the following day and returned in triumph. 'To this day no one knows how he got permission,' Deedes wrote. 'Anyway he did it; took 50 photographs, 300 yards of film and got a first class story. Being shot at by the Italians over Adowa and having a bullet hole in the wing improved the story.'

Waugh paid up – and painted Knickerbocker into his novel as Wenlock Jakes, the Nobel prize-winning, highest-paid American reporter who had overslept in a train taking him to a Balkan revolution, woken up in the wrong capital, a peaceful one, but, undeterred, had caused a revolution there with his graphic account of blood and rioting in the streets.

By the end of November 1935, with no war copy emerging from Addis Ababa, editors in London, New York and other capitals were weary, if not angry, with the whole exercise. In any event, the Italians had finally unleashed the correspondents from Asmara and they were providing some graphic war coverage.

Herbert Matthews of the *New York Times* and Luigi Barzini of *Corriere della Sera* had come under fire in an Abyssinian ambush of an Italian flying column and their vivid accounts gave the world the first glimpse of the fighting on the ground. They were swiftly joined by others and it gradually dawned on the world's editors that it would have been far wiser, more economical and rational to have sent their correspondents to cover the Abyssinian war from the Italian side.

In Addis Ababa, the authorities finally agreed to allow the correspondents to leave the capital and a few ventured out to Harar in the south-east and Dessye in the north. (They were still unable to find any military action.) Several applied for permission to change sides. This was refused. Many others, aware of the Addis ennui in their offices, left for home or other more promising theatres of war. Waugh, Emeny, Knickerbocker and others finally made it to Dessye. There were plenty of Abyssinian warriors but no sign of the war. In any event, there were no facilities for filing copy. The Emperor also finally made it to Dessye with the full panoply of his court – but his intention was not to lead his men into battle, only to say farewell.

The day after he arrived, Waugh received official word that he had been sacked by the *Daily Mail* and resolved to fulfil a long-standing ambition to spend Christmas in Bethlehem. Bill Deedes and George Steer had ventured to Harar in the hope of catching some action on the southern front but they, too, were disappointed.

'Each morning we wake up here and send up a prayer to be bombed but the opposition are too infernally humanitarian,' Deedes wrote to his foreign editor. Sir Percival Phillips and O'Dowd Gallagher had been reassigned to China and had already left the country.

Noel Monks hitch-hiked towards the southern front and was rewarded only by hearing the artillery fire in the Ogaden. He secured a lift on a camel train crossing the desert and ended up in Berbera in British Somaliland. Hoping to get to the action by covering the war from the Italian side he bought a passage on an Arab dhow to Djibouti. The Italians thought he was a spy and refused him accreditation.

As it became clear there was little chance of any 'live' war copy from the Abyssinian side, the press corps dwindled rapidly. George Steer was among those who stayed. Steer had been sympathetic to the Abyssinian cause from the start and as the war progressed became more and more committed. He had waged a ceaseless campaign to convince an increasingly uninterested world that the Italians had

been using gas against tribespeople. He and a British Legation official went to the northern front to distribute gas masks. In May
1936, Emperor Haile Selassie bowed to the inevitable defeat, caught
the train to the coast and took a steamer into exile.

As the mobs took to the streets, Steer sought refuge in the legation compound and there married a fellow correspondent, Marguerite de Herrero of *Le Journal,* Paris. She died in childbirth less
than a year later. (Steer was later to marry Esmé, Sir Sydney Barton's daughter, the lady who had dashed wine into Waugh's face.)

The victorious Italian forces entered Addis Ababa on May 5th,
accompanied by fifteen correspondents. Matthews was among them
and broke the news of the end of the war with a cable to the *New
York Times*: 'ERA OF INDEPENDENCE THAT LASTED SINCE
BIBLICAL TIMES ENDED FOUR THIS AFTERNOON WHEN
ITALIANS OCCUPIED ADDIS ABABA.' The Italians refused
cabling facilities to the four correspondents who had remained in
Addis and, when they managed to file a joint dispatch on the legation radio, they were expelled. Many of those of the *Scoop* generation of correspondents went on to achieve journalistic, military and
other distinction. George Steer – that 'brave little South African' as
his colleagues called him – was soon to send the first vivid (and controversial) dispatch to *The Times* about the bombing of Guernica in
the Spanish Civil War. He was commissioned in the intelligence
corps and had the pleasure of being assigned to accompany Haile
Selassie on his triumphant return to his throne in Addis Ababa
after the Italians were defeated by British forces in 1940. Steer was
to die in a tragic accident in India before the war ended. He was not,
as we shall see, the last correspondent to become emotionally
involved with a cause in an African conflict.

The other South African, O'Dowd Gallagher, was sent by the
Daily Express to interview Haile Selassie in exile in the King David
Hotel in Jerusalem. In that newspaper's great egotistical tradition,
his interview was headlined 'GALLAGHER SEES EMPEROR'.

Gallagher went on to a distinguished career as a Fleet Street
war correspondent, surviving the sinking by the Japanese of HMS
Repulse in the South China Sea in 1941 and the bombing of the
King David Hotel by the Stern gang in 1946. Gallagher had learned
well that early lesson from Sir Percival Phillips. He was never beat-
en to a story again.

After unsuccessfully trying to find the Abyssinian war, Noel
Monks was invited back to Australia by Keith Murdoch, his former
proprietor (and father of Rupert). It was a notorious newspaper tradition to deflate immediately any illusions a returning correspon-

dent might have and Monks found himself assigned to cover a conference of the Women's Christian Temperance Union in Melbourne
Town Hall. (The *Telegraph* was also good at this. Within hours of
returning from what I thought had been a successful stint in the
Middle East I found myself writing up the world weather and the
high tide times at London Bridge.)

Monks was soon back in Fleet Street – on the *Daily Express* –
and joined some of his old Addis colleagues in covering the Spanish
Civil War. He, too, went on to distinguish himself as a war correspondent in World War II. Early in the war, he met and married
Mary Welsh of *Time* magazine who was later seduced by Ernest
Hemingway while Monks was in the Far East theatre. (Hemingway
was so jealous of Mary's earlier marriage that he threw a framed
picture of the couple into the bowl of a toilet in the Ritz Hotel in
Paris and blazed away at it with a German sub-machine gun,
destroying the hotel plumbing system as well as the photograph.)
Monks' son by his first marriage, John Monks, was later to become a
distinguished *Daily Express* foreign correspondent whose exploits in
Africa will appear later in these pages. Noel Monks was to have a
final interview with Emperor Haile Selassie in somewhat unusual
circumstances. In 1954 the Emperor was on board the cruiser, HMS
Nigeria, in the Mediterranean en route to Britain for a state visit.
Monks, as ever anxious to be first with the story, was aboard the
escort destroyer, HMS *Constance.* He persuaded Admiral Earl
Mountbatten to have him hoisted by jackstay to the Nigeria and he
was received warmly by the Emperor. They talked of the Italian
occupation and its aftermath and the future of Africa. Monks was
hoisted back to the destroyer where he wrote and filed his exclusive
interview. After all that enterprise, it never appeared. There were
no national newspapers published the following day because of a
dispute with the printers.

Herbert Matthews of the *New York Times*, who had covered the
Abyssinian war from the Italian side, was one of the Rome-based
correspondents detained – in relatively luxurious conditions – by
Mussolini's men for five months early in the war. Bill Deedes was
commissioned and served with great distinction, winning the Military Cross in France in 1944. After the war he managed two successful careers – in politics and journalism. He was MP for the Ashford division of Kent for many years, ending a long political career
as Minister without Portfolio in Harold Macmillan's cabinet. He
resigned all political offices when he was appointed editor of *The
Daily Telegraph* in 1974, one of the most popular of all Fleet Street
editors. On his retirement at the age of 72, he became Lord Deedes

but continued to travel extensively and write a lively column for the *Telegraph*. He spent much time in Africa and he, too, will reappear in this book.

Evelyn Waugh was one of the very few to return to Abyssinia during the Italian occupation. He had no assignment from a newspaper, merely a writer's curiosity and a great admiration for the 'civilising' influence of the Italians.

To Africa correspondents of several generations, *Scoop* became more than a brilliant satire of the trade. It can be – and frequently is – dipped into, like a Gideon's Bible, when the going gets rough. In it one finds a cynical but accurate mirror of all that goes on in any given African situation when the press descends en masse. All of the characters and most of the situations in the novel are recognisable to this day.

Emperor Haile Selassie was to preside over his tattered empire for another 32 years. As an egregious figurehead, he also presided over the decolonisation of Africa and was to sit proudly in the place of honour at the annual conferences of the Organisation of African Unity which headquartered itself, symbolically, in Addis Ababa. No matter that emergent leaders railed against 'imperialism' in his presence, Africa was free. Or was it?

In 1972, Haile Selassie, like so many other African leaders before and since, was overthrown by radical revolutionaries in his own armed forces and put to death. Ethiopia, like much of the continent, has been awash with blood and fraught with famine ever since.

Bill Deedes of the Morning
Post *with Ethiopian chauffeur
– Abyssinia 1935.*

*The 22-year-old Bill Deedes
on the* Scoop *assignment in
Abyssinia in 1935.*

The original cast of Scoop – *the correspondents sent to cover the Italian invasion of Abyssinia in 1938 are entertained by the Emperor's men. The journalists present included Evelyn Waugh, O'Dowd Gallagher and Noel Monks.*

Noel Monks of the Daily Express *returns to Abyssinia with Emperor Haile Selassie after the war.*

CHAPTER THREE

WHOSE UHURU?

*T*he small aircraft chartered by the foreign press descended through the Kalahari desert haze and began to circle Gaborone. It was September 1966 and few of them had ever heard of the place. Only a year before it had been a tiny, remote tribal village in the British Protectorate of Bechuanaland. Now it had been proclaimed the new capital of the new Republic of Botswana and the Africa correspondents were on their way to cover the independence celebrations. They peered through the perspex in the hope of formulating descriptions of the world's newest city. There was not much to see. The hasty transition from kraal to capital was still in progress. From the air, there were visible piles of sand, cement, bricks and scaffolding but precious little else. Donald Wise of the *Daily Mirror* exploded. 'Good God! They're giving independence to building sites these days!'

Wise's reaction was not so much a jibe at the new republic as an expression of scepticism. He and the other Old Africa Hands had spent the previous decade covering a plethora of independence celebrations in unlikely corners of the continent. The rush to decolonise was, if anything, far more unseemly than the notorious scramble for Africa in the late 19th century. Then the European powers had laid claim to vast tracts of Africa (with scant consultation of the people living therein). Hinterlands penetrated only by missionaries, explorers, adventurers and slave traders were carved out of maps and coloured pink, yellow, green or mauve to denote each European power's sphere of influence. Chancelleries vied with each other in demarcating outrageous boundaries which took no account of demography, topography, race, tribe, ethnic traditions or even geography.

One of the most bizarre examples, perhaps, is the Caprivi Strip, a 300-mile finger of territory that divides present-day Botswana from Angola. In 1893, the British ceded this strip to give German South West Africa riparian access to the Zambezi River. Germany's imperial aim, however, was to try and link its West African colony with German East Africa. They failed to take into account the difficulties of navigating the Victoria Falls, and Cecil John Rhodes was able to press on with his rose-coloured vision of British Africa extending from the Cape to Cairo without the hindrance of a trans-continental German corridor. The Caprivi Strip (named after Count Leo de Caprivi who had succeeded Bismarck as German Imperial Chancellor) remains an outlandish extension of the newest African republic of Namibia.

After World War II much of an exhausted Europe was only too eager to rid itself of increasingly troublesome and troubled African colonies and protectorates. The potential of exploitable resources was being outweighed by the prospects of the increasing fiscal burden of providing administration and infrastructure. Besides, the awful hangover of Hitlerian fascism and its excesses had struck a mortal blow to the imperialist ethic. To a post-war generation of liberal-minded Europeans the idea of one nation dominating others had become anathema.

Not a small part of the problem with Africa was the simple fact that there were very few areas so arbitrarily delimited that could call themselves 'nations' or display any attributes or homogeneity that might pass for 'nationhood'. Nations would therefore have to be created and some of the brighter sparks among the native leaders would have to be groomed for eventual leadership.

In cosy Hampstead drawing rooms, such prospects excited a form of indulgent paternalism that was to become more despised by Africans than even the more grotesque forms of racialism displayed by white settlers. In draughty London bed-sitters and Manchester working men's clubs, a much more insidious plot for the future of British Africa was being hatched. Professional Soviet agents like George Padmore and I T A Wallace-Johnson were assiduously cultivating and preaching revolution to aspiring African leaders. Among their protegés were: Kwame Nkrumah, a law student from the Gold Coast, Hastings Banda, an elder of the Church of Scotland from Nyasaland who had built up a respectable and respected medical practice in England and Jomo Kenyatta, a Kikuyu opportunist who had whiled away the war working in a Sussex market garden. Disparate as these three men were in background, personality and outlook, each was soon to earn the ultimate acclaim among African nationalists and revolutionaries: a spell in a British colonial prison. Each of them, too, was to succumb to the temptation of assuming the mantle of Africa's messiah, the personality cult of that soon-to-be familiar figure, the African dictator.

Kenyatta was the first to return to his homeland. He arrived in Kenya in 1946, leaving behind his English wife and a son. He was already 50 years old and he was going to have to move quickly if his ambition to become the first leader of an independent Kenya was to be fulfilled. Moreover, Kenya's white population was expanding rapidly with an influx of post-war settlers seeking a sunny, spacious alternative to grim, bomb-shattered British suburbia. Kenyatta had acknowledged that the British would not be ousted from Kenya without 'a bloody insurrection' which, he insisted publicly, 'Africans do not want'. They got it anyway – within a few years of Kenyatta's return. As was the focal point of conflict in many other African colonies, agricultural land and its apportionment provided the impetus for the political discontent of Kenya's blacks, notably the Kikuyu people in the White Highlands north of Nairobi. The return of more than 70 000 Kenyan troops who had fought with the Allies in the Asian theatre contributed to a militancy that had grown in tandem with white intransigence and insensitivity to the land issue. The upshot was the birth of Mau Mau, a Kikuyu secret society, bound by sexual and bestial blood oaths, which in 1952 turned to brutal, unnerving violence. White farms and farmlands were torched at night, cattle were maimed and slaughtered and intimidation of chiefs and village headmen became widespread.

Within a few weeks of his arrival as Governor, Sir Evelyn Baring declared a state of emergency. British troops were flown in from the Middle East, suspected Mau Mau ringleaders were detained and finally Kenyatta himself, who, in white eyes, had played an ambiguous role in the African nationalist political momentum that had accompanied Mau Mau, was arrested.

It was the arrest of 'the Saviour' as Jomo had been hailed by the Kikuyu, that brought the focus of the world's press back to Africa. International reporters inundated the tiny schoolroom at the remote outpost of Kapenguria, 300 miles north of Nairobi, where he was brought to trial. The British press was particularly well represented. Here in the dock, accused of fostering a sinister and evil cult that had white farmers cowering behind firearms and fences, was the cheery, avuncular black man who not many years earlier had enjoyed a couple of evening pints in his Sussex local. In vain did the authorities attempt to keep Kenyatta's five-month trial at a criminal level. The press and the accused ensured that it became a political cause célèbre.

The British government had been convinced that Kenyatta's incarceration would bring a swift end to the Mau Mau rebellion. The evidence was, to say the least, flimsy. Much later a key prosecution witness admitted receiving bribes and it was revealed that the magistrate had received an ex gratia payment, ostensibly to compensate him for having to leave Kenya to avoid repercussions. Kenyatta was duly sentenced to the maximum seven years imprisonment with hard labour to be followed by indefinite restriction. He was to serve his sentence in one of the more inaccessible corners of Kenya, the north-western desert far from his beloved Kikuyu heartland. Far from intimidating the Mau Mau, Kenyatta's removal marked the starting point of an upsurge in terror and terrorism that was to last for four years. John Redfern of the *Daily Express*, then doyen of African correspondents, covered the entire Kenyatta trial and found it 'very unsatisfactory...a travesty of British justice'. Redfern, a canny Derbyshire man, was one of Arthur Christiansen's discoveries and had justified his editor's instinct with fine coverage of the campaigns of the British and Canadian Armies in North Africa, Sicily, Italy and North-West Europe during which he was mentioned in dispatches. He had met Kenyatta before his arrest at the funeral of a local chief who had been gunned down. He drove Kenyatta back to Nairobi and invited him to tea at the New Stanley Hotel.

'Kenyatta flung out his arms and roared "It is not possible... you are a white man and I am black". He declined with thanks and disappeared down a side street. When I mentioned my invitation to the New Stanley manager he also roared. "If you had, I'd have had to have thrown you both out...Kenyatta in our lounge would have caused a riot."' A few years later, Redfern arrived back at the New Stanley to find the head porter organising the laying of a red carpet from the pavement to the reception desk. Who was the honoured guest, John inquired. 'President Kenyatta, Bwana...we are very proud.'

Redfern recalled that the prosecution's evidence was unconvincing and that Kenyatta's counsel sought to turn the hearing into 'a political show trial'. As the magistrate passed sentence on Kenyatta and his co-accused 'there was a dramatic thunderstorm overhead during which Kenyatta declared, prophetically, "We shall return".' Dr Louis Leakey, the Kenyan anthropologist, was appointed official interpreter as many of the witnesses spoke only Kikuyu. The Leakey family had been brought up with the Kikuyu and spoke the language fluently. Denis Pritt, KC for Kenyatta, accused Leakey of adding to the replies of witnesses. Some time after Kenyatta had been sentenced, a Mau Mau gang burst into the home of David Leakey, Louis's brother, just as he and his family were sitting down to supper. Mrs Leakey and the servants were butchered on the spot. David Leakey was force-marched to the foot of Mount Kenya where he was ritually tortured and murdered, then buried head down with a spear through his heart.

'Even among the hardened settlers of Kenya, the cold-blooded brutality of that murder sent a shiver down their spines,' wrote Sandy Gall, then Reuters man in Nairobi.

During the entire Mau Mau emergency, as it was officially known, some 15 000 people died, fewer than 50 of them Europeans. Yet it was a difficult conflict to cover. Donald Wise, fresh from hunting terrorists while serving with the Parachute Regiment in the Malayan jungle, found it frustrating. 'You could go out with the British troops but you were lucky if you saw anything. It was almost always a follow-up and reaction story...chasing out to a farmstead that had been attacked the previous night and getting a second-hand account of the carnage.' Sandy Gall joined a British army patrol in what was intended to be a dawn attack on a Mau Mau camp in a forest above Nyeri. With a young officer, two soldiers and six men of the King's African Rifles he drove to the edge of the forest and followed the patrol as they set off stealthily through the trees.

'I was nervous and jumping at every sound. At one point there was a sudden crashing in the bush just ahead of us and I immediately thought we had run into a band of Mau Mau. "It's all right," the officer whispered. "We've just disturbed a herd of buffalo." The Mau Mau also heard the buffalo and melted into the forest. When the patrol reached the camp at first light it was deserted.'

It was left to the feature writers rather than the newsmen to capture the essence of the Mau Mau campaign. Graham Greene, like Evelyn Waugh, undertook risky assignments for newspapers and magazines to provide himself with background for possible novels. Greene spent some time in Kenya – staying at a mission in Kikuyuland – at the height of the Mau Mau insurgency in 1953. Regrettably no novel emerged but he drew a vivid, compassionate picture of the conflict in a report.

Looking out from the mission station 7 000 feet up in the White Highlands, 'I could see the forested slopes of the Aberdares, the stamping ground of the chief enemy "General" Dedan Kimathi...two miles ahead of me across the Chania River was the Mau Mau-ridden Fort Hall Reserve from which attackers had come to the mission a year before; fifteen miles behind me was the scene of the Lari massacre, where 150 wives and children of the Kikuyu Home Guard were hacked to death.' In Indo-China and Malaya, Greene had found 'something approaching a frontline' but here, in Kenya's Central Province, 'the war was secret: it would happen the day after I left or the day before I arrived. It was a private African war which could be hidden so easily from white eyes, just as seventeen strangled bodies lay for weeks unnoticed in a squatter's village on the outskirts of Nairobi, a mile from the highway and the houses of officials.'

Greene's account was admirably objective. He felt for the white farmers who had 'a hard enough struggle without Mau Mau', their cattle plagued by locusts, rinderpest, wireworm, fluke and foot and mouth disease. 'Fear of ruin was to most farmers worse than the fear of death, for their whole life had to be lived here. This was their burial ground. They had been settled, in some parts of Kenya, a third as long as the Kikuyu. In England they would be exiles.' And of the Mau Mau: 'It would be easier to draw Kimathi as a heroic figure if we could put out of our minds those bestial ceremonies with the living sheep and the dead goat and the naked woman, or the pictures of mutilated bodies...for over and over again one was moved by the simplicity and pathos of this savage enemy.' So elusive, ephemeral even, was the Mau Mau campaign that, outside the odd foray to the White Highlands 'war zone', foreign correspondents happily indulged themselves in the very good life that beautiful country afforded. The Thorn Tree terrace and the Long Bar at the New Stanley Hotel in the centre of Nairobi became the waterholes where hacks, resident or transient, could be found day and night.

'One could sit and get gently plastered in the sun at lunchtime, which is what we usually did,' according to Sandy Gall, then as now one of the most congenial colleagues to have around.

Gall and Wise were the only two resident correspondents at that time but there was a constant stream of 'firemen' passing through Nairobi from their bases in the Middle East or South Africa: Eric 'Strangler' Downton and Douglas 'Doormouse' Brown of *The Daily Telegraph,* Roy Lewis of *The Times*, Len Ingalls of the *New York Times* and James Cameron of the *News Chronicle.* In addition there was always a reservoir of competent and convivial expatriate journalists working on the *East African Standard,* many of whom were to go on to make their names in international journalism.

In those days, too, Kenya attracted a kaleidoscope of characters who, in turn, attracted or were attracted to the press corps. Remnants remained of the country's notorious 'Happy Valley' set of champagne-swilling, wife-swapping aristocrats and pseudo-aristocrats. There was also a lively diplomatic circuit. Don Wise affectionately recalled gubernatorial parties at which Sir Evelyn Baring's aides-de-camp (including Charles Douglas-Home, later to become editor of *The Times*) staged cabaret acts, including a 'wonderful parody' of how Sir Evelyn had saved an Indian girl from drowning off the coast of Mombasa.

'It was a very bright and breezy Government House. The garden parties were extraordinary...there would be people standing around in full Ascot kit – grey top hats and silver cravattes listening to an enormous Kalanjin tribesman with a billiard ball in his lower lip and a bloody great glass of whisky in his hand.' Donald, who would be the first to admit to a sharp, life-long eye for the fairer sex, found Kikuyu women singularly unattractive. 'It was a long time before they acquired any dress sense. They used to hang around in British Army surplus greatcoats with cylindrical cigarette tins dangling from their ears...don't think this female circumcision thing helped 'em a lot.'

Wise shared the white Kenyan affection for the Masai, the towering, unpredictable nomads: 'Very colourful, although worthless from a story point of view. They would tramp up and down, twirling their spears. If they got a sudden rush of blood to the head it was prudent to accelerate out of the area.'

Evelyn Waugh, visiting Kenya in 1959, found the Masai tailored to his *Scoop* predictions. 'They had a lovely time during the Mau Mau rising. They were enlisted and told to bring in all the Kikuyus' arms. Back they proudly came with baskets of severed limbs.'

The emergency in Kenya, coupled as it was with the heyday of the Great White Hunter and the spurious glamour of the Happy Valley set, began to lure American film stars, writers and adventurers, all of whom were to provide good off-beat copy for the hacks. John Redfern returned to the New Stanley in the early hours of the morning to find his old friend and contact, John, the head porter, in a state of high agitation in the darkened foyer.

'Bwana, bwana,' he whispered. 'Mau Mau in the kitchen.' Sure enough, there was a flickering light coming from the hotel's large kitchen and the sound of someone moving around. Redfern summoned Brian Burrows, the new manager, who emerged in his pyjamas wielding an enormous revolver. The three men moved cautiously and nervously towards the kitchen door, finally kicking it open and cowering behind the wavering barrel of Burrows' gun.

'There, standing over the stove and clad in an apron, was Frank Sinatra,' Redfern remembered. 'He said something like "Hi guys... point that thing the other way and gimme a hand here." He was not the kind of bandit we had been expecting.' Sinatra had flown unexpectedly to Kenya to visit his then wife, Ava Gardner who was on location with Grace Kelly and Clark Gable making the movie *Mogambo*. Ava had awoken in the middle of the night craving fried bacon and eggs and Sinatra had found his way to the New Stanley kitchen to oblige.

Such films, coupled with works like Robert Ruark's *Something of Value* and *Uhuru,* overdramatised the Mau Mau period... 'And then, suddenly, Mau Mau began to rape and terrorise and turn smiling Africans into primitive savages...' Little wonder that Ruark was declared a PI – a prohibited immigrant – shortly after the real Uhuru. Like Ernest Hemingway, another regular Kenyan visitor, he was more swash than buckle.

'They call me an old Africa hand because I date back to the Bwana Mkubwa days, when colonialism reigned and everything was huntin', shootin', drinkin' and fishin', and when you yelled "Boy!" everybody came running,' growled Ruark. Curiously, after he had been tipped off about his impending arrest, Ruark escaped the New Stanley through the very kitchens where Frank Sinatra, not that much earlier, had been preparing Ava's midnight feast.

Ruark cultivated friends among the correspondents, notably Peter Younghusband and Jack Nugent of *Newsweek.* 'Just as well,' says Big Pete. 'Ruark would more often than not get smashed out of his skull and we'd have to carry him to his bed in the New Stanley.' Under drink, Ruark's obsession with Hemingway would come pouring out. He was a better shot, a better hunter, a better womaniser and, ultimately, a better writer than Hemingway, in his befuddled mind, at least. Younghusband remembers that Ruark lived in mortal terror of an ex-wife, so much so that he entitled one of his novels *The Honey Badger* after a particularly fearless African mammal that tends, wisely, to go for a hunter's testicles when cornered. Hemingway, of course, loomed large over the East African landscape, or more specifically from either luxurious safari camps in the bush (well away from Mau Mau territory) or his usual suite at the Norfolk Hotel. He was probably unaware of the curses being directed his way by the tired and emotional Ruark from the New Stanley down the road but a curse there seemed to be.

In 1953 he treated 'Miss Mary', as he coyly called his wife (in copy, anyway) to a Christmas present – a light aircraft flip at low level over some of Africa's more spectacular scenery. At Murchison Falls in Northern Uganda, the Cessna 180 ducked under a flight of sacred ibis and caught an old telegraph wire, crashing close to a herd of elephant. Mary suffered two broken ribs and 'Papa' Hemingway a dislocated shoulder but they survived the bush for a few days before being rescued by a launch. At Lake Albert they accepted the offer of a flight to Entebbe in a de Havilland Rapide which, in turn, crashed on landing. Mr and Mrs Hemingway were once again unscathed – except for the loss of a bottle of Grand MacNish whisky which exploded on impact.

Much of the world's press already had the Hemingways dead, once the news of the first crash had seeped through the bush. A German newspaper had a vivid description of Hemingway attempting to land the aircraft on the summit of Mount Kilimanjaro. As a result, Hemingway developed a passion for reading clippings of his own obituaries, an addiction which stayed with him until he committed suicide eight years later.

Literature's close call was journalism's gain. Donald Wise had just joined the *Daily Express* in Nairobi when the Hemingway crashes occurred. He was already too canny a reporter to swallow the rumours that the writer and his wife had perished. He swiftly made his way to Entebbe and was among the first to get the full story from Papa himself. 'That gave my career a tremendous lift-off...the office thought I could do no wrong and gave me free reign to operate out of Nairobi all over Africa, the Middle East and elsewhere.' Donald got on well with Hemingway, not surprisingly as his background had that blend of machismo and diffidence that the writer so admired in himself.

Wise, the son of a successful South African businessman, was public-schooled in England and went up to Oxford – with an eye on a future career in journalism. Higher education was cut short by the outbreak of the Second World War. Young Donald volunteered and was soon on a troop ship bound for Singapore. He had what he calls 'a rather useless war', being wounded and captured in Singapore. He spent time in Changi Prison before being sent as a Japanese prisoner-of-war to work on the Burma railway. 'We took a lot of casualties... about 3 800 dead out of 7 000 in eight months.' Not surprisingly, perhaps, he found after the war that the young bride he had married before joining up in Britain had given him up for dead and had married an American. He returned to South East Asia with the idea of becoming a rubber planter but soon found himself caught up in another war – the Malayan Emergency. He led a tracker team looking for Communist terrorists in the jungle... 'up to 20 days at a stretch without a bloody bath'. Journalism still called, however. After a stint on the *Rand Daily Mail* in Johannesburg he made his name as a stringer for the *Daily Express* in Nairobi and was soon appointed as a roving correspondent.

'At school I had read a couple of books about a foreign correspondent and thought "This is for me". It had to be the greatest time out...staying in first-class hotels, witnessing the most exciting things happening, eating the best food and drinking the best wines, meeting superb soignée women...and somebody else pays for it. That summing up of the job was for me accurate and remained so in my years as a foreign correspondent.'

Wise looked and sounded the part (and, at the time of writing, still does, well into his 70s in semi-retirement in France). He reminded me always of David Niven, although he was that much more rugged than the actor. Donald had actually been there and back on numerous occasions. Tall, with a trim military moustache and bearing, he had all the grace, charm and wit of his celluloid look-alike. Women fell at his feet (literally, on more than one occasion). He possessed a glorious turn of phrase and a wicked sense of fun which made him a wonderful colleague and companion on any story. He enlivened the dull periods and made the dangerous ones that much more interesting. As one old friend put it, Donald's arrival on any given story was 'just like opening a bottle of the best champagne'. He could be as competitive as the next man but was unfailingly helpful and considerate to younger colleagues or newcomers to a scene with which he was familiar. In a notoriously back-stabbing trade, you would be hard put to it to find anyone who disliked Donald Wise.

His officer's mess demeanour gave him his nickname, 'The Colonel' and on many occasions Don strode paths that others feared to tread because guards, doormen and flunkies automatically assumed he was top brass. It was a career littered with legends, some of which will unfold in these chapters. One of the favourites: Donald was reprimanded for sending a letter to his London editors in which he had used some bad language which had 'offended the secretaries'. Irritated by a cable from London demanding something outrageous he wanted to cable back a one-liner saying 'BALLS!' Mindful of the secretary's sensitivity he cabled instead 'ROUND OBJECTS!' There was a puzzled pause before London responded: 'WHO ROUND AND TO WHAT DOES HE OBJECT?' Apart from the Kenya story itself, Don Wise and other correspondents found Nairobi an ideal jumping-off point for trouble spots elsewhere in Africa and the Middle East. Wise recalls: 'Wonderful base in those days...good air links, excellent communications and plenty of local colour stuff like Joy Adamson wrapped in lesbian embraces with Elsa the lioness...the Wajir Yacht Club where the boats all had wheels because it was in the middle of the desert.'

Young Sandy Gall, tall, urbane and charming with, even then, what colleagues called a 'lived-in face', was able to indulge to the full his predilection for attractive women. When he was obliged to share hotel rooms with colleagues they would invariably find themselves awoken by giggles and grunts from beneath Sandy's mosquito net. When a young Princess Margaret visited East Africa in 1956, he wheedled an introduction and gazed into her 'stunningly blue eyes

...flashing fire'. But, as always, more onerous duties called. Sandy had just flown 'with a couple of the women reporters' for a weekend at Malindi on the Indian Ocean coast when Reuters tracked him down with that most inconvenient of missives, a 'movement message' instructing him 'PROCEED ADENWARDS SOONEST'. Female sighs could be heard on the African breeze as he winged his way northwards.

Donald Wise could not understand the sexual success of young Gall 'who in those days, unlike now, was never well tailored'. He recalled a cocktail party thrown by Sir Roy Welensky, Premier of the Central African Federation, in Salisbury, when Sandy arrived late 'scruffy as hell with his hair sticking up on end.' Sir Roy turned to Wise, who always managed to remain fresh and dapper in the most hair-raising circumstances.

'Who is that man who looks as if he's fought his way through every bar in town to get here?' Sir Roy demanded.

Wise, of course, was no slouch when it came to women. In Mogadishu, then capital of Italian Somaliland, an immaculate, well-groomed Wise decided to pass an evening at a darkened night club called Croce del Sud – the Southern Cross – known to transient hacks as 'the sweaty crutch'. Donald spotted an equally dark beauty sitting alone in a corner. He did the gentlemanly thing and asked her to dance.

'To my horror when she stood up I thought she was a hunchback but I was committed and off we went slowly around the floor. I suddenly realised she wasn't hunched at all, she had a baby strapped to her back. This little bugger came up under my armpit looking for nosh...gave me quite a turn.'

Back on the Thorn Tree Terrace in Nairobi, an elegant, cravatted Donald greeted Oliver Woods, then foreign editor of *The Times* who had arrived to interview the Governor, Sir Evelyn Baring.

'Splendid chap, Oliver...won an MC during the war...but he emerged from the front door of the New Stanley wearing carpet slippers, a pair of baggy old grey trousers and an old tweed jacket with holes in the elbows and stuffing poking out of the shoulder pad, peering through his granny glasses and carrying a battered old music case. I was aghast. 'You're not going to see the Governor like that?' I asked. He looked puzzled and rushed off. A couple of beers later he was back, assuring us that he'd had a very interesting chat with the Governor. Just shows you...if I'd have presented myself at Government House dressed like that they'd have thrown me out on my ear.'

The Mau Mau troubles continued for four years before being subdued. A beleaguered Dedan Kimathi, the Mau Mau leader who

had been subjected to a two-year personal manhunt, finally crawled
out of a forest on the slopes of the Aberdares and was wounded and
captured by a British soldier who, in the half light, mistook him for
a leopard.

The statistics of that period, now written into African history as
the first black African 'war of liberation' are revealing. The hard
corps of Mau Mau guerrillas probably numbered no more than 15
000 confronted by 25 000 British infantrymen and paramilitary
police backed by ground-strike aircraft and thousands of black auxil-
iaries. The death toll of Mau Mau and their supporters was officially
given as 11 500. At least 2 000 Africans who fought with the security forces were killed. Most telling of all, the number of white civilians killed in four years of terror and savagery aimed specifically at
them: thirty-two.

But the power of the panga had asserted itself beyond the numbers game. White settler resistance to black advancement had been
undermined by British involvement in the Emergency. When it
ended in 1956, agrarian reform followed apace and three years later
land ownership in the White Highlands was open to all. By 1960
Kenyatta was still in restriction (and condemned by Sir Patrick
Renison, the new Governor, as 'the African leader to darkness and
death'). A year later, Kenyatta was allowed to return to his home at
Gatundu and to campaign openly as president of the Kenya African
National Union (KANU).

Legend has it that he had been allowed a daily bottle of brandy
in prison in the hope that he would drink himself into darkness and
death but 'Mzee' – the old man – emerged at the age of 70 full of
spirit of a different kind. In 1963 he won the pre-independence election hands down. By the end of that year, as the first black prime
minister of Kenya, he was preaching reconciliation and forgiveness
to farmers in the White Highlands.

The foreign press corps in Nairobi, repeatedly accused by the
settler community of sympathising with black aspirations, was
impressed by Kenyatta's transformation from the embodiment of
unspeakable evil to the chummy, conciliatory pragmatist. From the
start, Mzee had realised the power of the press and was only too
willing to receive visiting and resident journalists. Jack Nugent,
Newsweek's first African correspondent, drove out to Gatundu on
the day restrictions were lifted. 'Every fifteen minutes Kenyatta left
his crowded porch to stroll around his freshly seeded lawn waving
his fly whisk and shouting "Uhuru! Uhuru!" The forests echoed with
the roar of his people responding "Uhuru na Kenyatta".' Nugent,
like Donald Wise, thought Kenyatta had quickly proved himself a

'great statesman' but the *Newsweek* man was soon to learn that 'freedom for the people' did not necessarily mean Uhuru for the press. His editors commissioned a cover story on Kenyatta to coincide with independence. Nugent sought and secured another cheery interview with Mzee at Gatundu. American news magazines practise what I regard as a rather risky editing process. A correspondent's file is supplemented by a mass of information garnered from other bureaus and sources. All is then woven together by a New York editor in the snappy house style. In my experience, the procedure leaves much too large a margin for error.

Nugent was to suffer from the inclusion in his cover story of a colourful snippet picked up by *Newsweek*'s London bureau: Tom Mboya, the bright, ambitious and very vain Minister of Justice in Kenyatta's government owned 110 tailored suits.

Jack Nugent and his wife had built a reputation for throwing lavish, generous parties. In the middle of one Jack was called to the 'phone to be told that the newly formed National Union of Kenya Journalists was demanding that he be deported forthwith as a result of the *Newsweek* cover story. As far as Jack was concerned the copy had looked favourably on Kenya's independence and on Kenyatta's stewardship. The journalists' union included very few journalists and he was inclined to dismiss its influence. But within days he received a formal government notice advising him that he had been declared a prohibited immigrant and ordering him to leave the country.

Having had three happy years in Nairobi with his family, Nugent was not going to quit that easily. He pulled every official and diplomatic string he could think of to stall the deportation – and to try and find out what had upset the Kenyan authorities. He was harassed by police, threatened, denounced publicly by the government and told that the cabinet had taken the decision to throw him out.

Kenyatta himself, he learned, had taken exception only to a small aside in his story which alluded to his new wife, Ngina, as 'a shy girl'. Kenyatta did not regard her as 'shy' (and nor did anyone else in later years in Kenya when she was discovered to have organised and run a massive ivory poaching business from the protection of State House). Finally he learned that Tom Mboya, he of extravagant sartorial taste, was his main antagonist, having been needled by cabinet colleagues and diplomats about his wardrobe. Finally the deportation order was withdrawn and Nugent was granted another exclusive interview with Kenyatta before leaving Africa, voluntarily, a year later.

Tom Mboya, a member of Kenya's second largest tribal group, the Luo and a man widely favoured to succeed the ageing Kenyatta, was assassinated by a Kikuyu gunman in a central Nairobi street in 1969. An unknown Kikuyu was soon arrested, convicted and executed for the crime but no motive was ever established. This did not prevent widespread conflict between the Kikuyu and the Luo people who believed Mboya had been a victim of tribal hegemony.

Usually regarded as a smooth, personable character, Mboya had astounded me a few years earlier when we were introduced. He proffered his hand and I reached out to shake it when he heard our host add 'from the London *Daily Telegraph'*. He snatched his hand back and made as if to spit on mine.

Such was the price, I supposed, of working for what Malcolm Muggeridge, a former deputy editor of *The Daily Telegraph,* had called 'the repository of the soul of the Tory party'. African politicians were – and are – extremely sensitive to overseas press criticism and tended to monitor it carefully. The *Telegraph* leader writers, tucked in Fleet Street cubby holes blissfully unaware of the perils in the field, would invariably give some African leader both barrels just as I tippy-toed into his country with smiling obsequy. In such circumstances it was essential to remember what one was supposed to call an African with a rifle. The correct and only answer: 'Sir'.

To his credit, Mboya had made no secret of his views on press freedom. 'Because the leaders are trying hard to create unity, they become sensitive to anyone who appears to act as though he constituted an opposition and did nothing but criticise the government's efforts,' he had written. 'Freedom of the press in a new country has, therefore, got to be limited.' The state radio, Voice of Kenya, took his words to heart. When he was murdered, the radio did not report a word for fear of inciting anti-Kikuyu feeling.

Richard Beeston, *The Daily Telegraph* staffer in Nairobi in the early sixties, was a victim of an anti-Kenyatta editorial in the newspaper. Dick was relaxing at his Nairobi home one morning, tuned into the Voice of Kenya on the radio. The lead item announced that 'Mr Richard Beeston, Nairobi correspondent for the fascist *Daily Telegraph* of London has been deported from Kenya...'

Sure enough his deportation had been ordered as soon as Mzee had heard the *Telegraph* editorial relayed on the BBC World Service that morning. Dick was a popular figure in East Africa and his spontaneous farewell party spilled from the New Stanley to the Norfolk and thence to Embakasi Airport where he was to be escorted on to a London-bound BOAC airliner.

Fully aware of the international convention which demands

that a deportee should have his fare paid by the deporting state, Dick calmly asked his escorts for his ticket. Consternation! No one had thought of that! Officials ran around in ever decreasing circles, the pilot of the aircraft begged and pleaded for a compromise and passengers already on board sweated and fumed. Dick stuck to his guns and continued drinking with his chums in the airport lounge. Finally, a ticket was produced, Beeston boarded and Kenya had restored its honour.

Deportation was to become the most pleasant fate to befall an offending African correspondent. Imprisonment, beatings, death threats and much worse awaited foreign journalists covering other, less considerate, emergent African states. Big Stanley Meisler, Africa correspondent for the *Los Angeles Times* in the 60s and 70s, collected no fewer than 13 deportation and PI orders – and he was one of the more thoughtful, sober and compassionate correspondents. I managed to be barred from only six countries.

The message soon became clear in Kenyatta's Kenya: foreign newsmen were in no way discouraged from visiting or even setting up indefinite base in Nairobi as long as they did not write anything disparaging about Kenya itself or, more particularly, criticise Mzee or those members of his government he did not want criticised. This unwritten code suited most African correspondents admirably. Nairobi was a pleasant capital to work from. There were excellent air connections to most parts of the continent and to Europe. Kenya's scenic splendour, from its game parks to its tropical coastline, made it agreeable to wives and families.

Kenyatta created a happy-go-lucky, free-wheeling, free-enterprise society (despite, or perhaps because of, his early schooling by the Comintern). There were few shortages, plenty of good restaurants and rarely a 'troublesome' story in Kenya itself which might disturb the peace. Kenyan officials merely shrugged when Nairobi-based correspondents filed gory stories about other parts of Africa, even the damning tales emanating from its East African Community neighbours, Uganda and Tanzania. Much of the unfolding horror story of Africa was filed from Nairobi, whether or not it carried the dateline of the Kenyan capital.

All the major news agencies – Reuters, Associated Press and United Press International – ran their African operations out of Nairobi. Their correspondents were under strict, if tacit, instructions not to rock the Kenyan boat. There were some not prepared to play ball. I treasure the memory of a very good Reuters man, an Australian, who filed a story which had upset one minor and very pompous Kenyan official. The official complained to an old friend who was a notorious Reuters editor in London. Up on telex from London to the Reuter Bunker, as it was known, in Nairobi, came a rocket and the instruction to the correspondent to apologise personally to the government man.

The Australian hit the roof, adding many new dimensions to the substantial lexicon of antipodean expletives. When we calmed him down slightly he picked up the phone and purchased on the office account a first-class fare to Sydney. He then sat down at the telex, opened a line to London and tapped out (you could almost hear the Australian accent) a message to the editor: 'EYE UNLICKING BLACK BACKSIDES FOR YOU, REUTERS OR ANYONE ELSE STOP UPSTUFF JOB ARSEWARDS'.

In diplomatic terms it rivalled the approach of Norman Luck, a Fleet Street heavy normally confined to London crime beats for the *Daily Express*. By some quirk of journalistic fate, Luck found himself, briefly and slightly bemused, in Nairobi. That day, Charles Njonjo, Kenya's extraordinarily urbane Attorney-General, educated at the London School of Economics and called to the bar at Gray's Inn, met the visiting press. 'Charles Njonjo,' he said, holding out his hand as Norman shuffled forward. Luck jabbed at his own chest. 'Me Norman', he announced loudly.

It says much for Kenya that the country's four daily newspapers remained under private control for many years after independence. Other African countries nationalised their newspapers and turned them into obsequious, often crude, propaganda sheets. Ironically, the press in Africa rapidly reverted to its genesis which began (in Sierra Leone in 1801) with the publication of the dust-dry official government gazette.

Ali Mazrui, one of the continent's towering intellectuals, wrote: 'It is not for nothing that the word for newspaper in Swahili is "gazeti"...the Adam and Eve of newspapers in Africa were government gazettes.' Sadly, nearly two hundred years on, many of them still are. Kenyan editors, however, were only too aware of the perils of publishing unflattering comments or reports of either Mzee or his ministers. The pressures were constant, sometimes subtle, often not so subtle.

Tom Mboya's murder in 1969 ignited Kenya's most serious crisis since independence. Tribal tensions were never very far from the surface. Antipathy between the Kikuyu and the Luo – Mboya's tribe – was marked not least because of political rivalry between Kenyatta and Oginga Odinga, the colourfully controversial 'Double O' leader of the opposition (when Kenya had an opposition).

Few hacks in Nairobi were surprised to discover that the first journalist on the scene of the Mboya assassination was Mohamed

Amin, the Kenyan-born son of a migrant Punjabi stonemason. Mo Amin, soon to become one of the most famous news cameramen in the world, had as always received an early tip-off and was on the scene of the shooting within minutes. He organised the ambulance and jumped in the back with Mboya to film the dying minister on the way to hospital. The film won him a British TV Cameraman of the Year award – and confirmed once again to his colleagues that Mo had an uncanny – some said highly suspicious – sixth sense when it came to being first on the spot.

The tribal implications of a Kikuyu being convicted for the assassination of a leading Luo were quick to surface. There were ugly clashes between Luo mourners and police and the mood in Luoland on the shores of Lake Victoria remained volatile. Kenyatta moved quickly, appointing another Luo to replace Mboya and promoting two others to prominent government positions. Kenyatta had been recuperating from a stroke at the time of the shooting but his hypersensitivity was as sharp as ever. George Githii, editor-in-chief of the *Nairobi Nation* was bundled into exile after writing a report which alluded to Mzee's 'mild indisposition'. Kenyatta recovered swiftly as the tribal tension persisted. He stomped the country preaching unity and denouncing tribalism. As part of his whistle-stop he was billed to address a gathering at Kakamega, a peaceful area and a harmless-sounding trip which most correspondents thought could be happily left to the Kenya News Agency.

Mohamed Amin sensed or learned that there was a secret plan for Mzee and his entourage to peel off from Kakamega and head down the escarpment to Kisumu on Lake Victoria in the still-seething Luo heartland. He confided this to John Platter, an old friend and then head of the UPI bureau in Nairobi (and later to become one of South Africa's best-known wine farmers). To Platter, Kenyan born and bred, it made sense. He knew that Oginga Odinga was due to open a new hospital in Kisumu (with funds provided by the Soviet Union). He knew also that it would be totally in character for Mzee to make an unannounced visit to Kisumu to upstage Odinga and demonstrate both to the Luo and to Moscow who really ruled the roost.

Well before dawn Amin and Platter set out from Nairobi and caught up with the presidential cavalcade at Kakamega. Sure enough, a last minute announcement was made that Kenyatta was, indeed, to make a surprise visit to Kisumu and the convoy headed towards Lake Victoria. Platter recalls that thousands of Luo people were gathered outside the new hospital where Odinga, in his usual beaded cap, knee-length gown and Mao collar, was greeting the

Russian ambassador. 'Kenyatta and Odinga smilingly exchanged pleasantries through clenched teeth as they took their seats on the dais.'

The feared paramilitary presidential guard, the General Service Unit, were strung out along the perimeter fence where the Luo crowd had started to chant ominously, but several hundred locals had gained entry to the hospital compound and were mingling with the VIPs and guests. As Kenyatta moved towards the public address system, mayhem erupted.

'Within a few feet of the president people began smashing each other with broken chairs. Odinga and the Russian ambassador scurried into the hospital but Mo was already filming and taking stills, close enough to the action to have to wipe flecks of flying saliva off his lens,' Platter wrote. Kenyatta's bodyguards immediately formed a circle around the president (who, as always, remained remarkably calm). They then opened fire, moving backwards to protect the old man.

Amin and Platter instinctively and wisely gained access to the protected circle, the cameraman filming all the while. A berserk official spotted Mo, shoved a pistol into his face, twisted his shirt and shook him. 'Open that camera! Give me that film!' Amin, at his apologetic, submissive best, obliged and handed over a film.

It was, of course, not THE film. 'Mo was far too old a hand for that...seconds after the first shots were fired and the bodies began to fall, he had changed films repeatedly, handing me the reels for safe keeping,' Platter remembers. The UPI man ducked behind some officials, yet another Mohamed Amin scoop tucked in his pockets. More nerve-wracking moments were to follow. An enraged Kenyatta reached for a microphone and began to speak. As he did so, Odinga and the Russian ambassador emerged sheepishly and took their seats. Medical orderlies began to carry away the dead and wounded. The Luo crowd was as incensed as Mzee but, as they say in show business, he had the microphone. 'He reciprocated the Luo jibes and launched into them in his raunchiest, anthropological best...Odinga butted in and tried to grab the microphone...the battle raged on.'

John Platter decided it was time to disengage, although he had problems persuading Amin they had enough of the amazing scenes. 'By now the GSU and the presidential bodyguard were literally shooting a pathway out of town. Dust and the crowd's jeers enveloped the scene. We retrieved my car and weaved into about sixth place behind the president, Mo filming the Luo crowds on the rampage. Even two policemen trying to hold back the mobs were shot. One in starched khaki, his head partly severed, reeled over the curbside to the left of us. Mo was leaning out of the car trying to capture the carnage on film. He wanted me to stop. I had to remind him that my car wasn't insured for this kind of thing.'

Platter and Amin made it back to Nairobi with an exclusive story, film and photographs that went around the world. The casualties from Kenyatta's surprise visit to Luoland: fifteen dead and eighty wounded. 'Had any hospital ever had such an opening?' Platter wanted to know. He was also full of admiration for Amin's uncanny news sense. 'How, among all the photographers based in Kenya, was Mo once again alone on the scene? No Mafia set-up. No luck. It was straightforward planning, foresight and hard work. He'd sniffed out a possibility and while others were content to dismiss a routine presidential trip and take off for a weekend at the coast, Mo was ready to rise with the sparrows and head the other way.'

I was in northern Botswana with freelance photographer Mike McCann when I got what we know in the trade as a 'call-back' on Platter's story. We were trying to put a magazine feature together on Southern Africa's 'freedom ferry', a rickety raft that plied across the Zambezi to Zambia, occasionally carrying South African dissidents to what they hoped was going to be liberty and enlightenment.

Earlier, we had been delayed on a remote road by an enormous herd of buffalo making its way to the river. While we gave them right of way, McCann fashioned a cleft stick from a thorn tree sapling. As a joke, we gave it to a Motswana friend and instructed him to use it to deliver any urgent messages. With a huge grin, he loped through the night to our bush camp, carrying the cleft stick with a message a colleague had relayed from Salisbury to Kasane, the nearest village in Botswana. As he swigged what was left of our whisky I read the message from *The Daily Telegraph* foreign desk 'VIEW UPI TRIBAL CLASHES KENYA ASSUME YOU NAIROBI-WARDS SOONEST.'

Moving as fast as I could from a pretty remote spot in the bush, I made it to Nairobi within 36 hours, but still got the 'What kept you?' reaction from Ricky Marsh on the foreign desk in London. Only a couple of inches on the DT map of Africa, old boy! In the meantime, Kenyatta had also moved fast. He had outlawed the opposition and put its leaders, including Odinga, under house arrest. That achieved, he then named the date for Kenya's first general election since independence.

All this, by now, was pretty routine stuff in an African democracy but Nairobi was abuzz with much more alarming rumours: the Kikuyu were once more indulging in the more sinister forms of their oathing ceremonies. Now, there are oaths and oaths. The Kikuyu have a recorded 700-year-old history of oaths and Kenyatta had written, with passionate affection, of the rituals of brotherhood in his book *Facing Mount Kenya*.

In Kiambu, one of their tribal strongholds, I was persuaded by a charming and intelligent young government official to ask whatever I wanted to know about oaths. ' Are you a Freemason and have you taken the Mason's oath?' he asked. The answer to that was 'No' but I took his point. Oathing was a traditional, harmless ritual by which brotherhood and goodwill were bonded, he said. What about the savage, obscene and bestial oathings that had brought out the worst in the Mau Mau? He laughed.

'That was war...a war of liberation...and you British were the ones who taught us that all is fair in love and war.' What about the rumours in Nairobi that the young man convicted of murdering Tom Mboya had come straight from an oathing ceremony? What about the murder of a church minister who had refused to take an oath? The charm and the smile dropped as one. His eyes narrowed perceptibly. 'Rumours are not good for brotherhood and goodwill... rumours are not good for journalists.' In the time-honoured tabloid phrase, I made my excuses and left.

Back in Nairobi I sought out an old friend, Eric Marsden, a former Fleet Street man who was then Assistant Editor of the *East African Standard*. Eric had lived and worked in Kenya for many years. He loved the country and the people and had made a study of their customs and traditions way beyond the call of duty. He confirmed what the Kiambu official had told me: there was a great range of Kikuyu oaths and most of them were no more malevolent than those of Manchester Masons. But the Standard's non-Kikuyu black staff were in an extremely agitated state. They had heard that much more war-like oathings were taking place among the Kikuyu. Worse, there was evidence to suggest that they were taking place, with the consent and knowledge of the owner-occupier, at Gatundu, Jomo Kenyatta's shrine-like residence north of Nairobi. Eric gave me a friendly backgrounder. There was no question of my quoting him, or even using in my copy much of the speculative information he had imparted. I filed a report which merely referred to the upsurge of tribal tensions. Not being happy about Kenyatta's alleged involvement, I left it out of my copy. Unbeknown to me, however, other visiting firemen had picked up the Gatundu oathing story and it was splashed heavily in several Fleet Street newspapers. I was on an early flight to Johannesburg to chase another story when Mzee heard on the BBC World Service that London newspapers were linking him with Mau Mau oathing ceremonies.

Peter Hawthorne, himself an old Kenya hand, greeted me in Johannesburg with a cheery 'So you got out of Nairobi just in time, Novvo!' What did he mean? Hadn't I heard? Eric Marsden and two other highly respected white journalists, Alan Chester and Michael Chester (unrelated) had that very morning been served with deportation orders and unceremoniously bundled aboard a London-bound airliner. I was astounded. Neither of the Nairobi newspapers for which the three men worked had made any reference to the renewal of oathing ceremonies, let alone any mention of Kenyatta. Nor had they been quoted in the foreign press stories.

From all later accounts, it appeared to be one of those decisions emanating from the impenetrable labyrinth of Kenyan politics. Mzee had, in a fury, sent word down that publicity about oathing must cease at any cost. The off-with-their-heads command had reached a senior official in the Information Ministry who had a long-standing antipathy to the three men for their refusal, on other occasions, to toe the official line. They were the easiest targets of opportunity and out of the country they should go.

It is relatively painless for a transient journalistic fireman to be expelled from a country. If he has any sense, he will wait until he has already departed before filing a critical report on a sensitive situation anyway. It is more disconcerting for a foreign staffer, who has established family, friends and contacts and set up temporary home and base. It is devastating for an expatriate hack who has probably put down roots and identified fully with his new country.

Such was the case with Alan and Mike Chester and Eric Marsden. Of the three, Eric had the best Kenyan government contacts and the greatest desire to return to Kenya, a country for which he had great affection and where his two children had been born. The Chesters resigned themselves to alternative destinations but Eric wheeled and dealed from London for his deportation order to be rescinded. Eventually it was, ostensibly with the imprimatur of Mzee himself.

A year later he was allowed to return and resume his trade. But the dark side of Africa has a long and unforgiving memory. He received a succession of anonymous, threatening telephone calls, menacing notes and, finally, awoke one morning to find the mutilated body of a black man on the doorstep of his home. As a widower with two young children to care for, he finally agreed to accept a standing offer made by his old friend and colleague, Harold Evans, to join the *London Sunday Times* as Jerusalem correspondent. Understandably, the Nairobi press corps, foreign and local, was unnerved by the arbitrary and rather mysterious expulsion of three colleagues. Perhaps that was the aim of the Information Ministry, if not State House. It certainly contributed to the rather subdued coverage given to Kenyatta's next move: the threats to expel the country's large and influential Asian community. It was low-profile time for the press of East Africa and correspondents in the Kenyan capital settled once again into the cosy routine of reporting the all-too-numerous tragedies and travesties elsewhere in Africa.

Several prominent Kenyan politicians who had the temerity to question the existing order disappeared, were disgraced or murdered but the country retained a pragmatic political front that held Western affection and a glamorous tourist image that attracted that rarest of African commodities – foreign exchange. In his dotage, Kenyatta fed his chickens and pigs, took to strange theological ramblings and to constructing the complex riddles so beloved of the Kikuyu. A remarkable man by any standards, he died in August, 1978. A testimony to his distinction among politicians worldwide, particularly in Africa, is that he died in his sleep at a ripe old age. As our television colleagues are fond of saying when they sign off their dispatches: 'Only one thing is certain…nothing will ever be the same again.'

Following Page: ➡

Top: *Peter Webb of* Newsweek *in Nairobi with all the foreign hack of the sixties needs – typewriter, radio and fags.*

Bottom: *John 'Ali Bin' Osman of the BBC interviews Kenyan President Daniel Arap Moi.*

'I know there's a war on, waiter, but this can't be your best brandy' –
Tony White of Reuters.

Following Page: ⫸

An officer and a gentleman – Donald Wise in Kenyan badminton rig.

'No photographs please... this is an undercover assignment' –
Ian Colvin of The Daily Telegraph in Nairobi 1969.

CHAPTER FOUR

WINDS OF
FLATULENCE

*T*he late and much lamented George Gale had many attributes but an ear for music was not among them. Even if he had been musical, it is doubtful if he would have recognised the Ghanaian national anthem. It was 1961 and the country had been independent for only four years. The national anthem was not the catchiest of tunes. When a band struck up the opening bars in the Black Star Hotel in Accra, George was enjoying a drink or two with his Fleet Street colleagues in the hotel lounge. Then a roving correspondent with the *Daily Express*, George was in Ghana covering the visit of Duncan Sandys, Commonwealth Secretary at the time.

Those who remember him – and there will be many millions of British radio listeners and TV viewers who will not forget his programmes in the 1970s and 80s – will recall that unmistakable, gravelly growl which carried like a foghorn to the corners of any building he graced. When that building was a bar or hotel, the decibels rose in direct proportion to the liquor downed. This was one such occasion. George was holding forth to the delight of his colleagues but also to the intense interest of several young Ghanaians dotted around the lounge, studiously pretending to examine newspapers through those large, one-way dark spectacles which are as characteristic of the African secret policeman as a crew-cut used to be of the CIA agent.

It is doubtful whether these young 'spooks' could follow George's gruff wit and insulting erudition but they were under orders from their boss to watch for any signs of subversion from these foreign journalists. Gale, of course, obliged. Not for nothing had he been the genesis of *Private Eye*'s parody of the raging Fleet Street hack, 'Lunchtime O'Booze', or that magazine's more specific 'George G Ale'.

He was at his vociferous best when the band struck up the anthem, barely noticed those in the know rise to their feet out of respect and continued to roar out his story from his armchair. The spooks had all they wanted. They reported to their boss, one Krobo Edusei, a sinister Ashanti appointed as Minister of the Interior to Kwame Nkrumah, the 'Redeemer' of Ghana and, in his own eyes, at least, the saviour of emergent Africa.

Krobo Edusei – inevitably to be dubbed 'Crowbar' by his many detractors – was a kind of eminence noire to Kwame Nkrumah. He adopted the self-satisfied smugness coupled with a rather dangerous paranoia that befitted a minister who doubled as head of a 'secret' police force answerable only to a man who frequently compared himself to a black Christ. His agents posted at the Black Star conveyed the tidings he wanted to hear. This raucous, red-haired English newspaperman, showing all the colonial arrogance of his caste, had demonstrated disgusting disrespect towards the Ghanaian national anthem, to the newly liberated people of Ghana and, therefore, to The Redeemer himself. He would have to be dealt with.

A badly hung-over and totally bemused George Gale was awoken the following morning by a couple of Interior Ministry officials who served him unceremoniously with a deportation order. He was to be on the next plane to London that evening. His offence was that he had shown 'gross disrespect' to the leader, the government and the people of Ghana by not standing up for the national anthem. This 'hostile attitude' would not be tolerated. He had to go. George, basically a gentleman, although he would never admit it, apologised profusely. 'I didn't know the tune,' he insisted.

The phrase 'tone deaf' does not translate well into Ashanti. Anyway, Crowbar did not want to hear any excuses or apologies. Nor did the British High Commission, of course. Ghana was Britain's showpiece former colony and thus 'Osagyefo' – The Redeemer – and his men could do no wrong, certainly not as a result of abominable behaviour by this blustering, bombastic chap from Fleet Street. George was duly deported – with a good story for the *Daily Express* and an even better one for the lunchtime circuit at El Vino. As was rapidly becoming the tradition, his colleagues in Ghana chipped in for an alcoholic wake. Stung by taunts about his lack of musicality George composed – and sang in duet with John Ridley of *The Daily Telegraph* – an impromptu tribute to The Redeemer. To the tune of 'I got plenty of nothing' from *Porgy and Bess,* Gale and Ridley belched out 'I've got qualms about Kwame... and Kwame's got qualms about me...' all the way to Accra international airport.

The hacks were not the only ones to have qualms about Kwame. By the time the Gale incident occurred, Nkrumah was manifestly leading Ghana and much of Africa down the slippery slope to dictatorship, oppression, enforced hero worship and a personal interpretation of socialism which insisted that Ghana's basic wealth be distributed equitably – among his own family. Specifically for providing him with palaces and personal Swiss bank accounts.

Tom Stoppard, an unsuccessful hack (he never made it beyond a trial period on the *Bristol Evening Post*) but a highly successful playwright, must have had Osegyefo in mind when he had one of his characters, an African dictator, refer to 'relative democracy'. It was a system soon to be all-too-familiar in Africa whereby the members of one's family benefit from one's elevation to the top job by being awarded the best ministerial portfolios, the most influential civil service posts and monopolies on the only lucrative businesses in town.

Before the war, Nkrumah had been an ambitious young schoolteacher in the British colony of the Gold Coast (so named because of the lucrative nature of its slave trade rather than any rich geological seam). He showed some initiative studying at various paternalistic American academic institutions, by working as a ship's steward, a Harlem fishmonger and a soap factory labourer. He dabbled in theology and left-wing politics in Pennsylvania, New York and latterly London where he was the most fanatical of the little group of communist pupils of George Padmore, the pipe-smoking West Indian revolutionary and Comintern agent.

When he left America, according to his own writings, he noticed the Statue of Liberty 'her arm raised as if in personal farewell to me'. He would not rest, he wrote, until he had taken the message of liberty to Africa. He was soon to build his own statue, a 20-foot high effigy of himself, in bronze, in the centre of Accra but 'liberty' was not its name.

Nkrumah returned home in 1947 and soon established himself as a national and international hero, campaigning for self-government, organising trade union movements and leading demonstrations against British colonial rule. The British obligingly put him into gaol for a brief period, thereby assuring his status as a leader in waiting. Nkrumah was to wear with pride his convict's cap embroidered with the letters 'PG' for prison graduate.

The Gold Coast had already been earmarked as the first British African possession to be decolonised as the new state of Ghana. Alone among tropical colonies it had large resources of natural wealth and was the world's largest producer of cocoa. Its people were cheerful, friendly and relatively well-educated. It had a rich history and a quaint, if crude, democratic system wherein chiefs could be 'enstooled' instead of enthroned, or 'destooled' instead of dethroned. This chap Nkrumah was a bit of a firebrand but, by gosh, he was popular and was being acclaimed by anti-colonialists across the globe as a 'modern Moses'.

The acclaim that greeted Ghana's independence on March 6, 1957, was astonishing in the general mood of euphoria it generated about Africa's 'bright new future'. Delegations came from sixty nations. The Duchess of Kent represented Queen Elizabeth and Richard Nixon, then Vice-President, the United States. Nixon was effusive about 'the kind of colonialism that can produce a Ghana'. Nkrumah was borne shoulder high to Parliament Square, performed an impromptu dance and then burst into tears. Everyone was reported to be deliriously happy and all British newspapers reported that the crowds 'sang and danced in the streets throughout the night in joy'.

This line about happy Africans dancing through the night was to become a standard intro to the stories filed by correspondents about the rash of independence celebrations that were soon to follow Ghana's example. There was one flaw, however.

Independence invariably came at midnight, long after the final deadline of European newspapers. Most of the hacks on the spot filed these glowing accounts hours before the event and then, being sociable types, went on to enjoy the flood of free food and booze without actually checking to see if the citizens were actually that happy.

It was left to reporters with the less demanding deadlines of weekly journals to sound notes of doubt. Walking the streets of Accra long after the new Ghanaian flag had been hoisted, one such correspondent saw no dancing, heard no singing. He found the locals in bars and night clubs subdued and apprehensive about the future. 'Africans were much more hard-nosed and realistic about what independence portended,' he wrote. 'Rosy dreams were left to the departing colonial masters and the metropolitan press.' A few years later at Nigeria's independence celebrations, David Williams, then editor of the authoritative *West Africa* magazine, found 'desultory groups wending their way home'. His companion, a correspondent for a liberal newspaper, harangued the Nigerians. 'Dance, dammit, dance! You're supposed to be dancing.'

In Ghana, it was not long before the African reality began to emerge. *The Daily Telegraph*, under Sir Colin Coote, managing editor, maintained a hawk-like surveillance of emerging Africa. Sir Colin persuaded his friend Walter Elliott, a Tory minister, to write about his visits to West Africa and Elspeth Huxley to give her impressions on East Africa. He also 'caused staff correspondents to be sent in succession and without respite to every accessible corner...the paper became known as the Bush Telegraph!'

Sir Colin made a point of meeting African leaders visiting London, Hastings Banda, Kenneth Kaunda and Kwame Nkrumah among them. He recorded in his autobiography: 'It is not the least use expecting them to behave or think like Westminster parliamentarians. Independence does not mean to them the right of free discussion – how should it? What it means to them is power. Similarly, to them a civil service does not mean a body of trained administrators – it means a bunch of nominees subservient to them.

'As a result of its pertinacious interest in African affairs, *Daily Telegraph* correspondents have been in trouble in Ghana, East Africa and to a lesser extent in the Union of South Africa. I never find it surprising that inexperienced governments should be touchy, or that they should have a lot to hide. To get expelled is the occupational risk of a correspondent and if he is expelled for telling the truth, that is a feather in his cap. Expulsion does far more harm to the expeller than to the expelled – it can be compared with children locking nanny out of the nursery. They will, notwithstanding, have to learn table manners one day.'

Sir Colin warmed to the theme: 'African leaders will learn in due course not to ape the Roman emperors with a claim to divinity and infallibility. If they don't learn, a period of collapse and relapse into barbarism will come and will be longer. Meanwhile, the British press must report facts. *The Daily Telegraph* correspondents always do so, about apartheid as well as about embryo Prester Johns.'

In independent Ghana, it did not take long for the African reality to emerge, although a surprising number of foreign correspondents were initially enamoured of Nkrumah. John Redfern, of the *Daily Express*, had met and interviewed him as early as 1948 and had found him 'a complicated character...extremely charming one minute and coldly ruthless the next'. Redfern was known to colleagues as 'The Bishop' because of his strong Christian faith and his penchant for examining churches and mission stations while bullets flew and beer flowed around him. (He was later to become religious affairs correspondent and a member of the Church Information Committee of the Church of England.)

Redfern approved of what appeared to be Nkrumah's austere lifestyle at that time – no alcohol, no smoking and frugal food – and referred to him in copy as 'an African Gandhi'. The man who would be The Redeemer was suitably flattered when he heard this relayed – on Redfern's own radio – by the BBC World Service. Nkrumah ordered that the sobriquet be taken up (along with many others) as a rallying call for his party. At the independence celebrations, Redfern was the obvious choice to offer Nkrumah the good wishes of the foreign press. The *Express* man had heard that the main bedroom of Nkrumah's home was being refurbished. Was he contemplating marriage? he asked. 'Not just yet,' Nkrumah replied 'but if I do I shall, of course, consult you.' A few months later he chose an Egyptian bride from a series of photographs supplied by families in Cairo. He did not consult The Bishop.

One journalist who, at no stage, was fooled by Nkrumah's charm was Ian Colvin of *The Daily Telegraph*, a leader writer, roving correspondent and a first-class, if slightly eccentric, investigative and interpretive reporter. The remarkable story of Ian Colvin has, amazingly, still to be written fully, although his African experiences appear in these pages. When Kwame Nkrumah attempted to impose his will on the foreign press he could not have chosen a more implacable adversary. Among Colvin's many claims to fame was that he had once been told by Winston Churchill – jokingly, of course – that he had been the man who had started the Second World War.

He was a worthy heir to his father, also Ian Colvin, a famous leader writer on the *Morning Post* whose skilful, satirical pen had been the scourge of successive British governments. Colvin Senior had made his name on the *Cape Times* in South Africa and commemorated this happy period of his life by christening his son Ian Goodhope Colvin. Colvin Junior entered journalism and within a remarkably short time was appointed the *News Chronicle*'s correspondent in pre-war Berlin at the age of 23. The range and depth of his contacts in Berlin was so great that he learned authoritatively and early on of Hitler's plans to attack Poland. In March 1939, on his own initiative, he flew back to London and sought an interview with Prime Minister Neville Chamberlain. He believed that the British Ambassador and Whitehall officials were either suppressing or minimising the bad news before it reached the Cabinet. He first saw Lord Halifax, the Foreign Secretary, and told him of the imminent threat to Poland. Halifax took him to Chamberlain's room where he was asked to give his appraisal of the situation in Germany. He established his bona fides by mentioning plans by senior Germans to overthrow Hitler had a war developed over the 1938 Munich crisis. Three of the men he named were later executed by Hitler.

Eventually, Sir Alexander Cadogan, head of the Foreign Office, asked him: 'What would be the effect if we guaranteed Poland?' The young Colvin replied 'It would help the situation in Germany'. Soon afterwards, Chamberlain contacted Warsaw proposing an Anglo-Polish guarantee that was immediately announced in the House of Commons. Six years later Colvin, who had served with distinction in the Royal Marines and had commanded a landing craft flotilla, called on Winston Churchill. 'So you have survived the war,' Churchill told him. 'And it was you who started it with that Polish guarantee.'

Churchill was to pay fulsome tribute to Colvin in his War Memoirs. 'I gathered and contributed a great deal of information from foreign sources. Ian Colvin was the *News Chronicle* correspondent in Berlin. He plunged very deeply into German politics and established contacts of a most secret character with some of the important German generals and also with the independent men of character and quality in Germany who saw in the Hitler movement the approaching ruin of their native land.'

Colvin was to follow this coup with a painstaking and diligent investigation in the early 1950s which revealed one of the most astonishing stories of the war. He learned that the British secret service had objected to a novel called *Operation Heartbreak* written by Duff Cooper who had been a wartime Minister of State. He resigned his job and travelled throughout Europe researching the clues of an amazing wartime espionage trick.

In 1943, the body of a Royal Navy officer who had recently died from drowning was floated off the Spanish coast. The body had been furnished with a set of documents to mislead the Germans just before the invasion of Sicily. Rommel's papers were to show that the German secret service had been well and truly duped. Colvin's analysis published in 1953 as *The Unknown Courier* was to form the plot for the spy story and later the film *The Man Who Never Was*.

A distinguished, rather scholarly figure, he was to publish another half a dozen books on politics and intelligence matters but his professorial habit of peering over the top of his half-moon spectacles and dozing off in the middle of press conferences – particularly after a goodly lunch in the tropics – belied his toughness, humour and sense of adventure.

It is doubtful whether Kwame Nkrumah was aware of Ian Colvin's background when he decided to throw his newly acquired weight around with the foreign press. Ghana had been independent for only five months when Colvin, who had just joined the *Telegraph* from the *Sunday Express* where he had been foreign editor, was dispatched (no doubt with Sir Colin Coote's words ringing in his ears) to see how the new nation was faring. He found the atmosphere in Accra 'strange and mistrustful' and 'I sensed that the carefree, laughing Ghanaian way of life was going into eclipse'. Part of the cause was Nkrumah's willingness to deploy his newly acquired citizenship and deportation laws to bully would-be or real political opponents.

The law was being tested for the first time in a case in Kumasi, in Ashanti heartland, against two Moslem leaders of the National Liberation Opposition whose deportation had been ordered by the authorities. They had won an injunction against deportation and the state was to demand that the injunction be ruled invalid. Colvin flew to Kumasi on the same aircraft as Geoffrey Bing, QC, the British barrister acting as constitutional adviser to Nkrumah. Colvin took an instant dislike to Bing 'an assiduous, perspiring and ingratiating figure'. It was Bing, not Ghana's attorney-general, who had taken it upon himself to demand the deportation of the two Moslems.

There was a tense atmosphere in Kumasi and extra police and troops had been deployed in the area. Colvin reported that the police had used batons to keep angry crowds away from the courtroom. Bing's arguments against the injunction were upheld by the judge and the two Moslems were taken into custody and driven to Accra. Colvin reported the angry scenes after this had happened. 'This afternoon thousands of Ashantis surged through the city roaring their defiance of the Nkrumah regime.'

This reference to manifest disenchantment with his government infuriated Nkrumah. In the classic tradition of 'shooting the messenger', he ordered Bing and 'Crowbar' Edusei to take action against the troublemaking press. Writs of attachment were granted by the Supreme Court against Colvin and against the editor of the *Ashanti Pioneer,* a pro-opposition daily published in Kumasi, which had also reported the riots. Bing, a former Labour MP, argued that the reports amounted to an attack on the impartiality of the judge and could bring hardship to the Englishmen connected with the case, including himself.

Colvin was called in to police headquarters where a CID man with the wonderfully colonial name of Carruthers advised him that criminal charges were being contemplated against him. He was asked for his passport but 'on my undertaking to remain in Ghana pending further decisions', Carruthers accepted his word instead, warning him that he would be arrested if he attempted to leave the country.

Colvin, of course, was as good as his word. He spent the three weeks before his case was to be heard probing the general mood of the people of Ghana and finding it one of bitter disillusion. The ancient rivalries of the Moslem north with the Ashanti kingdom against the Coast Colony had been accentuated by attempts to dominate from Accra. People were beginning to realise that Nkrumah's party had come to power on a 'colossal fraud' promising houses and cars for all. But 'from the patched tin roofs and slum street gutters of Bukom Square the people look up at a few nine-storey show pieces...they have seen no spread of wealth, no abatement of police powers and no easier justice since independence.' Colvin was to write this later. In the meantime he was charged with contempt of court.

The Daily Telegraph was suitably indignant about the treatment of its correspondent. It retained Christopher Shawcross, QC, another former Labour MP and brother of Lord Shawcross, to represent Colvin and flew him to Ghana. With him, to report on the proceedings and lend moral support, went another senior *Telegraph* correspondent, George Evans. When the case opened on 10 September in the Supreme Court in Accra, Mr Shawcross went for Mr Bing's jugular. The application was 'incompetent and should not be entertained', he told the Acting Chief Justice, Mr Quashie-Idun. Mr Bing, who had by now been sworn in as Attorney-General, was solely responsible for the application against Colvin which smacked of Star Chamber methods, said Shawcross.

Shawcross accused Bing of 'perpetrating a monstrous outrage upon the tender and infant freedom of Ghana' by bringing the application against Colvin out of personal spite. The two QCs were frequently on their feet at the same time protesting to Mr Justice Quashie-Idun who finally intervened to make them shake hands 'to resolve this matter in the native custom'. After three days of acrimonious legal wrangling, the Supreme Court decided it had no jurisdiction to hear the application and ruled that the case should have been heard in the Kumasi Divisional Court.

Colvin was ordered to appear before the Kumasi court a week later and left Accra for Nigeria. In the meantime, Christopher Shawcross, who had also popped across to Nigeria, was refused permission to re-enter Ghana and was declared a prohibited immigrant. Krobo Edusei, the Interior Minister who had taken to giving press interviews from a massive gold-plated bed he had ordered from Harrods, said Shawcross had been barred 'in order to maintain peace and stability in the country'.

Ghana was just as free as Britain, he insisted, and 'she cannot tolerate British lawyers coming here to abuse the elected government'. *The Daily Telegraph* then instructed Colvin not to return to Ghana, saying that his defence had been 'intolerably handicapped' by the banning of his counsel. The issue now became a diplomatic cause célèbre. There were questions in the House of Commons and a reluctant Foreign Commonwealth Office was obliged to lodge a formal protest with the Ghanaian government. Colvin was thoroughly enjoying himself. He promptly slapped writs on Nkrumah, Bing and the Police Commissioner, claiming damages for unlawful detention and slander.

A few days later, Nkrumah announced in a broadcast to the nation that the case against Colvin would be dropped 'to clear the air and remove misunderstanding'. He wondered if Ghana's critics fully appreciated the internal security problems in Ghana 'where we have to deal with a complex relationship of feudal, tribal and other factors and fight against inspired rumours and vicious misrepresentations'.

Colvin was declared a prohibited immigrant but this did not stop him from making strenuous efforts to recover the 250 guineas costs awarded to him by Accra Supreme Court. (Donald Wise remembers, with great delight, Colvin's attempts years later to have Geoffrey Bing and a Ghanaian government aircraft attached when it landed at Salisbury Airport. 'It caused an awful diplomatic tizz because he was perfectly within his rights.') The *Manchester Guardian* gave 'Dr Nkrumah and his colleagues credit for their second thoughts while *The Daily Telegraph* thought the Ghana Government 'still has a long way to go before belief in its devotion to democratic principles is re-established'.

George Evans was also refused permission to re-enter Ghana after a visit to Nigeria but this was rescinded once he returned to Lagos and he once again returned to Accra. There, in the foyer of the Ambassador Hotel, he bumped into 'Crowbar' Edusei who gave him a long, rambling interview. 'If I had my way you wouldn't have been allowed here,' he told Evans with a smile. 'But Kwame Nkrumah is a gentleman. If you wish to come to Ghana you must not misbehave.' He boasted that he too had been a journalist for seven years and lectured Evans on the ethics of journalism. 'We shall rule for 25 years because we know how to organise effectively and we tell people the truth,' he added.

I have never been able to understand why so many African politicians, black and white, insist on forecasting the duration of their power when most of them have been, and will be, fortunate to see out the current year.

Years later I was present when Ian Douglas Smith boasted confidently that there would be no black rule in Rhodesia – 'not for 1 000 years'. Edusei's forecast to George Evans was sixteen years adrift. Nkrumah was soon to become totally paranoid. He locked up opposition leaders like Dr J B Danquah and Joe Appiah, survived numerous attempts on his life and retreated more and more to the seclusion of his castle or his palace where Russian officers commanded his personal guard.

From the fastness of his retreat, Nkrumah pressed on with his 'vision' for pan-African unity, the defeat of white settler rule by pan-African forces and promoted himself as a statesman by offering to mediate in international crises. As once-wealthy Ghana sank into poverty around his feet, he ordered the construction of a massive palace, complete with luxurious residential suites, banqueting halls and soaring fountains. All this to house one single conference of the Organisation of African Unity. Perhaps a measure of his standing among fellow African leaders was the fact that only 13 heads-of-state turned up.

Corruption flourished unchecked among his faithful and obsequious henchmen like Crowbar Edusei who owned fifteen properties, a lease on a London flat, six foreign bank accounts, a fleet of expensive cars and, of course, the gold-plated bed from Harrods. Nkrumah pointedly ignored evidence of such blatant corruption presented to him. Honest police officers knew why: The Redeemer, the Messiah, the Modern Moses, the would-be ruler of united, socialist Africa was the biggest crook of them all. He had amassed a personal fortune of more than two million pounds in foreign bank accounts and indulged his own love of luxury with such whims as a six-million pound 'frigate' built on the Clyde which was nothing more than an armed, floating gin palace.

It was not so much this self-indulgence that caused his downfall as his obsession with raising an army to defeat the Smith regime in Rhodesia. Under the guise of training for this operation, senior army officers prepared for a coup d'état. In 1966, while Nkrumah was on his way to China 'to find a solution to the Vietnam problem', he was overthrown with little resistance. The market mammies of Makola danced in the streets, his statue was torn down and the ubiquitous portraits that had adorned every public building and many private homes were defaced. The new regime sent this self-same portrait to Interpol in the 'Wanted – Dead Or Alive' tradition.

The military leaders who had staged the coup gave way to an elected government three years later, but it was not long before the chain-smoking, whisky-swigging general seized power. He was toppled by his chief-of-staff, a lieutenant-general, who was in turn overthrown by a junior air force officer, Flight Lieutenant Jerry Rawlings.

Rawlings obviously had a strict upbringing. His remedy for rampant corruption and graft was to seize the military top brass and other senior government men, have them blindfolded and strapped to posts and executed by firing squad. Rawlings surprised many by handing over to civilian rule, but, in 1982, he returned in a rather bizarre coup attempt in which soldiers rampaged through Accra looting the very little that was left in shops and private homes. At the time of writing, Ghana, that once proud pilot show-piece of British decolonisation in Africa, is an economic and social wasteland ruled by fear, graft and the gun.

Nkrumah, with his family, had gone into exile in nearby Guinea where his old friend and admirer, Sekou Toure, made him co-president. The Redeemer was, however, kept under close wraps. No foreign journalist was allowed into Guinea to get his story. He died of cancer, a forlorn but never-to-be-forgotten figure, in 1972. From the earliest days of his power, it had been clear in which direction he was going to push Ghana. His treatment of Ian Colvin and other correspondents was evidence of despotic, corrupt and disastrous rule.

And yet the British government persisted apace with a policy of handing over, with unseemly haste, its remaining African colonies and protectorates, most of them far less prepared than Ghana had been for self-rule. Historians have suggested that Whitehall's conviction was that communism would make huge inroads into Africa if black nationalism was resisted. History suggests that Whitehall was, not for the first time, horribly wrong. Ironically, it was the 'last of the Victorians', Harold Macmillan, who set out for Africa shortly after being elected Prime Minister of Britain in 1959, to articulate his government's willingness to heed Tom Mboya's advice and 'scram from Africa'.

He started his six-week safari in Ghana and found Nkrumah 'an engaging, charming character' despite the latter's rantings about colonialism. It was in Accra that he first referred to the 'wind of change' sweeping through the continent, although it was not until he repeated the phrase in a keynote address to the South African parliament in Cape Town in February 1960, that it had the desired impact.

Macmillan spoke of 'the strength of this African national consciousness' and went on: 'The wind of change is blowing through this continent, and whether we like it or not, this growth of national consciousness is a political fact. We must all accept it as a fact and our national policies must take account of it.'

The phrase had actually been bandied around Westminster and Whitehall for six years before Macmillan's speechwriter thought it might be an apposite theme for his safari. It was left to Henry Fairlie, then the most celebrated of Fleet Street political columnists who was accompanying Macmillan, to pluck the 'wind of change' from the text and turn it into an ever-resounding catch-phrase. But it was his great friend and colleague, George Gale, drawing on his own African experiences, who got it right. 'Wind of change?' roared George. 'Even in 1960 it was more of a long, windy and very wet fart!'

In those early days of Uhuru in Africa, foreign press interest was still remarkably limited, given the drama that was unfolding. As far as American correspondents went, there were the few 'name' transients who passed through, but few African-based correspondents. An American correspondent, in those days, was obliged to tell his readers where Africa was, and what, why and when it mattered before he could even begin to tell the story. French interests in Africa were vast and vital but the correspondents who visited Africa were either inhibited by the deep-rooted Quai d'Orsay restrictions on press freedom or were naïve revolutionaries propounding the African revolution in unheard-of underground publications. Portuguese, Italian and Spanish newspapers had similar fetters. The German press had still to find its post-Nazi feet.

The British colonies, especially those with large expatriate communities, like Kenya, the Federation of Rhodesia and Nyasaland and South Africa, always yielded stories that had a 'home' rather than a 'foreign' interest. 'Major Oliver Jackson, a 56-year-old retired gunner from Stowe-on-the-Wold, faced the painted, spear-wielding Mau Mau tribesman in Kenya's, misty terrorist-troubled upland'...that type of thing.

The impulse was very much that of the editor of the *Aberdeen Press and Journal* in 1912 when he received a report of a tragedy involving a passenger ship in the North Atlantic. Among those who perished was a Scot from Aberdeen. Having been brought up in the old school of 'get the local angle first and foremost' he made up the front page with the headline 'Aberdeen Man Lost At Sea'. Underneath, the subsidiary, or strap line read 'Titanic Sinks'.

All this was greatly acceptable fodder to Fleet Street's more widely circulated newspapers, yet to be known as the 'popular press'. The *Daily Mail, Daily Express* and, to a lesser extent, the *Daily Mirror* pitted their correspondents against each other in a bid to get the first man on the spot with the most graphic account of how he got there, what horrendous experiences he underwent to do so and how, finally, against all odds, got the story out just to tell YOU, the *Daily Beast* reader, as Evelyn Waugh would have had it, what is really going on in the crumbling empire.

In this context the first-person 'I was there...' introduction was almost compulsory. It was before television techniques had been perfected to beam the reality of assorted horrors directly into post-prandial sitting-rooms in glorious technicolour. This was the age of the newspaper, propped against the cereal packet in the Pocklington (Yorks) kitchen, hopefully to bring forth the comment 'My, what a cock-up...I hope that this chap's being paid well for going to a place like that'. (The answer to that, by the way, was 'Not very much but they told me the expenses were good.')

This style had its great exponents like Peter 'Bigfoot' Younghusband, John 'Piggy' Monks and Donald Wise, who was so much larger than life that an adhesive nickname eluded him. These men – and a host of others – would happily admit that their style and approach to the African transition was unashamedly gung-ho when it came to a story. It was a case of getting there early and projecting the personal pronoun into the 'I was the first reporter to break the siege of...' or 'Today I flew low over the rebel headquarters...'

The story, preferably, had to be full of bravado (and often was). It was expected to draw a vivid picture of the people and terrain and only then add a few pars – or paragraphs – of background and analysis in case the sub-editors wanted to pad it out a little. The fact remained that the competition and rivalry were so intense that, more often than not, these correspondents were there first and their accounts, colourful and hyperbolic, were the most graphic and the best news available in the days when electronic news-gathering, satellite television was unknown.

Ranged against the Monks, the Wises and the Younghusbands were the African 'commentators' most of whom were committed, equally unashamedly, to the 'cause of African emancipation' and the justness of 'liberation movements'. They tended to cultivate African leaders as personal friends rather than as contacts or interviewees and became deeply involved in any given 'cause'. Their reports to newspapers like *The Guardian* and *The Observer* would appear to be learned and well-informed but there was always the danger that readers would be hearing what any given president and his party wanted them to hear rather than what was really going on.

Doyen of the 'Africa experts', perhaps, was Colin Legum, a South African and a former Johannesburg City Councillor who had exiled himself in London, a refugee from the early purges of the Nationalist government's apartheid policies.

Colin had developed close friendships with many future African politicians while they were being fêted on London's then fashionable left-wing cocktail circuit. As Commonwealth Correspondent of *The Guardian* he was to become a familiar, if rather sinister figure, disembarking from private presidential aircraft or being publicly embraced by life presidents at public functions. His aloofness and his disdain for the more rumbustious hurly-burly of lesser African hackery did not make him the most popular of colleagues. His surname, coupled with his damp, limp handshake quickly earned him the sobriquet, 'The Vegetable'.

Legum had his rivals, the Canadians Clyde Sanger of *The Guardian* and Patrick Keatley and, later, several of his young acolytes. It was a school dismissed by the likes of Donald Wise as 'whimpering liberals', but their contrasting views of the age of Uhuru gave British newspaper readers, at least, a different perspective. More than a few white South African exiles became apologists for the 'new Africans' and persisted in springing to the defence of despots and dictators, especially if they espoused socialism, even when their excesses were revealed. Ronald Segal, a Capetonian who like so many others had fled South Africa 'one jump ahead of the security police' was enamoured of the African revolution and its exponents. Kwame Nkrumah, he wrote, had ensured his place in African history as 'a leader who has done the most concretely to further the ideals of Pan-Africanism.' Sekou Toure of Guinea was 'the most significant figure on the continent', Julius Nyerere's one-party socialist rule in Tanzania 'may produce a more vivid and deeply-rooted democracy than the Westminster pattern'.

While such commentators were trying to hawk the vision of African socialism, others were digging into the perpetuation of chilling African reality. John Osman, then a roving correspondent for *The Daily Telegraph*, was assigned by the new *Sunday Telegraph* to investigate – in 1961 – the very touchy subject of human slavery. Osman had already come across various forms of slavery in the Sudan and knew how sensitive the subject was. Under the pretext of making flying visits to the countries which straddle the Arab-Africa parallel, he began an investigation that was to take him six months and which disclosed that human slavery was still being widely practised. For his efforts he was awarded honorary membership of the Anti-Slavery League.

Osman started in newly independent Mali, formerly French Sudan, where he pointedly asked Modibo Keita, who was then negotiating a political association with Kwame Nkrumah, why he had not signed the Anti-Slavery Convention. He bounded his way through Upper Volta (now Burkina Faso), Niger, Chad and Sudan. Osman is as English as a pub but his Islamic-sounding name gave him access, that would have been otherwise denied, to Moslem leaders and officials. The slavery trail led to Saudi Arabia. There he befriended the then Crown Prince Faisal who readily admitted how difficult it would be to get rid of slavery because of its economic implications. Every Moslem had a duty to go to Mecca or Medina on Hajj. 'The reality was that African tribal chiefs going on Hajj would take whole rows of black men and women and cash 'em in like traveller's cheques to pay their Saudi bills.'

Faisal called in the Saudi public executioner, an enormous man who had been seized in Ethiopia and sold into slavery some forty years before. He showed Osman his special executioner's sword and boasted about his special pay. 'He cheerfully told me about his career,' John recalled. 'He had got it wrong on his first execution and the crowd had booed but he had become much better with practice and had successfully beheaded some 300 people without a hitch. He went on to ask me to send him some Lipton's tea and told me how much he enjoyed the BBC's Arabic Service.'

In Dubai, Osman befriended a British political agent who ran an official barge to show the flag around the Gulf states. 'He had an Arab crew which he provided with smart uniforms and drilled RN style...one morning he emerged from his residence to find one of his crew with his hands clasped around the flagpole. It turned out that the man was a slave owned by an old Arab sheik. He was quite happy to give his master his pay but when the old bugger took away his uniform he decided to seek manumission in a time-honoured way by clasping his hands around the flagpole of the nearest British diplomatic mission.' Osman's *Sunday Telegraph* series rebounded through the United Nations and beyond. When Faisal became the Saudi King he abolished slavery but, thirty years on, Osman points out that many thousands of black Africans still go on Hajj 'and not all of them came back'.

The publication of Osman's findings coincided with the independence of another British colony in West Africa. Sierra Leone had been under the British flag since the 16th century when English slave traders started raiding Africa's bulge. Unlike East Africa, where the slavers were mostly Arabs, West African tribal leaders ran their own trade, exchanging their own people for guns and other goodies supplied by European shippers. The Union Jack was struck in April 1961 in the capital, Freetown, so named as the country had been the home for freed slaves for a century (like contiguous Liberia founded by freed slaves from America in 1847 as Africa's first republic). Independent Sierra Leone got off to a quietish start but when the first prime minister, Sir Milton Margai, was succeeded by his younger brother (shades of relative democracy) in 1964 there came rumbles of discontent from the mountains and forests of the hinterland.

These reached the ears of *The Daily Telegraph*'s foreign desk which dispatched one of its younger foreign correspondents, David Loshak, to Freetown. Loshak found more than rumbles. Sir Albert, a barrister and amateur boxer was throwing his weight around the little country. A militant, fiery personality, he had quickly acquired a reputation for corruption and self-aggrandizement that was causing a surge of political and other opposition in the tiny country.

Loshak called on the information minister who told him, 'This is Freetown and the whole of Sierra Leone is a free town. This is not Ghana which deports journalists or Guinea which excludes them. You can write what you like – as long as it is fair.'

The atmosphere in the capital was such that David took the rider to be in the nature of a warning. He discreetly set out to interview one of Margai's most outspoken critics, Dr Raymond Easmon, who had written of the country's mood in a local opposition weekly newspaper and was convinced he would be arrested as a result. Loshak had checked into the same hotel which Graham Greene, based in Freetown as a British secret service agent during the war, had immortalised in *The Heart of the Matter*. It was there that he slipped some paper into his portable typewriter and began to compose his piece on the tensions in Sierra Leone. The paper happened to be some blank sheets of British Information Services and British High Commission stationery that he had picked up on his rounds. Later much was to be made of that trivial detail by the authorities. He took his copy to the cable office and sent it – press urgent rate – to London.

A few nights later, three plain-clothes policemen came to his hotel room with a search warrant. 'To my amazement it gave them authority to search on the grounds that I was believed to be in possession of cut or uncut diamonds. I had to laugh outright at this and bid them good luck but it quickly became clear that the sparklers they were looking for were my notebooks, cuttings and copies of my cables to the *Telegraph*.' It was the beginning of what he described as 'an Orwellian experience replete with flimsier pretexts and stonier stonewallers'.

His passport was impounded, but on the following day he was served with an expulsion order signed by Sir Albert himself. The police commissioner then told him that he would be placed in custody until he could be 'conveniently' put on an aircraft. He was detained in a barred and bolted office in police headquarters and remained there for six days and seven nights without being given any indication of his fate. All his requests to contact the British High Commission or his wife and family in London were refused. 'It was a time of fearful imaginings and miserable uncertainty.'

Finally he was formally charged with sedition and 'publishing false statements likely to injure the reputation of the Sierra Leone government'. By this time, the *Telegraph* was alert to his plight and a lawyer and a barrister were on their way to Sierra Leone. Accompanying them was Guy Rais, the *Telegraph*'s most senior reporter and one of Fleet Street's best-known and legendary characters. There are, of course, talkers and listeners. Guy was not of the latter ilk. Guy talked, muttered, cursed, cajoled, wheedled, growled, shrieked, sang and expostulated – and all of this when he was on his own. It was not so much a case of liking the sound of his own voice as of suffering, for him, the unbearable lightness of silence. A conversation with an automatic bank teller would be less one-sided than a chat with Guy Rais. And yet he was a first-class reporter.

Back in the home newsroom we listened in constant amazement as he prattled, joked and crackled down a telephone to some hapless interviewee only to emerge with a lengthy verbatim account from the hapless soul at the other end of the line. Guy was also loud. Despite the pipe clenched between his teeth and sucking lips, his voice carried to the four corners of the newsroom where other, less confident colleagues were attempting a more subtle approach in telephonic interviewing. It could be extremely irritating. To David Loshak, incarcerated for a long, lonely week in his police cell somewhere in hostile West Africa, the umistakable, gruff voice of Guy Rais demanding immediate access to his colleague was 'the voice of angels...a heavenly choir...the finest sound I've ever heard'. In the finest foot-in-door tradition, Rais was at the cell door, expostulating to an emotional Loshak about 'these silly old fools' running the police station, the country, Africa and, for good measure, the editors of *The Daily Telegraph*.

There was, of course, still the trial. The accused Loshak duly appeared in the dock of the Supreme Court of Sierra Leone on charges of sedition and others which, if proven, could have rendered him the least free man in Freetown. Mr Godfray Le Quesne QC appeared for Loshak and Mr Berthan Macaulay QC, the Nigerian-born Attorney-General of Sierra Leone, led the prosecution. The windows of the steamy courtroom were open and the noise from passing traffic, coupled with an excited buzz from 300 local people jammed into the public gallery, made it extremely difficult to hear any submission or interjection. But from the brass-railed dock, David distinctly remembers hearing Guy Rais muttering loudly 'Silly old fool...silly old moo!'

The seriousness of the charges belied the mood in the courtroom. The public gallery frequently erupted into delighted laughter.

'By their murmurings and shufflings and occasional hissing when the Attorney-General was worsted in argument or interrupted the defence they made it obvious where their sympathies lay...with their backslappings, greetings and spontaneous demonstrations of support for me in the court, in the streets and in my hotel, the citizens showed that the power-hungry politicians were not going to have things all their own way.'

As the trial dragged on, it became clear that the state case was based only on what David had written. There was no suggestion of inaccuracy even, let alone sedition. He had merely reported that there were rumours of the impending arrest of opposition figures. The attorney-general attempted to put sinister connotations on Loshak's use of British High Commission notepaper and on such trivia as the routine time-slug with which he had started his cable to London. The key witness was Dr Easmon – quaintly described by the prosecution as 'the opposition controversialist'. Sir Albert Margai was among the prosecution witnesses but had little to offer.

At the end of the hearing, Loshak was found guilty on four counts of sedition and 'publishing statements likely to injure the reputation of the Sierra Leone government'. He was fined the equivalent of 100 pounds which was paid immediately by the *Telegraph* solicitor and, to his great relief, deported. In London, the *Telegraph* afforded him what then passed in those hallowed halls for a hero's welcome. An editorial pointed to the difficulties of a correspondent's work in 'less stable states' and added 'Mr Loshak's trial may be regarded as a sort of battle-honour'. It was scant comfort to Loshak to learn that a year later Sir Albert Margai, despite strenuous ballot-rigging efforts, had lost an election to Siaka Stevens. Even less comfort for the people of Sierra Leone was the immediate military take-over followed two days later by a counter-putsch by the army and then another coup which replaced Siaka Stevens. Mr Stevens established a one-party state, imposed four states of emergency and survived numerous coup and assassination attempts before 'retiring' in 1985 to be replaced by yet another military regime. Sierra Leone remains a corrupt and bankrupt military dictatorship, repeatedly defaulting on its interest payments on massive loans from the International Monetary Fund.

Britain's post-colonial legacy was not looking too good in West Africa. Only The Gambia, those highly improbable banks of the Gambia River which intrude for 300 miles into the interior of Senegal, managed to stay out of the headlines. Poverty-stricken but cheerful, Gambia managed to keep its first popular president, Sir Dauda Jawara, for a quarter of a century. Correspondents visiting 'smuggler's creek' (the country subsists on a large measure of illicit trade with Senegal) found the friendliness and informality a delightful contrast to other parts of Africa. Jawara was always good for a 'colour' piece. He would give interviews while trimming his suburban hedge and took great pride, as a Glasgow-trained veterinary surgeon, of knowing the name of every cow in his domain.

Whitehall, followed meekly by Westminster, looked to the mighty Federation of Nigeria, Africa's most populous and potentially wealthiest state, for some remedy to the post-colonial hangover. Harold Macmillan, riding his ill wind in 1960, called in on Nigeria on the eve of its independence and recorded 'the sense of fun and merriment' for which West Africans were renowned. Perhaps his brief had failed to inform him that some of Nigeria's leading politicians had been sounding dire warnings about the federation's lack of viability. Abubakar Tafawa Balewa, the first federal prime minister, had said twelve years earlier that Nigerian unity was 'only a British invention'. At the same time, a Yoruba leader had written 'Nigeria is not a nation. It is a mere geographical expression.'

And, of course, so it was to prove. In the six years following independence, the country was wracked with pain and turmoil. There were two military coups, an abortive attempt to create a unitary state, and inter-tribal rioting which left thousands dead. Foreign correspondents were arbitrarily deported (including the hapless David Loshak of the *Telegraph* who was becoming a little paranoid about West Africa and accepted a posting to India). In the Nigerian civil war that was soon to follow the military takeovers, journalists were to be shot at, beaten, traumatised, agonised, wounded and, in one tragic case, killed, in the course of duty. But that is for another chapter.

In sharp contrast to Britain's botched and disastrous retreat from West Africa, France carved up its vast sub-Saharan empire with relative prudence, panache and success. The 'relative' must be emphasised. Paris had long since regarded its mission in Africa to be a civilising one. Small groups of bright Africans were nursed and nurtured into 'black Frenchmen' who would return to lead their countries into what General de Gaulle liked to refer to as *la plus grande France*.

In 1940, with Paris under the swastika, de Gaulle had taken his Free French administration to Brazzaville, the steamy, sultry French Equatorial African town on the north bank of the Congo River. There he was visited in 1941 by Ben Lucien Burman, a roving war correspondent with the Scripps-Howard newspaper chain and the *Reader's Digest*. Burman swallowed his distaste for de Gaulle – 'there was an intellectual arrogance...a disdain for the rest of

humanity' – to boost Allied war morale with some purplish dispatches: 'Here, astride the Equator, France miraculously survives...This
is no longer the heart of darkness...this is the Congo, the cradle of
New France.' Arrogant he most certainly was but de Gaulle felt sufficient gratitude towards his wartime African hosts to call a conference of colonial administrators in Brazzaville to discuss Africa's
post-war future.

The Fourth Republic brought some major concessions for France's
African territories and the system of creating black elites yielded men
like Leopold Senghor of Senegal and Félix Houphouet-Boigny of the
Ivory Coast who were to play influential roles in the following fifty
years in Africa. When de Gaulle returned to power in the wake of the
chaos caused by the Algerian war, he came up with a characteristic
solution to the mounting demands for emancipation in Africa: each of
twelve territories would vote 'Oui' or 'Non' to a large measure of autonomy which would leave Paris in effective control of defence, economic
affairs and foreign policy. It was take it, or leave it.

Eleven of the twelve states voted overwhelmingly in favour of
community with France and, in 1960, became independent, nominally
at least. Under the influence of Sekou Touré's radical rhetoric, Guinea
rejected the idea. The French reaction was immediate. French aid was
cut off and expatriate advisers, civil servants, teachers, engineers, doctors and businessmen were withdrawn. They took with them all
French government property that could be transported, and destroyed
that which could not. The telephone system was ripped out and even
the law books were removed from government offices. It was de Gaulle
at his vindictive worst.

By contrast, France showered magnanimity on the community
countries. Financial and technical aid was swiftly made available,
military advisers moved in and military units were strategically
deployed to some of the states. To all intents and purposes, de
Gaulle had achieved his wish for *la plus grande France*. Flurries of
rebellion in former French colonies were invariably put down by
French paratroopers, although the tiny state of Togo had the dubious distinction of becoming the first of many 'free' African countries
to suffer a coup d'état. President Sylvanus Olympio refused to
absorb into his army some 60 Togolese soldiers demobilised by the
French after the Algerian conflict. They shot him dead outside the
gates of the American embassy as he clawed for asylum. In Congo-
Brazzaville and Gabon, paratroopers broke up faction fights after a
disputed football international.

In Guinea, Souke Touré turned immediately to the Soviet Union
which promptly built an enormous runway and claimed the offshore

fishing rights for their trawlers while providing utilitarian aid such as porcelain toilet bowls and a few combine harvesters.

All foreign correspondents were barred en masse for many years but David Lamb, of the *Los Angeles Times,* persisted with visa applications and was finally invited to interview the 'Clairvoyant Guide' as Touré chose to call himself. Lamb found utter dilapidation and desolation in Conakry. Many thousands of Guinean dissidents had been gaoled, tortured and/or killed, including two dozen of Touré's former ministers.

Some two million Guineans – 40 per cent of the population – had fled into exile. Lamb's 'interview' turned out to be a crudely stage-managed stunt merely to have a distinguished American foreign correspondent being filmed by the government television network sitting next to the president. He was whisked away before he could ask any questions. Touré later telexed stock replies to questions he had posed to the *Los Angeles Times* bureau in Nairobi. Touré's death from a heart ailment in 1984 led to a swift military coup and a cautious move towards a renewal of old trading relationships with the West, including France.

George Gale of the Daily Express. *Ghana 1961*

CHAPTER FIVE

HEART OF DARKNESS

*F*rom the earliest recorded period, the vast West African region which became the Belgian Congo, and later Zaire, had inspired many of the myths and legends of darkest Africa. Here in genuine jungles and on the banks of rivers alive with crocodiles were to be found the pygmies, the cannibals, the witchdoctors, the mumbo-jumbo, the tarzans, the apes, the potted missionaries and all manner of wild, lurking, hostile creatures. Its sinister steaminess was perpetuated by powerful writers from Joseph Conrad in *Heart of Darkness* to V S Naipaul in *A Bend In The River*.

In 1960 the world suddenly realised that it was all too true. Belgian monarchs had governed the Congo like a vast country estate (eighty times the size of Belgium) for nearly a century. It was known as the 'silent empire' as the colonists drew an almost impenetrable veil over their exploitations of the region. The odd missionary or traveller emerged from the depths with stories of the natives being driven ruthlessly in quest of rubber and ivory – and of their being put to death or imprisoned if quotas were unfulfilled – but Brussels was able to brush aside such tales to an international community otherwise preoccupied with its own calamities.

The Belgians had created their own tiny class of assimilated blacks known as *evolues,* but political parties were banned, there was no press freedom and any whiff of dissent was crushed by the Force Publique, a colonial force of 25 000 men officered by whites. Brussels clearly hoped that the wind of change would dissipate itself in the stifling humidity of the Congo basin. It was not to be.

In January 1959 riots erupted in Leopoldville leaving dozens dead and several hundred people, including whites, injured. The cause, it transpired, had been the refusal of the authorities to allow a march of unemployed workers organised by an evolue schoolmaster named Joseph Kasavubu and his tribally based movement, Abako. This group and others, like the Mouvement National

Congolais led by another evolue, a post office worker named Patrice
Lumumba, had been spurred into political protest by General de
Gaulle's visit to Brazzaville, just across the river, and his take-it-or-
leave-it offer to French colonies in Africa.

By African standards, the Leopoldville riots were modest in
intensity and duration but they totally unnerved the white population and caused panic in Brussels. Unrest spread to outlying areas.
The Congo's ever-present tribal tensions erupted. Whole villages
were massacred and Belgian colons and their families started to flee
hurriedly through Leopoldville and the Congo basin ports.

Eric Marsden, then a roving correspondent for the *East African
Standard* and a stringer for major British newspapers, and Homer
Biggard of the *New York Times*, were the first journalists to break
the story of the impending chaos. 'We interviewed a Roman Catholic
bishop who gave us absolutely horrifying accounts of what was
going on in the interior,' recalls Marsden. 'We were both shocked as
none of this had come out. I remember Homer kept saying to the
bishop "Hey, is this on the level...are you expecting us to believe all
this?"' Marsden and Biggard confirmed the bishop's account.
'Belgian civilians were besieging Leopoldville airport and jostling at
the docksides. The unthinkable was happening. We had always
regarded the Belgians as the toughest and least perturbable of
Africa's settlers and yet here they were panicking on the turn. It
was clear that Brussels was going to pull the rug and quit the Congo
very rapidly.' The two correspondents filed the first of the Congo
horror stories that were soon to bring hordes of foreign newsmen
into the country. In the next few years, the Old Africa Hands were
to become a lot older and many of the newer chaps would be blooded
– sometimes literally – in the ways of independent Africa.

Initially, the Belgians tried to deny the Congo panic. The
Belgian Consul in Nairobi complained to the British governor about
Marsden's story. As Eric's wife was Belgian his denials caused
something of a diplomatic rumpus. But the decision had been made
by Brussels. Within a short eighteen months, the most chaotic of all
European decolonisations had taken place.

Sensing imminent 'freedom', the Congolese formed themselves
into a profusion of political movements, most of them based on tribal
affiliations which were to explode like a fragmentation grenade after
independence. The Belgian government hastily convened a round
table conference of newly emerged Congolese leaders, including
Kasavubu, Lumumba (released from prison especially for the occasion) and the shrewd, highly personable Moise Tshombe who, in col-
laboration with Belgian and other business interests, was already

planning the secession of the southern Katanga province, with its copper the wealthiest and most viable of the Congo's regions.

Faced with the prospect of committing itself to an Algerian type of war or granting shamefully swift independence, Brussels chose the latter. Even the pre-independence elections were chaotic, throwing up a pastiche of twelve rival parties with the volatile, unstable pan-Africanist, Patrice Lumumba, as the country's new prime minister, and Kasavubu, with his dreams of recreating the 16th-century empire of the Kongo, as president.

Lumumba aimed his barbed rhetoric at King Baudouin when the Belgian monarch came to Leopoldville to haul down the flag on 30 June 1960. 'Who could forget the hangings and shootings in which perished so many of our brethren?' he intoned. Any hopes harboured by the Belgians that they might wield Gaullist sway over their former colony were dashed by Lumumba.

'We have experienced contempt, insults and blows. We knew the law was never the same for whites as for blacks.' The new prime minister, 'his eyes glittering with hatred and venom', according to a Belgian commentator, went on to threaten Europeans living in the Congo. Even British and American journalists present found Lumumba's independence address chilling. King Baudouin was to suffer further humiliation. As he drove away from the ceremony in the back of an open car, a black youth rushed forward, grabbed his ceremonial sword and disappeared into the crowd, brandishing the weapon above his head. The incident added that much more menace to Lumumba's warnings.

Reuters had sent Nigel Ryan, one of their bright, up-and-coming young men who was later to become head of Britain's Independent Television News network, to Leopoldville. He was backed up by Serge Nabokov, an elderly white Russian from the Brussels bureau who found the heat, humidity and hints of impending horror too much to handle.

Correspondents in the Congolese capital were having to take turns on a creaky Creed telex machine to get their copy out. Nabokov's turn came to punch out a Reuters 'snap' – a brief, urgent news message – on the snatching of Baudouin's sword when he 'froze'. It is a condition not unknown among the finest and most experienced journalists, rather like an actor forgetting his lines on the opening night.

The conditions and circumstances of a situation suddenly crowd in, paralysing the thought process and other functions necessary for a journalist to operate under pressure. It happened to Serge Nabokov that day in Leopoldville. Nigel Ryan had to pull him away from the machine and complete the story himself. He then told Serge to rest and contacted Sandy Gall, who had just arrived in secessionist Katanga from Reuters' Johannesburg bureau, and asked him to get to Leopoldville to help out.

Gall duly arrived and checked into the Memling Hotel which was soon to become the base for the foreign press corps covering the Congo upheavals from the capital. All world crisis spots have their 'press centre' hotels – the Ledra Palace in Nicosia, the Crescent in Aden, the Commodore in Beirut, the Caravelle in Saigon and, of course, the 'Hotel Liberty' in *Scoop*'s 'Ishmaelia'.

They have advantages. Government officials, opposition and dissident groups, church, military and business interests, anyone with any point to make, knows where to find the international press (if not in the lobby, then certainly in the bar). Hacks can keep an eye on each other and, usually, on rival copy and contacts. The fact that the secret police can too is one of the disadvantages.

Only a few days after independence, the Memling was run-down and showing all the signs of indifference and torpor. 'The dank heat of the tropics invaded the lobby, overpowering the air-conditioning…the staff were sullen and listless.' But the bar was crowded with journalists from a dozen countries. There were the familiar sounds of Fleet Street at the front, including the raucous roar of George Gale. The hotel was abuzz with reports of the bloody mutiny among the Congolese soldiers of the Force Publique. Discontent with the Belgian officers and a crisis of expectations fostered by politicians had led to a country-wide rebellion by the rude soldiery. Drunken and drugged troops had turned on their officers and had then rampaged through the civilian areas, killing, maiming, looting and raping.

In his usually helpful way, Lumumba accused the white officers of inciting the rebellion themselves. A totally bemused Brussels finally dispatched some 10 000 troops to put down the mutiny and protect the 80 000 Belgians in the Congo. A unit of Belgian paratroopers was landed at the port of Matadi in the Congo River estuary and was immediately involved in a battle with mutineers.

The Congolese turned on the white population and chose the softest target on which to vent spleen and other ejaculations: the missions and their complements of helpless nuns. The rape of the Congo nuns became the most emotive, headline-catching event of the entire crisis. It remained in memories for many decades and is still cited today as the type of horror that can become the white woman's burden in Africa.

Ed Behr, then a distinguished correspondent for *Time-Life,* had covered many upheavals, crises and wars but it was his Congo experience, particularly The Rape of the Nuns, that gave him the title for his eminently readable autobiography: *Anyone Here Been Raped And Speaks English?* Behr opened his Congo chapter thus: 'The sun was blazing hot outside, and even under the relative shelter of the aircraft hangars the humidity was intense. Packed resignedly inside, thousands of Belgian civilians, mostly women and children, waited their turn to be airlifted out of the newly-independent ex-Belgian Congo, out of Africa and to new lives in Belgium.

'Some had been driven out of remote, up-country towns by the excesses of Congolese soldiers and rebels on the rampage. Others had succumbed to an understandable fear psychosis and had fled mostly imaginary terrors, leaving everything behind save their pathetic bundles. Into the middle of this crowd strode an unmistakably British TV reporter, leading his cameraman and sundry technicians like a platoon commander through hostile territory. At intervals he paused and shouted, in a stentorian but genteel BBC voice "Anyone here been raped and speaks English?"'

It is a telling legend, and, like most of the yarns that journalists spin and retail about and against themselves, it gains with age and in being passed on, generation after generation like the verbal histories of pre-literate peoples, although in the case of travelling hacks, invariably embellished and enhanced across myriad saloons. Many of the anecdotes in this book are of that ilk. The version of this particular story that I tend to believe is that created in the Memling Hotel bar by George Gale when Sandy Gall returned with his account of the scenes on the road to Matadi where he had gone to find refugees from the excesses of the mutinous Congolese troops.

Sandy found a Roman Catholic mission whose Mother Superior took him to a room full of women, mostly nuns, their habits 'travel-stained and weary' after the long journey from Matadi. He had heard the stories of rape 'but it could be just another rumour among hundreds of others...not the sort of story that any reputable journalist would want to write without being absolutely sure of the facts'. The Mother Superior confirmed that, yes, the nuns had been raped but Gall was unsure how to begin. 'We did, somehow. They spoke quietly, haltingly and gradually their story unfolded. The mutineers had burst into their mission school near Matadi, drunk and waving their rifles about. They had ransacked the place, terrorised the sisters and then started to rape them.'

For the benefit of younger readers who have been exposed to the totally uninhibited approach of latterday hacks, it should be pointed out that this was 1960 and Gall, despite his reputation as a ladies' man, was one of the last of the gentleman journalists.

'I forced myself to be sceptical. "That is a very serious allegation. How can you be sure," I asked. "Because I saw it," one sister replied quietly. "And I was raped myself." I found myself stammering in disbelief and embarrassment. "You were actually raped yourself?" The sister replied "Yes," her eyes hard, her voice matter-of-fact. "I was raped...several times. They even raped a seventy-year-old sister, Sister Agatha. She's sitting over there." She turned and pointed to an elderly nun at the other side of the room, sunk in her own private misery.'

Gall found among the nuns the wife of a Belgian colonial official who had been murdered. She, too, had been gang-raped. 'Many questions came to mind but I could not bring myself to ask them...I was convinced beyond any shadow of doubt that I was hearing the absolute truth.' Back in Leopoldville, Nigel Ryan urged him to write the story for Reuters. 'But for God's sake be careful. London will be like a cat on hot bricks over this story.' Sandy tapped out his cable, with, as Reuters demanded, dates, times, names and places and authentication. It made headlines everywhere, creating an image of savagery and chaos that was to persist for a very long time. In the bar of the Memling Hotel, George Gale bellowed his cynicism. 'I suppose you wandered among these nuns asking if any of them spoke English and, by the way, had they been raped?'

Such is the stuff of the mythology of the foreign correspondent. The exclusive story, hard-won under fire and other unimaginable dangers, will automatically be debunked by colleagues. It is – or was – done in good humour and the affected disbelief and the teasing will be by way of congratulation from the only peer group that matters. They know. They have been there, they are with you and will be when the next hairy assignment comes your way, unlike editors, the sub-editors and the reading public who might flit through such stories from the comfort of a humdrum daily existence. Sandy need not have worried so much about his rape story. Within weeks such accounts were commonplace. As one cynical colleague put it: 'There came a time when you couldn't move in the Congo for raped nuns.' In fact, according to official Belgian figures, 251 white women were raped, 230 white people were severely assaulted and 15 were killed in the course of the Force Publique mutiny. Many thousands of Congolese suffered death, mutilation and terror when old inter-tribal wars erupted in the wake of the breakdown of law and order.

Nigel Ryan and Sandy Gall regarded the *Daily Express* team, George Gale and Geoffrey Thursby, as their most formidable rivals in covering the increasingly chaotic situation. These were the great gung-ho days of popular journalism and Beaverbrook demanded and got from his foreign staff – then the largest in Fleet Street – the dramatic 'I was there as...' stories. Just how competitive this team could be Sandy learned the hard way one morning when he heard that Congolese troops had seized Leopoldville's Njili Airport, trapping hundreds of frightened Belgian civilians waiting to flee the country. The word was that Belgian paratroopers had been sent in to rescue them.

The Reuters man called a number he had for the airport. It rang for a long time before a gravelly voice answered 'George Gale here'. He confirmed that the paras had landed and were storming the airport building but could add no more as he was lying on the floor. Gall rattled off his agency story but was infuriated when he learned how George had handled the story for the *Express*. Gale had described how he had been at the airport when the Belgian troops landed.

'In the middle of the battle,' he wrote, 'the 'phone rang at a desk near me. No one answered it so I crawled over and picked it up. It was Sandy Gall of Reuters. "Hello George! What's going on?" he asked.' It made Sandy appear as if he was way behind on the story, whereas Gale had been at the airport fortuitously on another mission when the battle broke out. There were no call backs from Reuters, however, and Gale bought Gall a couple of large drinks to assuage his anger.

Only in Katanga, where Belgian troops had quickly put down the mutineers, was there relative calm. Moise Tshombe reorganised the armed forces in his province and on 12 July – just two weeks after Congo independence – he declared Katanga's secession. Foreign journalists who had met and interviewed Tshombe were impressed by the man. The eldest son of a wealthy Katangese merchant, he had had a privileged start to life and had capitalised on it by deploying to the full his natural charm, fluency in several languages and a political shrewdness. He married into the royal family of the Lundu, the most powerful Katangese tribe. From an early age he set about consolidating regional political power.

Tshombe was cheerfully evasive to correspondents who had asked him about plans for secession. Smith Hempstone, Africa correspondent of the *Chicago Daily News* (and much later US Ambassador to Kenya), first met him a few weeks before independence. Tshombe joined him for a drink on the terrace of the Hotel Elisabeth in the Katangan capital a few weeks before independence. 'He was exactly on time...he wore a button-down white shirt, red tie, blue tweed suit and carried in his hand a black homburg with which he waved genially to passing acquaintances.'

Tshombe spoke warmly about the United States which he had just visited on a State Department grant and thought a similar federal system might work in the Congo. The Congo was too large and its people so diverse that only a dictatorial form of government could hold it together, he told the American correspondent. 'If a unitary form of government is imposed, the Congo will die,' he added, prophetically. Hempstone was impressed with his intelligence, bravery and racial tolerance. Sandy Gall found Tshombe 'warm and friendly and somehow vulnerable, with his music hall black man's face and manner'. Jack Nugent of *Newsweek* also succumbed. Tshombe was 'an absolute charmer...his round handsome face is capable of instant hurt...he pleads with his dark brown eyes'.

When he announced Katanga's secession, Tshombe found he had the support, for what it was worth, of the great majority of foreign correspondents covering the Congo, even though many of them were soon to suffer at the hands of his evil gendarmerie. Politically it was a different matter.

An infuriated Lumumba accused the Belgians (with some justification) of tacitly supporting Katangan secession and demanded UN intervention. Dag Hammarskjöld, the UN Secretary-General, was personally sympathetic to the concept of socialist pan-Africanism espoused by Lumumba and immediately mobilised a UN force to 'restore order' in the Congo and to bring Tshombe and Katanga to heel. Within weeks a polyglot array of troops was being deployed, adding several new dimensions to the confusion and chaos. In time the UN 'peace-keeping' force was to number some 20 000 men from 26 different countries.

According to Hempstone, the Congo's descent into chaos was the pretext, and not the cause, of Tshombe's secession. He 'assumed the posture' of anti-communism not because he necessarily thought Lumumba was of that persuasion but because he thought it would win him important allies in America, Britain, France and Belgium. He hoisted his green, red and white flag, printed currency and stamps. His reconstructed army, the gendarmerie under Belgian officers, had restored enough order in Katanga to persuade the copper mining giant, Union Minière, to reopen its plants and bring production back to normal. Shops in Elisabethville still sold a wide and attractive range of imported French luxuries and the food and wines were excellent. It was, for a brief period, an island of sanity, calm and order amid the maelstrom of the swirling, muddy, bloody Congo waters. Not surprisingly, the foreign hacks gravitated to Elisabethville, specifically to the Grand Hotel Leopold the Second, known to all with varying degrees of affection as the Leo Deux. Katanga had all the makings of a great story. Tshombe, as always, was affable and approachable, unlike the increasingly crazed Lumumba. Katanga appeared to be post-colonial Africa's most successful and viable secession and the living was relatively easy.

John Bulloch, *The Daily Telegraph* man who was to spend more time in the Congo than most other correspondents, recalls with some embarrassment the pro-Katanga partisanship of the press corps which gathered at the Leo Deux. 'We were all for Tshombe and, with few exceptions, violently anti-UN,' he recalls. 'When I come to look back on what I wrote in those days I realise that we were more polemicists than reporters. The Katangese were very good at propaganda and we were quite happy to accept what they fed us.'

Tshombe stood as firmly as he could against any UN presence in Katanga, predicting that 'in their luggage' they would bring 'anarchy, disorders, pillage, murder and misery'. He was right again but he was finally and reluctantly obliged to accept a 'token' presence of Swedish and Irish troops, a force that was 2 000 strong when the Belgian troops pulled out. Lumumba was becoming manic about the UN's refusal to put its forces under his command. He asked the Soviet Union for help and the Russians obliged, sending 200 technicians and 100 trucks and a fleet of Ilyshin transport aircraft. With the Americans providing all the air transport and other logistics for the UN force, a Cold War rivalry was added to the mess.

Secession suddenly became fashionable. In Kasai province, the eccentric Albert Kalonji proclaimed himself 'King' of a new, independent 'mining state' of south Kasai, in the heart of the Congo's diamond mining area. Peter Younghusband of the *Daily Mail* swam another crocodile-infested river to attend the 'independence celebrations' in Bakwanga in Baluba territory.

'There was His Majesty,' said Peter, 'complete with the statutory fly whisk of African authority, eyes glinting behind gold-rimmed spectacles waving a large rod which he assured us was invested with magical powers. He used the stick to draw a large, kidney-shaped map in the dust. That, he said, was the new state. We noticed that it embraced all the large diamond mines in south Kasai.'

Younghusband asked him about reports that Lumumba's army – the Congolese National Army – was marching on Bakwanga to end his secession. 'Ah yes,' said King Albert, 'I have an army which is entraining for the front as we speak. I shall lead them personally into battle.' Peter had seen nothing more military than a 'guard of honour' of some 20 men, most of whom were far from sober. But Kalonji led a procession to the railway station and there was a rag-tag group of soldiers loading crates of beer onto a train. 'The train pulled out with Albert's army which was never seen again,' Younghusband reported. Kalonji was, however. He quickly made his way to Elisabethville to seek succour from his old chum, Moise Tshombe.

Bigfoot Younghusband was giving George Gale a hard time in the 'I was there' stakes. The big South African was the master of the intrepid pen. In Katanga, he also had the advantage of a friend and contact, a Rhodesian bush pilot named Alan Kearns, one of the few fliers ready to risk his life and his Cessna to fly in and out of the Congo. In what Peter called 'a quiet period' he got Kearns, a tough, affable man, to fly him over positions reportedly held by Lumumba's Armée Nationale Congolaise now moving on dissident Baluba territory with its Russian logistical backing.

Peter recounted: 'Alan took the Cessna low over a large convoy of Russian vehicles and we took a couple of heavy calibre rounds through the fuselage. He was worried about his aeroplane. I was worried about my life. We high-tailed it out of the area. I had seen enough to give me a good story.' Bigfoot gave the experience the 'treatment' and it was splashed in the *Daily Mail* on the now classic lines of : 'Today I was shot at as I flew low over crazed Congolese troops advancing with their Russian armour on rebel Baluba positions...' Etc., etc. Prominent in the story was the account of the bullet 'ripping through the fuselage of the Cessna'.

Back in Elisabethville, a seething George Gale received a cable from the *Daily Express* foreign desk: 'MAILS YOUNGHUSBAND UPSHOT REBELS REDWISE STOP WHY YOU UNSHOT QUERY'. George tapped out a telex explaining that Younghusband had a monopoly on the only light aircraft available. The *Express* snapped back 'WHY YOU UNBUY PLANE QUERY EDITOR DEMANDS EXPLANATION STOP'. This was too much for the fiery Expressman. Bigfoot Younghusband would have to be out-scooped soonest.

Alan Kearns was prepared to fly anyone anywhere if the price was right and Gale had the Beaverbrook imprimatur to 'buy' an aircraft. He would not only fly over the advancing Congolese army. He would land in their midst and demand to know, loudly in English, what was going on. Sandy Gall and Dickie Williams were keen to go along and Kearns, with his intrepid, battered Cessna making more foreign exchange than even the shrewdest foreign hack, said he would give it a try.

According to Sandy Gall, who checked with a friendly Belgian military man, Bakwanga, the proposed destination and ostensibly the scene of the current battle, was still in the hands of 'King'

Kalonji's forces and would therefore be relatively amenable to the
sudden arrival of foreign journalists from Tshombe's breakaway
Elisabethville. The three hacks – the tall, young, scruffy Gall, the
chunky, roaring, flame-headed Gale and the shortish Welshman
with the wonderful BBC voice, Dickie Williams – were soon airborne
with 'bronze-kneed Alan Kearns gunning his little Cessna down the
runway' for 'bright African pastures anew'. Navigating with a map
on his knee, Kearns eventually found Bakwanga – a small town in
the middle of interminable bush country – and landed. Gale, Gall
and Williams climbed out, stretched their legs and unloaded their
portable typewriters from the hold. They were surprised to be
approached by a white man 'obviously English and obviously a journalist'. It was Tom Stacey, then a London-based freelance journalist,
who had flown to the town from Leopoldville. Stacey was horrified to
learn that the three had flown from 'rebel' Elisabethville. There had
been a major battle and the Armée Nationale Congolaise (ANC) –
Lumumba's men – were in charge. 'They're all very jumpy,' he
added, helpfully. To all intents and purposes, Gale, Gall and
Williams were in enemy territory.

Sure enough, an ANC officer with, as Gall noted, an ingrowing
beard, approached them. Hostile and suspicious, he demanded to
know who they were and where they had come from. The correspondents, realising that the mention of Katanga would not impress,
lied. They had come from Leopoldville. The officer examined their
passports and demanded to see the *laissez-passer* they would have
had if they had come from the Congo capital. His suspicion mounted
and he marched off to check their story. 'I did not like the sound of
that, but, knowing how inefficient communications were in the
Congo, I thought it might take all day or possibly longer to receive
an answer,' the optimistic Gall thought. Another officer moved forward and introduced himself. He was a Lieutenant Ali Trabelsi of
the Tunisian Army, commander of the United Nations troops in
Bakwanga.

Trabelsi was also nervous, but he offered the journalists a tour
of the town while their bona fides were being checked. He told them
that the ANC had arrived in Russian transport aircraft, quickly
routed Kalonji's 'army' and had then gone on the usual rampage of
killing, raping and looting the town.

Back at the airport, the angry Congolese confronted them. 'You
are spies,' he screamed. 'You are under arrest. Your plane is from
Rhodesia. Your pilot is Rhodesian. The penalty for espionage is execution by firing squad.' The hapless hacks and their pilot were driven to an army camp where drunken Congolese soldiers burst into

the guard room where they were being held and advanced on them with malice aforethought.

Sandy Gall describes the scene: 'The room was hot, crowded and noisy with the din of the soldiers' voices; the air heavy with the threat of violence. I was aware of a row of black faces in front of me and that we almost had our backs to the wall. Suddenly one soldier stepped forward and ripped the watch from my wrist. I saw other hands reaching out on either side of me. One soldier reached inside George's jacket and snatched his wallet. We were jostled and pushed back against the wall. Our shoes were torn off. "On your knees", they shouted. No, I told myself, stay on your feet, don't fall down or you may never get up again. On my right, a big brawny soldier wearing a pair of dark glasses – a status symbol among Congolese – his face shining with sweat, stepped forward. He held what looked like a heavy swagger stick in his right hand. Slowly, taking careful aim, he lifted it high and brought it cracking down on the slightly bald head of Alan Kearns. Alan uttered no sound at all. The soldier prepared himself for another blow. For a moment the scene froze on the retina, like a breaking wave caught by a camera shutter.'

The men were bracing themselves for what they were convinced would be an all-out attack by the mob when, as often happens in unpleasant African circumstances, an angel appeared, in this case in the guise of a venerable, grey-haired Congolese military policeman and two young assistants. 'The soldiers who had been pressing so close to us that we could smell their sweat stepped back and, quietly now, their voices barely audible, started to melt away out of the room.' The MPs had been sent by their new-found friend, Lt Trabelsi of the United Nations into whose custody they were now delivered. The UN officer was anxious to get them out of Bakwanga as soon as possible.

They were bundled aboard a UN Dakota and flown to Leopoldville where Nigel Ryan met them with instructions to take them to the British Embassy. In the classic tradition of the British diplomatic service in Africa they were harangued by a second secretary for 'making a thorough nuisance of yourselves' and 'giving the Ambassador a great deal of trouble'. Sandy Gall snapped back 'That's what he's here for'. They were told the Congolese authorities would agree to drop the 'spying' charges against them if they agreed to leave the country forthwith. At this stage, the hacks were only too pleased to comply. They filed their stories from the post office and, deportation orders in hand, caught the ferry to Brazzaville across the great brown Congo River. In this friendly French colonial town they dined off oysters and lobsters flown in from France, washed down with a couple of bottles of Puilly Fuisse. 'A foreign correspondent's life is hell,' mused George Gale.

Back in Elisabethville, their colleagues learned with relief that they were safe. All foreign hacks in the Congo had been badly shaken by news that an American journalist, Henry Taylor of the Scripps-Howard newspaper chain, had been killed by machine-gun fire in Bakwanga. Taylor, 33, had arrived in the Congo on a Wednesday and was shot three days later. The word was that he had been mistaken for a Belgian soldier. He had been wearing a khaki outfit which had a paramilitary look about it. His colleagues immediately started wearing brightly coloured clothing. Jack Nugent of *Newsweek* pulled on a brilliant red shirt and a pair of blue trousers. 'Now I could be shot only for bad taste.'

Life – and copy – for the press corps in Katanga was enlivened considerably by the arrival of white mercenaries. Tshombe and his backers – the moguls behind Union Minière – realised that sooner or later the United Nations would move against the secessionist province. They decided that the Katangese gendarmerie would be effectively bolstered by recruiting as many white mercenaries as they could. It was not difficult.

Southern Africa has always been a fertile breeding ground for soldiers of fortune. Tshombe's recruiters were soon in touch with a former British army major now seeking relief from the boredom of running a successful business in South Africa. Mike Hoare was soon in Elisabethville organising a motley crowd of ex-servicemen, adventurers, crooks and malcontents into what was to become his Five Commando. At the same time 'Colonel' Bob Denard, a tough, ruthless French soldier, was assembling his own band of desperadoes, officially to be known as Four Commando but soon labelled 'Les Affreux' for their appearance and their behaviour on and off the field of battle.

Foreign correspondents and mercenaries have much more in common than either group would like to admit. In Elisabethville it was not long before the hacks and the hired guns were socialising, drinking, womanising, exchanging banter and brawling together, much to the anguish of the Belgian proprietor of the Leo Deux. He had considered the newspapermen bad enough. One of them had nearly burned down his hotel. (Jimmy O'Driscoll of *The Daily Telegraph* had fallen asleep in a hotel bedroom with a smouldering cigarette in his mouth. He suffered second-degree burns but the rest of the damage was slight.) Now the manager had to cope with 'Les Affreux' – and they were armed. Mike Hoare was automatically dubbed 'Mad Mike' by the journalists, more for the sake of appealing alliteration in copy than because of his behaviour. (We did the same with Lt Colonel Colin Mitchell, of the 1st Battalion, the Argyll and Sutherland Highlanders, when he kept his promise to take a group of us with him when he recaptured the Crater district of Aden in 1967. At one stage he had us ahead of his troops to describe to us what they were about to do. From that night onwards, we called him 'Mad Mitch'.)

Hoare, in fact, was the perfect gentleman, courteous, considerate and charming. His mission, as he saw it, was to prevent communist encroachment in his beloved Africa and Tshombe's anti-communist posture – coupled with unlimited funds, arms and ammunition supplied by Union Minière – made Katanga an attractive proposition. His second-in-command, Alastair Wicks, a much decorated British soldier, also cut an imposing figure with his measured Old Harrovian drawl.

Hoare, Wicks and Denard were to loom large over the chaotic Congo landscape and to reappear frequently in other African upheavals in later decades. The mercenaries were to inspire books, films and legends. They were also to inspire fear and loathing among the pan-Africanists and their liberal promoters who saw them as 'racist thugs in the vanguard of neo-colonialism' – the catchy phrase coined by Moscow to disguise and dissemble its own intentions for Africa.

Mike Hoare had soon endeared himself to the Katanga press corps. He and his men provided an endless stream of copy – and some wonderful taproom tales. He lost one of his men – an Irish NCO – in a battle with Baluba tribesmen in the north-east of the Congo. One of his colleagues was due for some furlough which he intended to take in Ireland. Hoare asked him to convey the condolences of the unit to the dead man's mother in Dublin. He did so, seeking out a grieving elderly lady in a back street of that fair city to explain that her son had been a very brave man, a soldier who would have been much decorated in any regular army unit.

It was tragic, he went on, that he had eventually been caught and hung by the Balubas. 'Mother of God!' exclaimed the woman. 'Even the bloody English would have hanged him by the neck.'

Such black humour became commonplace in the bars of Elisabethville as the full extent of the crisis in the Congo became apparent. The trigger-happy mercenaries could not resist exchanging fire with the jittery Swedish troops of the 'token' UN force in Katanga and sundowner time on the terrace of the Leo Deux was punctuated with flurries of tracer and mortar fire. In northern

Katanga, a civil war broke out between pro- and anti- Tshombe elements of the Balubas. Reports of oathing ceremonies – uncannily similar to those during the Mau Mau period in Kenya – infiltrated the perfumed boulevards of Elisabethville. Ian Colvin, the *Telegraph*'s roving pundit, was one of the few journalists to get in and out of Manono to file the kind of story that was to stamp Africa in general and the Congo in particular as a true 'heart of darkness'.

Colvin found that the anti-Tshombe 'youth league' – the Jeunesse – had gone on the rampage in the town, killing hundreds of people who they deemed to be in opposition. Missionaries, miners, businessmen, doctors – anyone, black or white, who appeared to be part of the successful white establishment – had been killed in the most brutal fashion.

Victims were flayed with bicycle chains, were scalped, were castrated and – shades of South Africa 30 years later – were doused with petrol and set alight. Smith Hempstone of the *Chicago Daily News* described some of the killings: 'A ten-man patrol led by the local administrative officer, Gregoire Kulu, was ambushed by about 100 Jeunesse in Kabalo district. The patrol was overrun. The Jeunesse cut off Kulu's legs, jammed sticks into the stumps and forced him to run on them before burning him alive.

'A Belgian NCO accompanying the patrol had his legs cut off below the knees, his anus cut out and his arms and thighs skinned before his head was cut off...twenty-two men, women and children were massacred at Makulakulu, their hands were cut off, dried and attached to the hats of the Jeunesse leaders as trophies.

'The local witchdoctor is said to have demanded a finger and genital organs from each victim for use in making dawa – medicine for the oathing ceremonies.' In Manono, a local chief, Vincent Yangala, was condemned by a Jeunesse kangaroo court. 'Chief Yangala's genitals were cut off, gasoline was poured on him and he was burned alive. His penis was carried triumphantly through the streets of Manono on a spearhead.'

Hempstone and Colvin wrote these and other stories of atrocities in the region but they were dismissed by UN spokesmen as 'imaginative and far-fetched'. The fact was that the UN force in the area was composed of ill-trained and ill-disciplined troops from Mali who were so terrified that they confined themselves, very firmly, to their barracks.

'The list of atrocious killings which took place in northern Katanga makes sickening reading,' Hempstone wrote. 'The most common weapon used was the bicycle chain, fastened to a stick and its links honed to razor sharpness. A few blows from such a weapon

can tear all the flesh from a man's leg in a matter of seconds. Those
unequipped with bicycle chains relied on clubs, spears and sharpened sticks. Many victims were burned alive or impaled. The more
distinguished prisoners were castrated.' It was not until Mike
Hoare's Five Commando routed the Jeunesse a few months later
that some order and effective administration was re-established in
the Manono area.

Meanwhile Lumumba was becoming more and more manic in
his utterances and erratic in his actions. He fulminated against the
UN, called Hammarskjöld a 'colonial stooge', demanded the withdrawal of all white UN troops, declared a state of emergency and
expelled the Belgian ambassador. His Congolese army began a
series of attacks on UN troops. He was dealing unilaterally and
directly with the Russians, a move which rang alarm bells in
Washington. By September it was clear he would have to go. On
5 September in a radio broadcast the idle and ineffective President
Kasavubu announced that Lumumba had been dismissed for plunging the Congo into civil war. Lumumba rushed to the radio station
to announce that he had sacked Kasavubu. Into this void stepped a
little-known 31-year-old Congolese army sergeant-major, Joseph-
Desire Mobutu, who seized power himself, ordered the immediate
withdrawal of all communist embassies and missions and established a 'government' of university graduates.

For a time, Lumumba took refuge in the prime minister's residence in Leopoldville, guarded on the inside by Ghanaian troops of
the UN (Nkrumah had been an early inspiration for and a strong
supporter of Lumumba). He would make occasional drunken forays
into the town, making impromptu speeches in bars and night clubs.
Ed Behr of *Time-Life* and a middle-aged Indian journalist found
themselves in the same bar one evening. Lumumba singled out
Behr, the only Westerner present, for an anti-imperialist harangue
and added, inconsequentially, 'The white men crushed the revolution in India. The white men killed Gandhi'. This remark infuriated
the Indian journalist. To Behr's horror he suddenly screamed 'The
whites didn't kill Gandhiji you bloody fool. We killed Ghandhiji!'
There was almost a riot. Lumumba's bodyguard pulled out a pistol
while the *Time-Life* man sought to restrain his Indian colleague.
Lumumba himself ended the incident. Swaying unsteadily on his
feet he declared 'I am going out to die like Ghandi....fetch
Kasavubu...fetch Mobutu...tell them Lumumba challenges them to
a duel. Tomorrow.'

Soon after this incident, Lumumba fled from his Leopoldville
refuge and made a dash for Stanleyville, ostensibly to join his sup-

porters there. His deputy, Antoine Gizenga, had established a rump Lumumbist government in the town. He might well have made it had he not chosen to stage yet more impromptu political rallies in the towns and villages en route. He was caught by Mobutu's troops at Port Franqui in Kasai province, beaten up and brought back to Leopoldville in chains. He was to undergo further beatings and torture in Thysville barracks where the Congo tragedy had started a long six months before with the mutiny of the Force Publique. But even the incarcerated, bruised and bleeding Lumumba retained his rhetorical powers and remained a threatening political figure. Before long word reached Mobutu that fellow-prisoners, gaolers and troops at Thysville were being swayed to a Lumumbist point of view and a decision was taken to move him.

The who, how and why of what happened next has been debated and disputed ever since. What is known is that Lumumba and two of his senior followers were taken from Thysville barracks on 17 January 1961, and put aboard a flight which finally landed at Elisabethville airport. He arrived in a bad state, having been again beaten to a pulp by his captors aboard the aircraft. Soon afterwards he was murdered.

Sandy Gall of Reuters was one of the few foreign journalists in Elisabethville when the word went around that a captive Lumumba was in Katanga. Tshombe's government initially protested ignorance but a Swedish journalist who had contacts with the Swedish UN troops guarding the airport confirmed it. The Swedes said Lumumba had been beaten so badly with rifle butts on the flight that the Belgian captain had remonstrated with his captors. Lumumba had been dragged off the plane roped and bleeding. 'They threw him into the back of a Jeep like a sack of potatoes and drove off.'

The Katangese finally announced that Lumumba was being held at the request of the Leopoldville government, although rumours abounded that he had been murdered shortly after his arrival. A month later, Godefroid Munongo, Tshombe's Interior Minister, issued a communiqué saying Lumumba and his two aides had been 'shot by villagers while trying to escape'. Munongo took a group of journalists to a shack in the bush where he said Lumumba had been held. There was a hole in the wall through which he had escaped, he said.

Ray Maloney of UPI was among the correspondents who were openly sceptical of Munongo's version. Where had Lumumba been buried? At a 'secret location' to protect the villagers from possible retribution, was the reply. Would Minister Munongo comment on widely-circulating reports that the former Congolese prime minister had been murdered by his guards on the day he had arrived in Elisabethville. Munongo's face remained impassive behind his large, one-way dark glasses. 'Prove it!' he challenged the hacks.

No one, apart from those actually present, could be sure, although a United Nations report later that year found 'in all probability' the murder had taken place in the presence of Tshombe and Munongo and two Belgian mercenaries. One witness, the UN said, had claimed that Munongo himself had plunged a bayonet into Lumumba's chest. Much later, a former Belgian mercenary claimed he had been a member of the firing squad which, under the direct orders of Munongo, had shot Lumumba. Tshombe and Munongo, of course, denied all the allegations of involvement.

The death of Lumumba had international repercussions. Demonstrations and protests took place outside the UN in New York, where the Security Council was meeting on the Katanga issue, and at Belgian embassies in a dozen countries. Anti-Tshombe feeling ran high, particularly among the radical Afro-Asian countries. In the heat of the moment, the Security Council passed a resolution demanding the immediate withdrawal of all Belgian and foreign military personnel and advisers, a move which brought Tshombe and Kasavubu together in a makeshift alliance against the UN. The explosive situation brought the foreign correspondents scrambling back to the Congo. The bars at the Memling in Leopoldville and the Leo Deux in Elisabethville were once again ahum with hackery.

Competitiveness among Fleet Street's finest in Africa extended beyond getting there earlier and sending back the first account. It had long since become a race for the most eye-catching dateline – the name of the spot from which the story is filed and the day on which it is sent. It is a practice long since abandoned by most newspapers which is a pity because the dateline had from the earliest days of newspapers given some romance to the story.

In 1900, for instance, the *Daily Mail* carried a chirpy account which it had received by runner and telegraph from Winston Churchill's aunt in Mafeking during the siege. 'NOW EATING STRAY DOGS,' the headline proclaimed. 'SIGNS THAT MAFEKING HAS NONE TOO MUCH FOOD' and then the splendid byline and dateline 'From Our Special Correspondent, Lady Sarah Wilson, Mafeking (Feb. 19) (via Plumer's Camp, Feb. 25).'

Some 60 years later, the dateline stakes among foreign correspondents had been enlarged to include the most arresting first sentence or paragraph – the 'intro' – of the story which followed. At one stage, the inimitable Donald Wise held the African award for the fetching intro. Donald had arrived in Luanda, capital of what was then Portuguese colonial Angola at a time when the black population was getting politically restless. As was his wont, his first move was to enjoy a cerveja or two, the local beer and a bowl of freshly caught shrimps served at the – then – delightful pavement cafés of the – then – delightful Angolan capital.

Donald had taken only a couple of sips as he absorbed the atmosphere in Luanda when 'there came the sounds of clamour' followed by a sickening thud as an African body thumped bloodily onto the pavement beside his table. 'Fair put me off me beer,' he said. 'Chap had been chased across the rooftops by the old Porko commandos and had fallen – or been pushed – off the roof above me.' But it gave Wise his award-winning intro for that day's story: 'The first African to be killed in Portuguese Africa nearly fell into my beer today...'

Peter 'Bigfoot' Younghusband, the gigantic South African who had been inducted into the same school of snappy intros had, by that time, worked to death the crocodile-infested rivers of Africa. During a quiet period, Big Pete had taken himself to Swaziland, one of Africa's most appealing black kingdoms, where a weary African hack could always be sure of finding a colour story or two to justify his posting. There was little going on to merit a cable but the Swazi ruler, the venerated and venerable King Sobhuza the Third was reported to have quelled a minor insurrection. The old, grizzled monarch had assembled the dissidents near his kingdom's airport which was – and still is – nearly always shrouded in mist. 'Do you see that aeroplane?' he demanded of his captive audience. 'When you can build an aeroplane, you will rule. Until then, I will rule.'

For Younghusband it was a good story but one which needed something more to attract the attention of his bosses on the foreign desk of the *Daily Mail* in London. It was feature, rather than 'hard news' copy. He had studied a map of Swaziland and had found an intriguingly named kopje called Sheba's Breast. (There are literally dozens of conical outcrops in Southern Africa so named, but Bigfoot was the first journalist to realise its value as a dateline.) He duly filed his Swaziland story: 'From Peter Younghusband, Sheba's Breast, Swaziland, Wednesday' and underneath his intro, which captured the award from Donald Wise, was 'I like it here...'

In the Congo of the early 1960s it was open season on datelines, as well as deadlines, bylines and the traditional interchange of cablese messages with one's office in London, Paris, New York or Washington. With Lumumba dead, the leaders of a dozen regions and spheres of influence in this vast country had ganged up in a haphazard fashion against the UN forces. In the Memling Hotel in Leopoldville, a young British journalist, Peter Hawthorne, who had worked in Kenya and the Rhodesias had kept his eye on a Congo estuary port through which much of the United Nations logistical support had been shipped. Its name was Banana.

Banana, an old slaving centre in thick mangrove swamps, is a port on what is now Zaire's coastal access to the Atlantic in the Congo River delta. With nearby Matadi, where Sandy Gall had found his ravished nuns, it was the main seaborne access for UN supplies by sea. Both towns had been garrisoned by UN troops and, in March 1961, were threatened by Congolese troops who now saw the world body, as it is still called rather grandiosely, as its enemy. In that month, the Congolese attacked Matadi and captured the UN garrison manned by bewildered Sudanese troops. At the same time, they stormed ashore from boats to seize the port of Banana.

Young Hawthorne was aware of the dateline contest between the 'Fleet Street heavies'. He was aware, too, that if ever the phrase 'banana republic' deserved a home it had to be in the Congo of that time. He was also anxious to prove himself with the hot-shots from London and, in the Memling bar, he mentioned the situation in the port of Banana ɔo a few of his friends. Peter has the instinctive humour of I.   native north-west England and the fact that the unbridled Co␣␣ ␣lese forces had chosen a Sunday to mount their attack on the port appealed to him.

Donald Wise immediately realised the potential for the 'absolutely marvellous, unbeatable dateline' of 'From Donald Wise, Banana, Sunday' and made his plans accordingly for a *Daily Mirror* exclusive on the derring-do of its intrepid correspondent. Peter Younghusband was also appraised of the dateline potential and was on his way. Walter Partington, a newcomer whizz-kid from the *Express* was late to latch on but made arrangements to travel to this wonderfully named port. This was going to be the scoop of the century. A dispatch with the dateline 'Banana, Sunday' would, without doubt, be the winner.

Wise had a problem. He had been wooed – by the promise of a better salary and expenses – from the *Daily Express* to the *Daily Mirror* whose readers he affected to despise – 'They must move their lips as they read' – and the sub-editors who, he was convinced, were 'a disgruntled bunch of failed journalists who commute from Orpington, don't know what the hell is going on but insist on changing one's copy because they wank on the fact that they are handling the copy of one who is actually at the frontline.'

In an effort to thwart the dreaded 'subs', Donald was given to throwing in a line on his copy filed to the *Mirror* which read 'Suddenly a horseman on a white charger rode down the street.' As Donald explained 'It had no relevance at all and was completely untrue but I tossed it into my copy from time to time just to keep the buggers in the subs room on their toes. Sometimes it appeared in the newspaper without so much as a raised eyebrow or a reader's query.'

The *Mirror* subs, some of whom did live in Orpington, had become aware of the antagonistic eccentricities of Their Man in Africa and were used to blue-pencilling the references to the ubiquitous 'white horseman'. When Wise filed his report from 'Banana, Sunday' – genuine as it was – the Chief Sub-Editor of the *Mirror* roared with laughter and told his subs to make sure the deadline was Leopoldville which they knew existed. 'Donald is up to his old tricks again!' The fact that he wasn't and that the dateline was genuine never occurred to them.

Younghusband was hot on the heels of Wise and sent a long, graphic dispatch from Banana which the *Daily Mail* appreciated. There were, however, other good stories breaking around the world and Bigfoot's dispatch was put 'on hold'. It was used finally on the Tuesday, appearing eventually under the dateline 'From Peter Younghusband, Banana, Monday'. The point was lost. Walter Partington of the *Express* had succumbed to his new-found penchant for the charms of black ladies – more of which later – which diverted his quest for the dateline championship. He found the 'most wonderful woman in the world' – a large, thrice-married mammy in Matadi who suddenly and briefly mattered more to Walter than the Banana dateline.

There had been a genuine story in Banana. It had taken place on a Sunday. But the hacks, for one reason or another, had failed to make the dateline they had sought. 'Banana, Sunday' was to remain the unrecorded award-winning African dateline. Many years later, Hugh Davies of *The Daily Telegraph* arrived in Banana having accompanied a footsteps-of-Stanley Congo River expedition. He got the name under his byline in the newspaper, but by this stage the practice of adding the actual day had ceased. He had to be content merely with 'Hugh Davies, Banana'.

'Look what the buggers have done to my copy' – John Bulloch of The Daily Telegraph.

Following Page bottom: ⫸

Correspondents in Katanga in 1961 celebrate the founding of 'Royal Uhuru Airlines' run by bush pilot Alan Kearns (seated). The bearded George Clay (centre) of ABC was killed soon after this picture was taken. He was shot by a sniper on the road to Stanleyville.

Ian Colvin 'the man who started World War II' in the Congo.

Keeping up appearances in the Congo – Tom Stacey, Daily Express.

Peter Hawthorne of Time *magazine – he saw potential in a port called Banana.*

CHAPTER SIX

WHY YOU UNSHOT?

*E*lisabethville had to be the story. Moise Tshombe was now fully under siege. His secessionist Katanga was unrecognised, not even by his shrewd supporter to the south, Sir Roy Welensky, premier of the Federation of Rhodesia and Nyasaland, or his new-found ally Joseph Kasavubu, still nominally president of the independent Congo, with whom he had agreed on a stance against the United Nations.

Vilified across the globe for what was generally accepted to be his role in the murder of Patrice Lumumba, he was beleaguered and came swiftly to depend on the support and succour of his white mercenaries. 'Mad' Mike Hoare, the languid Alastair Wicks, 'Colonel' Bob Denard and 'Les Affreux' generally became the men to be reckoned with in the Katanga of 1961.

Down at the bar of the Leo Deux, the assembled hacks were, as always, enjoying themselves while attempting to work out which way the totally chaotic Congo story was going and which location might give them the most dramatic dateline. Filing the daily story – getting whatever they had to send to their editors – meant a queue for the telex at the Cabine Publique in the Elisabethville Post Office. This entailed the punching of a telex tape on a 'blind' Creed machine – one which did not give an automatic printout – and the handing of the tape to one of the Belgian operators who, depending on the generosity of the correspondent, would transmit it to London, New York, Paris or Tokyo 'as soon as possible'. Frequently the lines were 'down', more often the operators were hungover, bored or frightened, or all three.

There were some scenes at the Cabine Publique in Elisabethville which did no credit to the honourable gentlemen of the Fourth Estate. One esteemed correspondent was infuriated when he found that his bribed telex operators were sending before his copy long messages from the British consul or, worse, some 10 000 words from the Russian agency, Tass, which was Moscow's horribly ill-informed 'intelligence' network in the region. He was a big man and his well-aimed kick at the central plug put out the entire communications system for a time. 'They're all fucking commies!' he cried as his colleagues carried him up the stairs of the Leo Deux to bed.

At this time, the *Express* was scoring on communications points, not least because of the energy, efforts and perspicacity of their Foreign Desk man, Jimmy Nichol, to my mind one of the most sympathetic foreign editors a man in the field could ask for. Not only would Jimmy find you, wherever you were, but he would talk you out of your accumulated neuroses, persuade you back to your wife, insist gently that you file a complete and exclusive story and take care of all outstanding family problems and details. Unfortunately I never had the chance to work under him, but I came to envy the *Express* men who did. Messages from the *Telegraph* were invariably bland and cold. 'ASSUME YOU FRONTWARDS FASTEST STOP EARLY COPY ESSENTIALIST.'

Nichol reached a simple solution to the communications logjam. The London office would dial into the Elisabethville telex at given times and 'speak' to the correspondent who would then be able to convey his copy without expense or hassle. That was the theory. This system was quickly picked up by other correspondents. The incoming telex would be greeted by cheers from the assembled correspondents who would shepherd their man to the machine, usually with instructions to 'MOM' – hang on after his copy had been sent – while another journalist would come forward with his pre-punched tape for 'onpassing soonest' to his own office, even though it might be a rival newspaper.

But this was the Congo and hiccups were bound to occur. On one occasion there had been no incoming or outgoing telex from the Cabine Publique for a couple of days. The frantic hacks, their hands wrapped with telex tapes punched on the 'blind' machine, were screaming for their copy to be sent. The machine suddenly burst into life. Up came the *Telegraph* foreign desk with a brief message for Jimmy O'Driscoll, currently their man on the spot who was duly led to the telex by his colleagues to answer his master's voice and then ask for onpassing facilities for his colleagues. The telex clattered out the message: 'ASSUME YOUR KEEPABLE SHORTS FOR EARLY PAGES' – and was then cut off immediately. It was merely a routine message from the foreign desk to correspondents worldwide.

The 'keepable shorts' referred to newsy, off-beat stories that could be set in type and used as fillers in parts of the newspaper set in type early. By some fluke, the telex operator in London had managed to connect with the Elisabethville post office. Having got the answer-back, he presumed all was well and shut down the machine to go for a drink, not knowing that five thousand miles away a dozen hacks were screaming for a link with the outside world. O'Driscoll went to get drunk, justifiably, and his colleagues made sure, this time, that he extinguished his cigarette before he passed out.

Communications are much more important to any journalist, particularly one on a foreign assignment, than anything else. The most dramatic exclusive, crafted into mellifluous prose, will not reach the Kansas City milkman or the chap on a London bus – or even the ephemeral posterity of a newspaper cuttings library – if it cannot be filed, or sent back in some way to the office. 'Getting it out is much more important than getting it' was the rule. It was never more apposite than in Elisabethville in Katanga in 1961.

Tshombe had cause to regret deeply his decision to allow a 'token' – and white – UN force into Katanga. The nervous, pallid Swedes had taken control of Elisabethville's airport and were to prove themselves as lacking in discipline as Tshombe's own gendarmerie. The Irish contingent had become a walking, talking embodiment of one of their own jokes, believing in some mysterious fashion that they were merely continuing the 'stroogle agin' the fookin' English'. They had arrived in Equatorial mid-summer in heavy, serge greatcoats (which many retained, sharing a belief with Baluba witchdoctors that such cladding of the body would deter the fookin' spiritual evils that abounded in the region).

Then came the UN's Indian contingent, more meticulous than the British in their attention to the right form, manner and demeanour of officers and gentlemen. The Indian Air Force, which had obviously studied all the right Battle of Britain movies, was also there. They got on famously with the press corps, many of whom had served, as they had, in World War II. They shared the jargon and the camaraderie of the mess – until the crunch came.

The UN, operating with that same incandescent naïveté that characterises to this day Europe's approach to Africa's problems, decided that the removal of Tshombe was a good idea. They arrested him on his return from a Congolese peace conference. He was soon released, to the bemusement of the furrow-browed Swedes, at the insistence of the people they assumed to be his protagonists, Colonel Mobutu and President Kasavubu. The furrows in those heavy Scandinavian brows became even deeper when Kasavubu's newly appointed Congolese Prime Minister, Cyrille Adoula, requested them to subjugate Katanga with all means at their disposal.

It was most confusing, not only to most of the foreigners in the Congo at the time (certainly to the UN personnel and the foreign press) but to the great majority of Congolese who were being pushed and pulled in all manner of tribal directions. Even with hindsight, the only exact science, did it become clear that a major power struggle was under way among the Congolese. It could be understood only by the key players and they did not include the Americans, the UN Security Council, the Swedes, Irish and Indians, the Russians, the Chinese or, least of all, the Congolese villagers themselves who were about to swamped by genocide, fratricide, suicide and just plain good old homicide – in the most brutal and prolonged manner imaginable.

To head the UN 'token' force in Katanga, the UN sent as its representative Dr Conor Cruise O'Brien, an Irish intellectual, wit and would-be diplomat who, no doubt, saw his mission as one of bringing peace and harmony to this troubled land. He was an instant hit with the press corps, not least because he had been a journalist himself and understood the demands of the craft. He established residence in Elisabethville only a mile or so from Moise Tshombe's official residence and was given to chatting with seeming erudition and charm to hacks outside his residence.

O'Brien had already decided that Tshombe, his gendarmerie and his mercenaries would have to go. He had, unilaterally as it turns out, issued orders for the subjugation of the Katangese secessionists. As befits an Irish diplomat and wit, he was nearly a victim of his own order. Tshombe had aloft an ad hoc 'air force' consisting of two Fouga Magisters, light trainers flown by Rhodesians which had the fire power of angry African bees.

As Conor Cruise was giving one of his impromptu press conferences, one of the Fougas droned overhead. The UN diplomat and wit immediately dived into a trench which his security men had thoughtfully dug in his garden. He was only seconds ahead of Lee Griggs, a gigantic *Time* correspondent, who landed on top of him, hurting him far more than a stray round from the buzzing Fouga Magister would have done. This bizarre scene was captured by Terry Spencer, one of the great photographers of the period, who was on assignment for *Time-Life*. Terry was a former Battle of Britain pilot and knew that the Fouga overhead was of little consequence. His picture of the spreadeagled Griggs on top of O'Brien in a foxhole made the front page, at which point the Irishman's sense of humour deserted him.

O'Brien had arrived in Elisabethville with his then mistress, later to be his wife, a lady of immense charm. *The Daily Express*, still then overseen by the ageing Beaverbrook who was insisting on a violently anti-UN line, heard of this and the command came down: 'Get this story of mad Irishman, his command of UN forces in Congo and his illicit affair.'

The hapless hack on the receiving end was Michael Parkinson, a Yorkshireman who was later to become one of the most popular personalities on British TV. Parkinson's views on his early days in journalism have been well-documented and broadcast but this instruction turned his stomach. He had been sent to cover a war in Africa and was immediately asked to 'expose' the private life of a diplomat.

John Bulloch, probably one of the most cynical men in the business, was impressed. 'He refused outright. He sent a message to the *Express* saying it was none of his business, that he was perfectly happy to cover the war but not probe into perceived misdemeanours of the people involved.' Parkinson was recalled, fired from the *Express* and then found his metier in TV presentation. He was possibly the first, certainly not the last, of the African hacks who was prepared to put his life on the line – but not his principles – to get to the story. Not long afterwards, O'Brien flexed his own muscles. He ordered the UN troops, Indian units under a Sandhurst-trained colonel, to seize control of the key points in Elisabethville – the radio station, the telephone exchange and – disaster for the foreign correspondents – the post office. The Gurkha soldiers were particularly enthusiastic in destroying the post office. Watched by the hapless hacks, they put it out of action by pouring thousands of rounds of ammunition into the building and tossing a few Katangese soldiers off the roof.

During the action, Peter Younghusband proved to his colleagues that his heroics were not confined to his copy. Dickie Williams, the BBC man, had taken refuge from the crossfire in a doorway across the square from the Leo Deux. During what he hoped was a lull in the shooting, he made a dash for the entrance of the Leo Deux where his colleagues were huddled, watching him anxiously. When he was halfway across the square, there was another burst of fire.

Younghusband remembers: 'We saw the sparks as the bullets seemed to chase Dickie and then he fell with a shout and lay there, writhing in agony. I was convinced – as he was – that he had been shot and I made a mad dash to get him out of there.' The risk was real as bullets were now cracking all around the square. Bigfoot Younghusband picked up the relatively slight BBC man and carried him back to the hotel. Dickie was still groaning and in obvious agony but his solicitous colleagues could find no sign of a bullet wound. He was nonetheless rushed off to the hospital where it was discovered he had snapped his Achilles' tendon. 'Thanks Pete,' he said when he emerged on crutches a few days later. 'I'm so sorry...it did sound just like a shot.'

The press corps was to get its own back on Dickie, unintentionally and in a rather macabre way. Williams died – of natural causes – a few years later at his base in Nairobi. He was cremated and, in accordance with his last wishes, his ashes were returned by a fellow hack to London to enable his widow to scatter them over the Essex countryside. The colleague duly arrived in London clutching the urn containing Dickie's remains.

On the way to the BBC headquarters he was waylaid by other Old Africa Hands who insisted that their old colleague be given a proper send off. This, of course, meant a pub crawl from Portland Place to Fleet Street. Dickie's urn was toasted time and again until the party finally dispersed with closing time amnesia.

According to one version of the story, Dickie's ashes were never found again, despite a frantic search. Perhaps his remains still lurk in a corner of a London pub. Another version has a very efficient BBC secretary – a Miss Moneypenny figure – tracking the movements of the colleagues and the urn and retrieving it. When anxious BBC types forgathered to mount the search on the following morning she announced, witheringly, 'You will find Mr Williams' remains in the filing cabinet under "W".' Whichever version is true, there can be no doubt that Dickie Williams would have loved the story – and both endings.

Correspondents were now faced with a real dilemma in Elisabethville. The post office was out and the dubious camaraderie of the Cabine Publique was no more. The telephones had been exasperatingly unreliable anyway, so the UN seizure of the telephone exchange did not really matter. The problem confronting all of the sixty or so foreign hacks gathered in the now darkened and beleaguered bar of the Leo Deux was how to get their copy out. There seemed to be only one clear solution. The journalists would have to risk the long, 150-mile drive to the Northern Rhodesian border and to one of the Copperbelt towns of Kitwe or Ndola to transmit their reports.

Vehicles and fuel were scarce. Most of the hacks had hired cars in the Northern Rhodesian towns to make the risky journey to Elisabethville from one of a few expatriate entrepreneurs in those mining towns. Men like Charlie Bloomberg who 'for you, china' had a car available – and was prepared to risk its fate in neighbouring Congo strictly for cash on the nail, and in foreign exchange, preferably American dollars or British sterling. Charlie was coining it but he was to lose a few cars.

Also making money out of the foreign press shuttle from the Copperbelt to Katanga was Len Catchpole, Cockney proprietor and mine host at the Elephant and Castle in Ndola. Len had a wall-eye

and hammed up his horror film image on every occasion. His brother Jack was the official hangman in the territory and used to regale
the assembled hacks with stories about how he always made sure
'me clients were comfy' as he adjusted nooses around necks. His
favourite story involved a reluctant 'client' who 'grabbed me by me
bollocks just before he was due to drop'. Len used to introduce him
proudly to newcomers. 'Meet me bruvver...he jerks 'em to Jesus.'
Len had quite a few lucrative sidelines, like the local undertaking
business and an arms smuggling operation. On one memorable occasion he combined the two by running an arms shipment into
Katanga in coffins accompanied by mercenaries disguised as white
fathers.

In Elisabethville relations between the UN troops and the mercenaries became even more tense. Firefights broke out frequently in
the streets and moving around town became hazardous. The hacks
moved uneasily between UN units, the mercenaries and the
Katangese gendarmerie, now increasingly jittery after the departure
of their Belgian officers.

Donald Wise was at his manic best. Most of his colleagues had
scars or bruises to show for their derring-do but Wise remained
unmarked and, as always, unruffled. His turn came when he visited
an Irish UN contingent. While he was there someone accidently detonated an ammunition box. Donald returned to the Leo Deux in triumph. 'I'm wounded...at last I am wounded!' His colleagues chided
him in disbelief until he turned around and stuck out his backside.
There, sure enough, was a thin line of blood seeping through his
smartly-creased linen trousers. He had been winged in the left but-
tock by a piece of flying Irish shrapnel.

There were lunacies, as well as mayhem, which had to be covered. One relatively quiet morning, the press were summoned to
meet the new commander of the Katangese gendarmerie, General
Norbert Moke, at his barracks outside town. Surrounded by hostile,
armed troops, the hacks were herded into a stuffy room where an
earnest official introduced a vacant-looking black man who stared at
them with undisguised suspicion and hatred. The correspondents
had heard that Moke, a corporal before independence, could pick up
cigarette butts between his toes. It seemed to be his only claim to
fame.

The official explained that as Moke spoke no English, French or
Swahili he would translate his answers. It soon became clear that
Moke had no answers to give. Each question was greeted with a fur-
rowing of the brows, a long pause and a few grunted words accompanied by gestures. The translator would then rattle off a series of

platitudes unrelated to any point that had been raised. The pressmen swiftly became restless. This was just another Katangese propaganda farce.

Finally Donald stood up, stretched, yawned ostentatiously and
strolled towards the door. He turned and said loudly to the gathering 'Will someone please throw the general a banana'. The hacks collapsed with laughter and, as Donald's remark was translated to a
perplexed General Moke the press conference broke up in confusion.
Whether or not Wise's scorn got through to the commander, relationships between his men and the journalists deteriorated sharply
from then on.

Not least of the hazards in making the copy run to Northern
Rhodesia was negotiating roadblocks manned by wild-eyed, antagonistic and ill-disciplined Katangese soldiers. Always drunk and frequently drugged, the Katangese tended to view any white travellers
as a member of the hated UN.

John Monks of the *Express* and the *Daily Mail's* Younghusband,
ruthless rivals as they were supposed to be in newspaper terms,
shared a car to make the journey together. Monks – son of Noel
Monks who had made his name with Waugh in the Abyssinian campaign – was an Australian, and Younghusband a South African.
Hopefully, neither could be mistaken for part of the UN force.

'We had an uneasy but workable relationship with the
Katangese at the roadblocks,' Monks recalls. 'We would always
make sure we had a good supply of whisky and cigarettes to give
them. Big Pete's French was only slightly more atrocious than theirs
but we managed to get back and forth with bribes and a bit of forced
humour.'

One evening the two men were relaxing in the Edinburgh Hotel
in Kitwe having filed their stories. They were approached by a mild-
mannered American who introduced himself as Weldon Wallace of
The Baltimore Sun. He was that newspaper's music critic and had
been covering the opera season in Milan when the Katanga crisis
erupted.

'My newspaper noticed that I was the man nearest the spot and
asked me to pop down here to cover the story,' Wallace explained. 'I
have actually never been to Africa before and wonder if I could get a
lift with you to Elisabethville.' The two old hands pointed out the
difficulties of getting through the roadblocks and explained that as
he, Weldon Wallace, had an American passport, the Katangese
might easily pick on him as the US was involved with the hated UN.
'We felt a bit guilty about this, especially as he was such a nice guy,'
Monks said. 'But it really was becoming a hairy run and we knew

that having a stranger with an American passport could easily put us all at risk.'

Wallace appreciated their point but, unbeknown to Monks and Younghusband, he sought out two other newly arrived journalists, Arthur Bonner of CBS, a fellow American, and Lionel Fleming of the BBC who travelled on an Irish passport.

They agreed to drive to Katanga together on the following day. Weldon Wallace had heard that Africans across the border were starving and had thoughtfully loaded the hire car with cans of dried milk and sacks of flour. 'I thought if I distributed food to refugees it would generate a spirit of goodwill and enable us to pass through to Elisabethville,' he said at the time. He was soon to learn that there was precious little goodwill left in Katanga.

The three men set off early, negotiated the Northern Rhodesian border post and drove down the hill to the Katangese border a mile beyond. It was still early morning but the Katangese troops lounging around the border post were drunk and high on dagga. They could scarcely believe their eyes when three white men emerged from the car cheerfully waving their passports – two American and one Irish.

As the cry went up 'Americans! Irish! UN spies!...kill them...kill them!' the three realised their error and tried to get back to the car. They were beaten and dragged at gunpoint to a fetid shack about 100 yards away while other troops cheerfully ransacked the car and began bayonetting the bags of flour.

The shack had a floor of compounded cow dung and a tin roof. 'It was hot and very smelly but that was the least of our problems. We were being slapped, beaten and jabbed with rifles. As the man who appeared to be the sergeant screamed threats and insults at us, hands reached out and grabbed our wallets and watches.' Through a window Wallace saw a large white man approaching. It was a guardian angel in the unlikely form of Peter 'Bigfoot' Younghusband. 'When he saw what was going on an expression of astonishment crossed his face. He inclined his head in acknowledgement of our plight. My hopes rose.'

Monks and Younghusband had set out for the border shortly after Wallace and his companions. At the Northern Rhodesian border post they had exchanged pleasantries with a Federal Army officer, a major whom Monks, then based in Rhodesia, had known for some time. They were told that two Americans and an Irishman had just gone through. With mounting concern the pair approached the Katangese border.

'The first thing we noticed was this great cloud of flour hanging in the air. The troops were fighting over the spoils from our colleagues' car,' Younghusband remembers. 'It was an amazing sight. There were these crazed black men reeling around covered in white flour, their eyeballs rolling. We realised something pretty nasty was going on.

'A Katangese immigration official indicated that three white spies had been "taken for execution".' Monks and Younghusband made a swift decision. Younghusband would try to do what he could on the spot to find the men and calm the situation while Monks would dash back to the Northern Rhodesian border post to summon help from the Federal troops.

Bigfoot strolled as casually as he could towards the shack where he heard sounds of another commotion. He glimpsed the terrified face of Weldon Wallace through the window and then made his way to the door.

'I burst in and, trying to sound authoritative, I bellowed in French "Stop this immediately...these men are famous journalists who have come to see President Tshombe". I was armed with nothing more useful than a Katangese press card which I brandished wildly. It did not work.'

The Katangese officer, his face contorted with fury, stepped towards the big South African, knocked the press card from his hand and, screaming 'Spies, spies...you are all spies', slapped him repeatedly across the face. 'I was transformed from a liberal to an Afrikaner nationalist in thirty seconds flat,' Peter recalls with wry humour.

There was nothing funny about his situation at the time, however. He was pushed onto the floor with the other three. To his horror, a soldier dragged a Bren gun into the open door of the hut, spreadeagled himself behind it and pointed it at the men. The others chanted 'Kill them...kill them'. The Bren gunner suddenly rolled over onto his back and started to laugh.

'I sensed they were waiting for somebody. I urged the others not to try and show their fear, which was more easily said than done.' The Katangese immigration officer suddenly appeared in the doorway and spoke to the soldier in charge. He pointed to Younghusband and said he knew him as a British journalist. Peter was ordered to his feet and told to get back to the border.

Wallace, Bonner and Fleming were then dragged out of the shack and bundled into a vehicle which took them several miles down the road and swung off into a clearing in the bush. Wallace took up the story.

'The soldiers crowded around. They tore off our jackets and ordered us to remove the rest of our clothing. One of them said they did not want our clothes to show bullet holes. I was convinced this was the end. We were going to be executed there in the bush.' The half-naked trio were then pushed into a line. Once again the soldiers cocked their rifles.

Back at the border post Younghusband found John Monks with the Federal troops in armoured cars. The friendly major was talking urgently into a field radio. Monks had got through to his old friend, Sir Roy Welensky, the Federal prime minister, who had ordered his troops to do everything possible to rescue the journalists. They had driven to the Katangese border post where the major was now trying to reach his opposite number in the gendarmerie on the radio. He succeeded. A senior Katangese officer raced to the scene just in time to prevent the execution of the three men. They were given back their clothes and handed over at the border post. Bonner and Fleming were shaken but unhurt. Weldon Wallace had no injuries but was white and shaking and clearly in shock. Monks and Younghusband rushed him back to Kitwe and summoned a doctor from the nearby copper mine. 'Weldon was put straight to bed and heavily sedated,' Monks said. 'Just before he went under he kept muttering that he had to write a story for his newspaper. He had to file. We told him not to worry and then he went into a deep sleep.'

The two Old Africa Hands sat down at a typewriter and, under Wallace's name, composed a dramatic first-person account of what had happened. 'My American passport nearly cost me my life yesterday...' it started, and went on in punchy Fleet Street style. They then cabled it to *The Baltimore Sun* which ran it prominently with Weldon's byline and picture under the banner headline 'A Captive of Wild Katangan Troops'. By the time the newspaper's music critic came to in the Edinburgh Hotel, there was a pile of cables from his editors and his proprietor congratulating him on his escape and his story and advising him that he was being nominated for a Pulitzer Prize for 'a story written under great pressure'. He was totally bewildered. 'But I didn't write anything...what are they talking about?'

Monks and Younghusband tried to tell him that he had dictated his account to them before he was sedated, but he was not convinced. Younghusband: 'He went straight back to the US and we had a long letter of thanks from him. But he said that, under the circumstances, he could not possibly accept a Pulitzer nomination...a pity because that's the closest we ever came to winning a prize.' Monks' hometown newspaper, the *Melbourne Herald*, ran the story of his exploits under the memorable headline 'Australian Reporter Saves Three From Natives'.

On the same day that Weldon Wallace made his debut as an
Africa hand, another young newsman was making a name for himself in Katanga. Ernie Christie, a South African photographer later
to become one of the world's best known news cameramen, was
among several journalists accompanying Indian UN troops in action
against Katangese forces near Jadotville. John Osman remembers
the scene: 'The Indian troops were very jittery. They had been shot
at repeatedly by mercenaries and were twitching at every shadow.
Suddenly, down the road came a Volkswagen Beetle being driven at
high speed. An Indian officer moved half-heartedly to wave the vehicle down, but before any of us could do anything the troops opened
up and riddled the car with bullets.

'It slewed to a stop with punctured tyres, but the Indians continued firing for several seconds. I could see that there were two
women passengers in a bad way. Dennis Neeld of AP and I ran forward and dragged them out of the car but it was too late. They died
in our hands from dreadful wounds.

'There was an Alsatian dog with its nose shot off and a bullet
wound in its back. The driver, another Belgian, jumped out, his face
streaming with blood from flying glass, and screamed at the UN
men. "Soldiers of peace...look what you have done...you are murderers...murderers." Ernie's pictures of that scene created shockwaves
of revulsion. All the victims were innocent civilians. It was all very
ugly but not untypical of the Congo at that time.'

The copy run from Elisabethville to the Copperbelt was becoming increasingly hazardous. It was not only the jittery Katangese
but trigger-happy UN troops, particularly the Swedes, who were
causing problems. They established a machine-gun post on the outskirts of town and were given to shooting wildly at anybody they
thought might be mercenaries. One morning, the hacks prepared
two cars for the journey. The word 'Press' was inscribed in bold let-
tering front and back and Union Jacks were tied to the aerials.
Sandy Gall joined Monks and Younghusband in the first car. They
were no more than two miles from town when heavy-calibre
machine-gun fire cracked over the vehicle. Bigfoot, at the wheel,
took wild evasive action which nearly overturned the car, but they
accelerated away without getting hit.

The following car was not so lucky. The passengers were Jean-
Claude Favre, a Swiss financial adviser to Tshombe, Jim Biddulph,
then with the Rhodesian Federal Broadcasting Corporation and
Sanche de Gramont of the *New York Herald Tribune*. The Swedes
did not bother to check any credentials. They opened fire with a
bazooka which struck the vehicle on the driver's side and exploded.

The car careened all over the road before stopping.

Favre was killed outright. Biddulph had a severe head injury and de Gramont was wounded in the back and the legs. The Swedes left them by the roadside for more than an hour before finally taking the wounded men to a field hospital. Biddulph and de Gramont were eventually flown out of Katanga for surgery at UN expense, the only tacit acknowledgement by that organisation that it was in any way responsible.

The press corps was badly shaken by the incident. Clearly the risks of using the main road were now too great. To the rescue came Alan Kearns, the Rhodesian pilot who had shared those unpleasant experiences with Sandy Gall and George Gale in Bakwanga. Just 20 miles due west of Elisabethville was the small Northern Rhodesian border post of Kipushi. It was a long, arduous dirt road journey from Ndola, but Kipushi had an airstrip, a short, bumpy grass strip, but not one to deter the intrepid Kearns. He agreed to start an air shuttle service for the press corps in Katanga, flying an old Tiger Moth between Ndola and Kipushi to ferry copy and film. This was the birth of 'Royal Uhuru Airlines' one of the African carriers that was known only to its exclusive hack clientele – and to newspaper accountants who were frequently confronted with large bills on impressive, printed 'Royal Uhuru Airlines' stationery.

'Royal Uhuru Airlines' was one of the better-kept secrets of the battle for Katanga. It was not the only expense account fiddle of the Congo crisis but it was certainly one of the most successful. The hacks were putting their lives on the line every day, as were people who helped them, like Alan Kearns, Royal Uhuru's chief – and only – pilot. The rule of thumb, among the Fleet Street men in particular, was that if the job hurt, 'punish' the office with a big expenses sheet. John Ridley may have taken it to an extreme when, on one occasion, the car in which he was travelling with Monks and Younghusband broke down five miles from Elisabethville and the three were obliged to walk.

Monks recalls: 'Ridders was lagging a bit behind, seemingly muttering to himself. When I went back to see if I could help, he held up a languid finger to silence me and counted out a few more paces..."617, 618, 619, 620", stopped and explained that this was a hardship and he was counting every step."I will punish the *Telegraph* for walkage old boy," he boomed. "It will cost them half-a-crown for every yard I have to walk in this benighted continent."'

The stories in Katanga were coming thick and fast but so were the dangers and the frustrations. Press corps sympathy towards Tshombe and his secessionist cause was waning rapidly and his frequent press conferences in the heat of the tropical African summer afforded the few hacks who turned up an opportunity for a kip. John Ridley and Peter Lynch of UPI were regular press conference snoozers, although Lynch was blacklisted by Tshombe when he started awake and asked a colleague, within earshot of an English-speaking Tshombe aide, 'What's the fucking ape have to say today?'

Travelling anywhere became very dangerous. Jack Nugent of *Newsweek* and Ross Mark of the *Daily Express* were manhandled and shot at just outside the town. John Bulloch and Jack Starr of the *Daily Mail* limped back to the Leo Deux one day in a Volkswagen with its windscreen shattered and its bodywork riddled with bullet holes.

Tshombe's two Fouga Magisters still dominated the daylight skies, shooting up Conor Cruise O'Brien's residence and any other real or suspected UN target. David Halberstam, a young *New York Times* man, happened to be at Elisabethville airport when the Fougas had a go at the despised Swedish UN positions. With other correspondents he made a dash for the terminal building as the little planes swooped over spitting light-machine-gun fire.

Halberstam was hampered when his newly acquired tropical trousers suddenly dropped around his ankles and he tripped and fell. Halberstam was later to go on to a career as a famous reporter and writer during the Vietnam war but this was his undignified baptism of fire. As his colleagues dragged him to the safety of the terminal building he was heard to shout: 'I don't wanna die in any Goddam Mickey Mouse war'. Cyril Ainsley, one of the most distinguished of the old *Express* hands, was quite badly cut by flying glass when gunfire from one of the Fougas hit the terminal building.

John Bulloch knew the Fouga pilots well. 'One was a Hungarian called Sputnik who was a refugee then living in Rhodesia, and the other was a Rhodesian of dubious French origin. They used to come and drink with us – heavily – at the Leo Deux after their "missions". They had improvised on a bombing technique. They had empty beer crates which they loaded with hand grenades. Each grenade had a bit of string attached to its firing pin. They used to grip twelve bits of string in one hand as they came down low over what they hoped was their target, drop the crate and pray that none of the grenades exploded prematurely.

'Neither of them was too hot on navigation. When they arrived at the Leo Deux we used to have the maps spread out on the table on the terrace and ask them what they'd been trying to hit that day. When they told us we'd say "Jesus, you were way off course...you should have turned right here and gone in there." It was a farce, like everything else in the Congo – but, unfortunately, a bloody farce.'

The increasingly manic atmosphere led to confrontations amid the now firmly established camaraderie between the correspondents and the mercenaries in the Leo Deux bar. An intense Agence France Presse man repeatedly needled 'Les Affreux', the wild and bearded wonders of Col Bob Denard's French soldiers of fortune. They finally called him outside, formed a ring around him and fired pistol shots repeatedly around his feet, urging him all the while to keep on dancing. Wisely he did.

Other members of the press corps were prepared to match the 'mercs' on a macho-to-macho basis. One such was big Jim Howard, an Australian photographer for UPI who had been obliged to leave his home country after 'some mistake about a bank job in Perth'. Bearded and burly, Jim announced to a group of Les Affreux in an Elisabethville bar that he would bet $1 000 none of them could get past him to get out of the door. A massive Belgian mercenary took up the challenge and a prolonged, bloody battle ensued. Finally Jim picked up the groggy Belgian, spun him around over his head and hurled him – inadvertently – through the door. The mercenaries claimed their colleague had therefore made it outside and obliged the UPI man to pay up – at pistol point.

Howard eventually found frontline photo-journalism a little boring. After being thrown out of numerous countries – for a string of alleged offences from kidnapping (a 16-year-old girl) to espionage, he took to seafaring, wrecking a number of expensive yachts off the coast of South Africa. He was last heard of in the Southern Indian port of Cochin, denying any knowledge of a $100 million drug consignment which had been seized by US coastguards from a yacht he owned.

Dangerous as it was, the situation had its moments of pure farce. George Evans, the British Consul in Elisabethville had the questionable honour of living next to Tshombe's residence. He became accustomed to the odd and usually ineffectual UN mortar attacks on his neighbour's home. One night, however, he was awoken by a frantic tapping on his bedroom window. It was Tshombe, wearing his pyjamas and a dressing gown and looking extremely nervous.

'Come in M le President,' said George, opening the window wide. 'What can we do for you?' Tshombe clambered in, babbled on about the UN attacks on his home and asked for 'political asylum'. Consul Evans, at his diplomatic best, poured the Katangan leader a couple of large whiskies, lent a fatherly ear to his problems and escorted him back over the wall to his residence.

Down the road, the US Consul, Lewis Hoffaker, was preparing a cocktail party for a visiting American Senator, Thomas Dodd, Brian Urquhart, a senior UN official, and George Ivan Smith who had arrived to replace Conor Cruise O'Brien. The party moved on to the home of a Mobil Oil representative whose neighbour was the semi-articulate General Norbert Moke, head of the Katangese gendarmerie. Moke's guards saw the UN numberplates and assumed their chief was in danger.

They charged in and started to beat the guests with rifle butts and kicks. Smith and Urquhart, who suffered a broken nose, were dragged outside just as Hoffaker drove up with Senator and Mrs Dodd. The American Consul managed to grab Smith and push him into the car where the Senator and his wife were crouching on the floor. He drove away furiously to raise the alarm and finally secured the release of Urquhart, who had been held at gunpoint for several hours at a gendarmerie barracks.

Of all the UN troops in Katanga, the Irish contingent suffered the most. They had arrived in heavy serge greatcoats and thick uniforms totally unsuitable for Africa. Then the Katangese intercepted and plundered a huge consignment of Guiness sent to the lads by the Dublin brewery.

A considerate UN command topped it all by deciding to base them in the north of Katanga – in the heart of Baluba country, perhaps because the Balubas had an even greater reputation than the Irish for fighting ferociously any form of real or perceived authority. Worse, the Balubas had a great tradition of cannibalism which had stamped still more sinister overtones on the Congo crisis.

It was the Balubas' appetite for human flesh which gave rise to the greeting given to newcomers to Elisabethville: 'Welcome to E-vil and Meet The People Who Eat The People'. Cannibal stories were as abundant as they were apocryphal.

Bulloch and Ian Colvin travelled north to attend a press conference given by a Baluba leader, the Malopwe of South Kasai. It was said that when the Malopwe made his first journey in an airliner he had been handed a menu. 'No, no,' he said. 'This is no good...bring me the passenger list.'

At the press conference Bulloch noticed his colleague manoeuvre himself into a position where he was standing very close to the Malopwe, examining his face intently. Later Colvin leaned across to Bulloch. 'John...have you observed that mandible?... I'm sure everything they say about him is true.'

The Irish were involved in numerous running battles with the Balubas who were reputed to believe, despite the numbers who fell dead around them, that a secret potion turned the white man's bullets to water. The Irish took casualties, too, notably a brave machine-gunner whose position was finally overrun.

No trace of the gunner's body was ever found but the word seeped back to the Irish that his body had been borne away and eaten in its entirety as a mark of great respect for a brave warrior by other brave warriors. It didn't help their mood or morale much. The final humiliation for the Irish came when Baluba tribesmen and Katangese gendarmes besieged Jadotville north of Elisabethville. The Irish were obliged to surrender, a major setback to the psychology if not the substance of the UN offensive against Katanga.

John Bulloch and Jack Starr of the *Daily Mail* had visited the Irish in Jadotville just before the fall. 'They were all cowering in foxholes covered in black boot polish that made them look like the cast of a bad Black and White Minstrel Show,' recalled Bulloch. 'They were absolutely terrified that they were about to be eaten.' The journalists tried to cheer them up by telling them about the table manners of the Malopwe of South Kasai.

The hacks were to have their own Baluba experiences. Just east of Elisabethville was a camp housing some 35 000 Baluba refugees. They were supposedly guarded by the Swedes but word filtered through that they were becoming restless (not surprisingly, it turns out, as they had had no food or water for nearly two days and the sanitary conditions were non-existent). They tried to break out and were driven back by UN troops who killed at least 20 of their number.

Donald Wise and George Gale drove to the camp to investigate. Wise later described the scene to his colleagues: 'As soon as we drove in, they came at us like a swarm of hornets...big buggers, all starkers, with bows and arrows and axes. One of them had somebody's balls in his mouth. He wanted to show George the penis he had cut off some poor bloody Lunda. George thought they wanted to cut his off for their collection. At this point we began to realise that we weren't exactly welcome so we gave it full reverse thrust. They were coming after us, full gallop, holding these balls in their mouths like retrievers.'

Much as Donald's hyperbole was enjoyed over the bar, other hacks decided to investigate the situation for themselves. Smith Hempstone of the *Chicago Daily News*, Jack Nugent of *Newsweek* and Bob Targett of the *Sunday Times* set off in the direction of the camp. As they approached, they passed small groups of hostile-looking Balubas. 'Some of them carried spears, clubs or pangas. Others had bicycle chains fastened to sticks.' Suddenly they were obliged to swerve around a log which had been pulled across the road.

Smith Hempstone reported: 'We braked to a stop. Before we could turn around, a Baluba loped up, grabbed the handle of the door and began to shake a knife in the face of Bob Targett who was driving. Other Balubas started running towards the car. Targett quickly reversed. The Baluba at his window began to scream and make short jabs at him with his knife. Out of the corner of my eye I saw a squat Baluba dressed in ragged shorts and a dirty undershirt swing his panga in a gigantic arc. As the blow descended towards my closed window, I could clearly see the tendons knotting in his forearm.'

There was a crash and the car was filled with a cloud of milky, flying glass as the panga smashed into the window and bit deep into its frame. 'I was conscious of the fact that I was covered in blood from a score of superficial wounds. Targett had kept the car moving in reverse and we bumped over the tree and off the road. Other Balubas, howling with rage, went flying as we pulled onto the road again and sped away.' The Irish soldiers at a roadblock just stared as the battered car and its battered hacks sped past. Nugent was constrained to shout: 'You dirty bastards!'

As Hempstone wrote: 'That was the way it was in Elisabethville in September 1961. There was really no war. Just organised, large-scale murder. The situation was largely of the UN's making. Its nose had been bloodied and now it wanted peace.' That was a minority view. Most of the other correspondents believed that the UN – the military at least – wanted war and revenge – on Tshombe, the Katangese, the mercenaries and the Balubas. They wanted to get away from this clammy, homicidal and sanguinary centre of a hostile continent and return to the chilly climes of Dublin or Stockholm, or the spice and scents of India. The now battered and frightened hacks were getting just a little homesick themselves.

Dag Hammarskjöld was justifiably appalled by the shambles when he arrived in Leopoldville. He had been, undoubtedly, incensed by O'Brien's conduct and the events at Jadotville. He agreed to meet Moise Tshombe in Ndola. On the night of 17 September 1961, the UN Secretary-General boarded a Swedish charter DC6-B, *Albertina*, bound for Ndola in Northern Rhodesia to negotiate a truce with Tshombe. Presumably for security reasons, the Swedish pilot flew due east and then southwards down Lake Tanganyika. Six hours later, the pilot made contact with Ndola tower and began to descend. The aircraft flew over the airfield just after 10 p.m. and disappeared.

Many of the foreign correspondents from Katanga and quite a few others 'covering' the conflict from the safety of Northern Rhodesia had heard Hammarskjöld was on his way. They had assembled at Ndola Airport. The hacks were in a bad mood. Police would not allow them near the apron or in the buildings. For most, deadline time for the first editions of their newspapers had past. It would merely be a case of filing a quick 'snap' saying Hammarskjöld had arrived. An aircraft landed and, as far as the journalists were able to see, a group of civilians disembarked.

Donald Wise was one of the tallest hacks present and he craned to glimpse a tallish fair-haired chap among the disembarking passengers. 'That's Hammarskjöld isn't it?' he asked a policeman standing beside him. 'That must be him,' the policeman affirmed. Hardly a thorough check but there was no reason to suspect anything was wrong. 'A couple of others reached the same conclusion,' Donald remembers. 'It was routine stuff, so we thought. We all rushed off to file and enjoy what was left of the evening.'

All the major news agencies and most newspapers around the world carried the story that Hammarskjöld had arrived in Ndola and was locked in truce negotiations with Moise Tshombe. This fact added to the flood of international suspicion and recrimination that followed the discovery of the body of the UN Secretary-General amid the wreckage of the *Albertina* on a wooded ridge seven miles from Ndola Airport the following afternoon. The only survivor was an American security guard, Harry Julian, who died a few days later without regaining consciousness. Numerous subsequent investigations pointed to pilot error. The pilot's manual found in the wreckage was open at a page giving landing instruction for the airfield at Ndolo in the Congo. It contained no reference to Ndola in Northern Rhodesia.

But throughout that night and early the following day, with the Secretary-General's plane officially missing, diplomatic and government wires hummed with speculation, accusation and counter-accusation: the aircraft had been sabotaged in Leopoldville, it had been shot down by Tshombe's mercenary pilots or by Federal ground fire. The hacks awoke with egg on their faces, some with more than others. Clyde Sanger of *The Guardian* had not only landed Hammarskjöld but had managed to include a few pithy quotes from him. From that day on, Sanger, never the most popular of colleagues among the Africa press corps, was known as 'Snide Clanger'.

It was a little unfair. Donald Wise: 'They all tended to blame me and some chaps got quite angry, but we were all in the same boat and anyway we now had a cracker of a story.'

Wise and Ian Colvin chartered an aircraft to circle the area. They spotted the wreckage on the ridge shortly before the ground search party got there. Jack Nugent of *Newsweek*, who had flown in from Nairobi, had less luck. At great expense he hired a car and a driver to tour the surrounding bush.

His driver spoke no English, so Nugent tried to explain what he was looking for by flapping his arms and repeating the Swahili word for bird 'ndege...ndege'. Nugent: 'The man smiled and drove around and around. He stopped every so often and turned off the engine. If there were birds chirping in the scrub pine he smiled and pointed. He obviously thought I was nuts.' Hammarskjöld's untimely death seemed to signal the start of a long period of even more chaos, carnage and horror throughout the Congo. The UN, having been humiliated in Round One, reached a ceasefire agreement with Tshombe who remained tenuously in power in Katanga for another two years. Initially, UN troops even gave up the post office and radio station which gave the hacks in Elisabethville some brief respite from the Katangese and UN roadblocks.

John Bulloch and Jack Starr had found their own little communications goldmine – a young Belgian technician called René who with a bit of wizardry had rigged his own telephone to connect directly with the exchange in Ndola. The two hacks had befriended René and his family and found suddenly they had a way to get their copy out swiftly and with little risk. René was rewarded handsomely of course. Bulloch: 'Jack and I used to take separate and different routes to René's flat and arrive at different times. The rest of the hacks were livid. They couldn't work out how we were doing it.'

Their secret lasted for a week until Peter Lynch of UPI shadowed them one evening and burst through the door of the flat as they were dictating copy over the 'hot' line. 'Got you, you bastards!' roared Lynch. 'Either I come in and share the line or I'll go right back to the hotel and tell the others.' The syndicate was expanded.

For a time the Cabine Publique was back in action, but erratically. Correspondents were obliged to punch their own telex tapes on a 'blind' machine and hand them to an operator who would then try to transmit them. Bulloch and Mike Brown of the *Express* returned to Elisabethville one weekend after interviewing mercenaries in Albertville.

Bulloch: 'We both had good stories and rushed to the post office. We gave the tapes to the operator and waited impatiently for him to get through. He tried dozens of times. We tried. Nothing. No connection at all. We stayed all night trying every few minutes. The following day we were at it again. Still no connection. We were nearly in tears with frustration. We had tried bribing the operators, cursing them, offering them villas in Spain, everything. Suddenly this American UN guy comes in, chats to the duty man and a few minutes later we hear him screaming down the telephone, "Hi mom. How's everything...how are the kids?" He was talking to Los Angeles on the phone. We stared at each other and then advanced on the operator. Did he mean to tell us that the telephones were working and that we could 'phone London? "Mais oui...c'est possible." For 24 hours we'd battled to try and get through on telex without bothering to ask whether the 'phones were working!'

At another stage, when all the lines were down, the hacks found another Belgian technician who rigged up a morse key system. They tapped out a pooled story in morse and this was relayed to an air-craft flying overhead with a request for the message to be passed on. But the procedure was too complicated, too hit-and-miss to guaran-tee regular communications.

The truce between Tshombe and the UN broke down quickly. American Skymasters airlifted in reinforcements to the UN forces in what turned out to be Round Two, a second massive military drive to end Katangan secession. The Indians, Irish and Swedes were now reinforced by a battalion of Ethiopian troops. UN Canberra bombers, flown by Indians, gained control of the skies, shooting up everything and anything that moved on the roads, including civilian vehicles, peasant carts, villages, cattle, goats and pigs. Atrocity sto-ries abounded.

'We would meet wearily over breakfast to discuss the latest round of atrocities – committed by the Indians, the Swedes, the Katangese gendarmerie, the Congolese national army who were running amok in the north, the white mercenaries, the Balubas, the Belgians and everyone else you could think of. When we came to look into them, most of the stories were true.' Such was the hack's lot in a beleaguered and rather sad Elisabethville at the end of 1961. More unfortunately, it was the lot of the Congo and of Africa.

'The atmosphere in Elisabethville in those last days of fighting had a dream-like quality of unreality,' wrote Smith Hempstone. 'The streets were filled with rubble and lined with blasted palm trees and shattered cars, their tyres flat and their windows broken.' Most of the whites had fled but 200 were now huddled in the Leo Deux, sleeping eight to a room and on mattresses in the lobby and the cor-ridors. The UN was bombing and pounding the city with mortars. They hit the beauty shop, the French Consul's apartment, the Sabena Airways office, the Roman Catholic Cathedral, the museum, the zoo and many other strategic targets.

Katangan gendarmes under the command of the drunken and drugged Moke robbed, looted, tortured and terrified everyone and anyone they deemed to be Onusien – or a UN spy. UN troops looted (the Indians on a grand scale) all abandoned Belgian property and distributed shot and shell with equal abandon. The Congolese army, the dreaded ANC, simply went on an uncontrolled rampage. The Balubas continued to sever and consume remaining supplies of human genitalia. Other tribes seized the moment to settle old scores. The mercenaries swaggered and shot at anything that moved. And the hacks occasionally let off steam in the bar of the Leo Deux or in Michel's, the only restaurant left in town that could be relied upon for a passable chateaubriand bearnaise. 'It was not Africa or humanity at its best but we made the best of a bad bottle of Beaujolais,' said Wise.

All the Elisabethville pressmen remember one mercenary with great affection. Luigi was, despite the name, a Pole. He had once worked as a chef for the Governor of Rhodesia and his culinary skills had been greatly appreciated until the Government House silver disappeared mysteriously. He was a regular in the Leo Deux and Michel's, his combat fatigues always draped with bandoliers of ammunition and hand grenades, a machine gun slung over his shoulder and a natty red cravatt around his thick neck.

Luigi's duty for the Katanga cause was to defend the railway underpass just outside E-vil, a task he performed with astonishing zeal. John Bulloch remembers him standing on top of a truck firing a rifle at a Canberra bomber coming for a low bombing run on the railway. 'I asked him what the fuck he thought he was trying to do. "Listen," he said. "I'm frightened, but sitting in the cockpit up there is a little Indian. He can see me and he's frightened too. It puts him off his aim".'

Smith Hempstone recalled: 'We used to squat on the balconies of the Leo Deux with all the lights extinguished listening to the dull roar of explosions and the chattering of machine guns from the tunnel while tracer bullets burned across the night sky. Somebody would say "Luigi's catching hell tonight" or "Luigi will have a great thirst tomorrow". The tunnel was his personal real estate, his own small slice of Poland. He was the Polish baron standing up against the Huns and the Mongols. Without the tunnel, Luigi was just a squat little man who used to cook other people's meals.'

When the going got rough, Luigi's appearance at the bar would be greeted with cheers and backslapping from his highly relieved hack friends. 'Through the bloodied bandages he would roar with laughter at the madness of it all and get smashed with us on the strength of a status he deserved and treasured.' One evening Luigi failed to make his usual appearance for a pre-battle Pernod at the Leo Deux. Mortars rained down on the centre of Elisabethville that night. The hotel sang with shell fragments and the hacks dragged mattresses to what they hoped were protected corners to sleep.

The *Chicago Daily News* man reported: 'In the morning there was no food, water or electricity in the hotel. Mortars peppered the streets outside and acrid smoke poured into the lobby. Dogs ran about barking crazily. Wounded gendarmes, sullen and tired, streamed south towards the one remaining gap in the UN pincers. There were still a few gendarme mortar crews in the area and one went into action in front of the hotel, which indicated that the UN was no more than a few hundred yards away.' Incoming UN fire came from the direction of the tunnel and the correspondents realised that they were unlikely to be entertained by Luigi again. At best he had managed to flee to the border. At worst he was dead, defending a subterranean territorial imperative in a corner of Africa. He was not seen or heard of again.

Within days Tshombe had fled to Kitwe in the Northern Rhodesian Copperbelt and had agreed to an end to Katanga's secession. It was Round Two to the UN but the wily Katangese leader still had, as Donald Wise put it, 'several key cards sleevewise'. He was soon back in Elisabethville claiming that his deal with Cyrille Adoula, the Congolese leader, was imposed and therefore invalid. He held on for another year before the UN forces, with much mindless bloodshed and cruelty, finally seized Elisabethville in the name of a united Congo in January 1963. Moise Tshombe fled to exile in Spain, although he was still to play a major part in the interminable tragedy of this unhappy land. The press focus switched to Leopoldville and the dread, dank Memling Hotel. The hacks were having to double, and sometimes treble up in a room which inhibited – or in the case of one or two noted pederasts, enhanced – diversions sexual. John Ridley, as morose as ever, had once again been dispatched to the darkest continent to allow John Bulloch to foray into the hinterland. Bulloch was a little perturbed to be informed by Ridley on his arrival that he had shared a flight with 'an absolutely delightful young man' to whom he had offered a berth in the bedroom *The Daily Telegraph* men were sharing for a couple of days. Safety in numbers, Bulloch thought. He need not have worried. The 'charming young man' turned out to be Don McCullin, a young Cockney freelance photographer setting out to cover the first of many wars. He was – and is – as tough as they come and not quite Ridley's type.

Nor was Walter Partington, the young *Daily Express* correspondent sent out to back up Stephen Harper in Leopoldville and John Monks in Elisabethville. Ridley was fortifying himself for 'another ghastly African day' with a bowl of brandy at the Memling bar when Partington arrived, to be greeted enthusiastically by most of his colleagues. The young man's brashness and accent did not appeal to Ridley, who declined to even look around when someone tried to introduce him to Walter. Instead he boomed into his brandy bowl: 'Partington? Partington! Only BUTLERS are called Partington!' Not an auspicious start to Walter's colourful African career, but he was soon to establish a firm, if amusing, relationship with the *Telegraph* man, despite their widely divergent proclivities.

Revolt, rebellion and lawlessness swept most of the Congo. Rumours of atrocities by all forces now involved gusted through the Memling and sent correspondents scurrying into the heart of darkness, invariably to discover that most of the stories were true, or worse.

The UN was becoming totally disillusioned with the Congo. The crises had brought the world body to the brink of bankruptcy and had very nearly brought about its demise. With the news that the UN was about to pull out, rebellion and chaos swelled, not least in the eastern Congo among pro-Lumumba rebels, calling themselves, in the grandiose fashion of gangsters everywhere, the Simbas.

They massacred their way into Stanleyville, capturing this once most romantic of towns in August 1964 and established, wait for it, the 'People's Republic of the Congo' under Christopher Gbenye, a former Lumumba acolyte. Many thousands of people were systematically and ritually murdered, most of them in front of what was left of the 'public' at the foot of the numerous statues of the late lunatic, Lumumba. The condemned included teachers, health workers, civil servants, shop-keepers – anyone who might occasionally wear a tie or a jacket which would automatically brand him – or her – as a 'counter-revolutionary'.

The Chinese had seized the opportunity to establish an African identity for their 'people's revolution'. Peking's embassies and agents in neighbouring Burundi, Kampala, Congo-Brazzaville and Dar es Salaam – and from new found bases in Algeria and the United Arab Republic – were pouring money, arms, ammunition and other lethal accoutrements across Lake Tanganyika, across the turgid Congo River and across the Mountains of the Moon to back up the madmen like Gbenye and Pierre Mulele who had so swiftly established their own murderous despotisms in the eastern Congo. The increasingly beleaguered Leopoldville regime turned in desperation to Moise Tshombe, the exiled Katangan leader, who returned to become prime minister in Leopoldville. No doubt Washington had a major hand in this. The American concern about the degree to which Peking's influence was now exerting itself was palpable.

Tshombe knew what had to be done. He summoned back his old friend 'Mad' Mike Hoare and his Five Commando who, backed up by covert CIA air support, Belgian air force 'mercenaries' and other highly suspect forces like the Congolese army, the ANC, rescued some 2 000 whites being held hostage in Stanleyville and other Simba-held areas of the eastern Congo. History might record that the operation was a success but an awful lot of people were murdered, maimed and dehumanised in the process. The hacks, who had been covering the Congo carnage for four years, were also becoming a little hardened.

Jack Starr of the *Mail* had taken his life and his dateline to Kindu in Kivu province to investigate the story of thirteen Italian airmen of the UN force reportedly beaten to death in a rather horrible fashion by Congolese soldiers. He found that drunken Congolese had beaten the Italians over a prolonged period, then shot them and then dismembered their bodies. Starr found a demented World Health Organisation man who had actually been offered a severed hand from one of the Italians. He wrote a stomach-churning story of finding Italianate human limbs for sale in the local butchery. When, back at the Memling, cynical colleagues challenged him with the question 'How on earth could you know they were the Italians?' Jack took another swig of whisky and said, scathingly, 'The hands had long, white and very sensuous fingers.'

Stephen Harper of the *Express* and Ray Maloney of UPI had made their way to Bukavu, one of the Simba-held towns on the border of Ruanda-Burundi. There they found armed, drugged and drunken soldiers holding the townspeople in thrall. A young woman rushed up to Harper, slapped his face and screamed in English 'Clear off white man'. In a bar an elderly Congolese told them the whites were not the only people being terrorised. 'We get it much worse and nobody bothers about us. Soldiers act like conquerors with our women. They arrest us as capitalists if we wear a clean shirt or a tie.'

There was a blanket ban on pressmen accompanying the Belgian paratroopers who were dropped to relieve Stanleyville. Only one man, Ed van Can, a Dutch freelance cameraman, managed to get in, by locking himself in the toilet of a DC3. Sandy Gall, now working for ITN, managed to get in shortly afterwards – to find his Indian stringer from Nairobi being held by the Belgians on suspicion of being a Simba sympathiser. Sandy effected his release and filmed the devastation in the town. Most of the Simbas had fled across the Congo River and were being pursued by Mike Hoare and his mercenaries. Joyous residents emerged and began blowing up the numerous Lumumba statues in the town.

John Bulloch remembers dodging flying debris from the detonated statues. Jonathan Randall of *Time* magazine was not so quick. He was cracked on the leg by a lump of flying concrete and emerged in plaster and on crutches to be filmed and photographed by colleagues as 'a wounded survivor' of the Stanleyville massacres. 'We were all very grateful to Randall. Without him there wouldn't have been much of a picture,' Bulloch remembers.

Some of the old Elisabethville hands in the press corps cashed in on their good relationship with Mike Hoare and the mercenaries to get into action. On Tshombe's instructions, Hoare and his Five Commando were to mop up and send packing the Simbas from the areas they had held. John Bulloch wrote a major series on Hoare for the *Sunday Telegraph*, an assignment that entailed hours of commuting on American C-130 transports between Leopoldville and Stanleyville where the mercenary had his headquarters. Bulloch had been given the honorary rank of captain by Mike Hoare and got some first-class copy as a result.

'On one trip, Mike and I were flying in a C-130 on some mission when an American colonel came up and chatted enthusiastically to us. The Americans were supposed to be there on strictly humanitarian grounds, ferrying relief supplies and evacuating refugees, but this guy desperately wanted some of the action. He clapped me on the shoulder and said to me "Hey, captain! You get any shit down there, you just give us a call and we can give you air back-up. You'd be surprised what these fucking aircraft can do given the chance." I just didn't have the heart to tell him I was a hack.'

As always, it was the film and television journalists who ran the greatest risks. The scribe can always cower from the bullets, using his notebook and memory to do his work, but the photographers and cameramen have to be in the thick of it to get any results. The risk is often that much greater when they are obliged to use elongated lenses which have been mistaken by jittery troops for enemy weapons. Let nothing detract from the courage of the frontline cameramen.

As the Congo crisis reached its climax, news came through that a two-man television crew who had ventured into the north-eastern Congo from the Sudan were missing. The two men, Jens Albrektsen, a Dane, and Mohinder Maryara his Indian assistant cameraman, were both young freelancers, based in Nairobi. They had made their way to the town of Aba near the Sudanese border in the hope of making a film about the fleeing Simba rebels. Hans Germani, a German correspondent for *Die Welt*, was travelling with Mike Hoare's 'flying column' in the Aba area. (Germani was an Austrian-trained physician and was readily taken along by the mercenaries as their doctor.) He was also Nairobi-based and had worked with the two missing men. From a priest he learned that Albrektsen and Maryara had been denounced by the rebels as spies, tortured and hacked to pieces.

More sobering news for the Congo press corps came when Mike Hoare's column reached Stanleyville. George Clay, one of the most popular members of the African press corps, had been killed by a sniper. George, a large, genial South African, was one of the first all-round one-man-band journalistic operators in Africa and had covered the Congo débâcle from the first. He had been a stringer for *The Guardian* and then moved on to radio and television work. He joined the American Broadcasting Company, ABC, and with Ernie Christie as his cameraman had talked his way into joining Mike Hoare's convoy.

Clay and Christie were travelling in an open jeep in the convoy on the road to Stanleyville. With the roar and clatter of the vehicles nobody heard the sniper shot that killed George. The bullet entered his head and brain and it is doubtful if he knew anything about it. He stayed upright in the jeep and it was some time before Christie realised that he was not simply dozing. The young cameraman was shattered to discover his friend and colleague was dead. It was too hot and humid to risk decomposition. The mercenaries helped Christie to dig a grave in the bush outside Stanleyville where George Clay, wrapped in a blanket, was buried.

It was a sobering epitaph to the press coverage of the Congo crisis. Soon Tshombe was overthrown and General Mobutu, the army commander, once again seized power. Mobutu imposed a ruthless and corrupt regime but at least he brought a relative if disquieting measure of stability to his tortured land.

Most of the hacks left the Congo for other theatres, vowing that they would be happy if they never saw or heard of the country again. And yet there are very few correspondents who covered the crisis who do not recall their experiences as the most vivid and instructive of their careers. The Congo crisis is etched indelibly into African journalistic folklore.

Aust. Reporter Saves Three From Natives

NEW YORK, Jan. 4 (A.A.P.-Reuter).

— An Australian and an English reporter saved three journalists from drunken Katangan soldiers, it was reported today.

Weldon Wallace, of the "Baltimore Sun," said the Katangan troops beat him and his companions, Arthur Bonner of the Columbia Broadcasting System and Lionel Flemming of the British Broadcasting Corporation, and held them at gunpoint for five hours.

The three were trying to enter Katanga from Northern Rhodesia and were seized when they tried to pass a Katangan immigration post.

Wallace, in a dispatch from Kasumbalesa on the Rhodesia border, said they owed their rescue to Peter Younghusband and Australian John Monks, of the London "Daily Express."

John Monks, 32, married, with a daughter, is the son of the late Noel Monks, one of Fleet Street's most famous war correspondents.

He worked as a reporter with the "Melbourne Herald" for about nine years until three years ago when he returned to London to work with the "Daily Express."

Raced For Help

When Monks and Younghusband saw them held in a mud hut and recognised their plight, he said, Monks raced to the Rhodesian border by car and telephoned for help.

Younghusband tried to persuade the Katangan captors to release the three.

"Instead," Wallace said, "The Katangans turned on him, and seizing him by the arms, hurled him inside to become a prisoner with us."

Eventually a jeep raced up and an African jumped out and directed that they be freed.

Two Belgian women refugees died in the capture of Jadotville yesterday.

They were killed by a hail of bullets from Indian infantry as their car sped past a U.N. column approaching the town. Bullets smashed the back of the car.

The Indians continued firing at the car for at least a minute after it skidded to a halt with a punctured tyre.

Bullet In Throat

Reporters rushed forward and pulled out the bleeding woman.

One was already dead with a bullet through the throat and the other died 10 minutes later from multiple wounds.

The man driving the car, his face bloody from flying glass, screamed at the Indians: "Soldiers of peace, look what you have done – You are murderers."

Also in the car was an Alsation dog, whimpering in terror with blood dripping from its nose and a bullet wound in its back.

Another shooting was narrowly avoided when an Indian aimed his rifle threateningly at a man who drove a doctor to the scene.

How the Australian Press viewed Monks' rescue of Weldon from the Katangese.

John Bulloch of The Daily Telegraph *with the press corps' bullet marked car. Katanga 1961.*

Jack Starr of the Daily Mail *peers through the shattered windscreen of his car. Katanga 1961.*

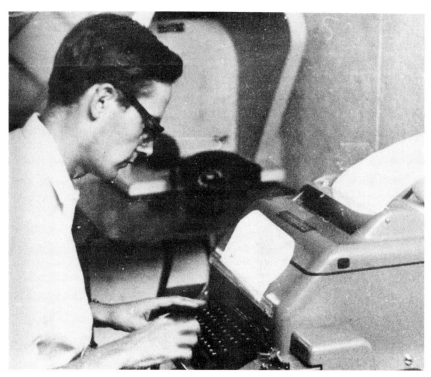

'Please send more money fastest'
– David Halberstam, New York
Times, on telex to his office from
the notorious Cabine Publique.
Elisabethville 1961.

Ernie 'Death wish' Christie, the
backstreet Johannesburg lad
who became one of the world's
best known and most fearless
war cameramen. He survived
conflicts from the Congo to
Vietnam, only to die in his home
town when he flew his aircraft
into a block of flats.

CHAPTER SEVEN

THE BROODING COLOSSUS

On the wall of Peter Younghusband's Cape Town office, from which he runs his freelance industry, his wine estates and sundry publishing interests, hangs a large poster. It depicts a pastoral scene, almost as idyllic as the Paarl Valley where his 17th-century farmhouse still boasts the large table on which the first dictionary of the Afrikaans language was compiled. The poster has an inscription, based as befits those weaned on the Old Testament, on a quotation from the Book of Psalms, slightly amended: 'Yea, though I walk through the valley of the shadow of death, I will fear no evil...for I am the meanest son-of-a-bitch in the valley.'

There are those, including some of his ex-wives and former Fleet Street colleagues, who might agree wholeheartedly with that sentiment. Younghusband could be the most formidable journalistic opponent, especially on a story – and in an era – that demanded the determination and derring-do of Your Man On The Spot.

His competitiveness was a compulsion. The demands of the foreign desk for him to be not only the first correspondent there but the one who had plunged into crocodile-infested rivers, perilous rapids, capsizing canoes in cyclonic storms on mysterious lakes, were met. Younghusband would emerge only slightly breathless with a local beauty hanging on to every limb, word and whim, to get the story and send it back to London, New York, Stockholm or Melbourne before anyone knew there was a problem in Xanadu or Zaire.

From my own experiences of working with – and against – Bigfoot, I can vouchsafe that many of the stories were true. I can also affirm that many of them were not. Like his great friend and colleague, Donald Wise, Younghusband was possessed of a healthy respect for his readers but not for the editors, sub-editors and other flunkies who 'flew desks' in cosy capitals and indulged in vicarious heroism by telling the mid-morning editorial conference (and, later, his impressed wife in Orpington): 'I've sent Younghusband to Timbuctou. He's on his way as I speak.'

Unlike Wise, whose excuse for pondering over a crisp three paragraphs for the *Daily Mirror* would be 'Remember, old boy, that I'm writing for people who move their lips when they read', Bigfoot never summoned the courage to show his contempt for the 'desk' by inserting the 'mysterious horseman on a white charger'.

Instead, he would, like Sir Percival Phillips in *Scoop*, read the right books, give it buckets of colour and apply the right dateline. A key factor was that Younghusband would have been there before, not necessarily at the critical period but recently enough to give any given story that wonderful touch of authenticity. Some of the most readable copy from one of the many flurries in Chad appeared under his byline some years ago. It was graphic, first-person stuff with a lucid analysis of the political and tribal background. Peter wrote it on the terrace of his vineyard near Cape Town. Younghusband is an Afrikaner, and very proud of the fact in the defensive manner of enlightened sons of the breed who have been pilloried for half a century for many of the world's evils. He is a big man, in stature, build, breadth and brawn. His father, like his grandfather, was a Van der Westhuizen but Peter was brought up by a stepfather whose name was Younghusband. He found it expedient not to dispute suggestions that his family might have been related to Sir Francis Younghusband, the mystic, philosopher and adventurer who came close to colonising Tibet for the British Empire. In fact, the Afrikaner side of the family cut him dead when young Peter went into journalism. Worse, he got a job with Tom Hopkinson's *Drum* magazine, which, in his grandfather's eyes, was produced for that most dangerous of African species 'the educated kaffir'.

Younghusband went on to work his way through the ranks of British provincial journalism in East Anglia, Darlington and Manchester before the *Daily Mail* discovered his talents and appointed him a foreign correspondent. His first foreign assignment for Fleet Street had been Katanga, not too far from home. An early task had been to nurse Henry Fairlie, then a distinguished political commentator, through the maze of South African politics.

Fairlie had demanded to meet a 'genuine old Boer of the veld' to find out what made the Afrikaner tick. Peter obliged by taking him to Sunday lunch with his grandfather, Oom Van Der Westhuizen, on the family farm at Moorreesburg in the Cape. It was a pretty stiff affair.

The family – 26 of them – had been summoned to pay their respects to this distinguished *rooinek*, the Boer's term for an Englishman. They gathered around the luncheon table with ill-disguised hostility. Peter was nervous. His family had not spoken to him since he started working for the English language press. Fairlie, plied with wonderful Cape wine and hospitality, soon became his lubricious self.

'Tell me, Mr van der Westhuizen,' he said loudly. 'Is it true that most Afrikaner families like yours have coloured blood?'

The horrified silence around the table was palpable. Forks froze on their way to large mouths. All eyes were on the old man. He masticated long and hard on his beef and then, finally, turned to his guest. 'If that is so, Mr Fairlie, then may I hope and pray that blood is Zulu.' The story tells more about the Afrikaner than it does about Henry Fairlie. And Bigfoot relates it with relish.

Younghusband's courage was never questioned by those who worked with him. His professional ruthlessness was as legendary as his exploits but he was, and remains, a man of immense compassion and humour that distinguished the African press corps of those formative and rather frightening years of the 'winds of change'. His on-the-spot opponent during that period was, invariably, John Monks of the *Express*. It was the heyday of the up-and-at-'em school of journalism and the competition was intense. The *Mail* and the *Express* were supposed to be at each others' throats at every turn when it came to getting the story. Younghusband and Monks stalked each other relentlessly. Every move was watched, every call monitored, every edition studied. Perhaps because of this professional relationship, which led to many shared dangers and adventures, the two men became firm friends, meeting the rival needs of their respective newspapers without impairing mutual respect and comradeship.

Monks had a daunting family tradition to maintain in journalism. His father, Noel, had been hailed as one of the most intrepid correspondents of World War II (having made his name, as we have seen, in Evelyn Waugh's Abyssinia in 1935). Noel had been an Australian swimming champion, had survived two air crashes on the same day, had worked his passage to and from Europe on tramp steamers and had found an enduring reputation as a newspaperman. John Monks had been force-fed through that very hard school of Australian journalism in Melbourne, his home town. Fair-skinned, chubby and always bustling and assertive (just like his father), he disdained equivocation on any given issue. It was either right or wrong, greatness or garbage, black or white. Never grey. Despite the bluster, he was also a man of great compassion, humour and competitiveness.

It was always amusing to hear Monks and Younghusband talk about each other out of school. 'Piggy Monks!' Peter would exclaim.

'Great guy! Heart of gold! Would help anyone, anywhere. Had to help him out so many times to save him from himself.' 'Youngers! What an operator!' Monks would expostulate. 'I suppose the big bugger is still conning his way to fame, fortune and a few more wives?' It was this kind of robust rivalry that gave Africa hacks one of their most memorable legends.

The island of Zanzibar, 22 miles off the coast of East Africa, had many legends of its own. In the 17th century the Sultans of Oman had extended their empire to include Zanzibar and its sister island of Pemba. For two hundred years it was the centre of a vast Arab trading empire, the main commodity being African slaves from the interior. 'When the flute is played in Zanzibar, all Africa must dance', ran an old Arab saying. The Arabs also established flourishing plantations of cloves and other spices, the aroma which greeted visitors by sea long before the island came into view. Britain established a protectorate in Zanzibar in 1890 but allowed the island to continue under feudal Arab rule. Burton, Speke and Stanley used Zanzibar as a base from which to prepare for their epic expeditions into the interior. The Sultan of Zanzibar indulged in a lavish lifestyle, commissioning luxurious ocean-going yachts, hunting wild boars and exacting royal rent to supplement the already substantial revenues from the clove plantations.

At the time of independence in December 1963 there were, perhaps, some 40 000 Arabs owning most of the land, a few thousand Asians running trade and commerce and 300 000 Africans, mostly manual labourers, farmhands or fishermen. Political awareness had manifested itself in the emergence of several African parties and a group of radical politicians who had made little secret of their revolutionary ambitions. Such was the contempt of the Arabs for their serfs that they failed to heed the warnings, even when a series of ugly race riots erupted in the years preceding independence.

When the revolution came just a month after Prince Philip formally hauled down the British flag, it took most people by surprise. Not only the Sultan's men but the intelligence services of the departing British and the Americans, who had a vested interest in the Project Mercury tracking station on Zanzibar, were caught napping.

The unlikely 'hero' of the revolution was an obscure African immigrant, John Okello, a semi-literate, psychopathic Ugandan. Styling himself 'Field Marshal' Okello had assembled a private army of a few hundred peasants. Armed with axes and spears, they attacked the police armoury in Zanzibar Town in the early hours of January 12th, 1964. Firearms were distributed to the revolutionaries, the unguarded radio station was seized and Okello was soon on the air inciting the African population to turn on their Arab masters.

'Enemies of the state will be hung, chopped into 1 000 pieces and boiled alive,' he announced, accurately enough as it turned out for at least 5 000 Arabs, and many others were humiliated, tortured and put to the sword in the massacres that followed. The Sultan had unceremoniously been bundled onto his royal yacht, the *Salaama*, and had fled into exile.

Okello's first broadcast had been monitored by startled Western intelligence agencies and alarm bells were sounded in their embassies in Dar es Salaam. Zanzibar was a valuable strategic prize. The Russians and the Chinese had made little secret of their ambitions to establish a base on the island from which, like the British explorers a century earlier, to make acquisitive forays into the African interior.

Not suprisingly, the New China News Agency was first with the news of the Zanzibar coup, probably because their 'correspondent' in Dar es Salaam was Abdulrahman Muhammed Babu, a fun-loving Zanzibari whose Marxist Umma party had been proscribed on the island a week before. Babu had been seen dancing in a Dar nightclub on revolution's eve, but he was soon back in Zanzibar as Minister of Defence and External Affairs for the new People's Republic. As news of the massacres of Arabs began to waft on the clove-scented breezes, foreign correspondents and cameramen poured into Dar es Salaam, clamouring to get to Zanzibar. Younghusband and Monks were among them. The scheduled flight from Dar had left that morning but had been turned back by the revolutionaries, now in control of the island's airport. Okello's increasingly hysterical broadcasts made it clear that any unauthorised aircraft or vessel approaching Zanzibar would be destroyed.

No air or boat charter would go near Zanzibar. Hacks and television crews who managed to persuade private pilots to fly them over were warned off by revolutionaries waving machine guns at them from the runway.

Peter Younghusband knew his territory. He took a taxi to the old slave port of Bagamoyo, 45 miles north of Dar, knowing that the old dhows still plied regularly to and from Zanzibar. Trudging up and down the beach, he found few dhow skippers interested in making the journey, even for the large wad of dollar bills he waved under their noses. Finally he was directed to a little hut near the beach where, he was told, an ageing owner was prepared to sell his equally ageing dhow. By the light of a flickering candle, he negotiated a deal with the old man. 'We were using bits of Swahili, a lot of hand-signals and much waving of wads. Making things a little more difficult was the fact that he had no nose at all and very little left of his mouth. Someone had obviously once taken a swipe at his face with a panga.'

Younghusband finally agreed to pay the equivalent of $800 for the purchase of the dhow and for the services of the skipper and his crew. They would sail at dawn. He spent a sleepless night on the beach, being bitten by sand flies and keeping an eye out for marauders who might have heard about the cash he was carrying. At first light he was wading in his underpants to his newly acquired dhow moored some 50 yards offshore, carrying his clothes, passport, camera and portable typewriter above his head.

He surveyed his new command with distaste. It was rickety, leaking, creaking ominously in the slight swell and there were many holes in the leg-o'-mutton sail being hoisted by the crew – all of whom looked as if they had stepped off the set of a bad pirate movie. 'Hardly what I would have chosen for the first and only boat I've ever owned, but it was the only hope I had of getting to Zanzibar.'

As the sun rose, Younghusband heard a familiar voice hailing him from the shore. 'It was Piggy Monks, pink and shining with sweat. He was desperate and begged me to share my ship. I negotiated a quick joint ownership of the dhow and we pulled him aboard, panting and puffing.' Slowly, the dhow nosed out of Bagamoyo in the vague direction of Zanzibar, some 30 miles to the east. But there was little wind and it took an age for the mainland to disappear behind them. By this time the Equatorial sun was high. There was no shelter and the two Fleet Street men were both perspiring and cursing in the back of the ancient craft.

Monks, with his fair skin, started to burn (just as his father had on a dhow trip off this same coast some 30 years before). Their small supplies of soft drinks were long since exhausted. The only thirst-quenching alternative was to share the old paraffin can of fresh water which the evil-looking crew were passing among themselves. 'It tasted base and foul. Monks was convinced he was going to catch syphilis by taking a swig but it was our only salvation. We held our noses and drank.'

Eventually a wind rose, the tattered sail filled and our heroes were making progress towards the spice island. Monks: 'It was a great relief all round. For the first time in hours we started to cool down a little. We were convinced this motley crew were going to slit our throats, but now they had their work cut out to keep this bucket afloat.' By dusk, they picked up the unmistakable and very pleasant aroma of cloves and suddenly there was Zanzibar. As the jetty of the dhow harbour came into view, a motor patrol boat cut through the water towards them. 'It was full of goons with guns who made our crew look like angels. They told us to drop anchor right there. We shouted to them that we had come to report on their glorious revolution but they waved their guns menacingly and we stayed put.'

The *Mail* and the *Express* rode at anchor in the gathering gloom, 300 yards or so from the end of the jetty. Younghusband's patience ran out. 'We had no drink, no food and we were both suffering. Monks's face had cracked like old parchment and I thought it was time for a decision.'

Bigfoot stripped down to his Y-fronts and plunged into the sluggish water, striking out towards the jetty. 'I hadn't realised the tide was going out. There was a heavy swell and a vicious undertow and I was already exhausted. I seemed to be getting nowhere. At one point I managed to grab on to the mooring chain of some other vessel and hung on to regain my breath. After what seemed an age I finally got to the jetty. Had it been another ten yards I just wouldn't have made it.'

The big South African hauled himself up the side of the pier and collapsed panting and heaving on the deck. 'I was prodded up by the end of a bayonet. There was a sentry, a large black man with a manic grin who had watched me battle my way through the sea. "You, white man, you are under arrest," he said. A couple of his chums came over and seemed to take great delight in slapping and beating me around a bit. I was getting used to it by this time. "The sins of the fathers shall be visited upon the sons," I thought to myself as they prodded and punched me towards a shed at the end of the jetty.

'The white man's dignity was severely lacking. I was dripping, sweating, totally exhausted and standing there in my underpants. For a moment I pondered on this glamorous career I had chosen, but they threw me inside this hut and slammed and locked the door. As I regained some composure I took in my surroundings. There was a chair, a couple of filing cabinets and a desk. And there on the desk – I had to shake my head to ensure I was not hallucinating – a telephone!'

Younghusband scrabbled in the desk and found a Zanzibar telephone directory. He found the number of the British Residency but there was no response. He tried several other numbers with no success. He then dialled zero and a very nervous voice answered. 'It was an operator in the exchange in Zanzibar Town. He had locked himself in when the revolution started and was as desperate as I was. "Help me, please help me," he pleaded. "No, you help me, please, and perhaps we can help each other".' Younghusband gave him the number of the *Daily Nation* in Nairobi and asked him to try it. To his amazement he was through within minutes and was talking to his old friend, John Bierman, the editor. Bierman, a well-seasoned hack, realised the situation and quickly took down the story Bigfoot dictated to him: 'From Peter Younghusband, Zanzibar, Sunday...Last night I swam the shark-infested waters of the Indian Ocean to the revolution-torn shores of this ancient spice island...'

The *Daily Mail* loved it. 'I think they were getting a little weary of my crocodile-infested rivers – but sharks were something new and exciting.' Younghusband had only just finished when the door of the customs shed was opened and there was Monks. The *Express* man had flagged down a rowing boat and had arrived at the jetty with Younghusband's clothes, passport and professional tools. 'Piggy had regained his exuberance and bluster. He had convinced the sentries that we were the most important journalists in the world and were in Zanzibar at the personal invitation of Field Marshal Okello who wanted to see us as soon as we landed.

'These desperadoes were not sure what to do but we finally convinced them to take us to their leader. With guns jabbed into our ribs, we were whisked into town. There was the occasional shot and the occasional scream. There were bodies lying in the streets and the unmistakable smell of terror.' As they were driven through the gates of the Red Fort, the military headquarters, the two hacks were busy working on the next move: convincing their captors that they were, indeed, on the island at the invitation of Field Marshal Okello of whom they had hardly heard, let alone met.

In the courtyards were hundreds of terrified Arabs – the lucky ones who had been arrested rather than slaughtered on the spot. The area was littered with loot stolen from the dozens of 'freedom fighters', some in their early teens, who were dressed up in saris, firemen's outfits, Arab headdresses, who ran around prodding their erstwhile oppressors with a variety of weapons. It was like a demented children's fancy dress party, except that the screams emanating from the continuing torture and execution sessions in the Fort were very real. Retribution for centuries of African humiliation and enslavement was at hand, and, as always, it was the kids who were enjoying it most.

Monks and Younghusband were bundled through this gory, smelly chaos into an office where they were told they would be interrogated personally by the man they had claimed had invited them: Field Marshal John Okello. Younghusband: 'A scrum of goons started to body-search us. I remember Monks, now purple with rage and sunburn, screaming "Don't you dare touch me there," as they clutched at his trousers. We were pushed into another office. There sat the blackest African I have ever seen. He had his feet in unpolished boots hoisted on the desk, dangled a large Colt .45 from his finger and he had that vacant look which meant that he was as high on marijuana as his men.'

Okello took his time examining his prisoners, the towering exhausted Afrikaner and the puce-coloured, enraged Australian. 'You, gentlemen, are spies,' he said. They protested. 'We are here to report your glorious revolution for the world's press.' He chose not to believe them, but Younghusband's luck had not deserted him. The telephone at his side rang suddenly and Okello answered it, with astounding respect. The hacks never discovered who was on the other end, but after a brief conversation Okello hung up, smiled at them and said, 'Welcome to our people's revolution...this is a peaceful revolution and we wish it to be given prominence in the press of the world. Where would you gentlemen like to go?'

Scarcely daring to believe this change of mood, the two men chorused 'To the English Club', the centre of British imperial rest and relaxation, which they knew from previous visits. Sure enough they were led out of the fort and dropped off at the English Club, with its neatly trimmed sward and the Union Jack still fluttering next to the Sultan's flag. Inside, some 200 British residents and their families were taking shelter from the mayhem in the streets. 'It was all very stiff upper lip,' said Younghusband. 'A large matron was rushing around bellowing "Don't panic. Remember we are British." Another younger woman snapped at her "Nobody's panicking...get me another nappy".'

Monks was furious when he discovered that his colleague had already filed his story. He rushed off to file his own account which duly appeared in the *Express* under the headline 'I Was A Prisoner In The Island Of Revolt'. It paled a little alongside Younghusband's 'I Swim To Foil Rebels' dispatch in the *Mail*.

Monks wanted to pre-empt any possible comeback from the *Express* asking 'WHY YOU UNSWIM SHARK-INFESTED SEAS?' so he sent a covering memo, sardonically apologising for not having been beaten up. He received a cabled reply from Jimmy Nicoll on the *Express* foreign desk: 'GLAD YOU UNUPBEATEN STOP AUSTRALIA WAS DASH BY SEVEN WICKETS THIS MINUTE'. The weary Australian managed a wry chuckle, despite the bad tidings of the cricket test. 'Bloody poms...that made my day!' Britain's *Private Eye* found the Monks-Younghusband accounts from Zanzibar irresistible. The *Eye* carried its own dispatch from its own Man-On-The-Spot, the immortal Lunchtime O'Booze. Under the headline 'I Am The First Transvestite In Terror Isle', this version read:

'I am the first British journalist to enter Zanzibar disguised as a young girl, cables Lunchtime O'Booze from the revolt-scented, spice-threatened island from which several British holidaymakers have already been evacuated in case.

'My decision to get into the "island of fear" at all costs was taken after seeing what my colleagues, Peter Younghusband of the *Daily Mail* and John Monks of the *Daily Express*, were doing to the situation.

'Younghusband and Monks, names that will be remembered so long as El Vino's stands, went to Zanzibar in a boat. An "Arab dhow".

'What other sort of boat do you take when you are in a place where the seamen are Arabs and their boats are dhows? Readers in Maidenhead realised for the first time that there are places without cabin cruisers.

'They sailed the seas for 18 hours, were then conducted into Zanzibar harbour by some kind of patrol boat.

'Then they were asked to wait for a bit before going ashore – police and customs formalities.

'Younghusband stripped off and swam a quarter of a mile. Monks, a quieter type, waited to go ashore in the ordinary way.

'Both ended up being examined by the police, who told them they could go anywhere they liked, said they were welcome and offered them a military escort.

'I sensed the undercurrents of dark menace beneath these seemingly routine procedures.

'I hired an Indian scow and was soon heading across the Indian Ocean in the direction of the island of nutmeg menace.

'As I gazed eastward I could not forget that only a couple of thousand miles over there and then first on the left lay China, which seems to me more or less of a brooding Colossus.

'Shortly before arrival I assumed my feminine disguise. I was determined to foil these people at all costs.

'A police officer said to me – and I could sense the hidden menace beneath his words – "Excuse me, sir, but is it the new custom for Fleet Street chaps to wear skirts? Just the other day we had one come ashore half-naked." I knew better than to speak in an island where the panga, the tonga and the bongo drum may mean death.

'Significantly the police officer himself said "Lots of death on the roads". He pretended to be talking about Kent, England, but I understood the threat behind the smiling badinage. I asked him to call me a taxi and drove through streets full of spice-scented menace to an hotel where excellent accommodations were available, the entire American colony having just been evacuated for fear of a Chinese invasion.

'As I sipped a cup of spice-scented Indian tea, I looked westward and sensed that somewhere was the mainland of Africa.

'A brooding Colossus.'

It was one of O'Booze's most brilliant dispatches and copies are treasured by Monks and Younghusband. The situation on Zanzibar, however, was pretty menacing, as other correspondents soon discovered. Back at Bagamoyo on the Tanganyikan coast, dhow skippers were now doing a roaring trade. Dennis Neeld of AP and Mohamed Amin forked out a small fortune to hire a much more efficient boat than their colleagues. They, too, were intercepted by one of Okello's motor launches, but one of the revolutionaries on board recognised Amin – he had visited the island regularly to take photographs and shoot film – and towed them into harbour.

Amin also knew Abdulrahman Babu, now a minister in the new revolutionary regime. Babu had in fact tipped off the cameraman about the impending coup. Now he enlisted Amin to take the first official photographs of the revolutionary council. In return he gave Amin an official pass – scribbled on a bit of cardboard torn from a detergent packet – enabling the pressman's chartered aircraft to ferry his film to Dar es Salaam. Amin's grisly news film of hastily dug mass graves and of Arab bodies being dumped from small boats to feed the sharks was used extensively by CBS, ITN and Visnews.

The Royal Naval frigate, HMS *Owen*, had been sent to Zanzibar to evacuate the British citizens. Amin was at the wharf filming them being loaded onto a launch when two revolutionaries armed with machine guns grabbed him and tried to snatch his cameras. He fought them off and made a sudden decision to leave the island by leaping into the launch. He was challenged by British marines but as the launch pulled away towards HMS *Owen*, Mohamed reached into his camera bag and produced his British passport. It was good enough to gain his passage to Mombasa. The two Zanzibaris on the dockside pointed their machine guns at the retreating launch but thought better of taking on the marines. Had they known the cameraman better they would have realised he would soon be back in Zanzibar in any event.

Jack Nugent of *Newsweek* was also bargaining for a Zanzibar-bound dhow at Bagamoyo. Nairobi-based Nugent had been in Dar es Salaam on another story at the time of the coup. He had, in fact, bumped into Babu in the Dar nightclub the night before. He had met the USS *Manley* when it arrived in Dar to offload the American citizens from Zanzibar and had been lucky enough to find an old friend among them, a young man named Peter Rand who had been on Zanzibar writing a 'last island paradise' story for an American magazine. Nugent had met his *Newsweek* deadline from Dar and now needed to get to the island. He and Rand had heard about the Sinbad run and, at Bagamoyo, the two Americans negotiated their passage to Paradise Lost.

Nugent persuaded his skipper to leave at midnight in the hope, John Wayne style, of 'hitting the beaches at dawn'. Nearly 20 hours later, drenched from a heavy swell, blistered by the sun, hungry and parched, they arrived off Zanzibar. They hove to alongside HMS *Owen* riding at anchor. 'I would not advise going into the harbour tonight,' an officer shouted from the deck.

'I heard that two British journalists went in last night and have not been heard of since. Come on board and have a cup of tea.' Nugent and Rand 'now a brilliant poinsettia-red, rheumy-eyed and feverish', guessed that the 'missing' journalists were Monks and Younghusband. The invitation to a little RN hospitality was too enticing. They opted for a few cold beers in the mess and gratefully spent the night on board the British ship.

At dawn – two days later than planned – Nugent 'hit the beach', or rather the jetty, where he and Rand were immediately surrounded by extremely hostile revolutionaries. An evil-eyed gentleman with a Castro-style beard, a black beret and a cocked machine gun spat at their feet. 'You are imperialist spies,' he snapped. 'Search them.' They grabbed the hacks' notebooks and pocket books, becoming extremely excited when they found Nugent's American *Express* card. 'Spies!...American spies!...' they screamed. The Americans were bundled off to the Red Fort. Unlike Monks and Younghusband a day before, they did not have the pleasure of meeting Okello. Instead they were rescued by Fritz Picard, the harassed American Charge d'Affaires who dropped them off at the Zanzibar Hotel.

There were now a few nervous foreign correspondents at the hotel who reported that they were tailed every time they left the building. A censor had also been installed to vet all copy, 'a black man with a big gun but very little brain'. Sitting under a hastily scrawled sign which read 'Yankees No, Zanzibaris Si', the censor pored over every line submitted to him, his eyes alighting only on the word 'communist' which he slowly cancelled out with a red crayon. Nugent's personal guard – the man with the Castro beard – was given to bursting into his room at all hours and threatening him with his machine gun, still cocked. The *Newsweek* man managed to slip some uncensored copy to his stringer in a toilet in the hope that it would somehow get to New York.

Politically, the situation in Zanzibar was changing rapidly. The teenaged revolutionaries in their fancy dress were still killing Arabs on the streets but 'Field Marshal' Okello disappeared as quickly as he had arrived. In his place emerged a brawny, street-fighting politician, Abeid Karume, who proclaimed himself Chairman of the Revolutionary Council of the People's Republic of Zanzibar. Karume, a former merchant seaman, had neither an education nor a sense of humour, even though he assumed the title 'Sheikh'. The harassed correspondents in the Zanzibar Hotel were summoned to his presence late one night in the lobby.

'Karume was perspiring heavily. He was wild eyed. He charged up to Picard, the American diplomat, and spraying him with beery saliva shouted "Why are you interfering in our internal affairs? You are under arrest. So are all these American journalists – particularly Nugent." Jack was paying the price for spreading the word about Babu having been seen in a Dar nightclub on revolution's eve. Babu eyed him beadily and ordered the armed rabble: "Lock them all up. We have no time to waste with Americans." Picard protested loudly, the correspondents shouted and bellowed – except for the wily Dennis Neeld of AP who had opened a telephone line to his office in Dar and was dictating "live" a story about the wild scene from beneath the reception desk.'

Down the road at the English Club, a plump Australian and a gigantic South African enjoyed a pleasant meal after dictating their stories to London from the secretary's phone. Most of the English residents had been evacuated to HMS *Owen* and they had a quiet evening.

In the Zanzibar Hotel, Picard had been dragged off and placed under house arrest. The Americans had been put under 'hotel arrest' and guards were posted outside their rooms. On the following morning Nugent was led at gunpoint to the hotel courtyard and placed against a stucco wall. 'The guards raised their rifles into firing position. I tried to smile. I dripped sweat and had a fuzzy, uncertain feeling. I think I said a fast prayer but I'm not sure now.' There was a rapid clicking sound. Nugent thought the Zanzibaris were pulling the well-established mock execution trick (which was always preferable to the real thing). But the clicks came from a large camera wielded by a giggling government photographer. The regime was about to deport the Americans and wanted their photographs in case they decided to sneak back.

Back in the hotel the harassment of the hacks deemed to be 'CIA spies' continued night and day. Their rooms were searched. They were followed by scruffy youngsters with guns wherever they went. The group included Bill Smith of *Time*, Bob Conley of the *New York Times*, Robert Miller of the *Toronto Globe and Mail*, Priya Ramrakha, a Kenyan Asian on assignment for *Life* magazine, Clyde Sanger of the *London Guardian* who had a Canadian passport, and Nugent and his friend Peter Rand, who was accredited to the *New York Herald Tribune*.

At lunch on the patio, the guards would peer at them constantly from behind the bougainvillaea. 'Not too many people wanted to sit near us. That would be guilt by association. We were pariahs.' Nugent remembered with horror that he had a US Defence Department accreditation pass in his luggage. It took him several attempts to flush it down the toilet.

'In eight out of ten countries in Africa, American identification can be a liability. I was picked up half-a-dozen times because of my passport. I've often wished that big gold eagle insignia on the out-side, with "United States of America" in big, bragging script, would be removed. I first scratched mine off in Katanga despite the notice which states you can lose your passport for defacing it. Better the passport than me.'

Nugent's office and family were trying unsuccessfully to get through to him by telephone and cable but the *Newsweek* man received only one telegram. It was from an old friend working for Capitol Records in Hollywood. 'CAPITOL WANTS ORIGINAL CAST ALBUM RIGHTS MUSICAL VERSION YOUR ZANZIBAR STORY.' It gave the hacks a few grim laughs. 'How many revolutions per minute do they expect for the record?'

Four days later, the 'American spies' were rounded up and dri-ven to the harbour – by way of a freshly dug cemetery which was indicated pointedly. Thankfully, they clambered aboard HMS *Owen* where Nugent was greeted by his pipe-puffing RN chums. 'Thought we might see you back again...have a cup of tea.' Capitol Records did not get their musical version of the Zanzibar story, but Nugent, back in Nairobi, heard he was starring in a radio adaptation of the episode. Radio Zanzibar put on a dramatisation of how the freedom fighters had caught the Yankee spies. The anti-hero was based on the *Newsweek* man who, in grovelling Swahili, finally broke down and confessed to being a CIA colonel sent to the island by dhow to organise a counter-revolution.

There was another sequel. Into the *Newsweek* office in Nairobi a couple of months later strolled a dapper figure in a smart suit and silk tie. It was former Field Marshal Okello, the man who had branded all the journalists as spies and given them a hard time on Zanzibar. Would *Newsweek* like to buy the rights to his life story? Nugent's answer was short, sharp and to the point. Okello looked crestfallen. Could the bwana then pay for his night's lodgings? Nugent relented and picked up the revolutionary leader's hotel bill. On behalf of *Newsweek*, of course. 'AWA!' he intoned to himself. It was the incantation of Old Africa Hands. It is acronymic, standing for 'Africa Wins Again!'

Okello eventually found a publisher for his short, bloody memoirs. In it he boasted that 13 635 people were killed in the few days he was in control of Zanzibar. He described how he had personally issued an ultimatum to the Sultan: 'You are allowed twenty minutes to kill your children and wives and then kill yourself.' On hearing that the Sultan had escaped, Okello described his reaction: 'I became enraged. I ordered my soldiers to fire in all directions and to kill whomever came before them, men, women, children, disabled persons, even chickens and goats.'

The text was predictable, perhaps. That it found a publisher in the 1960s, is not surprising. There were many 'liberal' publishing houses in which any black thug posing as an anti-colonialist revolutionary could find a sympathetic ear or two. What did startle his colleagues was the fact that the foreword to Okello's confessions was written by Clyde Sanger, *The Guardian* man who, with Nugent and other American correspondents, had been given such a hard time by the Zanzibaris.

Under Karume's rule, the purge of the Arabs continued. The youthful revolutionaries were unleashed to murder, maim and torture anyone they thought might be a counter-revolutionary. Chinese, Russian, Cuban and East German 'advisers' poured into the islands and rapidly established an advance base for what they hoped would be the new scramble for Africa. Like Cecil John Rhodes they wanted the map of the continent to be painted red – but for different reasons and ends. Communist Bloc ships were monitored (by the Israelis' highly efficient intelligence network in East Africa) slipping into Zanzibar waters and unloading supplies of arms and ammunition in quantities far greater than would ever be needed to defend Karume's regime.

Most of the African correspondents were quite happy to quit Zanzibar for good within a week or so of the revolution. Like *Private Eye*'s O'Booze they had sensed the spice-scented menace and preferred more hospitable parts of the brooding Colossus. Not, however, Mohamed Amin. The young photographer was building his reputation and bank balance rapidly and he knew he had to take risks to maintain the pace.

Amin was back in Zanzibar a few weeks later to cover a very brief visit by Duncan Sandys, the British Commonwealth Secretary. It was so brief, that the cameraman felt he would not have justified the expense of his trip unless he shot some hard news film. He had heard the Aga Khan's old house on the island was being used as one of the many detention camps for the thousands of Arab prisoners. He tried to persuade the revolutionary guards to let him through by shooting film of them posing, grinning, with their guns. It worked, until a senior man arrived and ordered the immediate arrest of 'the imperialist spies'. Amin and his two Tanganyikan friends were held for two days, beaten, slapped and kicked, before being deported. His brand new camera was confiscated.

Despite his PI status ('prohibited immigrant' – the badge of any self-respecting Africa hand at that time), Amin was back in Zanzibar several more times. In April 1964, the island formally united with mainland Tanganyika to form the People's Republic of Tanzania. It remained under the Karume knuckleduster, however, and Mohamed sneaked back in to film for CBS Russian-run training camps for young revolutionaries from throughout East and Central Africa. Colleagues warned him that his brashness was bound to catch up with him – and it did in 1966. He flew to Zanzibar again, to cover the visit of the President of the United Arab Republic, Gamal Abdel Nasser.

He was given a one-day visa at the airport but was picked up within hours and thrown into Zanzibar's now infamous Kilimamigu Prison. He was in solitary confinement for 16 days, sleeping on a concrete floor, eating one plate of porridge a day and drinking water from a lavatory cistern. He was interrogated – by East Germans as well as Karume's men – regularly. His cell mates included a minister in the revolutionary government who was soon taken outside and shot. He plotted with others to make an escape bid but, presumably thanks to pressure applied by CBS and the Americans, was suddenly released after a month's ugly incarceration and deported. He had been in the slammer for 27 days and had willingly signed an untruthful statement saying he had not been maltreated before being put on an aircraft for Dar and then home to his family in Nairobi.

In gaol in Zanzibar he was convinced he was not going to get out alive. 'If I do there's no way I'm going to do this job again,' Amin promised himself. But the day after his return to Nairobi he was commissioned to do another story. 'Once I was out, I was quite happy to go back to what I had been doing before. You either have it or you haven't. If I were to stop doing news, I think I should probably feel miserable.' It was not the most lucid explanation of why good hacks continue to plunge into terrifying situations after experiences like that, but many colleagues are at a total loss for words when it comes to answering the same question. Zanzibar continued to be a 'no-go' area for Western correspondents in Africa for many years. Karume's reign of terror endured, despite his 'union' with Julius Nyerere's 'enlightened socialist republic' of Tanzania. When the last of the Arabs had been killed or deported, he started on his own people. The mysterious 'disappearances', the killings, the irrational hostility of illiterate 'revolutionary guards' made this once romantic isle a place to be avoided at all costs by tourists, businessmen and journalists alike. Its economy, based on cloves, was soon sucked dry to pay for Nyerere's disastrous socialist policies on the mainland. Even the Russian, Cuban, Chinese and East German ideologues became disillusioned with the unbridled brutality and arrogance of the revolutionaries.

Just what impact all the dramatic reporting and footage from Africa had on the public at large came home to me in Addis Ababa some six years after the Zanzibar revolution. I was in the Ethiopian capital to cover the annual gathering of the Organisation of African Unity, one of the world's more grotesque misnomers. African leaders, most of them military dictators, would vie with each other to put on the most lavish show of megalomania and thuggery outside the conference hall and espouse the most absurd doctrines, theories and justifications within.

At that time, I had a long-standing booking at the Addis Hilton Hotel, a fairly monstrous high-rise which was supposed to be reserved exclusively for OAU 'leaders', their relatives, acolytes, aides, bodyguards and the ever-increasing number of freeloaders who made up the presidential entourages.

By this time, I was supposed not to be surprised by anything Africa threw in my direction, but there was something intriguing about a small party of elderly Americans, obviously tourists, who were my only fellow non-OAU guests at the hotel at the time. Large black men in dark suits or uniforms, but always with those ubiquitous one-way sunglasses, would sweep through the lobby and in and out of the lifts, crowded around some unknown figure who would turn out to be the president-for-life of some equally unknown state. The idea was to out-intimidate their look-alike bodyguards from some other nonentity.

The elderly American tourists were fascinated. They waited by the lift doors and with box cameras snapped away furiously at any egressing or ingressing entourage. 'This is really INTEREST-ING...this is, wow, FASCINATING...Who ARE these guys?' Any attempt by me to explain who they were, where they came from and what they represented was met with a blankness matched only by the ill-disguised yawns from *The Daily Telegraph* foreign desk when I tried the same, slightly more trenchant, analyses of OAU gatherings on them.

Finally I found myself sitting next to the tourist party's courier in the lounge. He explained that his people were members of a septuagenarian travel club out of California. (The courier was himself a septuagenarian, he told me.) The previous year, they had 'done' India and next year they would 'do' South America. This was Africa's turn and his party was at the start of a 'toor of the whole Goddam' continent.' To prove it, he pulled out their itinerary. It was formidable. In six weeks they were going to cover an awful lot of territory. A reference to Rhodesia caught my eye. 'Here we arrive in exotic Salisbury,' the itinerary gushed. 'Centre of the Federation of Rhodesia and Nyasaland – a fascinating experiment in co-existence between the races here in the heart of Africa.' I was about to explain that this fascinating experiment had fallen horribly apart some five years previously and that the region was involved in a rather ugly little war when my eye caught the word 'Zanzibar'.

I read on. 'Thursday we arrive in Zanzibar, the romantic spice island in the balmy Indian Ocean, ruled by the benevolent Sultan and under the protection of the British Crown.' I looked at my friend. He was beaming proudly. 'Ain't that just great?' he demanded. 'And I promise you, sir, that all these grand old folk are going to enjoy every minute of this.'

I took a long swig of something, looked at members of his party who seemed to be having the time of their lives and asked him when this itinerary had been drawn up. 'Hey...we got a whole lot of experts in LA who work on these toors.' I tried, as gently as I could, to explain that not only was the information dangerously out of date but that he might be risking a few coronaries among his party if they pitched up, as planned, in Zanzibar. There was certainly no British protection, I told him, and the benevolent Sultan was, alas, no more.

'No Sultan...no Sultan?' he shouted, grabbing back the itinerary and pulling out a pen. 'Who's in charge of the place now?' I told him a gentleman named Karume was in charge and was none too keen on foreign visitors of whatever age. 'No Sultan!' he kept muttering, his pen poised. 'Okay, this guy Karroomy...whadda we call him when we get there?' I took another swig and thought for a moment. 'If you get to Zanzibar and meet him,' I said, 'I suggest you call him "Sir."'

The brooding colossus.
Peter Younghusband
not only swam Africa's
crocodile-infested
waters but occasionally
did so in suit and tie!

'A man's gotta do what
a man's gotta do.' Peter
Younghusband.

CHAPTER EIGHT

THE SCOURGE OF THE FLY WHISK

Membership of the Order of GOAHs – the Genuine Old Africa
Hands – was not restricted only to those who had spent time
in the gaols of 'emerging' countries, or to those who had been obliged, verbally at least, to promote from corporal to colonel or from private to 'sir' the wild-eyed young man wielding the rifle. It was also
necessary to have been fly-whisked. The fly whisk became one of the
status symbols of African presidents. There are many species of fly
in Africa, some of which have caused continental catastrophes and
tragedies. Fly whisks have yet to prove themselves as a way of dealing with the problems.

Nevertheless, the fly whisk was the orb and sceptre of a dozen
or so African leaders. Some of the instruments were elaborately
adorned with expensive handles and equipped with the most exquis-
ite tail hair of the most endangered beast. All were brandished, with
varying degrees of destruction, as an instrument of power.

A whisk, this way or that, would indicate an 'Off with his head'
or 'Directly to gaol and do not pass go', a signal for all to chant the
national anthem and songs of praise for the leader or, in the case of
Dr Hastings Kamuzu Banda of Malawi, a sign of presidential oppro-
brium towards foreign correspondents who may have written something about his regime that displeased him.

A brush across the face, a flap across the shoulder or a prod in
the ribs from the fly whisk of the life-president of Malawi was
enough to freeze the blood of the visiting journalist. It was invariably
done in public, with rent-a-crowd looking on, chanting and jeering.
Big, brave hacks were known to be reduced to jelly-like, red-faced
whimps when this little black man, always dressed in dark business
suit and a large black homburg hat, would swat, poke, flick and wave
his fly whisk under their noses while tearing apart their copy in ringing public denunciation. To paraphrase a well-known saying, when
you'd been fly-whisked by Banda you stayed fly-whisked.

THE SCOURGE OF THE FLY WHISK   173

Hastings Kamuzu Banda is one of many African leaders with the title 'Doctor' and one of the very few entitled to use it. He is a fully qualified medical practitioner and, for many years, was a successful, respected general practitioner in suburban Britain. By any yardstick, his life and career were remarkable – and, at the time of writing, remain so.

He was born of Chewa peasant stock near the trading centre of Kasungu in what was then British Central Africa. As a teenager, he had over a period of several years walked more than 1 000 miles southwards to find work, initially in Southern Rhodesia and then on the gold mines of South Africa's Witwatersrand. He had received some basic education from Church of Scotland missionaries and was received into that church despite having undergone a pagan ritual of manhood among the Chewa people.

One of the hoariest of Fleet Street legends about Banda arose with a cable received from the *Daily Express* by (who else?) Donald Wise as he sipped a quiet beer on the terrace of Ryall's Hotel in Blantyre. 'HOW OLD BANDA?' demanded his office. Wise expostulated once again at the incompetence of his hated sub-editors and immediately scribbled back a reply: 'OLD BANDA FINE STOP HOW YOU?' For once, Donald was not being facetious. Banda's precise age was one of Africa's great post-colonial mysteries. Banda himself had cultivated a cult of mystery about his early life, including his actual date of birth. He has variously and occasionally mentioned 1905 and 1911, but perhaps the most accurate assessment was made by Philip Short, who was the only freelance, indeed the only journalist, to work in Malawi during the years of Banda's purge of the local press and prohibition of the international press. It was a nerve-wracking and precarious existence, as Ngwazi – the 'chief of chiefs' – subscribed to numerous newspaper cuttings and press monitoring services and read every word written about his country and himself. Short curtailed his own freelance career in Malawi by writing a scholarly, seminal biography of Banda. He was obliged to flee the country before publication, not least because Ngwazi got wind of the intensive inquiries the journalist was making about his early life.

Short gives Banda's birthdate as 1898, and quotes a relative and two village elders who remember Kamuzu, 'the little root', being born in the year of the 1898 Angoni uprising in what was then Fort Jameson in Northern Rhodesia. Banda's sensitivity to such a disclosure can only be ascribed to his self-promoted image of immortality (he was the first African leader to make himself president-for-life). How old Banda? Old Banda fine – and still going strong in his mid-nineties.

Johannesburg brought the young Banda into contact with African politicians and trade unionists and with the black churches that, under the influence of American negroes, espoused the inalienable right of the black man to run his own affairs. American Methodists recognised his potential by inviting him to the United States to complete his education and by presenting him with his first ceremonial fly whisk.

In America he studied medicine, as well as history and political science, mainly at the University of Chicago. He graduated as a Bachelor of Philosophy in 1931 and then enrolled at a medical college in Nashville, Tennessee (where he witnessed the lynching of a black man by a white mob). He was awarded a Doctorate of Medicine at Mcharry Medical College in Nashville and then went to Edinburgh where, in 1938, he enrolled at the School of Medicine of the Royal College of Physicians and Surgeons and renewed his association with his beloved Church of Scotland.

From Edinburgh, with yet more impressive qualifications after his name and having been ordained an Elder of the Church of Scotland, Banda applied to return home to Nyasaland to fulfil a long-standing ambition to be a medical missionary. Few people could have been more suitable and yet a group of white nurses working at the Livingstonia Mission wrote to the Church saying they would not serve under a black doctor. He applied for a Nyasaland government medical post but the Colonial Office sought from him an undertaking that he would not seek social contact with white doctors. Given such racial snubs, it is surprising, perhaps, that in later years Banda did not intimidate whites with something a little more potent than a fly whisk.

In North London after the war Banda soon established a flourishing medical practice with a surgery, a white secretary and a house in a fashionable suburb. There he completed the image of the comfortable, middle-class English professional by adopting his homburg hat, tightly rolled umbrella, dark suits and ties. Such was the respect which he commanded among his mostly white patients that they automatically rose to their feet whenever he appeared in his waiting room. He remained in close touch with the rapidly developing political situation in Africa generally and in Nyasaland in particular where there was increasing discussion of amalgamation or federation with the more powerful Rhodesias.

He was every potent inch an African nationalist but baulked at the brand of Marxism espoused by men like George Padmore. Nonetheless, he voted Labour, joined the Fabian Society and became close friends with other Padmore pupils including Kwame Nkrumah and Jomo Kenyatta. His home in Brondesbury Park became a debating centre for African exiles, students, and left-wing politicians and intellectuals. Journalists like John Hatch, Colin Legum, Clyde Sanger and Patrick Keatley were regular acolytes at these Sunday political surgeries and their contributions in *The Observer* and *The Guardian* reflected the shared, heady vision of pan-Africanism that Banda appeared to symbolise. It was in his suburban London home that the first coherent opposition to the proposed Central African Federation of Nyasaland, Northern and Southern Rhodesia was organised. From here, too, Banda exercised his influence and authority over the fledgling Malawi Congress Party.

Banda's puritanism was, by this time, notorious. He was strictly teetotal and had expressed his dismay, on arriving in Edinburgh, at finding so many pubs in this, the home of the Church of Scotland. He was also shocked by the convention which allowed a man to hold closely the wife of another man in the pursuit known as ballroom dancing. He lectured all who would listen on the moral decay, the sloppy dress habits and the lack of manners and respect for elders that he perceived in post-war Britain. For such a man, the impact of the news he received in his surgery in August 1953 can only be guessed at. His English secretary's husband was suing her for divorce on the grounds of adultery. Hastings Kamuzu Banda was named as co-respondent. In that same month, the Central African Federation came into being. Within a few weeks, Banda had closed his London practice and moved to the Gold Coast, renounced all personal involvement in politics and established a small practice in Kumasi, the Ashanti capital. He was joined by his secretary and they lived as husband and wife in relative obscurity for the next three years.

The Federation of Rhodesia and Nyasaland – 'this fascinating experiment in racial harmony' as my American tourists were led to believe – was, many believe, doomed from the start. It was opposed by black nationalists in Nyasaland and Northern Rhodesia on the grounds that it entrenched 'settler hegemony' centred as it was on Salisbury, Southern Rhodesia. It was opposed by most whites in Southern Rhodesia who saw it as a Colonial Office ruse to prevent their own claims for full self-determination.

Sir Roy Welensky, the burly former railwayman and heavy-weight boxing champion of Rhodesia, who was the embodiment of the Federal concept, had considered federation second prize. He had wanted amalgamation of the two Rhodesias. Nyasaland was, in his view, 'a neglected Imperial slum' in no way ready for any measure of self-determination.

Pugnacious but fair, Sir Roy was used to fighting by the Queensberry Rules. The British government was not. As the

Federation tottered from one crisis to another and as Federal forces found themselves confronting nationalist-instigated uprisings in Northern Rhodesia and Nyasaland, it became clear that Britain was itself bowing to the winds of change and regretting its hasty agreement to the white-dominated experiment of partnership in Central Africa.

Welensky, son of a Lithuanian Jew and his Afrikaner wife who had trekked north from South Africa, was proud of his humble origins. As a boy he had, as he frequently said, swum bare-arsed in the Makabusi River with the piccanins and had left school at 14 to work on the railways. From the footplate, he became involved in politics through the white trade union movement and was soon one of the most dominant political figures of the region, becoming Federal Prime Minister in 1955.

As the Conservative Party government in Britain moved quietly to destroy the Federation, Welensky was painted by the press as the archetypal 'white supremacist'. His looks and manner – beetle-browed, jutting jaw and a muscular gait and turn of phrase – were gifts to cartoonists portraying the typical Rhodesian white settler. This was how he was presented by Colonial Office confidants to the diplomatic and commonwealth correspondents in London. The Africa-based correspondents had a totally different impression.Welensky was the most approachable and quotable leader in the Africa of the 1960s. He was, in a totally unaffected and relaxed manner, on first-name terms with most of the foreign correspondents based or passing through the region, even those who had displayed their personal distaste of him and his policies. His office door was always open and his home telephone number was available to any hack who might want to check something, however inconvenient the hour. Alone among African politicians of the day, he had an instinctive grasp of and interest in international affairs and maintained, through regular correspondence, an amazing range of contacts among politicians and statesmen worldwide.

Roy Welensky and Hastings Banda were bitter political enemies, the one committed totally to the Federal concept, the other, finally lured from his hermitage in Ghana to lead the nationalist movement in Nyasaland, implacably opposed to what he called 'the stupid and hellish federation'. Throughout Nyasaland he was hailed as a Messiah and he soon precipitated countrywide foment for total independence for his country. Welensky gaoled Banda in Rhodesia, thus giving him that status most desirous of African leaders of the day, that of Ex-Convict (Colonial).

Banda, released from prison a year later at British government insistence (and, of course, for purely British political advantage), set about destroying Welensky's dream. He succeeded, and went on to become one of Africa's most remarkable dictators. He did not forget but he forgave. He was to invite Welensky to be guest of honour at Malawi's tenth anniversary celebrations (along with the white man who was his gaoler). Welensky accepted and made a gracious speech.

The two old protagonists, the one with absolute power in his home country, the other in retirement with his second, young family in self-imposed exile in rural England, corresponded with each other until Sir Roy's death in 1992. Within the stormy relationship between these two headstrong men lies one of the most intriguing yarns of recent African history – and more than a few threads of truth about the past, future and present of black and white Africans.

Banda was still in gaol in Gwelo when Harold Macmillan made his momentous safari on the winds of change in 1960. The British prime minister had met Banda and had enjoyed his company, an unlikely companionship which flourished when they discovered a mutual liking for old English snobbery. Macmillan had been phased only momentarily when Welensky hit him with a political hook. The Salisbury street fighter had sent a Canberra reconnaissance aircraft to film a British military build-up in Kenya. Why had Harold sent forces, including long-range strike bombers to Nairobi, if he did not intend to counter with force the threat of the Federal government to go it alone? Why Harold? Macmillan paused only briefly.

'My dear chap,' he assured Roy, 'they are there to protect you. You are under threat and our chaps are ready to protect your interests.' Welensky smelled treachery and, of course, he was right. Macmillan had already decided that the Federation would have to go. In Blantyre, the British Prime Minister ended his brief visit to Nyasaland with a civic lunch at Ryall's Hotel of grouse – or was it pheasant? – flown in from his favourite moor in Scotland.

There was a state of emergency prevailing in the territory as a result of Banda's return and the resulting disturbances. Federal police, most of them ex-British bobbies who had volunteered for a life in the African sun, were on duty outside. Inside, the foreign press covering Macmillan's tour, whooped it up at the bar. They already had the wind of change story and here they were in Nyasaland, the heart of the Empire thus renounced, to confirm for their British readers that the times they were indeed a'changing.

In the Blantyre street outside Ryall's a crowd of people gathered, its numbers estimated variably from 200 to 2 000, organised by the Malawi Congress Party to protest to Macmillan about the continued incarceration of their leader. Demonstrators had concealed banners and placards under their clothing. As Macmillan arrived, he was greeted by boos, whistles and chanting. Scuffles broke out as the police grabbed the placards and began to tear them up. There were more scuffles as the police formed a cordon and some demonstrators tried to break through. The disturbance lasted no more than 40 minutes and ended when a cloudburst drenched demonstrators, police and onlookers alike.

By any standards, certainly by those of emerging Africa, it was a minor incident, perhaps one to be recorded in three or four paragraphs. But it had been observed by Fleet Street's finest from the Ryall's terrace. Apart from a few GOAHs, the Macmillan tour press entourage included such weighty editorial names as Peregrine Worsthorne, a *Telegraph* leader writer, Henry Fairlie of the *Daily Mail*, Sydney Jacobson of the *Daily Mirror*, Stephen Barber of the *News Chronicle*, René McColl of the *Daily Express* and Anne Sharpley of the *London Evening Standard*. Some were destined to become editors; most had long since forsaken, if not forgotten, the craft of reporting for the heady realms of political commentary.

There was not too much interest in the civic lunch, but here was a live demonstration of heavy-handed white colonial cops brutalising innocent black protesters. On their own evidence later, several of the heavyweights strolled among the 'rioters' without spilling a drop of the gins and tonics they still carried. The international wires buzzed that afternoon as the correspondents vied with each in dramatising the event.

On 'pack' stories like these, hyperbole has its own momentum. The reports had 'an ugly situation' provoked by 'a few young undisciplined policemen', a 'sickening spectacle as white police officers stamped with heavy boots on bare feet'. They spoke of 'the stupidity of the Nyasaland white police officers' who 'went berserk, swinging batons, seizing innocent Africans indiscriminately and bundling them roughly with punches and whip slashes into caged vehicles'. They spoke of 'hysterical white settlers' and of blacks being hurled, yelling and struggling, into Jeeps and Black Marias.

Tuned into the BBC World Service at his home that evening, one of the white police officers listened in astonishment to the report of the disturbance. 'They must have gone to a different incident.' An American missionary who had been in the area at the time was later asked about a riot. 'Riot, what riot?' he asked.The leader writers seized on the theme. 'Name these guilty men!' demanded the *Daily Herald*. 'Stop these bullies once and for all.' What had happened could not be denied because it had taken place 'under the eyes of experienced reporters'. The *Herald* went on: 'Name the plain-clothes officer who in a state of frenzy started the whole thing...Name the officer in charge...this brutal, bullying attitude of mind must be kicked out of the colonial administration...little wonder that hatred boils up in the hearts of friendly coloured folk when boneheads are let loose to knock them around with batons...Name these men!'

The *Daily Mirror* demanded 'an immediate end to this police state', the *Daily Mail* said a white policeman had struck and kneed Africans while a senior policeman had encouraged his men to stamp on bare feet. The *Express* was confident that a good-humoured London bobby could have controlled the crowd single-handed and dispersed it without incident. Even *The Daily Telegraph* agreed that the police had provoked the incident by tearing up the placards. Predictably, the Swedish *Stockholms Tidningen*, which did not have a reporter present, was among the most shrill. 'The Aggression Of White Police Frightens The British', screamed its headline. 'The black masses acted calmly and with restraint until white police started to tear their banners away and attacked them with their truncheons. With uncontrolled brutality they whipped the black women and men and received willing assistance from local white civilians.'

The storm reverberated through the House of Commons. Opposition spokesmen demanded action against 'stupid and truculent' police officers. Ian Macleod, Colonial Secretary, was obliged to set up an inquiry. Mr Justice Southworth of the Nyasaland High Court duly established a one-man commission. For four weeks and two days he listened to eighty-one witnesses give their version of what had occurred outside Ryall's, including ten correspondents who were flown to Blantyre at the state's expense to defend what they had written.

They did not do a very good job. Under cross-examination, some had to admit that they had coloured their reports. Others admitted a total lack of local knowledge and said they had based their reports on experience elsewhere.

Mr Justice Southworth, in his 125-page report, felt obliged to apologise for the expense involved in bringing the reporters concerned to Blantyre in order to expose their distortions. His report, its ponderous prose disguising His Lordship's dry, wry wit, stands as an indictment of Fleet Street's approach to African situations, particularly those involving 'white settlers'.

The judge found that the crowd numbered between 800 and 1 000, most of them onlookers. The demonstrators numbered between 50 and 80 people. There were thirteen policemen in all, with a Land Rover and a truck. The police had worn light walking shoes, not heavy boots. Seven of them carried swagger-sticks and several were former members of British police forces.

A small group of demonstrators broke out of the cordon into the road, led by five young ladies, including a Miss Phombeya who led an emotional dance. In the course of the mêlée someone trod on her big toe and she fell to the ground. She was helped to her feet by a police inspector. A photograph of this event had been used prominently in newspapers around the world with the caption 'Police slap down girl demonstrator'.

Mr Barr, the American missionary, told the inquiry that once inside the police van 'the girls and several of the boys were carrying on their dancing rhythm similar to a normal village dance'. Mrs Warr, a white lady onlooker, described the ladies in the truck 'giving us all a little dance, clapping their hands and seeming quite happy'.

Mr Justice Southworth concluded: 'In the course of the disturbance, two or three of the demonstrators kicked or struck European police officers and three European police officers kicked or struck demonstrators. One young lady had her foot trodden on by a police officer and sustained a slight injury. The two officers who kicked demonstrators say they did this to make the demonstrators let go of them when they were dragged into the crowd: and the officer who trod on the lady's foot has explained how this was done by accident, an explanation which on the evidence one would not be entitled to reject.

'One other young lady may or may not have had her foot trodden on this occasion, but if this occurred, it appeared to have been done accidentally by someone in the crowd. The distance between the furthest points between which the demonstrators moved throughout the course of the demonstration is about eighty yards. The entire incident took place on a straight stretch of road covering an area less than one-sixth the size of a football field and appears to have occupied not more than forty minutes.'

The judge's conclusion amounted to an indictment of the press: 'As far as can be ascertained the amount of skin lost by both police and demonstrators as a result of injuries received on this occasion would hardly cover an area of one square inch, probably no more than the area of a penny postage stamp: and it does not appear that the amount of blood that was shed would be sufficient to test the capacity of an ordinary mustard spoon.

'Contemplating the measure of the injuries sustained by the demonstrators, one cannot avoid the reflection that when the face of Helen launched a thousand ships, and brought Agamemnon and the great Achilles to the shores of Phrygia, it hardly achieved as much as Miss Phombeya's toe when it brought the paladins of Fleet Street in the aerial argosies of our day across two continents to appear before your Commissioner in the remote highlands of middle Africa.'

The inquiry itself received relatively little coverage in the foreign press. The judge's damning findings even less. The affair of Miss Phombeya's toe was soon forgotten in the British parliament. It was not forgotten, however, by the whites of the Rhodesias. The proven distortion and exaggeration of foreign correspondents was to remain in their minds and, as shall be seen, grow into rancorous loathing of journalists in the dramatic events soon to unfold.

A literary curiosity of the affair was that Nicholas Monsarrat's novel, *The Tribe That Lost Its Head*, published several years before, describes a remarkably similar incident, progressively blown out of proportion by newspapers. Monsarrat's plot had the matter raised in the House of Commons and a political uproar which swiftly led to genuine riots, murder and rape. Banda, of course, had no doubts about how to handle the press, local or foreign. Under British pressure, he had been released from Gwelo gaol after serving just over a year and had returned to Zomba. 'It was the best turn the British ever did for me,' was his most accurate comment. Within a year, as leader of the Malawi Congress Party, he had swept the polls, within two years Malawi had seceded from the Federation and a year later the country became independent. By the time Malawi became a republic in 1966, Hastings Kamuzu Banda, the Ngwazi, had stamped his persona, his mores, his convictions, his whims and his fancies on every aspect of life in his country.

Nothing happened and nobody moved without his knowing about it. It was far more than a personality cult – although airports, stadia, highways, hillsides, monuments, landmarks, all quickly bore his name – it was the shaping of the minds of all Malawians, the unabashed belief that he, and he alone, knew what was right for his people and his country. In addition to being president-for-life of Malawi and of its sole legal political party, he held the portfolios of defence, foreign affairs, justice and others.

'Everything is my business. Everything. Anything I say is law...literally law.' Ministers were peremptorily dismissed, usually after public humiliation, MPs were publicly admonished for drinking or laziness. He imposed strict dress regulations on citizens and visitors alike – no tight jeans, no mini-skirts, no long hair. I was earnestly 'advised' to get my hair cut by one of his officials before attending a presidential press conference, even though it was a fraction of the length of what was then fashionable.

Local journalists were browbeaten into complete subservience. The *Times of Malawi* (once edited by Donald Trelford, later editor of

The Observer) became a presidential mouthpiece, carrying little except the utterances of Banda on any given subject. Like most other businesses in Malawi the majority shareholding in *The Times* was held by a company of which Banda was the chairman-for-life. Eight of the best Malawian journalists were arbitrarily thrown into gaol under preventive detention in 1973 and remained there for more than ten years. When James Callaghan, British Prime Minister at the time, cautiously raised the subject of their continued detention during Banda's visit to London, the Ngwazi exploded with rage. 'If I hear anything more about those journalists they will stay in gaol for the rest of their lives.' Callaghan quickly changed the subject.

For a time, foreign correspondents were tolerated on the occasional visit, although elaborate arrangements had to be made beforehand. Banda usually arranged for visiting hacks to be at some public function at which he would remonstrate with them – with his fly whisk, of course.

John Ridley, with his loathing of all things African, was particularly incensed at having been fly-whisked by Banda on one occasion. He got his own back by slipping a racial jibe into his copy. Banda had arrived at a rally dressed, as usual, in his black hat and dark three-piece suit. Ridley described the scene and added: 'The president-for-life arrived, wearing his customary flesh-coloured homburg.' It got past the sub-editors.

Banda's press conferences invariably turned into harangues. Making a point to Donald Wise, he once brought his fist down on a desk with such force that dishes and a water jug flew into the air, showering the assembled aides with peanuts and water. 'He was a cabaret act really,' recalls Donald. 'I think hew knew we expected him to blow his top and enjoyed him throwing a wobbly.' John Bulloch remembers a press conference at which Banda was insisting that the Arabs were the first colonising power. 'He suddenly turned to a minister quivering beside him and screamed at him "Fetch me the large map, boy!" David Bonavia, then with Reuters, was granted an interview, but such were his youthful looks that Banda immediately ordered him away. "Tell Reuters I will not have schoolboys sent to interview me!"'

It was thus with more than a little trepidation that my request for an interview with the Ngwazi was granted in 1970. I had arranged it through one of his brighter young ministers, the charming and personable Aleke Banda (who was no relation). I had to submit my questions in advance to Aleke, then the minister in charge of the information department. On the appointed day, Aleke met me at State House, Zomba, looking more nervous than I felt.

'He is running behind schedule so I don't think you'll get more than twenty minutes,' he said. 'In any case, if he is wearing his dark glasses please don't ask questions ten to fourteen.'

In my prepared list I had started off with some inoffensive, anodyne questions leading gradually, I hoped, to some more pointed ones about sensitive issues: There had been a spate of gruesome axe murders in Blantyre's townships which appeared to have political undertones. In addition, the entire white judiciary in Malawi had resigned after Banda announced that traditional tribal courts would henceforth have the power to try capital offences. They were the kind of references that could cause a 'wobbly' as Wise put it, particularly if the Ngwazi was wearing his dark glasses which, Aleke intimated, indicated a bad mood. We joined a queue of diplomats, businessmen and senior officials waiting on the presidential verandah, every one of them looking a little apprehensive. From behind the door to the Ngwazi's office there came a sudden burst of laughter. Everyone relaxed a little. Banda sounded as if he was in a good mood. 'You certainly won't have time for those last few questions now,' Aleke said, looking relieved. I was beginning to think about leaving them out anyway, such was the intimidating ambience of State House.

Finally we were ushered into the office, a large, panelled room, a large table, several small chairs and one large, throne-like seat. I set up my tape-recorder – one of the old reel-to-reel types – in front of the throne and sat next to Aleke facing it. We jumped to our feet as an inner door opened and The Presence came in. He was not wearing his dark glasses! Silently he took his seat and stared at me.

Reaching across to turn on the recorder I muttered something about getting right on with the interview, appreciating that His Excellency was running behind schedule. He cut me short with an abrupt wave of his hand. 'Who are you?' he demanded. I looked at Aleke. No help there. 'Well I am Munnion, sir,' I stuttered, 'correspondent for *The Daily Telegraph*.' He cut me short again. 'No, no, who ARE you?' I started to stammer out a potted life history. Again he cut me short with a chopping movement of his hand. 'No, no...I want to know what kind of journalist are you? I want to know if you are,' – and his voice began to rise angrily – 'A Colin Legum? Are you a Patrick Keatley? Are you a CLYDE SANGER?'

I realised suddenly that he was using me to vent his spleen on those three journalists who had befriended him in London in the early days of the African revolution but had, in his view, turned against him when he, alone among black leaders, had established diplomatic relations with South Africa. I hastily assured him that I was not in that mould of journalism, that I was responsible, honest and upright. I was about to tell him that I had just had my hair cut when he seemed to relax. I switched on the tape recorder and referred to my sheet of prepared questions. To my horror – and Aleke's – Banda reached across and grabbed my list. 'What have we here?' he asked with a headmaster's rhetoric. 'So these are the "responsible" questions you wish to ask me.'

Once again I opened my mouth to explain. Once again – as he was to do throughout the next 90 minutes – he cut me short with that abrupt flick of his wrist. I was totally intimidated. Aleke was transfixed. Banda slowly read out my first question aloud. It was something about threats by the Organisation of African Unity to expel Malawi for its relations with Pretoria.

'Ha!' he shouted. 'Let them dare! Just let them dare! I do not care what they say in Addis Ababa – the Organisation of African Unity. I do not care what they say in London – the Commonwealth Secretariat. I do not care what they say in New York – the United Nations. Let them dare interfere with Banda!'

And so it went on. He took all of my allotted 20 minutes to answer that first question and then, reading out the rest one by one, launched in to long and loud harangues by way of response. At one stage, Aleke tried to sneak a glance at his wrist-watch. Banda froze him, snake-like, with a malevolent stare. The Ngwazi was approaching the more sensitive area of questioning when there came a timid knock on the door. 'Come in!' he bellowed. A shivering flunky entered bearing a silver salver on which there was a small slip of paper. Banda snatched it and read it. Suddenly he began to shake with anger, grunted and growled, screwed the note up into a little ball and hurled it at the messenger. 'Get out!' he screamed. The man disappeared swiftly through the door. Lucky fellow, I thought to myself, but worse was to come. Banda reached into his top pocket, unfolded a pair of dark glasses and put them on. 'Where were we?' he said, picking up my questions.

By now Aleke and I were totally resigned to a fate we both believed would be pretty terrifying. But Banda calmed down as quickly as he had erupted. He got to the question about the judiciary and explained, in almost fatherly tones, how African tribal justice was much fairer than the British system. 'I have sat in your courts and watched taxpayers' money being used to set a murderer free! That's not justice. Under our system – which is much superior – you must not defend a criminal, a man whom everybody knows has committed a crime. You must not.' He went on to tell me a long, rambling parable about how, in his boyhood, he had helped bring a murderer to book for killing a woman in a neighbouring village. 'Everyone in the village knew he was guilty.'

The axe murders were the work of criminals but 'political elements' were trying to take advantage of them to make propaganda. He referred to cabinet ministers who had fled the country after his purge shortly after independence and said they were trying to turn his people against him. He raised his voice again. 'Clyde Sanger of the *Manchester Guardian*...he was their pet...he supported them.' I was later to learn that his fury with the *Guardian* man was compounded by the fact that he had, in earlier friendly days, consented to be godfather to Sanger's son.

On the future of democracy in Malawi his system was, again, far superior to that in Britain. 'Everybody in the towns and villages picks several candidates for parliament. These are submitted to me. I go through the list and pick out this man, or that man, because I know he will make a good MP for his people. That is democracy.' Thankfully he got to the end of the question list and stood up. Aleke and I leapt to attention. 'Thank you, sir, for your time,' I gushed. He nodded and turned to retreat into his inner sanctum. In a surprisingly gentle voice he said over his shoulder: 'Remember, I am not a politician at all. I am just an African nationalist. That's all.' I filed a lengthy piece on the Banda interview but received one of those infuriating playbacks the following day stating merely 'YOURS OUTSQUEEZED', meaning other stories had taken priority. I persisted and the *Telegraph* finally ran an abbreviated version: 'YOUR BANDA INSIDE CONCISELY'. I was furious at having expended all that emotional energy for so little and gave copies of the transcript to Philip Short who was already researching his biography of Banda and to Peter Niesewand, then freelancing in Salisbury. Peter was working on a feature about the Malawian leader for a magazine, *Illustrated Life Rhodesia* and, rather foolishly, I told him he could use whatever he wished. An unflattering cover story about Banda appeared in the next issue of the magazine with my interview published in full under Peter's name.

Knowing that Banda would certainly see a copy and would know it was the interview he had given to a representative of *The Daily Telegraph*, I feared the worst. Sure enough, I had a formal letter signed by Aleke a month later informing me that the Ngwazi had 'been pleased' to declare me a Prohibited Immigrant to Malawi. Aleke Banda fared worse. Without his knowledge, a Zambian newspaper ran a story about him, portraying him as the obvious heir to Banda. He was rusticated in disgrace to Nkata Bay in the north of Malawi.

Soon afterwards, Banda placed a blanket ban on all foreign correspondents visiting the country. Unfortunately, Blantyre was the most convenient transit point for flying north from Rhodesia to East Africa and elsewhere. It meant changing aircraft at Chileka Airport and the connection was invariably overbooked. We overcame this problem by waving our portable typewriters at Inspector Soko, the beaming Malawian policeman always on duty at Chileka. Realising that if he allowed journalists to stay in Malawi he would risk his own job, he ensured that we always got a seat on the Nairobi-bound flight.

Banda had little time for the man who was emerging as a counterpart in the other Federal component – Kenneth David Buchizya Kaunda, leader of the United National Independence Party (UNIP) in Northern Rhodesia, even though the two men had much in common. To Banda, Kaunda was a 'misguided young boy' who flirted too much with subversive people and was given to 'ridiculous displays of public emotion'.

But Kaunda was also a teetotaler, a non-smoker, a man of profound Christian convictions, from humble beginnings in a remote African village (with a father born in Nyasaland), a professed believer in non-violence and an incredible political staying power. 'KK', as he was soon known, also had a strong streak of ruthlessness that he has disguised with a charm, warmth and apparent human concern which seduced Western leaders for years.

As it dawned on the hapless Welensky that the British government was tugging the rug from under his large Federal feet, African nationalists were organising and campaigning in Northern Rhodesia, not only for the end of the Federation but for the power of independence that they sensed was imminent. Bob Hitchcock, a former *London Daily Mail* man, got to know the leading nationalists well when he was based in Lusaka for the lamented Johannesburg newspaper, the *Rand Daily Mail*. There was Harry Nkumbula, the boisterous, chain-smoking former London School of Economics student who had been earmarked by his 'Africa revolution' contemporaries in London as the natural leader of an independent Zambia – and would probably have made it had it not been for his over-indulgence. Drink and women were to be the curse of Zambia – and many of the hacks who covered the country.

Hitchcock recalled long, liquid dinners with Nkumbula and Kaunda in the Ridgeway Hotel in Lusaka, at which the downfall of Sir Roy Welensky and the Federation was discussed and debated. 'Kaunda, the committed teetotaller, was invariably in the forefront of these discussions. In his quiet, smiling way he could present the black case far more lucidly and logically than most other Africans in the party. But it was always Harry Nkumbula's words, uttered with that tired Humphrey Bogart rasp and punctuated by hiccups and the hack of a chainsmoker, that were received with the most deference.'

The two men were to share a cell when they were arrested as agitators but fell out politically. Kaunda went on to serve another spell in prison before emerging to form the UNIP which won an overwhelming majority in the pre-independence elections. But the mild-mannered adherent of Ghandian non-violence showed the other side of his personality with some of his utterances such as: 'Mau Mau will seem like a child's picnic compared with the mass rising that will result if the British government and Welensky continue to frustrate the legitimate aspirations of the African people of Zambia.' Independence came in 1964 and Kaunda, at the age of 42, became President of the Republic of Zambia soon afterwards, moving into the spacious neo-Georgian mansion of former British governors.

No one underestimated the problems he faced. The sprawling, landlocked country, shaped like a pair of boxing gloves, stretched from the Zambezi in the south to the shores of Lake Tanganyika in the north. Its wealth was centred entirely on the Copperbelt, a 90-mile corridor in the centre of the country where seven mines were run and operated by whites, most of them of South African and Rhodesian origin. At independence half of the four million blacks were under 20 years of age. There was one single secondary school for blacks in the entire country. There were perhaps six black lawyers, four black doctors and one black engineer.

Among the white population of some 70 000 were many of the country's large-scale farmers – and most of them were of Afrikaner stock. Zambia had an enormous agricultural potential, with plenty of water, good rainfall and rich soil. It could and should have been able to feed not only itself but much of Africa. As the pre-independence parrot-cry had been, as always, 'the whites stole our best land' it might have been expected that liberated black Zambians would return to the soil. It was not to be. Zambians with half an education flocked to the towns to overpopulate a vast, unwieldy and totally unnecessary bureaucracy. In Zambia, Uhuru meant a job in the civil service, a tightly rolled umbrella, perhaps a car but certainly enough money to consume vast quantities of beer.

Banda may have managed to impose some of his abstemiousness on Malawi but Kaunda was spectacularly unsuccessful in persuading Zambians of the virtues of teetotalism. My abiding impression was of a country either completely awash in beer or enveloped in a sullen, collective hangover.

I first visited Zambia a few years after independence. It turned out to be a bank holiday and I was met by our then stringer, an eccentric white journalist who had long since embraced the country's alcoholic tradition. He decided that our best contacts would be found in every bar and night club in the vicinity of Lusaka. We met lots of jolly people who imparted raucous views on every subject under the sun but by around 11 p.m. I suggested, rather fuzzily, that I had not done much research.

'You'd better meet Sikota Wina,' slurred the stringer, referring to one of the brightest young men in Kaunda's cabinet. Sikota had been expelled from South Africa's Fort Hare University for political activities, had edited a newspaper on the Copperbelt and had become Minister of Local Government Housing after independence, dramatising his job by personally driving a bulldozer to demolish slums. At the time, it seemed a good idea. We weaved our way through the late night Lusaka traffic and arrived at a pleasant suburban bungalow. The door was opened by an attractive young black woman, casually but expensively dressed. This was Glenda Wina, Sikota's American wife. She did not seem to think it at all odd that two swaying white men had banged on the door at midnight.

Glenda apologised. Her husband was out but should be back at any time. Please come in, help yourselves to a drink and excuse me while I try and get the kids to sleep. She was absolutely charming, full of fun and laughter and, as she had been a journalist in America, the conversation inevitably swung into gossipy shop talk and the swapping of anecdotes. At some point, the stringer's eccentricity asserted itself. He was no longer in the room and then we heard the roar of his car engine. He was gone and I was stranded in an unknown town in an unknown country in an unknown minister's home with his wife. Don't worry, Glenda said. Sikota will be back soon. It was 2 a.m.

Glenda poured some more drinks, played some soul music and we danced and chatted for at least another hour before there came the sound of another car, loud voices, and into the room came Sikota Wina accompanied by none other than Harry Nkumbula, then out in the cold politically. They, too, had clearly spent the evening the Zambian way. Glenda introduced me and the two men collapsed with laughter when they learned that this little Englishman dancing with the minister's wife in his home at 3 a.m. was the representative of the 'fascist' *Daily Telegraph*, voice of the capitalist oppressor, enemy of the people of Zambia, etc., etc. (The *Telegraph* leader writers had been at it again.)

There was nothing unfriendly in their attitude. Far from it. They thought it a huge joke. Sikota poured more drinks and we sat and talked and laughed through the dawn as if we'd been old friends for years. Sikota finally summoned a Ministerial car and I was chauffeured back to the Ridgeway Hotel in time for a late breakfast. I was aware that I had been given much fascinating inside information on Zambia in my conversation with the two leading politicians but when I came to much later in the day I couldn't remember one word. That was Zambia.

Kenneth Kaunda, tall, as charming as ever, his hair always swept backwards and upwards as if someone had given him a sudden shock, cut a dash on the international scene. He and his wife Betty were both passable musicians and had entertained President Nixon and his wife at the White House with guitar and song. Kaunda was also a keen sportsman, with a good game of tennis, a better one of ping pong and a passion for golf. He constructed a nine-hole course in the sumptuous grounds of State House and was given to inviting any visitor, diplomat, businessman and sometimes hacks, for a round or two. He claimed his handicap was 18 but rarely lost a friendly competition.

He was always immaculately dressed, with a wardrobe of neatly pressed safari suits and a wide range of silk cravats. There was always a clean white handkerchief in his top pocket. Where Hastings Banda was rarely seen without his fly whisk, Kaunda was never seen without his handkerchief. It would be flourished frequently – and often used to dab his eyes as he made emotional points in his many ringing speeches. That he was easily moved to tears was considered by many an affectation but they might have thought again if they knew, as he did, that Zambia's economy was crumbling swiftly and creating powerful tribal and political unrest.

He had been able to use Rhodesia's declaration of UDI and his 'frontline' stand against white rule as a legitimate excuse but, despite massive injections of foreign aid, the thin fabric of Zambia's infrastructure was becoming threadbare. Against his undertakings to the contrary, his government seized control of the copper mines in 1969, a move that merely had the effect of undermining what little foreign investment confidence there had been. His tearful proclamations of 'Humanism', a half-baked quasi-socialist philosophy, had an increasingly hollow ring as food queues lengthened throughout the land.

Zambia switched from comedy to tragedy and back again with bewildering speed. One day there would be charm and laughter; the next a sullen, belligerent surliness. There would be moments of high farce. When Sir Arthur Bottomley, Harold Wilson's Commonwealth Secretary, paid his first visit to Zambia he slightly misread his map of Africa. 'It's a great pleasure to be here in The Gambia,' he declared. The Zambians were polite but got their own back that evening when the local radio news announced the arrival of 'Sir Arthur Commonly, the Bottomwealth Secretary'. There were moments of bitter tragedy, such as the shooting dead of two women tourists by Zambian troops at Victoria Falls and the government's insistence that they were 'Rhodesian troops on a sabotage mission'.

Kaunda's attitude towards the press was also ambivalent. He proclaimed his belief in press freedom but when Dunstan Kamana, one of the finest of African editors, ran a story in the *Times of Zambia* about some ministerial abuses, he was peremptorily removed from the editorial chair and sent into some obscure diplomatic wilderness. He frequently harangued me about the attitudes of the Western press in general, and the *Telegraph* in particular, 'always trying to point out that we would have been far better off if we had stayed under white rule'. But he enjoyed the company of Western correspondents and the feeling was mutual.

My next meeting with Sikota Wina was not so congenial. In 1970 Zambia played host to the summit conference of 'non-aligned nations', that ridiculous misnomer for yet another jamboree of West-bashing Third World countries and their leaders. For the occasion, the Yugoslavs built on the outskirts of Lusaka the Mulungushi Conference Hall and VIP Village, a splendid concrete and glass edifice with all mod cons. The foreign press, we were assured, would be most welcome, and a dozen or so Africa correspondents, most of us based south of the Zambezi, duly arrived in Lusaka.

All hotel accommodation had been reserved for non-aligned delegates but temporary digs were provided for visiting hacks at the university campus. I had been invited to stay with old friends, Ian McLean, and his family at their comfortable suburban home. Ian was a senior partner in a leading Lusaka law firm. His wife, Alison, an old schoolfriend of my wife, was the daughter of Mr Justice Harry Davies, then a senior judge in the 'illegal' Rhodesia. Her mother, D'Urban, was also visiting Lusaka but there was plenty of room for us all. It was to prove an embarrassing arrangement. With a group of colleagues I went to inspect the press facilities at the Mulungushi Hall. They were splendid – banks of telephones, most of which worked, a long line of telex machines, desks, press kits – and a large, well-stocked bar. We were duly accredited with large laminated passes decorated with our names, our mug-shots and our organisations, and adjourned to the bar.

There was a familiar face from Fleet Street sitting at the bar, a very disconsolate, rather grumpy Colin Lawson of the *Daily Express*. Colin, a burly, gingery man, was one of Arthur Christiansen's great dateline firemen. He had taken part in the Sicily landings, followed the Russian tanks into Czechoslovakia, been thrown into gaol in Cuba during the missile crisis, all with great gusto. He was then the *Express* man in Bonn and Europe was his bailiwick. What on earth was he doing here in Zambia?

'Zambia? Zambia? Is that where I bloody well am?' he growled. 'I knew it was somewhere in bloody Africa.' It transpired that Lawson had upset the foreign desk of his newspaper and, according to him, they had sent him to cover the non-aligned conference as a sort of punishment. He was getting his revenge by refusing to shave and going on a drinking binge for the duration.

He found the ideal soul mate, a young Zambian-based white journalist who was, himself, a natural rebel and an even more natural imbiber. They spent the afternoon sitting at a table in the bar, slugging their way through a great variety of liquor. Towards evening, the lounge began to fill with delegates, most of them black or brown. Suddenly, Lawson's young companion clambered on top of the table, waving a bottle of slivovitz and stamping his foot for attention. 'Gentlemen...gentlemen,' he cried. 'I give you a toast...a toast to the Third World.' Bemused delegates raised their glasses. The young hack took a swig from his bottle, emitted a great shout of maniacal laughter and shouted 'The Third World...you're all fuckin' kaffirs...'

There was a ghastly hush, broken by a sudden buzz of angry conversation as Third World delegates translated the insult and its import. Lawson may have been smashed but he took in the situation immediately, grabbed his companion bodily and rushed him through the door. Unfortunately the bar was on the first floor of the hall which meant he had to negotiate a grand, sweeping staircase. Towards the bottom he slipped and dropped the little hack and the tightly clutched bottle of slivovitz in an ungainly heap on the floor of the main foyer. Such was the pandemonium that colleagues managed to drag them out and into the night.

It was an inauspicious start to conference eve but worse was to follow. Across the road, on the campus, Sikota Wina, now Minister of Information, had organised a 'Welcome to the Press' party. The booze, of course, was free and the throng that had gathered included far more Zambian freeloaders than press freeloaders. It had been a long, hot day and it was a balmy evening. Thirsts were being eagerly slaked.

The minister finally stood up to make a speech. I don't remember a breeze, but he was swaying slightly. 'Gentlemen of the world's press, welcome to the summit of non-aligned nations,' he began. Sikota went on to extol the facilities provided for us at the Mulungushi Hall and ended with the fateful words, 'If any of you have any complaints about the press arrangements you must come straight to me...' Most of us were impressed by the facilities but three of our number were furious. Mike Keats, of UPI, Ken 'Fingers' Whiting of AP and Tony 'Roarer' White of Reuters, all bureau chiefs for their respective agencies based in Johannesburg, had discovered that most of the telex machines in the Mulungushi pressroom had been allocated to Tanjug, the Yugoslav news agency. The three largest news agencies in the world had been allocated just one machine between them.

At the end of Sikota's speech, the three men took him at his word and approached him with their problem. The discussion turned into a bit of a shouting match, particularly when the minister discovered that all three were based in Johannesburg. As he turned on his heel to storm away, he allegedly heard one of the journalists mutter an adaptation of Zambia's national slogan. Instead of 'One Zambia, One Nation', he heard instead 'One Zambia, One Fuck-up!'

During the night, plain-clothes policemen began rounding up the hacks. Tony White was staying at the Reuters house in Lusaka when he became aware of two black faces, wrapped in the ubiquitous dark glasses, peering through the window. Roarer (his nickname, bestowed by Keats, of course, derived from his ability to maintain a gentlemanly posture while vomiting) invited them inside for a drink. They accepted readily, then arrested him and whisked him to Lusaka Remand Prison on the other side of the city.

At the university special branch men picked up Ken Whiting, Dan van der Vat, of *The Times,* Ed Linington, of the South African Press Association and Ron MacDonnell, a freelance cameraman. They also burst into the room of Dr Hans Reinhardt of DPA, the German press agency. Hans was a much older man and not in the best of health. He had a heart attack as he was being arrested and was rushed to hospital.

Keats and Ernie Christie, the photographer, got early wind of the purge and moved quickly to a private address, evading arrest. I had enjoyed a family evening with the McLeans and was alerted to the arrests only the following morning. A telephone call from a colleague warned me that the Zambians seemed to be picking up all who were based south of the Zambezi.

My curiosity got the better of me and I went directly to the Mulungushi Hall. In the pressroom, I was nudged, winked at and whispered to by various colleagues. 'They've been looking for you...get out now.' I was making my way, as casually as possible, to a rear entrance when the conference hall loudspeaker system burst into life. 'Mr Moonyan,' it boomed. 'Please come to reception. Mr Moonyan, urgently to reception.'

I suppose it was a novelty to be arrested by public address system, and anyway their mispronunciation of my name was slightly more flattering than Lord Camrose's 'Minnion'. I scurried to the rear entrance where two large black gentlemen – in wrap-around shades – examined my laminated accreditation badge on my lapel. 'Ah, Mr Moonyan...this way please.' I was ushered, very politely, into the back of a large black limousine, trying to discourage a colleague, Matt White, from remonstrating with my captors. Matt was shouting lovely old-fashioned phrases like 'Unhand this man...this is outrageous' and, as he was South African, I thought he too would be arrested. Jammed between my two successful special-branch men, I was whisked through the Lusaka traffic to Immigration Headquarters and marched into the office of a senior man. He was also wearing wrap-around shades. Why, oh why, I wondered, do African heavies have to look like Hollywood's version of the Tonton Macoute? He demanded my passport. I had, of course, left it at the McLean's house. He flicked his fingers and I was once again in the back of the limo, giving them directions to the home of my hosts.

Now I was a little more concerned. Would they try and implicate Ian and his family, living happily in Lusaka and pillars of the community, in whatever misdemeanour I was charged with? Worse, would they discover that the other house guest, Alison's mother, was the wife of a hanging judge in the hated white republic of Rhodesia to the south? The car swept into the McLean's drive. The ugliest and largest of my guards leaned over. 'We would be grateful, sir,' he said, 'if you would fetch your passport please.' D'Urban Davies had seen my arrival and, with all the instincts of the wonderful white African lady she was, had dived into a large wardrobe.

Alison opened the door and raised an eyebrow. 'These gentlemen want to see my passport,' I said. 'I'll just fetch it and be on my way. Perhaps you could let Ian know?' I rushed to my room, threw my spare passports into a cupboard and grabbed the one with the Zambian visa. I pecked Alison on the cheek. 'See you later,' I said, hoping I sounded cheery. And then, *sotto voce*, 'and Ian a lot sooner I hope'. She winked. My special-branch chums had not moved from the car. The radio was tuned into some heavy Congolese music and they were jerking around in their seats to its beat.

One of them took my passport and flicked through it rather idly, then used it to tap out the Congolese beat on the car seat. We arrived at the Lusaka Remand Prison, a shabby, walled gaol with rusty barbed wire tumbling over its peeling, stucco walls like an obscene wisteria. The gates swung open and a couple of very smart prison guards came forward. My policemen solemnly shook my hand. 'Please come back again soon,' one of them said.

I was still pondering on that remark when I found myself in a scruffy reception office where one of the smart young prison officers insisted on the removal of all my personal effects – including my belt, my watch and my shoelaces. Routine, in fact. Anything that I might use to commit suicide with in the slammer. Everything was being scrupulously annotated on a form when in walked an obviously senior prison man. 'Good morning!' he beamed. 'Welcome to Lusaka Remand Prison. I'm sure you'll find everything in order here and will enjoy your stay with us.' I've had far worse receptions at five-star hotels. Despite the circumstances, I beamed back. He was super-smartly clad, with a swagger stick tucked firmly under his left armpit and a genuine smile on his face. 'Thank you,' I said, rather stupidly adding 'It's nice to be here.' He looked at my prison entry form. 'English!' he exclaimed. 'I know England well. Wakefield...how is Wakefield?' The scene was beginning to take on a dream-like quality, but as it happened I did know Wakefield, having once worked for the *Yorkshire Post*. The governor had been trained at Britain's top prison officers' school in that town. We chatted about it for a few minutes and then his training took over.

'Please fill in this form here and here.' The form asked me for my tribe and the name of my chief. I wrote 'Tory' and 'Edward Heath'. He beamed again. 'And your shoelaces, please.' I obliged. 'Please come this way...you will find some of your English colleagues already here.'

I was ushered into the spartan, dusty courtyard. Tony White leapt to his feet, twirling his moustache and hamming up his upper-English accent (he was a New Zealander). 'Novvo, my dear chap, how nice of you to come...now let me show you around...this is the new laundry block I asked the chaps to build.' Dan van der Vat, the man from *The Times* and a Hollander whose liberal inclinations were constantly assailed by people mistaking him for an Afrikaner, was sitting with his back to a cell block wall, conscientiously taking notes. Fingers Whiting, the lanky, laconic American from AP was stretched out in the dust feigning a doze. He raised a hand in greeting. 'AWA', he said – 'Africa Wins Again'. Big Ron MacDonell, the cameraman, was squatting on his haunches. 'Tis an ill wind...' he said.

White grabbed my arm and pulled me to one side. 'Ron's driving me mad...he's been speaking in half-finished maxims all bloody night.' Roarer and I found a comfortable place in the dust and sat down to play 'I Spy With My Little Eye'. There wasn't too much scope in the prison compound, but I beat him with an 'f' for 'faucet' – there was an old rusty tap in the corner – and he stormed off to 'win over a couple of these guard chappies'. Van der Vat was still scribbling furiously. The sun was now beating down. Whiting was genuinely asleep, snoring gently. I was discussing golf with Ed Linington when the doors swung open to admit a very disconsolate John Platter, the UPI man. John was furious. 'I kept telling them I am based in Nairobi...I'm not one of you racists from the south...' Big Ron yawned. 'The sins of the fathers...' he said.

Another hour or so went past before the doors swung open again. In came Justin Nyoka, a black Rhodesian journalist and an old friend and colleague who had an excellent personal relationship with Kaunda. 'Salvation!' I thought. 'Justin's squared it with KK. We'll be out of here in no time.' Such hopes were dashed when Nyoka emerged from the 'reception' office, minus his shoelaces and belt. 'Ha!' he shouted. 'They shall all hear more about this...I've told them to contact KK immediately...this is outrageous!' He, too, had been caught in the dragnet. We pecked away at some kind of stodgy mealie porridge served for lunch – except for Ron MacDonell who wolfed it down, muttering all the while 'Let us eat and drink, for tomorrow we die...' 'For fuck's sake! Ron, shut up!' we chorused. A guard loomed out of the sun. 'Moonyan...Moonyan...this way.' I was led to the office and there, grinning at me on the civvie side of the grille, was my friend, my host and my lawyer, Ian McLean. 'How are you?' he asked, as if I'd just pitched up for a lunch. 'Fine, just fine...get me out of here.' Ian grinned again.

'Do you know, I've been retained on your behalf by your stringer, by *The Daily Telegraph* in London, by the British High Commission and by your wife on the 'phone from Salisbury. That's four retainers just to help you!' I forced a smile through clogging remnants of porridge. 'Then help me, Ian. Get me out of here for God's sake!' He examined a piece of paper in front of him and then said, quietly, 'How do you feel about habeas corpus?' 'Habeas corpus, the Magna Carta, the Fifth Amendment, anything, just get me out,' I hissed.

'You know, habeas corpus has never been tried in Zambia,' he mused. 'We could make Zambian legal history.' Make Zambian legal history! What a host! What a friend! My reply, in an old British courtroom, would have been written on a piece of paper and handed to the magistrate. McLean disappeared from the other side of the grille with a happy, preoccupied grin on his face.

We had two more visitors in the course of that searing afternoon. A very nervous young man from the British High Commission arrived, sweating and uncomfortable. 'This really is most embarrassing,' he stuttered. 'The High Commissioner is most upset with you chaps and some of you are not even British passport holders!' My Kiwi, Kenyan, American and South African colleagues raised their eyes to the sky. By this time I was used to Her Majesty's diplomatic staff in Africa and their deep concern for Her Majesty's embarrassing subjects, so our man's reaction was no surprise. I tried a request for some cigarettes and soft drinks. Perhaps something to read? Our man was horrified. 'But you are prisoners. This is a gaol. Really! This is all most inconvenient!' He scurried for the exit. 'Don't count your chickens,' Big Ron advised me.

A few minutes later an even younger man from the American Embassy arrived, bursting through the gates and demanding to see his man, Fingers Whiting. He beckoned us all over. 'Okay, you guys, we got everything under control...the Ambassador's sitting on KK's doorstep right now, raising hell about you all. You'll be outta here in no time. Thought you might like some home comforts in the meantime.' He flicked his fingers and a couple of warders arrived with cardboard boxes crammed with soft drinks, cartons of cigarettes, magazines and paperbacks. 'Seeya soon, guys. Take care now.' The contrast was staggering. Our American food parcels immediately gave us star status among our fellow prisoners, some 200 blacks who had been a little apprehensive about the sudden arrival of this bunch of bwanas. Roarer White rushed off with some cigarettes to nurture his 'tame screw'. We distributed largesse among our grateful fellow inmates. When we realised we had no bottle opener, a giant of a man, big Mike Makombe, came forward with a big grin. He grabbed the bottles one by one and deftly removed the tops with his great white teeth, roaring with laughter between each easy wrench. Things were looking up.

When we were herded into a large, communal cell (standard British colonial, 36' x 18') for the night, we shared out blankets and gathered around to hear the stories of our fellow inmates. Justin Nyoka helped with the translations where necessary. Most were Africans from neighbouring states, picked up for minor immigration infringements, having been unable to pay the standard border guard bribe. A young teacher from Rhodesia had tried to cross the border to visit relatives in Zambia. A Malawian trade unionist had wanted to make contact with his opposite numbers on the Copperbelt. An itinerant Tanzanian faith healer had wandered across the border by mistake. Some of them had been in Lusaka Remand Prison for more than two years, with no recourse to, or contact with, anyone outside. Their families had no idea where they were and they had never been charged with any offence or appeared in any court. It all made non-sense of the non-aligned platitudes being postulated on the other side of town, but it made good copy.

It must have been about 9 p.m. when a voice from behind the high grille window startled us all with an urgent summons. 'Antonee...Antonee...It is me...Bring some cigarettes.' Reuters' Tony White, our self-appointed fixer, jumped to his feet and grabbed a couple of packets of our cigarette ration. 'This is my man, chaps. All is well. Stand by one.' He reached up to the grille, passed over the cigarettes, and held a whispered conversation through the bars. We all clustered around to hear whatever news the 'tame screw' had to impart. Except Big Ron MacDonnell. 'Don't cross your bridges...' he said. The tidings were good. A team of heavies had arrived at the gate and the bwanas were going to be set free.

Sure enough, we were summoned to reception where a line of sunglasses, glinting in the moonlight, checked our names against lists, handed us back our passports, our shoelaces, belts, watches and wallets and ushered us into the night. Big Ron opened his broad shoulders, threw apart his brawny arms and declared, 'None can love freedom heartily, but good men...' 'Aw shuddap! Ron,' we cried, dispersing into the Lusaka darkness.

There was still time – in those good old days of Gutenberg's hot metal presses – to make the first edition in London. I cadged and purchased a series of lifts to the McLeans' home. Ian opened the door. He was in his shirtsleeves and had an intent look on his face, which fell when he saw me. 'Oh, no!' he groaned. 'What are you doing here?'

I charged past him. 'I'm free, free...where's the bloody tele-phone?' I had to stumble across his study, now littered with opened, referenced law books. As I waited for the operator to put me through to the *Telegraph*, I watched my friend, my host, my lawyer, reluc-tantly gather up his legal tomes. 'Very unfortunate this,' he mut-tered. 'We could have made legal history in Zambia, you know.' With lawyers for friends, who needs enemies?

On the following day, we tried to establish why we had been arrested and why the Zambian authorities had incurred such a bad press, wilfully and for no apparent reason. Apart from a few drunken exchanges which were – and are – part of the daily tapestry in the country, there surely could have been nothing to justify such action? Answer came there none. As Ken Whiting would have put it 'AWA!'

Ken did not have time to make any point. He was ordered to leave the country forthwith. This was followed by deportation orders served on John Edlin, a New Zealand journalist then working for the Argus Africa News Service and based in Lusaka, and Michael Keats and Ernie Christie who had emerged from hiding once they heard we had been released. John Platter and Ed Linington had their accreditation withdrawn. How these decisions were arrived at remains, to this day, anyone's guess.

Zambia's High Commission in London put out a statement accusing us of 'abusing' the country's hospitality and, hilariously, of 'living the life too permissive for Zambian society'. We should have been so lucky! Kaunda, made to look a clown in front of his fellow third-worlders, reached for his handkerchief. We were told later by Zambian friends that there had been a 'cock-up over whites'. The offender they had been looking for was either the white young man who had screamed a racial insult at the delegates at Mulungushi, or either Whiting of AP or White of Reuters who had tackled Sikota Wina over the lack of press facilities, or perhaps Matt White, the locally based man who had courageously tried to come to my rescue, or even Eric Wightman, the dour Coloured man who was then Zambia's Director of Information. Whatever they had been looking for, they had not found it, but, in classic Zambian tradition, had rounded up the usual suspects.

I wrote to Sikota complaining about the treatment I had received and the lack of any form of apology or explanation. I received an effusive and apologetic letter back by return. There had been many misunderstandings and misinterpretations of the whole issue. Rest assured, I was welcome to return to Zambia at any time. P.S. Glenda sent her love. A few weeks later I was back in Lusaka on some other story. It was a brief visit. I was back on base when I started to receive 'phone calls from friends in the Zambian capital. What had I been up to now? Special branch had been looking for me all over town, knocking down doors, searching hotels and friends' houses and demanding to know where I was. One Zambia? One tragi-comic enigma.

*Sir Roy Welensky,
Prime Minister of the
Federation of Rhodesia
and Nyasaland, enjoyed
relaxing in the company
of Old Africa Hands.*

*Is it a bird or is it a
plane?* Peter Niesewand
of The Guardian, *Tony
Rider of the* Rand Daily
Mail *and the author
survey the Zambian
sky.*

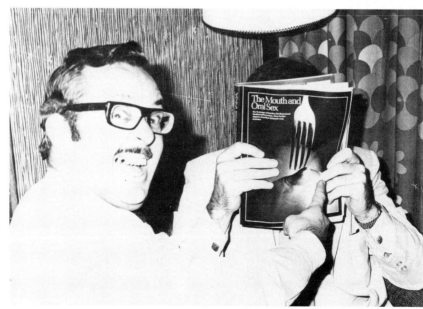

Reg Lancaster of the Daily Express *gives advice to young Zambians who had asked how man gets to the moon.*

◀▥▥ **Previous Page**

Top: *John Bulloch and namesake in Zambian bush.*

Bottom: *Go-getting Tony White of Reuters works on another exclusive.*

CHAPTER NINE

ARMAGEDDON IN THE ARMPIT

At that moment, even though we were right there, we did not know about the famine in Biafra. We were starving – in the cosseted sense of being bloody hungry. It had been 48 hours since we had last had a meal in Lagos. Now, 500 miles east in the ruins of Port Harcourt, which had just been recaptured by troops of Nigeria's Third Marine Commando Division, we were looking for something to eat and drink. Once Biafra's only access to the sea, Port Harcourt was devastated and seemingly deserted. A fetid blanket of mist and steam from the surrounding mangrove swamps hung over the streets, adding to the rather eerie atmosphere.

Col Benjamin Adekunle, commander of the Third Division, who earned the name 'Black Scorpion' with his venomous tirades against foreign pressmen who had the temerity to appear in his fiefdom, had accorded us his usual welcome. A burly sergeant had slapped, poked and pushed us onto the back of a truck and driven us at lunatic speed to the Cedar Palace Hotel in the centre of what had been town. The Cedar Palace had never been one of the greatest hostelries in West Africa. It had quickly become known as the 'Seedy Palace'. Like most other largish buildings in Port Harcourt, it had been shelled repeatedly over three months by the Nigerians as they advanced. Crumbling, reeking, and in complete darkness, it had no running water, electricity or plumbing.

But the door was open and using the portable lights carried by Phil Tibbenham's BBC *Panorama* crew, we found a few blankets and tried to make ourselves comfortable. A staff officer had arrived, saluted smartly, and told us 'Compliments of the GOC [Adekunle]. He regrets he is too busy fighting the war to see you immediately but asks that you avail yourselves of whatever facilities you can find.' We protested about the lack of any food or the facilities for obtaining any. 'The GOC is military governor in this region,' he said, waving his arm around the empty streets. 'His instructions are that you may help yourself to anything you can find.'

The *Panorama* producer, an energetic, restless young man, rushed off into the night. The rest of us, including Tibbenham, Michael Wolfers of *The Times* and John Barnes of *Newsweek*, gathered in the gloom of the foyer to make a plan. In the hotel kitchens I had made the mistake of opening every drawer and cupboard in the hope of finding a tin of something. My enterprise was rewarded only by great swarms of mosquitoes which emerged and dispersed, mission bent, through the hotel. They, at least, would not go hungry tonight.

A triumphant *Panorama* man returned from his recce to announce that he had located some tins of food and bottles of soft drinks. We followed him out eagerly into the darkened streets. A couple of blocks away there was a shop, a general store. Sure enough, through the window we could see shelves lined with cans of beans and peas and a few bottles of the ubiquitous Coca Cola. The trouble was that the shop was very firmly shut, locked, barred and bolted.

'We have Adenkunle's permission to help ourselves,' the producer cried. He grabbed a large lump of rubble and began pounding at the padlock on the door. In the cold light of day and in different circumstances, none of us would have even considered what we then did. We seized rocks and any other implement handy and began attacking the shop's fortifications with a manic frenzy.

We were stopped in mid-pillage a few minutes later by a quiet voice from behind us in the street. 'Good evening, gentlemen. May I help you?' Suddenly feeling very sheepish, we muttered something weak about having permission from the military governor. We then introduced ourselves to the stranger, a stocky Lebanese in his shirt sleeves who grasped our hands in turn and raised an eyebrow as we explained who we were.

'You are international journalists?' he enquired quietly. 'You come from these famous organisations like the BBC and *The Times*? Then tell me, gentlemen, have you come to report – or to loot?'

I shall never forget the shame and humiliation of that moment and nor, I'm sure, will my colleagues. Our new friend, of course, was absolutely right. We were attempting to break and enter – and loot. The Lebanese was the owner of the shop. He produced a set of keys and unlocked the door (our exertions had made very little impact on the locks). Quietly he served us, demanding outrageous prices for every item. I paid the equivalent of a couple of pounds for one small can of baked beans. We did not complain. How could we? We would happily have paid whatever he had demanded to expunge our guilt. We crept back to our fly-blown refuge at the Seedy for what must have been one of the quietest repasts in the history of hackdom.

The Nigerian civil war, 1967-70, was fought on two fronts: the bloody, bitter battles fought by brothers and cousins as the Federal forces, vastly superior in manpower and equipment, encircled the secessionist Ibos of Biafra, and the equally unscrupulous propaganda war fought by both sides. It thus became a war in which the journalists covering it were polarised, ensnared in conflicting allegiances, emotions and contradictory positions. Colleagues who were involved can still be found arguing acrimoniously among themselves about the rights and wrongs of 'the Biafran episode'. Some have never spoken to each other again. It was also the first African conflict in which television coverage had a major impact. Britain had retained great hopes for its African flagship when it gained independence in 1960 despite the fact that Nigeria, the most populous nation in Africa, with 50 million people, embraced an area twice the size of Egypt and had more than 200 tribes and all the built-in disadvantages that implies. Many of its leaders had been educated at Eton, Oxford and Cambridge and many of its officer corps had been to Sandhurst. There was an efficient and experienced civil service. Nigeria also contained some of Africa's most important natural resources – groundnuts, cocoa, tin, rubber, timber – and oil. A federal system had been assembled for independence, the country having been divided up into regions based on the main tribal groupings – the Yoruba of the West, the Ibo of the East and the Hausa-Fulani under their feudal Muslim emirs in the vast Northern Region.

Tensions soon began to stretch and strain this flimsy political patchwork. At one stage, police had to use teargas to break up a riot in the Federal Parliament in Lagos during which an Hon Member had tried to brain the Hon Speaker with the Mace.

Corruption was blatant, personal fortunes were amassed and regional and tribal rivalries surfaced throughout the land. Civilian rule came abruptly and violently to an end in January 1966 when a group of young, mainly Ibo, army officers attempted a revolution.

In Lagos, the rebels seized Sir Abubakar Tafawa Balewa, drove him out of the city, shot him and left his body in a ditch. In Ibadan, the Western Region capital, Chief Samuel Akintola died in a shoot-out with the rebels. In Kaduna in the north, Major Chukwuma Nzeogwu, Sandhurst-trained, led an assault on the official residence of Sir Ahmadu Bello, Sardauna (ruler) of Sokoto. The powerful Northern Region premier was put against a wall and shot dead. Africa's giant was in military hands and would experience only brief periods of civilian rule thereafter.

John Osman, recently appointed the BBC's Commonwealth Correspondent, had been in Lagos just before the coup, covering the first Commonwealth Prime Ministers Conference to be held outside

London. With a television crew he had then travelled to the northern region for a feature story and was within striking distance of
Kaduna when the Sardauna was killed. Osman was still getting
used to TV technique, but he was one of the most experienced and
competent reporters in the business.

He soon had Major Nzeogwu in front of his camera to explain
what had happened. The reaction to this straightforward piece of
journalism was to haunt him for months and stays a painful memory to this day. It is worth while, perhaps, giving the full transcript.

A cool, jaunty Major Nzeogwu: 'Well, when we went in there [the
Sardauna's residence], there were a lot of guards, policemen and some
of us. Naturally, they tried to shoot us, so we shot them first.'

Osman: 'Were there many casualties?'

Nzeogwu: 'Oh, not very many, no.'

Osman: 'Can you give me an idea?'

Nzeogwu: 'I don't know. On our side, yes, one...and our
injured...and the number of policemen, I think about three or four
have been killed.'

Osman: 'Did the Sardauna himself attempt to fight?'

Nzeogwu: 'No, we didn't see him until the time we actually shot
him. He ran away from his house when we fired the first few shots
from an anti-tank gun into the building. The whole roof was blown
off and the place was still alight. Then we went to the rear of the
house and there searched it from room to room until we found him
among the women and children, hiding himself. So we took away the
women and children and took him.'

Osman: 'Were the women and children safe, or did they die?'

Nzeogwu: 'Oh they were safe. No problem at all. We didn't bother much with them. We had to get them out in front because they
tried to surround him and protect him. They were mostly the women
of his harem, and children.'

Osman: 'There was one report that one of his wives died. Is this
true in fact?'

Nzeogwu: 'Oh, that is possible because we fired so many shots
and in the darkness, you know, accidents are bound to occur, yes.'

To Osman this was a routine, short interview with one of the
coup leaders. 'They were basic reporter's questions. He was the guy
in charge and we arrived raw, merely trying to establish what had
gone on. Of course the events he was describing were pretty horrific
but it certainly wasn't my job to express shock and dismay to this
young, pumped-up officer who was now clearly in charge of Kaduna.
It didn't cross my mind that I was conducting an interview in a way
that some people might find offensive.' John and his crew jumped

into a charter plane, flew back to Lagos and 'shipped' the film to the BBC on the first London-bound aircraft. It was carried prominently on TV news bulletins.

The reaction in Britain was fast and furious. The BBC switchboard was jammed with calls of protest, most of them abusive, about the way Osman had handled the interview. There were questions in the House of Commons, an outcry in the Lords and furious letters to Fleet Street. Sir Bryan Sharwood-Smith, a former Governor of Northern Nigeria, wrote to the editor of the *Telegraph* from his home in Bexhill-on-Sea, Suffolk, expressing his outrage.

'Sir...as scores of others must have been I was shocked to see on BBC television news the principal murderer interviewed, just as though he was a successful footballer, as he described the "operation" that he had conceived and carried out with so much ruthlessness and cunning.' Sir Bryan demanded to know, 'What effect is this apparent condonation of mass murder going to have on the more impressionable and less knowledgeable of its viewers in this country? Is this another example of BBC "realisms"? Is it suggested that this is merely the sort of thing that one can expect in Africa?' (Unfortunately it was to be just that, as Sir Bryan, as an Old Africa Hand, should have known.)

Another former expatriate who had lived in Nigeria wanted to know '...has political expediency reached such cynical depths that we accept without protest the most barbaric behaviour in the name of Commonwealth unity?' To his astonishment, Osman learned that a senior member of the BBC had also faulted him on the grounds that his manner 'seemed to take the murder for granted', although the BBC Board of Governors stood by him and sent him a message of congratulation.

The fact was that in 1966 people were genuinely shocked to see – as opposed to read – what kind of outrages were perpetrated in wars, coups and upheavals. It was the appearance and demeanour of Major Nzeogwu, coolly describing in front of the camera the murder of the Sardauna, not Osman's questions, that caused the outrage. Had Osman written up the same interview in a newspaper there would have been no protest. At that time, in the United States, millions of Americans were sitting at home in front of their television sets watching in technicolor just how sons, brothers and lovers were dying very nasty deaths in Vietnam. They were watching the gory, not reading about the glory. Such was the impact of television news film that the anti-war movement in America burgeoned into a potent force.

The BBC was to be involved in a number of controversies in Nigeria before the agonies of civil war were over but now it was the turn of the scribes. The major's revolution failed. Major-General Aguiyi-Ironsi, the army commander, rallied loyal troops, rounded up the rebels and established the first military regime and abolished the regions. In the north, the suspicion grew that the major's revolt and its aftermath were part of an Ibo plot to seize power. Many thousands of Ibos lived in ghetto-like conditions in the northern towns. By mid-1966, word was reaching Lagos of widespread massacres of Ibos in serious unrest in the north.

In June David Loshak, the *Telegraph* man who had been gaoled and charged with sedition in Sierra Leone, was arrested in Lagos after disclosing that the number of deaths in the north was much closer to 600 than the 92 admitted by the government. Loshak was interrogated 'most properly and politely' by the Nigerian police and held in a prison ante-room overnight before being deported on the next flight to London. An official announcement in Lagos said the *Telegraph* was free to send another correspondent to Nigeria, but that they should ensure he was a 'responsible person'. As with most deportations of journalists, it was a fairly safe bet that Loshak had come too close to the truth for the government's comfort. It was learned later that his estimate of 600 deaths in the north was, if anything, too modest. The Nigerian government's backhander in suggesting the *Telegraph* send a more responsible man was also mischievous. Within weeks, the Lagos government had expelled two of the most careful and responsible resident foreign correspondents, Walter Schwartz of *The Guardian* and *The Observer* and Lloyd Garrison of the *New York Times*. An unofficial, but onerous, form of censorship was also imposed.

Ironsi himself was not long for this world. In July, in a counter-coup by Northern army officers, he was whipped and then executed. Following more chaos, confusion and bloodshed, Lt-General Yakubu 'Jack' Gowon, a 31-year-old Northerner, emerged as Nigeria's leader and convened a constitutional conference. But in the Eastern Region, the military governor, Lt-Colonel Emeka Ojukwu, an ambitious Ibo officer and the Oxford-educated son of a wealthy Nigerian businessman, refused to accept Gowon's position or the invitation to the conference.

As the killing of Ibos in the Northern Region reached pogrom proportions, Ojukwu called on all Easterners to return home and took control of all Federal assets and revenues in the East. Many thousands of Ibos from all parts of Nigeria fled 'home'. In May 1967, Ojukwu proclaimed secession and the new state of Biafra – after the Bight of Biafra, the swampy, sweaty bay lapping the shores of this corner of the continent, known to Old Hands as 'the armpit of Africa'. The scene was set for a tropical Armageddon.

Nigeria was shaping up for a major story, but it was competing for newspaper space – and television and radio time – with other crises elsewhere in the world. I was covering the humiliating and shameful British withdrawal from Aden. (If Biafra was the armpit of the empire, I challenge anyone to name a more suitable candidate for the rectum than Aden, and yet its then strategic value was indisputable, as the Six Day War in the Middle East demonstrated clearly. Within months, Aden had been shovelled by a totally unnerved Whitehall into the Soviet Union's receptive backyard.) In international news terms, Biafra's secession and the inevitable, subsequent war had to compete with conflicts as diverse as those between the Israelis and Arabs, the Indians and the Pakistanis and Mayor Daley's police and demonstrators during the Democratic Party Convention in Chicago.

Correspondents who had been sent to Nigeria to cover the crisis there understandably became restless when no war broke out. Norman Kirkham, the bluff *Sunday Telegraph* man who had the bearing of a soap-opera Scotland Yard inspector and the genteel-shabby air of one of Graham Greene's less-successful, fictional British diplomats, had among others become bored with the limited delights of Lagos.

With other correspondents, Kirkham, fearing he was missing out on other more important stories developing elsewhere, cabled the *Telegraph* 'ASSURED WAR OUTBREAK UNIMMINENT STOP REBASING STOP REGARDS'. He and other hacks caught that night's VC-10 flight to London from Lagos. They arrived at Heathrow to discover that hostilities had, in fact, broken out in Nigeria during the night. They swiftly boarded a return flight to Lagos, arriving back in time to file quick cables 'IGNORE EARLIER STOP VIEW DEVELOPMENTS NATURALLY REMAINING LAGOSWISE'. It would be some time before the office accountants started puzzling over this day-return fare to West Africa on the air travel credit card accounts.

One correspondent who had not wearied of Lagos diversions was Walter 'The Butler' Partington of the *Daily Express*. Walter had discovered the delights and charms of black womanhood in the Congo some years before. In the nightclubs of Nigeria's capital he found the dusky beauties of the evening that much more obliging – and inexpensive. Worse, the stocky, fast-talking *Express* Man-On-The-Spot had a tendency to fall in at the flutter of an eyelid.

Most hacks shrugged off long, tedious Lagos nights by desporting themselves in the shower of their hotel rooms with the large-buttocked ladies from the Green Parakeet Nite Club and Bar down the road. (Night porters at the Federal Palace Hotel, the horribly misnamed 'five-star' hostelry which had become Nigeria's 'Hotel Imperial' would yawningly but obligingly chalk up an asterisk on the bill if a hack reeled in with a Parakeet poppet. She would appear on the hotel bill, cunningly disguised as an extra half room rate. Should there be any queries from the accountants it was 'Important contacts, old boy. There was a war on y'know'.)

Not Walter. He fell wildly and passionately in love with a sloe-eyed charmer on the Green Parakeet's tiny dance floor, and, being the English gentleman he was, asked her dreamily, around 2 a.m., 'My place or yours, loov?' The young lady was only slightly taken aback but nonetheless flattered. 'Oh, Walter, I would be honoured if you would come to my home.' It had been a long, hard day, but Partington, a tough, no-nonsense Yorkshireman, was in a hurry. He grabbed the lady and whisked her onto the street with one arm, hailing a cab with the other. Lagos taxis were not governed by the Hackney Carriage Act and were, thus, not quite up to the same standard of condition or service. Even so, a battered, spluttering, springless car responded to Our Man's imperial wave with amazing alacrity. By happy coincidence, the taxi driver turned out to be his new love's 'cousin' and the happy hack was whisked off into the Nigerian night for an evening of magic and madness.

Long after other kraal cocks had crowed on the following day, Partington came to under a reed mattress in a mud-and-wattle hut in a tiny village some 40 miles north of Lagos. Next to him, sloe-eyes snored gently. 'Jeezus! It's 10 a.m. Where the bloody hell am I?' It was a working day in a war zone and here he was 'in the middle of bloody jungle' with no signs of those most important of journalistic necessi-ties: transport and communications. There was no 'phone, no taxi, no bus 'and very few people who spoke a word of any known language'. A demented *Express* Man-on-the-Spot rushed around shouting and bully-ing, just like the crazy white men that the Yoruba had become used to in the old days of the slave trade. Finally, he located someone with a broken down truck who was prepared, after much haggling of the Nigerian kind, to negotiate a passage to Lagos.

Walter was suddenly overtaken by remorse for the erstwhile love of his life. He went back to the little hut, shook the young lady awake and explained that he thought she was absolutely bloody marvellous, that he would never forget that wonderful night, but that his Big White Bosses in London would want to know why he was not in Lagos, making some effort to cover the war that was going on. Trying to make it sound like an inconsequential after-thought, he added 'By the way, loov. How much do I owe yer?' From beneath the reed mattress, she averted her eyes, fluttered large lashes and said 'Oh, Walter, Walter...that will be five shillingis'. Partington, now consumed only by a passion to get back to Lagos and some form of communication with London, was startled.

'Five shillings? Five bloody bob!' he fumbled for his wallet. 'Here, loov, here's a fiver...buy yourself a new mud hut on t' *Daily Express*!'

Partington got back to Lagos and was one of the few to cover the war for his newspaper from both sides, not an easy feat. He did so, of course, in the rapidly outdating fashion of a Fleet Street swash-buckle that was being overtaken by the instant reality relayed by television. He was possibly the last of the first-person print heroes, but where there was a story, Walter was there, and his accounts remain a vivid tribute to his get-up-and-go approach to journalism.

His love of the earthier side of Africa and its winsome earth-lings was commemorated in a novel he dashed off after his last assignment in Africa. Its anti-hero was a young journalist who was constantly being beaten to the story by more cynical, older hands. There are many dusky, fairly explicit love scenes. It is a panegyric to West African womanhood. It was not a best-seller but must be some-thing of a collector's item. It was called *Screw*!

Despite the reticence of the hero of his novel, there was nothing self-effacing about Walter's abrasive approach to the story. In the Nigerian war, he was swiftly into battle – with the Black Scorpion, Colonel Benjamin Adekunle and the men of the Federal Third Marine Commando Division. In Port Harcourt, Partington became infuriated with the mercurial, unpredictable little officer. 'Are you really in control of your men, Colonel?' he demanded at an impromp-tu press conference. The Scorpion cast a beady eye over the assem-bled foreign hacks paraded in front of him. 'Is that Mr Partington of the *Daily Express*?' 'Yes!' said Walter defiantly. The Scorpion nodded slowly. 'I am reliably informed,' he said, 'that you lost your nerve the other day at the front.'

'I bloody well did nothing of the kind,' spluttered Walter.

'My soldiers tell me you funked it,' insisted the Colonel.

'Let me tell you that I was a tank commander in the last war while you were still in short bloody trousers,' Walter bellowed. 'And what's more I got wounded.' Adekunle smiled without his eyes.

'Ah, but that, Mr Partington,' he said, quietly, 'was a long time ago.'

In fact, Walter had far more reason to be upset at the slight. Only a few days before, he had been present when one colleague was killed and another badly wounded in action on the southern front. He had been lucky to escape injury himself.

Priya Ramrakha was one of several Kenyan Asians of the Mohamed Amin school of fearless photo-journalism. Tall, quietly spoken and humourful, Priya lacked Mohamed's ruthlessness but none of his courage. As one of the youngest photographers for *Time* magazine he had been shot up in the Congo, beaten up in Zanzibar and deported from a dozen trouble spots with his first-class film intact. The Asian correspondents frequently encountered more problems than their white colleagues. Nervous troops, officials, mercenaries or other obstacles to a journalist's progress were never really sure who they were. Like his good friend Amin, Priya had been through it all and emerged with a slow smile and a knowing shrug.

In October 1968, Ramrakha, still working for *Time*, was with a group of journalists accompanying Adekunle's 'commandos' on their jittery advance towards Umuahia, north of Port Harcourt. The hacks included Partington, Peter Sissons, then an ITN reporter, his cameraman, Cyril Page and soundman Archie Powert and a three-man CBS team. They were with an 18-man forward patrol which ran straight into a Biafran ambush and bursts of withering fire from snipers on three sides. Priya was shot dead as he ran for cover in a ditch. Sissons was badly wounded in both legs.

The BBC – 'Auntie Beeb' in those days to friend, foe and employee – was having more Nigerian problems. Frederick Forsyth, a self-confident but modest young reporter, had recently joined the radio department after one of those rather gruelling all-day tests the Beeb put their recruits through to assess ability, responsibility, resilience and, above all, resonance. Freddy's background was ideal: a good middle-class upbringing in Kent, an uninspired education at a minor public school, conscription in the Royal Air Force where he had learned to fly, and after the then obligatory service on a provincial newspaper, good foreign correspondent's grounding with Reuters, first in Paris and then in Berlin. He was possessed of a picaresque imagination which was to be invaluable in his future calling as one of the most successful thriller writers of the age but was of highly controversial merit in his shortish but colourful career as an African correspondent.

All good journalists have to have an imagination, and have to give it rein from time to time to make any given story come alive. Freddy, from the lofty heights to which his career as a novelist has taken him, readily admits to one overheated story he put on the wires as a young Reuters man in East Berlin which could have started World War Three.

Driving home late one night he found himself suddenly hemmed in by Soviet tanks, heavy armour, rocket launchers and mobile infantry carriers moving menacingly down Karl Marx Allee. He rushed to his telex to file a descriptive piece to the agency, coupled with an interpretive paragraph suggesting that a Russian assault on West Berlin was under way.

Lyndon Johnson in the White House and Sir Alec Douglas Home at Number 10 Downing Street, were awoken on the strength of the Forsyth flash. Older, wiser hands on Reuters London desk zapped back to Freddy, asking him to double-check that what he had seen was not merely a rehearsal for the imminent May Day parade in the city. He did. It was. He recanted, or as we say in the trade, 'rowed back', and the world slept peacefully, for a few nights at least.

With the Beeb, young Freddy had been pounding the domestic beat but straining at the leash to 'go foreign', preferably back to Europe where he had contacts, a few of the languages and good background knowledge. In the perverse way of British institutions, he was finally called in for his first foreign assignment. 'Africa, old boy, place called Biafra in fact...bit of a bush war...could be a fortnight's trip but take your toothpaste.' It was to transform young Forsyth's life but he was not that enthusiastic. 'I had never been to Africa before, apart from a brief visit to Tangier. I didn't particularly want to go. I only went on the understanding that I'd be there for a couple of weeks at the outside.'

Clearly it was out of the question to travel to Biafra via Lagos so Freddy took what became known to visiting hacks in those days as the Douala run – a scheduled flight from Paris to Douala, an old slave port on the coast of the Cameroons. From there it was a two-day drive to Enugu, the Biafran capital, or an hour's flight to Mamfe on the border and then into Enugu by road, a journey through secondary jungle made seemingly interminable by numerous roadblocks manned by what one hack called, memorably, 'amateur Biafrans', officious young men who prodded you with real guns or wooden replicas, demanded papers you could obtain only when you had arrived, and generally made themselves unpleasant.

Sandy Gall and his ITN crew were among the many who found the journey particularly onerous. In those days a three-man television news crew had to travel with up to fifteen aluminium trunks of equipment. The technology of the time was film, not tape. Large Arriflex or Auricon cameras, heavy tripods, large tape decks, lights and light stands and battery packs, large magazines of film, dozens of spares and accessories, made up consignments that could weigh up to a ton. Much of the equipment – long lenses and gun-microphones – looked like weaponry to untrained, suspicious eyes and added to the hazards and frustrations of moving in and out of war zones, particularly those in places with pretty primitive communications, like Biafra.

Few newsmen deserve higher accolades than the TV crews who had to manoeuvre all this equipment into war zones, stand up and move around in firefights to do their job, and then get their film, themselves and their equipment out again. All this against the clock. It made the average scribe's lot look simple.

Sandy and his crew, Cyril Page and Mick Doyle, were assigned to Biafra directly from the Six Day War in 1967. They chartered an aircraft to Mamfe and hired, at great expense, a vehicle of dubious reliability to get them through to Enugu. They were stopped at 'professional Biafran' roadblocks a dozen times, and obliged to unload and spread out their luggage all over the road in the dust while it was poked and peered over by young men who clearly had not got a clue what they were looking for. There is nothing quite so maddening as an African roadblock. It brings out the worst in any species. Gall and Co finally made it to Enugu and then attempted to get accreditation. Bits of paper were needed to negotiate the roadblocks. They were frustrated at every turn. The 'information director' was away, asleep, or in consultation. They were refused entry to the hotel in which they were staying. They did not have accreditation. In the apposite and pithy words of Cyril Page, 'What a fucking dog's breakfast.'

George de Carvalhao of *Life* magazine, organised a press 'council of war' in the deserted Enugu Hotel. He wanted signatures for a letter to Ojukwu complaining about the attitude of his Information Department and asking for facilities for the journalists who had taken the trouble to make the journey to cover the war from his point of view. All signed, including the newly arrived Freddy Forsyth of the BBC. Sandy Gall was 'fed up with the bloody Biafrans and their paranoid suspicions'. The situation was 'just like Katanga, but in Biafra nothing was easy, neither getting in nor reporting the war'. They were repeatedly promised interviews with Ojukwu but nothing happened. When they tried to get to the 'front' to film, they were harassed at every turn.

Gall and his crew finally got a few seconds of film at Nsukka before being threatened by a Biafran official. They were driven straight back to Enugu where, finally, Ojukwu emerged for his first press conference. The Biafran leader was 'dressed in a leopard-spotted battledress, his big black beard as big and as bushy as W G Grace's, and sat down in front of a Biafran flag depicting a huge rising sun against a black and green background,' Sandy recalled. 'He spoke slowly and in a rather monotonous voice but he undoubtedly had presence. He exuded optimism, saying he was quite sure his army would be able to hold off the Federal troops. I was not so sure, having just seen the nervous retreat of some of his men at Nsukka. Perhaps he was too British to trust the press. But I thought with the *New York Times* and *Life* magazine there for America, with the BBC and ourselves for Britain and with Reuters for the rest of the world, he had a remarkable opportunity to spread his message far and wide. But, in my opinion, he muffed it.'

Most journalists who went to Biafra in the early days felt, in the great tradition of instinctively supporting the underdog, that the cause was just and one that should be covered. But their experiences in Biafra, with its strutting, arrogant officials, its unpredictable mercenaries and its long-winded leader, made them anxious to use any excuse to get out of the place and into another theatre, any other theatre.

Freddy Forsyth felt differently. He was fascinated by Ojukwu and his ideals. He stayed on long after his colleagues, filing regularly for the BBC on the way the Biafran forces were giving as good as they got, and better. 'Ojukwu was a massively charismatic figure who enjoyed the support of 90 per cent of his people...their support was fanatical and they were fighting tooth and claw.' It was the romantic vision of the Biafran leader and his cause, but the young BBC man became increasingly and unashamedly committed to both.

Freddy later wrote: 'It was also clear to me that the Nigerian Army was a rabble, a shambles from beginning to end and that Gowon was no leader.' Having been involved with them both, I have no quarrel with that. 'I formed the view that this was going to be a very long affair and could potentially be extremely bloody. I filed that viewpoint.' It did not amuse the Commonwealth Office or the British High Commissioner in Lagos who flew to London to brief his superiors on 'the damage this callow young reporter from the BBC was doing'.

The message got through to the BBC hierarchy. John Osman, by now the Beeb's Commonwealth Correspondent and a friend of Freddy, was summoned by the foreign news desk, shown one of Forsyth's dispatches and asked to comment.

'It was a very good piece of reporting,' Osman remembers. 'Freddy had been with a Biafran unit which had ambushed some Federal troops. The copy was alive and rang true. Like many other correspondents, Freddy was incensed by the British government's support for the Federal side and had added an emotional tag to the effect that this had made him ashamed to be British. (In numerous subsequent African adventures I was to have precisely the same sentiment – and no inhibition about expressing it in my stories.)

'It was this that seemed to have upset the foreign desk. I explained that the guys in these circumstances obviously feel strongly about things, especially in a war situation when you're being shot at. I suggested we just cut out the last line and no harm would have been done. The foreign editor decided that Forsyth would have to be cautioned.'

Freddy had been sent to Biafra as a result of a message to the BBC from Angus McDermid. Angus, the GOAH, had sensed Ibo secession and probably civil war long before most other journalists. Realising that getting news out of a blockaded eastern region would be difficult, he set up the 'Douala run', slipping out of Lagos to the offshore Spanish island of Fernando Po and then through Cameroon. When secession came, Angus was the only journalist in the East. Most of the cable and wireless communications people were Ibos and had brought all their equipment back with them from other parts of Nigeria. They established telex and radio links with Europe and set up their own powerful transmitter which beamed Radio Biafra over a wide region.

It was a frustrating time for McDermid. He had the story to himself and efficient means of getting it out – but it was the time of the Six Day War and the problems of West Africa could not compete in news terms with another Middle East conflict. To his astonishment, McDermid then heard Radio Biafra announce that he had been declared *persona non grata* by the government in Lagos.

'To me it was very significant, because to be West African Correspondent for the BBC without having an entrée into Nigeria was a distinct handicap.' He slipped out of the Biafran back door to Douala and contacted the BBC who checked with Lagos and told him no such decision had been taken. He returned to the Nigerian capital and checked in with the Chief Information Officer (who, I remember, was a particularly unpleasant man, given to threatening correspondents with deportation or worse if they wrote anything he had not authorised). He told Angus 'You are always welcome in our country, but if you ever set foot in Biafra again, you will be declared *persona non grata!*'

The Radio Biafra broadcast had clearly been a cunning ploy by the Biafrans to gain for themselves a resident BBC correspondent. It would clearly be a major bonus in the propaganda war to have the world's major radio network reporting out of Enugu. Back in Lagos, McDermid realised that it was going to be impossible to cover both sides of the conflict on a daily basis. There had to be a man in place in each capital. The BBC agreed and sent Freddy Forsyth to Biafra. Thus were the journalistic battle lines drawn. From the start of the

war, antagonisms arose between correspondents covering the
Federal side and those who got into Biafra. The frustrations were
compounded by the lies and distortions pumped out by both sides.
Freddy was deeply upset by the message from the BBC. Back in
London he had a long session with the foreign news editor. Osman
remembers Freddy emerging from the interview white-faced and
enraged. 'John, I'm finished...Arthur's told me my reporting is too
emotive and that I need more political experience.' Forsyth was
given the job of assistant to the BBC's distinguished political correspondent, Peter Hardiman-Scott. 'We all thought he'd been treated
rather harshly,' said Osman. 'He was a first-class reporter and the
few flaws in his copy could have been ironed out with a few kind
words. But he was only 28 and the BBC political staff was certainly
no demotion.'

Freddy did not see it that way. In any event, the Palace of
Westminster offered none of the adrenalin-pumping excitement of
West Africa at war. After a few days, he simply packed a bag, shut
up his London flat and made his way back to Biafra to work as a
freelance. 'My main motive was anger at the cover-up. I'm a reporter
to my boot heels and don't like managed news. Someone, somewhere
was trying to tell us what we should read, what we should listen to
and what we should see. I didn't like that.'

Back in London, the Forsyth saga took a rather bizarre turn. An
increasingly concerned Beeb hierarchy, knowing just how upset
Freddy was over the Biafran episode, began to fear the worst. Later
that same day, two very senior BBC men, Godfrey Talbot and Allan
Wheatley, were sent to Freddy's Hampstead flat to try and find out
what had happened to him. Talbot was a famous World War II correspondent and royal reporter and Wheatley, the BBC's industrial
correspondent.

'When they got to the flat there was no sign of Freddy but all the
evidence that something was wrong...full milk bottles on the step and
newspapers and post piled unopened around the entrance,' Osman
recalls. 'We had seriously considered the possibility that he may have
shoved his head in the gas oven in frustration and rage and so these
two very distinguished BBC men put their shoulders to the door and
broke in. Freddy, of course, was not there and rather shamefacedly
Talbot and Wheatley tried to repair the door they'd broken. It was only
a few days later, when his copy started to appear in other newspapers,
that the Beeb realised he'd gone back to Biafra.' Back at the front,
Forsyth became the resident guru, consulted by the visiting hacks on
all aspects of the Biafran cause. A mischievous front-page story in the
Nigerian Observer carried the headline 'BBC MAN JOINS REBELS'.

To be sure, Freddy was putting the case for Ojukwu and his cause and was smarting from his perceived maltreatment at the hands of the BBC and the British establishment. But his lively mind was working on other things. One rainy day in Enugu, a group of visiting hacks was engaged in a rowdy poker game.

Freddy interrupted from a corner of the room. 'Don't make so much noise, chaps...I'm thinking about the plot.' His colleagues thought he was still brooding about what had happened to him in London. They were wrong. He was thinking about THE plot – the story of *The Day of the Jackal*, his first novel which was to become, almost overnight, a runaway best-seller and establish him as a world-famous writer.

The propaganda war between the Nigerians and the Biafrans obliged correspondents to pick sides. Those who found themselves with the Biafrans were scornful of colleagues covering the war from Lagos, suggesting that life was a jolly round of diplomatic cocktail parties and government handouts. Nothing could have been further from the truth. Most of us in Lagos were locked in constant conflict with obstructive and obnoxious Nigerian officials, trying to get permission to get to the front. As for the diplomatic circuit, the British High Commission maintained its great African tradition of making it clear reporters were a nuisance and an embarrassment.

The Nigerians imposed various forms of official and unofficial censorship. We did not all have McDermid's facility for dictating in Welsh. As in many African countries, the Nigerians seemed to believe that foreign governments exercised the same control over newspapermen as they did over theirs. Peter Enahoro, one of Nigeria's top journalists, had written cynically that 'all foreigners were held responsible for the actions of their governments at home'. John de St Jorre, who covered the war from both sides for *The Observer* and afterwards wrote by far the most readable and objective instant history, concluded that the news coverage was on the whole 'shallow, emotional and biased', although he concedes that the Federal Ministry of Information displayed 'truly, appalling inefficiency'. The press, particularly the British press, had a patronising attitude towards black Africans and did not take seriously 'their sovereignties and sensibilities'. For many news editors, 'strongly personalised crocodile-infested river and "cannibal" copy was all that they required from their reporters in darkest Africa unless, of course, their own nationals or other whites were involved.'

All the *Telegraph* wanted was coverage of the war, and the foreign desk would not have objected in the least if we had to swim among crocodiles and dine with cannibals to get it. In the early days, the Nigerian press and radio ignored the war entirely. In my room at the Federal Palace Hotel, I would tune in to the early local radio news in the vain hope that some mention might be made of what was going on at the front. The only oblique reference was the national slogan, chanted endlessly over the local air waves: 'To Keep Nigeria One Is A Task That Must Be Done.'

One morning, the radio bulletin began with the startling revelation that His Excellency Major-General Yakubu Gowon would be attending a school choral festival that very day. I yawned and turned over for a few more minutes in bed when the same bland voice, towards the end of the bulletin, said 'Early this morning, Russian tanks crossed into Czechoslovakia...' That was another of the problems in covering Nigeria at that time – there were too many competing, far more newsworthy crises.

The local office of Reuters slavishly bowed to the whims of the Federal government. The world's most famous news agency did not put out a story on the war unless it was contained in an official communiqué or uttered officially by a government minister. Reuters chief correspondent explained this away by pointing out just how much 'business' – the selling of communications equipment and 'news' services to the Federals – would be at stake if they did not toe the government line. The Reuters Number Two in Lagos, Sam Hall, was deeply ashamed of this attitude and expended much time and effort seeking out unofficial news of the war, only to find his copy spiked by his commercially minded superiors.

Our main method of obtaining news on a daily basis in Lagos was unorthodox. We would tune into Radio Biafra, knowing that its own version of events would be of highly dubious authenticity but at least pertaining to the conflict. We would then make a telephone call to Brigadier Hassan Katsina, the charming Northern aristocrat who was then Federal Chief-of-Staff, bounce off him the claims of Radio Biafra and from his bluff, hearty responses attempt to cobble together some coherent account of what was going on.

For most of the remainder of the time we chased from arrogant officials to hostile military men trying to get 'permissions' to go to the front. When the call came, it was usually a last minute rush to the military airfield and hours, sometimes days later to be invited on one of the leaky, creaky DC-6 transports flown by ageing American drop-out pilots who had a disconcerting habit of flicking hot cigar ash over pools of aviation fuel. The return trips were even more unnerving. We were jammed in with dozens of young, frightened, wounded Federal troops who were being 'casevaced' out of the war zone.

Some of them had been wounded by their own NCOs for show-ing cowardice in the face of the enemy. Some had literally shot themselves in the foot or leg to get the hell out of there. On one trip, as the lights of Lagos came into view, the maimed and wounded got very excited and began shuffling and hobbling en masse towards the rear exit of the old aircraft, anxious to end their ordeal as soon as possible. Just how the American pilot managed to keep his trim to land only God and Uncle Sam know. The problem arose when we came to a halt on the tarmac.

The rear-door panic had turned into a near riot as the young soldiers clamoured to get out. The DC6 was a nose-wheel aircraft and the skipper had to keep the engines revving at high speed to prevent the overloaded tail crashing to the ground. It took a full 30 minutes for two very tired Federal lieutenants with batons, drawn pistols and hysterical harangues to move forward so the engines could be shut down and we could disembark.

On one trip to the southern front, we landed at Port Harcourt to some good news – Lt Col Adekunle, the Scorpion and excoriator of the international press, was back in Lagos 'for consultation'. Our host would be his second-in-command, Colonel Godwin Ally, another Sandhurst man, of course, but a very different personality to the abra-sive, unpredictable Adekunle. Godwin was tiny, even by my modest standards, but had a very proper military bearing, a charming smile and manner and a strict sense of propriety. Port Harcourt remained its sad devastated and deserted self, but the officer corps of the Third Marine Commando Division had made themselves very comfortable at the Shell-BP Compound some five miles from town. It had its own generators and there was running hot water, electric lights and a goodly reservoir of supplies left behind by the fleeing oilmen.

It had been, as always, a bad trip but the news of Adekunle's absence and the round, beaming face of Col Ally was most welcome. Things really began to look up when he invited us to the Shell com-pound 'for a snifter'. His reception may, or may not, have had some-thing to do with the fact that our press party included a very tall, very assertive but, in a war zone at least, infinitely attractive German girl who claimed to be freelancing for the West German news agency, DPA. I shall call her Helga (it may even have been her name). Godwin Ally was certainly impressed. 'Gentlemen,' he announced without looking at us, 'and LADY' he added with empha-sis, gazing up at Helga's damp, statuesque figure. 'Welcome to the headquarters of the victorious Third Marine Commando Division.' In the officers' mess at the Shell compound, Helga became the cen-tre of attraction for the officers of the Third Division, visibly relaxing in the absence of the GOC. Soul music was played continuously on a record player and she was asked by several officers to dance, which she did, gazing haughtily into the middle distance. We were plied with beer before Col Ally announced, to our dismay, that there was no accommodation for us at the compound and that once again we would have to make ourselves comfortable at 'The Seedy' – the Cedar Palace Hotel.

'But you, my dear,' he said, smiling at Helga, 'cannot go with these ruffians. We will find a room for you here.' We tried to determine, silently, if Helga thought this was such a good idea and whether we should insist on her accompanying us, in the interests of professional camaraderie. She shrugged. 'Zat is very kind of you,' she said to Ally. 'I would like zat.'

We were bundled into a truck and taken to the derelict hotel. The following morning Helga arrived, spluttering and muttering. We couldn't wait to hear what had happened. She had danced some more and then asked Godwin to show her to her room. He had done so, and apologising profusely, showed her a bathroom which he regretted she would have to share with him. A few minutes later, she was in her nightdress, cleaning her teeth, when there came a tap on the bathroom door and in walked the tiny Colonel. 'I'm so sorry, my dear,' he said. 'I was afraid this might happen.'

To her horror he moved to the toilet next to the basin, dropped his neatly pressed trousers and squatted down for a long, noisy crap. Still apologising, he finally finished, pulled up his trousers and, bidding her a good night, disappeared into his room. Helga was horrified. 'Zis is vat you call Sandhurst military training?' she asked us.

From Port Harcourt, Adekunle's men were pushing northwards in a two-pronged advance to the key Biafran-held towns of Aba and Owerri. Some of us were taken on the road to Aba where, we were told, the men of the Third Division had that morning taken an important village. We reached a promontory overlooking the village at lunchtime to find that the 'dawn attack' had yet to take place. The young troops were sprawled under trees and bushes, looking nervous and tired. From a ridge, a lieutenant indicated the 'target' village below. 'The rebels know we are here,' he whispered proudly. I was not surprised. Since the previous day, the little roadside settlement had been pounded by shells from 103 mm howitzers (standard NATO) and 90 mm shells from British-supplied Saladin armoured cars on positions behind us. They had been screaming overhead as we reached this forward position.

At about 2 p.m. the lieutenant began screaming at his men, beating them into some kind of formation with a swagger stick fashioned from a golf-club handle. The 'dawn attack' was about to begin on the deserted village. We watched from above as the troops moved in from three sides and began a shack-by-shack search.

Quite clearly, the place had long since been evacuated, both by the entire civilian population and by any Biafran forces that may, or may not, have been there. Suddenly one the soldiers opened fire with his automatic rifle. The place erupted in deafening gunfire as possibly 100 troops, their rifles switched to automatic, emptied their magazines into the deserted houses and shops and into the air. There was no sign of any Biafran, or anything that could possibly have been identified as opposition. As the firing died down, our escort officer turned to us and announced, 'Gentlemen, you have just been privileged to watch another victory for the Third Marine Commando Division'. A victory over what, we wondered as we made our way back to Port Harcourt.

This turned out to be the pattern of attack by Federal forces on all fronts. Major-General Alexander, a British member of the observer team in Nigeria, recorded his observations in the *Sunday Telegraph* in 1969. 'Federal forces advance astride the road towards the town, and when they get to within three or four miles of it they halt. They then start building up their ammunition. Before the assault they subject the outskirts of the town to artillery and armoured car fire. The Biafrans do not carry out a staunch defence of this objective. Once they have decided that the Federals are about to attack they pull out, taking everything moveable with them, and the Federals move in firing every round of ammunition they have. After occupying the town, the Federal forces sit down and wait for their ammunition to be replenished, and the Biafrans carry out a counter-attack by fire. Ammunition control, as we understand it, is non-existent on the Federal side, and during an advance a Federal soldier fires every round in his possession, whether he is meeting resistance or not.'

That was the 'war' as far as I witnessed it. Conventional Sandhurst tactics deployed in a highly unconventional way. There was much saluting, British army style, and much use of swagger stick discipline but, on the ground, one group of very frightened teenagers with superior firepower would fire everything they had, to reassure themselves, as well as hoping the enemy, another group of frightened teenagers, would be unnerved by the noise and go away. By all objective accounts, it was much the same on the Biafran side.

Jimmy Wilde ('By name and nature') of *Time* magazine observed what he described as 'the code of Kipling'. He described Major-General Phillip Effiong, the Biafran chief-of-staff, as looking like a British staff general until the very end – 'a polished Sam Browne belt, a sword for ceremonial occasions and a chaffeur-driven, khaki-coloured English Humber car bearing a general's flag. His officers were similarly indoctrinated – moustaches, swagger sticks, batmen, officers' messes.'

This strange mixture of Sandhurst parody and African reality was embodied in the volatile, crisp and strutting figure of Colonel Benjamin Adekunle. On my first Port Harcourt run he singled me out with his swagger stick from a group of colleagues, turned to an NCO and said: 'This man must have a haircut'. We all thought it a great joke until the NCO, deadly earnest, approached me and said 'This way, sir'. I was driven to the Shell compound, taken directly to the camp barber and given a Nigerian army haircut. I've paid good money for far worse haircuts in New York and London. Later Adekunle insisted that we all be kitted out with Federal army uniforms and boots before accompanying his men 'into battle'. We protested in vain that this would compromise our journalistic impartiality.

(The Black Scorpion was thereby responsible for the first security scare in Rhodesia's Eastern Highlands in another war ten years later. I had used my Nigerian-made army boots on a trout fishing break in those wonderful mountains, forgetting that military boot patterns were very much part of anti-terrorist tracking techniques. A police counter-insurgency unit, on a routine patrol a few days later, were alarmed to find in the mud on the banks of the trout stream the clear imprints of military boots with their 'Made In Nigeria' insignia discernible to trained eyes. Fortunately they had the presence of mind to check with the fishing syndicate whether any member or guest could possibly have been wearing such footwear before raising a full alert.)

Adenkunle could and would switch in a matter of hours from the formidable military disciplinarian to Black Power advocate and then to thoughtful, chummy philosopher over a couple of drinks. He reminded me, in many ways, of a young Hastings Banda, although both men would spurn the comparison. On more than one occasion, Jack Gowon, the Nigerian head-of-state, had to apologise for the outbursts of his Third Division commander. The Scorpion took great exception to the arrival in his sector of the international observer team, questioning their military competence. At one stage he threatened to flog General Arthur Raab of Sweden.

The observers had been invited by the Federal government to check on Biafran allegations of genocide. In the Shell compound mess, Adekunle rounded on Lt-Col Edward Pinnington, of Canada, a twice-wounded veteran of the Korean war. 'Are you here to further your own promotion?' Pinnington bristled. 'We are not here to discuss my career, sir. But since you ask, I have probably jeopardised my promotion chances by coming to Nigeria at short notice.' Pinnington asked to be withdrawn. The observers had angered Adekunle by insisting on making a gruelling two-day journey to the front by plane, dug-out canoe and car to investigate Canadian newspaper reports that 500 'innocent villagers' had been slaughtered by his troops.

John de St Jorre records an episode in Port Harcourt in the same year when Harold Wilson, then British Prime Minister, was due to visit the Scorpion's sector. 'Waiting for Wilson to arrive, having threatened to arrest a group of us who were covering the event if we did not stay rooted to the spot when the prime ministerial plane touched down, Adekunle then went and actually locked up a Nigerian producer of the Federal TV network who was making a crucial publicity film on Wilson's Nigeria visit.' The producer was released eventually, only on the intervention of Brigadier Katsina, the affable chief-of-staff (who once confided to a startled group of hacks that he wanted to be a 'dashing Fleet Street journalist').

Gowon was finally obliged to instruct Yusufu Gobir, the top civil servant at the Defence Ministry, to call a press conference to explain Adekunle's approach. Gobir was frank. 'You all know what he's like,' he told the assembled hacks, who fervently nodded their agreement. 'During his lucid periods he is fine and he does not mean any harm to anyone. He has these outbursts but he is friends again soon afterwards.' The Scorpion was relieved of his post not long afterwards and put in charge of reorganising the congested chaos in Lagos harbour, a task he performed with speed, skill and efficiency.

Late in 1968, a series of incidents occurred in the Scorpion's sector which demonstrated the power and the perils of television journalism. An ITN crew filmed another noisy Third Division attack on an empty Ibo village on the road to Owerri. The young lieutenant in charge of the unit was clearly aware that he was being filmed. He strutted and postured in front of the cameras, haranguing his men in English and clearly disappointed that there were no rebels in sight.

Suddenly, there was a triumphant shout from some of his men. They had grabbed a young Ibo, no more than 17 years old, racing away from the village on his bicycle. He was wearing only a pair of blue shorts. Terrified, bleeding and his hands bound behind his back with wire, he was hauled before the lieutenant who immediately announced – to the ITN camera – that here was a Biafran rebel prisoner.

The young man's agony and terror was as obvious as the Federal officer's intent to kill him. John Barnes of *Newsweek* tried to intervene, pleading that, if the young man was a Biafran soldier, he should accompany us back to Port Harcourt as a prisoner of war. The lieutenant knew he was still on camera – and here, as he saw it, was his moment of triumph.

'This man is a rebel soldier!' he shouted, and then turned to the young Ibo blubbering in the dust 'Stand to attention!' The young man tried to scramble to his feet. To the horror of the newsmen looking on, the lieutenant turned to camera, smiled and said 'You see, he understands an order. He is a military spy.' He then lifted the automatic rifle under his arm and pulled the trigger. The shattered body of the Ibo was blown across the dusty road by the force of the blast.

It was a shocked and trembling press party that arrived back in Port Harcourt that evening. They had witnessed – and filmed – the cold-blooded killing of an unarmed man. The film went out from Lagos on the same airliner as John Barnes, who reckoned the story was too 'hot' to file from the Nigerian capital. Barnes intended to file his piece from neighbouring Accra, where the aircraft made a routine stop. Coincidentally, a fellow-passenger was Chief Anthony Enahoro, the Federal Commissioner for Information. Barnes was an old friend, and blurted out the story of the killing. Enahoro immediately realised what impact such television coverage would have on the Federal cause. He held up the airliner at Accra while he made a strategic 'phone call to Gowon in Lagos.

The order was relayed immediately to Adekunle in Port Harcourt: 'Find this lieutenant, try him for a war crime and execute him – and make sure the international press is there.' The Scorpion, of course, did just that. The newly arrived press party in his sector included David Tyndall of BBC TV and a crew which included a young, inexperienced soundman whose first foreign assignment it was. Others on the spot were Nick Lloyd of the *Sunday Times* (later to become the editor of the *Daily Express*) and John de St Jorre, by this time an old hand. On their first morning, after an uncomfortable night at the Cedar Palace, they were 'lined up like recruits on parade' outside Adekunle's office.

St Jorre: 'Out he comes, small, with a nipped-in waist, a starched and ironed uniform that is a work of art...He also wears a scowl and lectures us firmly on the iniquities of the Red Cross, the churches and of the foreign press. Finally, relenting, he says: "Gentlemen, you came down here for a story and a story you shall have. You will now witness an execution. Good morning." And we did.'

The press party were taken to a compound where, very quickly, the young lieutenant who had shot the Ibo was found guilty by a field court martial and sentenced to death. Still under military orders the press were driven to the playground of an abandoned school where the condemned man was securely roped to a tree and blindfolded. Nick Lloyd: 'I've never been able to forget it...it was part of the passing mosaic of horror...they read out his death sentence and he kept snapping out "Yes, sir!" all the time and behaving impeccably.' What happened then was to cause great controversy among newsmen and deep bitterness among the press corps covering the Nigerian war.

The firing squad had been brought to the ready and was waiting for the final order to fire, when the BBC's young soundman discovered a fault. He whispered to David Tyndall who instinctively blurted out 'Hold it! We haven't got a sound mike.' The firing squad was stood down for a few minutes while the BBC team fixed their sound equipment. The officer in charge was under strict orders to ensure that the press witnessed and recorded the execution to demonstrate to the world that justice was being done even in war. The firing squad was again brought to the ready, took aim and fired. The lieutenant's body quivered, jerked and then slumped against the ropes binding him to the tree. The whole incident had taken only a few minutes but the press witnesses were as stunned as their colleagues had been by the killing of the young Ibo a week earlier. As they left the scene, some were sympathetic to the obvious dilemma facing the BBC team in having caused a delay in the execution. Others were hostile and determined to file the episode as part of their stories. Associated Press put out the story on the world wires 'BBC MAN DELAYS EXECUTION'.

David Tyndall and his crew were recalled and reprimanded. He was condemned by one of the BBC governors and his career suffered for years afterwards. In cold print it looked bad and yet all the journalists on the spot had been dragooned into covering the execution in steamy Port Harcourt and knew how involuntary had been the anguished cry 'Hold it!' Very few correspondents with a similar problem would not have done the same thing in those circumstances, I suggest. The Federal authorities had obviously stage-managed the execution to counter the impact of the ITN film of the earlier killing. Whether they succeeded is doubtful. In most homes where the execution was seen on TV the revulsion probably compounded the conviction that Africa was one long horror story.

The Nigerians were clearly losing the propaganda war, not least because of the arrogance and incompetence of their Information

Ministry. (St Jorre, enraged by being told by a secretary that he could not get an appointment with the Director without an appointment, was only slightly mollified when he noticed a poster on the wall promoting a beauty contest for 'Miss Information'.) When Lagos-based journalists eventually managed to get to one of the fronts, there was usually a major snafu which backfired on the government.

On the road to Owerri one morning with an advance Federal patrol, a group of us came under shell fire – from Federal Saladin armoured cars which were supposed to be 'softening up' a Biafran position some way ahead. We all dived for cover. It was not my day. My ditch-mate turned out to be Michael Wolfers, the Africa correspondent of *The Times*. Michael was wearing the same safari suit he had had when I first met him in Aden two years before. I don't think he had changed since then. The suit certainly had not been washed. Earlier, Wolfers had nearly got the English journalists into trouble by accusing, inexplicably, a tough-looking French TV crew of being cowards. By contrast, the Biafran propaganda had been remarkably successful with influential and active lobbies in London, Paris and in Africa. Some of this success was attributable to a Geneva-based public relations company, Markpress, which was retained early in the conflict by the Biafrans. Markpress, linked to Biafra by telex via Lisbon, was soon bombarding 3 000 'opinion-makers' – politicians, journalists, businessmen and academics – with a steady stream of handouts under the banner of Biafran Overseas Press Service. As the first stories of the widespread starvation in Biafra began to stir the world's conscience, the name Markpress became synonymous with Biafra.

Famines are usually the result of natural circumstances or disasters but this one was caused by the civil war. Biafra had been under blockade since the start of the war. Then, as the Federal army stumbled ponderously towards the secessionist territory, Ibo civilians evacuated their villages and their traditional sources of staple food to move deeper into Biafran heartland. Catholic missionaries were the first to become aware of the sudden surge of kwashiorkor, the protein-deficiency, and began organising what relief they could. It was not until the summer of 1968 when Markpress organised the first party of foreign correspondents for a Biafran visit, that the starvation story began to have impact – and even then it was nearly missed.

Michael Leapman, then diplomatic correspondent of *The Sun,* was among the reporters on the trip. 'We'd spent about five days and done all the touring around. There wasn't all that much to write. The whole thrust was the Biafrans convincing us that they were surviving, resisting and winning the war, etc. We were taken to the airport to leave but no aircraft came and we had to spend another day.' Leapman met Alan Hart, then of ITN, who had been persuaded by a Catholic missionary to visit the hospital. There he had filmed the starving children and mentioned it to Leapman. As Hart would be taking his film out on the same aircraft, *The Sun* man and his photographer realised they could get the story out at the same time. They made a bee-line for the hospital.

'It was the pictures that really made that first story, pictures of kids in great distress. And talking to the doctor who said "This one here is going to die tomorrow". It was very moving stuff. I wrote it all down and reported it back. *The Sun* ran it as a series over about three days and sent me back about a week later.' *The Sun* in those days, of course, was the successor to the old *Daily Herald* and very much a socialist newspaper. It ran Leapman's story under the slogan 'The Land Of No Hope' and linked it with an attack on British arms supplies to the Federal side.

The story had great impact, coinciding as it did with the House of Commons emergency debate on British arms supplies to Nigeria. The *Daily Sketch* did a 'catch-up' campaign, sending out reporter Brian Dixon with half a ton of full cream dried milk from its readers. Dixon, of course, found starving Biafrans who had never even heard of London, let alone Fleet Street, saying to him 'God Bless the *Daily Sketch*'. Don McCullin, the Cockney photographer who had cut his combat teeth in the Congo some years earlier, was to take some of the most compelling and tear-jerking pictures of the Biafran war and its attendant famine. Don, commissioned by magazines like *Time-Life* and the *Sunday Times*, made several tours of the front. His personal reactions are movingly documented in his autobiography *Unreasonable Behaviour* (published by Jonathan Cape, London, 1990). McCullin's body was already beginning to show the pockmarks of shrapnel from the numerous wars he had covered right on the frontline but the scenes he witnessed and photographed as Biafra began to crumble stayed with him through the horrors of the Middle East, Vietnam and Cambodia.

He explained his commitment – and subsequent disillusion – with the Biafran cause: 'I went back to Biafra as often as I could. My access was due to the offices of a strange public relations firm called Markpress which operated out of Geneva. They used to vet people who were trying to go to Biafra. Unless you were wholly pro-Biafran you didn't get in. I became a so-called trusty of this organisation. At that time the machinations behind the scenes in this war still hadn't

become apparent, but with each visit my own belief in the sound-
ness of the Biafran cause dwindled.'

Uncharacteristically, he had even been moved to take direct
political action on behalf of Biafra when he was back in London. He
converted into a wall poster one of his photographs of a Biafran
mother trying to feed her child with her withered breasts. A colleague appended the caption 'Biafra, the British Government
Supports This War. You the Public Could Stop It.' Don, his wife and
colleagues fanned out around London to fly-post it. 'I paid special
attention to our own area of Hampstead Garden Suburb where
Prime Minister Harold Wilson, had his home.'

Back in Biafra he found that Ojukwu had already fled.
'Mountains of empty wine bottles outside the General Staff headquarters testified to the lifestyle the little echelon of top leaders had
pursued at the expense of their people's starvation. By now I knew
them as opportunist spivs.

'I was ravaged and confused by this war as never before, and
could see not the smallest justification for it. Or for my presence
here – unless it was to remind people, through my pictures, of the
futility of all wars. This was a man-made famine – made by the
secession and the response to it, made by greed and foolishness on
both sides and, most of all, by the dishonesty of the original conspir-
ators who created the breakaway state.'

For the record it should be mentioned that David Cairns, a
Daily Express photographer, had come across the starvation story
before any of his colleagues. But his office in London had shown no
interest. There was a suspicion in Fleet Street that the famine was
part of the now-notorious pro-Biafran hyperbole being put out by
Markpress.

The *Sun* and *Sketch* campaigns, with their pictures of starving
children with bloated stomachs, touched a public nerve which then
gathered its own momentum. Freddy Forsyth: 'There was suddenly
a tidal wave of applications from Fleet Street to the little office the
Biafrans maintained in London for space on a plane, for access. The
war itself would never have set the Thames on fire, but the pictures
of starving children put Biafra onto the front pages of every British
newspaper and from there to newspapers all over the world. People
who couldn't fathom the political complexities of the war could easily grasp the wrong picture of a child dying of starvation.'

There were demonstrations, collections and campaigns to 'feed a
Biafran baby' all over Europe. Biafra may well be completely forgotten as an unsuccessful attempt at African tribal secession but the
name is likely to live on as a synonym for starvation and famine.

Forsyth's caravan home in Biafra was besieged by visiting hacks who wanted to know how and why the war had started. 'The guys they sent down were not African experts. They were hard-nosed reporters who went out with no prior conceptions or emotional baggage. They were down there to report a story.' To help them out with background, he began to tap out on his battered portable typewriter what started out as a long article, then a pamphlet and finally a non-fiction book – his first – called *The Biafra Story*.

The dilemma of the correspondents assigned to cover the war was becoming acute. The genuine suffering was plain to see, but in reporting, filming and photographing it, the hacks were uncomfortably aware of being manipulated. Colin Legum, Commonwealth Correspondent of *The Observer*, could never be accused of reticence when it came to expressing his convictions in copy. He made no secret of his support for the Federal cause, not because he was in any way anti-Ibo but because he thought secession was a 'nonsense that would not work'. And yet it was a case of 'my heart bleeding for the Ibos but my head telling me something else'.

The *Sunday Telegraph*, a newspaper which would certainly fit the description of being 'Establishment-orientated', had supported the Biafran cause, particularly since the disclosure of the famine. In January 1970, in the closing stages of the Nigerian war, the newspaper had come by a confidential report compiled by Col Robert Scott, Defence Adviser to the British High Commissioner in Lagos, detailing the incompetence and corruption prevailing in the Federal army. The report contradicted many things Harold Wilson and his ministers had been telling Parliament, and Brian Roberts, The *Sunday Telegraph*'s editor, insisted on splashing it.

Special Branch officers interviewed him and 'after some unpleasant exchanges' he was charged under the British Official Secrets Act. After a four-week trial, during which the eccentric Roberts was led to and from the dock at the Old Bailey to sit on 'a kitchen chair once occupied by one of the Kray brothers' – the notorious British gangsters – Roberts was acquitted. (Roberts was a shortish man and Lord Hartwell loaned him a cushion on which to sit in the Old Bailey dock. It was never seen again.) The case had much more to do with the outdated Official Secrets Act than events in Nigeria, but the fact that the *Telegraph* management went all the way to back a story that was essentially anti-British Establishment and pro-Biafran demonstrated clearly the agonizing that went on in Fleet Street.

The end came for Biafra in January 1970. For the most graphic, accurate, on-the-spot reporting of the end of Biafra one had to read Richard Hall, a genuine Old Africa Hand if ever there was one, whose account for his own Gemini News Service was picked up, very wisely, by the London *Sunday Times.*

Dick Hall was taking a bath in Owerri when the Federal shells came over. 'Someone banged on my door and shouted "We are all going. You must go." I picked up my possessions, locked the door and went up the drive. I saw ahead that appalling, unforgettable sight, lit by the headlights of cars edging forward through the mass. It was the great exodus. The lines were endless, moving with a queer dream-like slowness. From this army of fear there was a muttering, indefinable but pervasive in the dark. The people went along with basins, suitcases, boxes, bedding all balanced on their heads. Small boys clung to their parents' hands. There were people wheeling bicycles without tyres. Now and then soldiers came by, stumbling amid civilians in a dazed way and helping each other. There were no orders given, everybody knew this was just the end for Owerri. It was to fall, as Port Harcourt had fallen, and Aba, Onitsha, Umuahia. There was no real place left.'

Ojukwu caught one of the last aircraft out and was given refuge in the Ivory Coast. There he was to make a fortune in the transport business. The end of the war did not bring the wholesale massacre by the victorious Federal troops but 'a profound feeling of relief and a sudden upswelling of compassion for the defeated Ibos'. John de St Jorre was among 80 journalists taken on a tour of the now non-existent Biafra a week after the end of the war. 'There was no "genocide", massacres or gratuitous killings; in the history of warfare there can rarely have been such a bloodless end and such a merciful aftermath...'

Possibly a million people had died in what had – then – been one of the bloodiest episodes in Africa's post-colonial history. And yet those deep wounds healed very quickly. Colin Legum went to the post-war army barracks at Onitsha. 'There in the officers' mess were the Biafran officers and the Federal officers drinking beer together as though it was the end of a cricket match. They'd fought it very sternly and they were now chums again, as they'd been chums before.' Nigeria's post-war story was not such a success, despite the remarkable spirit of reconciliation and the swollen rivers of oil revenues. Three more military coups with a brief return to civilian rule have left the country a restless giant. Emeka Ojukwu, allowed to return in 1982 and living in a prosperous Lagos suburb, describes Nigeria as 'an amorphous mass of individuals busy pretending to be a people'.

His old adversary, General Jack Gowon, was toppled in a military coup in 1975 while he was attending the African heads-of-state summit in Uganda – and he was given the bad news by John Osman of the BBC. The coup had been picked up by the Beeb's monitoring service at Caversham and a telex was sent to Osman, covering the OAU meeting in Kampala. It was intercepted by Ugandan intelligence who summoned a bewildered Osman to the foreign ministry whose officials questioned him about the Nigerian situation. Not having a clue what they were talking about, John was totally perplexed until he got through to London. Gowon took the news like the old soldier he was. Possibly he muttered to himself 'AWA!' – Africa Wins Again!

To the front driver! Ken Clarke (left) of the Daily Telegraph, *John Platter of UPI and Walter Partington of the* Daily Express *hitch a lift to the Biafran war with Nigerian troops.*

CHAPTER TEN

REBELLION AND REDOUBT

*T*he purple jacarandas were still in bloom in Cecil Square. These exotic but pretty trees criss-crossed and bordered the central park which was the heart of Salisbury, then, in 1965, the capital of Southern Rhodesia and until recently headquarters of the ill-starred Federation of Central Africa. Only from above could you pick out the pattern laid out by the colonial gardeners: the trees, shrubs, lawns and footpaths, even the oblong dimensions, amounted to a horticultural replica of the British flag, the Union Jack.

The square was named by the capital's founding fathers after the family name of the third Marquis of Salisbury – Robert Gascoyne Cecil – as Lord Salisbury, the Prime Minister of Great Britain in 1890 when the Pioneer Column of Cecil John Rhodes' British South Africa Company came to a halt after a trek from the south. (They had also made a mistake in locating the city there. It should have been another 35 miles to the north.) Lord Salisbury's great grandson was to become the first – and only – journalistic casualty of yet another ugly, prolonged war in Africa.

On November 11th, 1965, a Scottish butcher's son, Ian Douglas Smith, set the world back on its heels with a 'unilateral declaration of independence' – henceforth to be translated into a universally used acronymic, 'UDI'. It was the first manifestation of Africa's white rebellion. The BBC's live-wire, shall we say slightly eccentric, resident correspondent in Salisbury, Ronald Robson, had knocked around the continent long enough to know what was by now an established pattern of turbulent, wind-of-change Africa. But this was 'the white south' and he was not going to get on film any blood on the streets. He decided on a rather jocular approach that was to backfire on his colleagues for the rest of their days.

He took a freelance film crew to the edge of Cecil Square at lunchtime on the day after Smith's UDI. As always, there were many black office workers and others taking advantage of Cecil

Square's shade to take a nap from the burning, energy-sapping sun of the Southern Hemisphere's 'suicide month', just before the big rains come in huge, welcome thunderheads to drench the parched soil and mentalities with some form of sanity.

On the edge of the park, Ronnie Robson asked his cameraman to pan across the dozing black people resting horizontally in the shade. He announced over his microphone 'There has been another revolution in Africa...', his tone implying that the prone black figures were victims of yet another horror. 'But this has been a revolution with a difference,' Ronnie went on, describing how Ian Smith had declared independence unilaterally as his camera swung to Second Street, alongside the square and a normal bustling shopping scene. As Ronnie prattled over camera about the possible implications of UDI and its impact in Salisbury, the film swung back to Cecil Square to show 'dead' Africans waking up, stretching, yawning, getting up and going back to work. It was, he thought, a clever piece of television, but white Rhodesians thought and believed otherwise. They never saw the TV film or read any accurate account of how or why it had been taken. All they heard – and wanted to believe – was that the BBC had taken film of sleeping Africans in Cecil Square and had portrayed them as victims of the white rebellion.

To this day many 'ex-Rhodies' tell me this story with absolute conviction and get quite upset when I try to put them right. It is part of the immutable mythology of 'God's own country' as they liked to call Rhodesia and, these days, remember it from afar. Having spent many years living and working in that country, I would agree with their sentiments about its natural beauty and its slow, gloriously relaxed ambience.

My argument from Day One was, and remains 'Why UDI?' – a formal act which set the world against them automatically and inexorably led to war, tragedy and disaster. I have never received any cogent answer to the question. It was the emotion of the moment, the reaction to the conviction that Mother Britain was determined to 'sell out' Africa's whites by destroying the Federation – coupled with a fairly strong dose of the natural rebelliousness inherent in the country's pioneer history.

It had been founded by Cecil Rhodes' British South Africa Company, against the inclinations and wishes of a British government that was becoming nervous of too far flung an empire. By the time Ian Douglas Smith and his Rhodesian Front had taken power, its white population of 250 000 included thousands who had fought, like Smith himself, long, hard and gallantly for the Allied cause in World War II.

This was a new life in a wonderful new country with opportunity, privileges that they could never have gained elsewhere, one of
the globe's finest climates and, as Ian Smith kept telling them, 'the
happiest Africans in Africa'. The national ethos was to eschew vocif-
erously what they saw as the moral decay of the 'swinging England'
of the 1960s and the gutless, vacillating and double dealing men of
Westminster and Whitehall.

The white refugees had flooded in from Kenya's Mau Mau aftermath, from the horrors of the Congo and Katanga, from the absurd
posturings of the new Zambia, Tanzania and Uganda, from the evil
designs of the Communist Bloc, to fill the role in Africa so swiftly
and shamefully abandoned by the European powers. All very heady
stuff in the Rhodesia of the 1960s and, to their surprise, the rather
strange assortment of individuals that gathered around Ian Smith
to sign the UDI document on November 11th, 1965, got away with it
for a long time.

British colonial lore had it that whereas Kenya (then pronounced 'Keenyah') had been the 'officers' mess' of Africa because of
the breeding of the splendid types it attracted, Rhodesia (now pronounced 'Zimbabwe') had been the 'sergeants' mess', as its settlers
were perceived to be of lower middle-class order. It was not strictly
true, of course. The blue blood did not come any thicker than that of
James Angus Graham, Seventh Duke of Montrose, the Premier
Earldom of Britain, a Rhodesian farmer who was Good Ol' Smithy's
first Defence Minister.

Nor did aristocratic pretensions come any stronger than those of
Pieter Kenyon Voltalyne Fleming van der Byl, the lanky, languid
old Etonian, Oxford rowing blue and now, through marriage, eigh-
teenth in line to the throne of Lichtenstein, who was also a signatory
to the UDI declaration. 'PK' as he was universally known, and largely despised, had once declared memorably 'I am a Rhodesian' (he
was a South African Afrikaner). 'This is a breed of men the like of
which has not been seen for many a long age and which may yet,
perhaps by virtue of the example that it sets, go some way to
redeeming the squalid and shameful times in which we live.' Van
der Byl, as always, had his tongue, inter alia, firmly in his cheek.

Despite all this colourful colonial pedigree, Smith and his cabinet decided from the outset, like many emergent African leaders of
the period, that the press, local and international, was to be regarded as a potential enemy. His government immediately moved the
censors into the offices of the *Rhodesia Herald* and the *Bulawayo
Chronicle*, both South African owned, and any other publication that
looked as if it might challenge the 'white, Christian, civilised stan-

dards' that he proclaimed. Foreign correspondents, irrespective of
the editorial views of their newspapers, were not only treated with
disdain, suspicion and often outright hostility but were busily followed, filmed and photographed by Rhodesia's Police Special Branch
and Central Intelligence Organisation (both of which were infiltrated from top to bottom by British MI6 men).

The Department of Information was staffed by drop-out British
provincial journalists, most of whom had merely wanted to find a
quiet spot to soak up the sun and other good things, or reborn fanat-
ics like Harvey Ward. It was quite eerie for Old Africa Hands, arriving in rebellious Rhodesia to find their white 'kith and kin' government officials behaving towards them just like the lurching, non-too-
bright 'information' officers of newly independent black countries to
the north.

On my first visit to Salisbury, I had been rebuffed by the white
secretary of a senior government information man. 'He has much
more important things to do than see journalists,' she snapped. He
certainly had. Quite late that night, in a multiracial nightclub on
the backside of town, I was startled when a door opened and, amid
great whoops of laughter and rejoinders from the regulars, in came
the man I had been trying to see, bouncing a naked black lady on his
shoulders. He suddenly saw me, dropped his companion like the
proverbial hot brick and, adjusting his tie, came over with a watery
smile on his face. 'You've found me, then?' he asked with forced
brightness. 'Perhaps you would join me for a drink?' I did. Several,
in fact. He became a good friend, like most of his colleagues in the
Information Department. But I cannot remember one occasion over
many years when one of them was of any assistance whatsoever in
getting to the facts of any matter, or in any other informational
field. They were, without exception, the most conspicuous misfits in
a continent not known for a bespoke demography.

There was dear old Donald King, cheery, bouncy, eager to
please but absolutely clueless when it came to disseminating information or propaganda or anything else the ringmasters of this
absurd little circus cracked their whips for. Donald, English to what
was left of his toe-tips (he had shot himself in the foot, literally, trying to kill a snake in his bedroom), had come out to Rhodesia to
farm. He tried twice, but both farmhouses were burned to the
ground in accidents. We would have respected him more had we
thought they were 'insurance jobs'. They weren't.

Penniless, with a lovely family to support, he had turned to the
only job available to a failed farmer and herpocidal maniac – the
Department of Information. He had been there only a few weeks

when another disgruntled employee poisoned the civil service tea with a dose of arsenic. Most of the others had hangovers and declined that morning's tea ration. Donald had three whacking cups. Fortunately he got to hospital in time to be stomach-pumped, and recovered. He turned to cycling to regain his fitness. Head down one morning, he hit a stationary milk float head on and was back in hospital. I was very fond of Donald, but I resolved never to stand near him in a thunderstorm.

For information, in those early days, we correspondents had to turn to some of the more pleasant, and certainly more confident, men of the British South Africa Police, the 'force in the great tradition'. It was more of a regiment than a police force, having been formed by Cecil Rhodes' private company to spearhead the pioneer columns that moved into Mashonaland and Matabeleland in the late 19th century. It had a proud history – a couple of VCs included – and became a repository for the more adventurous, less academically endowed, sons of British families, You 'did your three in the BSAP' – the 'force in the great tradition' – and then settled in colonial style into something more comfortable and less competitive than might be found 'back home' which, of course, was Britain.

One of the more pleasant assignments of the Special Branch of the BSAP in the UDI period was to monitor the foreign pressmen – and women – who arrived in this white redoubt to report on the 'rebellion against the Crown' and its aftermath. The conventional wisdom at police headquarters was that all foreign hacks were subversive, either working for a hostile government (and, without exception, all governments were hostile to the act of UDI) or sympathetic to black nationalist aspirations. Salisbury, although a capital, was by no stretch of the imagination a city. It had the mood and atmosphere of an English market town. The most popular currency was gossip and its exchange rate never fluctuated. It was impossible to keep secrets, which impeded the work of Special Branch but made it a happy journalistic hunting ground. Like Nairobi in the 'Happy Valley' days, it giggled at the question 'Are you married, or do you live in Salisbury?'

In this milieu, Ian Smith's Special Branch men stood out like beacons. Most of them were only too happy to introduce themselves, explain that their job was to keep an eye on foreign journalists and enjoy the free drinks and meals that came with a Fleet Street expense account. Information was exchanged on a quid quo pro basis. At weekend parties in Salisbury's sumptuous suburbs, we frequently held impromptu pentathlons in which the newsmen foolishly challenged the policemen to contests – swimming, tennis, darts, billiards, table tennis and a wonderful game called 'liar dice'. It was always a matter of pride to the Salisbury press corps that we never lost a game of 'liar dice' against the 'spooks' as the plain-clothes men were called.

There were exceptions, of course, in this congenial company. Some SB officers took their tasks to paranoid extremes, following us everywhere, taking photographs and film of us on noisy 'concealed' cameras, hiding behind trees, lurking in the undergrowth and appearing suddenly in darkened bars and clubs. All you would know of their presence was a sudden flash of a fluorescent sock behind a pillar or a tree trunk.

'Hello Bill!' you would shout cheerily to the disappearing shadow. 'Lovely day, isn't it?' Considering that the forces of black nationalism, with more than a little help from their friends in Eastern Europe, were preparing busily for a war, the SB attention to the foreign press was slightly misdirected. It was, like much else in Rhodesia in those early days of UDI, a great joke. The town and its ambience combined to make it too small, too intimate, for it to be anything else.

I suffered, if that's the word, because my *Telegraph* predecessor had been John Bulloch, a GOAH who had made a name for himself during the prolonged Congo crisis. John had written a book about Britain's counter-spy establishment, MI5, and was naturally suspected by the keener Rhodesian spooks of being a senior British intelligence man. He wasn't, but Bulloch, a tall, aggressive Welshman and an instinctive newsman, had a wicked sense of humour and had hammed up his image as a tease.

In those days, we sent out copy on an old Creed telex from the local freelance agency, Afrinews, run by a Lancastrian named Ronnie Legge. Ronnie had a pointed beard, piercing eyes and was lacking only a pair of horns to make his appearance precisely that of a pantomime devil. However, 'dear old Ronnie' had made his journalistic name as a *Telegraph* war correspondent in the Western Desert and Italy. His first partner in Afrinews in Salisbury was Eric Robins, a superb writer and journalist and a former *Daily Mirror* man who had served as a British army intelligence major and had reported on the Nuremberg trials of Nazi war criminals for the *Daily Mirror*.

Robins had been an early casualty of Ian Smith's anxiety to rid UDI Rhodesia of those who may, or may not, have been 'subversive'. He retreated to Nairobi where he was for many years the grumpy doyen of foreign correspondents covering Africa. Dear old Ronnie went through half a dozen partners in his freelance business before it was realised that, despite conspicuous journalistic ability, he was intent on finding a 'partner' who would do the work and earn the money while he adjourned to Salisbury's New Club to play snooker. His partners had included Jim Biddulph, the former Federal Broadcasting man, badly wounded in Katanga, who was also expelled from Rhodesia in Ian Smith's early purge against the BBC.

The BBC as an organisation was banned from Rhodesia shortly after UDI. It was officially proclaimed *persona non grata* and ordered to 'withdraw its staff and impedimenta forthwith'. The Smith government's ire with the organisation was partly its own fault. Its diplomatic wireless service was a British government-funded branch of the organisation and was instructed by Harold Wilson's administration to establish an anti-UDI propaganda station in Francistown, 60 miles from the western Rhodesian border in Botswana. A massive two-million pound transmitter looming over the desert beamed a daily 'World and Rhodesia' programme to recalcitrant ,whites. It was one of Wilson's less inspired ideas. The programme, an agglomeration of appeals by 'liberal' Rhodesians and condemnations of UDI by the world at large, merely reinforced the rebellious resolve and drove into Smith's camp many whites who would not otherwise have supported him.

Contingents of British troops were sent to Francistown in relays to guard the transmitting station against possible attack by Rhodesian troops. They failed conspicuously to prevent a group of Bulawayo schoolboys entering the compound and attaching pro-Smithy banners and ladies' knickers to the mast. The troops quickly became bored. Francistown in those days was very much a frontier town where most of the brawny white miners and farmers had not acknowledged the independence of the former British protectorate of Bechuanaland. There were only two hotels in the town – the Grand, which wasn't, and the Tati, which was. Outside each of these hostelries remained genuine hitching rails, a reminder that it was not long since they were both used by African cowboys driving their cattle across the Kalahari wastes to the north. The main street was a dirt road, which, depending on the season, spurted up spumes of sand and dust or bogged down passing vehicles of all types. On one side were the Grand and the Tati set among lines of small, single-storey buildings housing general dealers, mining stores and other shops. The other side was formed by the main railway line linking the South African rail and harbour system with the Rhodesias and the Copperbelt.

There were perhaps 50 yards between the bars of the two hotels and the Francistown railway station on the other side of the road. In the brief, inglorious history of the BBC's propaganda radio station, high street Francistown frequently became a battleground between British troops supposedly guarding it and the white reactionary regulars of the bars.

When I visited the town in 1967, a company of Irish Guards had just been restored to their barracks by the Rhodesian police. They had fought, bare-fisted save for a few beer bottles, a running battle with the local whites which spilled from the hotel bars, across the main street, to the railway station, onto a train on its way north finally to be pulled off, still kicking and punching at Bulawayo Station some seven hours later. In the history of running punch-ups, it had to be one of the most memorable. The local police chief, his arm in a sling and his leg in plaster from trying to break up these daily confrontations, left Gareth Parry, then of the *Daily Express* and myself, in no doubt what he thought of the radio station, the troops on duty there and the British in general.

The mayor of Francistown was only slightly more conciliatory, but unbeknown to us or the citizenry of the town at the time he was about to decamp with the municipal revenues. In our copy, we described the Francistown propaganda exercise as Africa's largest white elephant. It was certainly counter-productive and led to much antagonism between the Smith government and the foreign pressmen attempting to cover the Rhodesia story.

Back in Salisbury, foreign correspondents were being harassed and deported. Smith shared the simple, colonial farmers' view that a free press was an unnecessary indulgence and that foreign correspondents were inclined to ask blacks for their opinion which was 'misguided, liberal and subversive'. When I first interviewed him – the *Telegraph*, of course, being one of the few foreign newspapers accepted, if not embraced, by Rhodesia's 'white rebels' – he fixed me with that cast-eye stare and told me with that unmistakable, flat-vowelled, nasal accent of the Rhodesian midlands 'Y'know, Chris, that most of your colleagues are workin' against the interests of my country. Any time I think you or your colleagues are workin' against the interests of my country I will not hesitate to make sure my people are ensurin' the security of the country and makin' sure my people are not exposed to this kind of thing – the lootin', shootin', burnin' and rapin' that's going' on all over Africa.'

Many foreign pressmen were banned or deported from Rhodesia in the first few years of UDI. Some deservedly so for sneaking into the country by posing as 'musicians' or 'ornithologists' and then skulking around black townships, patronisingly patting what they hoped were revolutionaries on the head and telling them to get on with the war. This small group was pathetically conspicuous in a town in which it was impossible to keep a secret for long.

The majority of banned journalists, however, had merely written pieces containing legitimate criticism of the Smith government or worked for publications which had done so in editorials and commentaries. I tried pointing out to officials that they were just aping the worst excesses of their despised 'black neighbours to the north' but they had their cosy little sinecures and sunny little suburban homes and were not going to risk all this by going into bat for a journalist.

Of those of us based in Salisbury, John Monks of the *Express* and myself were slightly more acceptable because of the general pro-Smith editorial line adopted by our newspapers. A regular visiting fireman from London was my friend and colleague Ian Colvin, then a *Telegraph* leader writer and special correspondent who had an almost obsessive interest in the Rhodesia story. Ian considered Ian Smith 'a political Titan' and was considering writing a book about the Rhodesian leader. When Colvin was in town, my stories often clashed with his, if not in content, in interpretation, but, to its credit, the *Telegraph* would run them side by side and let the readers decide which version they preferred.

It certainly never interfered with our friendship which endured until his death from a heart attack (typically, at the age of 62, he had just spent several arduous, uncomfortable weeks with the Kurdish rebels in northern Iraq). He had a haughty, schoolmasterish air and a thin, penetrating voice but was possessed of an immense charm, great journalistic perspicacity and, in relaxed moments, a wonderful self-deprecatory sense of humour and fun. One correspondent who had shared many moments of danger with him in many different theatres, said 'Ian Colvin was simply the bravest man I've ever met'.

One day in our office in Salisbury, Ian fielded a telex message from the *Telegraph* addressed to us both and asking us to send one joint story between us instead of separate pieces. 'You know, Christopher,' he said, 'I have never believed in the joint bylined story. It takes away so much and to my mind confuses the reader.' I did not share this view, although I thought to myself it might be difficult to reconcile my own straightforward, by-the-book style with Ian's infinitely personalised and eccentric flair. 'However,' Colvin went on, 'our masters have thus decreed and so be it. I suggest that on the morrow you check with your people and I'll scout around the corridors. We then should muster here at the office say at 1600 hours and whoever has the obvious lead should go ahead and we'll bring in the rest of whatever we've got.'

The following day was what we call a slow news day. Apart from a few odds and ends of gossip and rumour, I had nothing too much to contribute to any story that might seize London's attention. When I returned to the office, Colvin was already there, tapping furiously at an upright Underwood, occasionally stopping to peer at what he'd written over the top of his half-moon spectacles. 'I think I have our introduction, Christopher,' he said. 'I've seen Smith.' Now an interview with Smithy on a quiet day was an obvious lead to our joint story so I let Ian tap on. He pulled his first typed folio from the machine and tossed it over for my perusal.

Dutifully he had typed both our names at the top of the story but the intro started thus : 'Hello Ian! exclaimed Mr Ian Smith, recognising me instantly and pushing his way through a crowd of well-wishers outside his office in the centre of Salisbury to shake me warmly by the hand. The Prime Minister looked well and uncon-cerned...' Etc. I read on with amusement. Obviously Colvin had found nothing too newsworthy and had staked out Smith's office at the time he knew the Rhodesian leader would be leaving for home. It had not been an interview of any kind, merely the greeting that Colvin had described in that first paragraph. He continued typing.

I tried to remain deadpan as I pointed out that we had a slight problem with the story. He looked up. 'Well, Ian,' I said. 'If this is to be a joint bylined story it should read something like "Hello said Mr Smith recognising us both instantly and shaking us both warmly by the hands" and Smithy would certainly recognise me but he would not shake me warmly by the hand.' Colvin peered at his intro over his spec-tacles. 'Ah yes,' he said 'I see what you mean.' I couldn't contain myself any longer and burst out laughing. So did he, the wiley old hand. I hap-pily let him file his 'intensely personal story' with his byline alone. London never bothered to ask us for a joint bylined piece again.

Colvin, like many other *bon-viveurs* among the press corps, did have trouble keeping awake at post-prandial press conferences and interviews. I knew he also had sometimes used the technique to lull an interviewee into thinking he was not paying attention and hop-ing for a few idle indiscretions. One afternoon, after Ian had enjoyed a long working lunch at the famed La Fontaine restaurant in Salisbury's Meikles Hotel, he had an appointment with a leading banker and businessman. At about 5 p.m. I had a phone call from the banker's secretary.

'Could you please come and collect your Mr Colvin,' she said. 'He is fast asleep on the couch in the reception room.' 'Are you sure?' I asked. 'He often appears to be fast asleep when he isn't.' She paused. 'The Chairman is fully aware of Mr Colvin's techniques,' she said. 'But this time it took three security men to carry him from the Chairman's office. He was snoring then and he is still snoring.'

What Rhodesia lacked in professionalism in its Ministry of Information it more than made up for in the quality of its home-grown journalists, most of whom supplemented their meagre earnings from the local newspapers by stringing or 'moonlighting' for overseas publications. Rarely can there have been such a concentration of local talent in such a small colonial town. They included Ian Mills, the long-fingered, hyper-sensitive hypochondriac whose natural musical talents left his colleague's amazed that he chose journalism, Maureen Johnson, whose grandfather, Frank, had led the Pioneer Column (and through a misheard instruction founded Salisbury in the wrong place), Ian 'Bunter' Smith whose nickname I thought unfair until one evening when I mistakenly picked up his blazer instead of mine and arrived at a formal function looking like an ant in a bell tent, Peter Niesewand, Bill Mclean, Mike McCann, Justin Nyoka, Andy Kanyama, Robin Drew, John Spicer and many others. Most of them featured in the events, dramatic and droll, that were to unfold.

Unfortunately, their talents were often frustrated by the weak and vacillating editorship of Rhodesia's newspapers. Long after Ian Smith's blue-pencil men had left their offices, the *Rhodesia Herald* and, to a lesser extent, the *Bulawayo Chronicle*, imposed forms of self-censorship which went far beyond the bounds of prudence demanded by the situation.

Ian Mills was an early victim of editorial eccentricity. Mills was political correspondent of the *Herald*, a difficult row to hoe in those days of Rhodesian Front hegemony and arrogance. He was also the founder and leader of once of the town's best known bands, 'Sounds Anonymous,' which enlivened Salisbury's restricted night life considerably. Mills would compose, conduct and play superbly every instrument in the band from piano, to string, to brass to woodwind, with equal dexterity.

At his desk at the *Herald* one morning, an harassed Mills took a phone call from a Rhodesian Front MP, Andre Holland. Andre was one of the brighter members of Ian Smith's party and was particularly accessible to newsmen whom he delighted in showing around his cattle ranch, the improbably named 'Ponderosa' not far from Salisbury. It was a personal call to Mills. He was having a party at the ranch and was 'Sounds Anonymous' free to play on that date? Ian checked his diary. The band was not booked elsewhere and he named their rates. That was fine, said Holland making the booking.

A few days later, Mills was astonished and horrified to be called in by the *Herald* editor, to be dressed down and peremptorily dismissed. The editor received an invitation to Andre Holland's party which made it clear the event was to be a fund-raising effort for Ian Smith's ruling Rhodesian Front (a fact he had conveniently forgotten to mention to Mills). Music was to be provided by Ian Mills and 'Sounds Anonymous,' said the invitation. The editor ranted and raved. How could his political correspondent lend his name to a fund-raising party for the ruling party? All Mills' protestations that he hadn't known it was a political affair, that it had merely been a friendly booking for the band which was his hobby, were in vain. He was sacked.

Mills was not the only journalist to find himself caught up inadvertently in the politics of UDI. John Monks was a loyal *Daily Express* man but first and foremost, like his father, a newsman to his podgy fingertips. Monks was no liberal but he did not particularly like Ian Smith, his policies or his attitude towards the press generally. Monks was a close friend and confidant of Sir Roy Welensky and shared the former Federal Prime Minister's distaste for and distrust of Smith. It was therefore something of an embarrassment for him to receive a top-priority call from his office in London from his proprietor, Sir Max Aitken, son of the legendary Beaverbrook. 'Give Ian Smith my best wishes and tell him the *Daily Express* is completely on his side,' Sir Max ordered his man on the spot. Max Aitken had had a distinguished career as an RAF pilot during the war, as had Ian Douglas Smith. He had met Smith briefly when they were both serving with the RAF in the Middle East. 'I wasn't about to start arguing with the owner about the rights and wrongs of UDI,' Monks recalls. 'I made an appointment with Smithy and passed on the message.'

Little did the Australian realise at that time that this simple errand was to involve him in a totally invidious position of go-between in political manoeuvrings between the British and Rhodesian governments, a dubious role totally inimical to his status as a foreign correspondent and which led eventually to the ruination of his career as a Fleet Street journalist.

After the failure of Harold Wilson's first essay in warship diplomacy – the talks on HMS *Tiger* in the Mediterranean – Max Aitken took it upon himself to try and resolve the impasse between Wilson and Smith, his old RAF chum. Monks was to be the middle man.

Cryptic messages began appearing on the old Creed telex at Afrinews which were clearly unconnected with activities and interests journalistic. Monks, perforce, had to become more and more furtive in his day-to-day routine. As always, secrecy was impossible in Salisbury. Max Aitken's messages for Ian Smith came in on the

Afrinews telex which we all used. We quickly learned the simple code words which identified 'Hotdog' as Sir Max and 'Old Mate' as Ian Smith. When Lord Goodman, Wilson's personal solicitor, was brought into the act he was soon identified as 'Friend'.

Monks was a little peeved when colleagues from rival newspapers popped their heads around his door to tell him 'Message for you John...Hotdog says you must tell Old Mate that Sick Friend is on his way again.' The *Express* man was then asked to shuttle continually between Salisbury and London with messages, on one occasion making the 12 000-mile round trip three times in one week.

Even worse for Monks was the reaction of his foreign desk. They were kept in the dark about his role as diplomatic intermediary and his orders from Sir Max not to utter a word about what was going on. While we were happily filing stories from Salisbury about secret negotiations, Monks, who knew more than any of us, could not write about it. He started receiving angry messages from the *Express* foreign desk. Out of sympathy, Ian Colvin organised a coat of arms for our hamstrung colleague with the inscription 'I know all, but can say nothing'.

Monks recalls: 'It was a dreadful situation. On the one hand I was sworn to secrecy by the owner and on the other I had his foreign editor bollocking me for missing stories I knew all about but couldn't file.'

Another major headache for Monks came with the instruction from Sir Max to keep secret Lord Goodman's visits to Salisbury. Goodman, probably one of the best known lawyers in Britain, was of unmistakable bulk and girth with jowls to match and a pair of ferocious black eyebrows that made him a favourite of political cartoonists everywhere.

'Asking me to ensure that Goody's visits to Salisbury were kept secret was like instructing Adolf Hitler to keep a low profile at a Nazi rally at Nuremberg,' said Monks. He tried. Lord Goodman flew to Johannesburg and was picked up by Derek Robinson, the slow-speaking but shrewd Yorkshireman who was head of Rhodesian Special Branch. He was driven to a small, obscure hotel on the outskirts of Salisbury, not normally used by hacks or anyone else who might recognise him. It just so happened that Bill McLean, a reedy, bearded Scot then reporting for the *Sunday Mail*, had popped into that very hotel for a restorative beer (which he nearly choked on when Lord Goodman came panting and heaving through the door).

Goodman himself was to acknowledge later that he had been called upon to strive for 'miracles of anonymity of disguise which some might have regarded as nearly impossible'. He soon gave up and moved to Meikles Hotel while he was trying to persuade Ian Smith back to the negotiating table. Everyone forgot to remind his Lordship that Salisbury is at 5 000 feet above sea level, an altitude at which a man of his fighting weight was required to exercise little exertion. One evening, Monks received a late night phone call from Lord Goodman. He sounded as if he was being strangled. 'Get me a doctor quickly,' he gasped 'and tell him to bring his heart bag.'

Monks called a leading Rhodesian doctor and met him at Meikles where concerned staff were gathered around the heaving, prone form of the British peer dressed, as Monks clearly remembers, in an enormous pair of silk pyjamas with a coronet embroidered on the breast pocket. He was treated by the doctors who ordered that he be returned to a lower altitude as soon as possible. It took six Special Branch men to carry His Lordship up the steps of the first aircraft out – a Viscount airliner flying to Johannesburg. Monks accompanied him, making sure he had two seats over which to spread his considerable frame. 'The air hostess must have been new on the job. When Goody asked for some orange juice we hit an air pocket and she emptied the entire jug over his lap. As we were waiting for his connecting flight to London at Jan Smuts, a waitress came and upset a bowl of soup into his lap. Goody was, as always, philosophical. He merely growled at me 'It's obviously not my day, John'. I loaned him my tie which I'm sure he'll return some day. I would have given him my trousers but they would not have fitted and the South Africans would certainly have arrested me for public indecency.'

Despite his problems, Lord Goodman gave the 'Rhodesian problem' his best shot. He was always beset by unexpected hazards. At that time he was, inter alia, chairman of the trust which ran *The Observer* whose African coverage, as we have seen, was dominated by Colin Legum, its Commonwealth correspondent and the disgruntled former Johannesburg City Councillor whose personal mission was to advocate the downfall of white rule in Africa irrespective of what might replace it. Colin was, of course, a 'PI' in Rhodesia but had been impressed by the eagerness, enthusiasm and commitment of a young acolyte named Colin Smith who desperately wanted to become a foreign correspondent.

Smith, now one of Fleet Street's more legendary characters, was given his own 'secret' assignment to Rhodesia. Having been a regimental bandsman (his nickname in South East Asia is, after le Carré, the *Little Drummer Boy*) he thought it a good idea to enter the country as a 'musician'. The first time I heard of him came with a late night check on the Afrinews office. There was one of the more paranoid Special Branch men going through the filing cabinet (which contained nothing more incriminating than yellowing clippings from old newspapers and, if you were lucky, some of the negatives of Mike McCann's award-winning photographs).

I challenged the SB man in a joking way but he snapped back at me with: 'What are you supposed to be playing in the band?' I was totally mystified by this remark until I learned, on the following day, that Colin Smith, a youngster from *The Observer*, was in town under the guise of being a visiting musician. I took him to one side and advised him against pretending to be anything other than a journalist, whatever his mission. It was too small a town for that, I told him.

Undeterred, Colin sneaked off to Harare, then the main black township on the outskirts of Salisbury. He was followed by the SB. There he made contact with a young Ndebele whose name had been provided by Colin Legum in London. The SB made notes. The young black man offered to guide the *Observer* man to Rhodesia's own deep south – to the perimeters of Gonagudzingwa, a remote lowveld prison camp in which many of the black nationalist leaders were being held. With what he thought to be suitable rations for the bush, Smith left the capital early with his companion. Special Branch officers followed them.

Colin Smith and his friend overnighted at a bush motel, the Lion and Elephant at Bubye Bridge. Thinking, quite rightly, that he would not get decent accommodation for his black companion, Colin told his man to sneak around the back and make his way to his room. The two SB men thought this was hilarious and mentioned casually to the motel proprietor that 'some Pommy poofter has got a coon faggot in his room'.

The outraged management discovered the Legum contact in the *Observer* man's room and threw them both out, with many adjectives. Still undeterred, our intrepid Little Drummer Boy pressed on into the bush. The two SB men, by this time weary of their rare out-of-town assignment, realised that he was heading for Gonugadzingwa detention camp, that it was of no great subversive import, and notified the authorities concerned. They returned to the Lion and Elephant for a couple of drinks and waited.

Meanwhile, in the very hot and sometimes threatening thorn bush of the Rhodesian lowveld, the intrepid Smith and his companion pressed on. Finally they reached the perimeter fence of the detention camp. Smith found a convenient anthill for cover and crouched behind it to wait. The best version of what happened next came from Joshua Nkomo, then the leader of Rhodesia's ZAPU movement, still the putative black nationalist leader of the 'democratic Zimbabwe' envisaged by Britain, the retreating colonial power, and by the then fashionable socialist governments of Europe.

Joshua was a big man. He could have matched Lord Goodman pound for pound and I would not have put any money on a Sumo wrestling contest between the two men. As far as Nkomo was concerned, he was 'The Man', the future leader of an independent Zimbabwe with the stature and personality to join his old 'revolutionary' friends like Kenneth Kaunda and Julius Nyerere on their world tours, their wining and dining on the adulatory circuit of Western governments anxious to wean Africa's new leaders away from the Soviet Bloc.

Nkomo was a big, cheerful man, egocentric and cunning, but redeemed by a great sense of humour and fun. He was not particularly happy at the Gonugadzingwa detention camp, but he knew a prolonged stint in a colonial prison was an essential prerequisite to future African leadership. What he did not know was that Robert Mugabe, that young, intense 'professional student', as he called him, had from within the confines of the Wha Wha detention camp a few hundred miles away made his own successful bid for leadership of Zimbabwe's revolution.

On the morning that Colin Smith of *The Observer* and his young black guide had concealed themselves behind an anthill some 200 yards away from the Gonugadzingwa detention camp wire, Joshua and a couple of his lieutenants took their usual morning constitutional around the inner perimeter wire. 'It was a lovely morning,' Nkomo recalled later. 'As usual we soaked up the smells and sounds of the wild beyond the wire. Suddenly there was this distant cry on the breeze. We stopped and listened carefully. Sure enough it came again. "Mr Nkomo...Mr Nkomo..."' Joshua Nkomo's large frame shook with laughter as he related the story. 'If this little voice had come from above I might have dropped to my knees and prayed. But it came from the bush beyond the wire. "Mr Nkomo...Mr Nkomo." It came from behind a termite mound and suddenly there was this little white head popping up from behind it. "Hello," I shouted. "Hello," this little white head replied. "I bring you greetings from Colin Legum of *The Observer*." It was the funniest thing that had happened to us in Gonugadzingwa for a long time. We fell to our knees with laughter. The little man deserves a medal.'

Colin Smith did not get a medal. He was picked up by prison authorities, handed over to his Special Branch minders and escorted back to Salisbury. To the embarrassment of Lord Goodman, the *Observer* man was charged with being in a prohibited area but Smith was released after paying a modest admission-of-guilt fine.

The talks about talks faltered, spluttered and restarted. A Conservative government in Britain, with Sir Alec Douglas Home as Foreign Secretary, appeared to improve the chances of a Rhodesian settlement, and, indeed, an agreement was reached in 1971 which would have left Rhodesia under white rule until well into the next century. It required only a 'test of acceptability' among the black population and with most of the nationalist leaders safely in detention Smith was confident this would be merely a formality. But when 70-year-old Lord Pearce, a British High Court judge, arrived in Salisbury with a team of commissioners the black population had other ideas. Anti-settlement riots broke out in several urban areas while even in the remotest rural districts, the blacks were giving a resounding 'No'.

It was very clear to most of the correspondents who fanned out to follow the Pearce Commissioners that there would be wholesale rejection by the blacks. Most of us wrote it that way. My dear old colleague, Ian Colvin, was an exception. Colvin was so convinced that the settlement was the best hope for an honourable Rhodesian deal that he abandoned all objectivity. On numerous occasions he visited farming friends who insisted that their black labourers wanted to say 'Yes' and having convinced himself that this was so, he drove the bemused Africans to register their approval before the Pearce Commission. Even when Colvin, back in London, gained an early exclusive sighting of Lord Pearce's findings two months later he misread the conclusion.

In Salisbury at the same time I had received a very strong tip that the answer was 'No'. The *Telegraph* ignored my story and ran Ian's 'Yes'. I took no pleasure whatsoever in the fact that he was wrong. The bitterness that emerged after the Pearce findings were published manifested itself in the streets of Salisbury and elsewhere. White paranoia reasserted itself in an ugly fashion. Smith was furious and his officials began to cast about for scapegoats. Peter Niesewand was not the favourite journalist of Ian Smith or many members of his government. A South African of German ancestry, Peter had been brought up in Rhodesia, had been schooled there, had done his national service in the Rhodesian army and was a citizen. Despite this pedigree, he refused to be blinded by the patriotic paranoia of many whites. He was first and foremost a journalist and was acknowledged by all his colleagues in Salisbury as a very good one. He had returned from a spell with the BBC in London to establish a freelance agency in the Rhodesian capital, working for the BBC and *The Guardian* in particular. These two clients alone were enough to arouse suspicion and hostility in the Information Ministry but Peter also had a quick-witted, cynical approach to officialdom that some not-too-bright government men misinterpreted as arrogance.

He was hard-working and competitive to the extent that the Department of Information was convinced he was unpopular with his colleagues, a mistaken belief that was to contribute to the lowest point of relations between the Smith government and the press. His wife, Nonie, was a close friend of Denise, my wife. She had, in fact, introduced us. With the Monks family and other Salisbury-based journalists we socialised frequently. When Peter and Nonie were married at the Anglican Cathedral in Salisbury in 1969, most of the guests present were fellow hacks, many of whom had flown in from other news centres. One notable exception on the guest list was Desmond Lardner-Burke, Ian Smith's Minister of Justice, Law and Order who was widely regarded as one of the most reactionary members of the UDI Cabinet.

Lardner-Burke, an abrasive, rather arrogant figure who always wore a carnation in his buttonhole, had been in earlier days a close friend and neighbour of Nonie's family in the Rhodesian Midlands. He was not at all fazed by the presence of so many foreign pressmen at the reception. Far from it. At one stage he made a short speech in which he pointed to Peter and said to Nonie, 'If he gives you any trouble, just let me know and I'll have him locked up'. We all thought it a great joke at the time but he reinforced his point by taking Peter to one side and telling him directly that if he did not look after Nonie he would 'have him restricted'.

Niesewand began to realise how unpopular he was when Ian Smith lost his temper with the young journalist in a televised discussion programme. He was blacklisted by the Information Ministry and his home was searched by the police. Even then, he thought he had nothing to fear because he had nothing to hide. He was not a political animal and was certainly in no way 'subversive', even by the paranoid standards that were, at that stage, gripping Rhodesian officialdom.

The crunch came with a seemingly innocuous story Peter filed to *The Guardian* one quiet Sunday. He referred to Rhodesian troops crossing the border into neighbouring Mozambique to assist the increasingly beleaguered Portuguese forces in their battles with Frelimo guerrillas. That fact was not only well known throughout Rhodesia but had been written and published previously by several correspondents, myself included.

When a remarkably cool, angry Nonie Niesewand called to say that Peter had been arrested and taken to gaol on a detention order signed by dear old 'Uncle Des' Lardner-Burke the foreign press corps was stunned. Surely Smithy could not have carried his personal vendetta against Peter this far? There had to be something much more to it, we thought. Senior men assured me that Peter's detention had nothing to do with the Mozambique report and hinted darkly that it had nothing to do with journalism at all. Monks got precisely the same feed-back from his contacts in government. Was it possible that Peter had got involved in something more sinister? The foreign hacks held an emergency council. Impossible, we decided. We had known Peter long enough and well enough to have become aware in some way if he had been in any way committed beyond the bounds of journalism. From that point onwards, it was undeclared war between the foreign correspondents and the Smith government, the emotion and rancour of which persisted for many years.

The 'power of the press' is much vaunted and to my mind frequently overrated. However, when newsmen decide that a gross injustice has been inflicted on a fellow hack and work together to muster support, the results can be awesome, as we were about to discover. We rallied around Nonie upon whom great burdens now fell. The Niesewands had one baby son, Oliver, and Nonie was expecting their second child within a few months. There was Peter's freelance business to try and keep together, mortgage and bills to pay, a hostile and suspicious public to face and myriad other worries. In many ways, her predicament was worse than that of her husband, then sitting in solitary confinement in Gwelo, 300 miles away.

But Nonie Niesewand was no wilting violet. She was overtaken by an icy, frightening anger, a barely concealed rage that such a thing could have been inflicted on her husband and young family by her own people in her own country. Nonie was a very good journalist in her own right. She was highly articulate, very attractive and forthright. John Osman, then the BBC man based in Johannesburg, had used all his bouncy, boisterous diplomatic panache to persuade the Rhodesians to allow him into the country with a TV crew and he found Nonie 'the absolutely ideal interviewee in these situations... you couldn't have employed an actress or a model to put across a better case'.

Suddenly, Rhodesia was back on the front pages of newspapers around the world and Ian Smith was being pilloried as a little white dictator who would take arbitrary action even against one of his own white citizens if he looked like being a threat. It was not quite the way Smith had hoped this 'minor irritation', as he later called it, would turn out. Even Smith's staunchest supporters overseas were horrified. My newspaper, The *Daily Telegraph*, declared in an editorial that Peter's arrest and detention was 'another particularly ugly manifestation of the way the Smith regime is drifting...the Rhodesian government is stumbling from one blunder to another'.

Rhodesian officialdom panicked. They did not have any evidence but the international clamour was such that Niesewand would have to be charged and brought to court. Finally they decided to charge Peter under the Official Secrets Act – and to hold the hearing in camera, thus denying his colleagues access to the court or any record of the proceedings.

In closed court, Niesewand was found guilty and sentenced to two years' hard labour, one year suspended. Smith's government was trying yet another huge bluff, but it did not work. By this time we had gained access to the court proceedings and had learned that the only evidence against him was based on that one-off, 'quiet Sunday' report on the action in Mozambique. Our newspapers knew of the full circumstances, too. The condemnation of the magistrate's conduct and decision and of the Rhodesian government's handling of the entire case had been widespread. Sir Alec Douglas Home sent a message to Ian Smith saying the verdict would 'hardly improve the climate for any future political negotiations' – strong words, indeed, from Sir Alec. The *Sunday Times* said the 'savage sentence...illustrates not simply the tyrannical nature of the Smith regime but also its blind stupidity'. I reported for the *Telegraph* that Smith had called an emergency cabinet meeting to discuss how Niesewand could be released without exposing the details of the charges made against him. These, I reported, were of such a flimsy nature that the government would face a reaction of incredulity in Rhodesia itself.

He appealed against his sentence and the appeal was upheld by three judges and still the government wondered what to do. Peter was still in gaol, a detainee under the Emergency Regulations. Eventually he was told he would be released if he agreed not to say anything about the circumstances of his arrest or give details of his charge. He signed, and was whisked to Salisbury Airport to be put aboard a TAP airliner bound for London via Lisbon.

John Monks, the crippled Gordon Jeffrey – 'Captain Ahab' of the *Mirror* – and I had a prior tip that he was on that aircraft. We were too. It was a bad trip. Peter was, understandably, bitter and bemused. Gordon had, in the last-minute rush, left his pain-killing tablets in his stowed luggage and we had to call for any doctor on board to help. We found one, but he was too drunk to be of much help.

At our stop-over in Lisbon, we found an enormous, clamouring corps of our colleagues from Fleet Street competing with each other to get at our shattered hero. One reporter, claiming he was a 'minder' sent from *The Guardian*, of all newspapers, to 'look after Peter' tried to stop us entering the transit lounge. Jeffrey, who had retrieved his pain-killers from the hold, had to beat him into semiconsciousness with his walking stick to convince him we were friends of the family. In London, Peter found himself, to his total bewilderment, an immediate celebrity. Monks and I had a breakfast of kippers and poached eggs at the Savoy, reported to our respective offices, watched the FA Cup Final on TV and caught the next plane back to beleaguered Rhodesia.

Peter Niesewand had to fight off job offers with his new found fame. He settled for a staff job with *The Guardian* and went on to win several major reporting accolades, including two International Reporter of the Year awards for his coverage of the wars in Lebanon and Afghanistan. He wrote an 'instant book' about his experiences in Rhodesia, called *In Camera*, and it gave a remarkably dispassionate account of that traumatic period. He was shrewd enough to protect the many people who had helped and fought for him in that episode by not naming or alluding to them, but his love of the country and its people emerged. He was never to see Rhodesia again. He found enough success as an author of thrillers to retreat to Ireland to write novels full-time but was overtaken by cancer and died at the absurdly young age of 38.

John Monks had fought and won against the policies and prejudices of the *Express* proprietors to get them to support his friend and colleague. In doing so, he made an enemy of Ian Douglas Smith. Smith wrote a long and embittered letter to Sir Max Aitken about Monks' behaviour during Niesewand's farcical 'trial', blaming the *Express* man for 'failures of communication' between the Rhodesian and British governments. It was an unworthy gesture and it led to the end of John's career with the *Daily Express*. He was shuffled around in various posts, finally got the message and resigned to return to his native Australia.

Ian Douglas Smith would never admit it, of course, but I knew – and he knew – that the bungling of the 'Niesewand affair', his stupid personal vendetta against a young journalist who had caused him to lose his temper in public, had backfired horribly. The cause for which he had strived for so long – recognition as a responsible African leader trying to uphold 'civilised' standards – would no longer wash with international opinion.

Another Rhodesian freelance, Michael Holman, was selected by the authorities for 'special treatment'. Mike, a studious and quiet man who had been raised and educated in Rhodesia, specialised in financial journalism for overseas publications. An unabashed liberal, he made no secret of his distaste for Ian Smith's regime and its policies, although this rarely showed in his copy. Special Branch, holding a particular grudge against what they regarded as Rhodesian renegades, convinced themselves that Holman was 'subversive'. He was arrested on some spurious charge but he skipped bail and slipped easily across the border to Botswana and made his way to London.

Having known and worked with him for some time, I knew the 'subversive' charges to be ludicrous. I had many a furious row with police friends who refused to be convinced that Mike was not 'a Moscow agent'. Some time later, a Special Branch man collared me in a bar to tell me he had just received proof of Holman's communist links. 'He caught an Aeroflot flight from London to Moscow last week,' he announced triumphantly, giving me the flight number and the times of departure and arrival. I was taken aback and pondered on my own judgement of colleagues – until I bumped into Mike a few weeks later in Lusaka.

Over lunch at his cottage of the outskirts of the Zambian capital I told him of the Special Branch suspicions and asked about his flight to Moscow. He collapsed with mirth. In London, he had quickly decided to return to Africa to freelance and had chosen Zambia as the next best base to his native Rhodesia. Having been promised several stringerships, he shopped around for the cheapest flight to Lusaka. It turned out to be an Aeroflot offer from London, via Moscow where passengers were treated to a two-day Intourist tour of the city before flying on to Zambia. Mike Holman went on to become a distinguished African editor of the *Financial Times* of London.

So much for the suspected subversives. The real subversives were never detected or even suspected – and they included several senior government officials, including a few in the hierarchy of the Special Branch itself and the Central Intelligence Organisation in Salisbury. The only journalist involved in 'subversion', I learned much later, was a seemingly inoffensive Afrikaner correspondent who, for years, passed on details of sanctions-busting operations to the British. His ultimate reward was instant British citizenship and a British passport. He is now a lecturer at a provincial university in England.

Ronnie Robson of the BBC. His joke broadcast on the day of UDI in Rhodesia backfired.

Accused of high treason in Rhodesia – Peter Niesewand of The Guardian.

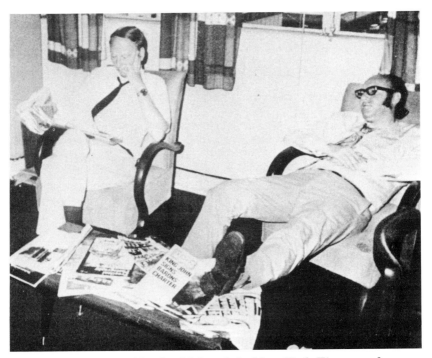

The waiting game – Charles Mohr of the New York Times *and Gordon Jeffrey of the* Daily Mirror *demonstrate that a foreign correspondent's life is hell!*

Heart of darkness – the author and Gordon Jeffrey of the Daily
Mirror *in a Salisbury nightclub.*

The Daily Express *takes the plunge – John Monks and daughter
with Sir Max Aitken, the* Express *proprietor who thought he could
resolve the Rhodesian crisis.*

'TELL THE QUEEN
I LOVE HER'

'**P**lease, please do not print this,' Idi Amin asked me, in a quiet, confiding voice. Nervously I reached across to my tape recorder to turn it off. 'No, no,' he roared, 'leave that on. This the world must hear. It is world news! Everyone must hear this!' In as respectful a tone as I could muster, I asked why he had asked me not to publish whatever confidence he was about to impart and then insisted that I keep the tape running.

'You must not be too clever with me,' he said, quiet again. I nodded my assent furiously. 'You must not think that because I say do not print this I mean that the world must not hear what I am going to say.' I decided that was very profound and I hoped my expression indicated that I was with him all the way, wherever that might lead to.

'The Israelis,' said Idi, still speaking slowly and quietly, 'are poisoning the Nile. They are flooding the Nile to poison our people. Do you understand that?' Of course I understood it. Why had I not realised before that Israel, a country which only a few months before had awarded this enormous, formidable black man, the coveted parachute wings of their airborne regiment, had poured millions of dollars into his tottering economy, had sent thousands of technicians to build ludicrous prestige hotels, halls and stadia in Uganda, had then decided to poison the Nile? Why had I been so stupid as not to see the plot that His Excellency General Idi Amin Dada, President of Uganda and soon to be Ruler of the World, was now revealing to me?

Being now the Old Africa Hand, the man who had had his hair cut on the orders of no lesser figures than Hastings Banda and Benjamin Adekunle, I knew exactly how to respond to His Excellency's revelations. 'Good heavens,' I said. 'Are you sure of this, sir?' Amin threw two enormous legs on his desk and laughed. It was not an unpleasant laugh, merely one of astonishment that this little white man could not have seen the transparency of the Israeli plot against him and his country. I confess I had missed it, but I scribbled busily into a notebook and, at His Excellency's insistence, the tape kept running. How, I wondered very secretly to myself, is the Great Zionist Plot to Poison the Nile story going to go down in London? Will they believe the straight quote or will they send me a message saying 'WHY YOU UNSAMPLE POISONED WATER NILEWISE?'

My immediate concern, however, was to get through this unsolicited interview with Idi Amin. I had been flitting through Kampala in quest of another story when Idi had heard I was in the capital. Charles Harrison, the former editor of the *Uganda Herald* and now a freelance, called me on one side with a wink. 'His Excellency will receive you,' he said. I started to explain that I had not requested or sought an interview with Amin. Charles was winking furiously. 'No, no, His Excellency will see you now.'

The mood and atmosphere in Uganda in 1972 was such that one did not make one's excuses and leave if His Excellency, Life President General Idi Amin Dada agreed to grant an audience, even though one had not requested it. There had been far too many reports and rumours of torture, murder and atrocities committed in the name of the military government. There had also been much evidence that at least some of these stories were true. Idi was not going to be an easy interview, but as Harrison was one of the elder statesmen of Old Africa Hands and had developed a serious attack of conjunctivitis, I knew I had no choice.

I was escorted to Amin's office at high speed by large gentlemen wearing, of course, the wrap-around sunglasses so beloved of African secret policemen. In the waiting room outside His Excellency's office, were several people I recognised. Most were cabinet ministers, civilian cabinet ministers like Charles Oboth-Ofumbi, the Minister of Internal Affairs, Joshua Wakholi, Minister of the Public Service, Alex Ojera, Minister of Information and Henry Kyemba, Minister of Health.

Most were to die rather horrible deaths within the coming months and from the subdued, highly tense atmosphere in Amin's waiting room that morning they seemed to know it. A secretary arrived with coffee. The rattling of the cups and saucers, the spilling of the sugar and milk and the nervous grins and quips told a story that I did not want to believe. Obuth-Ofumbi asked me if I had an air ticket out of the country. I did. He laughed, rather dryly. 'You are a very lucky man.'

This man Amin, I tried to tell myself, was surely not that bad. He had been a highly regarded NCO in the King's African Rifles. He had been Uganda's heavyweight boxing champion, had frequently proclaimed his love of Queen and Empire. Better still, he had, only a year previously, overthrown Milton Obote, to my mind one of the least appealing of Africa's emergent leaders who had led one of the continent's most attractive countries towards doom and destruction. But I found my tea cup rattling along with those of his cabinet ministers as, mentally, I tried to formulate some questions.

The preparation was unnecessary. As I was ushered into his enormous presence, he was asking the questions. 'You are from London?...How is your Queen? She is a very fine lady. I have served her as an officer in her army. The British are good people. Some of my best friends are British.' He then launched into his harangue against 'the Zionists' and brought their evil deeds up at every turn. It was only later that I learned his reconversion to Islam had taken place in Mecca and during a visit to Libya where Colonel Gadaffi had promised him millions of dollars worth of economic and military aid if Amin turned against the Israelis.

Amin was vague about the future of the 80 000 Asians in Uganda. He was investigating the corruption and banditry of the previous regime, he said, and some Asians had been involved. He gave no hint that within a few weeks he would announce their expulsion en masse and I believe that, at that point, he had not given the matter very much thought. He alternated between chummy confidences with his feet on the table – 'I want to be a farmer' – to explosions of rage against 'imperialist Zionists'.

Here, I thought, was an extremely unstable, rather frightening man. I was glad I was booked out that evening to Nairobi, little realising that I would soon be back in Kampala on indefinite assignment. As I was ushered out of his presence, Amin drew himself up to his formidable height, stood elaborately to attention and said 'Tell the Queen I love her'. I think he meant to say something like 'Give my best wishes to Her Majesty' but English had never been his strong point. In any event, I never had the opportunity to convey the General's felicitations to the Palace.

Before the advent of Idi Amin, I had always enjoyed assignments in Uganda. Churchill, after a visit in 1908, described it as 'a fairy-tale...a paradise on earth...a tropical garden'. A bit of poetic licence, perhaps, but it was a country of magnificent scenery and the people, particularly the Baganda of the south, were intelligent, charming and amusing. They could be particularly funny about Milton Apolo Obote, the self-opinionated, narrow-minded professional politician who had manoeuvred his way into absolute power shortly after Britain hastily imposed independence on Uganda in 1963. Obote had deposed by force the Kabaka of Uganda and was visiting his envy and temper on the Bagandans, the Kabaka's people.

Sir Edward Mutesa, the Kabaka, better known to his many friends in Fleet Street as King Freddy, was the traditional ruler of Uganda, being monarch of Buganda, the largest of the four kingdoms of the country. He had succeeded to the throne at the age of 15, had graduated at Cambridge University and had been given an honorary commission in the Grenadier Guards. Douglas Brown of the *Telegraph* remembered him as the 'perfect little black English gentleman' and even John Ridley, the lugubrious negrophobe, formed a close – very close – relationship with the Kabaka.

King Freddy had endeared himself to Fleet Street by repeatedly cocking snooks at British colonial authority, particularly represented by the snooty Sir Andrew Cohen, the Governor of Uganda. He had been exiled to Britain for pressing for Bugandan autonomy but was allowed to return in the run up to independence. At his thatched palace on Mengo Hill, one of the seven that make up the capital of Kampala, he poured large whiskies for visiting foreign correspondents, chatted about all things English (i.e. cricket and the weather) and won their support in his propaganda war against Sir Andrew.

At independence, to the mild surprise of the Foreign Office, Milton Obote, leader of the socialist Uganda Peoples Party, had agreed that King Freddy should be Uganda's first head-of-state. The wily Obote, however, guessed that Britain, only too anxious to scurry away from Africa's problems, would not interfere as he set about destroying the Kabaka and the Bagandan establishment to install himself as the president of the first republic of Uganda. He cultivated the support of the armed forces, notably a young officer named Idi Amin who, despite any semblance of an education, had proved himself loyal and ruthless.

Amin was a Kakwa, one of the northern tribes that spill over the border between Uganda and the Sudan, known to other Ugandans as the Nubians because of their warrior reputation – quite justified – as drinkers of the blood, eaters of the liver and mutilators of the corpses of their victims. Even while still with the venerated King's African Rifles there had been chilling stories about this seemingly genial giant of an NCO. Leading anti-cattle rustling patrols in north-western Kenya, Amin was reported to have personally murdered a dozen suspects, chopped off their private parts with a panga, and stuffed them into their mouths.

An inquiry established that these stories were almost certainly true, but Amin, because of his previous rank in the KAR, was one of the few Ugandans who could be promoted to officer status in independent Uganda and he received a 'severe reprimand'. As far as Obote was concerned, this uneducated peasant could be programmed like a robot to carry out the most daunting missions. Amin was sent secretly into the Congo during the Stanleyville crisis in 1964 to smuggle out gold and ivory, ostensibly to help pay for arms for the rebel Simba cause. The proceeds, in fact, disappeared and when Ugandan ministers alleged that Obote and Amin had been involved in corruption, the cabinet room was surrounded by troops and the dissidents thrown into gaol.

Obote them imposed his new constitution on the country, promoted Amin to army commander and ordered him to attack the Kabaka's palace on Mengo Hill. The palace was built like a fortified village on the side of the hill and the Baganda, forewarned, put up as stiff a resistance as they could. Big Dada led the assault personally, startling foreign press onlookers like Peter Younghusband and John Monks. 'This enormous man, grinning from ear to ear, drove in an open jeep to the foot of the hill, personally lined up a 122 mm cannon mounted on the rear and began blazing away at the palace.' The battle ended abruptly when all participants were drenched in one of the sudden cloudbursts for which Kampala is notorious. 'Rain stopped play,' Younghusband reported facetiously. 'The battle for Mengo Hill is expected to resume when the pitch dries out.'

It didn't. King Freddy took advantage of the storm to slip out the back, eventually to make his way overland to neighbouring Burundi and thence back into exile in Britain. There in a miserable bed-sitter in the East End of London, he was to die, ostensibly of alcohol-poisoning, four years later, a forlorn and lonely figure. Amin and his men – newly recruited Nubians who despised the southern tribes – ransacked the Kabaka's palace. Amin returned to Obote bearing gleefully the closest thing he could find to King Freddy's scalp – a ceremonial headdress. The foolish Obote, delighted with what he thought (and once described privately) as my 'faithful Kakwa guard dog', dispatched Amin's armed forces to conduct large-scale 'map-reading' exercises in parts of Uganda. He didn't want them lurking around the capital.

The semi-literate, peasant 'guard dog' chose the opportunity to build up his own power base. The Nubians, many of them Southern Sudanese from Amin's home area, not only dominated the army but were infiltrated into Obote's own secret police force, the General Service Unit which he thought safe in the hands of his rather sinister and very dangerous cousin, Akena Adoko. In retrospect, Akena was one of those African secret police chiefs who step from the pages of Graham Greene. Always immaculately dressed, his portly figure would appear at our sides in the most obscure nightclub or hotel anywhere in Uganda. The smile of greeting appeared genuine, but we could never be sure as his eyes were always, day or night, wrapped in sunglasses.

He had made himself known to me on an early visit to Kampala. 'Ah yes, Mr Moonyan of the reactionary *Daily Telegraph*,' he said. 'We have never met but I have been watching much film of you and your arrival.' I was flattered and told him so. Why on earth would he be interested in a film of a transient journalist? 'We know you "transient journalists",' he replied. 'We know that the things you discover might reach other ears.' He emphasised the point by tweaking violently at his left ear, briefly dislodging his sunglasses. He readjusted them quickly. 'Be sure Mr Moonyan we shall be seeing more film of you soon.' He left with two athletic-looking men, similarly shaded, detaching themselves from the wall and following him out.

The Bagandan barman grinned and winked at me, filling my glass unbidden. 'I see you know the President's cousin,' he grinned. 'He is a very important man, of course. He knows the President's wife very well, very well indeed.' I grinned my acknowledgement of his emphasis but grew a little uneasy as he went on to tell me a joke about Obote's notoriously vain wife, Miriam. 'Mrs Obote looks into the mirror long and hard,' said the barman.

'She says "mirror, mirror on the wall...who is the fairest of them all?" The mirror suddenly snaps back at her "It's still Snow White you black witch and don't you forget it."' He and other Bagandans around the bar collapsed in helpless laughter. I thought it a very funny story but there were still too many sunglasses around for comfort. In the finest traditions of Fleet Street, I made my excuses and left.

I returned again to Kampala in 1968 to make inquiries into the disappearance of one of the Kabaka's relatives, arriving on a Sunday. Not surprisingly, Kampala was officially closed down and enjoying itself at lakeside, in the mountains or at distant suburban homes. Trying to raise anyone who might comment one way or the other on a delicate matter of state was difficult, if not impossible. In frustration, from an upper floor of the Apolo Hotel, the grotesque 'five-star' monument to his middle name built by the Israelis for Milton Obote on another of Kampala's hills, I flicked through the local telephone directory, the old trick of *The Guardian*'s Harry Jackson. There was the home number of one Sam Odaka, Obote's foreign minister and, I had been told, a friendly, approachable character.

It was about noon, a hot and very sultry Sunday, but in those days I was keen enough to give it a whirl. The foreign minister answered the phone himself. He had, quite obviously, started his traditional, colonial lunch quite early but after I had explained who

I was and what I was after, insisted I come to his house, enjoy his hospitality and 'hear the truth'.

An official car was sent to the hotel to fetch me and I spent an extremely pleasant afternoon with Sam Odaka who gave me, between raucous introductions and greetings, a friendly, top-level run-down on what was actually going on in the country from a senior cabinet minister's viewpoint. It was a major exclusive ruined only by my inability to recall the pertinent points. Worse, when I pieced something together the *Telegraph* printers had gone on strike and I was filing into the void of the Fleet Street disease. But Sam's instant hospitality and the reception of his family and friends restored some of my faith in Obote's government, if not in the man himself.

Some time later, newspapers got excited when it was announced that Pope Paul had chosen Uganda for the first-ever visit by a reigning pontiff to Africa. The Pope had declared, unprophetically, that the evangelisation of Africa 'was an important phase in the divine plan for the salvation of humanity'. Uganda then had some three million Roman Catholics. The Apostolic Nunciatures had made it known that 'millions of pilgrims' were trekking to Kampala from all parts of Africa. We duly filed stories to this effect but had trouble agreeing on a figure of a few hundred thousand, topside, when His Holiness duly arrived and kissed the oily tarmac of Entebbe Airport.

Johnny Apple Junior, then the abrasive *New York Times* man in Nairobi, was one of nature's organisers. On those rare occasions in Africa when events did not need organising and were running fairly smoothly, you could guarantee that Johnny would be there, bull-horned voice booming and elaborate plans 'A' and 'B' and 'C' made which would be certain to fly in the face of any official arrangements. Apple Junior had taken it upon himself to organise special facilities for the foreign press covering Pope Paul's visit to Uganda.

The Pope was due to make one of the most interesting journeys in Africa – the 25-mile trip on a narrow tarred road linking Entebbe with Kampala. At the best of times, it is an exhilarating trip in either direction. The road twists and winds across the hills flanking the northern shores of Lake Victoria, suddenly widening and then narrowing as erratically as the locals who drive it regularly. It weaves through little settlements whose entrepreneurs have thrust their businesses half way into the road to attract one's attention. When one of Uganda's interminable conflicts was in progress, it was unusual not to see several bodies lying by the roadside or in the road itself. When all was peaceful, it was unusual not to see a body or two from a traffic accident lying similarly. One always had a sense of achievement at having negotiated the trip safely.

Probably His Holiness had not heard of this little Hell Run, but he was soon to learn. Johnny Apple Junior had organised a Press Bus. 'Hey, you guys, this is the fastest Goddam bus this side of the Nile. I've got the best Goddam driver in this Godforsaken town to drive us alongside the Goddam Pope, okay?' Okay, Johnny, we chorused, a little bemused by the energy and dedication devoted to such a routine story. It was not to be routine. Not with Johnny Apple Junior in charge.

His Holiness, having kissed the oily airport apron, was placed in the back of an open Mercedes, there to bestow, with the pontifical waves, blessings upon the waiting roadside throngs. 'Right, you guys, on the bus!' shouted Apple. 'We gotta get outta here ahead of the Goddam Pope.' We piled onto the bus. The driver had been assured by Apple that he had Formula One potential and Divine guidance. He set off to prove it, weaving through the lines of limousines laid on for the dozen African heads-of-state, each vying with the other for pole position. We were doing well. As we passed Entebbe's golf course, I noticed with envy some expatriates, obviously Protestants, examining the line of their putts. 'Where are these Goddam pilgrims?' screamed Apple, waving a brawny arm towards the deserted roadsides.

Pilgrims there were not, but the Papal Grand Prix was on. Presidential chauffeurs were being urged by their employers to ensure they were ahead of the field. Apple enjoyed the challenge. Sitting next to the increasingly nervous bus driver, he was bellowing instructions. 'Take the bastard on the inside...move over...now move it...Great! GREAT!...now take that gap and get through!' It was now getting a little hair-raising for us ordinary mortals hanging on grimly in the rear of this rather old bus. We scraped the side of a racing limousine and a Ugandan photographer who had unwisely positioned himself on the roof toppled into the road. We later learned that he had broken his arm and bruised his head but the Apple Express did not stop.

Finally, an escorting police car managed to manoeuvre itself alongside the bus. An enraged Indian police officer banged on the driver's door with his swagger stick, screaming at us to pull in. I felt for the driver. On the other side, Johnny Apple was screaming 'This is the Goddam press bus. We gotta stay ahead of the Goddam Pope.' To our relief, the driver succumbed to uniformed authority and swerved into the side of the road. I retain vivid memories of His Holiness passing us with the classic gesture of benefaction, wincing as he heard, as he must have done, Johnny Apple Junior screaming at the policeman, 'This is the fucking press bus and we're authorised to be ahead of the fucking Pope!'

It was not the best of Papal excursions. Pope Paul was taken to the shrine of Africa's first martyrs – eleven page boys at the Court of an earlier Kabaka. The lads had been ritually killed in 1886. They had been wrapped in straw mats and thrown alive onto a raging fire. His Holiness blanched visibly when Milton Obote confided to him that the 'martyrs' had been unfaithful sodomites to King Freddy's grandfather. Fleet Street and the Vatican have, at least, something in common. The 71-year-old Pontiff made his excuses and left Africa.

Uganda could always be counted upon to produce an intriguing story or two. In 1970, in company with other East African leaders, Obote had made unpleasant, veiled threats against the country's Asian community. Indian labourers had been imported by British colonialists to build the railway from Mombasa on the Kenyan coast to Kampala in the interior. It was an amazing venture, known as the 'Lunatic Express' to more sanguine observers, although Churchill described it thus: 'You climb up a railway instead of a beanstalk and at the top there is a wonderful new world.' Churchill rode on the cow-catcher of one of the first trains to make the journey, but it was the Indian artisan who built this iron beanstalk. The job completed, they settled throughout East and Central Africa to do what they know best: to trade, to fulfil the essence of the basic principles of supply and demand. The Indian community swiftly became Africa's middle class and, not least because they were unashamed to flaunt their wealth and status, more despised among the blacks than any European colonialist.

When the Asian community in Uganda began to feel Obote's hot breath they moved and manipulated to cover their options. Most were, by right, British citizens. The man in charge of the applications in the British High Commission in Kampala was Brian Lea, a genial, very relaxed former British Railways policeman who had made it his job to know and understand the problems of Uganda's Asian community and to try and balance these with the political fear in London of another sudden influx of non-white Commonwealth citizens.

Brian Lea's job was not an enviable one. Every day he was dealing with dozens of applications from Ugandan Asians to enter a Britain whose government, in its usual state of benign panic, was moving the goalposts on the cricket pitch. In turn, the Indians were used to getting their own way in a blatantly corrupt African society by persistent blandishment and bribery. Africa hands among the foreign press corps knew Lea well. He was unusually frank, for a British diplomat, about his dilemma. We responded, in turn, by pointing out in copy the dreadful anomalies and iniquities of immigration laws and the value (long since proven) of East African Asians to any community and culture.

It came as something of a shock when, in May 1970, we heard that Brian Lea had gone missing for three days and had then emerged unharmed to claim he had been kidnapped by a group of Asians who had taken him to a small island in Lake Victoria and held him to dramatise their plight in getting entry permits to Britain. By any yardstick it was a great story. Once again I was back in Kampala with John Monks and Peter Younghusband. The *Daily Mirror*, in its infinite eccentricity, decided to send its horse racing editor, Alan Gordon, to cover the story. Gordon, a plump, myopic, sun-suffering African novice, was to prove, once again, that a good reporter is as good as any story he is sent on.

We foregathered at Kampala's Apolo Hotel for the start of a judicial inquiry ordered by Obote to investigate Brian Lea's 'kidnapping' claims. We Old Africa Hands were muttering 'Nonsense...it's a set-up...dear old Brian could never have done something like this'. Alan Gordon, fresh from the turf of Epsom Downs and Catterick, demurred. 'What if it's true?' We shouted him down. 'Listen, old lad, we know this man and we know the country...they are framing him.'

We had a succession of visitors at the bar of the Apolo. Mr Akena Adoko, Obote's cousinly head of the secret police, popped in to tell us we were all on film. We made a mental note not to watch Mr Adoko's home movies. Bob Astles, the very strange British expatriate who was reputedly close to Obote, called by to accept our drinks and tell us we were all 'under surveillance' and that there was much more to the Lea affair than we realised. Mr Mohammed Hassan, a very good policeman who was then head of the Ugandan CID, made a point of looking us up to assure us that Lea was guilty of conniving at his own 'kidnapping' to cover up an investigation into allegations that he had been taking bribes from the Indians.

The public inquiry in Kampala's town hall took on all the trappings of a major criminal trial. Desmond Ackner QC was flown out from London to represent Brian Lea, Godfrey Binaisa QC the chubby and charming former Ugandan Attorney-General appeared, in effect, for the 'prosecution', and the whole affair was presided over by Mr Justice Robert Russell, a British-born Ugandan High Court judge. We didn't know it at the time but the inquiry was to last six weeks, hear evidence from more than 50 witnesses and bring to the fore a host of colourful Ugandan characters. It soon became a major public attraction, the best entertainment Kampala had ever experienced. The judge frequently threatened to clear the court as the public gallery fell about with helpless laughter as the evidence unfolded. Brian Lea, First Secretary (Consular) at the British High Commission, a former RAF fighter pilot, initially claimed that he had been lured to his office on a Saturday afternoon, forced into a car by an Asian, an African and a half-caste, blindfolded, driven to 'a jungle clearing' and held against his will.

The story became more and more improbable as witness after witness testified that they had seen Lea travel quite freely to Nkunze Island, four acres of fly-blown scrub, in Lake Victoria. There, they insisted, he had drunk whisky, desported himself with four young African maidens and, in the words of Mr Binaisa, 'basked in the sun on some lush island on a frolic of his own making'.

Desmond Ackner's abrasive and cynical courtroom manner was obviously brilliant in the Old Bailey but fell flat when he cross-examined primitive Lake Victoria fishermen. Mr Ackner learned very quickly that irony and sarcasm are totally ineffective in African communication. Half way through the inquiry, Brian Lea changed his story. He admitted a previous visit to Nkunze Island in the company of the three Asians who were allegedly his kidnappers. There he had 'made a fool of myself' with a young African woman. He had been 'cultivating Asian contacts' to assist his duties in allocating his quota of immigration visas to Britain.

It was bizarre. It was also good copy and we were getting a lot of daily space in our newspapers. But as the inquiry dragged on Monks, Younghusband and I began to feel the seemingly interminable boredom. I worked off some of the frustration by sending furious messages to London about the sub-editor who inserted the parenthesised explanation 'African chopping knife' after every mention in my copy of 'panga'. Monks imported an exercise wheel to reduce some of his flab. One evening, the carpet in his room slipped under his feet and with a great roar he shot forward on his wheel to become wedged in the balcony railings high above Kampala. It took us over an hour to dislodge him.

Younghusband became convinced that the young Africans who cleaned our rooms were spies for Akena Adoko. One morning, instead of following our usual routine of trooping down to the inquiry after breakfast, Bigfoot decided to sneak back up to his room. His enormous frame burst through the door to the sheer terror of the room attendant who was sitting at Younghusband's typewriter tapping out, on Apolo Hotel notepaper, a reference to himself. He had already managed to type 'To Whom It May Concern'. With a great Afrikaans roar Peter grabbed him by the collar, held him with one enormous fist over the balcony of the tenth floor and called the manager on the house phone.

Little Joe Kakere, the assistant manager, rushed to the room. 'What do you think of this Joe?' bellowed Younghusband, still holding aloft the terrified room attendant. Joe looked at the typewriter and the note. 'This is very bad, very, very bad,' he said, shaking his head. 'They are under strict instructions not to use the hotel notepaper.' Peter exploded. 'Sod the notepaper, what about my typewriter?' 'Ah yes,' said Joe, looking up at the squirming employee. 'What were you doing with the boss's typewriter?' You've got to hand it to the Ugandans for quick-wittedness.

'I saw some ants in the typewriter…I was just trying to get them out,' he said. Younghusband suddenly saw the hilarity of the whole episode. He dropped the room attendant and collapsed on the floor laughing. Little Joe and the ant-hunter did the same.

Little Joe was almost too obliging. The Apolo was one of those ghastly concrete and glass edifices that newly independent African governments insist on erecting like some phallic prestige symbol. It had an enormous lounge-bar area with appalling acoustics. A young Indian pianist had been imported to provide incidental music. He was not that bad, I suppose, but one evening, he got carried away and launched into a crashing crescendo of the Warsaw Concerto. We simply could not hear each other speak. We complained to Little Joe. 'Just tell him to keep it down a bit.' To our horror, Little Joe marched across to the pianist, slammed the lid down on his sensitive fingers and fired him on the spot.

As the crestfallen Indian, clutching his music sheets, started to leave, we rescued the situation. I persuaded him to return while Monks and Younghusband pleaded with Joe to reinstate him (with the proviso that he played quietly). The Indian maestro played on, meekly, for several months. Brian Lea, once the inquiry into his indiscreet frolic finally ended, was whisked back to London, never to be heard of again. Little Joe ran a good hotel for a couple of years before Idi Amin's thugs dragged him on to the hotel lawns and shot him.

I was among those who cheered the advent of Amin. The odious Obote was at a Commonwealth Prime Minister's Conference in Singapore when his army commander seized power in a coup d'état remarkable for its seeming lack of blood. There is much evidence to suggest that the hidden hands of British and Israeli intelligence organisations helped what they hoped was a genial buffoon to oust the conniving Milton Obote. Big Idi, trained in the great tradition of the King's African Rifles, seemed to be a much better prospect for Western interests in East Africa. How wrong could we be?

By the time of my interview, he had been in power just twelve months during which Uganda had been reduced to a state of terror.

Martin Meredith, then a freelance correspondent of *The Observer*, flew in with a list of contacts among political dissidents in Uganda, thoughtfully provided by Colin Legum, then Assistant Editor of that newspaper and an admirer of Milton Obote.

Meredith made his contacts as discreetly as he could, but this was the new, paranoid Uganda. He had boarded his return flight to Nairobi at Entebbe Airport when Ugandan police officers came on board and arrested him. He was held at Kampala's central police station on a formal charge of stealing a telephone directory from his hotel room. The questioning, however, had little to do with theft. His interrogators wanted to know who Meredith had seen and why. He was eventually released but rumours soon emerged that a number of people on the contact list were missing.

Meredith had been lucky that Amin had not yet purged the police force and replaced the British-trained detectives and special branch officers with his own, hand-picked assassination and torture squads. These were staffed exclusively by Nubians, sadists and psychopaths almost to a man. The squads were given innocuous-sounding names like the State Research Bureau, the VIP Protection Unit and the Public Safety Unit. There was little research, protection or safety carried out by these groups. They were responsible for the wave of killings that, we came to learn later, started shortly after Amin came to power.

During that first interview with Amin I was aware of one very sinister figure among the otherwise nervous officials attending the president. He sat slumped in a chair in a sloppy uniform. A grubby tee-shirt peeped from the neck of his unpressed tunic. His forage cap was perched above brutish features and totally expressionless eyes. Throughout the interview he never took his eyes off me. When I glanced in his direction, he would slowly slap a swagger stick against his indolently extended leg. Clearly he was not among those who lived in terror of Idi Amin. It was only a few months later that I learned this was Major Isaac Maliyamungu, probably the most vicious of the killers with which Amin was surrounding himself.

Major Maliyamungu was head of the 'VIP Protection Unit'. He would produce for Amin lists of prominent and other Ugandans ostensibly suspected of real or potential subversion but more often men who had some readily seizable assets or perhaps a coveted motor car, wife or mistress. Amin would point to various names on the list and say to Maliyamungu (whose name meant 'gift of God'): 'Give him the VIP treatment.' Straightforward assassination was not good enough for the major. A Ugandan schoolmaster from the once strongly Roman Catholic village of Masaka in the south gave me a chilling account of Maliyamungu's pacification methods.

He drove into the centre of the village and ordered his men to fetch the mayor, another schoolteacher who had been outspoken in his criticism of Amin's military. The man was stripped naked and hauled before Maliyamungu before the assembled, terrified villagers. Maliyamungu asked him in a loud voice if he wanted a cigarette. The teacher was too frightened to reply. The head of the VIP Protection Unit suddenly chopped at him with the ceremonial sword he always carried, severing the man's penis. He picked it up and stuffed it into the man's mouth.

My teacher informant, who was among the onlookers, was weeping as he continued the story. 'Maliyamungu said to the mayor: "There is your cigarette. I will light it for you" and made as if to light the severed penis. The man was collapsing but the Major's men held him upright. Maliyamungu then asked him if he had ever wanted to see the contents of his own stomach. He slit open his belly with his sword. This went on for what seemed like hours. To our shame, we were paralysed with fear and did nothing. We had no arms and nothing to fight with. We watched our friend being butchered in front of us.'

The mutilated body was finally hitched to the back of a Jeep and driven around the village by a triumphant Maliyamungu. The body finally fell in two halves, both of which were hung from prominent trees in the village. Masaka had been pacified by the VIP Protection Unit.

To our shame, perhaps, we in the Africa press corps knew little of such incidents in Amin's early days. There were rumours, of course, but Uganda had always been a political labyrinth and Amin seemed such a jolly, approachable soul. His buffoonery also made good copy. Then we lost an American colleague and the picture from Uganda began to take on a truly sinister pattern. Nicholas Stroh, the son of a Detroit brewer, had left his job on the *Philadelphia Evening Bulletin* to go freelancing in Africa. Nick, at 33, was one of the up-and-at-'em school of investigative journalists who had not been in Africa long enough to realise that such tactics could be unwise in the post wind-of-change era.

He had heard rumours of a massacre of some 1 000 troops of the Acholi and Langi tribes, the kin of the deposed Obote, at the Mbarara Barracks, 40 miles north of the Tanzanian border. Mbarara was the headquarters of the self-styled 'Simba' ('lion' in Swahili) battalion commanded by Lt-Col Waris Fadull Ali, another Nubian of unfriendly reputation, who had allegedly been responsible for disposing of the disloyal troops on Amin's orders. In Kampala, Nick Stroh hired a car and drove south. With him was a friend, Bob

Siedle, another American who was a lecturer in sociology at Kampala's Makerere University. Bob went along because he was interested in missionary church architecture and might have found some interesting examples on the drive to Mbarara.

Neither Stroh nor Siedle was ever seen again. Much later, it emerged that Nick had left Siedle at the Mbarara Hotel to drive directly to the Simba barracks to investigate the massacre reports. There he had gained access to Major Aiga Juma (only a year before, a Kampala taxi driver) who was at first startled and then angered by the table-thumping approach of the American reporter. Juma had Stroh seized and sent men to grab Siedle from the hotel in the town. The two men were beaten, bayoneted and then strapped to drums full of oil, riddled with bullets and then set alight. Their remains were dumped in a river. Their car was also burned and driven over a gorge.

The disappearance of the two men gave Amin the first diplomatic headache of his rule. The American Embassy in Kampala started to make loud noises. Amin then still had some civilian ministers and advisers who persuaded him to take action. He appointed Mr Justice Jeffreys Jones, a British judge of the Uganda High Court, to conduct an inquiry. Mr Justice Jones, in the circumstances, did a diligent job. He got very close to the truth and wrote his report implicating Col Ali and Major Juma in the murder of the two Americans. But such was the atmosphere of fear and intimidation that surrounded his inquiries that the judge fled to Kenya, booked himself on a ship out of Mombasa bound for Europe and posted his report just before the vessel departed. Amin received the report – and promoted Ali to Army Chief-of-Staff, later to provincial governor and then to Cabinet Minister.

Back at the Apolo Hotel – now renamed the International – the atmosphere was becoming increasingly strained. Every time we went out to talk to people, or to the bar, or upstairs to the Leopard's Lair nightclub on the top floor, or downtown for a meal, we were followed by the highly dangerous, amateur sleuths of the Public Safety Unit. These young killers were supposed to be a discreet squad of plain-clothes men, but all had taken to wearing vivid floral shirts, baseball caps and the ubiquitous reflective sunglasses of the trade. All carried Uzi sub-machine guns tucked into their belts.

Their method of 'shadowing a suspect' was to walk immediately behind you, occasionally treading on your heel. In a bar or restaurant they would push locals off stools and chairs and sit down immediately beside you. Like so much else in Amin's Uganda it would have been hilarious if it was not so dangerous. We knew these conspicuous young spooks had their own method of killing which began with the victim being stuffed into the boot of a car, driven to a remote spot, tortured for the fun of it and then dispatched by garotte, a sharp knife, or a sharp tap with the heavy end of a 20 lb sledgehammer.

At that early stage, they merely had orders to follow the foreign journalists and to monitor our telex messages and telephone calls. Knowing they were listening at the hotel switchboard to our calls overseas, we alerted our offices to the menace and, when we dictated copy down the telephone, took care to include exaggerated praise of Idi Amin. The foreign desks understood and removed the panegyrics from our copy.

But, once again, the menace had not been conveyed to the copy-takers, those lovely people sitting with headphones in London and taking down our deathless prose with loud yawns. A colleague got a cheerful Cockney copy-taker at one particularly sensitive moment. Aware that our minders were tuned in downstairs he began to dictate: 'His Excellency, Life President Idi Amin...' The Cockney interrupted. 'Oh Gawd!' he said. 'Wot's the old black baboon been up to now then?' My colleague immediately cut the line and fled his room down the fire escape.

Henry Kyemba, one of the few well-educated and trained civil servants who survived the early years of Amin's purges and tried in vain to keep his country on some kind of even keel, revealed later that even Idi feared Maliyamungu. Amin once told him that he thought the major 'might be going mad' but he was kept on and promoted. The British government, realising it had helped to create a catastrophe, took immediate remedial steps. It sent a senior military intelligence officer to 'train' Amin's goon squads. He resigned after a couple of months, telling Kyemba 'Obviously an intelligence officer needs some basic intelligence. These chaps have none.'

According to Kyemba, Amin had no idea of fiscal policy. The Israelis were urged to go ahead with myriad prestige projects – barracks, roads, airports and apartment buildings, including an elaborately guarded and bunkered Field Marshal Idi Amin Air Force Base at Nakasongola, 70 miles from Kampala. There were few aircraft to guard and, in any case, Amin could not bear to have them very far from his reach at Entebbe. There they crashed frequently into Lake Victoria as he ordered imaginary attacks on South Africa from his lakeside lodge which he named 'Cape Town View'.

When the accounts began to surface for these projects, he expelled the Israelis and denounced Zionism. As Uganda ran deeper and deeper into international debt, Amin began using the Bank of

Uganda as 'a personal petty cash box', Kyemba recalls. 'By his definition countries could not go broke because they printed money and
could always print more.' When Kyemba and others tried to persuade him of financial realities, he hit upon the brilliant idea of
expelling en masse Uganda's Asian minority, most of whom had
accumulated much wealth by instinctive hard work and diligence.

The impact of this announcement was immense. The British
government, whose record in Uganda was one of repeated bungling,
was sent into panic by the thought of 80 000 Asians with entitle-
ment to British Commonwealth passports descending on the
benighted islands. I knew as personal friends many Ugandan
Asians. I knew of the community's huge contribution to the economy
and culture of Uganda and of their potential value to my home country which had a clear obligation to accept them as Commonwealth
citizens.

It has to be recorded that the Ugandan Asians who were finally
allowed into Britain have proved the point: some of those who were
stripped of all their assets, humiliated and tortured by Amin and his
men, are now among the wealthiest people in Britain. Let it also be
recorded that the British Foreign Office put its best effort into pre-
venting any influx of Ugandan Asians into the country and that the
behaviour of British officials at the High Commission in Uganda at
this time was cowardly, naïve and, by any standards, totally despi-
cable. Like Freddy Forsyth a few years before in Biafra, I suddenly
felt very ashamed to be British. As a result of the political implications of such an influx into Britain, the Uganda story, hitherto just
another African basket-case, became major news. Our lives in
Uganda were suddenly enlivened by the arrival of dozens of 'heavies', experienced men – and women – who would not particularly
care about where they were but were keen to get, preferably by a
foot in the door, to the 'truth'. There were others, less experienced,
trying to make a journalistic name for themselves by being 'on-the-
spot' on a major news story. It was a 'major news story' only because
of its implications for Britain and Canada and other nations who
might be obliged to accept Asian 'refugees'. The interest in what was
actually going on in Uganda – the systematic killing and looting by
'Government forces seeking out the perpetrators of economic sabotage' – was of secondary interest.

Although his goons were following us everywhere, Amin initially appeared to revel in the attention of the press, particularly television. Peter Stewart, a tough, former Fleet Street tabloid investiga-
tor, led the first BBC TV team in to pit his wits against arch-rival,
Richard Lindley of ITN. Their rival quests for good 'visuals' led to

some ferocious competition. One morning, I was with Peter as he decided, on the spur of the moment, to waylay Idi Amin outside his Kampala base, a suburban home he had called 'The Command Post'. Anything less military it would be hard to imagine. Chickens and a couple of goats scrabbled in the dust, teams of women toiled over wash tubs and hung clothing out to dry, and children ran and screamed in the yard. But it was heavily guarded whenever Amin was in residence.

On this occasion he was. The goon squad immediately frisked us and demanded to know our business. Stewart was very good at handling thugs. 'Tell the General,' he ordered, 'that the BBC is at the gates'. He made it sound almost biblical. It worked. Suddenly an enormous shadow loomed up at the sentry box. Idi stared at us for a few minutes. He was fully aware that we were both journalists and was obviously making up his mind whether to adopt a friendly or hostile approach. Peter disarmed him.

'Good morning, General,' he boomed. 'It is a very hot day and we were thinking that we had not seen you at the swimming pool recently.' I had to admire Stewart's audacity. In those early days, Amin had occasionally delighted the TV boys by suddenly arriving at the International Hotel swimming pool and challenging them to a race or two. He was always ready to say a few, or more, words into the microphone afterwards. He took an elaborate look at his watch. 'I'll be there...ten minutes from now. I'll be there. YOU be there Mr BBC!'

He need not have asked. We rushed back to the International, rounded up Peter's crew and were quickly poolside. Stewart suddenly struck his head with his hand. 'Oh! For Christ's sake, I've forgotten my swimming trunks.' He was staying at a different hotel some way away and there would be no time to fetch them. Peter was determined that his TV exclusive would show him desporting himself in the pool with Idi. He needed some trunks desperately. We tried the pool attendant, the porter's desk, even the manager's office but no one had any suitable trunks. In desperation Stewart looked at me. 'You're staying here, Chris. You must have a swimming costume.' I had, of course, but Stewart was well over six feet tall with the build to go with it. I was not. I said I was happy to give it a try, so we rushed to my room. Stewart struggled and heaved himself into my tiny trunks and we rushed back to the poolside. Idi was already there, dressed immaculately in a towelling robe and wearing Olympic-styled, well-fitting, leopard-spotted bathers. 'Now Mr BBC man, let us see if your swimming has improved,' he roared, shedding his towelling robe and plunging in like a wounded hippo. Stewart paused only to make sure his cameras were rolling and joined Idi in the water. They swam a couple of lengths. Idi ducked the BBC man a couple of times and they emerged to camera. Stewart was handed a microphone and launched into a slightly breathless poolside interview.

There were several of us standing around, bemused hotel staff, watchful bodyguards, perhaps a couple of visitors. None of us noticed anything unusual, at least about the appearance of the two men. The interview lasted for about ten minutes. It was great TV, one in the eye for ITN. The film footage was canned and rushed to the airport for the first flight to London. It got back just in time to be aired on the following evening's 6 p.m. BBC TV news.

There, on millions of screens, was the 'beast of Central Africa', perfectly clad, being interviewed by the BBC's Peter Stewart, looking slightly uncomfortable in a very tight pair of swimming trunks. And there, peeking out from the BBC man's trunks, was the unmistakable shape and form of a large left testicle! When the BBC relayed to Peter the flood of complaints they had received about his improper dress, he sent back a one-worder: 'Bollocks!' Back came the riposte. 'No, old boy, only one!'

Also enlivening the Kampala scene at the time was Miss Mary Kenny, the very lively, very vivacious and very Irish feature writer, then working for the *London Evening Standard*. It soon became clear that Mary was interested not so much in the Uganda story as in one of our colleagues, Richard West, the author and freelance writer who had arrived a little earlier. Dick West was clearly a little intimidated and quickly moved to a small hotel on the outskirts of town.

Mary, knowing of West's fascination with Africa, bustled around Kampala's markets, buying exotic African female adornments, presumably as a form of local breeding plumage. She was so persistent in her questions about West's whereabouts that, to our shame, perhaps, we eventually shopped him, giving not only the location of his hotel but his room number and the name of the friendly porter who could be bribed to lend her the pass key. We saw neither of them for three days. A few weeks later they were married and, happily to report, have remained so ever since. It's an ill wind, indeed.

The mood in Kampala became much uglier as it became clear that Amin was determined to throw out all Asians, not just those who were non-Ugandan citizens. Worse, it was obvious that he made this blatantly racial ploy to appease his Nubian army and secret service men who freely began looting or seizing Asian shops and businesses. The atrocity stories multiplied. The atmosphere of fear, oppression and apprehension became palpable. Churchill's 'fairy-tale land' echoed to screams in the night and unexplained bursts of gunfire. I had never been able to shake off a perverse habit of reading the best fiction about the worst situations when on location. Listening to Idi Amin's new version of the sounds of the African night, I was re-reading V S Naipaul's *In a Free State*: 'You could hear them raising the hue and cry and you know they're beating someone to death outside. You should either stay away, or you should go among them with whip in your hand. Anything in between is ridiculous.'

Most of the foreign hacks, including me, began to feel a little bit of pressure. My problem was that the *Telegraph* had a long-standing policy of keeping a correspondent on the spot indefinitely, long after rival newspapers had pulled their men out, or at least relieved them. Any request for a break from an oppressive story would be met, automatically, with one back from the Foreign Desk: 'THANKS YOURS BUT INSIST YOU ONSTAY.' This policy had paid off on several occasions when the *Telegraph* man had been the only one on the spot for a counter-revolution or a counter-coup, but it was dispiriting to the man involved. Diversions, social and otherwise, became essential. In Kampala during 1972 I was lucky in having relays of colleagues arriving who were also good friends.

Michael Knipe, then the African correspondent of *The Times*, had been a friend for years. Always beaming through owl-like spectacles, well-scrubbed, pink and youthful-looking, Knipe was congenial company in the best and the worst of times. He had, as an unmarried man, the most complicated and confused love life. Attractive women were always braving the bombs and bullets to seek him out, usually finding him in the arms – or some other part of the anatomy – of another local beauty. Knipe always sought the assistance of his colleagues to help him find a way out of these dilemmas, a sometimes pleasurable, sometimes dangerous diversion. He was also a musician of some talent, and had been a semi-professional jazz drummer in an earlier life. He drowned the sounds of those Kampala nights with Scott Joplin tapes, played endlessly and mournfully in his hotel room.

Mike had adopted a diffident, almost absent-minded approach to difficult situations which worked in the most improbable ways to get him what and where he wanted. He had that great gift of self-deprecating humour that kept us amused in the more hairy moments. He had recently been on a rugged trip in the Ogaden Desert, returning thankfully after two weeks to the relative luxury of a Nairobi hotel room. He leapt into the shower to wash off the grime and dirt.

The most prized and closely guarded possession of the foreign hack in those days was the Air Travel Credit Card. This little green piece of plastic could be used to buy an airline ticket to anywhere, get seating priority in any class and the bill would eventually be sent to one's home office. Taking his second successive shower, Knipe decided to clean up his Air Travel Card, the indentations on which had collected some muck and grime. He reached across to his wallet, pulled the valued card and began to scrub it under the shower. Suddenly it turned to a fluorescent pink and began to flash, neon-style, 'Not Valid…Not Valid'. He had activated a built-in, anti-forgery safeguard. That took some explaining to *The Times* Foreign Desk.

To break the oppressive monotony of Kampala, I had found a friendly boatman in a village on the shores of Lake Victoria who was happy to hire out his motor boat for a few hours, especially for a few US dollars. We found it great fun to pack a picnic lunch, a bottle or two of warigi (a gin made from local bananas) and potter around the numerous islands on the northern shore of this great lake. These Munnion mystery tours usually took place on a Saturday morning, traditionally a 'quiet' time for newspapers and television networks. As long as we were back in Kampala by Saturday afternoon, no one was going to miss a story.

Mike Knipe took to these 'mystery tours' like a latterday Stanley. One Saturday, he took over the tiller and set about finding an island with a sandy beach that he had spotted on an earlier trip. We skirted around various small islands and then spotted his beach. It looked very pleasant, limpid waters lapping a stretch of sand fringed with quite thick jungle. An ideal spot for a relaxing picnic, but Knipe was in explorer mode. 'I am going to walk all the way around this island,' he declared, setting off energetically into the trees. An hour or so passed, and then another. There was no sign of the intrepid *Times* man. Three hours passed and some colleagues were beginning to get agitated. Some had work to do and we needed to get back to Kampala.

We split up into search parties, shouting out Knipe's name with mounting anger and apprehension. I found a small rise and clambered to the top. It certainly was a big island. There was no sign of any shoreline on three sides. Finally, an exhausted, puce-pink figure crashed through the undergrowth and collapsed on the beach. It was the Man from *The Times*, bleeding from giant thorn wounds and battered by branches.

'Christ!' he moaned. 'This must be a bloody enormous island.' He had walked for a couple of hours, vaguely following the shoreline, before realising that this wasn't going to be a jolly round-the-island stroll. In trying to take a short-cut back to the beach he had got lost and entangled in the jungle. We hauled him into the boat and made our way back to Kampala, hissing and muttering our displeasure. The joke was really on all of us. I found a Ugandan friend with a detailed map of the area. We had not been on an island at all. The attractive beach had been on the mainland and Knipe had been heading for the Rwandan border, some 200 miles away. He was thenceforth known as 'Knipe of the Nile'.

In Kampala our 'minders' were becoming more intrusive and aggressive. Most of the hacks had their rooms searched. We were followed everywhere and ears were flapping on our every conversation. Jolly John Osman, who had arrived for the BBC, accompanied me to look at the old Kabaka's palace. Two carloads of sunglasses and sub-machine guns pulled in behind and ahead of us. We tried to engage them in a friendly conversation about Uganda's recent history. Not a flicker. They followed us around the otherwise deserted site, fingering triggers and suddenly pushing in front of us to stare at us menacingly. Once again, we made our excuses and left.

Richard Stott arrived in the middle of this period for the *Daily Mirror*. It was his first foreign assignment in Africa and he soon picked up the menacing mood. What was left of his peace of mind was shattered when, unbeknown to him, the *Sunday Mirror* ran a full, front-page picture of Amin with a huge headline proclaiming 'He's Mad – Official'. The *Mirror* had found a tame psychologist in London to pronounce on Idi's mental state from his rantings. Stott received a phone call from an extremely nervous British diplomat.

'If you're the *Mirror* man, the High Commissioner advises you to leave Uganda immediately.' Richard was now understandably twitchy. He could raise no one on the *Mirror* desk. We advised him to make the usual tactical withdrawal to Nairobi until the heat was off. Instead, he headed straight back to London. We did not blame him, and although there were a few raised eyebrows at the *Mirror* at his sudden return, it certainly did not harm his career. He became editor of that newspaper a few years later.

Donald Wise, the old campaigner, flew into Kampala for the *Mirror* to instill his tonic-like humour into the jittery hack corps. Donald's advice to all and sundry, our minders included, was that Idi needed sexual therapy. 'What he needs is a good woman to go down on him like a Dacca crow,' he roared. Sandy Gall arrived to head up ITN's camera crew, Mario Rosetti, the large genial Italian, and his tiny soundman, also Italian, always attached to him by the microphone umbilical. Donald had christened this team 'Mario and his donkey'. I don't think we ever knew the soundman's name.

Don McCullin, now a famed war photographer, complemented the officer's mess demeanour of Wise and Gall with some classic Cockney sergeant's mess humour. Don had a highly individual way of working, a routine dictated by the Equatorial light. He was up at dawn to catch the sun's first rays or out in the even better late afternoon light. 'I ain't interested in chasin' fire-engines,' said Don. 'If the light's not right it's a bleedin' waste of time.' He produced his usual, brilliant off-beat images of Amin's capital. In between it was, for McCullin, poolside at the International with a warigi and tonic by his side. The drink was usually bought for him by Boris, the Tass-KGB man, who for some reason wanted to 'learn Cockney'. The *Daily Express* had sent reporter John Harrison and photographer John Downing, a lively, energetic and humourful team. John Fairhall of *The Guardian* and Nick Moore, Reuters bureau chief from Nairobi, were great colleagues to have along as both had been brought up in Kenya, spoke Swahili and were aware of the African ethos. Penny Tweedie, an attractive young freelance photographer, arrived and displayed much courage which brought out Downing's protective (rather than paternal) instincts.

I suppose it was not a great story from an American viewpoint. The only American correspondent was Andy Torchia from AP's Nairobi bureau. Thank God for Andy. When the going got rough for the foreign press, as it was about to do, it was, as always, the American diplomats, not the British, who put themselves to much risk and trouble to help us. It was a good press corps to be with. We all became close friends, not least because we were all aware that we were under siege and that Amin would be making some kind of move against us before long.

The crunch came early in September. John Osman and I had separately picked up reinforced rumours that Makindye Barracks, the military police headquarters, had become Amin's main killing field. Ugandans, black and Asian, who were perceived to be opposed to military rule were being killed daily, and nightly. One of the few former inmates to have been released – he bought his way out with an enormous bribe – had told us chilling stories of ritual killings at Makindye, of victims being forced to bludgeon others to death with sledgehammers before suffering the same fate themselves. Truckloads of bodies, they had said, left the prison every night to be fed to the crocodiles in the Nile or in Lake Victoria.

Such was the understandable panic and fear among the Asian community that, at first, we were loath to believe the tales of horror from here. Several sources, however, indicated a similar pattern of organised murder and disposal. Osman and I determined that the story was far too sensitive to file from Kampala. We would try to obtain further confirmation and fly to Nairobi to send it. Little did I think I would soon have the opportunity to investigate the Makindye reports first-hand.

Osman had recently married Virginia Waite, a former *Telegraph* journalist who had accompanied him to Africa on this trip. Vinnie had been commissioned to write a tourist guide to East Africa and that weekend she and John had travelled from Kampala to the Mountains of the Moon on the Burundi border, with an official Ugandan guide, to gather material – and enjoy an unusual, slightly delayed honeymoon. Sandy Gall, having been threatened by Amin at a reception, decided it was time to leave, but ITN insisted he 'onstay' in Uganda. He and his crew decided to weekend at another tourist spot, the Murchison Falls National Park. The rest of us went to the old Grand Hotel to hear Mike Knipe sit in as guest drummer with a very good local band in the basement nightclub.

That night, a small army of some 1 000 Ugandan exiles from Tanzania invaded the country across the southern border, engaging Amin's troops near Mbarara. We awoke to martial music being played on Uganda Radio and even more troops than usual rushing to and fro in the Kampala streets waving cocked weapons at everything and everyone. Fairhall, Harrison and I called the British military attaché, one of the few cool-headed types at the High Commission, and arranged to meet him for a briefing on what military dispositions might be available to either side in this little war.

We then adjourned for a pre-arranged Sunday lunch at the lakeside home of Charles Harrison, our unflappable resident stringer. Half way through, we tuned in to BBC World Service to hear the newscaster say that 'all foreign journalists in Kampala have been confined to their hotels'. We decided the best policy was to return to the hotel where, at least, we hoped we would have facilities to file.

It was a mistake. The hotel lobby was crawling with goons and armed troops. As Fairhall and I approached the reception desk to ask for our keys we noticed the clerk, normally a cheerful, helpful soul, wide-eyed and trembling with fear. We made our way to the lift doors, studiously ignoring a shout behind us. As we entered the lift, a rifle barrel was jammed between the doors forcing them to re-open. A soldier waved the rifle at us. He was also wide-eyed and shaking – but with rage. 'You are spies! Spies! Out! Out!' He prodded us at gunpoint into the lobby and ordered us to sit in two chairs. He was opposite us, waving the rifle under our noses. I tried to ask, as gently as I could, what the problem was but he cut me short with another snort of 'Spy! Spy! Shuttup spy!' I shut up.

Out of the corner of my eye, I saw one or two of our colleagues glancing towards our plight and, wisely, moving away. Not Sandy Gall. He and his crew had heard of the invasion attempt at Murchison Falls and had just driven back to Kampala through a few hostile roadblocks. To my horror, I saw Sandy march towards us, a rather forced smile on his face.

'Hello, chaps,' he said to us. 'Anything going on?' I knew Gall was trying to give us a bit of moral support and was grateful, but he was going to land himself in trouble with this approach. 'Piss off, Sandy,' I hissed out the corner of my mouth. 'We are under arrest.'

Our guard screamed at me, prodding me in the stomach. 'You, spy, shutupp, spy!' He turned to Sandy.

'Who are you?' Not for nothing is the tall ITN man named Gall.

'Good afternoon,' he said politely to the soldier, extending his hand. 'I'm Sandy Gall and you are...' The guard turned his rifle Sandy's way and screamed at him: 'You, go away...go away.' Sandy got the message, gave us a cheery wave and strode across the lobby. He was to be seeing more of us much sooner than he would have liked. Finally, our nervous young soldier was relieved by three plain-clothes men of the Public Safety Unit. They were unfriendly, unsmiling but at least the safety catches of their Uzis were locked. At gunpoint, we were led upstairs where, not much to our surprise, more goons were ransacking our rooms.

I was made to stand by the window with my hands on my head as a rather bizarre interrogation began. My room was littered with reams of paper – discarded intros, messages, cuttings, newspapers and the useless, anodyne press handouts issued by the Information Minister. (Unbeknown to us, Amin had at that moment ordered the execution of Alex Ojera, the Information Minister.) It was one of the official handouts that attracted the most attention. It was about five weeks old and announced merely that 'His Excellency Al-Haji, Field Marshal Dr Idi Amin Dada, VC, DSO, MC, the Life President' would inspect his glorious, courageous troops at Tororo barracks the following weekend.'

'Aha!' snarled one of the pairs of sunglasses. 'So you were planning to assassinate the President at Tororo? That is where you were going to kill him?' I was suddenly seized with an urge to shout with laughter, which I suppressed. It would probably have proved fatal. I had visions of myself pulling up a footstool to enable me to reach Amin's neck, put my little hands around that giant windpipe and squeezing. Better still, I could lend him my swimming trunks and put an end to the Amin dynasty. I merely stammered out an explanation that this had been sent to me by His Excellency's very own Information Ministry.

Another goon had found a letter from my wife, Denise, and was poring over it, moving his lips as he did so, in the great tradition of Donald Wise's readers. This was a little perturbing as I was then based in rebel Rhodesia. I should have had more faith in Denise's good sense. She had made no mention of anything that could link the letter to Rhodesia and posted it under cover to relatives in Britain who had sent it on. It had a London postmark. The goon giggled as he came to the terms of endearment. I made a mental note to stamp very hard on his windpipe when circumstances improved.

Finally, he held up the letter under my nose and pointed to the address in the top left-hand corner. It was one word: 'Umwindsidale'. It is partly an African name. The name 'Umwindsi' is that of a river which flows through a very pleasant rural area outside Salisbury (now Harare) where my wife's parents lived. 'What is this?' he asked. With as much assertiveness as I could muster, I lied to him: 'That, sir, is the address of my family home in England.' I emphasised the 'England' and pointed vaguely northwards to drive home the point. He seemed satisfied.

With some horror, I realised that, stupidly, I had retained in the notebook in my pocket all the military details given to us by our friendly neighbourhood military attaché that morning. If they were looking for anything to brand me as a spy that would be ready-made. It began to burn a hole in my pocket. I need not have worried. For some reason I was ordered outside my room while the search continued and told to lie on the floor of the corridor, my hands still on my head. At such moments, many thoughts flit through the mind but, I have found, Africa has a way of diverting the most fearful. One of the hotel deputy managers, a large, ape-like figure came shambling down the corridor towards me, prone on his carpet, and a goon with a sub-machine gun standing over me. He kneeled down to peer at my face which lit up when he recognised me as a guest of long standing.

'Hello, sir,' he said. 'Is everything all right?' I replied, realising for the first time that to speak through gritted teeth is quite possible: 'No, I think I am under arrest.' The deputy manager's face lit up. 'Ah! You must be one of the foreign journalists. They are arresting all of you.' He settled down on his haunches beside me.

'Tell me,' he said. 'I have always wanted to be a foreign journalist...can you help me to become a foreign journalist...you people have such a good life!' Inwardly I screamed 'AWA! AWA!' – Africa Wins Again!

'*Gimme an intro for this story*' – *Peter Younghusband in Kampala's Apolo Hotel 1969.*

Following Page: ⫸

Top: *Lake Victoria 1970 – Peter Younghusband surveys Nkunze Island where a British diplomat claimed to have been held by his Asian kidnappers.*

Bottom: *John Fairhall* (The Guardian) *Mike Knipe* (The Times) *Penny Tweedie (Freelance) Keith Graves (BBC) on Lake Victoria 1972.*

MAKINDYE PRISON CHESS MATCH
D.Telegraph 3   Guardian 2

The Guardian *cartoonist marked the release of correspondents from Idi Amin's notorious Makindye prison with his impression of the chess match between the author and John Fairhall in their cell. They made an improvised chess set from incriminating notebooks.*

John and Virginia Osman were thrown into gaol together by a considerate Idi Amin.

CHAPTER TWELVE

CALIBAN'S CONTINENT

At gunpoint again, I was led out to a military vehicle and bundled into the back. There was the broad, still-beaming face of John Fairhall who had shared the same experience but had concentrated his mind on his just-announced appointment as Education Correspondent for *The Guardian* (a job he was, happily, able to take up later with great distinction). He had made the mistake of exchanging a few words in Swahili with his interrogators. They had immediately accused him of being a 'Kenyan spy' and thumped him around the head. Then, before we moved off, two young white men, handcuffed and retching with terror, were thrown in alongside us. They turned out to be Lars Holmstrom, a reporter for Sweden's *Expressen* newspaper, and his photographer, Kenneth Johansen.

The two Swedes had left Stockholm two days earlier, having been given their first foreign assignment. 'Go to Africa, to Uganda and discover the TRUTH,' they had been told. 'Not these lies that are being put out by the agencies.' Excited and filled with a sense of adventure, they had arrived in Kampala that morning, unaware, of course, that there was an even greater state of emergency because of the invasion from Tanzania. They had checked into the International and had gone to the roof-deck to overlook this scenically attractive African capital.

Two young men in sunglasses appeared next to them. 'Hello,' said Lars, full of that patronising Swedish bonhomie that emerges instinctively from these strange Nords confronted by someone of a different hue. 'This is a beautiful city...you must be very proud of it...can you please point out to me the special sights we must see?' One of the goons smashed him across the mouth with the butt of his Uzi. They were both arrested and thrown into our truck. Huddled in the back of the police van, we decided mutually and tacitly that it was not the time for protest or an exchange of confidences. To my relief, we pulled up outside the Central Police Station in the centre of Kampala and were herded into the main charge office. There we were ordered to squat on the floor while policemen, some of them obviously remnants of Uganda's well-trained old force, argued and remonstrated, very bravely, with the brightly shirted goons who arrived at various intervals waving their sub-machine guns and pushing in a variety of totally bewildered white civilians, some with their wives and families.

This was a good sign, I reasoned. If Amin had ordered a general round-up of whites it was not a press purge but a general precaution against any white helping whoever was trying to overthrow him. There was strength in numbers, I thought. The more obviously innocent European families who arrived to join us the better. This would be a temporary measure, surely? It was not to be.

My heart sank as I saw a young, slim thug from the Public Safety Unit enter the charge office, give the sergeant-in-charge a backhanded slap across the face and move among the babble of seated prisoners. I knew him, and worse, he knew me. He had, over the previous months, frequently perched himself on barstools alongside me, refusing my offers of drinks with one of those eyeless smiles, suddenly plonking himself beside me at cafés and restaurants, saying not a word but listening to all conversations and somehow always being there. I feared him more than the others because he was obviously senior in rank in whatever absurd unit to which he was attached, because he had obviously 'targeted' me – and mainly because he never wore those ubiquitous sunglasses.

His eyes tonight were bloodshot and glazed. He moved down the lines of squatting whites, swiping out occasionally with a swagger stick. He reached our group and paused. I could think of nothing better to do than greet him. He smiled with his mouth and stained teeth only. 'You,' he said, tapping me on the head gently. 'And you and you and you and you.'

By this time our arrest party had been joined by Don McCullin, John Harrison and Andy Torchia. Our man knew who he was looking for and his tapping swagger stick was indicating to an accompanying party of goons just who they were to grab and manhandle into waiting vehicles outside. I do wish I had been a good enough reporter to get his name. I would very much like to meet him again, preferably on neutral territory. We were herded and prodded to the roadside outside the police station and I heard my 'friend' bark the order to the drivers and guards. It was one word – the last one I wanted to hear at that time and place. 'Makindye', he said to the driver. 'Makindye now!' Our guardians now were the real heavies of the Public Safety Unit. The public was far from safe and these men could, under no circumstances, be called a 'unit', but absolute power was theirs. The two military vehicles rushing us through the evening traffic had their flashing lights on, their sirens screaming. The drivers delighted in sending any other vehicles into ditches alongside the road as we screamed past. We started to climb out of town towards Entebbe. Lars Holmstrom whispered to me 'This is the road to the airport, no? They are going to deport us, no?' I didn't want to be facetious, but I had to tell him 'No'.

The vehicles roared through a series of gates into a compound. We were manhandled out and assembled in a very nervous huddle before a glazed-eyed, pot-bellied NCO. Leering soldiery in sloppy combat uniforms gathered around us. One of our escort officers rattled off what we presumed to be a list of our misdemeanours to the NCO. Suddenly we were clubbed to the ground with rifle butts. In the dust we were ordered to remove our shoes and double into the guardroom. Sweating soldiers kicked at us as we ran past and we tumbled on top of each other. A corporal, a cigarette dangling from his lips, ordered us to remove our socks.

Suddenly from outside came angry shouts and the sounds of slapping and kicking. A plain-clothes man brandishing the inevitable machine-pistol threw a young African civilian into the room. He fell on top of us, bleeding and blubbering. Finally, another corporal arrived and began to make a list of our possessions – wrist-watches, pens, cash, the usual prison list. I thought this a good sign. If they were taking the trouble to record our goodies, surely they could not be planning to kill us, not immediately anyway? Don McCullin was not so sure. 'This is it, mate,' he whispered. 'They're going to kill us all.' I learned later that Don, on one of his evening photographic excursions, had been picked up and brought to Makindye. He had been released after an hour or so but not before the NCO who had checked us in had warned him that if he ever came back he would not leave alive.

We were led out of the guardroom at gunpoint, through another gate and into the main prison, a series of 25 ft by 50 ft single-storey British military prison blocks. The ground was generally dry and dusty, but my bare feet frequently touched things soft and squelchy. A loud fluttering and shuffling on the tin roofs of the cell blocks drew our attention to a host of vultures gathering in the evening gloom. The omens were not good. As Fairhall, the two Swedes and I were pushed into Cell Block A-1 through a large iron door I heard McCullin mutter 'Cheers, mates. Good to know yer'. I supposed that Don was so full of shrapnel shot and shell from Vietnam and Cambodia that he had become a fatalist.

It was pitch black inside the cell but as soon as the heavy iron door had closed behind us, willing hands reached out and there were whispered greetings from all sides. A match flared briefly and then another. We met our cell mates – 21 Africans in all who seemed delighted to have *wazungu* – white men – as their new cell mates. We were offered a blanket each and Big Joe, a bulky and amazingly cheerful Togolese who was clearly the 'cell boss' (he had been there for more than a year) allocated us space on the bare, concrete floor. We became aware that four of our fellow inmates, who had greeted us and solemnly shaken our hands, had resumed a small prayer meeting in one corner of the large cell. They were on their knees in a little group, their hands clasped together. Low but repeated and anxious 'Amens' came our way. Big Joe whispered to us, by way of explanation, 'Policemen'.

My immediate thought was that they were police spies planted in our cell, but if that was the case why were they praying so earnestly? As a smoker, my only hope for a gasper was Big Joe. I crawled across the cell to talk to him in his prime position – six blankets in the quietest corner. If I had 'access to funds' he could provide me with as many cigarettes as I wanted. We made a deal. Joe was an itinerant 'businessman' from Togo who travelled throughout West, Central and East Africa organising 'deals', buying and selling anything he could lay his hands on. In any other society, I gathered, he could have made Paul Getty and Howard Hughes look like shopkeepers. He had made the mistake of driving his large, battered Cadillac into Uganda a year previously. The car had been coveted by Amin's troops at a roadblock. Joe had been hauled out, beaten up and thrown into Makindye. His prized vehicle, he assumed, had been 'appropriated' along with his samples and his personal possessions.

As we shared this whispered conversation in the dark I asked him about the 'policemen' praying in the corner. 'They are the Ugandan police force,' said Joe, 'the soldiers arrested them last night. They will be killed tonight and they know it.' I thought – or rather hoped – that he was exaggerating. He wasn't. While I had been hearing Joe's story, John Fairhall had joined the prayer meeting in the corner. In Swahili, he had asked them who they were. They were two inspectors, one superintendent and one sergeant from Kampala. Amin had suspected the remnants of the old police force would side with the 'rebels' who had invaded from Tanzania. They had been picked up by the Public Safety Unit and knew they would be killed, there and then, in Makindye that night.

I was having great difficulty in absorbing all this. My own basic terror was being sublimated in a concentration on doing the best we could in whatever circumstances arose. John was more philosophical. He went to join the police officers in prayer. I explained the situation as we knew it to the Swedes, Lars and Kenneth and we all went and joined the prayer meeting. There was something biblical about the scene which followed. At about midnight, there was the fearful sound of the cell's iron door being hauled open. An electric light controlled from outside was switched on, and, for the first time, we were able to see our cell mates clearly.

There was fear on every face, probably on ours, too. The soldiers had been drinking and were certainly high on something. A corporal came to the group in the corner and grinned malevolently at the prayer meeting. He spent some time examining four faces on the floor before tapping two shoulders with a swagger stick. 'You...and you...' he said. 'Up and out!'

The two designated men – the former police sergeant and an inspector – were bundled out of the cell accompanied by miss-aimed but vicious kicks from the soldiers. The door was hauled shut and locked. The light snapped off. The two remaining policemen dropped into fervent private prayer. The cell fell silent. Possibly a few minutes later, outside the cell, there was a sickening thud, a scream, another thud and a groan. A few minutes later, we heard a maniacal scream, another thud, a brief shout of laughter and then silence.

This, I thought to myself, has to be a nightmare. This is not really happening, I convinced myself. Some horribly perverted subconscious images were imposing themselves on my brain and I would awake in my hotel room to find another sunny Kampala morning. All such delusions were dispelled when, perhaps an hour later, there came the ominous squeak and groan of our cell door and, once again the light snapped on.

Our two remaining policemen – the inspectors – had known what was coming and were already on their feet as the staggering corporal came towards them. For one horrible moment, I thought that Fairhall and Lars Holmstrom were going to attack him. Both were large, gentle men but the reality of what was going on had struck home. Our new-found friends were being taken, two by two, from the cell.

One would be coerced into breaking his companion's head with a sledgehammer. His own head would then be bludgeoned by the guards. My two colleagues were, fortunately, restrained by the rifles carried by other soldiers, jabbed into their stomachs with the drunken, challenging looks of morons who know they have the edge in a bar brawl. We nodded goodbye to our policemen friends as they were led from the cell. The sounds, a few minutes later, were now familiar in a very macabre way. Thud, scream, groan, thud, groan, scream – and, worse, a shout of anger.

That was our first night in Makindye Military Prison. There were to be five more, but I had numbed myself with silent curses, incantations and imprecations to hitherto unknown Gods. How on earth had what I had been led to believe to be an honourable career in journalism led me to this? Fairhall was magnificent. After the hideous loss of our four cell mates, he continued the prayer meeting – and every single one of us in that cell joined him, even the cell-wise Big Joe from Togo. By dawn, Fairhall had organised cell-cleaning parties. With improvised brushes and dusters we cleaned the cell from floor to ceiling. There was, in one corner, a tap with a slim dribble of water running into a foetid drain. This was also our toilet. It was cleaned and cleaned again.

By full daylight, we must have had the cleanest cell on the block. Between Big Joe from Togo and Fairhall of *The Guardian* everything was organised. Most of our cell-mates were Ugandans, lesser civil servants and post office workers. There was David, an itinerant Kikuyu tinker from Nairobi who, again, had been stopped at a Ugandan military roadblock, had his car and goods stolen and had been thrown into Makindye. There were two cosmetic salesmen from Ghana who had been arrested at Entebbe when they arrived, sprayed with their own products and thrown into Makindye. The camaraderie in Cell A-1, Makindye Military Prison, was unbelievable. Fairhall and I made notes of each and every one of them, knowing that if any of us was going to be released it would be the *wazungu*. We, possibly, might be able to raise some kind of protest on their behalf.

Through Big Joe, I learned that McCullin had landed on his feet. He had been put in what Joe called 'the executive suite'. This was the cell housing Manubhai Madhvani, the wealthy Asian businessman whose interests were at that moment being plundered by Amin's men. Even inside Makindye, Madhvani still had enough influence to obtain for himself a bed with sheets, tea, cigarettes and other little luxuries. One less attractive feature of the cell was the presence of Bob Astles, the ubiquitous, rather sinister Englishman who had been an odd-job man for Obote, and was soon to perform similar functions for Amin. It was, nonetheless, a sight better than Cell 1-A. Harrison and Torchia were in a cell similar to ours.

Sandy Gall and Nick Moore survived another night at the International before they, too, were picked up and whisked to Makindye by the goon squad. They had a particularly rough time. After checking in their valuables, shoes and socks at the guardroom they were forced to run through the compound, being jabbed with rifles all the while. They were initially thrown into C-19, which they later learned was death row.

'The walls and ceiling were covered in bloodstains and pock-marked with bullet holes. We both concluded that we were not going to get out of this place alive.' In the course of the day, they heard a prisoner being beaten to death outside their cell and watched guards taunt and torture other prisoners in their cell. Finally, an officer arrived and appeared to think it was not a good idea for the two *wazungu* to be watching the activities in C-19. That night, they were transferred to the Madhvani cell with Don McCullin.

John and Virginia Osman were not enjoying much of a belated honeymoon at the Mountains of the Moon Hotel in Fort Portal. They had to drive through Mbarara, headquarters of the 'Simba' battalion which, unbeknown to them, was about to come under attack that night from the rebels invading from Tanzania. The troops were in a highly nervous state and rounding up Asians at gunpoint. When they got to their hotel, Osman dictated a story to Philip Short, then the BBC stringer in Kampala. In the middle of the night, troops burst into their bedroom, ripped off the bedclothes and started screaming at them, 'Where are the guns?' It took all of Osman's diplomatic skill to calm them down and assuage them with his accreditation and travel permits. They were bundled into a Land Rover with a captain as an escort officer who was told to take them back to Kampala forthwith.

At Mubende they ran into a a drunken, frightened rabble of sol-diers who pushed Osman around while Virginia cowered in the back of the vehicle. 'They were discussing among themselves whether to kill us or just beat us up.' Their escort captain finally persuaded the troops that his orders were to report directly to Field Marshal Amin and they were allowed to proceed. They arrived at Entebbe late in the evening and were put in a cell in the police station. 'Fortunately, one of the old-style police officers was in charge. He was terrified of Amin's secret policemen but when they left he allowed me to call the Entebbe Hotel to order some food. Would you believe that not long afterwards, a smart waiter, clad in a white uniform and a fez, arrived from the hotel with quite a good meal under large salvers? I thanked him profusely and reached for a tip. He looked at me, dead-pan. "Will that be cash, sir, or will you sign?" I immediately said I would sign. I scrawled across the bill "To whom it may concern...please call the British High Commission"'.

It was a bold move, but it backfired. Virginia had just settled back on a bare wooden bench to try and get some sleep when the door burst open and an enraged army officer came in screaming.

'Where are the bastards...they are trying to make fools of me...we are going to shoot them.' He crashed into the Osman's cell, uttering furious oaths in Swahili, and took a wild kick at the end of the bench on which Virginia was sleeping. Mrs Osman did not move. She remained prone on the bench, gazed up at the furious major, and said sweetly. 'Jambo, wapi simba?' She had been in East Africa only a few weeks and these were the only words of Swahili she then knew. They mean 'Hello, where is the lion?'

The officer stared down at her, his jaw agape. 'Wapi simba?' he repeated, astonished. 'Wapi simba?' He suddenly started to laugh, repeating the phrase over and over and staring at the still studiously prone Virginia. 'He had a mild form of hysterics. Doubled up with laughter he reeled out of the cell, never to be seen again.' Mrs Osman looked at her husband. 'Do you have any other good ideas for a honeymoon?' John took the point but, typically, replied 'Look, Vinnie, this is a bloody good story...if we ever live to write it!'

In the morning, a police inspector arrived, his face and uniform covered in blood. 'Look what our wonderful army has done to me,' he told the Osmans. They were driven to Kampala and to the guardroom at Makindye. But their luck held. A call came through and they were told they would be driven straight back to Entebbe Airport to be deported. There, to their delight, they found the ineffable presence of Donald Wise, Keith Graves, the BBC TV man, and other hacks who had been held briefly at Kampala's police station.

Donald had been arrested at his room in the Grand 'by an ugly dwarf with a shotgun'. At this time, he was based in South East Asia and his press passes for China, Cambodia and Vietnam caused great excitement, as did his short-wave radio marked up with all the wavelengths he needed to tune into foreign radio stations. 'That was it...I was a spy. They tossed me in a vehicle and this little bugger insisted on sitting on my face. They threw me into a cell, removed my belt and shoes and told me I'd be shot at dawn. I'm not sure if they actually mentioned "dawn" but the message was the same.' In the morning, he was allowed out to join the rest of the journalists, whites and other transients who had spent the night huddled in the main charge room. 'Bit of an amazing sight...kids running about with snotty noses playing, grub delivered from the Grand and a party of Japanese mountaineers in heavy clothing, hissing and bowing at everybody and not having a clue what was going on. They'd just returned from an expedition in the Mountains of the Moon.' Donald was surprised to see a 'whiter-than-white' face poke itself through the bars. 'British High Commission,' said the face. 'Can't stay long...how many people here?'

It was, as far as we could make out later, the only effort made by the British diplomats in Uganda to establish what had happened to us. I was infuriated later to read in the *Telegraph* that the British High Commission claimed we – six British citizens in Makindye Military Prison – had 'been interviewed and were being well-treated'.

Not one member of that miserable establishment came near Makindye while we were there. We were certainly not interviewed and we most certainly were not being well-treated. It was symptomatic of the grotesque parody of diplomacy that the Foreign Office applied to the entire Ugandan tragedy. The hacks, generally, can take care of themselves. But there were at least 22 000 Asians, holding British passports and full citizenship, who were being murdered, beaten, brutalised and robbed without so much as a peep from British officials on the spot. Worse was to come.

Wise, Graves and the Osmans were happily on board a British Caledonian airliner, en route to London, when we spent our second night in Makindye. Obviously, we had no knowledge of what had been going on outside. During our first night, John Fairhall had decided that we could keep our sanity only by formulating a rigorous cell routine. He was right. By dawn, we had improvised a chess board from the pages of my notebook – containing details of the military briefing – which had miraculously escaped the searches. We started our first game.

At 6 a.m. every inmate of Cell 1-A was allocated a cleaning task. We cleaned that large cell from top to bottom, thoroughly and repeatedly. Fairhall even managed to get the tap in the corner working more efficiently which meant that all our ablutions were that much easier and our waste that much more easily disposed of. Big Joe was enthusiastic about this project. He had a 'tame' guard who, miraculously, produced a bottle of vile after-shave lotion. We used it carefully, drop by drop, to help purify 1-A.

That morning, there came the dread sound of the key in the lock and the groan of the heavy iron door. Two young Asians were hurled through the door and sprawled on the floor in front of us, spilling blood. One had a split chin. He had been stopped at a military roadblock, his car had been seized, he had been beaten with rifle butts and he had been thrown into Makindye. We staunched the blood with the rest of my notebook. His companion, thin, slightly-built and shivering, had a permanent nosebleed. He had been beaten for 24 hours by soldiers who were convinced he was concealing cash that he did not have. We made them both as comfortable as we could. The Kikuyu tinker came over to me to chat quietly. He apologised for the 'brutality of Africa'. It was touching but the only way I could think of comforting him was to talk about the mayhem in Ulster.

An afternoon silence was broken by sudden, shrieked commands of guards outside the cell. Big Joe uncovered his 'spy hole', an old air vent that he had secretly restored. Through it, we could see prisoners being ordered from an adjoining cell block to unload possibly a dozen bodies from a truck. Clearly, the men had been badly mutilated. 'Big hammers,' said Big Joe. 'They use big hammers to kill them. If they shoot them it causes too much noise and too much trouble.' At that stage, I wondered whether I should applaud their sensitivity.

Not long after, the doors rattled and were unlocked amid much shouting, screaming and bellowing. This was the one and only eating time of the day. A large dustbin full of inedible, stodgy maize with a few pieces of rancid meat was tipped in our direction as we filed towards it. I was going to decline but Big Joe whispered urgently in my ear. 'Take all you can. Someone needs it.'

As I scooped up two handfuls of stodge, screams of agony came from the adjoining cell compound. The military guards were enjoying a little diversion. They were making two half-caste prisoners perform increasingly difficult athletic feats. The youngsters faltered and soldiers, spittle on their lips, brought down rifle butts on their heads. It was a sound we were getting used to.

Fairhall's regimen was, in retrospect, a life-saver. He had paced out the length of the cell and established that 250 lengths at a brisk stride would be the equivalent of strolling down Les Promenade des Anglais in Nice. Several times a day, the men from *The Guardian*, the *Telegraph* and *L'Expressen*, Stockholm, strode purposefully up and down Les Promenade des Anglais. The Asians thought we were mad but we were soon joined by Big Joe from Togo and the Kikuyu tinker who insisted we pointed out various sights to them, including the topless ladies on the beaches. Fairhall and I pursued our chess marathon on the improvised board with a vengeance. It became quite a needle match. The only time I thought John's admirable composure was going to crack was when I won Round Three.

We had calculated that our chances of surviving depended on the degree of success achieved by the invading rebels. If they appeared to be threatening Kampala we reckoned our military guards would get very nasty indeed and possibly panic. We had no way of knowing that the ill-planned, half-hearted invasion had been routed within a few hours. Amin was hamming up the war nerves to suit his own purposes, giving his troops even more arbitrary powers. On day three, another badly beaten Asian was hurled into our cell. After we had treated him as best we could, he told us that the rebels had been defeated. The atmosphere in Cell 1-A lightened considerably.

On Day Five, the great iron door creaked open to admit a beefy Nubian sergeant and several armed soldiers. The journalists were instructed to write down on a piece of paper he provided their full names, home addresses and 'the place you want to go to if you leave here'. I failed to notice Lars Holmstrom write down 'Back to Sweden – as soon as possible' but this was picked up as facetiousness by the guardroom officer. The Nubian sergeant and his men were quickly back in the cell. Lars was singled out, slapped around and made to lie on the floor. He was ordered to roll up and down the cell ten times. Rifle butts and boots were raised at his prone figure every time he rolled past. We were obviously not out of the fire yet.

Big Joe was convinced that we would soon be free. We busily collected all the personal details of our cell mates, promising to do what we could to notify relatives and friends and, where possible, their diplomatic representatives. That afternoon, the door creaked open once again and we were ordered out in single file to the guard-room. There, with some surprise and relief, we joined our colleagues from other cells. As we were marched towards the gate, a group of men under guard were being marched in, barefoot, bedraggled and fearful. All were Ugandan police officers, their badges of rank ripped off. Our hearts went out to them. There was no reason to suppose that their fate in Makindye would be any better than that of their colleagues who had briefly shared our cells.

Our belongings were returned to us. As we pulled on our socks and shoes for the first time in six days, an officious, thin-faced officer arrived with a sheaf of deportation orders. Once again we were lined up. 'Sign here,' he snapped. 'And don't ever come back to Uganda.' Sandy Gall could not resist the rejoinder 'Don't worry. We won't'. Thin-face exploded in shrill rage. 'You come back here,' he screamed at Gall. 'What did you say?' For one terrible minute we thought Sandy's crack would send us straight back to the cells. Gall grovelled and apologised and we filed out into the compound in silence. As we waited for transport, a group of Ugandan soldiers manhandled a screaming civilian through the gate. They pinned him to the ground while a large woman whipped him hard and unmercifully. The man was screaming. The soldiers were laughing. No one, least of all this chastened party of hacks, intervened. After a week in Makindye, the scene did not seem that abnormal.

A clapped-out bus arrived and we boarded. To our amazement, it diverted past the hotels where we were allowed to pack our bags and pay our bills. We began to breathe a little easier as the bus sped past the gates of Makindye and headed towards Entebbe Airport. The journey took more than an hour as there were military road-blocks every mile or so. We were still under military escort so were untroubled by the indolent soldiery. They were waiting for fleeing Asians who were systematically robbed of what few possessions they had tried to take with them. At the airport, the American Charge d'Affaires pushed his way through our guards to ask if we were all okay. He had made the risky journey to Entebbe with two medical orderlies to see if Andy Torchia in particular and the rest of us in general needed any treatment. I exchanged knowing looks with Sandy. There was, of course, no sign of any British diplomat.

It was nearly midnight when a British Caledonian airliner, out of Nairobi and bound for London, landed at Entebbe. We almost ran to board. It was only after we had taken off that any of us dared to believe that we were finally free. The captain kindly sent back several bottles of champagne for us and then announced the bad news: Heathrow was fogbound and we were diverting to Manchester. We chartered taxis from Ringway to intercept the breakfast-special express train to Euston and ate heartily for the first time in a week. We were unaware that we had become minor celebrities. John Osman and Donald Wise, deported two days before, had been on television to explain, cautiously, that we were being held in Amin's notorious military prison. At Euston, there were TV teams and reporters out in force to greet and interview us.

Nick Moore of Reuters, a gentleman to the last, succumbed to a TV interview and placed his suitcase on the platform beside him to answer questions. He had survived five days in Amin's hell-hole and had returned with his person and luggage intact. When the interviewer finished, Nick turned to pick up his suitcase. It was gone, stolen from the platform in broad daylight! Our stories from Uganda were graphic and accurate enough. They could hardly be otherwise, given that we had all experienced the horror first-hand. I arrived back at 135 Fleet Street to be locked into a small office on my own by Ricky Marsh, the Foreign Editor. 'Just let it flow,' he said. I did. Like all personal experience stories it wrote itself. I was interrupted repeatedly by phone calls from colleagues and TV producers demanding my story before I had written it myself. Jolly John Osman was on the line.

'We're having a Ugandan prison reform society gathering at El Vino's tonight,' he boomed. 'Be there.' That evening I called Nick Moore at Reuters to tell him of the gathering.

'I haven't written a word yet,' he said. 'I'm waiting for the word from on high.' Poor old Nick. Reuters had been totally unsympathetic about his incarceration, angry about his deportation and totally unconcerned about the theft of his suitcase at Euston Station. This world-renowned 'news' agency was more concerned about the possible loss of its 'business' in selling its service to the Ugandan government, irrespective of who was in charge. It had hardly been a hero's welcome. A senior Reuters man had buttonholed him on his arrival back in Fleet Street and demanded to know why he had been arrested and gaoled. Without waiting for a reply, he went on 'Don't tell me, Moore...you were mixing with journalists!'

East African states at that time had, despite poor relations between each other, maintained a rule that if a journalist was declared a prohibited immigrant in one he would automatically be debarred from the other. As Nick had now been PIed in Uganda, it put his job as Reuters bureau chief in Nairobi in jeopardy. Reuters top men went into a huddle to decide how Moore should write his story.

Finally, late in the evening, they decided he should merely draft a few anodyne paragraphs recording the fact that some foreign reporters had been released after being detained. No colour, no background, no drama and, above all, nothing that might upset the Ugandans. Moore did as he was told and then asked if anyone had made him a hotel booking. 'Hotel? Hotel?', the reaction of the senior man was one of horror. Nick felt like Oliver Twist. 'Surely you must have relatives in Britain?' Moore had an aunt in Guildford. The senior man pulled a pound note from his pocket. 'I'll lend you this...there's a good train service to Guildford.' So much for the hero's return.

Fleet Street's handling of the Makindye story had its low points. The *Daily Mail* had been very late off the mark, sending Les Watkins to Kampala after we had all been arrested. Les was arrested himself as he was checking into the Grand Hotel and deported immediately. He had been in the country less than two hours, but this did not deter the *Mail* from splashing his story under the headline 'Mailman Leslie Watkins flies back with the first full story from Uganda'. Of the *Express* team, John Harrison had been with us in Makindye while photographer John Downing had been in the much more relaxed atmosphere of the Central Police Station in Kampala. Downing had brought back photographs of the main charge room, including some of children who had been picked up with their parents playing in the cell corridor. The *Express* ran Harrison's horror story alongside Downing's pictures without making the distinction between Makindye and the police station. There was a flood of cynical letters from readers demanding to know how the two could be reconciled.

My cell-mate John Fairhall, immediately accepted the job as Education Correspondent of *The Guardian* and deservedly won an International Reporter of the Year award for his Ugandan coverage. Nick Moore returned to Nairobi for Reuters with no hassles from the Kenyans. After squeezing every drop of Ugandan copy out of me, the *Telegraph* sent me back to Nairobi to 'Amin watch' from there.

One of my first tasks, at the behest of *The Times* foreign desk, was to establish if their man, Mike Knipe, who was still in Kampala, was all right. Knipe's survival was one of the great mysteries of Amin's press purge. Mike had been in Kampala for as long as we had. He had been followed around by goons, as we had. I remember seeing him hovering around the foyer of the International when Fairhall and I were picked up. But throughout all the arrests, gaolings and deportations he had not so much as been questioned. He continued to file, guardedly, to *The Times*.

Jerry Kaminada, the Foreign Editor, asked me if I could make discreet contact on the telephone from Nairobi to ensure Knipe of the Nile was not under any undue pressure. I got through to his room at the International, disguising my voice. I used what they call 'veiled speech' to avoid compromising him in any way. A very cheerful Knipe assured me that all was well, he was enjoying himself and he now had a regular drumming gig with the band at the Grand. Yes, there was something I could do for him. Would I find out if it was possible to drive a Mercedes Benz from Kampala to South Africa without too many formalities? Amid the horror, Knipe had been offered a Mercedes at a give-away price by a fleeing Asian and was tempted. I assured *The Times* that their man was not only alive and well but steeping himself in East African culture.

When Knipe finally emerged (*sans* Mercedes) he had only one hairy moment to report. Amin had imposed an evening curfew. Mike was a little late for his gig at the Grand. A carload of VIP Protection Unit thugs pulled up alongside him and bundled him in the back. Where was he going? To the Grand. To the Grand they drove, escorted him to him to reception and demanded to be taken to his room. Knipe had to explain that he was not staying at the Grand but the International. Back in the car, the squad drove him to the International and searched his room. 'Why were you going to the Grand if you are staying here?' demanded the head goon. The *Times* man explained that he played the drums in the band at the Grand.

They clearly disbelieved his story. They marched him back to the car, drove down the hill to the Grand once again, and frog-marched him through the basement restaurant to the stage where the band had already started its evening entertainment. The place froze as the goon squad marched in. The band faltered and stopped. Diners fell silent. One of the goons pulled the stand-in drummer off the stand and pushed Mike into his place. The others commandeered a table in the front and glared menacingly at the assembled musicians. 'Play!' hissed the senior pair of sunglasses. Knipe gave the performance of his life, prolonged drum solos, virtuoso twirling of the sticks, studious syncopation.

'The sweat was pouring off me. "Gene Krupa eat your heart out," I thought. Soon the VIP Protection Squad relaxed visibly and even began tapping their feet in time to the beat. They swallowed several beers hastily provided by the management and left. I never saw them again...and I've never been able to play like that since,' Knipe recalls.

The full extent of Amin's reign of terror was now becoming apparent to all. His civilian ministers – those who survived the death squads – fled one by one to confirm the stories of mass killings of perceived tribal or other 'enemies of the state' or arbitrary arrest, torture and murder of the few remaining members of Uganda's professional and administrative classes. Mr Benedicto Kiwanuka, Uganda's Chief Justice, was arrested by troops who burst into his High Court chambers and dragged him away, handcuffed and barefoot, to be murdered. The Nubian army officers, most of them Sudanese, not Ugandan, were given the top jobs, seized the best property and possessions and robbed, murdered and looted at will.

Amin's excesses made him a figure of fun in Europe. Alan Coren of *Punch* made him a jocular cult figure in a series of articles and books. But there was nothing funny about Idi Amin for those living in Uganda. He was more like a feudal robber baron than a military dictator. The killings and the looting continued unabated.

British policy remained one of cringing appeasement. The government sanctioned the continuation of the so-called 'whisky run', a regular airlift of luxury goods from Stanstead Airport in Essex to Kampala. This merely enabled Amin himself to live in style and provide goods to his army officers. Ordinary Ugandans never saw any benefits from the British supplies. Amin declared himself 'Conqueror of the British Empire' and reinforced the point by 'persuading' a group of British expatriates to kneel at his feet at a reception and then carry him around on a litter. He also condemned to death Dennis Hills, a British teacher and author who had described him as a 'village tyrant' in his book *The White Pumpkin*. Hills was reprieved only when James Callaghan, then British Foreign Secretary, made a personal visit to Kampala.

Africa's reaction was even more predictable than that of the British Foreign Office. Amin was a hero among the *wananchi* – the masses. They knew he was responsible for terrible atrocities, murder most foul, torture, terrorism, and had reduced his country to economic and social shambles – but he was humiliating the white man and was making the British government cringe. As far as the *wananchi* were concerned, Idi Amin was The Man of the Moment. The Organisation of African Unity made him chairman in 1975. There can, surely, be no sadder commentary on the dilemma of post-independence Africa than that.

As far as Fleet Street was concerned, Amin was one of those amusing African diversions, a genial, bloody tyrant readily accessible to the new breed of columnists who had not the slightest interest in, and certainly no knowledge of, the catatonic complexities of post-colonial Africa. 'Go and interview the buffoon,' said the features editor. 'Of course,' they said, and happily trooped into Kampala to get their very colourful interviews with Idi Amin. As we used to say in copy, 'I watched in horror as...' (take in agency). He was not mad. He was not a fool. He knew, instinctively, how to play the game of public relations. When he was confronted by a journalist visiting for the first time, he would play the expected role. It was a different story with correspondents he knew. He would bluster, threaten and intimidate.

David Martin of *The Observer* had been monitoring Amin from his base in neighbouring Tanzania. When Martin dashed off a book about the Field Marshal's regime, Amin put a price on his head. He deported Philip Short, the BBC stringer. Peter Younghusband, now with *Newsweek*, had upset Amin with a cover story for that magazine – and by winning a challenge from the big man to stand back to back to see who was the tallest of the two. (Bigfoot Younghusband was, by a short head.)

When Amin attended an OAU meeting in Mogadishu he spotted Younghusband among a group of pressmen in the lobby. He marched over and jabbed his baton towards him. 'You!' he said. 'You! I am going to catch you.' Peter, knowing he was on neutral territory, tried a witty reply. 'Yes, Mr President, but I can run very fast.' Amin lowered his lids and kept his baton pointed firmly at Younghusband. 'Nobody,' he said, slowly, 'can run faster than a bullet.'

When the OAU, to its everlasting ridicule, decided Idi Amin should be its chairman in 1975, two Makindye Old Boys, John Osman and Andy Torchia, were asked by their organisations, the BBC and AP, to interview him. As both had been declared *persona non grata* with the rest of us, they made representations from Nairobi and were told they could come to Uganda where they would be 'received' by Amin. With some trepidation, they flew to Entebbe and were summoned to his presence. 'The nearest he came to apologising for having thrown us into jug was his opening remark "Gentlemen, it is all very different now".' At the end of their joint interview, Amin said he now wanted to ask them a question – and insisted that the tape recorders stayed on. He leaned across to Osman, tapped him on the knee and asked: 'Tell me, Osman, do you really think I am mad?' John gulped. 'Well, Mr President, I have never reported that you are mad...' Torchia cut in. 'Well it all depends on what you mean...there are people who are clinically mad...' Both correspondents floundered for the right thing to say as Amin watched them stonily. Finally he said: 'You know people say I am mad but I am really fifty years ahead of my time.'

When this interview was broadcast, Osman was again criticised in letters to editors for not taking up the position of world prosecutor. One angry major (retd) wrote that if he had been in Osman's position, he hoped he would have had the courage to say: 'No. You're not mad Mr Amin. I hope the day comes when you will be publicly tried, judged and executed.' Osman replied to the major, saying he was sure he could arrange for him to see Amin and pass on his message personally if he could make his way to Uganda. He received no reply.

Amin was always curious about the BBC man's name, as were Moslems all over the world. Osman is about as English as anyone I know, except perhaps that the mythical English 'reserve' has never found a place in his patriotic arsenal. His family can be traced back for centuries of yeoman service in Oxfordshire and Sussex. He wanted to join the Royal Navy but was turned down because he was short-sighted. He translated his love of water into becoming a swimming and diving champion, at one stage joining the West-super-Mare Water Wizards, a team of divers who, dressed in clown costumes, entertained at seaside resorts with antics from the high boards. His love for the English language took him into journalism, on the *Brighton Evening Argus* where he started 'for two quid a week plus one shilling and sixpence bicycle allowance'.

As a colleague on any given foreign beat, he was probably the most popular journalist of his era. Many a morning, as the hacks emerged bleary-eyed for breakfast, Osman would appear, bouncy, cheerfully enthusiastic and would readily divulge the details of three or four interviews he had already conducted before we had got out of bed. If the telex and telephone lines were down, John could be relied upon to fix up a radio link from the local radio station and to persuade the BBC to relay our copy to our newspapers. If he had a fault, it was an ability to sustain a verbal barrage of comment, philosophy and anecdote for hours on end, delivered as if he was broadcasting to the world without a microphone.

A legendary victim of this trait was Bill Humphries of Reuters. Humphries had been persuaded to make an exceptionally long drive through Botswana with Osman in the Beeb VW Beetle. As hour after hour and mile after mile rolled past, Osman boomed out his stories and philosophy, to the stage where the Reuters man, who was not feeling at all well, felt himself tensing unbearably at the din.

There was no question that John's stories were true. He had been in every corner of the world several times and had a huge repertoire of fascinating yarns. 'I told the bloody woman "Get back on your donkey...we've got to make the rebel camp before daybreak"...I said to the King "Excuse me, Your Majesty, may I use your phone?"... Then the bloody copy-taker asked me to spell bougainvillaea...' Great stuff, but after nearly four hours of it, Humphries' nerve-ends were fraying and his knuckles were whitening. Eventually even Osman began to exhaust his rhetorical reserves.

There was blissful silence for ten, perhaps fifteen minutes. Then a speck appeared at the roadside in the distance. As their car approached it, they could see it was one of those ubiquitous hoardings advertising Coca-Cola. It triggered Osman's memory once again. 'Look at that!' he exclaimed. 'Drink Coke in the middle of the bloody desert...that reminds of the time I was crossing the Gobi...'

Humphries snapped. He leapt from his seat, seized John by the throat and screamed 'For God's sake, shuddup!' To this day, John Osman, reminded of the Reuters man, will say 'Bill Humphries! Very nice chap...but he's got something against Coca-Cola!'

Among the GOAHs, Osman had a variety of nicknames 'Ali Bin', 'Osman Bey', 'Osman Pasha', 'Pasha Ofendi', etc. Idi Amin was always curious, rolling John's surname around his tongue and deciding, to the BBC man's embarrassment, that he liked him. 'He kept inviting me back to Uganda which became increasingly embarrassing as I was having to broadcast more and more about his misdemeanours and brutality.'

On one occasion, he drove Osman to Entebbe Airport, at high speed, in his custom-built Range Rover. 'On the way he suddenly glanced at his watch and said it was time to listen to the BBC. He tuned in and to my horror up I came with a piece I had done about Uganda a couple of days earlier. It was not particularly flattering but Amin listened in silence, still driving at high speed. I was trapped. When it finished he glanced across at me. My mouth was very dry. "Osman," he said. "You very good reporter." It was the most consoling compliment I've ever had.'

Amin's behaviour became more and more bizarre. As OAU chairman he hosted the annual heads-of-state conference in Kampala, laying on for the delegates a display of firepower by his air force. In the official programme, the event was called, intriguingly enough, 'The bombing of Cape Town'. The hapless aviators were instructed to bomb and strafe a deserted island in Lake Victoria on which had been planted a South African flag.

Amin and his guests watched the exercise from a specially constructed platform dubbed 'Cape Town View'. It quickly became clear that the air force was out of practice. Most of the bombs not only missed the island but some came perilously close to the distinguished onlookers. Amin was furious. The air force commander was relieved of his command – and his life – immediately. His mutilated body was discovered a few weeks later.

Osman was once again at the centre of a drama during the Kampala OAU Conference. The BBC's monitoring service in Caversham picked up the first broadcast from Lagos radio announcing the overthrow of President Jack Gowon, who was attending the Kampala meeting. The Beeb sent Osman a telex message which was intercepted by the Ugandan Foreign Office. Osman received an urgent summons to the Foreign Ministry in Kampala and was questioned closely about a message he had not received, and then about a coup in Nigeria which he had not heard about.

'It soon became clear that they had intercepted my message. At the conference hall, the Foreign Minister asked me if I could find out more and came with me to a telephone booth while I talked to the Beeb in London. They confirmed the coup and gave a few more details. The Foreign Minister then had the embarrassing task of breaking the news to General Gowon that he was no longer head-of-state.'

Jack Gowon, arguably the most pleasant man ever to rule in Africa, took the news like the gentleman he was. At a press conference, he quoted Shakespeare 'All the world's a stage...And all the men and women merely players...', wished the people of Nigeria well and flew to Britain to continue his university studies.

Idi Amin's greatest humiliation came less than a year later, as he was due to hand over the OAU chairmanship at the next summit in Mauritius. PLO terrorists hijacked Air France flight 139 out of Tel Aviv shortly after it took off after refuelling at Athens. Under the hijackers' guns, it was flown to Entebbe where the 258 passengers and crew on board were held as hostages with, of course, Amin's connivance. Idi revelled in the new limelight, parading and strutting before the hostages cowering in an old airport building at Entebbe.

One wonders at the state of mind of those hostages. Not only had they undergone the terror of a hijacking but were now here at the mercy of the whimsical butcher of Central Africa. In the most audacious, brilliant military operation of the age, Israeli commandos flew to Entebbe on the night of Saturday, 3 July 1976, seized control of the airport and its environs and rescued the hostages – with one exception.

Mrs Dora Bloch, a 70-year-old passenger who held dual Israeli-British citizenship, had been taken to hospital in Kampala the previous day with a piece of meat lodged in her throat. After the Entebbe raid, Amin ordered his State Research Bureau to kill Mrs Bloch. She was dragged screaming from her hospital bed, shot in the head and buried in a shallow grave in the bush outside Kampala. If ever there had been doubts about Idi Amin's status as a very dangerous psychopath – and, unbelievably he had his apologists among 'liberal' Western commentators – the murder of Mrs Bloch should have dispelled them. Idi Amin never recovered from the humiliation of the Entebbe raid. His army had been conspicuously absent from the airport when the shooting started and he himself had gone to ground, thinking it was an attempt on his life. With the true, unerring instinct of the thug, he became completely paranoid, lashing out in all directions.

Thousands more Ugandans, Bagandans, Acholi, Langi, Christian – anyone who might possibly pose the threats he saw emerge from every corner – were massacred, murdered, or merely 'disappeared'. He clung to his last lifeline, Col Gaddafi of Libya, declared Uganda to be an Islamic state and attacked the Christian churches. He denounced publicly Anglican Archbishop Janan Luwuum for 'hiding arms of war' and organised his murder, along with those of two government ministers, in a faked 'car accident'.

Idi Amin survived another year before being overthrown. His paranoia was so advanced that an assassination was not only difficult but would have left Uganda under the 'control' of his Nubian army, most of them manifestly thugs and bandits. President Julius Nyerere of Tanzania succumbed to pressure from numerous sources, not least fellow African leaders, to organise an army to topple his neighbour.

There was no small irony in this move. Nyerere, the self-styled *Kwalimu* – or teacher – had brought his own once-beautiful country to bankruptcy and ruin with the ideological terror of *ujamaa*, a half-baked Marxist scheme to force peasants into areas of concentrated agricultural production. But he was playing host to many thousands of Ugandan refugees and when they formed a force to march against Amin, he allowed the formation of an army of 40 000 men to invade Uganda. Amin got wind of the plot and, typically, staged an abortive counter-move. In 1978, he sent his army into the Kagera Salient in Northern Tanzania. They 'fought' in the manner to which they had become accustomed. They massacred hundreds of civilians, looted, raped, and plundered homes and farmsteads and then withdrew back into Uganda. It was the excuse Nyerere had been waiting for. His hopelessly ill-trained, ill-disciplined rag-tag army invaded southern Uganda. It met with very little resistance once the Nubians realised their opposition had some fire-power. The Tanzanian troops looted, plundered and raped their way northwards towards Kampala.

This, one hoped, had to be 'emergent' Africa at its nadir. The year was 1979, nearly 20 years after Macmillan's 'wind of change' warning. A semi-trained, hastily assembled army from one East African country was invading its neighbour in horrible disorder to overthrow an illiterate cannibal who had held his country in thrall with unimaginable brutality and terror with the support of black mercenaries of other religious beliefs from another African neighbour. And spare a thought for the thousands of totally innocent Africans who, as always, got caught up in this rolling, confused morasse of gunfire and armed youths who understood only that their *raison d'être* was to seize property and rape and kill anything that stood in their way.

I was in Zambia when I got wind of the Tanzanian plans for the invasion of Uganda. Eric Marsden, now the *Sunday Times* Africa correspondent, had picked up the same tip. Eric and I caught a scheduled Air Zambia flight to Dar es Salaam to see what we could discover. Knowing how sensitive Nyerere's men were about 'hostile' journalists – i.e. those who refused to find repeated excuses for Nyerere's disastrous *ujamaa* policy – we telexed ahead to tell the Tanzanian Information Department about our impending arrival and to ask for accreditation. It was a mistake. Special Branch officers were waiting for us at Dar airport.

I was escorted politely but firmly from the arrivals hall to the departure lounge and ordered back onto the same aircraft, which was returning to Lusaka. No explanation was given. The pilot, one of the Australian drop-outs then used by Air Zambia, had already locked his doors and started his engines. My escort was trying unsuccessfully to get through to the control tower to instruct him to let me on board. I decided that aircraft was not going to leave without me. I did not want another spell in a Tanzanian gaol.

I ran onto the tarmac, stood in front of the airliner's nosewheel and looked imploringly up at the impersonal cockpit perspex. The pilot relented finally and dropped his gangway. To cheers from amused onlookers on the terrace, I clambered on board, hot, frustrated but relieved. 'Have a scotch, Chris,' said a soft-spoken American voice in the seat beside me. It was one of the CIA's better known African operatives, a young professor whom I had met in the most unlikely places at various times. I accepted the drink gratefully while my friend confirmed that Uganda was about to be invaded by an army of exiles and Tanzanian troops. I gathered that Western intelligence agencies had helped to organise and finance an operation against Amin.

Poor Eric Marsden had a much rougher time. Special Branch missed him at the airport and he made his way to a hotel in Dar. He was just reporting my instant deportation to the British High Commission when the police caught up with him, burst into his room and escorted him straight back to the airport. He had, of course, missed the Air Zambia flight and the next foreign-bound airliner was Aeroflot to Moscow. Eric resisted being put on that flight but was obliged to camp for two days and nights in Dar's miserable little terminal before getting on an aircraft bound for Cairo.

Tanzania allowed only a handful of sympathetic correspondents to accompany its invasion army, including Tony Avigarn, a young American freelance and Nyerere apologist. Not surprisingly, the stories of the wholesale plunder and looting carried out by the invading forces did not emerge until much later. Poor Uganda! As Amin's thugs began to flee they were replaced by equally ill-disciplined looters and rapists. Such was the confusion in Uganda that most hacks chose to cover the invasion from the Intercontinental Hotel in Nairobi. There John Bulloch established an 'operations room' with a large-scale map of Uganda and a powerful short-wave radio with which to monitor the rival claims of the Ugandan and Tanzanian state radios. As far as lively copy was concerned, Amin did not disappoint. He put his fifth wife, Sarah, at the head of his First Mechanised Suicide Revolutionary Battalion. She had been a go-go dancer with that unit when he first met her. She was quickly dubbed 'Suicide Sarah' and her antics, as relayed by Uganda Radio, made bizarre reading.

Old hands knew it would be extremely hazardous to venture into Kampala with Amin under siege. He was dangerous enough in 'normal' circumstances. At bay, he would be lethal. So it proved. Against all the advice of their more experienced colleagues, two young Swedish journalists and two Germans working for *Stern* magazine, hired a boat from Kisumu on Lake Victoria and made their way across the lake to Jinja. They arrived just as Amin and his heaviest bodyguard were fleeing through the town, in retreat from Kampala. The four journalists were shot in cold blood shortly afterwards.

Only when the Tanzanians were clearly in control of Kampala did the press corps make their way to the ravaged Ugandan capital. In Amin's former residences and the headquarters of his death squads, they found a mass of evidence of the atrocities committed under his regime. David Lamb of the *Los Angeles Times* found his way to Amin's 'Command Post' residence.

'His bedroom, like that of a child, was covered with pictures of military aircraft, scotch-taped to the walls. There were cartons of hand grenades under Amin's bed and bottles of pills for venereal disease on his bureau. One closet was stacked with reels of Tom and Jerry cartoons and a file cabinet was stuffed with photographs of tortured Ugandans, gaunt, maimed creatures who hardly resembled human beings at all.'

Brian Barron of BBC TV and John Osman ransacked the files they found at State House and at the headquarters of the State Research Bureau where most of the slaughter of the dissidents had taken place. Mohammed Amin, the Kenyan freelance cameraman, 'liberated' a stack of film of Idi Amin taken by his official cameraman during the last, crazed days of the dictator. Hacks happily helped themselves to souvenirs lying around official buildings, including the numerous medals Amin had ordered from Spink & Son, the Royal-appointed medal makers of St James, London.

Idi fled the country, first to Libya and then to Saudi Arabia where his convenient conversion to Islam served to afford him a refuge. At the time of writing he is still there, occasionally sought out by hacks for off-beat interviews during the quiet 'silly seasons'.

Mo Amin, filming for Visnews, was the first to track him down at his hideout near Jeddah. Brian Barron squeezed the first interview with Mo's film but the Kenyan cameraman was infuriated when the BBC ran the piece without crediting him. It was billed solely as an exclusive interview by Brian Barron. It was not the first, or was it to be the last occasion on which others had taken the credit for Mohamed Amin's professional diligence.

David Lamb telephoned Amin at his refuge near Jeddah. 'That's what Uganda needs – democracy,' Amin told the startled *LA Times* man. 'Democracy would not work immediately in Uganda. It would take two or three years. Security is very bad there now, and there are many problems, but a tough person with military knowledge like me could teach the people discipline and prepare them for democracy.'

There was to be no democracy for Uganda, with or without Idi Amin. Trigger-happy Tanzanian troops, having exhausted pillage, turned to manning indolent roadblocks at which, depending on their mood, they would rob or rape any Ugandan. A series of civilian governments collapsed, including, mercifully, a return of Milton Obote. Anarchy replaced tyranny. Screams and gunfire continued to haunt the Kampala nights. Nobody really knew who was in charge in which area or which attitude to adopt at any given roadblock. Uganda's nightmare continued.

Less than a year after Amin's downfall, I was ordered back to Uganda on a whim of Peter Eastwood, the *Telegraph*'s then managing editor. It was not a trip I relished making, knowing just how difficult it was to find fresh water let alone edible food among the chaos. I assured the Foreign Desk that I would obtain a visa from the Ugandan High Commission in Nairobi. After a couple of pleasant days looking up old friends in the Nairobi capital, I ventured to the Ugandan visa office. A stern-looking Ugandan lady, large and bespectacled, was handling visa applications. I was well-armed to ensure that she would not grant me one.

I handed over my passport full of South African entry and work-permit stamps. 'You will notice that I am based in South Africa,' I said, emphasising the name of the hated 'apartheid regime'. She nodded and continued to thumb her way through my passport. 'I do work for the London *Daily Telegraph*,' I shrilled, with mounting panic. 'You know it is a very reactionary newspaper, not very sympathetic to African aspirations?' She nodded and continued to examine my forms. I produced my trump card. Unfolding the large, official form proclaiming me to be a Prohibited Immigrant presented after my deportation by Amin, I told her that I felt obliged to advise her that I was *persona non grata* in Uganda. She examined the PI order closely and, to my horror, picked up her visa stamp and gave me a two-week entry permit. 'Have an enjoyable stay in our country,' she said.

'AWA,' I muttered to myself as the aircraft droned towards Entebbe. There were few other people on board. At the airport, there was no sign of any bus or taxi. I flagged down a large four-wheel drive smothered with Oxfam logos. A pimply-faced Englishman half wound down the window but as soon as I explained that I was a journalist trying to get to Kampala he drove off at high speed. It was not the first time I had cause to curse this top-heavy charity.

A well-dressed Ugandan lady standing by the terminal building approached me and said, very quietly, 'I have a taxi. This way.' My saviour turned out to be a Bagandan schoolteacher. Her husband, also a teacher, had been forced to flee Uganda during Amin's reign. He had returned but could not get a job. She was moonlighting as an illegal taxi driver to make ends meet and help feed their family of four. My new friend proved invaluable at the numerous roadblocks we encountered.

The leering, drunken Tanzanian troops were at first hostile, but soon melted when she got out of the car and – totally out of character – flirted outrageously with them. 'I told them that you are a very important United Nations man and that I would come back and see them as soon as I had taken you to the UN offices,' she explained. 'I tell them the same story every time I go to the airport but they are always too drunk to remember.' She laughed loud and long. So did I. Not once was I asked for my non-existent UN passport. When we reached the British High Commission in Kampala I gave her triple the fare she asked for and asked her to give her children a treat.

Such very brave people found in the most unlikely circumstances in Africa always restored my faith in the people and the continent. My luck held. The British Consul, George Anderson, turned out to be that rarest of species, an intelligent, courageous British diplomat with an empathy for the task of a foreign hack, a profound understanding of the history and culture of the country in which he was serving and a great sense of humour. I'm afraid the British Diplomatic List, naming only such serving members, would be one of the world's slimmest volumes, as most of my colleagues would testify.

We had never met before but George, a pugnacious Scot, immediately offered full hospitality at his home. In the Uganda of those days, a clean bed, a shower, drinking water and a working deep-freeze full of food and drink was bloody luxury. Not only that, but the remaining diplomats, aid workers, UN officials and others trying to keep their fingers on the pulse of anarchic Uganda dropped by at all hours of the day and night. There was little happening that escaped George, and my notebook. I travelled the confused countryside with Consul Anderson who ran roadblocks, manned by indolent Tanzanian soldiers or whoever, by revving the engine of his 4x4 and pointing aggressively to the British flag flying from a pennant on its bonnet. It worked every time.

George told me a wonderful story about his pennant. He was an amateur photographer of considerable talent. He had, after months of patient negotiation with missionaries, managed to secure permission to interview the monarch of an ancient African kingdom high in the Ruwenzori Mountains on the border with Zaire. It had to be a secret trip. First Obote and then Amin had tried to bomb the king out of existence. They had failed. George got to interview and photograph him brilliantly but had to make a three-day hike on foot up the mountain.

When he returned through the mists he found a grizzled black man, huddled under a soaked greatcoat, camped by his vehicle. George greeted the old man and climbed into his 4x4 to start the engine. To his annoyance, the elderly African stood in front of his vehicle, pointing angrily to his pennant. 'That is the Union Jack,' bellowed George. 'That is the flag of my country, Great Britain. Now please let me pass.' The old man refused to move. 'No! No!' he kept shouting.

Exasperated, George climbed out into the mist and tried to explain to the man in a mixture of Swahili and heavily accented Glaswegian what the flag represented. Patiently the old man listened. Then he turned to George.

'Why I say "no", sir, is because it is not the Union Jack. It is the Union Flag. The jack is the pole upon which it flies. And why I say "no", sir, is because you have it here upside down.' He was correct in every detail. George was staggered. Here, literally in the heart of Africa, was an obviously poor, old derelict who had waited for possibly four days to tell him his British flag was upside down. It transpired, of course, that the man had served for years in the King's African Rifles and knew only too well what the penalties could be for calling the flag the 'jack' and, more important, for hoisting it upside down. AWA!

Idi Amin was not the only robber-baron who had held sway in some former African colony, vaguely defined, of course, and hastily shed when it was realised the natives were getting restless. The French had split up their West African territories. From the jungle of what had been French Equatorial Africa they created the Central African Republic, poised with steaming unease between Arab-dominated Chad and dictatorial Congo. Its intended leader, David Dacko, aged 28, was quickly overthrown by Jean-Bedel Bokassa, his cousin.

Bokassa was a seemingly jovial little man who had served for 23 years in the French army. Like Amin, he was full of animal cunning and suffering from delusions of grandeur. His undisputed bravery as an NCO in French trenches in World War II and in Indo-China saw him emerge with the rank of colonel. Soon after seizing power he appointed himself President-for-Life but even that title was not grandiose enough for this vicious little despot. In 1977 he proclaimed himself 'emperor' of the 'Central African Empire' and began preparations for a lavish coronation, modelled on that of Napoleon.

A third of his impoverished little country's budget went on elaborate Parisienne costumes and gowns, the imperial robe was to be encrusted with two million precious stones and the crown with 2 000 diamonds. For the convenience and comfort of 3 500 invited international guests, he imported fleets of Mercedes limousines and BMW motor cycles and many tons of air-freighted champagne, caviar and other feudal fripperies.

Much of this largesse came courtesy of Paris, and particularly President Giscard d'Estaing of France. The French leader and his family had been the beneficiaries of some of the finest diamonds mined in the Central African Republic. Giscard, who prided himself on his hunting skills, had been given unlimited licence to slaughter game in the country's supposedly protected game reserves. The d'Estaings of course, were among the VIPs invited to the coronation.

The French media, realising that this absurd spectacle in the jungle would provide a unique photographic opportunity, secured what they hoped would be exclusive rights to cover the event. They failed to acknowledge the ingenuity of the Old Africa Hands who were not going to be excluded from such a colourful story.

Michael Goldsmith, a veteran AP man based in Paris, flew into Bangui early to cover the elaborate arrangements being made for Bokassa's coronation. Mike was an old hand. He had covered wars in Asia, the Middle East and Africa. He should have known that the art of covering African dictatorships is to ensure, where possible, that you fly to an indifferent neighbouring country before filing any story that might be interpreted as unfavourable to the man in charge. The Bokassa story was, Goldsmith thought, too good to delay. He garnered all the details of the ludicrous spectacle about to take place and went to the Cabine Publique to file by telex. His article was highly unflattering to the dwarfish despot. When he could not raise Paris on the line, he tried the AP office in Johannesburg. A mistake. He got through and filed his copy for relaying to Paris and then New York. Bokassa's security men monitored a garbled version in which the South African relay answer-back was prominent. His Imperial Highness was not amused. Here, surely, was a South African spy in his midst.

In the middle of the night Goldsmith was summoned from his room at the Rock Hotel in Bangui by security men. He was taken for an unrequested audience with the emperor in one of a dozen imperial palaces around the capital. Bokassa greeted him like an old friend, then raised his imperial sceptre and cracked it across the AP man's head. He fell to the floor, his spectacles spinning across the marble floor. As security men kicked him into unconsciousness he was aware of the imperial boot stamping on and shattering his glasses.

He came to in a foetid cell where he was to remain, his wounds untreated, for more than a month. AP finally cajoled a reluctant French government to apply enough diplomatic pressure to secure his release. He was finally treated, allowed to wash and hauled once again before Bokassa who hugged him, kissed him on both cheeks and had him escorted to the airport to catch the next plane to Paris. When France finally became alarmed at Bokassa's excesses, they sent a senior diplomat to Bangui to urge moderation. He, too, was whacked on the head with the imperial sceptre. Bokassa insisted that all pressmen covering the coronation should be properly dressed – full morning suit with top hat and tails. As the emperor had a way of enforcing his wishes by personally chopping off the ears of those who disagreed, it was one of the smartest press turn-outs in the history of journalism.

James Pringle, *Newsweek*'s man in Nairobi, and Mohamed Amin, commissioned to cover the event for AP, hired their morning suits from Nairobi's Donovan Maule theatre. Pringle had to have his specially adapted to fit his squat, short frame. When they arrived in Bangui, fully dressed for the occasion, the temperature was into the 100s. 'We looked absolute fools. The immigration officers were falling about laughing, so we had no problem getting into the country.'

At the Ministry of Information they were told that they would not be accredited as the French had secured sole rights. All hotel accommodation had been booked so they spent the night in a church. On coronation day they had no trouble getting into the palace.

'We were so well dressed that the security guards just assumed we were diplomats or state guests.' Mohamed, his cameras around his neck, edged towards the throne, informing the curious that he was merely a guest from Kenya keen on taking a few snaps. Then one of the French cameramen recognised him and mobilised his colleagues to try and throw him out.

Mo Amin is not easily ejected from anywhere and an unseemly scuffle was taking place just as the trumpets announced the imperial arrival. Mo's leg 'inadvertently' caught the tripod of a French camera and it tumbled to the ground.

'Desperate to get the camera back on its stand to film Bokassa they stopped hustling me. After that, everybody was too busy trying to get their own pictures to worry about me.'

At the church, Amin made his way to within a few feet of the emperor, clicking away furiously. Security guards pounced on him but Bokassa signalled them to leave the photographer alone. AP got the best pictures of the coronation. The Nairobi hacks returned with some very colourful copy – and their ears intact.

Bokassa was allowed to inflict poverty and misery on his country for nearly fourteen years. But in 1979, even Paris thought he went too far when the emperor personally led a brutal attack on schoolchildren who had been herded into gaol for refusing to buy uniforms decorated with his portrait. Eighty of the children died. While Bokassa was on a state visit to Libya, French paratroopers landed in Bangui and restored David Dacko to power. Bokassa was tried, *in absentia*, for murder, cannibalism and fraud, and sentenced to death. He lived on, of course, in exile, initially in France and then in the Ivory Coast. He was eventually returned to Bangui to face trial on numerous charges, including massacre. He was sentenced to life imprisonment. Many theories have been advanced for the outrageous behaviour of dictators, not least Lord Acton's oft-quoted dictum that 'power tends to corrupt and absolute power corrupts absolutely'. Africa's numerous despots have added several new dimensions to the definition of corruption. I still wonder at the number of psychopaths who find themselves at the top of their particular patch of the continent.

Far less publicised in his remote corner of Africa, but with a record far worse than those of either Idi Amin or Jean-Bedel Bokassa, was President Francisco Macias Nguema of the former Spanish West African territory of Equatorial Guinea. For eleven years he turned his tiny nation into a concentration camp for its unfortunate inhabitants. Uncounted thousands were executed, tortured, dismembered and simply left to starve in overcrowded prisons. In most cases, the reasons for such primitive brutality seemed to be merely the presidential whim or predilection. Among the ten ministers in his first 'government' was a foreign minister personally clubbed to death by Macias at a 'cabinet meeting'.

He executed the governor of the national bank and insisted that all state funds be delivered to him personally to be stored in one of his numerous palaces. He persecuted all Roman Catholics, dismantled what education system there had been and brazenly looted and raped what was left of the citizenry. (At least one-third of the population managed to flee into neighbouring states.) His behaviour eventually persuaded Spain to engineer a coup.

He was tried for 'genocide, treason, embezzlement and systematic violation of human rights' in 1979. Local troops refused to carry out his execution as they feared their bullets were too weak to kill his spirit which would 'return as a leopard'. A Moroccan firing-squad was flown in to do the job.

The only journalist I knew who secured an 'interview' with this charmer was Roly Carter who was allowed to see him on death row. 'There was the "Great Maestro" and the "Great Miracle" as he styled himself cowering in the corner of his cell, crumpled and pathetic,' Carter recalled. 'But those eyes still had that maniacal stare that had sent countless thousands to their death. I did not prolong the interview. All a trifle chilling.'

When a 28-year-old Liberian army master-sergeant named Samuel Doe burst into the presidential bedroom in Monrovia and killed the long-standing head-of-state William Tolbert in his bed in 1980 there were still enough African apologists to acclaim him as a 'saviour and a redeemer'. It was later learned that Doe and his cohorts had first tortured the president vicariously, gouging out his right eye and disembowelling him slowly before shooting him three times in the head. Even so, Doe was praised in some international circles for retaining his NCO rank as the new Liberian president. The semi-literate sergeant was soon driving around the centre of Monrovia, personally ordering the arrests of former ministers and officials and supervising the erection of telegraph poles on a nearby beach for a series of public executions.

David Lamb of the *LA Times* was among the 40 correspondents in the capital for the coup and its aftermath. The hacks attended the kangaroo trials of the former ministers and were then summoned to Master-Sergeant Doe's first presidential press conference. 'He strode into the ballroom of Tolbert's mansion wearing a wide-brimmed army ranger hat, crisply pressed fatigues and combat boots,' Lamb recorded. 'He carried a ceremonial sword, a .375 magnum revolver and a walkie-talkie. In halting English he read a prepared statement, handled two brief questions and sat down. "Ladies and gentlemen," his new information minister announced in a casual voice, "you are invited to some executions at two-thirty."'

Outside, drunken soldiers danced around the mini-bus in which the condemned men were locked. They pounded on the windows and kicked at the doors, jeering and tormenting the men inside. 'Hey, there, Cecil boy,' one soldier shouted to the former foreign minister. 'I'm going to get the first shot. If I don't kill you, don't worry too much. We'll let you die slow.' On the beach, the men, clad only in their underpants, were bound to the poles. A jeering chanting throng continued to tease them while awaiting the motorcade of Sergeant Doe. For three minutes, the squad fired at the men, most of the bullets missing their targets. After 20 minutes or so, a soldier stepped forward and finished them off with bursts of machine-gun fire. The mob cheered. At least five correspondents vomited violently on the spot.

John Edwards, one of Fleet Street's finest foot-in-the-door operators, had not had much experience in Africa. He found it difficult to believe he was not in the middle of a ghastly nightmare. For some reason, Doe took a liking to Edwards and invited him to meet his mother in his home village. 'We went in convoy through the jungle to this little tin-roofed shack with chickens running around our feet. I was introduced to his mother. As we huddled round this oil lamp she told me what a wonderful son he was. Doe was on his radio-telephone ordering the execution of another ten ministers.'

Not long afterwards, Henry Reuter (no relation to the founder of the news agency), when roving correspondent for the Argus Africa News Service, turned on his radio in his hotel room in Monrovia to hear a live broadcast of Master-Sergeant Doe giving a pep talk to Liberia's national football team. The hapless soccer players had lost their previous three matches and were due to play Togo on the following Sunday. After hearing each man give his explanation and excuses for their failures, Doe addressed them.

'What this team needs is some incentive,' he said, slowly. 'Unless you win against Togo on Sunday, you will all be shot.' Fortunately it was an away match. It was a draw, but few of the footballers bothered to return to Liberia.

CHAPTER THIRTEEN

SOLDIERS OF MISFORTUNE

My banker friend sounded a little cautious on the phone. He had something that might interest me. Could I call at his office after business hours? Bulawayo was going through a relatively quiet period and I was about to leave for more newsworthy parts. He greeted me, led me in to an inner sanctum, locked the door behind us and lowered his voice. 'You spend some time in Nigeria...I wondered if this would be any use to you?'

He pulled one of two large, battered tin trunks towards him and lifted the lid. It was packed with banknotes, Nigerian banknotes of all denominations in large, hastily assembled bundles held together with elastic bands and string. 'I haven't counted it properly,' my friend whispered apologetically. 'But there is at least two million here.' It was a breathtaking sight. I realised how the Great Train Robbers must have felt when they realised just how much loot they had got away with. This fortune, however, was potentially much more dangerous.

It was towards the end of the Nigerian civil war. The federal government in Lagos had belatedly changed the country's currency in an attempt to prevent rebellious Biafra from using cash they had liberated early in the war to pay for mercenaries and expensive public relations companies. To be caught with one single old Nigerian note in Lagos now would be fatal, I explained. You would be immediately branded a saboteur or a spy or both and put up against a wall. My friend's face fell. 'Such a pity,' he sighed, taking one more wistful look at the booty before closing the lid.

He was admirably reticent about explaining how so much Nigerian cash had found its way 3 000 miles southwards to a Bulawayo vault, but I could guess. Rhodesia had a small but colourful band of flying mercenaries, pilots who not only kept aloft ancient aircraft which should have been condemned years before, but landed them in the most unlikely spots. I knew that Jack Malloch, chief pilot and pirate of this group, had been hired by the Biafrans to fly in and out of Uli airstrip. One of Jack's ageing Constellations had been impounded in Togo, allegedly full of Biafran contraband. I had no doubt that the Bulawayo millions I had just been shown were connected to this adventure.

Perhaps it is not surprising that the paths of Africa correspondents and those of sundry spies and mercenaries should criss-cross frequently – and sometimes merge. Post-colonial Africa has provided fertile soil for soldiers of fortune. They have been thick on the ground in most of the wars, upheavals and turmoils of the two decades of Uhuru. Some of the most famous – or notorious – cut their teeth in the Congo: 'Mad Mike' Hoare, 'Black Jack' Schramme and Bob Denard among them. Mike Hoare was a particular favourite with the hacks. Always polite, friendly and accessible, always there with a stiff-upper quote or quip – and always good copy. Michael Brown of the *Daily Express* was the first to dub Hoare 'Mad Mike' after accompanying him on one particularly hair-raising trip. The Colonel resented the nickname but never held it against Brown.

John Bulloch, then the *Telegraph*'s correspondent, became very close friends with the mercenary. Bulloch spent months with Hoare and his men researching a profile for *The Sunday Telegraph*. 'I became Mike's political and literary adviser. I took to wearing a uniform and held an honorary rank. I used to get saluted by the men.' Too close to the subject? 'I don't think so. I was getting the story the paper wanted. It was great fun.'

Hans Germani of *Die Welt* got even closer to Hoare. Hans had a medical degree from the University of Vienna and although he had never practised medicine he volunteered to accompany Hoare and his mercenaries throughout the Congo as their doctor. Hans was later to become a figure of fun among Africa hands, not least because of his habit of scratching his private parts while inveighing, in a parody of a German accent, against the evils of communism. He was also given to carrying a large Luger – and using it at the most disconcerting times. Even so, I always found him to be a kind colleague and a brave and diligent journalist.

Hans related his participation in mercenary battles with unrepentant frankness in a book *White Soldiers in Black Africa* published in Frankfurt. He had arrived in Albertville shortly after Mike Hoare's column had recaptured the town from the rebels. This was 'the saga of the men who came to the Congo as adventurers, vagrants, fugitives from justice, drunkards and idealists and who became the White Giants. This expression devised by superstitious rebels and spread by fear, dominated the fighting in the Congo. How often was I to hear the muffled drumming in the night, through forests and savannahs, "Flee, the White Giants are coming!"'

Hans clearly revelled in the mercenary's life. He frequently rode shotgun as Hoare's jeeps raced through rebel-held territory, joined in long sessions of drinking liberated champagne, brandy and whisky, and taught his companions to sing 'Lili Marlene' in German. He treated their wounds, staunched their blood and tried to prevent them from dying. He also treated wounded rebels and innocent villagers, often distributing and administering serum, advising them on nutrition and delivering a few babies. When Hoare returned for his second tour with Five Commando he sought out the German correspondent again.

'Hans, I am not forgetting how you once dressed my wounds. Would you like to join us on this campaign? You would be the only journalist I would take. I could use you for medical purposes and as an interpreter.' Hans accepted enthusiastically. On one excursion near the Tanzanian border, Germani spotted what he thought was a bush pig at the side of the road. 'I opened fire with my automatic rifle. Little dust clouds formed at a distance and the pig trotted away. No wonder – I had been shooting with sight 800. The pig turned up again and got its bullet. It was not a bush pig at all but one of the very similar domestic pigs.' He compensated the Baluba owner but never lived down the story among his mercenary friends.

He volunteered to accompany all of the frontal attacks and gives graphic accounts of the skirmishes and battles and the conditions in the rebel-held Congo at that time. He was with John Peters, the big Yorkshireman who was to become another mercenary legend, when they ran into an enemy motorised column.

'Peters moved his Jeep beside the armoured patrol truck. Both machine guns opened fire. Some heavy machine guns replied from the enemy side and the tracer bullets swooped over our heads. Both our machine guns had loading trouble but Peters quietly continued to direct the fire of the automatic rifles. Suddenly a hostile vehicle caught fire and the return fire stopped. The enormous flames lit up the tropical night like daylight, ammunition exploded and fantastic fireworks of splashing red balls raced through the air. As if on parade, Peters ordered the soldiers to get off and advance in double file. He went ahead of them all in the centre and in the red glow of the fire I saw his face shine with the joy of fighting. The man was enjoying every moment.'

Hans remained unashamedly proud of his days with Mike Hoare's mercenaries in the Congo. In later years, as his own health began to fail, he told me that it had been the high point of his life 'as a man, as a non-practising doctor and as a journalist'. His dispatches to *Die Welt*, although sporadic, included some of the most vivid and accurate accounts of the Congo crisis.

Fifteen years after the Congo, Hans joined Alex Morrow-Smith, then with *The Star* in Johannesburg, and myself in a quest to locate South African mercenaries who were reportedly being recruited by Holden Roberto's FNLA movement in northern Angola. Alex, a chunky, aggressive Scot who had served in one of that nation's toughest regiments, had heard that recruiting was taking place in the basement bar of a Johannesburg hotel on Saturday afternoons. The three of us were thinking of mercenaries as we descended into the crowded, smoke-filled bar and so the silence and the strange stares that greeted us did not seem unusual. The entrance had been heavily labelled 'Men Only' but that, too, was not unusual in South Africa.

The throng fell silent as we entered. Hans, scratching his arse, pushed forward. 'If any of zee old Congo boys are here I vill recognise zem,' he declared. Behind him, I became a little perturbed when I noticed that a few of our 'mercenaries' were wearing frocks. Suddenly Hans jumped into the air. Two strange hands had joined him in scratching his arse. Behind me there was a roared Caledonian oath as someone pinched Morrow-Smith's backside. Alex fought a gallant rearguard action as three chastened hacks battled their way back up the stairs. Unwittingly, we had ventured into one of Johannesburg's more notorious gay bars. We retired, with only slight harm to dignity, to a better-known watering hole.

'Perhaps zey were zee Gay Hussars,' cackled Hans. 'More like the bloody Queen's Own Light Infantry,' suggested Alex. We learned, later still, that, had we gone to the upstairs bar at the same hotel, we would have found our mercenaries.

The over-glamourised image of the white African mercenaries, created by Mike Hoare and his aristocratic, bemedalled Number Two, Alistair Wicks, in the Congo of the early 1960s, and propagated by colleagues like Bulloch and Germani, was to be as short-lived as most of the regimes the lads were supposed to be supporting. Daniel Carney, a very close friend of mine for many years, helped to foster the myth. Danny, son of a British diplomat, had suffered from dyslexia as a youngster and had been dispatched to Rhodesia to 'do his three in the BSAP', in other words to make a man of himself by serving the regulation basic three years with the British South Africa Police in Rhodesia. After his service, Danny became a successful businessman, but with typical courage fought his early affliction with his determination to become a novelist.

With his Irish romanticism, guts and application he succeeded. His first novel *Whispering Death* was an improbable story about an albinoid terrorist kidnapping the willowy blonde daughter of a white farmer. It was taken up by a German film company who finally produced a dreadful movie (financed largely by Danny's own company). I was invited to watch the filming at a Rhodesian beauty spot one night where *Whispering Death*, the albino played by a German actor, was to be filmed standing atop a dramatic balancing boulder, waving some kind of scalp and leading a hundred or so African extras in the chanting of 'Kill...kill...kill the whites...Kill...kill...kill the whites'. Etc. The extras were armed with plastic spears and replicas of automatic weapons but were brandishing them with realistic verve around their roaring fire.

Apparently the German director had been trying to get this scene right for the previous three nights. The extras could not get the hang of continuity and were improvising enthusiastically but with different movements at every take. The German film crew was going berserk. 'Cut...cut!' screamed the exasperated director. 'Tell zem zey haff to do exactly zee same war dance they did zee first time. Tell zem!' This went on for several hours until the patience of the extras was also exhausted. Yet another take was ordered. It was unsuccessful. The director slammed his head in his hands in despair. 'Cut!...Cut!' he cried. The Africans continued to leap around waving their spears and chanting 'Kill...kill...kill...' Again the director screamed 'Got in Himmel!...CUT!' only to be met by louder and slightly more menacing chants from the extras 'Kill...Kill...KILL the whites...' The German, the cameramen and crew, even Whispering Death himself, finally realised that the extras had taken the chant to heart and seemed to mean every word. In panic they fled down the hillside, leaving the Africans dancing around the fire.

Danny's next novel was much more successful. He called it *The Wild Geese* and based it, very loosely, on the exploits of Mike Hoare in the Congo. This, too, was bought and made into a film, this time by Hollywood professionals. It starred Roger Moore, Hardy Kruger, Richard Harris and Richard Burton. Mad Mike was hired as 'technical adviser', although I'm not sure the Colonel was too flattered by the sight of a puffy and rather overweight Burton, playing the mercenary leader, clambering clumsily in and out of an old Dakota.

So successful was the movie, though, that the producer bought the rights to another of Danny's books, *The Square Circle*. It was about the springing of Rudolph Hess from Spandau Gaol and had nothing to do with African mercenaries. That failed to stop the producers hiring the same stars and calling it *Wild Geese II*. By that time, Mad Mike Hoare was getting involved in what was to prove his rather sad swan song as a mercenary, but more of that later.

Carney was something of a protégé of Wilbur Smith, possibly the best-known and certainly the best-selling of African adventure writers. During the Rhodesian bush war, Smith expressed an interest in researching the situation for his next novel. Danny was back in uniform, having been drafted into the police reserve. He arranged for his superior, a police intelligence man I shall call Jock, to look after Wilbur. Jock was an avid Wilbur Smith fan. He had read all the author's work and clearly thought he could prove himself to be a good role model for the next dashing hero. I was invited to join Wilbur and Jock as we set off early one morning for what was then known as 'the sharp end' – the north-eastern farming areas where guerrilla activity was at its most intense.

We sped from command post to command post as Jock sought to please his hero with some 'real action'. I was becoming increasingly nervous. We were in a small Japanese saloon car which would hardly have withstood the blast of one of the boosted land-mines that were not that uncommon on the farm dirt roads. We had only Jock's service revolver to counter any incoming AK-47 fire. It was only slight comfort to notice that Wilbur was beginning to pale a little and crouch down into his seat. Jock, to his delight, suddenly heard the unmistakable sounds of a 'contact' – a clash between the security forces and a guerrilla group – crackle over his radio.

'Here we go, Wilbur,' shouted Jock. 'Here's some real action for you!' To our horror, he steered our little yellow car down a bush track, bouncing over boulders and swerving through thick patches of dust. A fire-force helicopter, its heavy machine gun blazing, seemed to touch our roof. Bullets whistled, whined and cracked all around us. A wide-eyed, camouflage-clad figure clutching an AK-47 darted across the track in front of us and disappeared into a thicket. Jock screamed to a halt and waved his .45 at a circling helicopter.

'He's in there, lads...go get him,' he screamed at the sky. And then to Wilbur: 'This is what it's all about Wilbur...this is what you came for...this is our little war.' Crouched with Wilbur on the rear floor of the car I could see from the look on the author's face that he was thinking there was a time for in-depth research and that much of it could be done in a comfortable library somewhere.

As always, my nerve cracked first. 'For fuck's sake Jock! We've seen enough...let's get out of here.' He grinned at me. 'Opening time at Meikles, eh Chris? You journalists are all the same.' The jibe was countered by the look of sheer relief on Wilbur's face as Jock gunned the car towards the nearest tarred road and we turned and headed back towards Salisbury. The helicopter gunship made a couple more passes above us, merely to reconfirm that we were, after all, misguided, if not mad, tourists. It was opening time at Meikles – and Wilbur accepted a couple of stiff brandies before the colour returned to his cheeks.

The day of the novelist in Africa was only just beginning. Freddy Forsyth had emerged from his beloved Biafra without a job and, in his own words, was impeded from working in Fleet Street because the BBC had discredited him. Unable to get a job, and penniless, he was 'obliged' to dash off *The Day of the Jackal*, made a few million in what could easily pass for overnight success and fame and needed never to put byte to word processor ever again.

But, to the relief of his many millions of followers, Freddy continued to write – one blockbuster after another. He has always insisted to the colour supplement harpies that journalism runs thick still in the veins. Africa and all its moods and menaces is, quite understandably, close to his heart. A novel with an African setting was therefore inevitable. Hence *The Dogs of War*, his second bestseller.

It is a story of cold-eyed white mercenaries who, at the drop of a big business bank draft, plan and execute a coup against some despotic West African regime or other. Most Forsyth fans I know thought it his worst book. I considered it his best, not least because I recognised his descriptions, many of his thinly disguised characters, and the mood and atmosphere of a West African country in thrall of a vicious, ruthless dictator attempting to hold Western business mineral interests to ransom rang only too true.

Freddy, who had quit the BBC in a fit of pique and taken himself back to Biafra as a freelance to liaise between Col Ojukwu and journalists who ventured into rebel territory, had got to know the mercenaries who signed up for the Biafran cause. In his first ever published work, *The Biafra Story*, a potted panegyric to Ojukwu, he recorded the following thoughts about the mercs:

'Despite all that has been said of hundreds of mercenaries, the score over the first eighteen months has been forty Frenchmen in November 1967 who left in a hurry after six weeks, when they decided it was too hot for them; another group of sixteen in September 1968 who stayed four weeks before coming to the same conclusion. Those who have actually fought with the Biafran forces have been a small handful comprising a German, Scot, South African, Italian, Englishman, American, two Flemings and two Frenchmen. Another half-dozen individual soldiers of fortune have drifted in for varying periods of one day to three weeks.

'With rare exceptions the difficulty of the combat conditions, the enormous odds against, and a rooted conviction that there must be easier ways of earning a living have kept most visits down to a short duration. The only two men who ever completed their six-month contracts were the German, Rolf Steiner, who suffered a nervous breakdown in his tenth month and had to be repatriated, and the South African, Taffy Williams, who completed two contracts and went on leave in the first few days of 1969. Ironically, the Biafran war story, far from consolidating the position of the mercenary in Africa has completely exploded the myth of the Congo's *White Giants*. In the final analysis, the contribution of the white man to the war on the Biafran side must be reckoned as well under one per cent.

'Most have been revealed as little more than thugs in uniform, and the riff-raff of the Congo did not even bother to volunteer to come to Biafra at all. Those who did fight at all, fought with slightly greater technical know-how but no more courage or ferocity than the Biafran officers. The lack of contrast between the two is underlined by Major Williams, the one man who stuck by the Biafrans for twelve months of combat, and the only one who emerges as a figure worth employing. "I've seen a lot of Africans at war...but there's nobody to touch these people. Give me 10 000 Biafrans for six months and we'll build an army that would be invincible on this continent. I've seen men die in this war who would have won the Victoria Cross in another context. My God, some of them were good scrappers." His assessment of most of the mercenaries, notably the French, is unprintable.'

Freddy is himself an adventurous fellow and an experienced hack. He is also on record as saying that it is the research of the plot of a novel that appeals to him far more than the actual writing of the book. But in journalism, there is nothing guaranteed to make you more unpopular with your colleagues than winning an award or, much worse, making a fortune as a novelist. When *Jackal* hit the jackpot for Freddy, his name was mud in the bars of Fleet Street. Had he remained an impoverished hack, pilloried for his principled, if unprofessional, commitment to a distant despot, he would have been welcomed as a hero. As it was, he made a quick fortune with a lot of guts and talent and was therefore a legitimate target.

The real dogs of war were soon at it. The London *Sunday Times Insight* team were sniffing the lampposts as his second novel was published. 'The novel *Dogs of War* made half a million pounds for its author, Frederick Forsyth. The world regards it as fiction; a small band of mercenaries know it is largely fact. They took part in a real-life attempted coup which Forsyth financed. *Insight* tells how it was planned – and how, unlike the novel, it met an ignominious end.' Thus ran the blurb introducing the exposé on Freddy's alleged involvement. It was gripping stuff, in the 'We name the Guilty Men' tradition.

According to the intrepid *Insight* team, the story had emerged from the diaries left by a former Congo and Biafran mercenary named Alan Murphy, who had shot a London bobby and then himself in the East End of London. 'From Murphy's ex-comrades – scattered now in Europe and South Africa – we have pieced together the story of the most remarkable of those known assignments: the attempt in 1972-73 to overthrow the regime in the west African state of Equatorial Guinea, a coup master-minded and financed by the millionaire novelist Frederick Forsyth. Our conclusion is startling. Forsyth's best-selling novel, *The Dogs of War*, is in fact a thinly disguised account of that operation.' So ran the intro to the *Insight* investigation.

'There is, however, one major difference. After a daring sea assault, Forsyth's valiant band succeed in their objective of taking over the West African state he called Zangaro. In real life, Forsyth's mercenaries were arrested by Spanish police 800 miles from their target and ignominiously packed off home.' So far, so good. Nobody in Africa, least of all the hapless citizens of Equatorial Guinea, a former Spanish colony, would rue the downfall of Life President Francisco Macias Nguema who had proved himself the kind of despot who might give Idi Amin and Jean-Bedel Bokassa a bad name. The *Sunday Times* claimed that Forsyth had started planning a coup against Macias within months of his return from Biafra. His 'confidant and adviser' was one Alexander Ramsay Gay, a mercenary who had commanded 3 000 men in Biafra. Their target was the island of Fernando Po where Macias spent most of his time in a fortified palace. During the Nigerian war, Fernando Po had been a staging post for flights into beleaguered Biafra.

According to *Insight,* Gay reconnoitred the region and came up with a plan whereby a dozen mercenaries, backed by 40 or so former Biafran soldiers, could seize Fernando Po. The cost, he estimated, would be £50 000 which Forsyth had provided. Gay acquired the arms and the men and finally the boat, a 64-foot coveted fishing vessel, appropriately named the *Albatross,* anchored in the Spanish resort of Fuengirola. The *Albatross* sailed for Malaga where the arms supplied by a Hamburg dealer were supposed to be loaded.

Things started to go wrong when Spanish officials refused to issue an arms export licence. While Gay and Forsyth tried to save the operation, the Albatross sailed to Lanzarote in the Canary

Islands. There officials, on orders from Madrid, impounded the vessel and questioned the mercenaries. The operation was aborted at a final total cost of £100 000 but as Forsyth was already at work on *The Dogs of War* which netted him half a million – using the planning of the *Albatross* operation as a basis for his plot – the *Sunday Times* calculated cheekily that he had made a cool £400 000 on the whole exercise.

Insight went a little further. They suggested that Forsyth planned to install his old friend, Gen Ojukwu, the ex-Biafran leader, on Fernando Po. Ojukwu had lawyers send a stiff letter to the *Sunday Times* denying any connection with the plot or the mercenaries. Freddy Forsyth declined flatly to discuss with the newspaper the allegations of his involvement and has remained silent on the episode ever since. Why not? An aura of intrigue and mystery is certainly not going to do any harm to a thriller writer.

Mercenaries have always attracted more human dross to their ranks than glamorous adventurers, none more so than the unhappy band assembled by the Englishman, John Banks. Banks, a former Parachute Regiment unarmed combat instructor, is probably the most publicised 'secret' security adviser, as he liked to style himself. His attempts in London in 1975 to raise a mercenary army to invade Ian Smith's Rhodesia on behalf of black nationalists had all the elements of a farce. Having advertised in the *Daily Mirror* and the *Daily Mail* for 'ex-commandos, paratroopers, SAS troopers' to take part in 'interesting work abroad', Banks seemed surprised when the British press followed his every move and attended all the 'secret' gatherings of his would-be mercenary force. The press was on hand, too, when Banks' 'army' of 20 hand-picked heavies assembled at Heathrow's Skyline Hotel pending their supposed departure for Zambia. When their promised advance pay failed to materialise, the mercenaries brawled and drank themselves into a collective stupor. That was the end of Mr Banks' first African adventure – which had been watched with hilarity by Rhodesian intelligence and with anger by Joshua Nkomo's ZANU men in Zambia who were infuriated by the presumption of these drunken Englishmen that they could fight a black man's war. Unfortunately for Africa, it was not the end of Banks' interest in the continent or in mercenaries.

In Angola, the rag-tag forces of Holden Roberto's FNLA movement were in disarray and retreat from the MPLA-Cuban offensive in the north, despite half-hearted help from the CIA and the Zairois. Roberto had turned in desperation to his unofficial representatives in Britain to find mercenaries who might help to turn the tide. By mid-1976, at his headquarters in Kinshasa, Zaire, he had four ex-

British Paratroopers, including a young Greek Cypriot, a small-time crook named Costas Georgiou, whom a psychiatrist had concluded was a 'textbook example of an aggressive psychopath'. In his wisdom, Roberto had appointed Georgiou commander of the mercenary force he was raising. Georgiou gave himself the *nom de guerre* 'Colonel Callan' after a British TV hero of the day.

Roberto made a further mistake. The man hired to assemble the mercenary force in Britain was none other than John Banks, 'Walter Mitty' as the press had dubbed him. As if Angola did not have enough problems! Banks hastily assembled 25 young ex-soldiers, most of them out of work or on the run from the police. Tony Geraghty, a *Sunday Times* reporter who had been closely monitoring mercenary activity in London, heard about the contract but offered to keep it under wraps if he was permitted to accompany the men to Kinshasa. Banks and company debated whether they should 'liquidate' Geraghty there and then, but decided they would dispose of the reporter once they got to Africa. There would be fewer questions. Tony had no need to worry, even had he known he was on the 'hit list'. It was clear to all that anything Banks touched was doomed to failure.

In any event, Geraghty was not the only hack with the story. The *Sunday People* exposed the presence of the 'force' at London's Tower Hotel where they had gathered as 'The Manchester Sporting Club'. Their departure from Heathrow was fully reported and as a result of the photographs that appeared in the following day's papers, police issued several warrants of arrest for those of our heroes wanted on a variety of criminal charges. Tony Geraghty pitched up ready to accompany them only to be told that his 'accreditation as a war correspondent' had been withdrawn. On board were at least three criminals, including a convicted safe-cracker, whose mission was not so much to help a beleaguered African liberation movement as to get their hands on as many Angolan diamonds as they could.

Inevitably, the Banks operation in Angola turned rapidly from farce to fiasco and then tragedy when the mercs arrived in Africa. Most of the bewildered young British tyros thought the heat that greeted them as they disembarked from their VC-10 in Kinshasa was a back-blast from the aircraft engines. None of them was prepared for the intense damp heat. That, unfortunately for them, was not all they were not prepared for. Within 24 hours they were in the hands of a manic Greek-Cypriot ordering them to perform unimaginable feats with outdated, hopelessly irrecoverable weapons and equipment. 'Colonel Callan', alias the Greek-Cypriot waiter, was Costas Georgiou. To their horror, Callan had already taken to the

cold-blooded torture and murder of any black Angolan soldier, supposedly serving under him, who stepped in his path. Sometimes he
summoned a black soldier serving under him merely to test a
weapon he had found at his disposal.

The outcome was also inevitable. 'Callan's' men, few of whom
had managed to hold on to their rank of "private" in the British
army, reverted to the street-fighter's basic cunning of self-survival
at all costs. Holden Roberto's dreams of a British-led salvation for
his ill-motivated, ill-led and understandably terrified (more by
Callan than by the enemy) troops were dashed. None of this would
have mattered particularly to the outside world. That the Russians,
with massive Cuban surrogate support on the ground, had moved in
to seize Africa's most bountiful territory in the name of the least
popular group in the country – the MPLA – was immaterial. It did
not seem important. Just another African punch-up.

The fact that it was a brilliant, swiftly executed strategic coup
for the Soviets was understood only by the CIA, and the French and
the British – and, of course, the South African – intelligence services. All had been wrong-footed by the speed and efficiency of the
Russian operation to back the MPLA against its 'impure' rivals,
Jonas Savimbi and his UNITA movement in the south-east and
Holden Roberto (brother-in-law of Joseph Mobutu, who is still president of Zaire) in the north with his FNLA 'army', perhaps no more
than a few hundred dedicated men in charge of a rabble of loyalists
from his Bakongo tribe.

Enter Callan and Banks and a few dozen British chancers and
misfits and the scene was set for tragedy. Encamped in miserable
conditions among terrified locals in a small pocket of north-western
Angola, they bickered, fought and thieved among themselves, taking
out their frustrations by killing vicariously any black civilian or
'friendly' soldier who got in their way. After a few bloody weeks in
which they had two brief skirmishes with the real enemy – the
Cubans and the FAPLA forces of the MPLA – 'Colonel' Callan
ordered the 'execution' of 14 newly arrived British mercenaries for
alleged desertion.

The crime took place near the small town of Maquela in
January 1976. They were killed in the most sadistic and brutal fashion by their fellow mercenaries, their bodies being left in the soggy
Angolan bush to rot. They included a 52-year-old Scot who had been
signed up by Banks as a non-combatant who 'spoke Russian' and
might be able to help 'interrogate Russian prisoners'. They also
included a 22-year-old former soldier from Birmingham who stepped
forward dutifully to admit to Callan that he had made a mistake.

'Callan held up his pistol. "This is the only law here," he said, and shot Davies in the forehead at close range, pumping a further two bullets into his head as he fell groaning against the wall. "The rest of you strip or you'll get the same," Callan told the other non-coms who were staring in disbelieving horror at Davies' exposed brains and the spreading puddle of blood around his head.' That is the testimony of one of the British mercenaries present, a man who took part in the massacre and lived to tell his tale and make a lot of money from the paperback rights.

To our shame, perhaps, there was little interest among the Africa correspondents in the arrival of a handful of British mercenaries in northern Angola. The circus of their recruitment and departure from London had been well covered at that end and there were quite a few major stories breaking elsewhere in Africa. There were a couple of exceptions.

Neil Davies of NBC, one of the most professional one-man-band television-radio reporters in the world, sensed a good story in northern Angola and parked himself in Kinshasa to monitor the comings and goings of the mercenaries. Davies, a Tasmanian, was way off his beat. He had made his name as a cameraman in Vietnam and had an abiding passion for South East Asia. But having been shot, shot at, tortured and gaoled in three continents he was sharp enough not to rush headlong into Angola. He recognised the mercs as 'dangerously inexperienced cowboys'. As a young, fit white man he would certainly be linked with them if things went wrong – and Davies sensed, correctly, that things were about to go horribly wrong.

No such inhibitions inflicted themselves on Robin Wright, then Africa correspondent of the *Christian Science Monitor*. Robin was young, extremely attractive, and far from inexperienced in Africa's vicissitudes, but as a woman reporter with a knowledge of Portuguese, she calculated that her chances of getting into Angola and getting out with the mercenary story were good. She very nearly miscalculated.

Robin hitched a lift into northern Angola with Holden Roberto and stayed on for a couple of days as a guest of the seven British mercs whom Callan had posted at Santa Antonio de Zaire, a small fishing village on the broad estuary of the Zaire River. As a precaution, the mercenaries had requisitioned a motor-powered fishing boat which they kept at the ready for a fast get-away.

With astonishment and horror, Robin listened to the story of Callan's massacre of his own men. She had an exclusive story, but she swiftly realised that getting it out, as always, was not so easy. To get back to Kinshasa she would have to get to San Salvador to

get a lift by road or, better still, a ride on the light aircraft that supplied the mercs. As far as she knew, Callan would be in San
Salvador and would not be too happy to help a reporter get out of
the country to publicise his activities. The problem was solved for
her by the FAPLA forces which, undetected by the mercenaries, had
moved on their position overnight.

Their Angolan comrades reported that FAPLA forces in tanks
and armoured cars were on the edge of town. The mercs were
inclined to dismiss this as overreaction as they had recced the road
south the previous day. But as an armoured car drew up outside the
colonial mansion they were using as headquarters and began dis-
gorging heavily armed men, they realised they had been caught.
They were hopelessly outnumbered, outflanked and outgunned. All
made a frantic sprint through the torrential rain to the nearby jetty
and the primed boat at the end – their only hope of escape. They
fired off their FNs as they ran but were taking heavy machine-gun
fire in return.

Robin Wright, terrified by the suddenness of the turn of events,
fled with them, running and ducking beside the burly figure of
Derek 'Brummie' Barker, the oldest and most experienced of the
mercs. Robin could have stayed put and declared her neutrality as a
foreign correspondent but a couple of years previously she had had
very unpleasant experiences at the hands of the MPLA in Luanda
and chose to take her risks with the fleeing mercs.

There was bedlam as they reached the jetty. Dozens of Angolan
residents of the little town were also scrambling for the boat. A
FAPLA armoured car chased them all the way, firing its heavy
machine gun. Half a dozen people, including one of the mercs, were
gunned down. To her amazement, Robin found herself cowering in
the bottom of the boat, shaken to the core but uninjured. The terror
was not over. The machine gun raked the boat, killing several
Angolan civilians around her. One of the three remaining mercs
managed to get the boat started and moved out into the estuary.
Robin watched as Brummie Barker, who had chosen to make a
stand at the end of the jetty, faced up to the armoured car with his
FN.

Brummie, a broken-nosed ex-Para and notorious pub-brawler,
who had taken a fatherly interest in the young American reporter
during her brief stay in San Antonio, finally dived into the water in
an attempt to swim to the boat. The vessel could not wait, however.
Several 90 mm shells from the armoured car rocked the little craft
as it started to disappear into the heavy mist. Barker swam back to
the jetty and was captured.

Robin Wright, shivering with cold and fright but still able to jot down a running commentary of the events in her notebook, was scarcely able to believe her luck when a jetty on the Zaire side of the estuary came into view. It was the little port of Banana. THE Banana!

There to meet them were two young Americans with the unmistakable haircuts and demeanour of the CIA, the clandestine sponsors of the entire British mercenary fiasco in northern Angola. Robin was flown to Kinshasa where she checked into the Intercontinental Hotel, intent on taking a long, hot bath before filing the amazing stories she had acquired. She was greeted immediately by Neil Davies, who had picked up whispers of the Maquela massacre but did not have enough confirmation to file.

Professional as she was, Robin could not help blurting out to Neil all she had been told and experienced in Angola. Neil Davies, also professional to his extremities, made sure she was comfortable and relaxed – and broke the story of the Callan massacre, through NBC, to an astounded world.

Until that news broke, the MPLA in Luanda had no previous knowledge of the ghastly disarray and disasters that had overtaken the mercs in the north. It was manna from heaven. They had thought they were up against a highly organised, CIA-backed international force. The FAPLA army moved in quickly for the kill. Commanders were ordered to capture as many white mercenaries as they could. Angola's propagandists – Michael Wolfers, formerly of *The Times* and Jane Bergerol, once with *The Guardian* – recommended that a show trial of 'reactionary bandits' would be good for 'the cause'.

Thanks to 'Colonel' Callan, John Banks and the totally inept mercenary operation sponsored by the CIA, the communists running the show in Luanda were treated to a free lunch. The captured mercenaries included not only Callan himself but a couple of American soldiers of fortune who had arrived belatedly on the scene. Unfortunately they also included the brave Brummie Barker who had saved Robin Wright's neck on the jetty at San Antonio, and a couple of very young British adventurers who had been 'into action' for only a few hours. All were duly 'put on trial' in Luanda. In the great tradition of such regimes, all 13 captured mercenaries were pronounced 'guilty' by an Angolan government spokesman long before their trial. It transpired that their respective sentences had also been predetermined by some central committee or other.

The international press was invited to cover the 'trial'. Most of the reporters present were experienced enough to realise they were taking part in a travesty of justice – but the Callan killings were too meaty, in terms of British home news, to miss. Better still for the London tabloids, Callan's sister, Panyoiota 'Blondie' Georgiades, fell in love with her brother's chief interrogator and torturer, one Victor Fernandes, trained by the KGB and later to defect. The foreign press was given full facilities, for obvious reasons, to cover the 'trial'. It dragged on a bit and there were loud mutterings of discontent when it was discovered that any kind of liquor was in extremely short supply in Luanda's hotels. Not only that, but the food in this once graceful capital was appalling. The Angolans laid on a trip to a game reserve to appease the visiting press, but as most of them were dedicated street-pounding crime reporters from London, few were impressed. Finally, the court reached its predetermined verdict: all 13 mercenaries were guilty. Callan, Brummie Barker, an American, Danny Gearhart, and a British newcomer, Andy McKenzie, were sentenced to death – a sentence finally carried out by a very nervous, inexperienced firing squad with some difficulty. The others received long terms of imprisonment.

There was no question of 'justice' of course. The whole show was as childish as the original mercenary exercise. The hacks, however, were only too glad after a month or so in this boozeless capital to clamber on board a Lisbon-bound TAP airliner. Five of them, who shall remain nameless, booked into first-class and quickly rendered themselves motherless.

So delighted were they with availability of booze in the first-class compartment of the Jumbo that they failed to notice their airliner was in fact being hijacked.

A desperate Portuguese resident of Luanda, who had found himself an AK-47, had walked through the assembled hacks on the upstairs deck of the aircraft, pointed his gun at the head of the pilot and ordered him to fly to Lisbon. The pilot tried to explain, very gently, that they were scheduled to fly to Lisbon anyway. The man jabbed his rifle at the pilot's head, told him to do as he was told and just to take off for Portugal. At Lisbon's international airport, the hijacker gave himself up, explaining that he was merely a desperate refugee from Angola who wanted to get back to his homeland.

Our colleagues stumbled off, totally unaware of this drama, and caught a connecting flight to London. One of them had just the presence of mind to ring his foreign desk. 'Oh, good, old boy,' said the deskman. 'I'll put you on to copy so you can dictate the story about the hijacking of your airliner.' It was the first any of them had heard about it.

Costas Georgiou, the Greek psychopath with a lethal chip on his shoulder, had done for the legend of the African mercenary, the

'White Giants', what Idi Amin had done for any semblance of democracy in Africa. The American mercenaries were a little late in catching up with the scene, but when they did, it was with a vengeance. As the Vietnam war ground to its defeat for the massive and superior US forces, an entire generation of young, battle-hardened Americans sought the world for some release from their humiliation and their military skills, unappreciated and even ridiculed, by the great American public. Many of them headed for Africa. It was suitably exotic. It held out the promise of easy money, loot and booty. And, even better, at any given time, there were a dozen wars in progress. Lt-Colonel Robert K Brown, a former Green Beret officer with a shrewd eye for business, had recognised the frustrations of many thousands of young American soldiers whose experience and skills honed in Vietnam had gone unrecognised and vilified in their own country, a super-power confronted with defeat at the hands of a distant, lesser army.

For this legion of the damned, Bob Brown founded and published a monthly magazine, *Soldier of Fortune,* which billed itself as a journal 'for the professional adventurer'. When I was first shown a copy, I thought it was a spoof. The format and style were modelled on the better-known, glossy soft-porn magazines but instead of sex there was violence.

There was a pull-out centrefold, but instead of a busty, naked lady there was a young Vietnam veteran, swathed in bandoliers of ammunition, a large hunting knife clasped in his teeth and carrying an automatic weapon above his head, wading through a swamp in Equador. He was real, or at least had been. They gave his name, his service record and carried a eulogy to his dedication and courage. He was 23 years old and he had died fighting with anti-communist insurgents in that country. Presumably the mercs were supposed to plaster their bedroom walls with this kind of poster instead of a pin-up.

There were articles on knives, which described their handling in the way that *Playboy* might describe foreplay. There were features on sabotage techniques, underwater knife-fighting and the comparisons between the effectiveness of different types of high-velocity bullets. In the letters page, a corespondent who listed an awesome CV of battle experience and expertise in unarmed combat, sought the editor's advice. He was taking his wife to Paris, Rome and London on vacation and wondered what additional fighting techniques he should master to protect his lady in the cultural jungles of Europe.

Deadpan, Bob Brown advised him how to deal with the skinheads of London, the foot-fighters of Marseilles and the flick-knife fiends of Naples. It was clever stuff. Not once was the word 'victim' used in the thousands of words of mayhem. It was always 'assailant'. In other words, if anyone should ever ask, the magazine was devoted to the art of self-defence. It sold – still sells – more than 200 000 copies a month and has made Lt-Colonel Brown an unrepentant millionaire.

Not surprisingly, Bob Brown became interested in Africa and the prospects its wars might open up to his readers. His Africa correspondent, Al J Venter, was the right man for the job. He had covered most of the wars and conflicts on the continent, was not lacking in military knowledge or contacts, and had a reputation for a gungho approach to any given problem, journalistic or otherwise. My first exposure to the real world of *Soldier of Fortune* came one evening in the Quill Club in Salisbury, just about the time when 'Colonel' Callan and his keystone clan were appearing before the kangaroo court in Luanda.

The Quill Club was the Rhodesian press club. Its progenitors had been called, as they are in most other countries of the world, 'The Press Club', but they had gone bankrupt under that name and the 'Quill' was adopted to keep creditors from the door. Not that much was kept from the door of the Quill. Situated on the first floor of the Ambassador Hotel in the centre of Salisbury it was housed in two small rooms which tended to attract, correspondents apart, an amazing and volatile backwash of human flotsam and jetsam that found itself for one reason or another floating around central Africa.

Thus I was not unduly surprised when Al Venter strode in one evening to ask me if I would sign in three American visitors he had accompanied to town. They were, he assured me, journalists of high standing. It would not have mattered anyway. It was a relatively dull evening at the club and any friends of Al's could be guaranteed to provide a remedy for that. We were not disappointed. The three visitors were intriguing even by Quill standards.

Lt-Colonel Robert K Brown, editor and publisher of *Soldier of Fortune,* was a tall, laconic man of unmistakable military bearing but a deafness in one ear caused him to stoop disconcertingly to hear what was being said to him. Ted Donovan was straight out of a comic strip. He was of bear-like build with enormous arms held permanently akimbo. His head was completely shaven, which emphasised the closeness of his eyes which darted suspiciously from one face to another and then over his shoulder as he spoke. He was introduced by a straightfaced Al as the 'Sabotage Editor' of the magazine. The third visitor was Ralph Huggins, known to his companions as 'The Arab'. Short but squat and powerfully built, The Arab had a built-in expression of suspicion and hostility. He repeatedly flexed his shoulders and muscles, giving the impression of being wary and alert, like a man constantly on the run from something or someone. He was, we were solemnly assured, the Knife-Fighting Editor of *Soldier of Fortune*.

Other members of the Club settled uneasily back to their drinks. We were used to heavyweights, freebooters, vagabonds and toughs. Indeed, our membership included quite a few in those categories. But these men were not only clearly armed but were distinctly uneasy in the company of journalists. Al tried to introduce light conversation. 'Bob!' he bellowed into Brown's good ear. 'Tell Chris about the Bay of Pigs.' I was later to learn that Donovan and Huggins had been involved in that abortive attempt to invade Cuba and overthrow Castro but The Arab thought this was not the time or place to tell the story. His fat hand shot across my shoulder and a large, stubby finger planted itself on Al's upper lip.

'You just button that lip, Al, boy!' he demanded with a menacing rasp. 'Just button the lip.' Al tried to make light of the gesture. We were among friends, he insisted. People who understood about these things and respected confidences. The Arab was unconvinced. He kept his extended finger on Al's lip and turned to me with an eyeless smile. ''Scuse me,' he said. 'You speak Spanish?' I assured him hastily that I did not but when he turned to Col Brown and shouted something like 'Mucho importante nao parliamo na journalista,' I felt obliged to make light of the scene.

'Don't worry,' I said to him, foolishly. 'Nobody ever wants to talk to us journalists.' He seized me by the collar, lifting me towards his narrowing even more suspicious eyes. 'I thought you said you didn't speak Spanish!'. In vain I tried to explain to him the benefits of a classical education. At the other end of the bar, some colleagues were being enthralled by the Sabotage Editor who was assuring them that he had two entries in the *Guinness Book of Records*. He'd got himself the biggest Alaska Brown bear, he said, not saying whether he used a gun or one of his huge fists. He had also once held the absailing record, naming some incredible height of the building which he had descended by rope. One of our keener sporting members was interested. 'That's very good...how many pairs of gloves did you use?' Donovan stared at him angrily. 'Gloves?' he demanded, unfolding huge gnarled hands. 'Gloves? Whaddya mean, gloves?'

Venter had arranged a hunting trip for the *Soldier of Fortune* trio in north-western Rhodesia. The guerrilla war was particularly intensive in the area and they were all aware that the hunters could become the hunted at any given time. The Sabotage Editor and the

Knife-Fighting Editor were particularly disappointed when towards the end of their trip they had experienced neither sight nor sound of 'the gooks'. So disappointed were they that on their last day Al had to dissuade them from laying ambush to a gang of innocent African railway workers repairing the main Bulawayo-Victoria Falls line. Col Brown stayed on for some time in Rhodesia. He liked the country, the people and the war – and it was very good for business.

Soldier of Fortune began carrying advertisements for 'adventurous Americans' to volunteer for the Rhodesian forces. The response was amazing. The distinctive accents of Texas, Louisiana, Kentucky, California and Oregon began to permeate the bars and clubs of Salisbury. Most claimed prolonged combat experience in Vietnam. Some were genuine and good at their job, others were chancers and con men and the CIA, always at the losing end of the Cold War in Africa, had its own men among them.

There were, perhaps, 300 Americans fighting with the Rhodesian forces towards the end of that war. Many of them sooner or later gravitated to an organisation called 'The Crippled Eagles', supposedly a 'social and support' club for Vietnam veterans who thought all their efforts and risks to contain the communist threat had been thwarted by 'limp-wristed liberals' in Washington. If they were not to be allowed to fight this war in South East Asia, they were sure as hell goin' to fight it in Africa. And they were not discouraged by the Rhodesian army recruiting department which did not include many men of liberal bent, and even fewer with limp wrists.

Yet another author was responsible for setting up the 'Crippled Eagles' organisation for American mercenaries in Rhodesia. Robin Moore had made his name as a popular writer of racy books on what were then regarded as racy topics: *The French Connection* (drugs), *The Happy Hooker* (prostitution) and *The Green Berets* (anti-commie militarism). Robin and his vivacious wife, Mary-Olga, bought a presumptuous house in one of Salisbury's more affluent suburbs and declared it the 'unofficial American Embassy'. Hospitality and charm oozed out of every air vent in this mansion. Every American mercenary in Rhodesia was automatically a 'crippled eagle' – because of his instinctive urge to get out there and fight the 'commie bastards'. All sooner or later ended up at one of the lavish parties thrown by the unofficial American ambassador.

Journalists, too, were attracted, not only by the free flow of booze, but by the bizarre stories the American mercs had to tell of their war experiences and their reasons for fighting for white Rhodesia. There was also an unmistakable presence of CIA agents among their number, always good for a laugh, if not for information.

At this juncture of the war, Rhodesia was attracting a lot of what the old hands called 'rucksackers' – young would-be journalists with little experience who hoped they could break into the big-time by taking themselves off to a war situation and volunteering for the hairiest assignments that more sanguine staffers would spurn. Vietnam had spawned a whole new generation of rucksackers. A few of them were to become very good, distinguished journalists. Most of them were junkie chancers or shameless opportunists or both.

Among the less popular rucksackers who arrived in Salisbury at this time was a young, unprepossessing American named J Ross Baughman, claiming to be an 'investigative photo-journalist'. The self-aggrandizement of the claim to be an 'investigative journalist' has never ceased to amuse me. By its very nature, newspaper work requires that one makes inquiries and conducts investigations. Here was one of the first of the breed to appear in our midst. From his brash, rather arrogant manner and ridiculous views, which he aired loudly and frequently, I branded him as a chancer. Baughman, however, had soon ingratiated his way into the unofficial 'American Embassy' and at one of the many bashes therein had convinced a fellow-American, Mike Williams, of his bona fides as a photo-journalist and a good, racist right-winger.

Mike Williams held the rank of major in the Grey Scouts, one of the proliferation of Rhodesian army 'special' units which was mounted on horseback to facilitate its movement at speed through the bush. Williams gave Baughman permission to join a Grey Scout patrol in Matabeleland. The patrol rounded up ten black youths in an abandoned school near a village. This was Baughman's subsequent account of what followed:

'W asked his name and when he did not reply hit him over the head with a bat. Soldiers then pulled down the underwear of Ncube's daughter and whipped her. Her mother was also whipped and then was tied to a bed whose metal springs had been heated over an oven. Later...Ncube was stripped and subjected to this form of water torture which he resisted, spitting out the water. He was kicked in the ribs and a wire was attached to his genitals and his daughter was forced to pull it, partially mutilating him. W then yelled at Ncube and fired a shot from his pistol five centimetres from his head. "God I hate doing this," said W, walking to his truck. "This war makes me sick".'

Baughman also took photographs – depicting the captives doing press-ups at pistol point, a soldier beating a captive with an interrogation bat and another with a rope around his neck. Three months after this incident, J Ross Baughman left Rhodesia and sold his picture story of the atrocities to Associated Press. It received wide coverage and, not unnaturally, caused an international furore. The Rhodesian government instituted an inquiry and offered Baughman immunity from prosecution if he would return to give evidence. He declined. An officer and three men of the Grey Scouts were demoted and fined as a result of the investigation. For this 'investigative endeavour', Baughman was awarded a Pulitzer Prize for feature photography in 1978.

There were, however, several disturbing aspects to this tale. Baughman claimed he had 'ingratiated' himself to the men of the unit by 'pretending' to share their views. But there had seemed to be little pretence about the extreme right-wing views he had expressed to his colleagues in the press. He had also worn a uniform and carried a weapon.

There was also a prolonged and unexplained delay between the dates of the incident and Baughman's dispatch. Perhaps there is more to this 'investigative journalism' than I thought. The Overseas Press Club in New York thought so too. They questioned the authenticity of the photographs and suggested they had been posed. The chairman of the Pulitzer Prize photography committee said they were unaware of any questions surrounding the pictures when they made their decision.

The 'journalism of participation' has been with us since the early beginnings of newspapers. From the examples set by some colleagues in Africa, it seems to be on the increase. The motive may be to increase personal reputation or to make a fast buck, but it does little for professional credibility. The worst examples, of course, were colleagues who succumbed to involvement in espionage. Most of those I know did so for financial gain rather than any sense of idealism. They were highly dangerous to their bona fide colleagues. When unmasked, they jeopardised the work, and sometimes the lives, of genuine journalists. Spies proliferated in Rhodesia after UDI in 1965 and the imposition of sanctions. Sanctions-busting, not surprisingly, became a national obsession. Foreign governments and rival commercial and industrial interests vied with each other to discover who was buying what from the beleaguered Rhodesians. Being a very small community had its advantages and disadvantages, depending on your purpose. It was extremely difficult to keep any secret in Salisbury. All newcomers were kept under scrutiny as a matter of routine.

It came as no surprise, therefore, to be advised by a friendly Special Branch man one day in 1969: 'There's a new CIA man in town'. The American government had, for a few years after UDI, maintained a 'skeletal' diplomatic mission under a consul-general. It maintained a small staff, all of whom were well known in Salisbury, socially as well as diplomatically. Thus the arrival of Col Irl Smith as a 'political officer' was a little too obvious. His advent coincided with great panic in Washington over the discovery that a shipload of a strategic mineral, then vital to the space programme, had found its way from a Rhodesian mine to Communist China by way of Beira and Macao.

Mike McCann, to my mind one of the best news photographers of his day, decided it would be a good idea to have a few 'stock' pictures of Irl Smith for his files. Smith was horrified by the idea, flatly refused to pose, and went to great lengths to avoid the photographer from then on. Rather odd behaviour for a diplomat, we thought. Smith had reckoned without McCann's persistence. Mike parked himself on his motorcycle outside Smith's residence in a leafy suburb and waited to snatch a photograph of the American as he left for work.

The colonel learned his house was being staked out, got his servant to open his gates and shot out into the road at high speed, ducking low over the wheel. Mike, as good a biker as he was a cameraman, gave chase, chuckling to himself at the absurdity of the situation. Smith threw his car around corners and up side streets, but the grinning figure of McCann was always on his tail. Finally, he spotted an African constable on a bicycle, screamed to a halt and bellowed at the bewildered policeman 'Arrest that man! He is harassing me!' Mike suddenly remembered he had forgotten to license his bike and decided to make a tactical withdrawal.

A few days later I agreed to help Mike get his pictures. With his cameras at the ready he spreadeagled himself in the back of my station wagon which I positioned near the entrance to the car park by the American consulate. Irl Smith duly arrived, parked his car and looked around suspiciously for any lurking photographers. He could see none. As he got out of his car and reached into the back seat to get his jacket, I reversed towards him. Mike released the back flap of the station wagon and began snapping away furiously. With a roar of rage, Smith suddenly realised what was happening and began advancing menacingly towards my vehicle. 'Go!' shouted Mike. I was momentarily held up by passing traffic but just as Smith was about to reach out and grab McCann, I found a gap and shot forward, nearly ejecting the photographer. Back at the office, McCann processed his film. He had a memorable series of photographs of the CIA man, the final one showing Smith's snarling, livid face a few inches from the camera. He was also soon to have numerous clients clamouring for them.

At police HQ, Smith had also been making himself conspicuous. Two senior detectives, Peter Moores and Mike O'Meara, had difficulty believing the evidence that was piling up on their desk. Smith had rented a number of post office boxes outside the post office in one of Salisbury's most gossip-laden suburban shopping centres. Black detectives posing as onion sellers had recorded with concealed cameras those people who deposited material in the American's boxes. Two well-known faces leapt out at Moores and O'Meara: Alfred Trevor Gallagher, a lawyer and a leading member of Ian Smith's Rhodesian Front party and Roger Nicholson, Financial Editor of the *Rhodesia Herald,* hotly favoured to become the next editor of that newspaper, and a highly respected journalist locally and internationally.

They, in turn, were watched and the packages they deposited in Irl Smith's post office box were intercepted, copied and returned. They were detailed reports on Rhodesian sanctions-busting activities and the general economic situation, information that would be useful to any government supporting the sanctions policy. The policemen discovered that Gallagher used to dictate his spy reports to his secretary and that Nicholson had swiftly established a substantial credit balance at the Chase Manhattan Bank in New York. In the homes of the two men, they were astonished to find materials like 'secret writing ink' and other spying accoutrements more suited to a schoolboy thriller than a CIA operation. 'The whole thing seemed so childish, so amateurish that we really thought we were being led into a ridiculous hoax,' Peter Moores told me later.

Hoax it was not, they finally decided, although the arrest of Nicholson had its humorous side. Nicholson was seated at his desk in the *Herald* office when he saw Moores enter and head for the editor's office. 'Hello, Peter,' he said breezily. 'Come to arrest the editor? Not before time!' Pete smiled thinly. 'Wait and see,' he replied, popping into the editor's office to advise him that he was about to arrest one of his senior men for espionage. Nicholson's joviality vanished when he saw the big detective advancing towards his desk with a warrant in his hand. 'You've been a naughty boy, Roger,' he said as he searched the journalist's desk and found yet more incriminating evidence.

The arrest and subsequent trial of the two men caused a minor sensation, although the 'foreign power' for whom they had spied was never mentioned by name. Eventually each was sentenced to four years' imprisonment, a surprisingly light sentence in the view of many Rhodesians. Within a few weeks the American and Rhodesian governments reached a clandestine 'understanding'. Nicholson and

Gallagher were taken from prison and escorted to an airliner bound for Europe. Both had the proceeds of their spying activities intact and both were able to pursue successful careers elsewhere.

Back in Salisbury, however, Nicholson's involvement had caused a closer, suspicious scrutiny of all journalists. In the middle of this episode, to my horror, the telex sprang to life with a cheery message from *The Sunday Telegraph* advising me that they were planning a major series on sanctions-busting. Could I please provide them with all the background I could? My answer was short and sharp, although I did point out that a colleague was at that very moment hanging by his thumbs in a Salisbury prison for doing just that. There was silence for a day or so and then a mysterious message instructed me 'LIKE YOU BEIRUTWARDS SOONEST PROMEET TELESUN EVANS'. In other words, make my way to Beirut to consult with George Evans, *The Sunday Telegraph*'s Assistant Editor.

In Beirut I was happy to meet up with George, an old friend and much experienced colleague, but perturbed to hear that the newspaper was determined to go ahead with the sanctions-busting series. They had already paid a substantial sum to a sanctions-buster for his story. They would reconcile the series with the paper's pro-Rhodesian stand by saying that as they had shown how easily sanctions were circumvented, they should be removed forthwith.

I pointed out that my posting in Salisbury, if not my freedom, would be jeopardised if I was seen to be involved in any way. George pondered for a moment and then had a bright idea. I would go to Nairobi for a few weeks on some pretext or another and there give *The Sunday Telegraph* all the background on sanctions-busting I had. Meanwhile, John Miller, a colleague then based in South Africa, would go to Salisbury and make it clear to all and sundry that he was *The Sunday Telegraph* man investigating sanctions.

For a few pleasant weeks I sat in Kenya pounding out thousands of words of background. George had demanded 'buckets of colour' so I threw in as much detail as I could remember, including the trivial fact that if there was one thing Harold Wilson had in common with Ian Smith it was a love of HP Sauce. Smithy ensured that he got a regular sanctions-busting supply of this famous relish. In Salisbury, John Miller played his part well. He was a Russian speaker and so attracted SB men like flies with a few throw-away Muscovite phrases. The series ran with no adverse reaction to me in Salisbury.

Then I had a routine lunch with Derek 'Robbie' Robinson, the deputy head of the Rhodesian Central Intelligence Organisation. He remarked that the *Sunday Telegraph* series was 'interesting' and expressed surprise that such a pro-Rhodesian newspaper would choose to run it. I agreed. 'Thank God they didn't involve me,' I said. 'They sent in their own man, John Miller, to do the dirty work.' Robbie, a canny, slow-speaking Yorkshireman looked at me for a long moment and then chuckled. 'We were fooled by that for a while, Chris,' he said. 'Then I saw that reference to the Prime Minister's liking for HP sauce. I was the one who told you about that some time ago.'

The mercenary business was revived spectacularly as the Rhodesian war intensified. Even with every able-bodied (and many not so) man in uniform, the Rhodesian security forces were desperately short of manpower to control the vast areas which opened up as guerrilla fronts. They had conscripted the over 40s (who became the 'Salusa Scouts' after a well-known brand of middle-age fortification tablets) and even the small Indian community (who, of course, became the 'Samoosa Scouts'). They were still woefully short. By the time Major Nick Lamprecht, the energetic and imaginative recruiting officer, had got to work there were perhaps 4 000 foreigners fighting with different Rhodesian units. When the war ended and Rhodesia became Zimbabwe in 1980, this group of soldiers of fortune was doubled by the number of disgruntled Rhodesian professional soldiers who simply could not get warfare out their system. It was a formidable army looking for a cause – with cash – to fight for.

Even with this new generation of wild geese, it fell to the old gander himself to organise and plot the most spectacularly disastrous mercenary venture in Africa's colourful history. At the Old Vicarage at Hilton in the misty green hills of Natal, Colonel 'Mad Mike' Hoare had been tending his orchards and occasionally practising his secondary, sedentary profession as a chartered accountant. At the age of 64, he could have been forgiven for thinking of retirement.

He was doing no such thing. He had been approached by Seychellois exiles acting for James Mancham, the first president of the independent Seychelles Islands in the Indian Ocean. Mancham had been overthrown by a young socialist named Albert René who had swung these idyllic islands firmly into the Soviet sphere of influence. The combination of a communist threat, an unpopular regime and what appeared to be an ill-trained, indolent defence force backed by a few Tanzanian troops, stirred the blood of the old war horse. Moreover, his old rival from the Congo days, Bob Denard, had taken over the Comoros Islands, another Indian Ocean paradise, a few years earlier, and was enjoying the fruits of a different orchard. Mike Hoare carried out his recce and confirmed his theories of the military possibilities. A force of 200 trained, well-equipped men, he thought, could easily subdue any opposition, remove the government, reinstall Mr Mancham and take thunderous applause from a grateful Western world for wrenching the strategic archipelago from the hands of Moscow. There was no shortage of recruits but, as planning progressed, it became alarmingly clear that there was a serious shortage of money. His original idea was to recruit from Europe and elsewhere, as South African involvement could prove politically embarrassing. But as the budget began to shrink so did Mad Mike's ambitions. He ended up with the cellar of the Old Vicarage crammed with weapons provided clandestinely by the South African Defence Force (mainly AK-47s they had captured in their own foreign adventures) and a hotch-potch force of 35 men, many of them South Africans.

One of Mike Hoare's failings, as he readily admitted later, was that he believed in sweet, old-fashioned virtues like loyalty. He recruited his brother-in-law, an ex-jockey, to set up a 'safe house' near Victoria, the Seychelles capital on the island of Mahé. He roped in several of his old Five Commando hands from the Congo days, some of whom were getting a little long in their tearaway teeth. He trusted the word of several recruits who turned out to be agents of security forces whose interests were not necessarily those of the ageing colonel. It was, in his own words much later, going to be a 'cut-price coup'.

One of the first men he had approached to join him in the Seychelles caper was Peter Duffy, a tough, personable Scot who, as a young man fresh from tough public schooling at Gordonstoun (where he was a fellow-pupil of Prince Charles), had joined him in the Congo as a captain. Duffy was a born leader and a natural adventurer. He had walked across Siberia 'to see what it is really like', spent two years in Japan qualifying as a judo black-belt instructor, farmed in East Africa and had made his home in Durban where he followed a career, very successfully, as a press photographer. To Hoare's surprise and disappointment, Duffy turned him down. His freelance business was doing very well and had just won a journalism award. He was too polite to say so, but the money Mike was offering was not that attractive anyway.

Duffy finally changed his mind. It was not that he believed in the 'journalism of commitment' or 'participatory journalism'. He just could not resist the adrenalin pump of real adventure. A grateful Mike Hoare immediately appointed him Number Two and Peter was committed. He had growing misgivings as the planning progressed. The recruits included several men he would not have trusted to feed his parking meter. Worse, Mike's budget was now so tight there was no question of getting arms in by boat, as per the original plan. The main body of mercenaries was to fly to Mahé as 'Ye Ancient Order of Froth Blowers', a genuine old British sporting-drinking movement which raised money for children's charities.

Their baggage would be so labelled but concealed in polystyrene false bottoms, beneath genuine fluffy toys for the underprivileged children of the Seychelles, would-be AK-47 assault rifles. They would fly as a sporty group on a scheduled Air Swaziland flight to Mahé, regroup themselves as a fighting force and seize control of the islands. A government-in-waiting of Seychellois exiles would fly in from Kenya and Mad Mike's last mission would, he hoped, enable him to bow out as the field-marshal-of-fortune in a blaze of glory. It was doomed from the start.

By the time the mercs landed in Mahé, many of the 'Froth Blowers' could safely be charged with overacting. They were pissed. One had a fully assembled AK-47 poking out of his luggage. It was discovered. He panicked. A fire-fight broke out there and then at the airport terminal, the Froth Blowers grabbing their bags, hastily assembling their weapons and deploying as best they could. In the first burst of fire, one of the mercenaries still in the customs hall was shot dead, probably by a colleague. One group tried to attack the adjoining barracks and was repelled. Another tried to set up a roadblock on the main route to the capital. Two others tried to seize the control tower. There was panic and confusion all round. A Seychelles Defence Force armoured car arrived and got stuck in the mud. Instead of capturing it for their own use, the mercs shot it to pieces and killed one of the occupants. A few of the mercs fled into the surrounding hills.

In the control tower, the two mercs heard an Air India pilot, flying a scheduled Boeing 707 from Zimbabwe to Bombay, asking for permission to land. He was making an approach for a refuelling stop in the Seychelles. They did not know how to respond in the formal language. In the terminal building Mike Hoare was trying unsuccessfully to get through to the pilot of the Air Swazi plane that had brought them in. He was told about the approaching Air India flight. As there was mortar, heavy machine gun and other fire flashing across the airport he told his men to instruct the pilot not to land. It would imperil his aircraft and all on board. His men had other ideas and, in any event, the Air India pilot was committed to his landing approach. To everyone's amazement, Captain Saxena brought the Boeing into a sharp but perfect landing, avoiding a stricken vehicle on the runway.

With the responsibility of his scattered force, some 80 innocent passengers and officials huddled in the terminal building, and now a Boeing-full of transit passengers on his hands, Mad Mike was in a pickle. He managed to get through on the phone to President René. Would he call off his men's fire while the civilian airliner refuelled and took off. René would – if he had Hoare's word as an officer and a gentleman that neither he nor his men would be on board. Mike gave his word. By all accounts he would have kept it but for some of his tougher lieutenants who realised the game was up and that the Air India flight was the only way out.

He was finally persuaded, only at half gun-point, to get on board with most of his group. Captain Saxena 'agreed' to fly back westwards, to Durban, in fact, where most of the mercs thought they stood a better chance of getting away with something. Behind them they left seven of the mercenaries and the back-up group, most of whom were quickly captured, tortured, put on trial and sentenced to death. The sentences, of course, were never carried out. After a couple of years on an idyllic 'prison' island, they were released and sent home. The South African authorities, despite their covert support for the coup attempt, were obliged to put on a show of judicial indignation for a sceptical world. There was, after all, a very sensitive question of air hijacking involved.

There is nothing quite so pathetic, nothing more calculated to encourage ridicule and induce lack of compassion than a failed mercenary. The Froth Blowers had to endure all this and more. Peter Duffy, who by every account had shown remarkable qualities of leadership and courage under the circumstances, was sentenced to five years' imprisonment. He served his time in Pretoria's Central Prison. Among other attributes, Duffy is a talented chef. In gaol, he knew he would never get near the best job – that of chef to the officers' mess – if he requested it. Prison does not work that way. Instead, he drew attention to himself and screamed at the bemused warders to do their worst – as long as they did not put him in the kitchens. They put him in the kitchens and he served his time as chef to a delighted officers' mess. He emerged to continue his successful journalistic career in Durban.

Other Froth Blowers served sentences ranging from two years to a few months before an embarrassed South Africa felt able to release them. They had lost one man at Mahé Airport, probably shot inadvertently by one of his colleagues in the panic. The Seychellois had lost an officer in the armoured car. At the bars and clubs where the dogs of war gather to discuss what job prospects are available, there was considerable fury. Mad Mike's last stand had totally disrupted at least two, possibly three, other coup attempts being plotted against Albert René's regime in the Seychelles.

Mike Hoare fought his last battle in the courts of South Africa, his home country. He lost. As chief scapegoat, he was sentenced to ten years' imprisonment and served nearly three years before being released. He wrote a vivid and moving account justifying his final campaign and departed on a long pilgrimage to Lourdes. The guns have disappeared for good from the cellar of the Old Vicarage in Hilton, Natal. There is a much more spiritual atmosphere there now.

The Seychelles débâcle was also a sorry story of 'the scoop that wasn't' for Peter Sharpe, the Africa correspondent of Independent Television News of London. Peter, an anxious and hyperactive reporter in a highly competitive medium, had finally been persuaded by his wife, Sue, to take a well-earned, delayed, get-away-from-it-all honeymoon. They opted for the Seychelles.

'It took a good ten days in paradise to get him to unwind completely,' Sue recalled. 'By that time we were due to get back to the rat-race.' They spent their final day at a luxurious French-owned hotel on a hilltop on the island of Praslin which offered wonderful views of the Indian Ocean and, on clear nights, a distant view of the main island of Mahé. As the Sharpes sipped their sundowners, Peter suddenly stood up with a start. The distant lights of the international airport on Mahé had suddenly snapped off. He could have sworn he saw the unmistakable pattern of tracer bullets in the evening sky. He made a dash for the telephone. Sue groaned. She thought his imagination was working overtime. 'The last night of our honeymoon and he was already back at work.'

Sharpe's instincts were good, however. He had actually had a distant view of the battle between the Frothblowers and the Seychelles military at the airport. Word of the mercenary attack spread quickly through the islands and reached the staff of the Praslin hotel who passed it on to the ITN man. Within an hour, President René was on radio confirm it. Sharpe was frantic. Here he was, on the spot, with a sensational story but no TV crew to back him up. He commandeered the hotel telex and began dialling the ITN number in London. When he finally got through, the automatic answer-back signal was on repeat, indicating that no one was in the office. He tried again, and again, and again with no response. His wife found him slumped from sheer frustration and exhaustion over the telex machine at 3 a.m. He was not to know that ITN's London headquarters had been brought to a standstill by a technicians' strike.

His bad luck did not end there. All flights to and around the islands were cancelled but he persuaded government officials by phone to Victoria to send a military aircraft to fly him to Mahé. Having thwarted the attempted coup, Rene's government was only too keen to show off their captured mercenaries to the international media. Peter had exclusive access to the hapless mercs – but still no crew.

By now an experienced GOAH, Sharpe knew that there was one – just one – Lear jet for hire in East Africa, an aircraft capable of getting to the Seychelles swiftly and, better still, onwards to South Africa, then the location of the only facilities for a satellite 'feed' of TV film from the continent. His rivals would be obliged to charter piston-engined aircraft, make a long, droning journey to the Seychelles and back to Nairobi where their film would have to be 'shipped' on a scheduled airliner. He would still have a full day's 'beat' on other TV networks.

ITN obligingly chartered the sole Lear jet in Nairobi and a TV crew clambered aboard for the flight to the Seychelles. On Mahé, Sharpe gnawed his fingernails waiting for them to arrive. Hours passed. Nothing. Eventually a tiny speck appeared on the horizon over the airport. It was a charter flight from Nairobi. But it was a piston-engined aircraft and landed a full team of BBC TV men. The boys from the Beeb quickly filmed the scene, the captured mercenaries and interviews with René and all others involved before clambering back on their plane and heading back to Nairobi.

By now, Sharpe was reduced to tears of rage and frustration. His exclusive had disappeared before his very eyes. The Lear jet never made it to the Seychelles. It had called at Mombasa to fuel-up for the longish haul and had been mysteriously detained by Kenyan customs officials for 'irregularities'. Rumour had it that a BBC man based in Nairobi had a distant cousin who was, conveniently, a senior customs official at Mombasa Airport. Such is the cut-throat rivalry in the TV game that no hack doubted those rumours.

AP photographer Jim Howard – he took on the mercenaries single-handed – and won.

'Where did I leave those prize-winning photographs?' – Mike McCann, news photographer extraordinaire.

A LUTA CONTINUA

*H*e was an old friend and drinking companion. His name, shall
we say, was Eddie. The eyes were bloodshot with the tell-tale
blurred roll that always reminded me of the black minstrel money
box I had treasured as a child. They indicated he was fully tanked
up already. Yet he had been the first black friend I had made in
Africa. I was pleased to see him again. He had been fired from a
good job for drunkenness some years before and rumour had it that
he had perished in some remote area from cirrhosis of the liver
induced by whisky and self-pity. Eddie indulged unstintingly in
both.

Ten years previously he had told me that the days of the whites
in Rhodesia were numbered. Black resistance to white rule, he
insisted, had begun with the first white incursion, the Pioneer
Column of Cecil John Rhodes which colonised this beautiful land,
not in the name of Queen Victoria but for a grasping, profit-making
concern, the British South Africa Company. Having mugged up on
my Rhodesian history, I was not going to argue with that. The rebel-
lions in Mashonaland and Matabeleland in the 1890s were well documented as were the reasons for them. But we were now five years
into UDI, a white settler rule that had been condemned by the
world, with little sign of resistance from the black population.

True, there had been one or two incursions from Zambia and a
couple of farmers ambushed and murdered, but Ian Douglas Smith
was uttering, without much fear of contradiction, his immortal 'We
have the happiest Africans in the world'. Eddie was adamant. There
would soon come 'an event' which would herald the end of white
rule, not only in Rhodesia but in the whole of southern Africa. He
was one of those drunks who became more articulate with every sip.
I sensed he was not alluding to some African mumbo-jumbo but
knew something interesting that I did not. I decided to stick with
him to find out what 'the event' might be.

I suggested we continue the discussion in a nightclub that was notoriously whites only. He snorted his scepticism and offered me a bet that he wouldn't get past the door. I accepted. If I got him into the club he would tell me about 'the event'. I was on safe ground. The owner was a friend who owed me a favour or two. Eddie was impressed when we were welcomed warmly and shown to the bar.

To my horror, two enormous, very drunk Afrikaners on their first visit to Salisbury parked themselves alongside us. With glazed, hostile looks they intruded in our conversation. They wanted to talk to Eddie. Sensing trouble, I tried to make light of the situation and move on but it was too late. Eddie was already involved in a heated debate about his African origins, his right to go wherever he wished in his country, and his desire to visit South Africa to see just how badly his fellow Africans were being treated 'down there'. With mounting apprehension I was dragged into the debate.

The 'boere' learned that I was a British journalist. Their pent-up venom was then directed at me. We were responsible for all of Africa's problems. We poms. We had been nothing but trouble since we set foot on the continent. If we had not interfered, our 'boet' here – slapping Eddie around the shoulder – and us would have sorted out the problem, eh Eddie? Eddie agreed vehemently, giving me one of one of those long winks with his bloodshot right eye.

I tried to make a joke and encourage Eddie to make his excuses and leave. We were, I said, going on to the black township of Highfield to a black nightclub, Mutanga's Modern Nightclub. 'Hey, man,' said one of the Afrikaners. 'That sounds just great. We can come too?' It was not really a question. These two enormous, very drunk Afrikaners were going to come to Mutanga's Modern Nightclub. Eddie was insisting they did. Frik and Hannes, for that is how they introduced themselves, weighed down the back end of my rented Toyota as we headed out through the balmy darkness of the Rhodesian night towards what was then Salisbury's main African township.

The last time I had been to Mutanga's was in the company of the distinguished Ian Colvin, then *The Daily Telegraph*'s elder statesman. With his ineffably aristocratic air, half-moon spectacles on the end of his nose, Ian had jumped into the deep waters of this cavernous hall, with its deafening decibel level and its dance floor packed with gyrating, sweating bodies, like a seasoned high-board diver. I introduced him to the proprietor, Mutanga the Greater, so called because he was reputed to have poisoned his elder brother to gain control of this very profitable club. Mutanga had never been very far from Salisbury in his life but he recognised a distinguished guest when he saw one. Two young ladies were immediately installed at the best tables in the joint.

Colvin interrogated them about their life style, their views on the political situation in Rhodesia and, memorably, their views on Harold Wilson's administration. They giggled, glanced at each other nervously and sucked their beers from the neck of the bottles. Ian beamed over his half-moons. 'Would you care to dance?' he asked the lady sitting nearest to him. Her surprise subsided before mine and there was my esteemed colleague on the dance floor. His partner was hoping to bob and twirl. Ian insisted on a waltz, although the pounding beat emanating from the bandstand was hardly conducive.

Mutanga the Greater was at my side, looking apprehensive. 'Mr Chris...the snatchers are here...they will go for your friend.' I knew what he meant. A highly professional gang of pickpockets and bag-snatchers who operated around the hotels of central Salisbury would come to Mutanga's after a hard day's work and spend their winnings at the bar. If there was an obvious 'mark' in the club, they had no compunction in putting in overtime. I caught Ian's attention in the throbbing, milling throng and indicated it was time to leave. 'Nonsense, dear boy...this is great fun.'

He continued to dominate the dance floor with his partner – a compromise between the foxtrot and the twist. I saw one of the young snatchers join the leaping mob, move closer towards Colvin's jocund figure and suddenly reach, expertly, for his back pocket. Without breaking rhythm, Ian turned grabbed his hand and, to the young thief's astonishment, led him around the dance floor. The patrons collapsed with laughter, then cheered and roared their approval. That was Mutanga's. That was Ian Colvin.

Now I was re-entering this raucous chamber with Fast Eddie (so named because of the speed with which he consumed liquor) and two drunken Afrikaners from the racist 'white south'. Mutanga the Greater greeted us all like long-lost brothers, provided a table and some beers. The all-inclusive ladies appeared immediately and with great roars of delight our friends from 'down south' hauled them onto the dance floor. Eddie thought it a great joke. I reminded him that I was calling in the bet. He grinned. 'Give me a lift home and I'll tell you everything.' It was very late and I felt an absurd respon-sibility for Frikkie and Hannes. They were oblivious to everything except their two 'lekker kaffir meisies', the music and the beer. They gave us cheery waves as we left Mutanga's and I drove Eddie back to his home in Mufakose township, a long way from town.

He pulled a couple of dusty beers from the cupboard in the sparsely furnished two-roomed box that he called home. He had insisted on waking his wife and introducing – or rather showing her – to me, to my intense embarrassment. She sat with their two babies incomprehendingly at one end of the room as Eddie, more lucid than he had been at the start of the evening, began to tell me of 'the event'.

'You have been in Mozambique, Chris...and in Angola?' He knew full well I had, covering the 'liberation struggles' against the Portuguese colonial authorities in those two elephant-ear territories of southern Africa. 'The Portuguese,' Eddie said quietly 'are soon going from Africa. They will leave. The boys will move in and that, my friend, will be the end of Smith and Vorster.' I scoffed loudly. The Portuguese, under a succession of dictators including Salazar, had built their colonies into a quasi-philosophical imperial mission. The Portuguese authorities and military forces in Angola and Mozambique had had very few problems in confining black nationalist guerrillas to very remote areas of both countries and appeared firmly in control. Eddie was now seemingly sober and deadly serious. I was enjoying neither condition. 'You wanted a story. I am telling you that the Portuguese are going to leave Africa within a few months and that the struggle for us will be over.' I was still chuckling about Eddie's prediction as I drove back to my hotel in Salisbury. As far as I was concerned, I had been conned by my old friend into buying many drinks and giving him a lift home. On the morrow I had forgotten most of the events of the previous evening, including the forecast of the imminent collapse of the Portuguese empire.

It was a mistake. I had been in Africa long enough to know that there was some substance to what early travellers had called the 'bush telegraph'. There is an uncanny awareness in the remotest areas of what has happened way beyond the reach of modern telecommunications, coupled occasionally with a rather chilling prescience of what is about to happen. Whether my friend Eddie was acting from superstition, from an educated guess or from wishful thinking I know not. But he was right.

Less than a year later, at 2 a.m. on the morning of 24 April 1973, the 'phone next to my bed in Johannesburg screeched ominously. To foreign correspondents all late-night phone calls are ominous. I had been in bed for less than an hour, having spent the night covering the very predictable results of a general election in South Africa. Jolly John Osman, boisterous and disgustingly jolly, was on the other end of the line.

'On your bicycle, chum,' he boomed. 'There's been a coup in Lisbon.' I uttered a blurred thanks and sank back on the pillow. A coup in Lisbon! My mind began to race over the implications for Africa. Mozambique? Angola? Their demise as colonies would alter the entire face of the subcontinent, not least in Rhodesia and ultimately in South Africa. My half-awake mind recaptured my night with Fast Eddie. This was the 'event' he had predicted. I spent the rest of the night trying to reach him on the telephone and then, as the calls from London started to come in, work out where I would be better placed to cover the story. Should I go to Luanda or to Lourenço Marques, as it was still called? What about the 'creeping coup' against Emperor Haile Selassie in Ethiopia? That was still a major running story on my patch.

'We'll leave it to your experienced judgement, old boy,' said *The Daily Telegraph* Foreign Desk. 'Go where you think the best story will be but make sure we are covered on all of them.'

The following weeks were a nightmare of difficult travel throughout Africa, trying to stay on top of all the stories now breaking in all corners. We had a reliable stringer in Mozambique so I decided to try for Luanda, the (then) very graceful capital of Angola. Portuguese bureaucracy was still firmly in place. A visa was required with forms completed in triplicate, in special ink and submitted three months in advance of a proposed trip. A ridiculous condition for a hack on the move. I tried an old ruse. I tapped out on the telex machine a fake message, ostensibly from my London office advising me that the Portuguese authorities had granted me permission to proceed to Luanda without let or hindrance. The lady checking me in for the TAP flight to Lisbon via Luanda did not even ask about a visa, but as I was walking away jubilantly from the queue, a traveller collared me to indicate that I was wanted back at the desk. There was Mr Grobelaar, an airport official from head to toe, asking quite politely to see my visa. I showed him the telex. He shook his head. 'I'm afraid we cannot allow you on this flight with this,' he said. 'We are responsible for your passage and the authorities in Luanda will not accept this as a visa.' I tried for the following day's flight on South African Airways but the looming figure of Meneer Grobelaar remained unimpressed by my credentials or protestations.

In desperation I accepted a suggestion from Lee Griggs, the *Time* correspondent, who was known – and loved – as 'the Colonel' for his languid, easy-going demeanour in difficult situations. Lee accompanied me back to Jan Smuts Airport. I was clad in schoolboy gear, complete with little peaked cap and shorts. Lee had fashioned a sign which he draped around my neck. (In those days I appeared young enough to get away with it – just!) It said 'This child to be met and collected in Luanda'. Mr Grobelaar was lurking around the check-in desk but, as I pulled the school peak low over my eyes, he didn't give me a second glance.

Colonel Lee was insisting that I was looked after on the flight. Solicitous air hostesses shepherded me to the aircraft and fussed around me as we took off. Only when we cleared South African air space did I dare order a double Scotch on the rocks. When I propositioned the most attractive hostess, most of them realised it was a ruse and appreciated the joke. My proposition was not accepted but the crew played along when we landed at Luanda. I was escorted through immigration and customs with very few problems. Retribution occurred when I checked into the Hotel Tropicana in Luanda in my schoolboy kit and was immediately identified by colleagues already ensconced. It took some living down, but at least I had made my destination.

Luanda in those not-so-far-off days was one of the most attractive capitals in Africa. The Portuguese had a way of recreating the architecture and ambience of their own cities in their colonies. Beneath a 16th-century fort on a promontory overlooking the harbour, wide boulevards boasted colourful, lively pavement cafés with some of the finest seafood to be had in Africa.

The wars of liberation being fought by the FNLA in the north, the MPLA in the centre and UNITA in the south had rarely impinged on the easy-going life in the capital. Visiting journalists, once approved and admitted, would be given lavish hospitality by Portuguese government officials given a budget for that very purpose.

Trips to the 'front' were equally grand: aircraft were laid on to some distant headquarters where some charming general or brigadier would offer similar hospitality, wave a hand airily towards the silent savannah or forest and insist that there really was no war. Only in furtive conversations with the troops would one learn that there were in fact bodies in bags and mutilations caused by the occasional but bloody skirmishes. The Portuguese conscripts were bitter, too, about an enforced three years in hostile territory so far from home. This disillusionment was shared by their comrades in Mozambique and combined to influence the events which led to the 1974 coup in Lisbon.

But in Luanda, all was seemingly relaxed. The wine and beer flowed in the bars and night clubs and even the agents of PIDE, the sinister secret police, would join visiting hacks for a tipple and a chat. Don Wise, sent to cover this 'forgotten war' (one of many of Africa's 'forgotten wars') found the city most congenial. Don settled himself in the sun at a pavement café and ordered a drink. This was the kind of war he preferred to cover. He had taken but a couple of sips when from above him two shots rang out. The body of a black man plunged from the roof of a four-storey building and splattered on the pavement beside him. Donald raised an eyebrow. His PIDE companion shrugged. 'We have the occasional bandit,' he explained. Donald was not so easily misled. That afternoon he filed that first 'frontline' dispatch to the *Daily Express*. 'The first casualty of Angola's bloody war nearly fell into my beer today...'

The Lisbon coup had little initial impact in Luanda and yet behind the scenes the three liberation movements began manoeuvring and jostling for position to take over this, potentially Africa's wealthiest nation. The new Portuguese administration made it clear it was hell-bent on getting rid of its colonies willy-nilly. A Yul Brynner look-alike named Admiral Rosa Couthino was installed as the last Portuguese governor, charged with handing over to a coalition of the three guerrilla movements as soon as possible. Couthino soon made it clear why he was known as the 'Red Admiral'. His sympathies clearly lay with the Marxist MPLA which soon found itself occupying the best positions, equipped with the most modern weapons and in touch with the Soviet and Cuban agents who recognised the potential of this African foothold far sooner than their Western counterparts.

Within days of Angola's official independence, the MPLA moved against its two coalition partners, the FNLA and UNITA. Both were outgunned and outmanoeuvred. Suddenly Luanda itself became a battlefield. Bigfoot Younghusband and I were on our way to chat to a diplomatic friend one morning when all hell broke loose in a city centre street. Automatic rifle fire cracked above our heads and ricocheted off the buildings. It was coming from both ends of the street. We dived into a doorway as the battle, presumably between two of the rival armies of the coalition, raged for nearly an hour. Concrete and glass splinters showered our cowering figures (mostly Peter's as I was using his huge frame for cover). The ground shook as one of the adversaries brought up some heavier artillery, a rocket-launcher at least. 'What the fuck are we doing here,' Peter groaned. The age-old cry of the hack under fire. 'You should talk!' I shrieked. 'You're the one who can retire to your Cape wine farms. Some of us have to do this for a living.'

Luanda was no longer fun. Shooting would break out in the centre and the suburbs at any time of the day or night. The pavement cafés closed. The graceful walls of the old town were suddenly daubed with the ubiquitous graffiti of the revolution. Suburban villas housing rival political groups came under heavy fire. Hotels were suddenly crowded with heavy-lidded Russians and swaggering Cubans.

Soviet freighters queued to get into Luanda harbour to unload thousands of tons of war materiel for the MPLA who very quickly gained the upper hand. Jonas Savimbi tried to hold the coalition together but he and his men were forced to flee back to the vast south-east of Angola from whence he had waged war against the Portuguese colonists. The FNLA retreated northwards towards their base in neighbouring Zaire. The FNLA's last stand in Luanda came with a gallant stand in an ancient fort, Sao Pedro da Barra. There for three days they held out against an enormous barrage from MPLA forces. From the end of the spit that extends into the bay I watched the lethal fireworks display with Michael Chapman, an Englishman freelance journalist who had lived and worked in Angola for 15 years. As a series of heavy shells tore apart the walls of the ancient fort, Chapman sighed. 'If you thought Portuguese rule was bad, wait until you see what this lot is going to do,' he said, with prescience. Chapman left the country for good shortly afterwards.

Soon Luanda – and therefore the new government of Angola – was in the hands of the MPLA. Strutting young commissars demanded papers and passes, seizing companies and businesses in the name of the revolution. Arrogant young gunmen of 'the people's army' swaggered the streets, harassing and bullying all who could not produce a party pass. Worse, the inevitable camp-following 'journalists' of the left wing arrived to witness the people's victory. They included such absurd practitioners of the 'journalism of commitment' school as Jane Bergerol, my old friend, Michael Wolfers, and the Australian Marxist, Wilfred Burchett.

Wolfers soon squeaked his way into a job with the revolutionary government, training 'people's journalists' no less. The death of Luanda was movingly chronicled by a young Polish journalist, Ryszard Kapuscinski, sent by his news agency in Warsaw. He described the panic as the Portuguese traders packed all the stocks from their shops and businesses and their possessions into wooden crates and waited at the dockside for ships to take them to Lisbon, Rio, Cape Town – anywhere.

'I don't know if there had ever been an instance of a whole city sailing across the ocean, but that is exactly what happened. Before they left they had still managed to build the wooden city in Luanda, into which they packed everything that had been in the stone city...'

Kapuscinski described vividly the rapid decay of the city. Water ran short and then the pumps ran dry. 'I walked around dirty, needing something to drink so badly that I came down with a fever and saw orange spots before my eyes.' The policemen left, the firemen left, the garbagemen left and mountains of garbage began piling up in the streets. 'You could walk through some streets only with great effort and disgust. In this climate the excess of sun and moisture accelerate and intensify decay, rot and fermentation. The whole city began to stink. One morning the cats started dying, having poisoned themselves collectively on some carrion. After two days they puffed up and swelled to the size of piglets. Black flies swarmed over them. The odour was unbearable.'

He described a young MPLA soldier standing amid the rubble, smiling and saying, 'They've taken everything from us but we've got a home now. They left us what's ours.' He then emptied the magazine of his automatic rifle into the air in jubilation. Luanda had been 'liberated' but in the vast expanses of the hinterland *a luta continua*...and was to do so for many more very bloody years.

On the other side of the continent, Mozambique's liberation was no less disheartening or bloody. Immediately after the Lisbon coup, the buzz went around the Africa press corps that the man to contact was a Portuguese officer I shall call Louis who was based in the town of Nampula in the far north of Mozambique. I made the journey with Dennis Gordon of the *Rand Daily Mail* and Ken 'Fingers' Whiting of AP. To our surprise, Louis turned out to be a young, roly-poly man with a ready smile and sharp wit. In his civilian shirt-sleeves and sneakers he was a complete contrast to the rather sinister, manicured, eye-shaded Portuguese security officers who had been in place only a few weeks before.

Louis poured us generous slugs of white port (it was 8 a.m.), perched himself on the edge of a desk and asked us, in immaculate English, what we wished to know. Naturally we began by asking what he knew about the future of Mozambique but he waved the questions aside. 'Your story at the moment, gentlemen,' he said, 'is what has been going on in Lisbon'. He then launched into a detailed run-down of the background to the revolution in the Portuguese capital, giving dates, times, places, names of all those involved and a masterly analysis of the overthrow of the Salazar dictatorship. We were staggered. Here, in the middle of the African bush, we were being given a full briefing on the cause and effects of a coup in Europe.

The detail was amazing. He told us that the plotters were aware that several of our colleagues based in Lisbon were in the pay of PIDE, the secret police. It had been arranged to ensure that all of them were out of Lisbon on the due date. This had been done by offering them generous facility trips to Portugal's colonies. 'You chaps can never resist a free trip,' he laughed. 'There wasn't one foreign journalist in Lisbon at the time of the coup.' Everything Louis told us turned out to be uncannily accurate – including the names of respected colleagues who, it turned out, had been acting as agents for Salazar's secret police. My foreign desk wanted to know how, from the depths of Africa, I could give them so much background on events in Lisbon. I could not enlighten them. We never discovered precisely who Louis was or what his role had been. He had clearly been in on the plot from the start but what on earth was he doing in a tiny northern Mozambican town? Another African mystery.

As in Angola, the Portuguese had been fighting a brutal but remote war against freedom fighters in Mozambique. In the case of the east African colony there was only one reasonably organised and armed movement, known by its Portuguese acronym of FRELIMO. Based in Dar es Salaam, FRELIMO had been formed in 1962 and quickly found itself under the leadership of Eduardo Mondlane, a charismatic and highly personable doctor of sociology. Mondlane's door was always open to visiting journalists, even those whose newspapers' policies opposed his revolutionary guerrilla policies.

For years, FRELIMO's guerrilla activities had been confined to the far north of Mozambique, hit-and-run raids across the Rovuma River border from Tanzania, planting mines on roads used by Portuguese patrols and nocturnal indoctrination of villages. In the early days, they had given the Portuguese little to worry about. Mondlane's most effective weapon was his flair for public relations. He insisted that FRELIMO had liberated large parts of the rural north and had set up its own schools and social services.

'Come and see for yourself,' he would say, donning combat fatigues, strapping on a pistol and leading the hapless hack into the bush. Sure enough, with suitable drama, Mondlane would lead his man across a large river and take him to a village full of happy people enjoying schooling and social services rarely seen in any African villages. What he never told the visiting correspondent, of course, was that the river was not the Rovuma and that the villages they were shown were still within the safe borders of southern Tanzania.

It worked so many times that many of the world's most distinguished newspapers carried glowing reports and pictures from 'liberated Mozambique'. The trick so angered the Portuguese that PIDE were ordered to assassinate Eduardo Mondlane, which they did with typical ruthlessness, a parcel bomb which killed him at his desk in Dar es Salaam in 1969.

FRELIMO was bigger than one man, however. By the time Salazar was overthrown in 1974, its guerrillas did control large areas of the far north. The Portuguese military were becoming increasingly hard-pressed, so much so that they had been obliged to swallow Latin pride and seek assistance from Rhodesian forces. Even so they had not reached the northern port of Beira or even seriously threatened the critical Beira-to-Umtali railway link. In Lourenço Marques, the capital 800 miles to the south, very few local people had even heard of FRELIMO. The war was so remote that the only uniforms seen were those ceremonial dresses when innumerable generals paraded through the town. Correspondents arrived in droves in the wake of the Lisbon coup to await the transition. They waited, and waited, but of any kind of revolution, liberation or even transition there was little sign. Never mind. The pink-washed colonial splendour of the Polana Hotel, with its views over the Indian Ocean and its sizzling piri piri prawns and chilled sangria on the lawns around the pool compensated for the journalist waiting game.

There were still the usual visa problems, of course, but these were assumed to have been relaxed. Or at least I assumed they had been relaxed. I flew in with John Osman visa-less and was startled when the white immigration man flicked swiftly through my passport. 'I have no visa I'm afraid,' I apologised. He leapt from his cubicle and danced a little angry jig, shouting to his colleagues: 'No visa...no visa...this man, he has no visa'. Other immigration people jumped from their boxes and took up the cry. Behind me, Osman boomed that he was from the BBC and would they please let us pass without let or hindrance.

Finally we persuaded them to let us through and we arrived at the Polana to find many of our colleagues had had similar hassles. Such was the ennui of the press corps that we began to devise a musical show around the situation. It is not uncommon for a gathered hack corps in moments of boredom to make up songs relating to any given predicament.

I would rate our show 'Viva Mozambiqua' as one of the best. As always, the melodies and tunes were plagiarised. We began with a scene at the airport in which the immigration man leapt from his cubicle chanting 'No Visa! No Visa! My God, he has No Visa' to be joined by a chorus line of his colleagues taking up the refrain. In the waiting queue of passengers, Jolly John Osman would, in booming baritone, provide the counterpoint (to the tune of 'Let's face the music and dance') 'I have a circuit tonight...I have a circuit to London tonight...'

Our colleagues entered into the spirit of the 'musical' with more enthusiasm than I had ever seen them deploy on a story. There was only one telex machine at the Polana which meant that one's copy was seen by everyone else. Hence, to the tune of 'When You're Smiling' we had 'When You're Filing...When You're Filing...The Whole World Files With You'. We were finally issued with pink press cards which were supposed to give us unlimited access but, as usual, were totally useless. No matter. It gave us another number: 'You can go wherever you want with your little pink card...(soprano chorus)...little pink card...'

Wilf Nussey, head of the Argus Africa News Service, thought this whole affair was frivolous and, initially loftily, refrained from making a contribution. Finally even Wilf succumbed. One evening, he made a grand entrance through the swing doors of the Polana lounge, flanked by two of his assistants, Deon du Plessis and Tom Roy. Wilf is a tall man. Deon and Tom were bigger. They suddenly went into a soft-shoe shuffle routine singing tunelessly: 'We are from *Argus*...From *Argus* are we...We all work for WILFRED NUSSEY'. The hacks cheered. The immaculately clad Portuguese ladies choked on their coffee.

So keen did we become about our 'musical' that we seriously thought of suggesting that we stage it at the independence celebrations, when and if they ever took place. On the assumption that Samora Machel would become the first president we were to have finished off, to the tune of 'Grenada', a grand chorus rendition of 'Samora...You've got us under your skin...' (which he certainly would have done had we ever performed in public).

Martin Meredith of the *Sunday Times* discovered a bowling green in the grounds of the hotel and the British hacks took enthusiastically to another diversion. We were given advice by a resilient group of expatriate lady bowlers who, clad in their immaculate whites and regulation hats, were competing at the other end of the green.

Two American colleagues, Charles Mohr of the *New York Times* and Bill 'Mutters' Mutschmann of CBS scoffed at us from the sidelines until they realised there was a certain ball skill akin to baseball. Suddenly they were interested and an Anglo-American challenge ensued. Mutschmann got a little carried away as his wood curled across the sward. He added a new dimension to the lexicon of crown green bowling by yelling at the top of his voice 'Roll on, motherfucker...roll on!' The expatriate ladies at the other side of the green gave us no more advice.

This bizarre 'phoney war' period had many light-hearted moments. When one well-known correspondent was discovered *in flagrante* beneath an exceptionally large lady hack, he found a note in his room saying simply: 'Some are born great, some achieve greatness and some have greatness THRUST upon them'. There was a kangaroo court trial of a hack who committed the cardinal sin of filing a story to his newspaper about the exceptionally high black market foreign exchange rates that could be – and were – obtained on the Indian market. Black market money exchange was one of the time-honoured ways by which the hacks doubled their money. To write about it was to kill the goose that lays the golden eggs.

Perhaps a fitting end to this period came with a rumour 'confirmed by the highest authority' that Lourenço Marques was being renamed 'Kanfumo'. No one was quite sure where the name had come from but the dearth of copy was such that every one of perhaps 100 correspondents from all corners of the globe dutifully filed stories under the new dateline. For three days, Lourenço Marques, to become Maputo, was known to the world as 'Kanfumo'. Just as the revolutionaries in Lisbon had little idea of what they were going to do about Mozambique, FRELIMO had made no plans to organise or conduct any political activity in Lourenço Marques or anywhere south of Beira. As it was obvious that sooner or later they would be asked to form a government, John Osman and I flew to Dar es Salaam to ask about their plans. We found ourselves answering questions instead of asking them. What was Lourenço Marques like? What were the people saying? Was the climate similar to that in Tanzania? Someone finally produced a battered, outdated tourist map of the city and John and I pointed out the various points of interest.

It did not augur well for the future of Mozambique. Months later, when they had put together some skeletal semblance of an organisation in the capital, a bewildered population attempted to express their support by scrawling the graffiti on the occasional wall. They even got the name wrong: 'Viva Ferlimo' or 'Viva Fremilo' or 'Viva Femilio'.

The white population, unlike their counterparts in Luanda, felt no panicky urge to quit. There seemed to be no threat. They formed their own resistance movement 'Fico' – 'we stay' – and defiantly drove around offering a single raised-finger salute. The Portuguese army garrison was under orders merely to keep the peace and avoid involvement in any form of political activity. The crunch came when a group of whites rushed the radio station and took over the studios and transmitters. Under the melodramatic name of 'The Dragons of Death', they declared UDI on behalf of white Mozambicans.

For several days, their broadcasts became more shrill and racist. Fico supporters took to the streets carrying firearms. In the teeming townships surrounding Lourenço Marques, black concern

turned to anger and then exploded in violence. Mobs set up improvised roadblocks, hauling whites from their cars, beating them,
burning their vehicles and with increasing ferocity killing, clubbing
and stabbing them to death.

Bigfoot Younghusband and I once again found ourselves swimming against the tide. We had been ordered in from South Africa to
cover the situation. As the airport had been closed at the first sign
of violence we had to drive. At Komatipoort, the border post, we
were lucky enough to be offered a lift with Stan Maher and Les
Bush of the *Rand Daily Mail* who had an office car loaded with supplies in case of a siege situation. It was approaching dusk as we set
off on the 40-mile journey to Lourenço Marques. We had just heard
on the radio that the 'Dragons of Death' had relinquished the radio
station and sought the protection of the Portuguese army garrison.
The indications were that the mobs were in control of the approach-
es to the city and some parts of the city itself. Confirmation came
quickly as convoys of oncoming vehicles flashed their lights and
waved us down. Terrified Portuguese screamed out of their windows. 'Don't go any further...they are killing all white people...they
are burning everything...turn back and drive for your lives.' It was
slightly unnerving. Stan Maher who was driving, slowed down as
we held a discussion on the wisest plan. Bigfoot suggested that we
proceed very slowly. If there was the slightest sign of trouble on the
road ahead we would turn and get back to the border. Stan knew
there was a Portuguese army post just before the outskirts of
Lourenço Marques and suggested that if we could get that far we
could seek refuge there. With stomachs knotting almost audibly, we
agreed.

We could not have been travelling at more than 40 mph when
we came around a blind bend. It was now dark. The huge shape of
an articulated truck, stationary lengthwise across the road, loomed
in the headlights. Stan wrenched the wheel and skilfully avoided
missing the rear end of the truck. But we were now on the wrong
side of what we realised with horror was a hostile roadblock. A mass
of angry faces emerged from the gloom, pressing around the car and
beating on the roof and windows with sticks, clubs and spears. 'Out!
Out! Out!' We had no choice. We clambered out and were manhandled against the side of the car.

'Journalista...Ingles...Imprensa,' we chorused. We were roughly
body-searched by some while others tore open the boot and began to
scour through the provisions. I guessed there must have been at
least 200 blacks manning the roadblock, many of them extremely
hostile. They were not interested in stealing our provisions, our

watches or wallets. They were searching for weapons. I prayed that none of my colleagues was carrying so much as a pocket knife.

After what seemed an age, they pushed us back into the car and told us to drive on. Stan Maher, very wisely I thought, indicated that we would be very happy to turn back but they angrily waved us forward. It was a very sweaty foursome that proceeded down the darkened road towards LM. The darkness suddenly disappeared in a flash of flame to our right and we were suddenly enveloped in smoke. It was another roadblock. This mob had just overturned and set fire to a car carrying fleeing Portuguese. The bodies of the two occupants lay inert, illuminated by the flames. Once again we were spreadeagled against the car. Once again we were searched thoroughly. Once again we were waved onward.

We got to the gates of the army post which were firmly locked. A very nervous sentry refused our pleas to be allowed in to talk to his commanding officer. The gates suddenly swung open to allow an armoured car to emerge. A subaltern poked his head from the turret. His advice was to go back but under no circumstances were we going to run those roadblocks going the wrong way. 'Follow us, but don't stop,' he said.

Stan tucked the bonnet of our car into the rear of the armoured car and we sped towards the lights of Lourenço Marques, now clearly visible. The military vehicle suddenly slowed and then stopped. Another roadblock; this one manned by possibly a thousand men. They swarmed around us and, now used to the routine, we emerged with our hands held high. To our consternation the armoured car pulled away and sped down the road. We were on our own again. The search was even more thorough and this time we had to part with our cigarettes and whisky. The mood of the mobs appeared to be getting uglier.

There were two more roadblocks before we crossed the causeway which leads to the centre of the city. Our troubles were not over. There was a vast milling throng blocking the road and we could see several whites being chased and beaten. As we reached the periphery of the mob, a sheet of flame engulfed a small block of shops at the side of the road. Looters carrying boxes of goods and anything they could carry leapt through the flames and smoke. Part of the crowd turned on our car and began hammering on the roof. A small black man, bespectacled and sweating, leaned through the window. 'You must go back now, immediately...they will kill you!'

Stan Maher needed no more persuading. He slammed into reverse and we shot backwards onto the causeway. What now? None of us felt like renegotiating all those roadblocks back to the South

African border. It seemed we could go neither forward nor backward without serious risk. I looked at the water below. It was calm. Across the bay the lights of the Polana district twinkled enticingly. Bigfoot and I were fully prepared to swim, although it was a good two miles.

We were pondering this option when another car screamed to a halt beside us. One of three young coloured men inside shouted, 'If you want to get into the city follow us.' They roared off and, with his usual great presence of mind, Stan followed. Just before the roadblock at the other end of the causeway the car in front swerved onto a track, bumped over a stretch of waste ground and finally picked up a street which seemed to lead us north of the city. We sped past two, possibly three, abandoned roadblocks and on two occasions rocks bounced off the roof. Our new found companions kept driving at speed. We followed. Finally we reached a well-lit main road, thankfully deserted, which led us into the centre of the city and on to the Polana.

It was time for a very large whisky. And another. Our colleagues ensconced in the hotel told us we could relax. All telephones and telex lines were down indefinitely. There was no way of getting our copy out – unless someone felt like driving back to the South African border. No one volunteered. More whisky and much reflection on the sheer terror of having a white face in the middle of a very hostile black mob. Groups of colleagues arrived through the night. Jolly John Osman, of course, had had the very bright idea of catching the train which ran regularly from Komatipoort to LM. It was a slow journey. At one stage the train broke down and Osman and his colleagues helped to push start it. 'Another first,' boomed John. 'First time I've had to push a train to war.' But there were no roadblocks and they got through. Hans Germani and his wife, armed to the teeth, drove through all the roadblocks in the early hours of the morning firing wildly in all directions. 'I'm sure I got some of zem,' shouted Hans, waving his Luger around the Polana lounge.

But for all the ingenuity, heroics and stupidity we were all stuck. We had no communications. Peter Hawthorne and Bigfoot Younghusband decided bravely that they would make a copy run by road back to South Africa at dawn the following morning. They reckoned that the mobs would have dissipated or drunk themselves into stupors – and they were right. Carrying copy for everyone, they had a trouble-free run to Komatipoort, opened up a telex line from the local hotel and sent thousands of words around the world about the situation in Mozambique.

Over breakfast on that following morning, the press corps froze in disbelief when that strange sound – the ringing of a telephone – echoed across the terrace. There was a scramble to see if the phones were working. They weren't. But here was an incoming call – and it was for me. It was my wife, Denise, calling on a party line from her parents' smallholding outside Salisbury in Rhodesia. All the subscribers to this party line – about 30 of them – had discovered that with a certain method of tapping one could get trunk calls out free of charge. Denise had heard there had been trouble in LM and had given it a try. My colleagues watched enviously as I dictated my story to her with instructions to relay it to the *Telegraph*.

Then the ever-enterprising Osman arrived at the hotel. As always he had been up before everyone else and had been to the local radio station. There he had found a frightened but bribable technician who had managed to arrange a radio link with the BBC in London. John would take everyone's copy, dictate it to the BBC who would oblige all by relaying it to the London offices of the newspapers.

Communications remained down for another 24 hours but we had got the story out. The *Telegraph* foreign desk sent my wife a herogram for her assistance – and sent me a rocket. They had received my story – the same one – from three different sources: from Hawthorne and Younghusband in Komatipoort, via the BBC and from Denise. 'Communications most expensive, old boy. Please watch costs on duplication!'

That particularly grisly week, in which more than 100 Portuguese had been murdered by the mobs, inevitably provoked the exodus of Mozambique's white community. It was another of Kapuscinski's 'wooden cities', as the Portuguese loaded their belongings and crates, deserted their properties and fled by sea to Lisbon or by road and rail to South Africa.

By the time independence came in 1975, the depressingly familiar signs of decay had already overtaken the once sedate, somnolent capital of Lourenço Marques, now officially renamed Maputo after a local chief. The cafés and bars were locked and bolted, the shops were sparsely stocked, garbage and litter gusted around the boulevards and the infantile scrawls of revolutionary graffiti smothered the walls of once graceful buildings.

Township dwellers simply broke into suburban houses and apartment blocks and moved in. The better houses and apartments were appropriated by the legion of civil servants, party officials and the influx of Russian, East German and other 'friends of the revolution'. Samora Machel, a manic-eyed, diminutive figure, clad himself in Castro-style combat fatigues and harangued endless rallies with meaningless rhetoric. He allowed himself to be advised by an inner circle of white Marxists who busily set about ruining what remained of the economy.

Foreign journalists, unless they were of the dubious breed with commitment to the revolution, were discouraged or forbidden entry. On one occasion, I managed a brief visit in the slipstream of a visiting British politician. The city was dirty and ineffably depressing. I passed a shop in one of the main streets which was completely empty, save for three disconsolate-looking assistants lounging behind the counter. Intrigued, I called in to ask what they would be offering if they could obtain it. After a few bemused shrugs, one lady said: 'Anything, but we have nothing.' I learned it had been a prosperous clothing and shoe store only a couple of years earlier. For those who had foreign exchange, or a senior party card, there was the ridiculously labelled 'duty free shop' where reasonable, imported consumer goods could be obtained. This, of course, was out of reach to the people. They had to join the interminable queues for bread, vegetables or even once-abundant fish, when available.

They had excuses, of course. The country was besieged by 'enemies of the revolution' and was at war. A couple of the 'enemies' were the obvious ones – Ian Smith's Rhodesia whose forces frequently crossed the border to strike at ZANU guerrilla bases, and South African commandos raiding ANC units in Maputo and elsewhere. Others were less obvious, like the Western agencies which set out to disrupt Soviet plans to construct a deep-water port at Nacala to take warships pointing into the Indian Ocean. And then came RENAMO, or the MNR, the Mozambique Resistance Movement. The brainchild of Rhodesia's Central Intelligence Organisation, RENAMO was a rag-tag force of blacks who had fought with the Portuguese, renegades, and disgruntled former FRELIMO fighters.

Rhodesian intelligence men gave them rudimentary training and sent them back into the Mozambique bush to cause as much havoc as they could and, hopefully, distract FRELIMO from giving assistance to ZANU guerrillas now threatening Rhodesia's entire eastern flank. In their haste, they omitted to give RENAMO any form of coherent political policy or leadership, a factor which enabled Machel's government to brand them, with some justification, 'bandits'. In turn, Machel frequently forgot to pay his own army which was sent into the bush to tackle the rebels. Disgruntled soldiers either joined RENAMO or set up their own bandit groups, raiding and plundering villages, stores, convoys or anything that would provide them with a living.

When Rhodesia became Zimbabwe, the South African Defence Force took over as RENAMO's benefactor, providing large quantities of arms and ammunition and some semblance of political leadership in the shape of the totally nondescript Afonso Dahlakama. Rural

Mozambique, in fact anywhere outside the limits of the main towns, was overtaken by anarchy. Machel's fiefdom was confined to the decaying, dying city of Maputo and the port of Beira. Refugees fled into neighbouring Malawi, Zimbabwe and South Africa. Famine and fear were pervasive and remained endemic for many more years.

Angola's civil war swiftly took on a much more sinister and dangerous dimension. The Russians and their Cuban surrogates had moved quickly to consolidate their foothold, having backed the MPLA in its seizure of sole control from the independence coalition with the FNLA and UNITA. Angola was a rich prize for the Communist Bloc: deep water Atlantic ports, strategic aircraft landing facilities, an abundance of oil in the Cabinda enclave and lucrative diamond fields in the interior. The US had been caught on the hop and the CIA was embarrassed and displeased. Angola was about to become the last major superpower battlefield in Africa. Even the collapse of the Soviet empire and the end of the Cold War failed to bring peace to this troubled land. Jonas Savimbi rejected the results of the first democratic elections, supervised by the UN, and his UNITA forces fought on.

The CIA initially preferred the FNLA, not least because the movement was based in Zaire. The corrupt dictatorship had long since been 'bought' into the American sphere of influence. Jonas Savimbi had modelled his UNITA forces on vaguely Maoist lines and principles and seemed a little suspect. Savimbi, however, was soon to prove himself the arch-pragmatist and by far the more reliable and powerful force ranged against the Marxist MPLA and its rapidly swelling Cuban 'task force'.

Even the collapse of the Soviet empire and the end of the Cold War failed to bring peace to this troubled land. Savimbi rejected the results of the first democratic elections, which had been supervised by the UN and which accorded victory to the MPLA. UNITA forces returned to battle formation and the civil war continued at still greater intensity.

Savimbi had a natural flair for public relations. Hacks attempting to cover the situation in Angola were meeting great resistance from the government in Luanda which, if they approved a visa, would lay on a strictly regimented 'programme'. The South Africans were similarly discouraging about visits to the northern border of Namibia and Angola. The flamboyant and vain Savimbi found foreign correspondents only too willing to visit him in the territory he controlled and, inevitably, to put across his case and his views.

Savimbi's publicity-consciousness was soon to lead to a serious security breach. Two British journalists, Fred Bridgland of Reuters and Michael Nicholson, the intrepid ITN correspondent, became regular visitors to UNITA-held territory, courtesy of a small fleet of aircraft which shuttled between Lusaka and towns in southern Angola. Bridgland, based in Lusaka, had made a point of interviewing Savimbi on several occasions and was unabashedly impressed by the man, his political fluency, his aims and his policies.

Shortly after Portugal's swift and shameful retreat from Angola, Bridgland had noticed a number of fair-haired white soldiers among Savimbi's men gathered around a Panhard armoured car. When he spoke to them they declined to say where they had come from but their heavy South African accents told the reporter all he wanted to know. It was not hard enough evidence for a Reuters dispatch but Fred was now commuting regularly into Savimbi territory and the evidence began to pile up. At one stage he and Nicholson cadged a lift on Savimbi's private jet (on 'loan' from Lonrho) which to their amazement made a refuelling stop at a top-secret South African base in northern Namibia. There they saw convoys of Panhards and Hercules C130 transport aircraft whose destination could only be Angola.

A few days later, the two reporters were in Benguela, a key port on the Atlantic coast south of Luanda. Nicholson's cameraman managed to sneak some film of a Panhard and a number of white soldiers in the vicinity of the town. Later they questioned Savimbi about the use of South African troops and armour in his proposed push towards Luanda. Savimbi's replies were ambiguous but gave enough away to convince the newsmen that their story was accurate. Bridgland's story led to Nigeria rejecting UNITA and switching its backing to the MPLA. The CIA was furious. The South African forces, until then billed by newspapers as the mystery column, pushed on relentlessly towards Luanda.

A gaggle of hacks descended on Benguela to confirm the involvement of the South Africans. Savimbi hedged again and diverted our special correspondents by sending them on a very special railway journey – a 200-mile ride along the Benguela Railway which UNITA then controlled. Bridgland reported that the journey 'seemed to be divorced from reality which, with hindsight, was indeed so'. A large Glasgow-built steam locomotive pulled a column of freight cars packed with UNITA soldiers. 'At the back we reclined in an ornate private passenger carriage with a rear viewing platform.

'We correspondents stood on the platform and gazed across the great African plateau at a breathtaking sunset as fiery in its redness as the war which none of us had managed or would manage to see at first hand.' The man from the *Wall Street Journal* was unimpressed. 'What a goddam country. You know you can't get a single statistic in this place? No figures on coffee production, no banana tonnages...' Feeling a little guilty about not getting so much as a glimpse of the war they were supposed to be covering, the hacks persuaded a young Portuguese railwayman to take them on an electric-powered rail inspection car to view the remains of a rail bridge across the Lumege River blown up by the MPLA on their retreat from Luso.

'We approached the twisted wreckage of the bridge at what seemed far too high a speed...our party was composed mostly of Britons indoctrinated in the virtues of the stiff upper lip: we said nothing. At the last moment the driver slammed on the brakes. It was much too late. The rail car skidded on at great speed. We plunged down the remnants of broken rails on the bridge towards the river bed. We were halted in mid-dive towards oblivion by a twisted girder. We hung precariously in mid-air, above the water.

'An imperious, booming voice from the dangling end demanded "Nobody panic...let us have no panic." It was "General" Max Hastings of the *Evening Standard*, marshalling the troops. He need not have worried. No one was panicking. The hacks hauled themselves up a hanging rail to safety and dubbed UNITA's territory The Land With No Brakes.'

Disclosure and confirmation that the dread South Africans were helping Savimbi was akin to the kiss of death for the UNITA leader. Support from influential African states dissipated. The US Congress panicked and the CIA's clandestine backing for the South Africans was withdrawn. Just as its forces reached the outskirts of Luanda, Pretoria got cold feet and ordered a retreat, to the cold fury of the South African commanders and troops. The MPLA and the ever more numerous Cuban forces, heavily equipped, moved southwards. Savimbi and his dwindling supporters marched deeper into the bush, there to languish and regroup quietly for nearly two years.

For a time, the world all but forgot about Jonas Savimbi, and would have done so completely had it not been for Leon Dash, a black correspondent for the *Washington Post*. For journalistic enterprise and courage, Dash's venture into the interior of Angola to find Savimbi is rivalled only by Stanley's search for Livingstone a century earlier.

The American entered Angola from Zambia, crossing the Ninda swamps with his UNITA escort, wading naked with their clothes on their heads. This two-hour trek left him with severe lacerations to his legs which turned to running sores. It was the beginning of a eight-month assignment during which he walked more than 2 000 miles, fell ill several times, lived for a time on grubs, watched UNITA go into battle, came under fire on several occasions and observed Savimbi prepare to fight his way back into the Angolan political arena. His dispatches, when he finally emerged, were models of reporting an African bush war.

A year or so later, Mike Nicholson and his ITN crew achieved the feat of gaining the permission of the South African Defence Force to cross the border from Namibia in search of Savimbi. Soon after the crossing the truck in which they were travelling was ambushed by the MPLA. Nicholson and his crew were obliged to flee with UNITA men into the bush. Unwittingly, his timing was bad. The South Africans decided, for reasons of political expediency, to close the Namibian border. Nicholson's attempts to return were repeatedly rebuffed. For four months he and his crew wandered for hundreds of miles through the Angolan bush, dodging MPLA patrols and ambushes. Finally his editors in London persuaded the South Africans to make contact with UNITA and to arrange for Nicholson and his team to be flown from an isolated air strip to safety.

As Savimbi rebuilt his forces and regained his confidence and some new foreign backing, invitations to correspondents to visit the 'land with no brakes' were widely distributed. Invariably, these press facilities turned into endurance tests for the hacks. Jack Foisie – 'Uncle Jack' as he was affectionately known to all his colleagues – looked like a benign, dotty grandpa from an American television sit-com. Slightly built, bespectacled and slow of speech, he maintained an air of detached amusement even in the most hair-raising situations. The *Los Angeles Times* veteran, however, had one of the sharpest journalistic minds in the business. He had survived two aircraft crashes in the course of duty – including one in which the aircraft in which he was a passenger was shot down in Vietnam. 'Another one for the memory book!' Uncle Jack would say in such circumstances.

Foisie enjoyed his visits to Angola – as did his colleagues who looked forward to the verbal sparring matches between the *LA Times* man and Savimbi. Jonas got his own back by sending Jack on a 300-mile trip to a newly captured town. It was supposed to be a two-day journey. It took ten days. 'Vehicles frequently broke down, overheated or suffered flat tires as they struggled through the sandy waste or plunged into deep brush to hide when the drone of aircraft was heard,' Foisie reported. 'In one ten-hour stop due to an engine breakdown, the driver and the cook chopped out the top of an empty 45-gallon drum and pounded the metal into a radiator fan to replace the broken one. When the fan belts broke, UNITA soldiers were lined up and the one with the narrowest belt sacrificed it as a replacement.' Another one for the memory book, Jack!

Fred Bridgland had, by his own admission, become obsessed with the Angolan saga. Perforce, he had spent practically all his many weeks in Angola over a period of eight years with UNITA and had established a rapport with Savimbi which was similar to that Freddy Forsyth had with Ojukwu during the Nigerian civil war. It was hardly surprising that Bridgland should find himself the first reporter to be invited to witness a major battle – the UNITA attack on the garrison town of Cangonga. He invited a freelance camera-man, Gwynne Roberts, to join him. Bridgland's account of the battle was as honest as it was graphic – and highlighted one of the terrible dilemmas that can, and all too frequently does, confront the war correspondent. 'We were about three kilometres south-west of the town when the mortar and cannon fire began,' Bridgland wrote. 'Huge flames shot up in the distance, outlining buildings. Then we began to hear the crackle of Kalashnikovs. Walking in strict single file along a path charted by reconnaissance guerrillas through a field of anti-personnel mines, we at last reached the Benguela Railway, crossed it to the north and began closing on the town from the west. The adrenalin pumped harder as we walked down the line towards Cangonga and its water tank on high steel supports came into view.

'Then as the staccato of the Kalashnikovs grew more persistent, and louder, we were pulled off into another mine-free route through the undergrowth and we finally entered Cangonga at the western end of the airstrip. To our right, huts surrounded by giant sunflow-ers were ablaze. To the left, a building that was clearly the MPLA's arsenal was burning and exploding periodically with great violence, prompting us to hit the ground in case flying shards of metal scythed us down.

'The centre of the town was under UNITA control but firefights were continuing in every direction amid the crumps and crashes of mortars and rockets. At the eastern end of the runway we stopped. Then all hell broke lose. Concentrated firing came from huts about 30 yards to the right. Some MPLA soldiers had regrouped and launched a direct counter-attack against the command party. Gwynne stood filming in the direction of the firing before he was smashed to the ground in a mass rugby tackle by UNITA officers. He cursed them as they pinned him down. I was already trying to burrow into the earth like some demented ostrich as bullets whooshed overhead and the arsenal erupted with increased fury.'

As the reporter moved into the centre of the town 'three UNITA soldiers appeared, dragging a body with the kind of respect normally accorded a stuck pig. The body moved and emitted a groan of agony: the MPLA soldier, a boy who was barely 18, had a gaping head wound which looked fatal. I shouted to the soldiers to put the boy down: he was dying. Though they understood no English, they responded by laying him face down in the dust. If it's true that any man's death diminishes one, then being witness to callous treatment of badly wounded fellow human beings makes one feel unclean. As journalists we can claim we are only there to observe: but that cannot always be an excuse for inaction, for opting out of humanity.'

Bridgland and Roberts persuaded a senior officer to get help for the boy and were assured he would be given medical treatment and taken as a prisoner of war. Gwynne Roberts, a veteran of wars in the Middle East and elsewhere in Africa, recorded his own feelings in his diary. 'When I saw his face and head matted with blood seeping from a white wound onto his brown skin, pity swept through me and I was almost in tears as I filmed. This poor creature was in abject despair and terror. What had such a young lad done to deserve this – forced possibly by poverty to join the army? I felt sick at heart – half-disgusted with myself for being there to film this but hating everyone for reducing a human being to such misery. And UNITA is not just the guilty party. America, Russia, France, East Germany, Saudi Arabia, Cuba, Zaire, South Africa, Zambia – the list is endless and includes Britain and West Germany – all share responsibility. Their interests have little to do with the good of the Angolan people.'

The experiences of Bridgland and Roberts tellingly underscore the dreadful dilemma of foreign correspondents. All too often, we find ourselves obliged to stand and observe, or film, or photograph, the most horrific, agonising and moving moments of fellow men. To become involved or offer assistance is supposed to run contrary to our dispassionate, objective professionalism. Sometimes it is downright dangerous, counter-productive even, to do so. Often there is simply no choice but to remain a detached observer.

In Uganda's Makindye military prison, for instance, there was nothing I or my colleagues could have done to prevent our cell-mates from being sledgehammered to death in the yard outside. We would have met with the same fate, or worse. What we could – and did – do was to resolve to give as much publicity as possible to the brutality in the hope that world conscience might force a change. Once released, we also spent many days lobbying all who might listen and help to secure the release of other, less fortunate cell-mates who had little chance of outside assistance. I am happy to record that many colleagues in many grisly war and conflict situations around the world have forsaken 'professional detachment' to help victims where and when they could.

In Angola, Savimbi's successes were countered by yet another increase in the Cuban forces sent to help the MPLA. By the end of 1985, intelligence agencies estimated there were at least 35 000 Cuban troops in Angola supported by 3 500 Russian and East German advisers. The Angolan air force was re-equipped with the then latest Mig-23 fighter-bombers and Sukhoi-22 fighter-bombers. The US Congress voted to end its ban on assistance to Angolan rebel movements and Stinger anti-aircraft missiles were on their way to UNITA. South Africa was again heavily involved, striking at MPLA columns deep in Angolan territory under the pretext of carrying out 'hot pursuit' raids against SWAPO guerrillas infiltrating Namibia.

The MPLA government in Luanda began to feel slightly more confident about allowing Western correspondents to visit Luanda. Apart from friendly fellow-travelling Marxist reporters, few reporters had been allowed to visit the capital. (A notable exception was Xan Smiley, then editor of *Africa Confidential*, who got into Luanda posing as a sports writer accompanying an American baseball team.) As the restrictions relaxed, a group of British and American correspondents was invited to join a convoy southwards to see the MPLA's latest military successes and to be given proof of South African involvement with UNITA.

They got their proof sooner than expected. Three South African Air Force Mirages appeared overhead and shot up the convoy, sending the hacks scattering for cover in the bush. My old friend, Kenneth Clarke of *The Daily Telegraph*, was among them and ricked an ankle in his dive for safety. Coincidentally, I was on a press facility trip to a South African base in northern Namibia at the same time. I struck up a conversation with a personable young Mirage pilot who quite happily told me about his day's work in strafing an MPLA convoy.

'They were running in all directions like headless chickens, man,' he chuckled. Only later did I learn that one of the stricken fowls was my colleague and friend. For some reason, he has never forgiven me for the incident.

Fred Bridgland truly earned his spurs in Angola. From 1975, just before independence, until 1989, the Angolan story, in Bridgland's own words, 'dragged me along with it'. He took enormous risks, influenced the course of events on at least one occasion with his reporting, and developed a great affection for the people of Angola. Fred was frequently accused of being an apologist for Savimbi. While Bridgland made no secret of his admiration for

Savimbi and what he was trying to do, he was the first to identify and write about the dark side of the man, particularly his vicious and ruthless methods of disposing of those he perceived to be a threat to his position. Fred's Angolan reportage – and his two books on that war – shine not so much for analysis but the compassion with which he describes the Angolans caught up in what was essentially a superpower struggle.

No such journalistic heroes emerged from Mozambique's war, not least because it was extremely difficult to get to. The Marxist government in Maputo under Samora Machel and his successor, Joaquim Chissano, discouraged visits by any other than 'sympathetic' (i.e. left-wing) hacks. The rebels had little coherent leadership, policy or organisation. Intrepid correspondents venturing into Mozambique to locate RENAMO were just as likely to find themselves shot up by bandits or held as hostages.

Nick della Casa, an adventurous young cameraman, found himself a captive of RENAMO for eight months. Nick had served with Rhodesia's Grey Scouts, a mounted unit, during the guerrilla war but had been seduced by what he perceived to be the glamour and excitement of a foreign correspondent's job. With no training or experience but plenty of courage, he borrowed a camera and set off alone into the wilds of northern Mozambique.

He was soon captured by RENAMO who disbelieved his story that he was a journalist. The young Englishman had arrived out of the bush unannounced, wearing paramilitary clothes and had no credentials of any kind. For several days he was tied to a tree and interrogated endlessly. Finally RENAMO was convinced he was relatively harmless but thought he might make a useful hostage. After eight months Della Casa was released, having struck up a great rapport with his captors. They asked him to return to make a film about their activities and, a couple of years later, he did just that. Nick was young enough and headstrong enough not to let his Mozambique experience deter him. A few years later, with his new bride and his brother-in-law acting as his crew, he ventured into northern Iraq from Kurdish territory against the advice of all his colleagues. All three bodies were discovered later.

Pretoria was repeatedly blamed for RENAMO's continued activities and for supplying them with arms and ammunition, despite the signing of the Nkomati Accord of friendship and co-operation between Chissano and P W Botha the South African president. The rebels had many other backers, however. There was at least one wealthy American right-wing organisation which provided funds to former Rhodesian special forces men who, in turn, supplied REN-

AMO. Funds and supplies for the rebels were certainly provided by Arab oil states. No doubt the elements of the South African Defence Force which had been closely involved with RENAMO did not abandon their friends overnight. The conservative government of Daniel Arap Moi in Kenya emerged as a powerful African sympathiser with the RENAMO cause.

The problem in Mozambique is in identifying that cause. In a couple of meetings with the unprepossessing Afonso Dahlakama, the RENAMO leader, I and my colleagues have had great difficulty in establishing precisely what he stands for. A merely anti-communist crusade may have curried support a few years ago but today, with the Chissano government committed to a multiparty democracy and a free-market economy, it makes little sense. Mozambique remained a volatile, dangerous, poverty-stricken land, even after the uneasy peace pact, finally signed in 1992.

I can never write about either Mozambique or Angola without recalling that drunken evening with Fast Eddie in Mutanga's Modern Nightclub. In a few short, slurred sentences he had forecast accurately what was going to happen in Southern Africa: the Portuguese would leave Africa and that would presage the end of white rule in Rhodesia and South Africa. It had happened soon enough in Rhodesia, largely because of the collapse of Mozambique. The full impact of the superpower involvement in the war in Angola has yet to be assessed but it would be churlish to reject the notion that South Africa's abandonment of apartheid and moves towards democracy were not greatly influenced by events in both former Portuguese territories. Cheers, Eddie, wherever you are.

*Angola 1978 –
Dermot Purgavie of
the* Daily Mail *and
James Macmanus
of* The Guardian.

*Larry Heinzerling
(left) of Associated
Press and the
BBC's John Osman
help to push their
broken-down train
in Mozambique
1974.*

CHAPTER FIFTEEN

SUNSET IN THE
SERGEANTS' MESS

*J*ack Gaylard, tall, bulky, bespectacled, was Ian Douglas Smith's *eminence grise*. As Cabinet Secretary in Rhodesia through the UDI and war years he was a powerful but normally taciturn man. On this occasion – in 1976 accompanying Smith on a visit to South Africa – he let his guard slip a little to John Osman of the BBC. The news had just been received that FRELIMO was about to take over the government of Mozambique. 'By God! John,' said Gaylard. 'The bloody Portuguese have really uncorked the bottle this time.'

They had indeed. Gaylard realised immediately, even if it took his boss a little longer, that the take-over of his country's neighbour by the Marxist liberation movement effectively spelled the end of white rule in Rhodesia. Ian Smith's tough but tiny army had been hard pressed to contain guerrilla infiltrations from Zambia and the far north-east of Mozambique. Now another 800 miles of hostile frontier would open up. Mass infiltration by guerrillas would be difficult, if not impossible, to contain. So it was to prove.

In the early post-UDI years, to have called the Rhodesian conflict 'low-intensity' would have been to overstate the case. Joshua Nkomo's ZAPU in the north-west and ZANU in the north-east had made sporadic and largely ineffectual forays which had been dealt with quickly. The guerrillas then were ill-organised and under-trained. They also lacked that most essential ingredient for successful insurgency – support and succour from the local population.

At that stage, it was certainly one of the less perilous of Africa's wars to cover as a journalist. The main difficulty was in finding the 'front'. A rumour of a 'contact' – a clash between the security forces and a marauding band of intruders – would dispatch a convoy of hacks to flounder around the bush trying to find the action, usually unsuccessfully.

John Bulloch devised a wicked scheme to counter the ennui of such occasions. ZAPU attacks usually took the form of hit-and-run forays across the Zambezi River or Lake Kariba. When there was a whisper of an incursion, Bulloch would send a message to Fleet Street advising the foreign desk 'PROCEEDING TERROR-STRICK-EN ZAMBEZI VALLEY STOP PLEASE ARRANGE WAR ZONE INSURANCE.' We would then make our way to Victoria Falls or Kariba for the weekend, there to wine, dine, gamble and enjoy some of the finest scenery in the world.

Slowly, but inexorably, the war intensified. In the early 1970s the first attacks occurred on white farmsteads in the far north-east of Mashonaland. There was now a frontline. The tobacco farmers on the escarpment in the Centenary and Mount Darwin areas were obliged to fortify their homes and take precautions against a sudden onslaught in the night. The pattern was the same: a long-range barrage with mortars, rifle-grenades and AK-47 assault rifles before the attackers disappeared into the bush, leaving a couple of land-mines buried in the farm roads.

Coverage was relatively easy. We secured invitations to stay with farmers in what was then called 'the sharp end'. They and their families were only too happy to have company and dispensed hospitality on a grand scale. You became accustomed to your hosts wearing side-arms and carrying rifles as you gathered for sundown-ers. The crackle of the Agric-alert – the radio network linking remote farmsteads – would occasionally interrupt supper. It was no more than slightly nerve-racking. I sustained my first injury of the Rhodesian war by cracking my head sharply on a bath tap whilst staying on a Mount Darwin farm. Relaxing deep in the suds, I was suddenly startled by a sharp crash. A cat had jumped through the bathroom window, dislodging a soap dish.

Fortunately I was never lucky enough to choose a farm that was attacked, although I came close. In the Centenary district one week-end, a farmer proudly showed us his elaborate security system. He had installed rifles, shotguns and home-made claymore mines in trees and outbuildings around his home. All the triggers and deto-nators were linked by a system of wires to the farmer's bedroom. The idea was that his night-guard, if alerted by sounds of an impending attack, would pull a string attached to the farmer's big toe. The farmer would activate his arsenal with a tug of the wires, hopefully convincing the would-be attackers that they faced a small army of defenders. That was the theory.

In the middle of a Sunday night we were awoken by an incredi-ble cacophony. Explosions, flashes, bangs and sustained gunfire erupted all around the house. This, I was convinced, was it: the night attack. Intrepidly, I dived beneath the bed, quivering and quaking. Only much later, when I heard the farmer remonstrating angrily with his night guard, did I emerge. The hapless employee had been startled by an avocado pear falling onto a tin roof. He had pulled the string and activated the formidable defence mechanism. Of guerrillas there was no sign.

Rhodesia was still one of the more comfortable assignments for the foreign correspondent, and certainly one of the most pleasant places in Africa to be based. Despite the paranoia of the Smith administration and the general hostility towards the press, the country offered, as Zimbabwe still does, some of the most spectacular sub-tropical scenery in the world. Its restaurants, bars and hotels were well-run and stocked. Pretty girls were a'plenty and hospitality on the farms and in the suburbs was unceasing.

Salisbury was a small capital. A leisurely stroll in the morning would enable the hack to cover the full range of contacts and repair for a good lunch and a snooze before filing. Everyone knew everyone else and everything that was going on elsewhere, anyway, so it was unlikely that the most indolent of journalists would miss a major story. The story itself – a white settler's rebellion against the dwindling might of the British Empire – was a good one. What a contrast to Vietnam, Bangladesh, Aden, Nigeria, Beirut, Iran and those other hell-holes without home comforts! Little wonder so many colleagues opted to cover the Rhodesian saga.

The collapse of Portuguese rule and the inevitable intensification of the guerrilla war with its implicit threat to bring an end to white rule sharpened world press interest in Rhodesia. The resident press corps multiplied. By 1976, the government's animosity towards and suspicion of the media had largely dissipated. The war was being reported mainly from their side anyway, as it was virtually impossible to make contact with the guerrilla groups involved in the fighting. The Salisbury-based press corps had developed close personal relationships with many in the government, in the police, the army and in the farming community which was bearing the brunt of the conflict.

Few journalists had any sympathy with the Rhodesian Front and certainly not for the politically suicidal act of UDI. They nevertheless indulged themselves to the full in the relaxed and hedonistic lifestyle of the capital. Large suburban houses, replete with statutory swimming pools, tennis courts and teams of servants, were the order of the day. Poolside parties lasted through the weekends. During quiet news periods, there were a dozen excellent golf courses in and around the city on which the hacks truly earned their self-deprecatory collective appellation.

James MacManus, of *The Guardian*, and Gary Burns, an Australian cameraman, shared one of the more sumptuous residences. MacManus was known as 'The Irish Lancer' because of his Celtic ancestry and his success with women. Flaxen-haired and blue-eyed, he had once been voted the most beddable man, in a private poll among the lady students at the University of Rhodesia. Burns, tough, taciturn and always sporting what these days would be called a designer tan, had an equally complicated love life.

The parties at their mansion were memorable. In renting the house they had 'inherited' a manservant, one Orpheus, whose wages they doubled even though they swiftly became aware that he was robbing them regularly of food, booze, cash and anything else they might leave around. Even so, Orpheus was willing and energetic and would impress their guests by staggering onto the terrace, clad in immaculate whites topped by a red fez, with a tray full of drinks.

On one occasion MacManus was perturbed to be told of the imminent arrival in Salisbury of a senior *Guardian* man whose disdain for all the trappings of white privilege was well known. The Irish Lancer deterred all female callers, switched off the underwater lights of the swimming pool and the floodlights of the tennis court and gave Orpheus the night off. The *Guardian* executive made no secret of his disgust at the size of the house as they crunched up the driveway. It was dark, but, over a small glass of sherry on the terrace, his gimlet eyes picked out the reflection of water. 'Is that, by any chance, a swimming pool?' he asked accusingly. MacManus, never usually lost for words, was fumbling for a dismissive excuse when, to his horror, the entire house and garden was bathed in brilliant light. Orpheus had risen.

Forgetting his night-off instructions he had realised there was a guest on the terrace. Instinctively he had switched on the tennis court floodlights, the underwater lights in the pool and also those illuminating the flowering shrubs in the grounds. And there he was, in his servile finery, bearing a silver tray laden with champagne, whisky and the finest brandy. The senior *Guardian* man had apoplexy. MacManus, not for the first time, had to do some quick thinking to keep his job.

Occasionally, a twinge of guilt – or boredom with the interminable political aspects of the story – overtook the hacks. This was the time to make an excursion to the increasingly troubled countryside. Both guerrilla armies, ZIPRA and ZANLA, had become bolder and much better organised. The authorities insisted on calling the opposition 'terrorists' but it was now an obvious, full-scale guerrilla war, reaching into every corner of the country and touching the lives of all its people.

Large Soviet-made land-mines began to make their presence felt. They were particularly effective in the thick sand and dirt that made up many of the rural and farm roads. Often they were boosted with extra explosives so that if you were lucky enough to survive the blast you were likely to be stone-deaf for the remainder of your days. There is no more buttock-clenching experience than driving along a dirt road that might be mined. Riding on the back of a truck in such circumstances would invariably find hardened hacks and soldiers with one hand covering their eyes and the other clutching their crutch (for all the good that would have done). The Rhodesians began to develop an amazing variety of mine-protected vehicles. They would still detonate the mine, but their wheels and bodywork were of such a shape that the occupants, in theory, would survive. Some of my more ballistic-minded colleagues worked out the weight required to detonate one of these mines was such that a lightweight such as myself, riding a small motorcycle, could ride happily over a land-mine without detonating it. A long-standing, important lunch engagement at Meikles Hotel prevented me from taking part in the experiment.

The most hazardous part of covering the war in those earlier days came when the guerrillas began to shoot up vehicles – any vehicles – travelling on main roads. They usually did so from some distance away, from high ground. The first indication that one was under attack would be a shower of sparks from the tarmac ahead as the AK-47s ranged in. Many a time a motorist would arrive at his destination unaware that he had come under attack until he found bullet holes in his vehicle. High speed was initially regarded as the answer. Then the conventional wisdom became that a vehicle bristling with weapons poked menacingly out of the window might deter the attackers.

This presented the correspondents with a dilemma. For a supposedly objective, impartial observer to carry a weapon in any war situation is, in my opinion, wrong and perilous. A gun-toting reporter is immediately identified as a combatant, abrogates his impartiality and can readily find himself put up against a wall and shot. A fierce debate raged within the Salisbury press corps. Finally it was decided that the problem should be put to our respective editors. They would have to decide for us.

The response was intriguing. The liberal *Guardian* instructed MacManus to arm himself immediately. James rushed off and purchased a Rhuzi, a lethal, local version of the Israeli Uzi sub-machine gun. He took a couple of lessons on the range but still frightened the hell out of his colleagues whenever he appeared brandishing the thing. The left-wing *Observer* man was told he could arm himself if he felt it would improve his safety. The right-wing *Daily Telegraph* sent me a sharp message instructing me not, repeat not, to carry arms under any circumstances.

Paul Ellman, the *Observer* correspondent, acquired a long-barrelled pistol of Spanish origin. I think it had last been fired in the Spanish civil war, but this did not deter Ellman from practising Clint Eastwood-type twirls and stances with the thing, usually after a few drinks in the Quill Club. Ellman was an excellent reporter but an unpredictable and volatile character. He had rapidly earned the nickname 'Paranoid' as one never knew what might upset him at any given time, sending him into blind, uncontrollable rage. On a sunny morning one would greet him with a routine 'Good morning, Paul. How are you?' only to reel under a snarled response 'What the fuck's it got to do with you?' Or a cheery 'Hi, Paul! Everything okay?' might be met by a face buckling into a menacing scowl. 'Just what do you mean by that?' he would demand. He proudly wore the tee-shirt we had made up for him with the inscription: 'Paranoid? Who, me?' In a good mood, he could be delightful and amusing company. There was no way of establishing the lie of the land.

Just after the call-to-arms decision, Paul and I shared a car to drive to the 'sharp end'. He was in a bad mood and was waving his Spanish pistol menacingly out of the window before we had cleared Salisbury's suburbs. Paul was muttering furiously to himself in the rear. I was at the wheel. Half way down the Mtoko road, two shots very close by startled and deafened me. I swerved from one verge to another for several hundred yards before regaining control. Ellman had discharged his pistol through the roof of the car. 'Just practising,' he grinned sheepishly.

It was, fortunately, a hire car. If ever an award was deserved for patience, fortitude and endurance it should have gone to the long-suffering car hire companies of Salisbury. The hacks were forever writing off vehicles in the bush war, either by rolling them at high speed or in taking evasive action from real or (more often) imaginary hazards. The record was held by Alain Dubos, a mercurial French freelance cameraman, who wrecked sixteen hire cars in two years. Dubos was an instinctively aggressive operator. In those days, cameramen had to carry the heavy CP-16 film camera with its bulky magazine protruding from the rear. On many occasions I watched Alain demolish his cine-competitors by wielding the rear end of his camera like a club while filming any given event.

The guerrilla war – the *chimurenga* or the 'war of liberation' as it was known to ZANU – began to assume a much more ugly face when it became clear that the infiltrating guerrillas were gaining the support of the villagers in the interior. In some cases this was achieved by brutal intimidation. In many others it was by politicisation and persuasion, midnight *pungwes*, or gatherings, at which the spirits of Shona ancestors were invoked and the people were told of their duty to continue the fight waged by the forefathers to drive the white man from the land.

Up to this point, the Rhodesians had relied mainly on the paramilitary police force, the British South Africa Police, to gather intelligence and contain the infiltrators. Once it was acknowledged that in many areas the 'boys' or the *gandanga* as the guerrillas were known, had won sympathy and support from the locals, the army was called in. Under the command of Major-General Peter Walls, the once largely ceremonial Rhodesian army slowly began to take control of the counter-insurgency operations from the police, and soon found itself a battle-hardened, experienced corps. The professional frontline soldiery consisted mainly of the two battalions of the Rhodesian Light Infantry, tough youngsters whose mixture of English and Afrikaans slang betrayed their genesis. They were backed by the Rhodesian African Rifles, modelled on traditional British colonial lines with black troops and NCOs under white officers. Then, in parody of the British regimental system, the special forces units proliferated, the Special Air Services Squadron, its bitter rival, the soon to be notorious Selous Scouts named after the 19th-century hunter-explorer Thomas Courtenay Selous and the Grey Scouts, a Dragoon-styled mounted unit. Despite the plethora of units, the combat strength was small compared to the vast territory they were supposed to cover and the increasing, seemingly-limitless recruitment potential of the enemy.

When Mozambique fell to FRELIMO and Nkomo's ZIPRA found sympathy and refuge for their fight in Botswana and the west of Matabeleland, the battle was really joined. Rhodesia was almost completely encircled by hostile territory, save for a relatively narrow border with South Africa, the routes to which were easily ambushed. The besieged government responded with increasingly desperate measures. The system of conscription was extended to embrace all able-bodied men up to 40 years and then to 50 and above. The days of Dad's Army had returned.

The Rhodesian Air Force, with its ageing Canberra bombers, Hawker Hunter fighters and helicopters, managed to maintain air superiority, but that did not count for much against an enemy that moved through thick bush at night and easily merged into tribal villages during the day. For transport, the Rhodesians relied on a small fleet of very old Dakotas, one of which had flown and survived the battle for Arnhem in World War II. A couple of these were converted to 'Para-Daks' which meant their rear door was removed to enable easy egress for paratroopers.

It chilled the marrow and the spine to travel in a Para-Dak. It was freezing at 16 000 feet and the dread currents from the open rear door meant hanging on for dear life to avoid being sucked out. On one facility flight, Deon du Plessis, the gigantic head of the Argus Africa News Service Bureau, decided he had to attempt a leak in the aircraft toilet – a can tucked in the rear of the fuselage. Grimly seeking hand-holds like a rock climber, he made his way towards the rear. Finally it was clear even he was not going to be able to resist the vacuum draught from the open door. It took half a dozen colleagues to prevent him being sucked into the blackness beyond. Deon leaked, but not in the can.

Atrocity stories abounded, unavoidably perhaps, given the nature of a war in which hundreds of thousands of peasants were being 'persuaded' at night by the *gandangas* and harassed throughout the day by increasingly desperate Rhodesian security forces. As in every modern war, it was the innocents caught in the middle who took the heaviest casualties. Of the 12 000 people who were to die in Rhodesia's eight years of bitter conflict, most were civilians.

With combat itself difficult to witness and cover, the hacks took it upon themselves to investigate the proliferation of massacres. These often took the form of the murder, pillage and rape of a village or a remote mission station. Each side blamed the other, of course, and it was difficult, if not impossible, to establish who was responsible. The Rhodesian forces, particularly the Selous Scouts, had adopted the practice of using 'pseud' gangs, soldiers disguised as guerrilla units, to infiltrate in the same way to gather intelligence and carry out atrocities to discredit the *gandangas*. ZANLA and ZIPRA soon picked up the tactic and would wreak revenge on a recalcitrant village, claiming the villagers to be Rhodesian security forces.

The army maintained the pretence, against all odds and evidence, that the Selous Scouts were merely a tracking unit. Lt-Colonel Ron Reid-Daly, a cheery, open-faced soul, looked more like someone's favourite uncle than the founder-commander of one of the most formidable special forces units in the world. He was, in fact, known to many as 'Uncle Ron'. Such was the sinister and menacing image projected by the Scouts that Ron decided a small facility trip for a few foreign correspondents might help improve the image of his unit. It was a confidence trick, of course, and we all knew it. We were going to be shown the Selous Scout training camp in the Matusadona Game Reserve on the edge of Kariba. There we would be shown the training and tracking techniques they used. We would see or hear nothing of the 'dirty tricks' operations the unit was primarily engaged in behind enemy lines.

It promised to be an interesting trip, however, and we would certainly get some colourful copy. Richard Cecil, a newcomer to the resident press corps in Salisbury, offered me a lift in his single-engined aircraft. Des Hamill of ITN joined us on a chilly morning at Mount Hampden airfield outside Salisbury.

Lord Richard Cecil, second son of the Marquis of Salisbury whose family had given its name to the Rhodesian capital, was bright, energetic and very gung-ho. After Oxford he had been commissioned in the Grenadier Guards, serving in the Middle East and in Northern Ireland where he was mentioned in dispatches. He had been seconded to the British SAS in Ireland and had carried out some extremely risky operations with that unit. He did not mind being teased about treading in the footsteps of the young Winston Churchill. He wanted to follow his career as a soldier with a stint as a war correspondent and made no secret of his ultimate ambition to enter politics.

Richard was determined to get to and report on the action at the front of Rhodesia's very shadowy war. Unashamedly he pulled rank – social not military – to do so. He had been befriended by P K van der Byl, Rhodesia's Minister of Defence who, despite his name and Afrikaner antecedents, had adopted all the affectations and mannerisms of a 19th-century English social-climbing snob. Lord Richard Cecil became the first reporter to accompany Rhodesian troops in action in 'contacts', or firefights, with the guerrillas. He had an occasional retainer from *The Times* who misused or failed to use his very good copy. He came to me, and *The Daily Telegraph* snapped it up. Here, after all, was 'live' copy from the front, no matter how it had been obtained.

I happily accepted his invitation to fly up to Kariba for the Selous Scout 'jolly' as facility trips were known. Richard had just obtained his private pilot's licence and did not have many hours, but he exuded confidence. I had no qualms as we took off and ran straight into a massive cloud bank. For nearly half an hour visibility was nil, but we seemed to be climbing in the correct mode. Sure enough, we burst through the cloud, high above the ground, in brilliant sunshine. 'Have you got a cigarette, Chris?' Richard asked. 'Sure,' I said, reaching for my packet. 'But you don't smoke.' He grinned. 'I do when I fly through a cloud bank like that without my commercial licence.' I exchanged arched eyebrows with Des Hammil in the rear seat.

On a clear day, navigation to Kariba from Salisbury was easy. One merely followed the power cables to the hydro-electric station at the dam. As we started to descend towards the small lakeside airstrip, Richard suddenly hauled the stick back, opened the throttle and headed across the dam wall towards the hostile Zambian bank.

'What the fuck are you doing?' Hammil and I cried in unison. 'Where the fuck are we going?'

My Lord Cecil grinned. 'Heard they've got some kind of Bofors on the Zambian side. Just seeing if they'll have a go at us.' Our screams of rage and fright were drowned by the aircraft's engine as Cecil made three low passes over the Zambian end of the Kariba Dam wall. To his disappointment we did not come under fire. I made a mental note not to accompany my friend to any war zone, anywhere, ever again.

Ron Reid-Daly met us at the Selous Scout training camp. Its unlikely name was 'Wafa Wafa, Wasera Wasera', he explained, which loosely translated meant 'If you manage to find this place you'll be bloody lucky to get out alive'. After our journey, I believed him. Uncle Ron insisted that we shake off the dust with a swim in the creek, an inlet from the lake. 'We'll just make sure Fred isn't around,' he said, barking an order at three Scouts who jumped forward and pumped several dozen rounds of FN automatic rifle fire into the water. 'Fred', it transpired, was the creek's resident crocodile who could be dissuaded from lunching on swimmers with such a fusillade.

Lunch was served under a mopani tree. Two brawny Scouts scattered the ashes of a fire and unearthed the head of a kudu which had been killed 'for the pot' the previous day. There was no pot. The raw head had merely been baked in the earth beneath the fire. 'Old Red Indian recipe,' said Uncle Ron. 'Have an eyeball...they're delicious.' The meal was disturbed only slightly when a corporal suddenly sprang towards the tree and grabbed a small but deadly snake from a branch. 'Show them how you milk the fangs,' ordered Ron. For one ghastly moment I thought we might be having snake venom for dessert. The corporal, gripping the reptile firmly behind its head, merely demonstrated how it could be detoxified by 'milking' the fangs.

For those seeking extra excitement, Ron invited the visiting hacks to make a tour of the Scouts' obstacle course, a monster, trap-laden endurance run of nearly a mile, embracing every possible hazard the African bush could offer. The press took three casualties.

Lord Cecil, being of recent SAS ilk, tried the toughest leg which involved swinging out over Fred's inlet on a long rope. The trick was to avoid returning to shore and hitting the very resilient trunk of the large tree to which the rope was attached. On his third attempt Richard smacked into the trunk with a sickening thud and cracked a rib.

Ian Black, a pugnacious Scot from the *Daily Express*, had also had recent military training and launched himself into a high-speed run over a variety of natural hurdles. He missed his footing on the fourth hurdle – a gigantic termite mound – and fell to the ground with a loud groan: one broken ankle. I tried the overhead parallel ropes strung between two tall trees. The idea was to swing across 50 yards using only your hands for support. 'Don't fall,' shouted Uncle Ron. 'We've piled thorn bushes underneath to encourage the lads to carry on.' I glanced down to take in the long, menacing white thorns protruding beneath – and dropped like a stone. I was still picking out the thorns and splinters and nursing scabrous punctures three weeks later. Chubby Clive Mocke of the South African Perskor Group managed to haul himself 30 feet up the trunk of another large tree when he suddenly froze with fear. Fortunately two Scouts were on hand to rescue him with ropes. 'You press chaps are not too fit,' Ron remonstrated. 'We must get you in shape.'

Demonstrations of sharp shooting, two-eyed shooting, blindfolded shooting, knife-fighting and throwing and surviving in drought-stricken bush by drinking one's recycled urine four times rounded off a perfect day. 'We shall sleep under the stars,' yawned Ron. 'Nothing like a kip in the great outdoors on a wonderful, balmy night.' Balmy night indeed! Two hours and three hundred mosquito bites later I crawled into the cab of an army truck and scratched myself into oblivion.We were awoken early by an ear-shattering squeal. The troopie ordered to prepare breakfast had grabbed an unsuspecting warthog by the tail and killed it with a couple of karate chops. 'Fried warthog!' announced Ron. 'Much better than bacon.'

It was tracking day. We would be shown just how efficient the Scouts were in high speed bush tracking techniques. We were introduced to Sergeant Zing, a massive Matabele whose feet, I thought, would leave tracks the size of meteorite craters and whose gleaming white teeth would reflect the sun at five hundred yards. With amazing grace and agility, Sergeant Zing manoeuvred through tall grass, over dusty tracks and through thick thorn scrub without leaving a trace or making a sound.

'Right,' barked Ron, I want three volunteers...you, you and

you...' I, of course, was one of them. 'You will be *gandangas* for the day.' The idea was that the three of us, accompanied by a young Scout who would be armed, would be given an hour's start to head off into the bush, using any device we could think of to cover our tracks. Sergeant Zing and his men would pick up our spoor and locate us in no time at all.

We set off at the cracking pace established by the young troopie, through high elephant grass and then deep into a mopani forest. The Scout suddenly lifted his hand for a silent halt. There was a powerful smell of wild animal and we realised we were surrounded by a large breeding herd of elephant, browsing almost invisibly in the trees around us. The Scout motioned for us to stay still and moved forward. He uttered a few grunts and whistles and there was a great crashing of branches and pounding of feet as the herd realised an enemy was in their midst. He had deliberately stamped-ed them to crush the undergrowth and conceal any tracks we may have left.

I was pondering on what might have happened had they stam-peded in our direction when an awesome, guttural bellow froze us in what would have been our tracks (had we been leaving any!). It came from behind a thick bush, some 30 foot below us in a gulley. Our Scout's rifle was at the ready in a flash. 'Don't worry,' I whis-pered to my colleagues. 'No elephant could get up that steep slope.'

I had hardly got the words out before the bush parted and an enormous cow elephant, clearly very angry, burst through and came up the almost vertical slope like an express train. 'Don't panic!' shouted our guide as we cannoned off each other like Keystone Cops. 'Jump!' In unison we hurled ourselves down the slope into the gulley and clambered into the branches of the tallest tree we could find. The elephant, ears aflap and head tossing, paused at the top of the ridge, snorted in disgust, and finally ambled off after the rest of the herd. Shaking with delayed shock we disembarked from the tree, wondering how we could have achieved such a speedy ascent in the first place.

Under the Scout's orders we concealed ourselves in a clump of bush. 'Zing and his men will be here any minute,' he said. No more than three minutes had passed when I jumped out of my skin at a sharp nudge in the back. It was the barrel of Sergeant Zing's rifle. He was grinning at us through the thicket. 'If it hadn't have been for that elephant we would have got you before you stopped,' he said.

My only consolation for that morning's hardship was that Colonel Reid-Daly, with the follow-up party, was stung on the head by an angry bee. That evening a group of Scouts was instructed to head off into the bush a catch an impala for supper. 'No shooting,' said Ron. 'Show them how you catch supper silently.' I was reluctant to volunteer for anything further, but I caught a wink from one of my new-found troopie friends and we piled into a truck. The Scouts thundered through the night, bumping across tracks and crashing through the bush. Suddenly I caught a glimpse of lights. It was the village of Kariba.

We piled into the nearest pub and began swallowing pints of cold beer. The Scouts broke every rule in the book, regaling us with hair-raising stories of blowing up bridges in Zambia and Mozambique, of killing 'gooks' bare-handed and planting their severed heads on poles in the middle of guerrilla camps *pour encourager les autres*. A tracking unit, indeed!

It was a merry party that crashed through the bundu back to Wafa Wafa. We were less than a mile from the camp when the Scouts realised they had forgotten to catch an antelope for supper. The problem was solved when a rabbit appeared on the track ahead, transfixed by the headlights. One of the troopies leapt off the truck, grabbed it and broke its neck. Around the camp fire, Reid-Daly was not amused. 'I send out the finest trackers in the world to grab a buck, you're away for three hours and you have the nerve to come back here with one measly little bunny rabbit!'

The war intensified sharply. What fun there had been at the 'front' in the early days dissipated swiftly. We were not to see or hear of our Selous Scout friends for a long time – unless it was a brief mention in the 'Deaths' column of the *Rhodesia Herald*. Any road out of town became a white-knuckled trip, day or night. The white community was small and close and every casualty was a friend, or a friend of a friend.

Humanity's conflict-littered history has demonstrated that a certain mania overtakes a community caught up in a war. In Rhodesia in the late seventies, a type of madness developed and embraced the resident foreign correspondent corps. A side effect – not unpleasant at the time – was that the hacks suddenly found themselves in great demand with the ladies of the town.

By this time, most able-bodied Rhodesian men were obliged to spend most of their time in the bush, leaving lonely and bored womenfolk to stave off the boredom as best they could. The correspondents constituted one of the few pockets of available male company. Better still, they had liberal expense accounts and access to imported wines, spirits and other sedatives and stimulants.

We were inundated with dinner and party invitations. Wild evenings would find the correspondents' combo in full swing: Martin

Meredith of *The Observer* on piano, Michael Knipe of *The Times* on drums and Ian Mills expertly playing anything else that came to hand. (Only Mills could acquire the sole French Horn to be found in Rhodesia.)

The ladies seemed to enjoy every minute of it, although there were some close calls. Knipe of the Nile's musical career came to an abrupt end when the enraged husband of a sultry lady he had been escorting discovered where he lived and hurled his prized drum set into the swimming pool. Peter Jordan, the *Time* photographer, awoke in a strange flat one morning with an equally strange lady asleep beside him. It had been a night of blissful amnesia, but the first rays of the morning sun through the curtains picked out one very large army boot, and then another. They did not belong to Jordan. 'They're my husband's, darling,' yawned the stranger next to him. 'He's the regimental boxing champion. You must meet him.' It was, Jordan recalled 'a rapid fire-escape job'.

W Rowlinson Carter, an ITN cameraman whose ultra-English drawl and affectations modelled on P G Wodehouse characters belied his modest South African upbringing, was caught *in flagrante* by his suspicious wife by the side of the other woman's swimming pool the morning after the night before. The lady in question worked for the government's Information Department and was known thenceforth as the 'Info Nympho'. Another visiting hack was delighted to be invited back to a flat by an attractive young woman he had met at a dinner party. She darted into the kitchen to make coffee while he took in the sitting room door, half hanging off its hinges, a wall pock-marked with bullet holes, a machete stuck in a wooden chest. Ammunition boxes were stacked on the terrace outside, and on another wall was a photograph of a young man in combat fatigues whose eyes indicated he might just have seen too much violence and mayhem in his day.

'That's Jack,' said the young lady emerging with the coffee. 'Forgive the mess but he and his Scout mates sometimes pitch up in the middle of the night and go wild with weapons they've taken from dead terrs.' It was, as Peter Jordan would have said, another rapid fire-escape job.

It must be recorded that the hacks took more casualties on the sexual front than they did in combat. Paul Ellman made a pass at the wife of a fellow journalist and had his skull split open by a heavy upright Remington typewriter wielded by the irate husband. A young lady reporter, always happy to share her favours, picked up something non-specifically venereal from a correspondent recently arrived from Vietnam. Notes were compared in the long queue outside the surgery of Salisbury's best-known pox-doctor. Most of the hack corps were there but also a fair sprinkling of government officials, soldiers, airmen and a well-known MP. *Private Eye* was rumoured to have the story in type under the heading 'Tree of Shame', but, mercifully for all those concerned, it never appeared.

The Quill Club became the hub of Salisbury's twilight social whirl. As Rhodesia's press club during the war years, it attracted a panorama of personalities and characters. Here, on any given evening, were to be found mercenaries, crooks, con men, spies, MPs, hookers, fun-loving farmers' wives, actors, muggers, buggers, bandits and, of course, the ladies and gentlemen of the Fourth Estate.

Special Branch men mingled with forced bonhomie amidst black politicians and journalists, many of them totally sympathetic with the guerrillas and 'the struggle'. It was as he left the Quill Club one evening, that a leading black activist, Edson Sithole, was abducted by unknown men, never to be seen or heard of again. It was from the Quill Club, too, that Justin Nyoka, one of the more experienced black journalists who freelanced for the BBC, left to visit his small farm in the south of the country, only to disappear for nearly two years. Justin was picked up by 'the boys' and had to do some very fast talking to convince them he was well known to their leadership. He was marched hundreds of miles through the bush into Mozambique. There he was persuaded to join 'the struggle' and, with typical Nyoka luck and cunning, eventually became a senior official in the Zimbabwe government.

At any given time, it was difficult not to find one of Africa's better-known journalistic characters doing his utmost to ensure the Quill Club bar did not go bankrupt. John Edlin was an unmistakable New Zealander, in accent, demeanour and behaviour. He had, however, spent more time in Africa than he had in his homeland, working as a freelance in Ghana, Zambia and Zimbabwe and travelling extensively throughout the continent. Edlin was known, with varying degrees of affection, as 'Shithead', presumably because of his semi-permanent beer-fuddled condition. He always – almost always – managed to meet his deadlines, whatever his condition. The legends of Edlin and his antics were as numerous as the beers he downed on any given day. Yet, as many of his friends would testify, he was one of the most generous of souls.

Just as the apes can never leave Gibraltar, or the rooks the Tower of London, Africa would never be the same without the maniacal, piercing cackle of Edlin resounding around the bars and beerhalls of the continent. One of his major faults was that his whispered asides could be heard even by the partially deaf within a 500-

yard radius. He once confided to me in a Mozambique nightclub crowded with Portuguese commandos who had just been told they had lost their war: 'The trouble with these Porkos, sport, is that they're all cowards'. He was quite surprised when the club fell silent and dozens of menacing stares were directed at our table. I managed to bundle him into the street before the full impact of his 'aside' had registered.

Edlin was a fatalist. He took great exception if his friends did not take a swing at him from time to time, or if his employers did not sack him occasionally, if his girlfriend or wife did not leave him, or if people who owed him money tried to pay him back. One of his great chums was Alex Morrow-Smith, one of several professional Scotsmen who graced the Salisbury hack corps. Alex was short, stocky and built like the proverbial brick privy. He was also one of the best-read journalists I knew and would always find an apposite literary quote while removing his spectacles to deck men twice his size with one blow.

Morrow-Smith and Edlin met in the Long Bar of the New Stanley Hotel in Nairobi. Edlin had just been fired by the Argus Africa News Service for being tired and emotional while giving a keynote address to senior executives of the Argus organisation. Morrow-Smith was working for the *Daily Nation* in Nairobi.

Alex loved Kenya. He had served there with his beloved regiment, the Cameronians, otherwise known as the 'Poisoned Dwarfs' because of their smallish stature and pugnacity. He had decided he liked Africa when he and several of his men appeared before an elderly white colonial magistrate for wrecking a bar in Mombasa. 'Lt Mowwow-Smith,' the magistrate had said sternly. 'You are a disgwace to your wace and your wegiment.' Each man was fined ten shillings.

Alex had popped into the Long Bar for a quickie and took an immediate dislike to a little, pasty-faced Kiwi holding forth on the iniquities of journalism and Africa at the end of the bar. In his own words, he 'banjoed' Edlin, knocking him to the floor with one short, sharp blow of his Glaswegian fist. Edlin rose unsteadily to his feet, bought Morrow-Smith a drink and the two became firm friends. That evening they caught the train to Mombasa and, much to the consternation of Mrs Morrow-Smith, spent three days and nights of drunken debauchery together.

This rather formidable friendship resumed when, a few years later, they found themselves in Rhodesia covering the war. Edlin was freelancing and his copy had caught the attention of a senior man from the *Wall Street Journal* who was most anxious to hire a

stringer in Salisbury. He asked after Mr John Edlin and was directed towards the Quill Club. It was a relatively quiet night in the club.
The first sight that greeted the *Journal* man as he walked in was of
a prone, shrieking figure lying on the floor of the bar with a stocky
man standing above him still holding aloft the bar stool with which
he had just 'banjoed' the stricken hack. 'I'm sorry,' stuttered the
American 'I was just trying to locate Mr John Edlin, the well-known
journalist'. A dozen fingers pointed to the crumpled, slavering figure
on the floor. Edlin did not get the *Wall Street Journal* job.

Morrow-Smith was, like so many other members of the
Salisbury press corps, a man of many moods. By this time he was
working for the Argus Africa News Service under Deon du Plessis.
Deon had asked him to go to Umtali, the town on the Mozambique
border that was coming under increasing attack from ZANLA. After
one particularly heavy mortar attack, Deon and I decided to drive
down and join Alex on the story. As usual the Cecil Hotel was full.
Deon insisted on sharing a room with his colleague and obtained a
key to Morrow-Smith's room. There was no sign of Alex. As he let
himself in, du Plessis groaned. 'Oh, my God...come and have a look
at this.'

The sheets and the pillows were covered in the blood, as were
the bathroom walls. There were chips of teeth in the sink and discarded clothing, also bloodstained, all over the floor. Had Alex been
the victim of a ZANLA mortar attack? No such luck. He emerged,
gap toothed, bruised but grinning. He had spent the previous night
in the bar of the Cecil involved in a heated argument about the
political situation with an SAS man and two Special Branch 'jim-
mies'. Alex had finally insisted they went outside to settle the
debate.

He had managed to grab a fencing pole and had broken the SAS
man's leg before being finally overpowered by the three men and, in
his own words, 'pulped'. (A few weeks later, the SAS man limped on
crutches into the Victoria Falls Hotel. He and Alex embraced each
other warmly and settled down to a beery reminiscence about the
details of the Umtali fight. As I said, everyone was slightly crazed.)

Chris Reynolds was the defence correspondent of the *Rhodesia
Herald*. A bearded, lurching and much-loved man, he was a popular
figure in the many impromptu military messes that had been estab-
lished at bases throughout the country. He travelled the now per-
ilous countryside regularly, accompanied by photographer Paul
Harris, a young Cornishman of piratical ancestry and appearance.
Well-fortified with whatever brew or distillation was to hand,
Reynolds and Harris would set out every day to find the war.

The risks they took, coupled with Harris' unerring ability to find a lady in the most unlikely setting, quickly earned them the nicknames 'Crazy' Reynolds and 'Dirty' Harris after the characters in a popular movie of the day. Harris' nickname had less to do with his personal hygiene than his method of approaching the fair sex. I once watched with awe and admiration as he introduced himself to a Dutch woman reporter who had just arrived. He immediately launched into a graphic – pornographic, in fact – description of what he would like to do to her. With a smile of anticipation on her face, she clasped him around the waist and they disappeared into the night. Edlin tried the same technique a few nights later. Once again, he found himself heavily handbagged to the familiar floor of the Quill.

If the foreign correspondents covering the Rhodesian war spent much time with bottle or glass in hand, there were excuses. It was an ugly, protracted conflict with no clearly demarcated frontline. Like most guerrilla wars, allegiances were blurred, the entire country was, by now, a combat zone and death and destruction lurked in every shadow. Crazy Reynolds had been to visit a newly established military base at a place called Ruda in the beautiful Honde Valley near the Mozambique border. He had, of course, helped to launch a newly constructed mess at the camp which had been heavily mortared during the night. Crazy immediately christened the mess the 'Ruda Wakening' and sent a message asking Paul Harris to join him to take some photographs.

Paul, CBS cameraman Bill 'Mutters' Mutschmann and I drove to Ruda in the expectation of capturing some frontline coverage. We arrived in the afternoon to find Crazy salvaging what he could from the bar stock. We helped while the troopies replaced the damaged roof. Towards sundown, Reynolds insisted that we drive on dirt tracks to see a military vehicle that had been destroyed by a boosted land-mine the previous night. It seemed like a good idea at the time. We found the blackened wreck by an enormous crater but it was too dark to take photographs or film. Relaxed as we were, the consensus was that we should head back to Salisbury. At speed.

There was a network of dirt tracks and we had taken several wrong turnings before we found the main road. It was completely dark by now, and moonless. There was no sign of any other vehicle on the road. Harris was at the wheel and had his foot flat on the accelerator pedal. I heard him exclaim 'Oh, shit!' as a line of sparks danced along the tarmac in front of us. Simultaneously the windows on the left hand side of the car shattered. In the rear, Mutschmann and I tried to bury ourselves in the floor as the vehicle swerved from one side of the road to the other. Miraculously, none of us had been hit although we found later the car had taken at least nine direct hits. Two of the tyres had been hit but Harris, wisely, kept his foot down. We weaved and screeched on naked rims for another 20 miles.

Just before we reached the village of Mrewa the front and rear windscreens shattered simultaneously. It turned out to be a single shot fired from behind us. I was back on the floor. Harris was cursing and wrestling with the wheel, Crazy Reynolds was singing some tuneless ditty. Mutschmann, infuriated by this second attack, had his Rhuzi at the ready and blazed away ineffectively into the darkness. We pulled into the Mrewa pub for the night. The car was a smoking, shattered wreck but we four were completely unscathed. That was the more familiar pattern of covering the Rhodesian war for the hacks.

Sooner or later, we knew, the press corps was bound to take casualties – war casualties that is. And so it was to be. Richard Cecil would appear in my office in Salisbury from time to time with vivid descriptions of the 'contacts' he had experienced at first hand. He had encouraged his old friend and former British SAS colleague, Nick Downie, to join him in Rhodesia to make a television film of the war. P K van der Byl had given them carte blanche to attach themselves to any unit they chose, to travel where they pleased and to film whatever they wanted. The army brass was not unhappy with the arrangement. Both men were experienced military officers, battle-hardened and were likely to be an asset rather than a burden in any tight combat situation.

Richard's copy was a little rambling and over-written but it took a short time to knock it into *Telegraph* news style and telex it to London. It was the only first-hand combat copy to appear in any newspaper. He and Downie parachuted in to 'contacts' with the Rhodesian Light Infantry.

'We jumped from 500 feet,' he wrote. 'The helicopter had gone in first and the fire-fight had already started.' The young RLI troopies, smeared with camouflage cream, jumped in rapid succession from the Dakota, Cecil following them. Just seven seconds later, through the pattern of tracer bullets crossing the drop zone, he landed in some soft dirt. The battle lasted for six hours and left twelve guerrillas dead. It was good, if dangerously acquired copy, by anyone's standards.

Cecil and Downie had shot most of the footage for their film when, on April 20th, 1978, they parachuted into a volatile area of the Mtoko Tribal Trust Land with A Company, 2nd Battalion, the Rhodesian African Rifles. Richard was moving with a flanking line of ten black soldiers towards a known guerrilla position. He was on the outer edge of his group moving through tall grass. A lone insurgent, presumably a perimeter sentry posted by the guerrillas, suddenly rose from the grass no more than seven yards ahead of him, firing his AK-47 on fully automatic. Richard was hit in the chest, stomach and legs. A ferocious fire-fight immediately ensued in which rockets were fired at a helicopter gunship and two guerrillas killed. A helicopter landed to casevac Cecil but he died within ten minutes of being shot.

News of Richard's death left the correspondent corps in Rhodesia in a deep state of shock. He had, of course, taken enormous risks but was a popular, enthusiastic and admired journalist. He was just 30 years old.

Nick Downie went on to finish the film which was screened by Thames Television later that year. Members of the Cecil family flew to Rhodesia and, like most of his colleagues, attended a moving memorial ceremony at the RLI barracks. His body was flown back to England and buried in the family cemetery at Cranborne, Dorset, with two buglers from the Grenadier Guards sounding the last post. P K van der Byl described him as a man 'possessing everything that made Britain great and built the British Empire'. More prosaically, but with no less feeling, his friend Major André Dennison, commander of Alpha Company of 2 RAR, recorded in his diary: 'Rhodesia and A Company lost a very good friend in Richard Cecil and his death was badly felt by all. He had been in five contacts with the Company and at all times had worked his way to the front, despite theoretically hanging back with Nick Downie.'

André Dennison, Yorkshire born, was, by general consensus, possibly the finest soldier in the Rhodesian army. He led from the front and was always first out of the aircraft on para-drops into combat. Better still, he was a great friend of the press. While recuperating from a severe leg injury sustained in action, he spent much time in the Quill (and on the golf course where, despite his wound, he would hole out long before Roly Carter and I had hacked our way past the ladies' tee). During his convalescence he developed a very close relationship with a willowy blonde American photographer, Sarah Webb Fairbanks Barrell.

Sarah had only recently arrived in Rhodesia to cover the war, but her reputation had preceded her. The story, probably invented by the numerous hacks whose advances she had rebuffed over the years, was that she had become a high-priced hooker in New York to earn the money to buy cameras and an air ticket to Vietnam to cover the war in that country. When her relationship with a journalist ended in bitterness (so it was said), she had thrown his typewriter and cameras into the Saigon River. From Vietnam she had moved to Cambodia, there again consorting with some of the tougher hacks and soldiers. For obscure reasons, her nickname was 'Sarah Dum-Dum', possibly after the specially-prepared bullet that does so much physical damage to the recipient.

I had heard on the hack grapevine that John le Carré had used her as a model for his character 'Lizzie Worthington', a beautiful, blonde press photographer in his novel *The Honourable Schoolboy*, set in South East Asia. When I asked the leggy Sarah whether she thought this to be true she refused to speak to me for a week. I declined to take the advice of Bigfoot Younghusband that 'if you play your cards right Munnion, you can go up on her'. I apologised profusely instead. Soon it was clear she was deeply in love with Major André Dennison, having accompanied his unit on several occasions and helped to nurse him back to health after his injury.

Alpha Company was deployed to the Fort Victoria area early in June 1979. André Dennison and a couple of his men repaired to the nearby Zimbabwe Ruins Hotel for drinks. In the course of the evening, a ZANLA group attacked the staff compound near the hotel. Almost instinctively, Dennison led his men at speed into the blackness to set up an ambush. A highly nervous police reservist, following behind them, saw a fleeting shadow and opened fire, killing Dennison at close range. His last words: 'Oh, fuck!' Sarah Webb Barrell was beside herself with grief. She inserted a memorial notice in the *Rhodesia Herald* to 'My brave and committed soldier. Love from Sarah', attended his full military funeral in Fort Victoria and returned to Salisbury where she locked herself in the flat where she had shared probably the happiest moments of her life with him. Two days later, she shot herself with a .38 pistol Dennison had given to her for her own protection. She was 33 years old.

Such tragedies were becoming all too frequent. It could be safely said that not one family in Rhodesia, black or white, had remained untouched by some form of death, destruction or mayhem caused by the war. That, as we have seen, included the rather strange 'family' of eccentric, manic characters that made up the resident press corps. Frustration and grief in such circumstances give birth so easily to rage and a desire for revenge. Hence a multiplicity of atrocities became a sinister and sickening aspect of the Rhodesian conflict, exacerbating the deep bitterness which was essentially racial.

Nkomo's ZIPRA forces had acquired from their Russian friends a consignment of SAM-7s, heat-seeking, ground-to-air missiles that were short range and sluggish, but which had proved deadly against low-flying, slow aircraft. One had been fired from the Zambian bank of the Zambezi at a tourist flight – 'the Flight of the Angels' – over the Victoria Falls. The pilot saw it coming and took evasive action. The missile peeled off and struck the newly built Elephant Hills Hotel and Country Club nearby, destroying the building but injuring no one.

We chartered a light aircraft to cover the story. There was no need to ask the pilot to take precautionary, highly aerobatic action as we came into land at the Falls. This scenic wonder was now, indeed, a war zone. Most of the hotels had been attacked by mortars and rockets. Notices in every room instructed guests what to do in the event of an attack. The only guests, in fact, were hacks covering the attacks and parties of hardy German tourists who were given to complaining if they did not come under fire during their stay. Many contented themselves by stealing the warning signs as souvenirs.

ZIPRA became more efficient in their missile deployment. In September 1978, the Air Rhodesia Viscount *Hunyani* took off from Kariba en route to Salisbury. The 56 people on board were all civilians, families, parents with children, businessmen and tourists. Five minutes out of Kariba a SAM-7 hit a starboard engine and exploded. The skipper wrestled to control the aircraft and almost made a successful crash landing in a cotton field in the Urungwe TTL. But the aircraft plunged nose first into a deep irrigation ditch, cartwheeled and exploded. Eighteen people survived the crash, ten of whom were soon shot dead in cold blood by ZIPRA guerrillas who arrived on the scene.

The news stunned white Rhodesia. Everyone knew someone who was on board. The shock turned to cold fury when, in a telephone interview with the BBC from the headquarters in Lusaka, Joshua Nkomo chuckled and boasted of a triumph for his 'freedom fighters'. Revenge was not long in coming. With increasing desperation, the Rhodesian forces had been striking at the guerrilla bases in neighbouring Mozambique, Zambia and Botswana, using the Air Force, the SAS and the Selous Scouts on the ground and air raids which were initially called 'hot pursuit' exercises and subsequently 'cross-border operations'. Although many were killed, these attacks acted more as morale-boosting exercises for the white population than as military operations that could alter the course of the war.

After the first Viscount attack, the Rhodesian forces mounted an air raid against a ZIPRA camp at a farm near Lusaka and other Zanu bases in Zambia. This was the audacious or atrocious, depending on one's point of view, 'Green Leader' raid.

The leader of a Rhodesian bomber group called up the controller in the Lusaka tower as the Rhodesian air force crossed the border, unchallenged. The sanitised Rhodesian version released later on cassette tape and played endlessly by gleeful whites ran 'Lusaka Tower this is Green Leader. This is a message for the station commander at Mumbwa [the main Zambian air base] from the Rhodesian Air Force. We are attacking the terrorist base at Westlands Farm at this time. This attack is against Rhodesian dissidents and not against Zambia. Rhodesia has no quarrel with Zambia or her security forces. We therefore ask you not to intervene or oppose our attack. However, we are orbiting your airfield at this time and are under orders to shoot down any Zambian Air Force aircraft which does not comply with this request and attempts to take off. Did you copy that?'

In a tone of voice which made the attack sound like a routine, everyday occurrence, the Zambian controller replied: 'Copy. Roger. Thanks. Cheers.'

The unabridged version of the conversation in the cockpit was soon doing the rounds and proving even more popular: 'Steady, steady...I'm gonna get them...yeah, steady now. Bomb's gone...they're running. Beautiful...Roger, just let me get onto the fuckin' tower and give them our bloody message. Where's this fuckin' piece of speech...I think it'll be better when we've climbed up...I'm just trying to get the fuckin' thing ready...That was mushi, fuckin' hundreds of gooks...there are fuckin' kaffirs everywhere...they like fuckin' ants running around there, eh? Jesus, there's a swarm of them...'

The fact that there were women and children in the camps was immaterial. Women and children were 'fully fledged insurgents' anyway. That there were refugees was also of little concern. Both ZIPRA and ZANLA ensured their bases in Zambia and Mozambique were enmeshed with genuine refugee camps to enable them to shout 'foul' in the event of such an attack. What mattered most to white Rhodesia was the avenging catharsis: the victims of the Viscount *Hunyani*.

Overnight, Green Leader became the national hero. Songs were composed and sung lustily, Green Leader tee-shirts and badges sold out rapidly and local newspapers carried paeans of praise for the bomber pilot, accompanied by cartoons parodying Zambian panic. Veteran AP correspondent Eddie Adams was one of those chosen by the Rhodesians to visit Mkushi camp in the far north of Zambia. The fact that the Rhodesians felt able to take correspondents from Salisbury deep into Zambia without so much as a by-your-leave indicates the level of confidence they had in this type of attack. In his dispatch, amended by military censors, Adams compared the scene at Mkushi to the early days of Indo-China. 'As American forces in the late sixties hit insurgent bases in Cambodia from Vietnam, now the warplanes of Rhodesia's unrecognised biracial transition government bombard bases in neighbouring Zambia of the guerrilla alliance stepping up the war.'

Comforting though such cross-border raids may have been, with their high enemy body counts and sense of military supremacy, the motive for their execution was born out of a sense of frustration. Even with every able-bodied man in uniform and the undoubted courage of the professional fighting forces, the Rhodesians were unable to get to grips with, or contain, the guerrilla offensive within the country itself. It was losing the war on the ground. White farmers and other civilians were being killed almost daily in the rural areas. It was only a few months later that Nkomo's men were able to demonstrate that Rhodesia's air superiority might be short-lived. Once again, in February 1979, another civilian Viscount airliner taking off from Kariba en route to Salisbury was hit by a SAM-7. It burst into flames and plunged into a ravine, killing the 59 passengers and crew immediately.

Ian Mills of the BBC was one of the many passengers at Kariba Airport that evening awaiting a flight back to Salisbury. Two Viscounts were laid on to cope with the load. The waiting passengers were issued with different coloured boarding passes to indicate which flight they would be taking. Mills greeted General Peter Walls, Rhodesia's military supremo, who was in the queue travelling as a civilian. Noticing that the general had been given a green card for the second flight, Mills also grabbed a green card to seize the opportunity to chat to the general on the flight. His journalistic zeal saved his life. The red card holders on the Viscount *Umniati* perished in the attack. News of the tragedy was whispered to Walls while Mills was chatting to him on the second aircraft. He had, briefly, an exclusive but it was one he felt in no condition to file. Again, everyone knew someone who had been on the stricken *Umniati*.

Atrocities multiplied on the ground. Missions and missionaries were murdered, tortured and raped. As many missionaries were unabashedly for the 'struggle', suspicion frequently fell on the dirty-tricks units of the Rhodesian security forces. By the same token, the guerrilla system, or lack of it, had spawned numerous little psychopathic warlords who took no orders from Maputo or Lusaka and ruled their patches with the arrogance and brutality of feudal barons. My own view, at the time and now, is that both sides shared responsibility for the numerous, ghastly massacres that were carried out in the last years of the war.

Foreign correspondents were quickly flown to the scenes of massacres by a fast-reacting Rhodesian propaganda department. They
provided grisly but graphic copy, inevitably slanted to implicate the
guerrillas. In later analyses of the coverage of the war, correspondents were criticised sharply by left-wing commentators (most of
whom were conspicuously absent in the heat of battle) for accepting
the Rhodesian version of such events. The fact was that on-the-spot
copy was very difficult to obtain, even by the hacks the government
regarded as 'on-sides'. When he was Information Minister, the drac-
uline P K van der Byl was once asked why so many reporters had
been deported. 'You should have asked why more journalists were
not deported,' he replied. 'There were far too few. I don't believe you
can defend Western Christian civilisation against Soviet expansion-
ism with liberal, laissez-faire policies. We were far too tolerant
about the whole thing.'

Two of my colleagues who could hardly be said to have been
sympathetic to the Rhodesian cause felt obliged to defend the way
we operated. Michael Kaufman, the Africa correspondent of the *New
York Times*, made the point that Rhodesians provided transport to
stories that newsmen simply could not ignore. The guerrillas and
their frontline state backers were hostile and suspicious of the
press.

'During the Vietnam war, how many reporters were able to get
the Viet-Cong's side of the story?' Kaufman asked. 'Not until certain
reporters managed to get invited to Hanoi late in the war did certain key facts emerge. The fact is that in any war, the side that
holds the capital has an advantage.'

David Ottaway, the highly respected *Washington Post* correspondent and later foreign editor of that liberal newspaper, con-
curred that the government was always quicker off the mark when
there were propaganda points to be made. 'The government, of
course, provides gory details about how the guerrillas kill pro-
government civilians, black or white, for propaganda purposes. It
does its best to hide the army's misdeeds and the risk to reporters of
digging them out is expulsion. The agony facing every reporter is
whether the story is big enough to risk being expelled and thereby
no longer being able to cover any part of it. You have to ask yourself
whether some news is better than no news. I have been kicked out of
enough African countries now to know precisely how this pressure
affects a reporter.'

Military censorship in Rhodesia was a joke. For the *Telegraph
Magazine* I spent a week with 'frontline' farming families to write

about their life under such stressful circumstances. Photographer David Goldblatt was commissioned to illustrate the article. On a remote dirt road in the combat zone we came across an African domestic servant, a tall, beaming man clad in pristine whites, a tall chef's hat perched on his head, carrying a silver salver of imported smoked salmon from one farmer to his neighbour. It made a superb picture of the contrast and contradictions of the situation. It was ruthlessly excised by a young army officer, the censor at Combined Operations Headquarters. 'Shows Rhodesia in a bad light,' he snapped, when we complained.

I came across this self-important prat a little later in the war. He had been attached to one of the more absurd branches of the Rhodesian security forces called the Psychological Operations Unit. From noisy 'sky-shouts' from aircraft fitted with loudspeakers to childish and crude propaganda, 'PSYAC' was charged with winning the hearts and minds of the African population. Our young subaltern censor convinced his superiors that the average African peasant believed the hyena was a manifestation of an evil spirit. The presence of a hyena in the vicinity of a kraal suspected of harbouring guerrillas would turn the inhabitants against the *gandangas*, he insisted.

They let him loose one dark night with a set of plaster casts of the animal's spoor and a pocket tape-recording of its eerie howl. On all fours he prowled around a suspect village, occasionally playing his hyena tape at full blast. After about half an hour he was stunned by a large rock which bounced of his head. This was quickly followed by a fusillade of stones and other missiles, some of which hit him as he limped off into the bush followed by a long harangue in Shona which, loosely translated, said: 'Piss off...we are trying to get some sleep here.'

The press corps had its own contingent of buffoons and a tradition of buffoonery. Mike Sullivan of the BBC was a regular visiting hack. Tall, lean and silver-haired, Mike had gone into journalism having failed to achieve his life's ambition by dropping out of the Hendon Police College. He fancied himself as a man of the great outdoors. Rhodesia offered unlimited opportunities for indulging in macho pursuits and 'Inspector' Sullivan took every advantage.

A fellow hack was a keen scuba-diver and offered to bring along his equipment to give Mike a few lessons in Ian Mills' ample pool. It was a Sunday and Mills was throwing a lavish lunch party for fellow journalists. Sullivan was duly kitted out in the frogman's kit and given a few basic tips. With back-strapped tanks containing enough oxygen for an hour or so underwater he plunged to the bottom of the pool. He appeared to have picked up the skill quickly and was soon swimming successive lengths in the crystal depths.

As often happened at hack social gatherings, the telephone rang. Some important story had just broken which required our attention immediately. Utensils were downed, final swallows taken of drinks and the place emptied as we rushed off to file the story. In our haste, we had completely forgotten about Sullivan, still swimming strongly at the bottom of the pool and thinking we were all standing above admiring his expertise. When he emerged half an hour later, he was unnerved to find an empty garden and house. 'It was like the *Marie Celeste*,' he said later. 'There were half-finished gins-and-tonics still fizzing, half-eaten salads and cigarette butts still smoking in the ashtrays. I thought it was a practical joke and padded around the bushes in my flippers in the hope of finding you all hiding and laughing. Very eerie.' I fielded a telephone call in the office. The voice sounded a bit like the man from Mars or a heavy-breathing obscene caller. I finally realised it was Sullivan, talking through his frogman's mask. 'Anything going on, old boy?' he wheezed.

Rarely has such a small hack given rise to so many legends in such a short time as Jacques Clafin who arrived in the middle of the war to take over the UPI bureau. A short, bearded Californian of French ancestry, Jacques was our very own Inspector Clouseau. He provided us with our own walking, talking *Pink Panther* series. Earnest, rather pompous but diligent and energetic, Clafin bestrode the story as if he had a distasteful smell permanently under his nostrils. He was perpetually suspicious, often with justification. He was of the school of tape-recorder scribes. A microphone was always in his hand, attached to a tape recorder which seemed to have been sewn to his suit. The mike would be thrust and jabbed towards anyone or anything that might make a noise. If the object or subject was silent, Jacques would bombard it with questions until his little machine registered a response.

When he first arrived in Salisbury, several of us were sharing an office. His first story was the official announcement that three convicted terrorists were to be hanged on the following morning. Jacques was immediately on the telephone to the Prisons Department, demanding a press seat at the execution. The expostulation at the other end of the phone was drowned by our own howls of derision. Clafin was miffed. 'I've witnessed and reported on a guy going to the electric chair in the States but I've never seen a hanging,' he complained.

Alan Pizzey, a Canadian journalist and one of the more kindly members of the hack corps, took Jacques under his wing. Pizzey returned from accompanying Clafin to the scene of a guerrilla attack on a village. The Canadian was a tough guy, having started his working life as a lumberjack, but he returned looking pale. It had not been the usual blood and gore that had upset him but Clafin's *modus operandi*. The hacks had been shown an African lady who had been violently raped by one of the attackers. Jacques had pushed his microphone into her face and demanded 'Did he ejaculate inside you?'

As a disgusted Pizzey pulled him away and remonstrated with him, Clafin objected. 'In California you have to have an ejaculation before it is statutory rape!' he protested. The African victim, fortunately, had not understood a word he had said.

Jacques soon developed the kind of relationship with Assistant Commissioner Mike Edden of the Special Branch that was uncannily similar to that between Peter Sellers and Herbert Lom in the *Pink Panther* film series. It began when someone made the mistake of pointing out Edden to Jacques as a senior spook. At the airport one day, Ian Douglas Smith was giving his usual bland comments to the media before flying off on yet another jaw-jaw mission.

Jacques seized a pause in the questioning to thrust his mike under Smithy's nose and ask 'Prime Minister, is Mr Edden going with you?' Smith was clearly bemused. 'Who?' he queried. Jacques' microphone, followed diligently by the assembled TV cameras, ranged over his entourage and finally pointed to the burly figure of Mike Edden, now trying to conceal himself behind an official. 'Oh, him,' said Smith. 'Well you'd better ask him yourself.' Undeterred, Jacques shouted the question across to the visibly embarrassed secret policeman.

Edden grabbed me after the press conference. 'Who the hell is that guy?' he hissed. 'He's just put me on international television. Just tell him to keep out of my way.' Only a few days later I was chatting by a door to Assistant Commissioner Edden as we waited for a briefing at Combined Operations HQ. From the corridor beyond, I heard the unmistakable clip-clop of the UPI bureau chief making his way to the briefing room. Jacques always wore built-up heels (what the Americans call an active compensatory factor) which were steel-tipped. Clafin swung through the door, microphone in hand.

'Have I missed anything?' he demanded. There was a howl of rage and pain from behind him, clearly captured on his tape. He had planted one of his heavy heels on Mike Edden's toe. 'Are you sick, Assistant Commissioner?' asked Jacques. 'You ought to see a doctor.'

He took his seat, oblivious to the look of obsessive hatred on the policeman's face.

Talks about talks about discussions that might or might not lead to negotiations that could, just possibly, lead to a political settlement became a tedious part of our duties in Rhodesia. Foreign politicians, seeking to enhance their own stature, came and went, usually shaking their heads in despair. They ranged from the smug, posturing David (now Lord) Owen, to the growling, Mafia-modelled Dr Henry Kissinger. With his strong-arm tactics, Kissinger finally twisted Smith's arm into a power-sharing concept with black leaders, notably the heavy-lidded Ndabiningi Sithole, the burly and not too intelligent Chief Chirau and the utterly ineffectual Bishop Abel Muzorewa.

The talks, which led to the establishment of the ill-fated Muzorewa government of Zimbabwe-Rhodesia, dragged on for weeks and then months at Government Lodge on the outskirts of Salisbury. Only one hack survived the first week or so of lobbying the daily discussions. Jacques Clafin of UPI kept a lonely vigil at the gate, hoping for a breakthrough quote.

One afternoon, close to deadline, Jacques was rewarded when the Rev Sithole, as always surrounded by his henchmen, emerged to climb into a waiting Mercedes which proceeded down the drive. As the car pulled up at the gate, Jacques pushed his mike through the driver's window and into the black leader's impassive face in the back seat.

'Reverend Sithole!' bellowed our man. 'How would you characterise today's talks?' Sithole lowered his lids. 'You could say,' he said slowly, 'they were fruitful, frank and full.' Jacques withdrew his mike quickly as the driver caught a gap in the traffic and sped off. It was getting late. Jacques shot his cuff to check the time on his new Rolex Oyster wrist-watch, a gift from his father in Los Angeles. It had gone, vanished in the few seconds his arm had been inside the car.

Clafin's telephone call to Mr Sithole, requesting his chauffeur and bodyguards to search for the watch 'which must have dropped off in your car' was one of the saddest, funniest conversations we had heard in the office. The Rolex, needless to say, was never seen again.

Sooner or later, the war was bound to come to Salisbury itself. It did so with a series of bomb blasts in public places, none of which caused much bodily harm. A Saturday lunchtime found a huddle of hacks in the Flagstaff Bar of Meikles Hotel. A farmer friend strolled in with his wife. I went to greet them. His wife had made no secret that she despised journalists and everything they stood for. To her, we were the proverbial vultures preying on the misery of others. 'I know why you lot are here,' she sneered, nodding towards my colleagues. 'You're just waiting for the next...' Her final words were lost as a massive explosion shook the building, shattering some windows and sending us all instinctively diving to the floor.

Ian Black dragged me from the confusion. 'Let's go!' he shouted. We ran into the street and followed the emergency vehicles converging on one of the largest office blocks in the centre. Less than an hour later, we had established that the bomb – a boosted land-mine – had been planted in a public toilet immediately behind the building. It had caused structural damage but, again, no casualties.

It was, however, a story and we were right on Sunday newspaper deadlines. In the office there was chaos. Only one telex machine was working (it sometimes took hours to get phone calls through to London) and it had been commandeered by the UPI man. 'Just gimme a minute,' howled Jacques. 'I just wanna get my flash out on UPI.' We acknowledged the agency man's needs but it didn't prevent our giving him a hard time as he tapped out a couple of quick paragraphs off the top of his head. His intro – still posted on the gaff boards of UPI offices around the world – read: 'A large bomb exploded in a men's toilet in downtown Salisbury Saturday – leaving an unmistakable smell and a large brown cloud hanging over the city.'

As always, bomb scares were far more frequent than actual explosions. The Rhodesians formed an over-trained anti-bomb squad which rushed around the city detonating all manner of 'suspicious' objects. To this very day, if you examine the ceiling of the foyer of Meikles Hotel, you can see discoloured pockmarks. These were caused by a couple of lipsticks, some mascara and a powder compact which were in a handbag left by an absent-minded housewife on a hotel chair and eagerly blown up by the bomb squad.

Bill Mutschmann was an early victim. 'Mutters' Mutschmann had been something of a figure of fun when he first picked up a camera. As a middle-aged American, he had first come to Rhodesia with the public relations department of an American mineral company which had interests in the country. When they withdrew as a result of sanctions Bill stayed, befriended the hacks and decided (quite rightly) that there was good money to be made in TV work. He was keen and amazingly energetic for his age, but his first efforts at news camera work were disastrous.

Bill was often in action before he had mastered the intricacies of the CP-16 film camera. On more than one occasion, during one-off filming opportunities, the film would be spewing from the back of the camera. Many times sympathetic colleagues loaned him copies of their own film to ship to clients as he had failed to focus properly or had misread his light meter. Mutschmann overcame these handicaps and became an efficient and respected frontline cameraman. Colonel Ron Reid-Daly was particularly fond of the grizzled, growling newsman and dubbed him 'Wild Bill Bourbon'. Mutschmann's favourite tipple, in fact, was an expensive American cocktail called the 'Silver Bullet'. A couple of these and he would start grunting and muttering angrily to himself.

His moods improved immensely when he met, courted and finally married the graceful and charming Captain Doreen Grey, the Rhodesian Army PR lady and a former actress. Rather late in life, he learned to fly. He worried the few colleagues who elected to fly with him by adjusting his spectacles at the end of the runway, peering myopically into the middle distance and uttering, without fail, 'Okay, as Wilbur said to Orville, let's aviate'. He did, however, fly a single-engined aircraft from Salisbury to his home town of Phoenix, Arizona, 'just to prove to myself I could do it'.

Bill had his share of adventures and mishaps on several war fronts in Africa but none so traumatic as that outside Ian Smith's residence in the centre of town. The hacks were gathered for some seemingly momentous statement when the buzz came that Smithy had sneaked out of the back entrance and was on his way to the airport. In the usual media scramble to follow the story Bill left his large equipment bag, containing an expensive back-up camera and other valuable and newly acquired accessories, on the ground outside the gate. Before he could get back to retrieve it, the bomb squad arrived, cleared the area and blew to smithereens several years worth of his earnings.

Roly Carter taught Bill the way to make money as a freelance cameraman. The powerful TV technical trade unions insisted that correspondents travelled with at least two assistants, including a sound man. Carter, who worked mainly for ITN, was a fully competent, all-round newsman. He disdained any assistance. To keep the technical union happy, however, he used to charge a daily rate for a mythical sound person. In his case, he listed the name of his pet bulldog, Mr Watkin. When Mike Nicholson arrived with a crew, Carter dispensed his usual lavish hospitality at his home.

Unbeknown to him, Nicholson's soundman was a fervent member of the TV technician's union which had nursed strong suspicions about Carter's operation for some time. In the middle of lunch, the door burst open and the bulldog skidded, slavered and farted his way through the guests. 'Watkin!' bellowed Carter. 'Watkin! Get out of here.' The soundman smirked with triumph. 'Gotcha,' he said, reaching for his union notebook. Later, Carter gazed at his pet wistfully. 'You,' he said to Watkin 'ain't nuthin' but a sound dog'.

The Rhodesian press corps left itself wide open to accusations of flippancy, of levity, of indifference even to the horrors we were supposed to be covering. The practical jokes, the parties, the striving to feature in the daily bulletin of anecdotes and apocrypha were, however, merely a release from the tragedy unfolding all around us. Coverage had become difficult and dangerous and accuracy was actively discouraged by all sides. Refuge was found in a press corps camaraderie that was to remain strong long after the Rhodesian story ended.

Apologists for Ian Douglas Smith and his diehards? Nonsense. I still treasure the tape-recording of my last one-on-one interview with him in his Salisbury office shortly after one of his ministers had confided to me that 'the wheels have really come off now'.

He was studiously relaxed. His feet were propped up on his desk. He was in his shirt sleeves. And he was totally unrepentant. One of those massive African thunderstorms was gathering over the high plain outside. He prevaricated and justified every move he had made in 15 agonising years. He knew he was lying, he knew that I knew he was lying and the storm beyond seemed to know. Each time he came out with an obvious untruth, there would be a flash of lightning and, as my tape testifies, an enormous clap of thunder.

Martin Meredith of the *Sunday Times*, a serious-minded stalwart of the foreign correspondents' corps, echoed the feelings of most of his colleagues in his definitive book on the Smith years, *The Past Is Another Country*. He wrote: 'There was an appalling complacency about the death and destruction that the last few years of white rule have brought to Rhodesia. It was not just the casualty statistics that mattered. By comparison to the Algerian war, for example, the figures were small. Officially, the dead inside Rhodesia numbered 15 705: 8 250 guerrillas, 954 security force personnel, 6 091 black civilians, 410 white civilians; thousands more had been maimed and injured. But beyond that there were the side-effects of war which affected the entire nation: an economy virtually bankrupted by the cost of the government services; abandoned farms, broken marriages, rising alcoholism. That too was part of Smith's legacy.'

The end of white Rhodesia was scripted by the least expected team: Margaret Thatcher's high Tory government and its shrewd and pragmatic Foreign Secretary, Lord Carrington. Carrington realised that the Muzorewa regime simply had too much white influence to gain international acceptance. He scrapped all the previous plans and theories and convened the Lancaster House Conference. With much manipulation, persuasion and persistence, Carrington finally secured an agreement on a new constitution that the Foreign Office devised. It had aspects that, in retrospect, were remarkable.

Rhodesia, for a period, was to return to British rule under a British governor. Supervised by a large contingent of international observers and independent electoral commissioners, a one-man-one-vote election would be held. A Commonwealth peace-keeping force – predominantly British – would hold the military line during the elections. The choice of governor was also surprising. The large, genial figure of Christopher Soames emerged from an RAF VC-10 in December 1979 admitting right away that he had little knowledge of African affairs or of the complexities of the Rhodesian situation. He was, however, soon to learn. For many white Rhodesians, Lord Soames carried some vicarious credibility because his wife, Mary, was the daughter of Winston Churchill. Nobody with such connections, they hoped, would allow this last outpost of the Empire to succumb.

The Union Jack was raised on the lawns of Government House in Salisbury for the first time in ten years. In the remarkable four months that followed, it became evident that the Foreign Office's hidden agenda was a plan to ensure that a Muzorewa-Nkomo alliance would emerge from the elections, thereby shutting out the Marxist Mugabe. The whispered buzz-word around Government House was 'ABM' – meaning 'anyone but Mugabe'. It was not to be, of course. Muzorewa's appeal had evaporated, not least because all the Queen's horses and all the Queen's men could not prevent wholesale intimidation of the hapless rural populations by Mugabe's men.

At midnight on 17 April 1980, Smith's Rhodesia which he had once boasted could last for 1 000 years, became the nominally Marxist People's Republic of Zimbabwe. Watched by Prince Charles and with musical accompaniment by reggae exponent, Bob Marley and the Wailers, the Union Jack was struck for the last time in Africa.

Following Page: ⫸

Mike Sullivan of the BBC, an amateur cartoonist, summed up the dilemma of journalists in Rhodesia on whether they should arm themselves.

LISTEN — YOU GOTTA RECALL ME TO
LONDON —— THIS TRIP'S GONE ON
TOO LONG!!

The author and Sue Sharpe accept a snack from Sally Mugabe, wife of the Zimbabwean President, at the country's independence celebrations.

'Comrade Max', a renegade guerrilla in Rhodesia, shows the hacks how he operated. From left: Peter Taylor, Sunday Telegraph, *Richard West, freelance, Rowly Carter, ITN, James MacManus,* The Guardian, *Chris Reynolds, the* Rhodesia Herald, *Peter Sharpe, ITN.*

CHAPTER SIXTEEN

FINAL EDITION

*T*here was a surfeit of symbolism in the lowering of the last Union Jack in Africa that night in Salisbury. The flag's final flutter was wreathed in teargas as riot police outside the stadium tried to disperse some over-enthusiastic Bob Marley fans. There were tears of joy from Zimbabweans who thought the millennium would dawn in the morrow's Harare; tears of grief from white Rhodesians for the finale of an epoch of rearguard colonialism and tears of nostalgia from a handful of foreign hacks who were quietly acknowledging to themselves the end of a very special era of journalism.

The last days of empire in Africa were coinciding with a worldwide revolution in newspapers, in journalism, in communications – life-blood of the craft – and, most dramatically, in the way news was defined, interpreted, conveyed and expressed. Even though we were many thousands of miles away from our headquarters, caught up in the turmoil and traumas of another continent's wars, those of us who were weaned on printer's ink were aware that a 'new order' was in the making in our own profession.

The colonisation of Africa had coincided with the development of newspapers and the concept of newspapermen. Its demise was coinciding with 'new technology', as computerised printing and publishing techniques were called, with the age of electronic news-gathering, of satellite television and with a public depending increasingly on instantly transmitted flickering pictures. The few seconds allocated to the most dramatic story on television news would create the received perception of the event.

No longer would the lord of the manor unfold his crisp *Times*, neatly ironed after delivery by the butler, to read a dispatch from Abyssinia which had reached the Thunderer by fast-packet steamer from Djibouti. No longer would the man on the London omnibus or the Kansas City milkman, those two most famous of newspaper readers, absorb the derring-do of the Stanleys, the Hemingways or the Younghusbands as they swam crocodile-infested rivers and fought off tropical diseases to transmit, possibly by carrier pigeon, that fascinating first-person account.

For the British correspondents, the newspaper revolution portended the end of their spiritual and professional home, that rather grubby London thoroughfare connecting the City with the West End synonymous worldwide with journalism and known as Fleet Street. If London was a collection of villages, then Fleet Street was one of the most homogeneous. The annual visit (if he was lucky!) by the foreign-based hack was a ritual of homecoming. From the end of the Strand to Ludgate Circus there would be dozens of familiar faces. Colleagues would drag you into foetid pubs in vile alleyways, happy to listen with cheerful cynicism to your tales of the great beyond as a good excuse for another drink.

In the newsroom, a familiar face would dash past, take a second glance and shout 'Hello there, old boy...haven't seen you for yonks...been away?' even though your byline and exotic dateline might have been all over the front page for the previous six weeks. There was always the thrill, too, when the floor began to vibrate beneath the feet as the mighty rotary presses in the basement began to spew the first edition.

More often than not, in the 1960s, your home leave would coincide with yet another industrial dispute. The printers wanted another £100 a week because there were a couple of extra pages on a Friday, the electricians were out because they had caught a sub-editor changing a light bulb in his office or the journalists were holding a compulsory chapel meeting in St Bride's in sympathy with an expenses dispute at the *Essex Chronicle*.

Never mind; a kindly compositor would break off from the picket line to give you a lift home in his Jaguar, possibly taking you via an expensive nightclub for a nightcap. The malpractices and overt corruption of Fleet Street's printers would have made the most profligate African dictator blush. Their graft and greed, coupled with weak, vacillating managements, had written Fleet Street's epitaph long before that village died.

All these reminiscences crowded in as Rhodesia became Zimbabwe on that balmy night in 1980. For thirty or so eventful years in Africa, the world had relied largely on the printed word for news of the continent's painful shedding of its colonial skin. The Genuine Old Hands had rushed from riot to revolution, from the back-of-beyond to the front, from palaces to prisons to telegraph office, telex, phone, pigeon-post and many other ingenious ways to get the unfolding story of imperial retreat back to their newspapers.

It had always been frenetic, often fun and sometimes frightening but there was the certainty of the camaraderie of the hack-pack on a good story, especially in the tighter corners. Like any other village, the pack had its vicious gossip, bitchiness and personal confrontations, but the correspondents could always be confident of support and succour in adversity.

That era was now ending. The television crews, with their tons of equipment, hypnotic camera lenses and chartered Lear jets on standby were the new tin gods. African politicians were among the first to be flattered by the prospect of posturing on the magic box in simultaneous global hook-ups. 'Think visual,' my television colleagues would shout. 'It's gotta be moving. If there's no action there's no television.' From the Sudan to South Africa I watched African mobs learn quickly to ham it up for television, sometimes gleefully waiting for the cameras to arrive before committing a premeditated killing or vicious assault or starting a bloody riot. There were spin-offs for humble scribes. Late one evening I fielded a phone call in Lusaka from a TV colleague in Lagos. She wanted to ask about certain logistical problems about getting a crew into South Africa. 'By the way,' she added casually. 'You might be interested in this.' She then proceeded to give me a highly significant story of the moment, gleaned from a chat with a visiting US State Department official. 'Surely you've put this out?' I asked. 'No ways,' she replied. 'It's all talking heads crap. No visual back-up. This is show-biz, baby. New York would shoot me for a waste of satellite feed.'

Then there were the cut-rate, sometimes free rides to and from the story in the TV company's chartered aircraft. The massive budgets of a television news-gathering operation opened up a new, luxurious world for the notebook-and-biro brigade. The TV men had to get in and out quickly with a mass of equipment and a cast of thousands to catch their satellite times. Expense was no object. Good chums in the TV business would always find a spare seat for an old-fashioned scribbler who would offer no competitive threat to their deadlines or interpretation of events. On some running stories, one TV company would have a couple of jets, hired at thousands of dollars per hour, on permanent standby to ferry film and tape to the nearest transmission point.

One bright morning we touched down in an ITN Lear jet at a remote airstrip in Botswana to be besieged by thousands of screaming, singing, chanting people waving flags and dancing and tumbling in traditional greeting. They fell silent suddenly as the aircraft disgorged a gaggle of bleary-eyed, bestubbled hacks lugging cameras and tape recorders. The Prince of Wales, for whom they had been waiting, landed an hour later in a modest piston-engined job.

TV, of course, had its many disadvantages. Princes, presidents, prime ministers, pimps and perverts would always give preference to the men with the cameras. Press conferences, like major sporting events these days, were arranged for the convenience of transmission times, not for the people present. The scribe's little tape recorders were pushed to one side by banks of phallic microphones, the front seats were reserved for the TV front men so their cameras could cut away to close-ups of that noble left profile as they posed the question that would reveal all. Bustling technicians would entangle one with wires and cables. Searing arc-lights would melt one's chocolate bar iron rations in one's pocket. Sensational disclosures would be delayed as politicians and their TV interrogators preened, primped and primed themselves for the cameras.

The hapless hack would spend hours tracking down his quarry only to be told: 'I've given a full statement to the BBC. You can take what you want from tonight's *News at Nine*.' As my friend had said, this was show business, baby. The end result would be an almost subliminal flash across screens, but this was how multiplying millions of people would now get their news.

Back on the plus side, there are times when a story can be covered by the writing journalist far more efficiently by watching the TV footage shot by colleagues in the visual media than by being on the spot himself. The cameras can, from better vantage points, capture sequences, scenes and quotes that will go unseen and unheard by the hack in the middle of any given mêlée. Alistair Cook, that most respected of commentators on American affairs, readily ascribed his own brilliant reportage of the assassination of President John F Kennedy to the mass, instant TV coverage. He did not travel to Dallas. He watched the drama unfold, minute by minute, in his New York apartment.

During the township riots and upheavals in South Africa in the 1980s, there would be so much happening in so many different areas that it was merely a matter of luck if you happened to find yourself in the right area at the wrong time – or the wrong area at the right time. A quick visit to the offices of one of the networks to view their footage would frequently yield good descriptive copy. Then there were always those many hours to be whiled away waiting in remote spots, relieving the boredom by watching on a TV monitor a blue movie smuggled in by a thoughtful crewman...

Journalistic accolades, as I have said before, should, if at all, be accorded to the TV news cameramen and their sound persons (those scurrying figures linked to them by electronic umbilical cords). They are the hacks that have to take the risks. The scribes can pick it up in the hotel bar, the TV correspondent can (and often did) do his piece to camera in front of a suitably dramatic backdrop long after the event. But when the bullets, rocks and teargas fly, the camera team has to be right there, fully visible and carrying equipment that in the heat of battle can appear convincingly ballistic.

Those South African riots could be very unnerving. No matter that you had large 'Press' signs plastered over your car, no matter that you we were with black colleagues capable of communicating in half a dozen vernaculars, no matter that you were able to give all the correct raised-fist gestures or utter the right slogans: you could suddenly find yourself surrounded by an enraged mob bent on mindless, irrational destruction, or a riot police unit only too happy to open fire with tear smoke, rubber bullets or shotguns. Alan Cowell of the *New York Times* had his car totally written-off by rocks and iron bars hurled and wielded by teenage 'activists' in Katlehong near Johannesburg. He, remarkably, emerged unscathed. Michael Hornsby of the *Times* is still plucking pellets of riot police buckshot from his backside eight years after a riot in Cape Town's Crossroads.

It was odds-on that in those flourishes of fury a journalist would be seriously hurt, or killed.

George De'Ath, a young South African, had already made a name for himself as a courageous frontline cameraman in the township wars of the 1980s. He was filming the troubles in the KTC squatter camp in the troubled Crossroads area of Cape Town for Britain's ITN. More than 60 people had been killed in faction-fighting between the ANC-supporting 'comrades' and conservative vigilantes known as the 'witdoeke' because of the white headbands they wore. There were repeated allegations that the vigilantes were being supported by the South African riot police.

Accompanied by soundman Andile Fosi, George had made his way through the shantytown to film riot police firing teargas at a group of comrades. They were suddenly confronted by an angry mob wielding axes, pangas and clubs. Andile later said he made the tragic mistake of thinking they were 'comrades' and greeted them as such. The mob immediately began attacking them with shouts of 'Kill the dogs!' The cameraman and the soundman huddled together and tried to explain who they were, but George received a vicious blow on the head from an axe and dropped to the ground. Andile made a dash for a police vehicle a couple of hundred yards away. He escaped with slight wounds. When the police reached George he was almost dead. He had been repeatedly hacked and stabbed and was slumped across his camera.

The 34-year-old award-winning cameraman lay in hospital in a coma with extensive brain damage for days before dying. There remain unexplained circumstances surrounding his murder. Andile Fosi claimed in a later court hearing that George's film of the attack had been tampered with. Other newsmen testified that the police had never interfered with the 'witdoeke' during the township violence and had been tardy in getting George to hospital after the attack.

There were similarities between De'Ath's killing and the cold-blooded murder of Tony Joyce, an Australian Broadcasting Corporation television reporter in Zambia in 1979. Kenneth Kaunda had placed his armed forces on a 'war footing' after repeated Rhodesian attacks inside Zambia. Joyce and cameraman Derek McKendry, both experienced in covering war situations, notably Vietnam, flew from London to Lusaka and immediately set about arranging government accreditation and finding out where the action was. John Osman and Brian Barron cautioned the Australian team about the volatile situation in Zambia. 'The security forces are very jittery and trigger happy,' Osman warned. 'They believe every white man is a Rhodesian mercenary.'

Joyce was eager to get some film quickly. He and McKendry hired a taxi to drive them 40 miles east of Lusaka where the Chongwe Bridge had been blown up by Rhodesian commandos two days earlier. The Australian reporter did two pieces to camera, McKendry captured some footage of the damaged bridge, and they climbed back into the taxi, asking the driver to return to Lusaka. Less than a mile from the bridge a single shot fired from the bushes at the side of the road hit the Peugeot taxi. The driver screeched to a standstill. Three men emerged from the bush, ordered the men out of the car and told them to put up their hands. They complied. One man, bare-chested and wearing only a pair of black trousers, waved a 9 mm Browning automatic pistol in their faces. They were variously accused of being white imperialists, Rhodesian rebels and spies. McKendry guessed that their captors were members of Joshua Nkomo's ZIPRA, the organisation that had been the main target of the Rhodesians.

To their relief, a white police car arrived and two uniformed Zambian policemen emerged to inquire what was going on. After much heated discussion, the policemen said they would take the journalists back to Lusaka to establish their true identity. They were ordered into the back of the police car. McKendry recalled: 'There were about a dozen men in all, mostly in Zambian militia uniforms. The one in black trousers seemed to be in charge. He was obviously a lunatic, very agitated and obviously high on something.

I thought the situation was mildly dicey but not too serious as long as we stayed very cool.

'We told them were were there to tell the world what dastardly things the Rhodesians were doing and were going to make sure that every Australian knew. Our friend in the black trousers suddenly fired a random shot. I felt a slug whistle past my head. I turned and saw it had hit Tony high in the forehead from a range of about 20 feet. I thought he was dead. I climbed out of the car and shouted "You motherfucker, you killed him". He said "Yes and now I'm going to kill you". He pointed the Browning at my head and I suddenly thought I was about to go to the great newsroom in the sky.' The police restrained the gunman and McKendry jumped back in the police car to find his colleague was still alive – just. He urged them to drive to a hospital in Lusaka. The cameraman was taken to Lusaka central police station where he was held in a cell for the next five days.

Joyce, in a teaching hospital, was in a bad way. The bullet had lodged in his head and he had lost a lot of blood. An English missionary doctor managed to keep him alive, but it was obvious he needed highly specialised treatment. ABC executives flew to Lusaka only to be met with hostility from Zambian officials and indifference from the British High Commission. (Joyce was an Australian citizen but had been born in England.) Contact was eventually made with Malcolm Fraser, the Australian prime minister and a personal friend of Kenneth Kaunda. Permission was finally granted for Joyce to be flown to Britain. He was rushed to St Bartholomew's Hospital where, despite the best possible medical attention, he died five weeks later.

All the evidence gathered by the British police and diplomats confirmed that Joyce had been shot in the police car in cold blood. Kaunda promised a full inquiry but the Australian government never received a satisfactory response. Nevertheless, the Zambian leader was fêted at a Commonwealth meeting in Melbourne later that year.

While the Old Africa Hands attempted to adjust to their secondary role to television as gatherers and purveyors of news, there was a new breed of print journalists bursting into editors' offices, fresh from the universities of America and Europe. Many of them had made career decisions after the highly dramatised success of Messrs Woodward and Bernstein in bringing down the Nixon administration after the Watergate scandal. Some had PhDs in journalism, a grotesque contradiction in terms if ever I heard one. Most were 'computer literate', which meant that they could feel their way around modems, multiplan worksheets, databases, bytes and formats but could not necessarily be expected to spell 'bougainvillaea'.

The sharper, more ambitious graduates of this new school emanated from the new-tech foreign room 'work stations' to join the gentlemen of the road in the world's flashpoints. Instead of the old hack's greeting, 'Hello, old boy...anything going on?' they tended to wave the cigarette smoke aside with disgust, recoil at the whiff of whisky or beer on the breath and rush off to the nearest university for a definitive, erudite, if highly one-sided analysis of the given situation. They would return to hunch over their word processors, a diet coke and a hygiene-wrapped sandwich at one side. Their eyes would betray no concern for what the reader, or even the foreign editor, might want. Instead, the narrowed eyebrows and intent expressions said 'Take me to your Pulitzer Prize committee'.

They would not be seen dead at the older hacks' favourite watering-holes. You might be unlucky enough to be invited to an early vegetarian supper at which our New Man would hold forth on the needs of a newspaper as an information-gathering system or on the interaction of journalistic ethics and social responsibility. Glib boasts about 'advocacy', 'investigative' and 'committed' journalism would slide into the conversation and be explained paternally to older hacks and non-hack guests. During a sip of post-prandial herbal tea, I longed to hear the echoes of Donald Wise's old saw, 'Remember, old boy, I'm writing for people who move their lips when they read'.

There is, these days, an entirely new lingo whenever foreign correspondents forgather. Gone are the long, liquid evenings of unlikely yarns, of the room number of that sloe-eyed air hostess on the inbound flight or the best local black market exchange rate. Instead, the conversation is more than likely to be one of bauds, parameters and modems. Pocket screwdrivers have replaced pocket pens; alligator clips and adaptors have taken the place of notebooks and hip-flasks. The *Washington Post* had the grace to publish a lament for the good old days of the battered typewriter and the long hours in front of dinging, clattering machines. It was written by Eugene Robinson who covers South America, but it applies with equal aptness to Africa. 'By now the world is used to time-conserving, labor-saving technological advances that end up requiring more time and effort than ever before. But computer transmission has gone further, at least among journalists in this part of the world, bringing many of us to the point of obsession. The medium has become not message but master.'

Robinson complained that clean transmission by laptop computer was a complex process, especially in the Third World where most 'phone systems were based on the tin-cans-and-string principle. 'Sending home the news requires ingenuity, persistence and the willingness to commit minor acts of vandalism. Clean transmission requires direct, wire-to-wire connections, and since the phones do not have modular jacks this means removing the switchplate on the hotel room wall and delving into the spaghetti of grey wires, searching for the two – and only two – that work.'

A compulsion had now taken hold of correspondents who would dial a dozen times in a row, peering anxiously at the screen, delighted like children at Christmas when the computer gives its message of hope ('CONNECT'), crestfallen at its message of failure ('NO CARRIER'). He recalls that Paul Knox of *The Globe and Mail* of Toronto had been on an Amazon excursion in 1992 when front-page news erupted in Colombia. He rushed from the depths of the jungle to Bogota – without his computer. He filed stories by typing them out and dictating them over the phone. 'It was so retrograde, so sad. But the strange thing was that he always finished filing his story much earlier than everyone else. He confessed to feeling "liberated". And he actually had interesting things to talk about at dinner.'

Computer technology is a wonderful breakthrough for journalism and for foreign journalists – when and if it works. I would like to challenge Eugene Robinson and the Latin American press corps to a wager that however primitive they believe the South American communications systems to be, they are as efficient as the Tokyo Stock Exchange compared to their equivalents in most African countries. And I have still to find a new technology boffin who can explain to me why, with this computer miracle into its second or third generation, deadlines have advanced by four or five hours. Daily newspapers in London, for instance, demand copy by 3 p.m. their time. In the bad old days of hot-lead composition and pernicious print unions we could still get our copy comfortably in the first edition by filing at 8 p.m.

Thank goodness that most newspapers have retained that cynical, infuriating but oh-so-reliable homo sapien – the copytaker, or telephone reporter or 'dictationist', as the Americans insist on calling the breed. The phones may be bad, agonisingly slow and full of static, but once the connection has been made there is a human voice, as opposed to a mechanical or electronic signal, to assure you that some form of copy has been received. The best of them are able to put together an intelligible story even if they hear only one out of five words.

Modern science and technology have not altered the age-old golden rule of journalism: the correspondent is only as good as his lines of communication. The most earth-shattering exclusive, the finest, carefully honed piece of deathless prose, the definitive exposé are all completely useless unless you can get them quickly back to the office. Nothing – satellite hook-ups, lap-top computers, facsimile machines, modular telephones – has changed that rule.

In the heyday of the Old Africa Hands there existed a deity worshipped by every hack from Cape Town to Cairo. His name was Edmund van der Merwe, known with affectionate awe as 'Fingers'. As a young man, Van der Merwe managed to secure a job with South Africa's Post and Telecommunications Department. Like many Cape Afrikaners his ambition was to own his own wine farm. On a post office salary that seemed like a pipe dream, but he quickly established a reputation for being the fastest telex operator in the south. Once challenged, like an old Wild West gunfighter, to prove it, he matched his skill at a blind telex keyboard to keep up manually with the transmission of a tape by a high-speed Creed machine. He won, with a large loop of tape between the machines and word-perfect copy at the other end. Hence 'Fingers'.

During stints as a PO operator in the Parliamentary Press Gallery in Cape Town his skills – coupled with an uncanny empathy with the needs and requirements of journalism and deadlines – came to the notice of foreign correspondents then based in that fair city. He was hired on a part-time basis to transmit copy for hacks who found, after a good lunch, that their own fingers got stuck between the keys of the telex machine.

With a glimmer of grapes growing and glowing in his own fields, Fingers took the plunge, resigned from the post office and established his own communications business. Such was his skill, reliability and reputation that within a few years Van der Merwe had a highly successful business. He would personally travel with the press corps to trouble spots all over Africa to set up and ensure communications. Only a few years later he was in a position to buy his first wine farm near Paarl but, by now, the excitement and adventure of hackdom ran thicker than wine in his veins. He continued, fortunately for us, as the Great Communicator.

My faith in Fingers was confirmed late one night in Quelimane in northern Mozambique during FRELIMO's war with the Portuguese. I had a good story. I had found a telephone. But I was suffering dreadfully from amoebic dysentery and the phone was working only erratically. Getting through to London or Lisbon was out of the question. Finally, I managed to get through to Fingers in Cape Town, dragging him from his bed. The line broke almost immediately but not before I had managed to blurt out my number.

Within a matter of minutes, Fingers was calling back, using his post office contacts to get a reasonable connection. The line broke regularly but he picked up one word in three, intuitively put the rest together, and the telex tape was running to London before I had finished dictating.

Fingers maintained his operation in Harare well after Zimbabwe independence. His best customers there were the three correspondents of the Soviet news agency, Tass. They were, however, tardy in paying their communications accounts. Repeated requests for payment were referred to the Russian Embassy in London. It so happened that Van der Merwe was planning a trip to Britain anyway. He had already dug out his 'London suit', a lime-green, double-breasted number that made him as conspicuous in Britain as a stick of biltong in a health bar. He was given the name of the Russian embassy man who would deal with his problem and duly made an appointment.

Having announced himself as Van der Merwe from South Africa, he was placed in a waiting room for some time, slightly disconcerted to have people peering around doors to study him curiously. Finally, he was ushered into the senior man's inner sanctum. A large tape recorder was switched on and three stenographers stood poised at his shoulder to record every word. Fingers suddenly realised that his true purposes had been mistaken. They thought he was a defector from Pretoria.

'Now, Mr van der Merwe,' asked the senior man. 'Tell us how you think the Russian people may help you.' Fingers slapped a thick wad of bills on his desk. 'You can pay these outstanding accounts right now, man!' he said. 'And in South African rand if you wouldn't mind.'

Zimbabwe was not, of course, the last of the African states to shed the colonial yoke. There remained the vast slice of territory, flanked by two deserts and known variously as German South West Africa, South West Africa, SWA/Namibia and finally, in March 1990, the Republic of Namibia. Anyone seeking a palpable definition of space and light should put Namibia on their itinerary. It is a wild, beautiful land of rock, canyon, giant sand dune and endless spans of deserted, treacherous Atlantic shoreline (most of it known, aptly, as the Skeleton Coast). Its deserts, the coastal Namib and the Western Kalahari, teem with unique flora and fauna. I make no apologies for the travelogue. The country deserves it. It is also unique in Africa, certainly, and most other parts of the globe, because its 320 000 square miles are inhabited by just over one million people.

It has a history as colourful as its population. For centuries the only occupants were sparse communities of Bushmen, Hottentots and Herero, hunter-gatherer and pastoral communities who rarely troubled each other. A century ago, the land was largely unknown to the European. The Kaiser's Germany annexed the territory in the scramble for Africa, decimated the Herero people for their presumption in putting up some resistance, discovered diamonds, and built wonderful buildings, including opera houses, in the middle of the desert. German rule ended with their defeat in the Great War. The then League of Nations granted the then Union of South Africa the mandate to govern the territory until the inhabitants 'can stand on their own feet in the arduous conditions of the modern world'. The UN, the League of Nations' successor, attempted by political and legal means to relieve South Africa of its mandate. South Africa defiantly continued to govern the territory as a fifth province until the 1980s when the war in Angola and redoubled pressure from a now largely independent Africa obliged Pretoria to cede. In the many hundreds of reference books on Africa you will find scant reference to Namibia or South West Africa. Despite its beauty, its intriguing past, its economic importance (diamonds and uranium) and the intense international wrangle over its future, it could not be 'sold' as a story to any newspaper in the world. It was not for want of trying. I knew few African correspondents who did not enjoy visiting Namibia and spent long hours attempting to convince foreign editors that it was a 'sexy' story.

(The only overt sex in Namibia was, in fact, the back page of the *Windhoek Advertiser* which carried naked pin-ups of local girls long before Fleet Street's *Sun* had a Page Three. The *Advertiser* was founded and run, alone, by Hannes 'Mad Smitty' Smith, one of the world's most eccentric, resilient editors. His newspaper was compulsive, compulsory reading.)

The sixteen years of one of the most half-hearted and inept guerrilla wars in history was waged, almost exclusively on the northern border with Angola by SWAPO and its predominantly Ovambo following. The tribe was more Angolan than Namibian, but having long since been recognised by the UN as 'the sole, authentic voice of the Namibian people' SWAPO had little trouble in swinging the independence election. To get to the 'war' meant relying on the South African Defence Force to lay on a military aircraft to fly to one of the remote bases on the Angolan border. I know of no reporter who saw anything that could remotely be described as 'battle' between SWAPO and the South Africans in sixteen years and dozens of facility trips to the border.

We resigned ourselves to the fact that editors throughout the world automatically spiked any story that mentioned Namibia. The obligation to summarise where and what the territory was about in crisp journalese did not help. 'This vast troubled, mineral-rich former German colony ruled as a fifth province by South Africa in defiance of a withdrawn United Nation's mandate'. Etc., etc. We could hear the copytasters yawning from thousands of miles away.

Freelance Ray Kennedy, who knew the country well, had the rare distinction of once persuading London's *Daily Mirror*, a popular tabloid, to carry a story about Namibia. Ray had interviewed a genial local politician, a Dr Afrika, leader of the Rehoboth Baster (literally 'bastard') people who had set up their own little republic in the middle of the desert. Dr Africa held strong conservative views and expressed them forcefully. Back at his hotel, Kennedy sat muttering over his typewriter. How on earth was he going to capture the attention of *Mirror* readers with such esoteric material? Finally, he broke into an evil chuckle and tapped out his intro: 'Dr Afrika is a right Baster.' The *Mirror* used it.

My own impression was that South Africa had no intention, certainly within the previous 20 years, of attempting to hold on to Namibia as an additional province. Pretoria held on with all the diplomatic, political and military resources at its command merely because they feared the threat of a Cuban-backed Marxist government on its extended Orange River border. The withdrawal of Cuba's task force from Angola and the collapse of communism in Eastern Europe removed that threat. The South African government, particularly its exchequer, was certainly not unhappy to greet independence in Namibia, even if its new government was led by the buck-toothed, none-too-bright Sam Nujoma.

None other than the effervescent Pik Botha, now Foreign Minister, told me fifteen years ago that South Africa had no intention of trying to make Namibia a fifth province of his republic. Pik played hilarious host to a week-long tour of the territory laid on for foreign correspondents. In Windhoek he had laid on non-stop successive press conferences with the leaders of no fewer than 22 political parties. They approximated to the various tribal and ethnic groups in the country – whites (English-speaking), whites (German-speaking), whites (Afrikaans-speaking), Basters, Bushmen, Caprivians, Damaras, Hereros, Kavangos, Coloureds, Namas, Tswanas and Owambos.

It was a very long, hot day. By mid-afternoon most of my colleagues had slipped away to the swimming pool or the shops. Only Peter Hawthorne and I remained to interview the Damara cabinet. The Damaras speak with a distinctive, normally attractive 'click' language but every question, however innocuous, had to be debated at length by the entire cabinet before they answered. It sounded like a convention of crickets. Both Peter and I dozed off waiting for one answer. We were shaken awake gently by the Damara leader. 'Thank you, gentlemen of the international press, for your very kind attention,' he said without sarcasm – and in perfect English.

The tour ended with the lavish hospitality of Consolidated Diamond Mines and the De Beers Corporation in their 'forbidden' diamond area north of the Orange River. A silver-tongued PR man insisted to us that they had never had any trouble with their black labour force and that SWAPO was unknown on this patch. Clive Small of the BBC tape recorded a joke interview with me pretending to be a SWAPO activist, saying we were about to seize control of the diamond fields. Small later played the tape to CDM officials and caused a massive security scare. Pik thought it was great fun.

Throughout the tour – including one memorable night when he had performed his own tribal dance in his underpants in the middle of a spectacular thunderstorm – the future foreign minister had insisted that South Africa was only too anxious to rid itself of the responsibility of Namibia – once the 'communist threat' had been removed. 'Namibia's a very pleasant name,' he said as we flew back across the Orange River. 'Much better than South West Africa.' Several years later, South Africa's attitude towards Namibia was spelled out as clearly by General Jannie Geldenhuys, then commander of the South African forces in Namibia. A gentle, thoughtful man, Geldenhuys invited Nick Ashford of *The Times* and myself to supper at his home. Late into the night he discussed with us South Africa's dilemma over Namibia. He showed us copies of the hand-written letters he felt obliged to send to families of his men killed in action. He described his agony in having to do so. 'Every single one of my men knows that this is not really our war,' he said. 'It would be different if we were defending South Africa on the Orange River. That is our own country. This is like a colonial war and our history shows just how deeply we resent any form of colonialism.'

South Africa and its long and volatile relationship with the press, international and local, does not fall within the parameters set for this story. According to successive generations of Afrikaners who have ruled that very strange society since 1948, they fought Africa's first successful war against colonialism. They resent – as do millions of non-Afrikaners – any suggestion that their great problems are in any way colonial. Detractors who refer to Africa's 'last remaining imperial question' at the southern tip of the continent are mistaken, they say. The South African saga is so utterly different to those of other African countries that its coverage by foreign correspondents merits at least one volume of its own.

Yet so many of the Old Africa Hands were obliged to cover aspects of the South African story (indeed, many were born there and others based there) that its influence, particularly in the way its government reacted to foreign pressmen, demands a reference here. My own experience convinces me that South Africa got a far fairer hearing from correspondents who had spent time elsewhere in Africa.

An all-round experience of the continent and its problems afforded a balance and lack of hysterical affront to which many hacks who covered only South Africa were – and still are – prone. Reaction against apartheid and all its many iniquities and absurdities meant that the South African story would yield a daily flow of copy for the morally outraged hack. There can be no question that similar injustices, discrimination and sophistry perpetuated daily in other African states received but a fraction, if any, of the coverage accorded to South Africa.

Not the least of Pretoria's problems in coping with foreign press coverage was the number of South African journalists who secured jobs and stringerships for foreign newspapers and used these positions from which, at best, to expatiate their own guilt feelings for being of the 'hated apartheid state' or, at worst, to pursue ruthlessly fame and fortune by pandering in their copy and demeanour to the knee-jerk enthusiasm with which most of the world's editors greeted stories that were not just anti-apartheid but anti anything South African.

There is a sizeable index of South African journalists who built their reputations by condemning themselves to self-righteous exile or by 'fleeing' the country (sometimes when there was no reason whatsoever for them to 'flee'). Even so, successive South African governments and their cumbersome, bumbling bureaucracies were their own worst enemies when it came to dealing with newspapers, newspapermen and, later, with television. Local editors needed phalanxes of lawyers on call to cope with more than 200 laws on the statute books governing what they might or might not publish.

Editors and journalists were repeatedly hauled before the courts, harassed and sometimes gaoled. Reporters and photographers were beaten up, shot at, spat at, kicked, banned and banished. Some suffered mysterious nocturnal attacks on their homes and threatening, anonymous telephone calls. And they were the lucky ones. Relations between the press and the police were probably the worst. The South African Police seemed to recruit from Hollywood's Central Casting department. Watching them in action, it was difficult to believe they were not taking part in a parody of themselves and all that the outside world believed they were capable of.

I'll never forget the reaction of the police commissioner at a press briefing shortly after the first of the major township upheavals in Soweto in 1976. Charles Mohr of the *New York Times*, not one of nature's liberals, wanted to know why police had used live ammunition against the demonstrators. Had the South African riot police not heard of tear smoke, water cannon and rubber bullets, he asked. The commissioner's weatherbeaten face puckered with distaste. 'Rubber bullets?' he replied. 'Rubber bullets? Let me tell you, sir, that when they start throwing rubber rocks at my men I might, just might, decide to issue them with rubber bullets!'

Foreign journalists would get a foretaste of the South African experience when they applied for entry visas. Interminable waits at embassies, hourly telephone calls, endless questions and form-filling – and finally, if they were lucky, a one-week permit. To be based in the country entailed an elaborate procedure which would culminate in a temporary permit being issued for a period up to a maximum of six months depending on whether your copy was deemed, by some faceless committee, to be 'positive' or 'negative'. Deportations of foreign hacks were commonplace, rarely with any reason being given. At one stage, the government attempted to exercise control over the Foreign Correspondents Association. At another, they seriously toyed with the idea of establishing a 'register' of journalists. To obtain a parliamentary press pass involved the completion of a heavy portfolio of forms which demanded such details as the colour of your grandparents' eyes.

The upshot was that even journalists who genuinely appreciated the immense and complex problems facing the government were instinctively rendered if not hostile, then certainly 'negative'.

Holger Jensen, otherwise known as 'Captain Wilderness' or 'The Hulk' because of his carefully cultivated macho persona, his love of hunting and the exaggeration of his naturally burly build by the platform cowboy boots he always wore, was *Newsweek*'s Southern African correspondent for several years. He was a lot brighter than his adopted appearance suggested, and a widely experienced war correspondent and foreign hack. Unlike most of his colleagues, he spoke Afrikaans, having been brought up in South Africa.

When he returned to America he wrote a critique of Pretoria's press management techniques – and of the 'new wave' of less experienced correspondents attracted to the South African story. 'The new crop of American journalists does adopt the bandwagon approach,' he wrote.

'They all try to leap on it whatever direction it is going in lest they be left behind and thus be seen as "missing the story". Often the bandwagon is going the wrong way. For example, the story put across to Americans, generally speaking, is that South Africa should be governed by blacks because they are in the majority and have been suppressed by the white minority. Scant attention is given to what sort of black government would emerge or the concerns of white South Africans who fear that their well developed and fairly advanced nation may be ruined like Angola and Mozambique. All these are valid criticisms, particularly when applied to the foreign press. But Pretoria must share the blame for its plight. Its treatment of the press is often as stupid and shortsighted as the treatment of South Africa by the press.'

The press in South Africa remains the most free and vigorous on the continent. There was marked improvement in official attitudes under the F W de Klerk administration, coupled with protestations by the putative incoming government of the African National Congress that it upholds fully the concept of a free and unfettered press. There are unhappy indications, however, that an incoming, democratically elected black government will not readily abandon the habits of backstage media manipulation and menace adopted for so long by South Africa's Afrikaner rulers.

The foreign press, in the 1990s, has revealed, unwittingly, the inverted racism that has underpinned its own approach to the South African story. The rest of Africa – some 50 nations covering an enormous land area of the planet – rarely rates more than a few brief paragraphs per week in the more serious newspapers and even fewer seconds of TV time per month on international networks. There are exceptions, of course. The most notable in recent years was the 'discovery' of Ethiopia's devastating famine by our old friend Mohammed Amin and Michael Buerk, then BBC TV's South African correspondent, in 1984. Numerous journalists had been aware of the appalling suffering being caused by that famine for the previous three years. Many had written about it, only to find their copy spiked. The film made by Amin and Buerk for *Visnews* was first shown on BBC TV news and then around the world. It provoked an immense and immediate response. Viewers around the world emptied their pockets. Bob Geldorf's Live Aid concert and Sport Aid's Race against Time raised many millions. Publicity begot publicity and for months financial and much other assistance poured into Ethiopia. It helped to alleviate the problem, certainly not to cure its causes. Amin and Buerk, though in their own words, 'just doing our job', were fêted as heroes and celebrities. Some prat even suggested it should be called 'Buerk's famine'.

The fact remains that famine is endemic throughout the parched Sahel region of north-central Africa and many other regions. Old Africa Hands had written not only about the famines of the 1980s, but of those in the 1970s and the 1960s. John 'Shithead' Edlin covered the 1984 calamity for AP. On his own initiative, he raised money from friends and colleagues to fund the establishment of an orphanage in Ethiopia. The authorities recognised his effort by having made a commemorative plaque which hangs on the wall of his Harare home. (True to Edlin luck, his name was misspelt. The plaque thanks 'Mr John Edline'.) It was not Shithead who got the headlines, however. It was the men who made the television film. Without detracting from the professionalism or compassion of Messrs Amin and Buerk in any way, it was moving pictures of famine victims and their circumstances that had the impact. It was visual. It was 'good television'.

Aids is a much bigger and much more serious problem throughout Africa. It has, by comparison, received very little coverage. Locally based scribes are aware just how bad the situation is but in most African countries they have been warned by the authorities that they write about it at their peril. International TV is aware of it, too. But the dread disease does not lend itself to good visual material. And, one suspects, there is a certain 'African tragedy' fatigue setting in among TV viewers – and newspaper readers – in the rest of the world. It could signal a farewell to alms for the continent.

The exception, at present, is South Africa. Most of the world's major news-gathering organisations have only one bureau or staff correspondent in Africa. With few exceptions they are in South Africa.

Could it be that this interest is because South Africa is still ruled by white people and that white interests are at stake? In 1989, Charles Moore, then Editor of *The Spectator*, wrote: 'If and when South Africa finally goes the way of the rest of the continent and is ruled by its black majority, I predict that our interest in it will quickly wane. Not only because our hopes will be disappointed (though they will be) but because we, the whites, will have left the stage.'

Should that turn out to be true, I can only be thankful that I was young enough to be sent to cover Africa at a stage when there was enough foreign interest in the continent to enable me to become an Old Africa Hand. To borrow an intro from Charles Dickens, one of journalism's more distinguished sons: 'It was the best of times; it was the worst of times.'

ACKNOWLEDGEMENTS

So many friends and colleagues volunteered their time to give help, hints guidance and advice in the course of researching and writing that it would be invidious to list them all. Many more readily allowed me to dip freely into their memories, their libraries, scrap books and their own work to paint as detailed a picture as possible. I must mention the Editors of *The Daily Telegraph, The Sunday Telegraph,* the *Sunday Times, The Observer, The Times, The Guardian,* the *Daily Express,* the *Daily Mail,* the *Daily Mirror,* the *New York Times,* the *Washington Post,* the *Los Angeles Times,* Reuters, Associated Press, United Press International and others for the help and liberties taken with their libraries, their goodwill and the endeavours of their staff, past and present. To all of them a heartfelt, old-fashioned message: 'Multithanks'. In particular, thanks to *Private Eye* for permission to quote in full Lunchtime O'Booze's seminal dispatch from Zanzibar, and to those colleagues and their publishers who gave permission to quote from their own eminently readable books, namely Sandy Gall and Hamish Hamilton (*Don't Worry About the Money Now,* London, 1983), Smith Hempstone and Faber and Faber (*Katanga Report,* London, 1963), Phillip Knightley and André Deutsch (*The First Casualty,* London, 1975), Brian Tetley and Moonstone Books (*Mo — the story of Mohamed Amin,* London, 1988), Don McCullin and Johathan Cape (*Unreasonable Behaviour* London, 1990), Ed Behr and Hamish Hamilton (*Anyone Here Been Raped and Speaks English?* London, 1981), Paul Harrison and Robin Palmer and Hilary Shipman Ltd. (*News Out of Africa,* London, 1986), John de St. Jorre and Houghton Mifflin (*The Brothers' War,* Boston, 1972) and David Lamb and Random House (*The Africans,* New York, 1983). Others opened their doors, made up the spare bed, offered me boundless hospitality and ferried me to and from airports, often in the middle of the night. In this respect I owe special debts of gratitude to Mike and Sybil Keats and Don and

Daphne Wise in Hong Kong, David Storey in Bangkok, John and Di Monks in Melbourne, Gary Burns in Sydney, Ian Black in Malibu, George and Margo Gordon in New York, Jonathan and Gail de Leighton Squires in Connecticut, Mike and Lindsay Hooper in Washington DC, Ken and Gill Clarke and Nat and Helen Gibson in London, Bill and Hilary Deedes in Kent, Ron and Theresa Squires in Wiltshire, John and Virginia Osman in France, Peter Younghusband and Peter and Jessie Hawthorne in Cape Town and, in Natal, Mike and Joan Shuter, Richard and Carole Wood and John and Erica Platter. At William Waterman, there was the detonation of ideas and enthusiasm, encouragement and timely help. There was also constructive, professional criticism from Jennifer Crwys-Williams who edited. And a very special acknowledgement to my wife, Denise, who endured yet another prolonged absence by her husband before suffering the much greater hardship of having him permanently in the house, hunched over the word processor, grumpy, preoccupied and uncommunicative.

BIBLIOGRAPHY

Behr, Edward, *Anyone Here Been Raped and Speaks English?*, Hamish Hamilton, London, 1981.

Blake, Robert, *A History of Rhodesia*, Eyre Methuen, London, 1977.

Bridgland, Fred, *The War for Africa*, Ashanti, Gibraltar, 1990.

– *Jonas Savimbi, A Key to Africa*, Macmillan, Johannesburg, 1986.

Caute, David, *Under the Skin, The Death of White Rhodesia*, Allen Lane, London, 1983.

Clapham, Christopher, *Haile-Selassie's Government*, Longman, London, 1969.

Collier, Richard, *The Warcos*, Weidenfeld and Nicolson, London, 1989.

Colvin, Ian, *The Rise and Fall of Moise Tshombe*, Frewin, London, 1968.

Coote, Colin, *Editorial*, Eyre and Spottiswoode, London, 1965.

Crwys-Williams, Jennifer, *South African Despatches*, Ashanti, Johannesburg, 1989.

Davidson, Basil, *Africa in Modern History*, Allen Lane, London, 1978.

Dempster, Chris, and Tomkins, Dave, *Firepower*, Corgi, London, 1978.

Dumont, René, *False Start in Africa*, Deutsch, London, 1966.

Forsyth, Frederick, *The Biafra Story*, Penguin, London, 1969.

Gall, Sandy, *Don't Worry About The Money Now*, Hamish Hamilton, London, 1983.

Germani, Hans, *White Soldiers in Black Africa*, Verlag Ullstein, Frankfurt, 1966.

Gray, Tony, *Fleet Street Remembered*, Heinemann, London, 1990.

Gunther, John, *Inside Africa*, Hamish Hamilton, London, 1955.

Harrison, Paul, and Palmer, Robin, *News Out Of Africa*, Hilary Shipman, London, 1986.

Hart-Davis, Duff, *The House the Berrys Built*, Hodder and Stoughton, London, 1990.

Hempstone, Smith, *Katanga Report*, Faber and Faber, London, 1962.

Hoare, Mike, *Congo Mercenary*, Hale, London, 1978.
– *The Seychelles Affair*, Transworld, London, 1986.
Kapuscinski, Ryszard, *Another Day of Life*, Pan, London, 1987.
Knightley, Phillip, *The First Casualty*, Quartet, London, 1975.
Lamb, David, *The Africans*, Random House, New York, 1983.
Listowel, Judith, *Amin*, IUP, London, 1973.
Martin, David, *General Amin*, Faber, London, 1974.
Martin, David, and Johnson, Phyllis, *The Struggle for Zimbabwe*, Faber, London, 1981.
McCullin, Don, *Unreasonable Behaviour*, Jonathan Cape, London, 1990.
Meredith, Martin, *The Past Is Another Country*, Pan, London, 1980.
– *The First Dance of Freedom*, Hamish Hamilton, London, 1984.
Mondlane, Eduardo, *The Struggle for Mozambique*, Penguin, London, 1969.
Naipaul, Shiva, *North of South*, Deutsch, London, 1978.
Niesewand, Peter, *In Camera*, Weidenfeld and Nicolson, London, 1973.
Nugent, John, *Call Africa 999*, Coward-McCann, New York, 1965.
Pakenham, Thomas, *The Boer War*, Weidenfeld and Nicolson, London, 1970.
– *The Scramble For Africa*, Weidenfeld and Nicolson, London, 1991.
Short, Philip, *Banda*, Routledge and Kegan Paul, London, 1974.
St Jorre, John de, *The Nigerian Civil War*, Hodder and Stoughton, London, 1972.
Tetley, Brian, *Mo-The Story of Mohamed Amin*, Moonstone, London, 1988.
Waugh, Evelyn, *Waugh In Abyssinia*, Longmans, London, 1936.
– *Scoop* , Chapman Hall, London, 1938.
Welensky, Roy, *Welensky's 4,000 Days*, Collins, London, 1964
West, Richard, *The White Tribes of Africa*, Jonathan Cape, London, 1965.
Wood, J R T, *The Welensky Papers*, Graham Publishing, Durban, 1983.
Young, Kenneth, *Rhodesia and Independence*, Eyre and Spottiswoode, London, 1967.

INDEX

Aba: 148, 220
Abako: 99
Abyssinia: 28-39, 41-45
Accra: 83, 88
Ackner, Desmond: 265-6
Adams, Eddie: 398
Addis Ababa: 22, 27-29, 30-32, 35-39, 41-46, 169-70
Addis Hilton Hotel: 169-70
Aden assignment: 21
Adekunle, Benjamin Lt-Col: 202, 211, 219-20, 222-24
Adoko, Akena: 260-61, 265
Adoula, Cyrille: 125, 145
Africa
    independence movements: 11
    diplomatic measures: 12-13
    foreign press corps: 14-22
African National Congress: 427
Afrika, Dr: 423
Afrinews: 237, 243-44
Aguiyi-Ironsi, Major-General: 207
AIDS coverage: 428
Ainsley, Cyril: 136
Aitken, Sir Max: 243-44, 252, 255
Akintola, Samuel, Chief: 204
Albatross (fishing vessel): 324-45
Albrektsen, Jens: 148-49
Alexander, Major-General: 221
Ali, Waris Fadull, Lt-Col: 269-70
Ally, Godwin, Colonel: 219
Amin, Idi: 13, 256-60, 267-75, 298-301, 303-308
Amin, Mohammed: 67-69, 163, 167-68, 307, 312-13, 427-28
Amin, Sarah: 306

Anderson, George: 309-10
Anglo-Boer War 1899-1902: 9-10
Angola
    independence: 352-54
    mercenary recruitment: 319, 325-28
    war: 355-57
Apolo Hotel, Kampala: 261, 265
Appiah, Joe: 86
Apple, Johnny, Junior: 262-63
Armée Nationale Congolaise (ANC): 109-16, 144
Ashanti Pioneer: 84
Ashford, Nick: 424
Asmara
    reporters: 40, 41, 44
Associated Press, Nairobi base: 65
Astles, Bob: 265, 290
Avigarn, Tony: 306

Babu, Abdulrahman Muhammed: 157, 163-65
Bagamoyo: 157-58, 163
Bakwanga: 107, 108, 109
Balewa, Abubakar Tafawa: 96, 201
Balfour, Patrick: 35
Balubas: 138-40, 144
Banana (cargo port): 118-19
Banda, Aleke: 182-85
Banda, Hastings Kamuzu: 52, 81, 173-77, 181, 182-86
Banks, John: 325-27, 330
Barber, Stephen: 178
Barber, Wilfred: 34
Baring, Evelyn, Sir: 53, 56, 61
Barker, Derek 'Brummie': 329-31

Barnes, John: 203, 224
Barrell, Sarah Webb Fairbanks: 395-96
Barron, Brian: 307
Barton, Esmé: 39, 46
Barton, Sydney, Sir: 39, 44
Barzini, Luigi: 45
Bate, Henry, Sir: 5
Baudouin, King of Belgium: 101
Baughman, J Ross: 336-37
BBC television news: 206, 272-73
    radio departure: 211-12, 214, 217, 224-25, 231, 238
Beeston, Richard: 64-65
Behr, Ed: 102-103, 114
Bello, Sir Ahmadu: 204
Benguela Railway: 367-68
Bergerol, Jane: 355
Berry, Michael: 7
Bey, Wazir Ali: 38, 42
Belgium
    rule in the Congo: 99-102
Biafra: 1-2, 4, 202, 204, 207, 212-18, 221, 226-27, 229-31
Biafra Story: 322-23
Biddulph, Jim: 134-35, 238
Bierman, John: 160
Biggard, Homer: 100
Binaisa, Godfrey: 265-66
Bing, Geoffrey: 84-85, 86
Black, Ian: 386, 405
Blantyre demonstration, 1960: 177-78
Bloch, Dora: 304
Bloomberg, Charlie: 128
Bokassa, Jean-Bedel: 310-13
Bonavia, David: 182
Bonner, Arthur: 131-33
Botha, P W: 373
Botha, Pik: 423-24
Botswana: 51, 69
Bottomley, Sir Arthur: 190
Brazzaville: 96, 100, 110
Bridgland, Fred: 366-67, 370-73
Britain
    diplomatic embassies in Africa: 12-13
British South Africa Company: 233, 236
British South Africa Police: 382
    Special Branch: 236-37
Brown, Douglas: 56

Brown, Mike: 142
Brown, Robert K Lt-Col: 332-34
Buerk, Michael: 427-28
Bukavu: 147
Bulawayo Chronicle: 234, 242
Bulloch, John: 19, 107, 120, 127, 136, 138, 139, 142, 144, 145, 147, 148, 151, 182, 200, 237, 306, 317, 376-77
Burchett, Wilfred: 355
Burman, Ben Lucien: 96-97
Burns, Gary: 379
Burrows, Brian: 57
Burton, Richard: 320

Cablese: 37
Callaghan, James: 182
Cameron, James: 13-14, 56
Camrose, Lord: 7
Cangonga, attack on: 37-71
Caprivi Strip: 51-52
Carney, Daniel: 319-21
Carrington, Lord: 407-408
Carter, Roly: 314, 406, 410
Carter, W Rowlinson: 389
Catchpole, Len: 128-29
Cecil, Richard, Lord: 10, 384-85, 394-95
Cecil Square, Salisbury: 233
Cedar Palace Hotel, Port Harcourt: 202-203
Central African Republic: 310-11
Chamberlain, Neville: 82
Chapman, Michael: 355
Chelmsford, Lord: 9
Chester, Alan: 71
Chester, Michael: 71
China, intervention in Congo: 146
Chirau, Chief: 404
Chissano, Joaquim: 373-74
Christie, Ernie: 134, 149, 152, 192, 198
Churchill, Winston Spencer: 9-10, 82-83, 116
Clafin, Jacques: 402-405
Clarke, Ken: 231, 372
Clay, George: 121, 149
Cohen, Sir Andrew: 259
Colvin, Ian: 82
Colvin, Ian Goodhope: 76, 82, 83-86, 113, 121, 138, 141, 240-41, 248, 349-50

Computer journalism: 417-19
Congo
    attacks on nuns: 102-104
    independence: 100-102
    mercenaries: 317-19
    rebellion: 102-18
    riots: 99-100
    under Belgian rule: 99
    UN peacekeeping force: 106
Congo-Brazzaville: 97
Conley, Bob: 166
Cooper, Duff: 83
Cooper, Tom: 4-5
Coote, Colin, Sir: 80-81
Coren, Alan: 299
'Crippled Eagles' Organisation: 335
Cuba
    intervention in Angola: 366, 372

Dacko, David: 310, 313
Dahlakama, Afonso: 365, 374
Daily Express
    news coverage: 89-90, 228
Daily Mail: 89-90, 134
Daily Mirror
    news coverage: 89-90
Daily Sketch
    Biafran coverage: 227-28
Daily Telegraph: 4-5, 8-10, 14, 47, 64,
    80-81, 93-95
Danquah, Dr J B: 86
Dar es Salaam: 1
    British High Commission: 12
Dash, Leon: 368-69
Davies, Hugh: 119
Davies, Neil: 328, 330
Dawson, Jim: 5
Day of the Jackal: 322
Deakin, George: 31
Deakin, Ralph: 37
De 'Ath, George: 415-16
de Bono, Emilio, General: 40
de Carvalhao, George: 213
Deedes, W F 'Bill': 26, 33, 34, 35, 36,
    38, 39, 41, 43, 44, 45, 47, 49
de Klerk, W A: 427
Dennison, André, Major: 395-96
d'Estaing, Giscard, President of
    France: 311
de Gaulle, Charles, General: 96-97,
    100

de Gramont, Sanche: 134-35
de Herrero, Marguerite: 46
Della Casa, Nick: 373
Denard, Bob 'Colonel': 111-12, 123,
    317, 341
Dessye: 45
de St Jorre, John: 217, 223, 226, 230
Dodd, Thomas: 137-38
Doe, Samuel: 314-15
Dogs of War: 322
Donaldson, Teddy: 5
Douala: 212, 215
Douglas-Home, Charles: 56
Downie, Nick: 394-95
Downing, John: 278, 297
Downton, Eric: 56
Doyle, Mick: 213
Drew, Robin: 242
Dubai: 92
Dubos, Alain: 381
Duffy, Peter: 342, 344
du Plessis, Deon: 392

Easmon, Dr Raymond: 93, 95
East African Standard: 56
Eastwood, Peter: 308
Edden, Mike: 403
Edlin, John: 15, 198, 390-92, 428
Edusei, Krobo: 78, 84-87
Edwards, John: 315
Effiong, Phillip, Major-General: 221-
    22
Elisabethville: 106-107, 108, 111, 112,
    123, 124-129, 125, 126 142, 143,
    145
Elliott, Walter: 80
Ellman, Paul: 15, 381, 389
Emeny, Stuart: 31-32, 35, 39, 43, 45
Enahoro, Peter: 217, 224
Entebbe raid: 303-304
Enugu: 213
Equatorial Guinea: 313, 323-25
Eritrean Liberation Front: 22
Ethiopia: 28, 33, 48
    famine: 427-28
Evans, George: 86
Evans, Harold: 71, 137

Fairlie, Henry: 88, 178
Faisal, Crown Prince of Saudi Arabia:
    91-92

Fairhall, John: 278-79, *283*,-85, 288-90, 293-94
Favre, Jean-Claude: 134-35
Federation of Rhodesia and Nyasaland: 175-76
Fellowes, Larry: 10
Fernandes, Victor: 331
Fernando Po (island): 324-25
Fico (resistance movement): 360
Five Commando: 111, 146-48
Fleming, Lionel: 131-33
FNLA: 325-26, 353, 354, 355, 366
Foisie, Jack: 15, 369
Forbes, Archibald: 9
Forsyth, Frederick: 211-14, 215-17, 229, 322-25
Fosi, Andile: 415
Fouga Magisters: 136
Four Commando: 111
Fox-Movietone film crew in Addis Ababa: 35
France
  African diplomatic mission: 12
  African empire: 96-97
Francistown: 238-39
Freetown: 92, 93
FRELIMO: 357-58
Froth Blowers: 343-44

Gabon: 97
Gaborone: 51
Gale, George: 77-78, 89, *98*, 103, 104, 105, 108, 109, 110, 111, 139
Gall, Sandy: 55, 56, 60-61, 102-104, 105, 106, 108, 109, 110, 115, 134, 147, 212-13, 277, 279, 281, 290, 295
Gallagher, Alfred Trevor: 339-40
Gallagher, O'Dowd: 31, 32, 33, 37, 38, 40, 45, 46, *50*
Gambia: 95-96
Gardner, Ava: 57
Garrison, Lloyd: 207
Gatandu: 70
Gay, Alexander Ramsay: 324
Gaylard, Jack: 376
Gbenye, Christopher: 146
Gearhart, Danny: 331
Geldenhuys, Jannie, General: 424
Georgiades, Panyoiota: 331
Georgiou, Costas 'Colonel Callan': 326-31

Germani, Hans: 148, 317-19, 363
Geraghty, Tony: 326
Ghana: 78, 79, 80, 81-87
Githii, George: 67
Gold Coast: 79
Gobir, Yusufu: 223
Goldblatt, David: 401
Goldsmith, Michael: 311-12
Goodman, Lord: 244-45
Gordon, Alan: *23*
Gordon, Dennis: 356
Gowon, Yakubu 'Jack', Lt-General: 207, 218, 222-23, 230, 303
Grand Hotel Leopold the Second, Elisabethville: 106-107
Graves, Keith: *283*, 291
'Green Leader' raid: 397-98
Green, Maurice: 7
Greene, Graham: 55-56
Grey Scouts, Rhodesia: 336-37, 382
Griggs, Lee: 15, 126, 352
Guardian, The
  news coverage: 90-91
  cartoon: *284*
Guinea: 97-98
Gwynne, H A: 33

Halberstam, David: 136, *152*
Hall, Richard: 229-30
Hammarskjöld, Dag: 106, 114, 140-41
Harar: 45
Hardiman-Scott, Peter: 216
Harper, Steve: 21, 147
Harris, Paul: 392-94
Harris, Richard: 320
Harrison, Charles: 257
Harrison, John: 278, 279, 286, 297
Hart, Alan: 227
Hawthorne, Peter: 118, *122*, 363, 423-24
Heinzerling, Larry: *375*
Hemingway, Ernest: 47, 58-59
Hempstone, Smith: 105-106, 113-14, 139-40, 143, 144
Hills, Dennis: 299
Hitchcock, Bob: 186
Hoare, Mike: 111-12, 114, 123, 146, 147, 148, 149, 317-18, 320-21, 341-45
Hoffaker, Lewis: 137-38
Holland, André: 242-43

Holman, Michael: 252-53
Holmstrom, Lars: 285, 287, 295
Home, Sir Alec Douglas: 248, 251
Houphouet-Boigny, Félix: 97
Howard, Jim: 137, *347*
Humphries, Bill: 302
Hunyeni Air Rhodesia Viscount,
    attack on: 397
Huxley, Elspeth: 80

Ibadan rebellion: 204
Ibo rebellion: 204, 207
Indian High Commissioner, Kampala:
    13
Ingalls, Len: 56
Insight investigation into Equatorial
    Guinea plot: 323-25
Intercontinental Hotel, Nairobi: 306
Israel
    African diplomatic missions: 12-13
    assistance to Uganda: 271
Italy, policy in Abyssinia, 1928: 31
    war in Abyssinia: 40, 41, 45, 46
ITN: 212-13, 223
Ivory Coast: 97

Jacobson, Sydney: 178
Jadotville siege: 139
Jawara, Sir Dauda: 95-96
Jensen, Holger: 15, 426
Jeffrey, Gordon: 251, *254, 255*
Jeunesse rebellion in Katanga: 113-14
Johansen, Kenneth: 285
Johnson, Maureen: 242
Jones, Jeffreys, Mr Justice: 270
Jordan, Peter: 384
Joyce, Tony: 416-17
Juma, Aiga, Major: 270

Kampala: 274-77
Kaduna rebellion: 204
Kakere, Joe: 267
Kalonji, Albert: 107-108
Kamana, Dunstan: 190
Kaminada, Jerry: 298
Kanyama, Andy: 242
Kapuscinski, Ryszard: 355-56
Kartoum, battle of: 9
Karume, Abeid: 165, 167, 169
Kasai Province, Congo: 107
Katsina, Hassan, Brigadier: 218

Kasavubu, Joseph: 99, 100, 114, 116,
    125
Katanga Province: 101
    civil war: 113-14, 123, 124, 125-30,
        131-33, 134, 135-43, 144, 145
    mercenaries: 111-12
    secession: 105, 106, 107
Kaufman, Michael: 400
Kaunda, Kenneth David: 81, 186-87,
    189-90
Kearns, Alan: 108, 109, 110, *121*, 135
Keatley, Patrick: 91
Keats, Michael: 15-16, 18, *23*, 192, 198
Keita, Modibo: 91
Kennedy, Ray: 423
Kenny, Mary: 274
Kenya: 53, 54, 55, 56, 57-62, 63, 64,
    65-72
Kenya African National Union
    (KANU): 62
Kenyatta, Jomo: 52, 53, 54, 62-63, 64-
    72
Kenyatta, Ngina: 63
Khan, Aga: 6-7, 168
Kiambu: 70
Kikuyu: 53, 54, 57,
    oaths: 69-71
Kikuyuland mission: 55-56
Kilimamigu Prison, Zanzibar: 168-69
Kimathi, Dedan: 61
King, Donald: 235-36
Kipling, Rudyard: 9
Kipushi: 135
Kirkham, Norman: 207
Kisumu, Kenyatta's visit: 67-68
Kitchener, Lord: 9, 10
Kiwanuka, Benedicto: 299
Knickerbocker, H R 'Red': 32, 44, 45
Knipe, Michael: 275-77, 279, *283*, 298-
    99, 389
Komatipoort: 363
Kruger, Hardy: 320
KTC squatter camp, Crossroads: 415-
    16
Kumasi, case against National Libe-
    ration opposition: 84
Kyemba, Henry: 257, 271-72

Lagos: 204, 208-10
Lamb, David: 98, 307, 314
Lamprecht, Nick, Major: 341

Lancaster House Conference: 407
Lancaster, Reg: *201*
Lardner-Burke, Desmond: 249
Lawson, Colin: 191
Lea, Brian: 264-67
Leakey, David: 54-55
Leakey, Louis, Dr. 54
Leapman, Michael: 226-27
Legge, Ronnie: 237
Legum, Colin: 90-91, 229, 230, 245
Leo Deux Hotel, Elisabethville: 111,
    112, 116, 123
Leopoldville riots: 99, 100-105, 110,
    146
le Quesne, Godfray: 94
le Sage, John: 8
Lewis, Anthony: 20
Lewis, Roy: 56
Liberia: 314-15
Lindley, Richard: 272
Linington, Ed: 192, 198
Lisbon, coup 1973: 351-52
London Daily Mail: 10
Lourenço Marques: 358, 360-64
    renaming as Maputo: 364
Loshak, David: 93, 96, 207
Luanda: 352-56
Luck, Norman: 66
Luigi (mercenary): 144
Lumumba, Patrice: 100-102, 106, 107,
    114, 115, 116
Luo (tribe): 64, 66, 67
Luoland, Kenyatta's visit: 67-69
Lusaka Remand Prison: 194-97
Lynch, Peter: 136, 142
Lynch, Peter: 142

McCann, Mike: 69, 242, 338, *347*
McCall, René: 178
Macaulay, Berthan: 94
McCullin, Don: 145, 227-28, 278, 286,
    287, 290-91
McDermid, Angus: 1, 2, 3, 4, 15, *24*, 215
McDermid, Myfanwy: 4
MacDonnell, Ron: 192, 195, 197
Machel, Samora: 364-65
McKendry, Derek: 416-17
McKenzie, Andy: 331
McLean, Alison: 190, 192-93
McLean, Bill: 242, 244
McLean, Ian: 179, 190, 192, 195-97

McManus, James: 17, *375*, 379-80,
    410
Macmillan, Harold: 88, 96, 177-78
Madhvani, Makindye: 290-91
Mahé Airport, battle: 343-45
Maher, Stan: 361-63
Makındye Barracks: 278
Makindye Prison: *284*, 287, 288-95
Makombe, Mike: 196
Malawi Congress Party: 175, 177, 181
Malawi, independence: 181-186
Mali, slavery investigation: 91
Maliyamungu, Isaac, Major: 268-69,
    271
Malloch, Jack: 316-17
Maloney, Roy: 115, 147
Mancham, James: 341-42
Maputo (formerly Lourenço Marques):
    364
Margai, Sir Albert: 93, 95
Margai, Sir Milton: 92
Mark, Ross: 136
Markpress: 226
Marsden, Eric: 70-71, 100, 305-306
Marsh, E H 'Ricky': 4, 69, 296
Martin, David: 300
Maryara, Mohinder: 148-49
Masai: 57
Mashonaland
    attacks on farmsteads: 377-78
Matadi: 118
Matthews, Herbert: 41, 45, 46, 47
Matusadona Game Reserve training
    camp: 384-88
Mau Mau insurgency: 53-58, 61-62
Mazrui, Ali: 66
Mboya, Tom: 63-64, 66-67, 88
Mbarara, Barracks massacre: 269
    war: 279
Meikles Hotel, Salisbury: 404-405
Meisler, Stanley: 65
Memling Hotel, Leopoldville: 102, 104,
    116, 118, 145
Mengo Hill: 260
Mercenaries
    Americans: 332, 335
    Angolan operation: 325-31
    Congo War: 111-12
    post-colonial Africa: 317
    Rhodesia: 341
    Seychelles: 341-46

Meredith, Martin: 268, 359, 407
Miller, John: 340-41
Miller, Robert: 166
Miller, Webb: 40, 41
Mills, Ian: 242-43, 389, 399
Mills, Jim: 39-40, 42
Mitchell, Lt-Col: 112
Mkushi Camp, Zambia: 398
Mobutu, Joseph-Desire: 114, 115, 125, 149
Mohr, Charles: *254*, 359, 426
Moi, Daniel Arap, President of Kenya: *73*, 374
Moke, Norbert, General: 129-30, 138, 143
Mondlane, Eduardo: 357
Monks, John: 15, *24*, 47, 90, 130, 131-33, 134, 135, *150*, 155-56, 158-64, 240, 243-45, 251-52, *255*, 260, 265-67
Monks, Noel: 32, 33, 37, 38, 40, 41, 45, 47, *50*, 155
Morning Post: 9
Monsarrat, Nicholas: 181
Moore, Charles: 428
Moore, Nick: 278, 290, 296
Moore, Robin: 355
Moore, Roger: 320
Moores, Peter: 339
Morrow-Smith, Alex: 319, 391-92
Mossman, James: 10
Mouvement National Congolais: 99-100
Mozambique war of liberation: 356-58, 364-66, 373-74
MPLA: 325, 327, 353, 354, 355, 366
    FAPLA forces: 327-28
Mtoko Tribal Trust Land: 394
Mugabe, Robert: 408
Mulele, Pierre: 146
Mulungushi Conference Hall, Lusaka: 190-92
Mungongo, Godefroid: 115-16
Murphy, Alan: 324
Mussolini, Benito: 31, 41
Mutanga's Modern Nightclub, Salisbury: 349-50
Mutesa, Sir Edward (King Freddy): 259-60
Mutschmann, Bill: 359, 393-94, 405-406

Muzorewa, Bishop Abel: 404

Nabokov, Serge: 101-102
Nairobi, African correspondents: 65-66, 69, 70, 71, 298
Namibia: 421-24
Nasser, Gamal Abdel: 168
National Liberation Opposition, Ghana: 84
Ndola: 135, 140, 142
Neeld, Dennis: 134, 163, 165
New China News Agency: 157
Newsweek: 166-67
Nguema, Francisco Macias: 313-14, 324
Nichol, Jimmy: 124
Nicholson, Michael: 367, 369, 406-407
Nicholson, Roger: 339-40
Niesewand, Nonie: 249-50
Niesewand, Peter: *199*, 242, 248-52, *254*
Nigeria
    censorship: 217-18
    civil war: 1-2, 4, 96
    independence: 80
Nigerian Civil War: 204-206, 208
Njili Airport, Leopoldville: 105
Njonjo, Charles: 66
Nkomati Accord: 373
Nkomo, Joshua: 246-47, 376, 396-97
Nkrumah, Kwame: 52, 78-84, 86-88
Nkumbula, Harry: 186-87, 188
Northern Angola
    mercenaries: 319
Northern Rhodesia: 186
Nugent, Jack: 58, 62-63, 106, 111, 136, 139-40, 141-42, 163-65, 166
Nujoma, Sam: 423
Nussey, Wilf: 359
Nyasaland
    demonstration, 1960: 177-81
Nyerere, Julius: 304-305
Nyoka, Justin: 195, 196, 242, 390
Nzeogwu, Chukwuma, Major: 204-206

O'Booze, Lunchtime: 162-63
Obote, Milton: 258-60, 264, 267
Oboth-Ofumbi, Charles: 257
O'Brien, Dr Conor Cruise: 126-27, 136
Odaka, Sam: 261-62
Odinga, Oginga: 66-69

O'Driscoll, Jimmy: 111, 124
Ojera, Alex: 257
Ojera, Alex: 279
Ojukwu, Emeka Lt-Col: 207, 213-14, 228, 230, 325
Okello, John: 156-57, 160-61, 165, 167
Olympio, Sylvanus: 97
O'Meara, Mike: 339
Organisation of African Unity: 169, 300, 303
Osman, John: 30, *73*, 91-92, 204-206, 214, 216, 230-31, 277, 278-79, *284*, 291-92, 296, 300-303, 307, 351, 358, 363-64, *375*
Osman, Virginia: 30, 279, *284*, 291-92
Ottaway, David: 400
Owen HMS: 163
Owerri: 226, 230

Page, Cyril: 213
Panorama assignment in Port Harcourt: 202-203
Para-Daks: 383
Parkinson, Michael: 127
Partington, Walter: 118-19, 145-46, 208-10, *231*
Past is another Country, The: 407
Paul, Pope
    visit to Uganda: 262-64
Pawley, S P 'Pop': 4
Pearce, Lord: 248
People's Republic of Tanzania: 168-69
Peters, John: 318
Phillips, Percival, Sir: 32, 39-40, 42, 45
Picard (American diplomat): 165
Pinnington, Edward Lt-Col: 222-23
Pizzey, Alan: 402-403
Platter, John: 67-69, 195, 198, *231*
Polana Hotel, Lourenço Marques: 358, 363
Poland, Hitler's attack on: 82-83
Port Harcourt: 202, 219, 223
Prince, John: 5
Pringle, James: 312
Pritt, Denis: 54
Private Eye
    account of Zanzibar: 162-63
Purgavie, Dermot: *375*

Quashie-Idun, Acting Chief Justice: 85

Quill Club, Salisbury: 333-34, 390

Raab, Arthur, General: 222
Radio Biafra: 215, 218
Rais, Guy: 94
Ramrakha, Priya: 166, 210
Rand, Peter: 164, 166
Randall, Jonathan: 147-48
Rawlings, Jerry Flight-Lt: 87-88
Redfern, John: 54, 57, 81-82
Reid-Daly, Ron, Col: 383-87
Reinhard, Dr Hans: 192
RENAMO (Mozambique Resistance Movement): 365-66, 373-74
René, Albert: 341, 344, 345
Reuter, Henry: 315
Reuters
    Biafra war: 218
    Leopoldville: 101
    Nairobi base: 65-66
    Uganda experiences: 296-97
Reynolds, Chris: 392-94
Rhodes, Cecil: 233
Rhodesia
    censorship: 234-35, 239-40, 400-401
    Department of Information: 235, 249
    mercenaries: 325, 335-40
    news coverage: 10-12
    spying activities: 337-39
    UDI: 8, 232
    war: 376-82, 393-400
Rhodesia Herald: 234, 242
Rhodesian African Rifles: 10, 382, 394
Rhodesian Air Force: 382
Rhodesian Front Party: 8, 233
Rhodesian Light Infantry: 382
Rickett, F W 'Bill': 32, 42
Rider, Peter: *199*
Ridley, John: 135-36, 145-46
Riley, Norman: 5
Ridley, John: 78, 182
Roberto, Holden: 319, 325-26, 328
Roberts (editor of *The Sunday Telegraph*): 229
Roberts, Gwynne: 370-71
Robins, Eric: 237-38
Robinson, Derek: 244
Robinson, Derek 'Robbie': 340-41
Robson, Ronnie: 233, *254*

Rosetti, Mario: 277
Royal Uhuru Airlines: 135
Ruark, Robert: 58
Ruda: 393
Russell, Edward: 33
Russell, Robert, Mr Justice: 265
Russell, William Howard: 9
Russia
    African diplomatic missions: 12
    intervention in Angola: 327,
        366
    intervention in the Congo: 107
Ryall's Hotel, Blantyre demonstra-
    tion: 177-81
Ryan, Nigel: 101-102, 104, 110

Salisbury: 10-11, 232, 239, 378, 404-
    405, 411
Sandys, Duncan: 168
Sanger, Clyde: 91, 141, 166, 167
Sao Pedro da Barra: 355
Saudi Arabia
    slave trade: 91-92
Savimbi, Jonas: 355, 366-69, 370
Saxena, Captain: 343-44
Schramme, 'Black Jack': 317
Schwartz, Walter: 207
Scott, Robert Col: 229
Segal, Ronald: 91
Selassie, Haile: 27-28, 29, 30, 31, 43,
    46, 47, 48
Selous Scouts: 382-88
Senegal: 97
Senghor, Leopold: 97
Seychelles plot: 341-46
Sharpe, Peter: 345-46
Sharpe, Sue: 410
Sharwood-Smith, Sir Bryan: 206
Shawcross, Christopher: 85
Short, Philip: 300
Siedle, Bob: 270
Sierra Leone, independence: 92-95
Simbas: 146-48
Sinatra, Frank: 57
Sithole, Edon: 390
Sithole, Ndabiningi: 404
Slavery investigation: 91-92
Smith, Bill: 166
Smith, Colin: 245-47
Smith, George Ivor: 137-38
Smith, Ian 'Bunter': 242

Smith, Ian Douglas: 8, 11, 16, 86, 87,
    232-34, 238-41, 243, 245, 248,
    250, 252, 376, 406-407
Smith, Irl Col: 338-39
Smith, Wilbur: 321-22
Soames, Christopher: 408
Soldier of Fortune (magazine): 332-35
South Africa
    relationship with the press: 424-
        428
    township riots: 414-15
South African Defence Force
    assistance to RENAMO: 365-66,
        373
    assistance to UNITA: 367-68, 372
Southworth, Mr Justice
    report on Blantyre demonstra-
        tions: 179-81
Soweto riots: 426
Special Air Services Squadron, Rho-
    desia: 382
Spencer, Terry: 126
Spicer, John: 242
Square Circle: 320
Stacey, Tom: 109, 121
Stafford, Robin: 29-30
Stalling, Laurence: 35
Stanley, Henry Morton: 8-9
Stanleyville massacre: 146-48
Starr, Jack: 136, 139, 142, 147, 151
Steer, George: 31, 32, 37-38, 39, 45, 46
Steiner, Rolf: 323
Stevens, Siaka: 95
Stewart, Peter: 272-74
Stoppard, Tom: 79
Stott, Richard: 277
Stroh, Nicholas: 269-70
Sullivan, Mike: 401-402, 409
Sun, The
    Biafran starvation coverage: 226-
        28
Sunday Telegraph
    serial on African liberation move
        ments: 11
    profile of Hoare: 317
    sanctions-busting series: 340-41
    slavery investigation: 91-92
    Biafra coverage: 229
SWAPO: 422

Taesas, Lorenzo, Dr: 38, 43

Talbot, Godfrey: 216
Tanganyika: 168
Tanzania
    invasion of Uganda: 305-309
Targett, Bob: 139-40
Taylor, Henry: 111
Taylor, Peter: *410*
Television, advent of: 413-14
Third Marine Commando Division,
    Nigeria: 202, 219, 221, 223
Thursby, Geoffrey: 104
Tibbenham, Phil: 202-203
Times of Malawi: 181-82
Togo: 97
Tolbert, William: 314
Torchia, Andy: 278, 286, 300-301
Touré, Sekou: 88, 97-98
Trabelsi, Ali, Lt: 109-10
Trelford, Donald: 181-82
Tshombe, Moise: 100-101, 105-108,
    111, 116, 123, 125, 126, 135, 136,
    137, 140, 142, 143, 145, 146, 149
Tweedie, Penny: 278, *283*
Tyndall, David: 224-25

Uganda: 258
Uganda, Asian community: 264, 272,
    274-75
Uganda, Asian population: 13
Umuahia: 211
Union Minière: 106, 111
UNITA: 353, 354, 366-68, 370
United National Independence Party,
    Zambia: 186
United Nations intervention in Congo:
    106-107, 109, 113-14, 116, 118,
    125, 126, 127, 129, 134-35, 138,
    139, 140, 142, 143, 146
United Press International: 15
    Nairobi base: 65
United States of America
    Africa diplomatic missions: 12
    intervention in Angola: 366
Urquhart, Brian: 137-38

Van Can, Ed: 147
Van der Bijl, Pieter Kenyon
Voltalyne Fleming: 234, 395, 400
Van der Merwe, Edmund: 420-21
Van der Vat, Dan: 192, 194

Venter, Al J: 333-35
Vereeniging, Peace Treaty: 10
Victoria Falls, attacks at: 397
Viscount airliners, attacks on: 397,
    399
Visnews
    Ethiopian famine: 427
Voice of Kenya (state radio): 64

Wakholi, Joshua: 257
Wallace, Edgar: 10
Wallace, Weldon: 130-33, *150*
Walls, Peter, General: 382, 399
Watkins, Les: 297
Waugh, Evelyn: 26-28, 29, 30, 32, 35,
    38, 39, 41-45, 48, *50*, 57
Webb, Peter: 20, *73*
Welensky, Roy, Sir: 61, 133, 175-77,
    186, *199*
Welsh, Mary: 47
West Germany
    African diplomatic missions: 12
West, Richard: 274, *410*
Wheatley, Allan: 216
Whispering Death: 320
White, Matt: 193, 198
White, Tony: *74*, 192, 194-95, 197, *200*
Whiting, Ken: 15, 192, 194, 196, 198,
    356
Wicks, Alastair: 112, 123, 319
Wightman, Eric: 198
Wild Geese: 320
Wilde, Jimmy: 221-22
Williams, David: 80
Williams, Dickie: 109, 127-28
Williams, Mike: 336
Williams, Taffy: 323
Wilson, Harold: 243
Wilson, Howard: 223
Wina, Glenda: 188
Wina, Sikota: 188-89, 190-92, 198
Winslade, Harry: 5-6
Wise, Donald: 18, *24*, 51, 55, 56, 67,
    59-60, 61, *75*, 86, 90, 116-19, 129-
    30, 139, 141, 182, 277, 292, 296,
    353-54
Wolfers, Michael: 203, 226, 330, 355
Woods, Oliver: 61
Worsthorne, Peregrine: 178
Wright, Robin: 328-30

Younghusband, Peter: 20-21, *23, 24,*
    58, 90, 107, 108, 117-19, 127,
    130-35, 153-55, 157-64, *171,* 260,
    265-67, *282-83,* 300, 354, 361,
    363

Zambia, cross-border raids into: 397-
    98
Zambia, independence: 187-88
    Chongwe Bridge incident: 416-17
ZANLA: 379
ZANU: 376, 381
Zanzibar Hotel: 165-66
Zanzibar, independence: 156-57
Zanzibar Town: 159
ZAPU: 376
Zimbabwe, declaration of: 412
Zing, Sergeant: 386-87
ZIPRA: 379, 382, 396-98
Zulu War, 1879: 9